JOHN RUSKIN

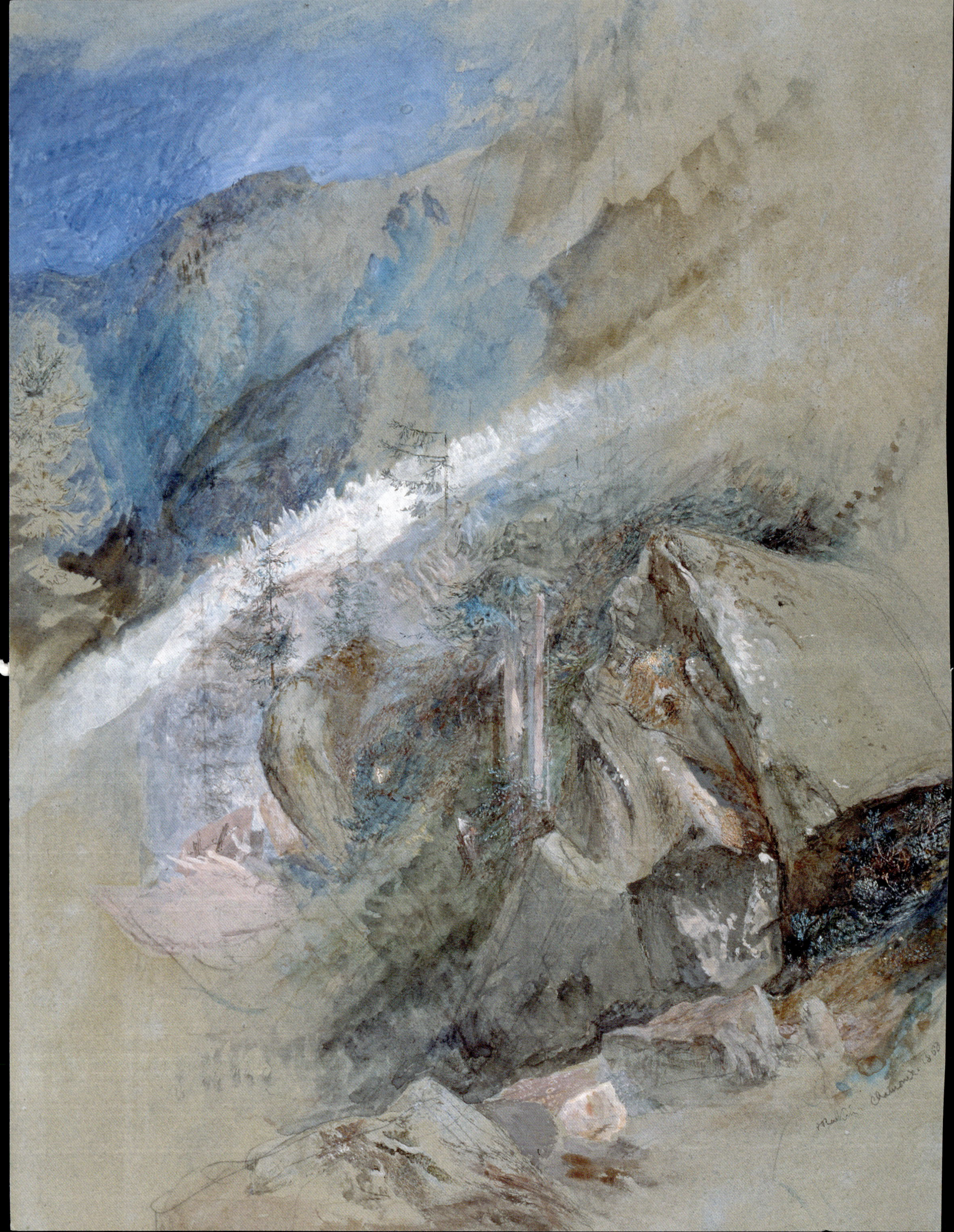

JOHN RUSKIN
Artist and Observer

Christopher Newall

WITH CONTRIBUTIONS BY
Christopher Baker, Ian Jeffrey
and Conal Shields

National Gallery of Canada, Ottawa
Paul Holberton publishing, London

Published in conjunction with the exhibition

John Ruskin: Artist and Observer

Organized by the National Gallery of Canada
and the National Galleries of Scotland,
and presented in Ottawa from 14 February to 11 May 2014,
and in Edinburgh from 4 July to 28 September 2014.

Published by the National Gallery of Canada, Ottawa,
and Paul Holberton publishing, London.

NATIONAL GALLERY OF CANADA

Acting Chief of Publications: Ivan Parisien
Editor: Caroline Wetherilt
Picture Editor: Andrea Fajrajsl

Printed in Verona by e-Graphic
Designed and typeset in Foundry Wilson by Laura Parker,
Paul Holberton publishing, London
Printed on GardaPat 13 Kiara

FRONT COVER *Rocks and Ferns in a Wood at Crossmount, Perthshire*, 1847 (cat. 72, detail)
BACK COVER *The Baptistery, Florence: Study of the Upper Part of the Right-hand Compartment on the Southwest Façade*, 1872 (cat. 35)
FRONTISPIECE *Mer de Glace, Chamonix*, 1860 (cat. 104, detail)

LIBRARY AND ARCHIVES CANADA CATALOGUING IN PUBLICATION

Newall, Christopher, 1951– John Ruskin: artist and observer / Christopher Newall; with contributions by Christopher Baker, Ian Jeffrey and Conal Shields.

Exhibition catalogue.
Issued also in French under title: *John Ruskin, artiste et observateur.*
Includes bibliographical references and an index.
ISBN 978-0-88884-919-9 (Canada)
ISBN 978-1-907372-57-5 (rest of the world)

1. Ruskin, John, 1819–1900--Exhibitions. I. Ruskin, John, 1819–1900
II. Shields, Conal III. Baker, Christopher, 1967– IV. Jeffrey, Ian, 1942–
V. National Gallery of Canada VI. Title.

N6797 R87 A4 2014 709.2 C2013-986007-X

CONTENTS

6 Foreword
8 Acknowledgements

12 Ruskin's Drawings
CHRISTOPHER NEWALL

30 Ruskin and Scotland:
The Intimacy of Landscape Art
CHRISTOPHER BAKER

44 Ruskin as Artist: Seeing and Feeling
CONAL SHIELDS

64 Fatal Praise: John Ruskin
and the Daguerreotype
IAN JEFFREY

Catalogue
CHRISTOPHER NEWALL

76 Architectural Detail and Ornament
114 Buildings
150 Towns and Topography
214 Geology and Foregrounds
260 Mountains and Skies
316 Nature Studies
348 Figures

362 Chronology
CHRISTOPHER NEWALL

370 Bibliography
373 Index of Works
376 Photographic Credits

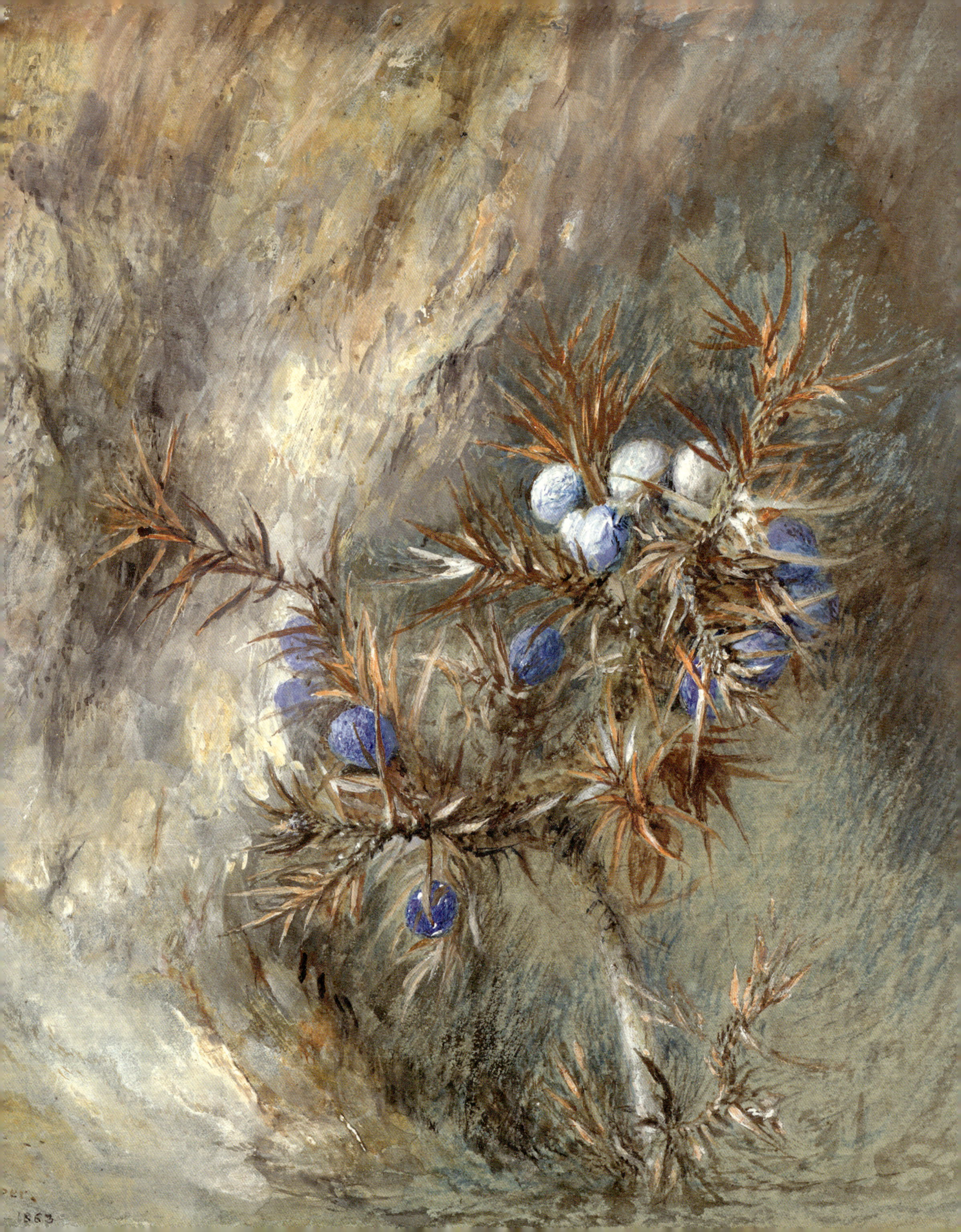
1863

FOREWORD

John Ruskin's drawings, with their lyricism and fluidity, meticulous detail and jewel-like colours, are a window into a brilliant and sometimes troubled soul. One of Victorian Britain's leading art critics and social theorists, known for the breadth of his subject matter and variety of writing forms, John Ruskin (1819–1900) was also a geologist, teacher and prolific artist. Although seldom exhibited during his lifetime, his drawings were the result of an intense and passionate artistic impulse.

John Ruskin drew to observe and comprehend. For him, drawing was a means of focusing his eye on the minutiae of nature and architecture in order to gather information and gain knowledge. He used photography – particularly the daguerreotype – as an aid to help reveal the hidden details of façades and stone carvings. To stand before one of Ruskin's highly expressive drawings, however, is not just to discover visual facts, but also to gain insight into the artist's complex world view and emotional state.

While previous exhibitions of Ruskin's drawings have explored their role as illustrations for his writings, *John Ruskin: Artist and Observer* is the most ambitious exhibition ever to focus on their inherent artistic qualities. Organized by the National Gallery of Canada in partnership with the National Galleries of Scotland, it brings together around 140 drawings, watercolours and daguerreotypes, representing Ruskin's entire career and diverse subject matter, including mountain views, observations of physical geography, and studies of intricate architectural ornament. With loans from important collections in Great Britain, Canada and the United States, the exhibition includes many of Ruskin's best-known and admired drawings, as well as others that are exhibited in public for the first time.

The exhibition and catalogue have been shaped in large part by Christopher Newall and Conal Shields. Newall's invaluable and perceptive essay on Ruskin's drawings offers an examination of the experiences that influenced his draftsmanship, while Conal Shields' essay astutely places Ruskin within the context of the art world. Ian Jeffrey has also contributed a fascinating essay chronicling the significance of the daguerreotype in Ruskin's work. We are grateful to them all.

Finally, we owe a very considerable debt of gratitude to the extremely generous public and private lenders without whom the exhibition and this publication could not have been realized.

MARC MAYER
Director and CEO
National Gallery of Canada

SIR JOHN LEIGHTON
Director-General
National Galleries of Scotland

CHRISTOPHER BAKER
Director
Scottish National Portrait Gallery

Cat. 119, detail

ACKNOWLEDGEMENTS

The success of *John Ruskin: Artist and Observer* is the result of the collective effort of a large number of people.

First and foremost we are immensely grateful to co-curators Christopher Newall and Conal Shields for their dedication, passion and detailed knowledge about Ruskin's art and life. Our thanks also go to the generous lenders to the exhibition and the people at these institutions who helped to facilitate loans: Abbot Hall Art Gallery, Lakeland Arts Trust, Kendal; The Alpine Club, London; The Ashmolean Museum, Oxford; Birmingham Museums and Art Gallery; The British Museum, London; The Fitzwilliam Museum, Cambridge; Ken and Jenny Jacobson, Great Bardfield; Harriet Joll; The Morgan Library and Museum, New York; Museums Sheffield; Ruskin Foundation, Ruskin Library, Lancaster University; Brian Sewell Collection, London; Victoria and Albert Museum, London; Whitworth Art Gallery, The University of Manchester; and Yale Center for British Art, New Haven.

For inspiring us to undertake the exhibition, our thanks in particular go to David Thomson, to whom we are indebted for the generous loan of works from his private collection.

Many individuals played essential roles in helping the exhibition and catalogue to take shape. We thank in particular Barbara Adams and Brian Barnes at the Archive of Modern Conflict; Christopher Brown and Colin Harrison at the Ashmolean Museum; and Stephen Wildman, Director and Curator of the Ruskin Library. We would also like to thank: Neda Babliku; Liz Brown; David Franklin; Mark Griffith-Jones; Vanessa Hall-Smith; James Holloway; Guy Peppiatt; Nick Rogers; Olivia Seligman; Rosy Temple; Bernadette Tsuda; Paul H. Walton; Helen Walton; and Clive Wilmer. We also thank the Department of Canadian Heritage through the Canada Travelling Exhibitions Indemnification Program for their support.

A book of such substance and beauty involved the combined efforts of many individuals. Our deepest gratitude goes to the authors, Ian Jeffrey, Christopher Newall and Conal Shields, whose insightful texts provide a fresh perspective on Ruskin's draftsmanship. The publication was expertly managed at the National Gallery of Canada by Ivan Parisien, Acting Chief of Publications. Our thanks go to our committed editors, Caroline Wetherilt and Mylène Des Cheneaux, to our meticulous translators and copy-editors for the French edition, Danielle Chaput, Sylvie Chaput and Christine Dufresne, and to Andrea Fajrajsl, Picture Editor, who dealt with all of the images. Our gratitude also goes to Paul Holberton and Laura Parker, for their vision and enthusiasm for the book.

At the National Gallery of Canada we wish to thank firstly Marc Mayer, Director and Chief Executive Officer, and Paul Lang, Deputy Director and Chief Curator, who have supported this project from the start. Our gratitude also goes to Karen Colby-Stothart, former Deputy Director, Exhibitions and Installations (now Chief Executive Officer, NGC Foundation), and Christine Sadler, Acting Director, Exhibitions and Installations, who oversaw the many elements of the exhibition and provided expert advice throughout.

We also extend our thanks to: Gordon Filewych and his Design department, especially Senior Designer Ellen Treciokas; Jonathan Franklin and colleagues in the NGC Library and Archives; Stephen Gritt, Director of Conservation and Technical Research, and his department; Jean-François Castonguay, Chief of Technical Services, and his crew; Jean-François Bilodeau, Deputy Director, Advancement and Public Engagement; Lisa Walli, Chief of Marketing and New Media, and her colleagues, along with Josée-Britanie Mallet, Senior Media and Public Relations Officer; Megan Richardson, Chief of Education and Public Programs,

Cat. 50, detail

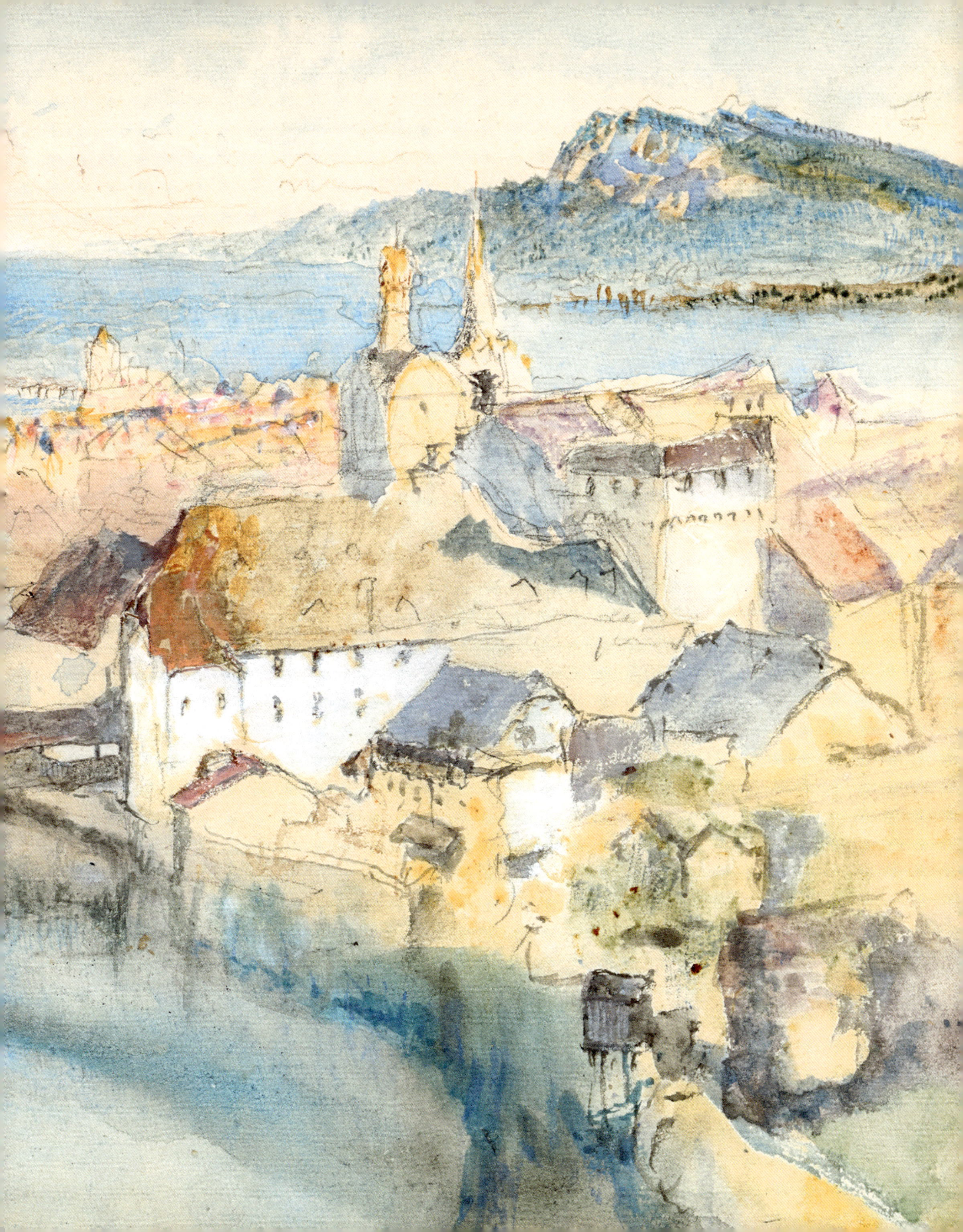

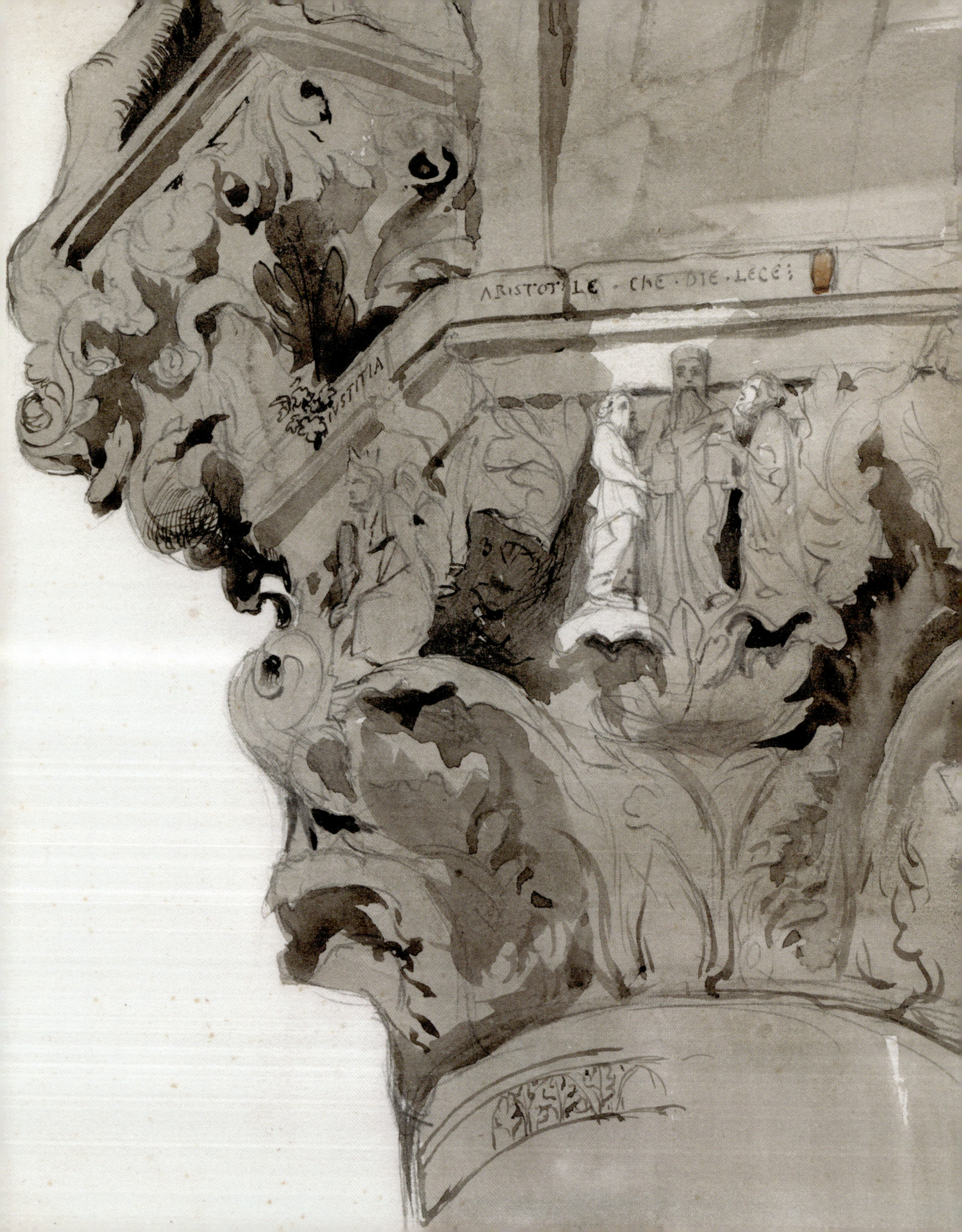
ARISTOTILE · CHE · DIE · LEGE
IUSTITIA

and her department; Marie-Claude Rousseau in Collections Management, and her team; and Katherine Stauble. And last but not least we extend our gratitude to our exceptional project manager Nelda Damiano, who along with Kate Beresford and other members of the Exhibitions team met the many organizational challenges of the exhibition with great commitment and humour.

At the National Galleries of Scotland we would like to express our thanks to everyone involved in creating the exhibition in Ottawa, for their professionalism and care. In Edinburgh key support has been provided by Sir John Leighton, Director-General of the National Galleries of Scotland; Michael Clarke, Director of the Scottish National Gallery; Samantha Lagneau, Head of Development; Patricia Convery, Head of Press and Marketing; Tessa Quinn, Content Manager (New Media); Siobhan McConnachie, Head of Education; Imogen Gibbon, Deputy Director; Julie Lawson, Chief Curator; Anne Lyden, International Photography Curator; Graeme Gollan and James Berry, Senior Paper Conservators; Rosalyn Clancey, Registrar (Exhibitions); Cassia Maria Pennington, Administration Assistant (Loans); Anne Backhouse, PA to the Director; Kim Macpherson, Curatorial Administrator; and Cavan Convery, Exhibition Designer.

The exhibition in Edinburgh has been most generously underwritten by Alex and Rhona Callander – enlightened and long-term supporters of the National Galleries' exhibition programme, to whom we are very grateful; it will be shown in the Robert Mapplethorpe Photography Gallery at the Scottish National Portrait Gallery, which is especially appropriate, as it includes some outstanding daguerreotypes; finally, the exhibition will be indemnified in Edinburgh through the Government Indemnity Scheme, courtesy of the Scottish Government.

ANN THOMAS
Curator, Photographs
National Gallery of Canada

CHRISTOPHER BAKER
Director
Scottish National Portrait Gallery

Cat. 8, detail

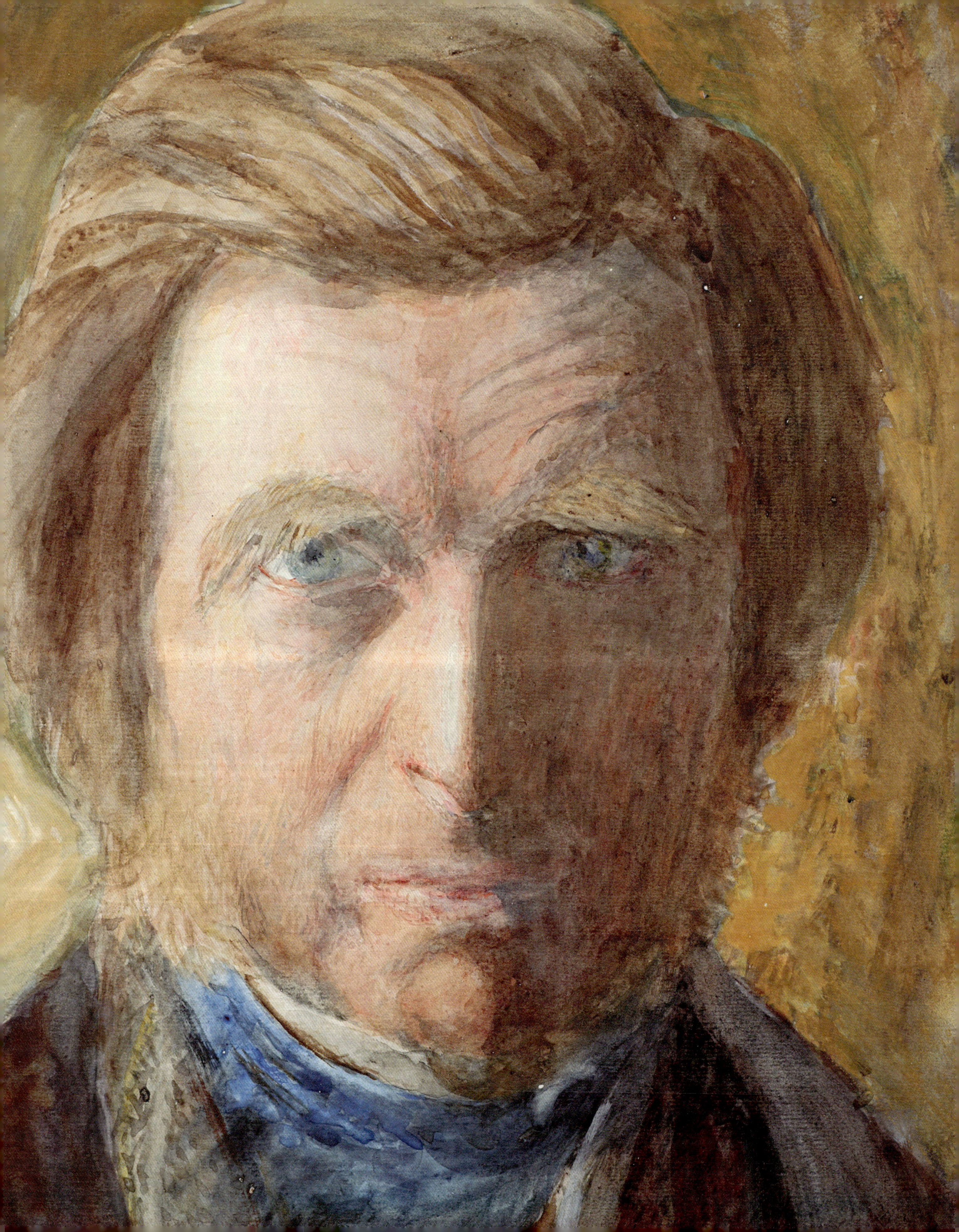

Ruskin's Drawings

CHRISTOPHER NEWALL

AS THE NINETEENTH-CENTURY French writer Théophile Gautier said of himself, "Je suis un homme pour qui le monde visible existe,"[1] John Ruskin was also one who was constantly aware of all that lay before him. Wherever he found himself – in familiar surroundings or when exploring places for the first time; in towns and cities and when studying buildings and works of art; or in the open air and at times when he sought communion with nature or attempted to comprehend the mechanisms that form the landscape – he was constantly and irresistibly drawn to the aspect of all that was to be seen. The faculty of sight was the starting point and basis of his intellectual life, and the delight that he experienced from the act of looking made his patterns of thought spontaneous and personal. By the very process of observation he gained perceptions about the sphere in which he existed and all that there was in it, and by the empirical inspection of phenomena of every kind he tested what he knew or had been led to believe, and refreshed his knowledge of the world.

Ruskin was gifted with extraordinary acuity of sight, and the directness and focus of his eyes as seen in his self-portrait watercolour (cat. 130) tell of a man for whom the exercise of looking was the foremost sensory function and one upon which he was utterly reliant. He seems always to have been intent on protecting his eyesight from damage or strain, even as an undergraduate wearing tinted glasses and later purchasing in London's Charing Cross Road spectacles with especially dark lenses for use in the mountains. He was perhaps also aware of how striking to others was the penetrating blue of

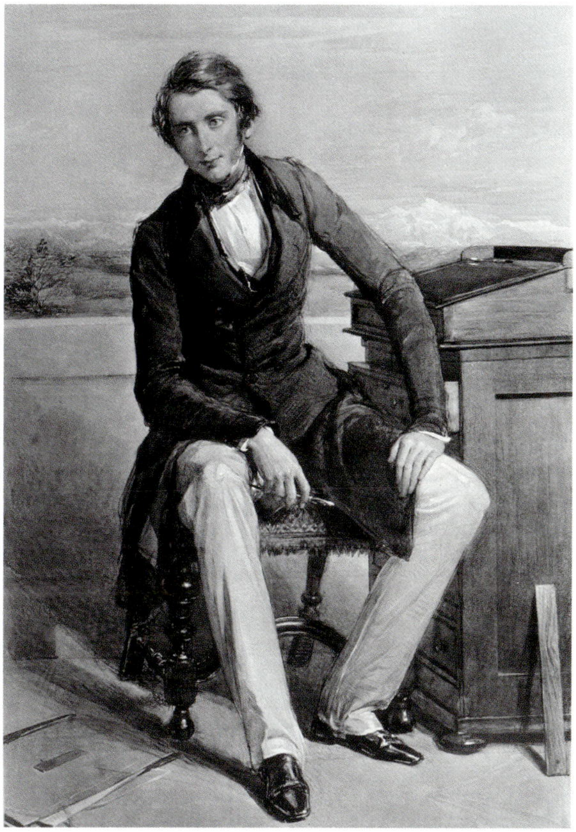

FIG. 1.1
after George Richmond
John Ruskin
Photogravure of a lost watercolour of 1843
Ruskin Foundation (Ruskin Library, Lancaster University) (RF 814)

Cat. 130, detail

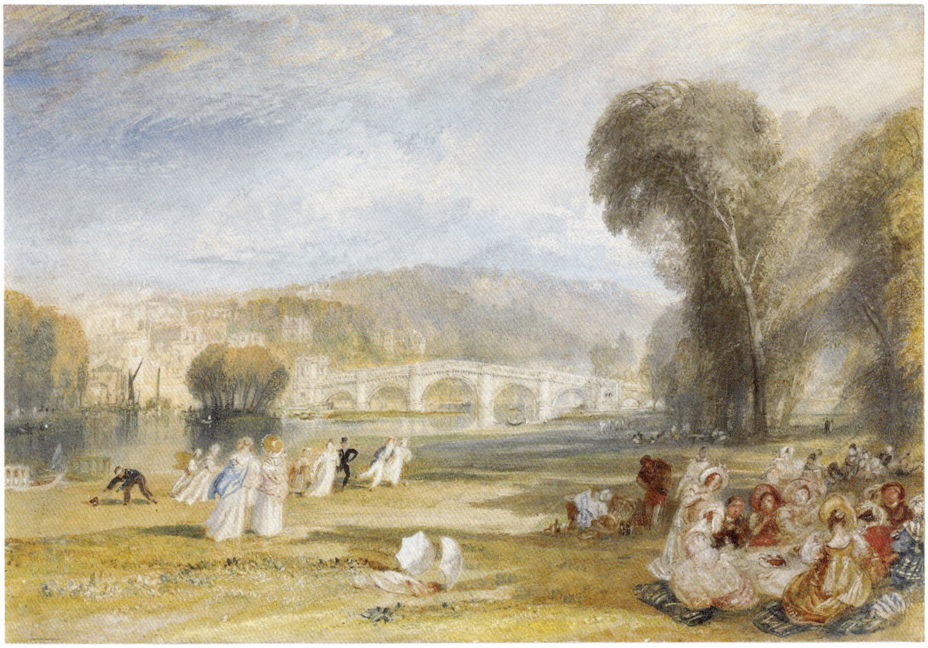

FIG. 1.2
J.M.W. Turner
Richmond Hill and Bridge, Surrey, c. 1831
Watercolour touched with bodycolour on paper
The British Museum, London (1958.0712.435)

the irises of his eyes, a colour that he seems to have deliberately matched in his choice of neckerchief or stock.

There were frequent occasions when Ruskin expressed anxiety about the state of his sight in his diary and correspondence and, as James Dearden has observed, the incidence of these concerns mounted in frequency in periods of mental instability and stress.[2] Only in the 1870s did Ruskin find that he needed to wear reading glasses, while his long sight seems to have remained sharp into old age, so that in 1886 he might proudly state that he could "see everything far and near down to the blue lines on this paper and up to the snow lines on the Old man – ... as few men of my age."[3] As he wrote in his autobiography *Præterita*, he had "a sensual faculty of pleasure in sight,"[4] while "the first vital principle [of drawing]," he believed, "is that man is intended to *observe* with his eyes, and mind."[5] The sheer delight that he took in looking at things, accounts of which experiences peppered his published texts, is pre-eminently evident in the vast corpus of his drawings. The functions of seeing and observing were key, and whatever work of art might follow was to be regarded as an incidental product. As he wrote in *The Elements of Drawing*, "I believe that the sight is a more important thing than the drawing; and I would rather teach drawing that my pupils may learn to love Nature, than teach the looking at Nature that they may learn to draw."[6]

Ruskin was taught to draw as a child and as an accomplishment that befitted an educated gentleman. His father, John James Ruskin, who was himself an amateur draftsman, employed a succession of drawing masters – Charles Runciman, Anthony Vandyke Copley Fielding, David Roberts and James Duffield Harding – to give his son practical instruction, and Ruskin learnt how to adopt, and subsequently dismiss, their methods. During this formative period and when his youthful style of drawing was dependent upon the example of older artists, he studied the architectural subjects of Samuel Prout, an experience that spurred him on to want to examine and draw buildings. The greatest impact of all, however, was that made upon him by the works of J.M.W. Turner. In 1832 Ruskin was given a copy of Samuel Rogers' book of poems *Italy*, illustrated with vignette engravings designed by Turner, which he lovingly copied and imitated. Ruskin's early watercolour technique, in which a

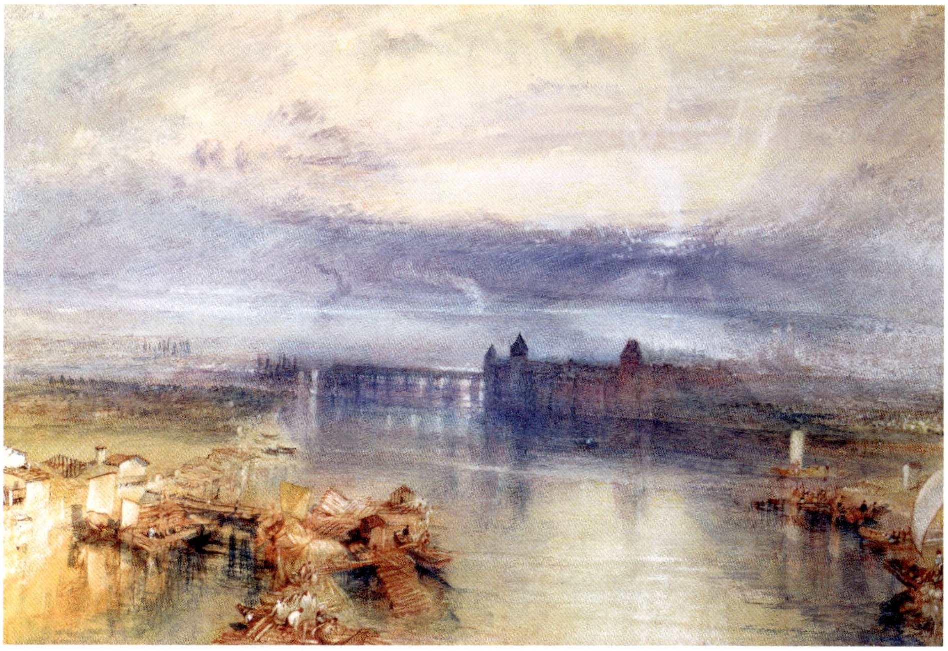

FIG. 1.3
J.M.W. Turner
Constance, 1842
Watercolour on paper
York Museums Trust (York Art Gallery). Purchased with the aid of a grant from the Victoria and Albert Museum Purchase Grant Fund and the Art Fund, 1983 (YORAG: R2476)

constant variety of surface texture stood for detail, owed much to his study of these illustrations. More or less consistently for the years to come, Ruskin idolized "the man who beyond all doubt is the greatest of the age; greatest in every faculty of the imagination, in every branch of scenic knowledge; at once *the* painter and poet of the day, J.M.W. Turner,"[7] as he breathlessly described him following what seems to have been their first meeting, at a dinner given by Turner's dealer and agent Thomas Griffith in 1840. From this time forward, Ruskin and his father began to collect works by Turner, starting with the watercolour *Richmond Hill and Bridge, Surrey* (fig. 1.2), and gradually the whole spectrum of the painter's genius was revealed. Griffith took an interest in Ruskin and showed him drawings quite different to the formalized vignettes of the *Italy* volume, sketches that were spontaneous, intuitive and unpolished, liquid in their forms and glowing with colour (see fig. 1.3). These Ruskin dubbed Turner's "delight-drawings,"[8] recognizing how they reflected the artist's love of the actuality of the landscape and admiring their emotional directness. He recalled how he "saw that these sketches were straight impressions from nature, – not artificial designs, like the Carthages and Romes. And it began to occur to me that perhaps even in the artifice of Turner there might be more truth than I had understood. I was by this time very learned in *his* principles of composition; but it seemed to me that in these later subjects Nature herself was composing with him."[9]

As significant as Ruskin's response to Turner's informal watercolour sketches may have been to his artistic development, also vital was his love of the engravings that formed Turner's *Liber Studiorum* (see fig. 1.4), which the artist had compiled between 1806 and the early 1820s, and which were gathered together in broad categories devoted to different types of landscape. The prints were generally made in mezzotint over etched line and printed in shades of sepia, and were regarded by Ruskin from the mid-1840s onward as among Turner's greatest achievements. He copied many examples and gradually devised for himself a style of drawing dependent on them, which relied upon carefully defined outline in pen and ink or the point of a brush, matched with washes of warm and earthy browns to denote the volumes of the landscape. By this method, Ruskin discovered how breadth might be instilled in

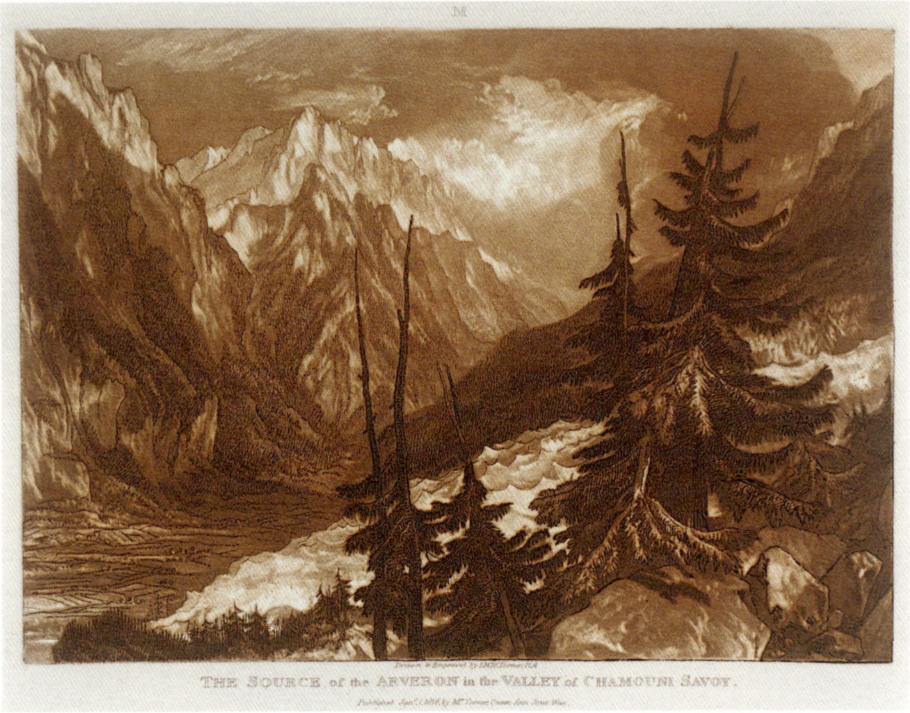

FIG. 1.4
J.M.W. Turner
The Source of the Arveron,
from *Liber Studiorum*, 1816
Etching and mezzotint on paper
Tate, London. Presented by
A. Acland Allen through the
Art Fund, 1925 (A01126)

his drawings by the simplified massing of light and shade, so that in 1852 he could write to his father that although works made on the basis of what he had learnt from the *Liber Studiorum* had "cost me great labour," it was by this process of self-education that he had "from that time ... understood the meaning of the words 'light and shade,' and have never since had any occasion to alter my views respecting them."[10] Monochrome drawings such as *Crossmount, Perthshire; Study of Crag, Tree and Thistle* (cat. 71) of 1847 are unimaginable without the example of the *Liber Studiorum*, while in 1857, in *The Elements of Drawing*, Ruskin recommended students to learn to draw landscapes by copying Turner's prints.

As important as this formative process of emulation certainly was, Ruskin's own early revelatory experiences of nature were crucial in his development. Two events of 1842 were described by Ruskin in *Præterita* as leading his emancipation from the influence of other artists. He came to regard these in retrospect as moments of epiphany when he saw clearly that it was his purpose to learn to describe nature with the closest possible accuracy. The first occurred:

> ... one day on the road to Norwood, [when] I noticed a bit of ivy round a thorn stem, which seemed, even to my critical judgment, not ill 'composed'; and proceeded to make a light and shade pencil study of it in my grey paper pocket-book, carefully, as if it had been a bit of sculpture, liking it more and more as I drew. When it was done, I saw that I had virtually lost all my time since I was twelve years old, because no one had ever told me to draw what was really there![11]

A while later, at Fontainebleau, he found himself "lying on the bank of a cart-road in the sand, with no prospect whatever but [a] small aspen tree against the blue sky." He described how, "languidly, but not idly, I began to draw it; and as I drew, the languor passed away: the beautiful lines insisted on being traced, – without weariness. More and more beautiful they became, as each rose out of the rest, and took its place in the air. With wonder increasing every instant, I saw

FIG. 1.5
James Duffield Harding
Twickenham, 1839
Chalk and watercolour on paper
Tate, London. Presented by the Art Fund (Herbert Powell Bequest), 1967 (T00996)

that they 'composed' themselves, by finer laws than any known of men."[12] Thus, Ruskin came to embrace the essential principle of direct and unaffected experience of the physical world.

Ruskin's drawings of the mid-1840s and 1850s go some way to fulfilling his own edict, which famously concluded the first volume of *Modern Painters* and stated that artists "should go to Nature in all singleness of heart, and walk with her laboriously and trustingly, having no other thoughts but how best to penetrate her meaning, and remember her instruction; rejecting nothing, selecting nothing, and scorning nothing; believing all things to be right and good, and rejoicing always in the truth."[13] During a succession of tours in France, Switzerland, Italy and Scotland from the mid-1840s onward, he advanced toward a style of drawing that was fully his own, in which his eye luxuriated in the textures and patterns of foliage and foreground and the fabric of buildings. Topographical conventions were abandoned and viewpoints chosen that allowed places and things to be seen afresh, with the surreal clarity of a dream. The degree to which Ruskin had departed from a conventional drawing technique, allied to his mounting indifference to the principles of legible composition, was apparent to him in 1845 when, in the Alps that summer, he compared his own works to those of his master James Duffield Harding (see fig. 1.5). It was Ruskin's

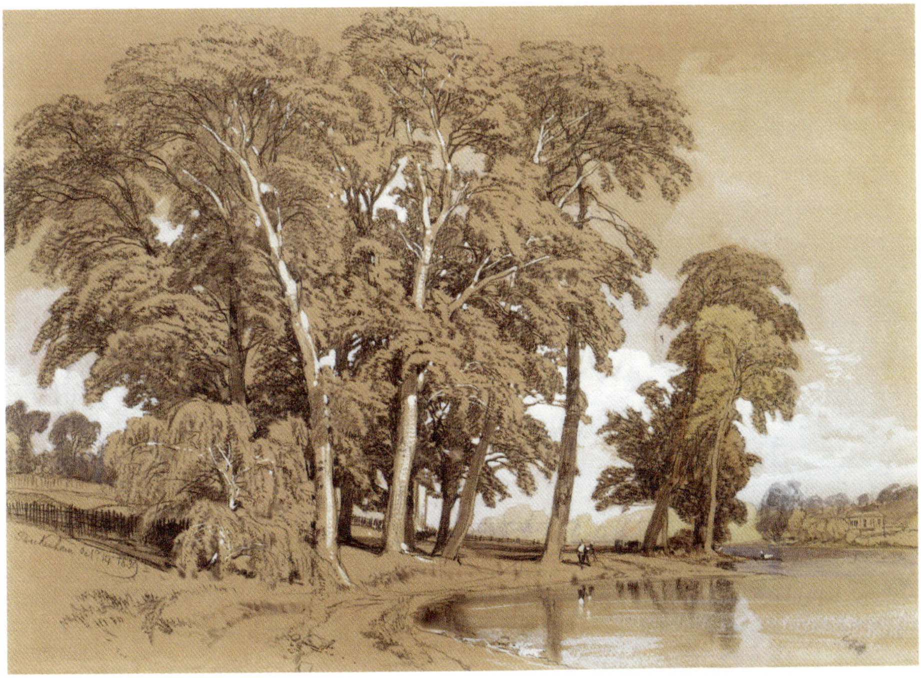

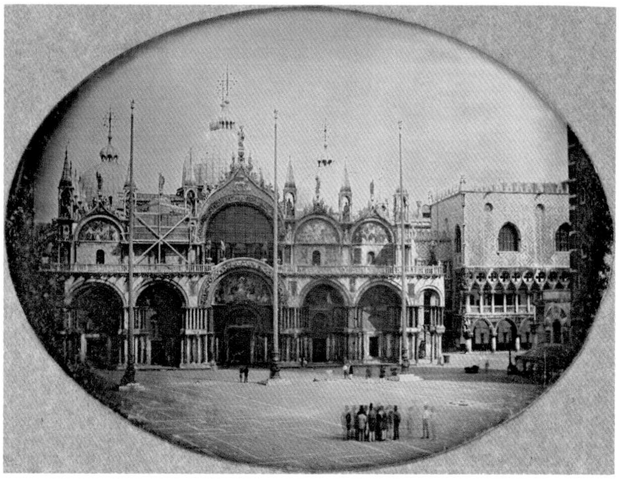

FIG. 1.6
Unknown French photographer
Venice. St. Mark's and the Piazza,
c. 1845
Daguerreotype
Courtesy of K. and J. Jacobson

conclusion that his companion's "sketches are always pretty because he balances their parts together, and considers them as pictures," whereas his own, by his own admission, were "always ugly, for I consider my sketch only as a written note of certain *facts*, and those I put down in the rudest and clearest way as many as possible. Harding's are all for impression; mine all for information."[14]

From the mid-1840s Ruskin's understanding of the possibilities of pictorial realism was led by his new appreciation of daguerreotypes. This technology of image-making, first introduced by French photographers in 1839, allowed unique records of places and things to be seen on the highly polished surface of a silver plate sensitized by iodine fumes and shown with a microscopic detail previously unimaginable (and which far exceeded in precision of replication the rival method of photographic enlargement from a negative, which from about 1860 superseded the making of daguerreotypes). Ruskin looked at the daguerreotype plates that he acquired – the first to enter his possession were a group of Venetian architectural subjects bought in 1845 (see fig. 1.6) – with amazement and wonder. To him, their example was – at least in the first instance – a spur to achieve ever greater degrees of minutely observed factual information in his drawings. It is clear that certain traits in his draftsmanship in the period were deliberate or unconscious adoptions of the way things look in daguerreotypes – in for example the tendency that early lenses had to flatten perspective and in the way the heightened effect of contrast in photographs made shadows appear especially dark and the forms of buildings to be seen as relief patterns of light and shadow.

Of course, Ruskin made daguerreotypes himself, or at least supervised their making, as well as buying them from professional photographers. Thus he built a collection of images of subjects that especially interested him – buildings, architectural details, mountain landscapes and geological formations being predominant – and he hugely valued them as documents of record. As regards their intrinsic worth as works of art, he offered different opinions, but seems eventually to have concluded that a drawing might convey a sense of emotional excitement and express the sensuous physical attraction felt by an individual for a place or thing in a way that a photograph could not. This was because a drawing was to be regarded as unique to particular circumstances and peculiar to the individual who made it (also true of a photograph, as Ruskin knew), but most importantly because the draftsman might more readily allow degrees of emphasis or even exaggeration, which would make such a work of art an even more telling response to what was seen.

A succession of references in his diaries and letters makes clear that Ruskin was an habitual draftsman. Wherever he was, at his homes in London or Lancashire, or when staying in Oxford or travelling in Europe, he had with him paper and drawing materials so that he might respond

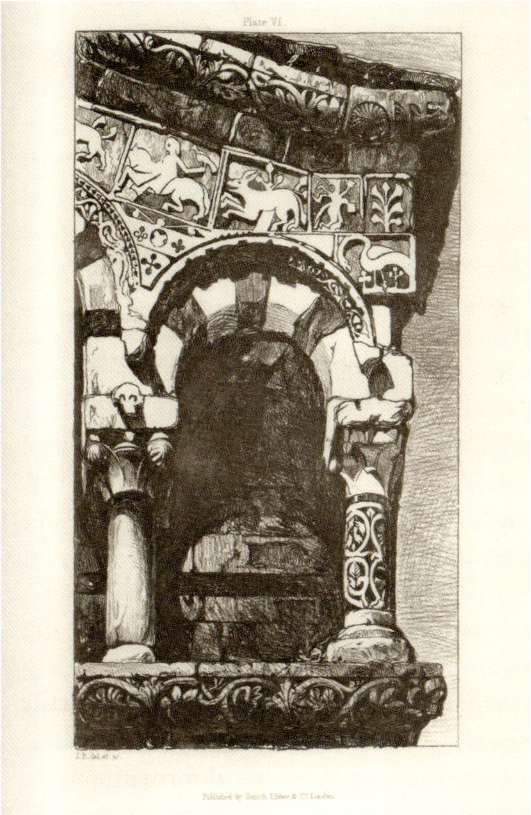

FIG. 1.7
John Ruskin
Arch from the Façade of the Church of San Michele at Lucca, 1849
Etching
From *The Seven Lamps of Architecture*, Library Edition, plate VI

without hesitation to the impulse to record what he saw. The sketchbooks and sheets that have come down to us provide an extraordinarily vivid notation on his experiences and the development of his patterns of thought, and also give documentary information about his great writing projects. In the first place, the making of drawings served a practical function in storing information about places and things to which he might subsequently refer. Views of Venice or Fribourg, for example, were made because he intended to write about those towns and because he knew that carefully made drawings of buildings or the wider topography would offer a level of recall equal to or beyond what might be instilled in a written account. On other occasions, he produced drawings of a diagrammatic character in which the exact profile of a carved moulding or sculpted patterning of a frieze or capital, or the precise formation of rock strata or shape of petals or stems in plants, or whatever else it might be, were recorded on the basis of measurement and meticulous observation – which again were put together for the purpose of recording data about the differences and variations of type for consultation at a time when those things might need to be specified in texts.

The studies and sketches that Ruskin made to provide the basis for intended illustrations in his books were entirely utilitarian. Countless architectural notations survive, for example those in connection with *The Seven Lamps of Architecture* (see fig. 1.7) and *The Stones of Venice*. With these, he was aware of the need for precision and careful instruction to the engraver so that the resulting plate would serve the didactic purpose of the text, although on occasions the person responsible for working up the finished illustration was sorely tested. Drawings of his were translated into line engravings for the manual *The Elements of Drawing*, but a degree of tentativeness is apparent in these that seems to simulate the search for ways to transmit truth of observation that was key to his instruction. On occasions, assistants were put to the task of working up sketches or even details of parts of extemporized glimpses of landscapes or nature studies to provide visual accompaniments to lectures. Different techniques and media lent themselves accordingly to the various applications to which drawings were put. Although there may be a temptation to regard Ruskin's work as an artist as something akin to a compulsion, done for its own sake and simply because he felt the need to draw, on many occasions works did in fact serve a practical purpose and were undertaken as part of a deliberate strategy to do with the gathering and transmission of information.

In 1871, when addressing the Metaphysical Society, Ruskin reviewed his own career as an artist-craftsman as one without any intellectual claim: "A painter," he said, "never conceives anything absolutely, and is indeed incapable of conceiving anything at all, except as a phenomenon or sensation."[15] A great difference lay between how he used drawing as a means of causing himself to look more intensively and the way in which so many professional artists treated the physical world as a mere pretext for the development of a commercially recognizable style. This divergence of purpose emerges starkly in Ruskin's relations with a younger generation of landscape painters in the 1850s; he, intolerant of their ambitions to paint and draw to please a contemporary audience and market; they, frustrated by his unwillingness to commend works that they had made in supposed adherence to his principles. Ruskin's own drawings have been regarded in some quarters as the works of an amateur, with whatever disparagement the term might seem to imply. In fact, as a corpus they are doubly extraordinary. In the first place, their variety of type and technique (on occasions obsessively concerned with exactitude of representation, on others apparently haphazardly indifferent to finish and legibility) would make them unimaginable as the work of an artist of the period seeking to his earn his living. Secondly, they show a constant engagement with Ruskin's own intellectual and emotional pre-occupations, a sense of urgency, and an avoidance of repeating motifs that places a gulf between them and the work of most amateur artists. Ruskin was of course privileged by his financial independence never to have had to consider the question of how to make his drawings attractive to potential buyers or acceptable in exhibitions (only once or twice in his lifetime did he sell a work or accept a commission, and the occasions when works of his were shown before the public were few); nor would it have crossed his mind that his own art might be subjected to the kind of critical analysis that he gave to works by contemporary artists in *Academy Notes* or *Fors Clavigera*.[16]

The value of his work as a draftsman was as a record of the intellectual and emotional engagement involved in the act of observation, even if the resultant drawings may have been marked by struggle and confusion. As he told readers in *The Laws of Fésole*: "If you desire to draw, that you may represent something you care for, you will advance swiftly and safely. If you desire to draw, that you make a beautiful drawing, you will never make one."[17] Looking at, and thus attempting to understand, the physical world was the essence of what he was doing; drawing was an invaluable stimulus to an ever-greater search for knowledge of what lay before him, but the work of art that resulted was, to his perception, of no intrinsic significance.

Ruskin drew under a powerful physical compulsion, which amounted on occasions to an uncontrolled and spontaneous response to the world. In 1852 he wrote to his father from Italy: "There is the strong instinct in me, which I cannot analyse, to draw and describe the things I love – not for reputation, nor for the good of others, nor for my own advantage, but a sort of instinct like that for eating and drinking." Pursuing the metaphor of bodily consumption and an appetite that might only be sated by looking and drawing, he went on: "I should like to draw all

St. Mark's, and all this Verona, stone by stone, to eat it all up into my mind, touch by touch."[18] Drawing was for Ruskin a means of intellectual engagement with the world, but also the expression of a physical need amounting to addiction.

Clearly, Ruskin was a man of obsessive interests, which when in full spate might take over his very existence. Whatever it may have been that preoccupied him in a given period, that object of investigation inevitably became something that he would seek to draw – and by doing so he would gain knowledge of the generality of whatever it was and, more importantly, the myriad variations and discrepancies that made natural form living and infinite. Geology and the shapes of mountain landscape were compellingly fascinating to him, and in his drawings of contorted strata and clefted ravines, aiguilles and glaciers, boulders and bedrock, he conveyed a sense that all that was to be seen in the physical world was to be regarded as in a relentless flux, which if observed would allow an understanding of how the landscape had originated and evolved, and how this would also lead to its inevitable dissolution. Skies and cloud formations, likewise, were studied because each moment in the emergence of a meteorological phenomenon was to Ruskin's perception a unique and unrepeatable conjunction and cause for reflection. Wild flowers, lichens and mosses, trees and their fruit and foliage similarly absorbed him because each part of nature, reduced to the tiniest fragment, was seen to be marked by minute variations, even when elements might superficially appear to be broadly symmetrical and consistent, and thus – in the process of their observation – a confirmation of Ruskin's constant search for the specific and individual, however obscure. The same sensibility, which might on the one hand manifest itself in a neurotic terror at the multiplicity of nature, and which took all things to be different from one another if scrutinized with sufficiently close attention, was applied in his study of architecture and topography. For Ruskin, the variations in the texture of carved stone, the incidental shapes and particular felicities of sculpted decoration, which seemed to him to be clues to the mentality of individual craftsmen, and even the beauties of wear and staining in the fabric of buildings, offered an overall patina that allowed a structure to be read as an organic whole. These were all elements that in their random combination might be seen as a kind of DNA to determine the identity and unique history of whatever it was that he was looking at.

Ruskin favoured things composed of parts approximately equal in size, where unity was achieved by rhythmic pattern. Purity of symmetry provided a sense of order and justice between elements, within which was permitted the expression of individuality; for above all else Ruskin was a man who believed that in whatever overall scheme of classification varieties of things might be placed there remained to be observed minute discrepancies of type in nature and the physical world. He was, in this sense, entirely in tune with the scientific understanding that led in 1859 to Charles Darwin's *On the Origin of Species*. Thus, were it in his drawings of geomorphic or sedimentary rock formations or the contortions of glacial flow, of specimens of wood oxalis or pine forests on mountain-sides, or of Romanesque capital sculptures or distant views of cities, Ruskin always looked for defining variations and inconsistencies. By drawing natural phenomena or objects constructed by man, any of which might be demonstrated to be unrepeatable, he was celebrating his own conscious existence and connection with the things he loved.

Certain artistic predispositions on Ruskin's part gave unity to his drawn compositions and allowed their elements to blend harmoniously and organically. Instinctively, he tended to mass forms from curved and interwoven lines, while the textures of his drawings depended on the constant variation of tone by the placing together of subtly differentiated points of colour and the avoidance of even surfaces of paint. As Peter Fuller wrote, "Ruskin argues that curved lines are more beautiful than straight lines, and that gradated shades and colours are more beautiful than plane surfaces, not just because that is the way things are in nature, but because the division of curves and gradated surfaces into an infinite number of degrees speaks of the infinity of God – 'a clear infinity, the darkness of the pure unsearchable sea.'"[19]

Ruskin had at his disposal a most fluent and instinctive way of drawing and one that allowed him to work quickly, when he wanted to, whether in pen, pencil or with the point of a fine brush. In addition, he sketched in chalk and painted in watercolour and gouache, and made prints in etching and drypoint. Certain works by him incorporate a whole variety of different methods and media – so that the forms become superimposed and mingled and are allowed to merge and melt into one another. Sometimes it is difficult to determine how a subject has been achieved in technical terms, as in for example one of the two views entitled *Ravine at Maglans* (cat. 74b), which has only on the occasion of this exhibition been recognized as incorporating a printed line beneath densely woven filigrees of gouache. That Ruskin so often drew in a way that suggests an absence of deliberation or forethought, but that may be regarded instead as being akin to a sensory submission to whatever it was he was looking at and as a kind of stream of consciousness, is indicated by his having often needed to abut further sheets of paper to allow a composition to extend into areas that he had not previously foreseen as requiring his observation.

In *Præterita* Ruskin pilloried himself for his "evermore childish delight in beginning a drawing; and usually acute misery in trying to finish one,"[20] but in fact it was his indifference to the tedious business of working up subjects so that they might be judged as works of art by the conventional standards of the day that made his drawings abstractly beautiful and always spontaneous. As a result, there hardly exists a drawing in Ruskin's entire creative output that may be regarded as finished; he was too impatient and cared too much about what lay before him to waste his time merely replicating and repeating elements of a composition, so areas were often left blank or blocked in with cursory lines while other parts were treated with the most minute attention. Thus his sense of urgency or impatience with the processes of dutiful record-making caused him on occasions to reduce his compositions to brilliantly drawn salients that seem to wind across the sheet with undefined areas between, but that are coherent and informative and have a wandering and colubrine beauty of calligraphy of their own. All was to be observed and inspected as found in its natural setting, in conditions determined

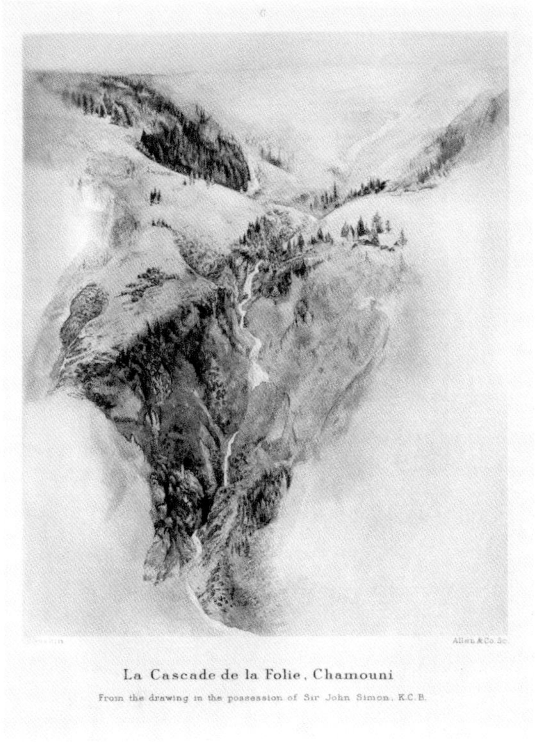

FIG. 1.8
after John Ruskin
La Cascade de la Folie, Chamouni
Photogravure taken from a lost drawing of 1849 or 1854
From *Modern Painters*, vol. 3, Library Edition, plate C

by the fall of light as it occurred at any precise moment (and with new sheets taken up as the sunlight shifted hour by hour) and with careful attention paid to the depth and direction of shadows. Points within the composition seem to drift in and out of focus and emerge from and become engulfed in ethereal infinity. Ruskin understood the need to reconcile overall impression with precision of detail, and in his intuitive and visceral observations he simulated the very act of seeing, whereby the eye concentrates on specific points within a field of vision and abstracts peripheral areas.

Ruskin's liberation from a supposed purpose of art to be legible made his drawings profoundly personal. It was their extempore and instinctive character – emerging as it sometimes feels subliminally and as if deriving from the artist's inner consciousness or id – that makes them unlike those of any of his contemporaries and marks his output as a draftsman unique. That his landscape drawings may be recognized on occasions as stemming from unfulfilled sexual desires, seen for example in the observation of geological forms unwittingly suggestive of female genital anatomy (see fig. 1.8), is an extraordinary demonstration of how Ruskin, who had no experience of physical love, found outlet for his untapped libido in drawing. In his observations of landscape foregrounds, he appears to have wanted to approach ever more closely, to draw with devotion and explore the actuality of nature. His sensory faculties of touch and smell, as well as of sight, seem to have been in a state of heightened receptivity as he drew, so that one may imagine the delight that he felt at crawling on hands and knees through a wilderness of grass and rock, and through the proxy of his drawing savour the sweet smell of moist moss and feel the warmth of reflected sunlight absorbed by and irradiated from exposed surfaces of stone. It was as if he sought a physical union with the landscape – to be enclosed within the forms of earth and water and rock and vegetation, to be invaginated by the physical world, so that, Hylas-like, he might himself be sacrificed in the epic struggle of conflicting mechanisms of growth and corruption and the elemental power of nature. Neither Ruskin, nor the guardians of his reputation in his lifetime and since, could possibly have contemplated such an interpretation of his drawings – he was utterly prudish about such matters and even invented a word of his own – "fimetic," i.e. to do with excrement – to describe works of literature (for example, Voltaire's *Candide*) that he found salacious. Yet in Ruskin's work as a draftsman he was emotionally unguarded and ingenuous in a way that makes his productions utterly compelling and hugely revealing.

Ruskin was the only child of parents who doted upon him to the point of suffocation and who sought to guard him against the world, but who also forced him by the pressure of their ambition on his behalf into a preternatural precocity. He was allowed few infantile pleasures and seems largely to have been kept apart from children his own age, and thus he grew up to expect to spend time alone and pursue solitary pastimes. In *Præterita* he gave an account of how he passed his days, "contentedly in tracing the squares and comparing the colours of my carpet; – examining the knots in the wood of the floor, or counting the bricks in the opposite houses,"[21] thus offering a glimpse of a state of mind that was already turning in upon itself and that in the course of time would find cause for demented fears in the appearance of things that would otherwise seem entirely innocent. During his early adult life he showed tendencies both toward petulance and emotional incontinence, and although he seems to have been agonized by the longing for companionship, he found great difficulty in maintaining friendships. With the seed of obsessive intensity sown in him at a young age, and in the absence of any person in his life with whom he might share knowledge and exchange new ideas and stimulus, on the basis of mutual intellectual respect, he gradually withdrew into an unhappy isolation. His neurotic frame of mind, which would now be described as that of a manic depressive, inflicted upon him bipolar extremes of mood, from emotional frenzy during which he exerted himself on whatever projects preoccupied him with stupendous energy, to bouts of profound despondency that left him incapable of applying himself as he sank in irresolution and self-pity. This was a psychotic tendency that manifested itself even when he was a young man, and was one that only became more relentless and cruel as he grew older.

Ruskin's drawings provide evidence of the emotional turbulence that he endured, as devastating to consider as any other account of his suffering. Perhaps the most remarkable stylistic divergence within the corpus of his work as an artist is the variation between opposite poles of meticulousness with the objective of painstaking detail, and wild and extravagant sketches the forms of which seem to emerge on the paper as a reckless, but at the same time wonderfully expressive, abstraction. The former objective was often achieved by close stippling of watercolour pigment to stand for the forms of landscape or architecture, or might be attained in microscopically observed pencil drawings; the latter by scrawled lines or blotches of colour that appear to be the work of seconds, but which result in drawings that are as beautiful and suggestive as anything he ever did. These two divergent paths mirrored opposite states of mind. The tiny, intensely detailed and coloured drawings of subjects such as feathers, flowers, twigs and stones stemmed from moods of manic despair and seem to represent his deliberate, even desperate, attempt to hold on to a connection with the physical world upon which he might rely and to retain information about what he could see that was to be trusted. As Kenneth Clark wrote of Ruskin in his later years, "He had stared fixedly at details all his life, and, as he grew older, to look into something intensively was like re-entering a lost Eden."[22] The second type of drawing, done at high speed and depending on a

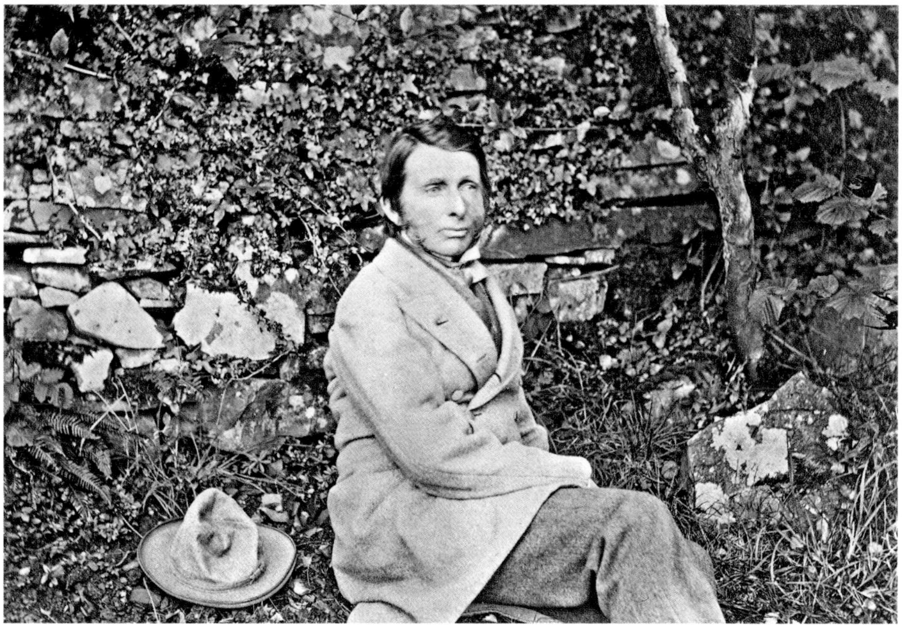

FIG. I.9
Frank Meadow Sutcliffe
John Ruskin, Seated on a Bank near Brantwood, 1873
Albumen print
Collection of the Guild of St. George, Museums Sheffield (CGSG00028)

command of medium that was painterly in its breadth, derived from moments of elation – as if Ruskin had recaptured for an instant the sensuous delight that buildings, landscapes and nature had given him in the past – glimpses that both relieved and exacerbated the grim despondency that settled upon him from the late 1870s onward.

The question of how Ruskin regarded his own drawings remains a conundrum. He made no claims for his own artistic production, insisting that the great majority of his works were mere sketches done for no larger purpose than to give fleeting glimpses of places and things, and on the grounds that only an individual who devotes his entire being to the vocation of creative artist might regard the output of his career as likely to have any value to following generations. In a lecture on the occasion of the opening of the Cambridge School of Art in 1858, he told students: "the best you can do in the production of drawing, or of draughtsmanship, must always be nothing in itself, unless the whole life be given to it. An amateur's drawing, or a workman's drawing – anybody's drawing but an artist's, is always valueless in itself."[23] In 1886, writing to Kate Greenaway, he offered a sad postscript on his life's work as an artist, in response to her enthusiasm for his drawings: "They are all," he wrote, "such mere hints of what I want to do, or syllables of what I saw, that I never think, or at least never thought, they could ever give the least pleasure to anyone but myself."[24] Yet, that Ruskin knew how important the making of drawings might be to others – spiritually, emotionally and intellectually – and how valuable the processes of observation that might lead to a drawing being made were – is testified by the fact that in his writing about drawing he addressed artists of all kinds, and with most generous encouragement to those who were to be regarded as amateurs. In his teaching he likewise believed in the universal usefulness of drawing, with the single reservation that students should restrict themselves to nature and landscape subjects, as he did, and not attempt to treat figurative compositions on the grounds that he did not think "figures, as chief subjects, can be drawn to any good purpose by an amateur," and that "as accessaries [sic] in landscape, they are just to be drawn on the same principle as anything else."[25]

That so many of Ruskin's drawings have survived, even including the slightest sketches, may be seen to indicate that they were at least put away by him for safekeeping. It is clear that he did occasionally inspect them in later years, as inscriptions were added – whether of dates (often incorrectly given) or locations – upon the sheets. There are accounts of visitors to Brantwood asking to see his drawings and of Ruskin's surprise – whether feigned or ingenuous – that they should be the object of attention. Ruskin's American friend Charles Eliot Norton encouraged him to continue to draw, noting in his journal on one occasion in 1872, "I use whatever power I have with him to keep him steadily and busily at his work,"[26] and writing to Ruskin to say: "Your influence will be made deeper, more permanent, and more helpful by patient work of this kind, than by your impassioned and impatient appeal to men who will scoff at your words."[27] In February 1879 Ruskin wrote to Norton to say that he had put aside a group of sketches that he wanted him to have, of "which I believe you may take pleasure in, partly in friendship partly in knowledge of the places," and which he thought "will be more useful in your hands than any one else's, – and perhaps of more in America than in England."[28] Many of the Ruskin drawings that are now in public collections in Boston and Cambridge, Massachusetts, were acquired by Norton in such circumstances. In 1879, an exhibition of Ruskin's drawings from Norton's collection was held in Boston and later in New York, in the catalogue of which their particular character was explained by their owner: "Few of these drawings were under-taken as an end in themselves, but most of them as means by which to acquire exact knowledge of the facts of nature, or to obtain the data from which to deduce a principle in art, or to preserve a record of the work of periods in which art gave better expression to the higher interests and motives of life than at the present day."[29] It was Norton who encouraged Ruskin to embark on the series of self-portrait drawings in which he is seen in introspective meditation, facing the reality of his own isolation.

In 1875 Alfred William Hunt, the professional watercolourist whose own drawings Ruskin had first commended in the 1850s, persuaded Ruskin to allow works of his to be included in an exhibition at the Society of Painters in Water Colours, prompting a bashful expression of regret that Ruskin had not felt able himself to appear in public. "My dear Hunt," he wrote, "I am very conceited about my sketches being placed, and could not behave with sufficient sangfroid at the private view [but] I shall peep in some day,"[30]– a letter that offers a glimpse of the gratification that Ruskin felt in finding that works of previous decades might be admired. Furthermore, he included many of his own drawings in the series of gifts made to the School of Drawing at Oxford, as well as to the museum of the Guild of St. George at Walkley in Yorkshire, in the belief that they might serve as useful examples to students and that they might inspire young people themselves to want to draw.

In the confusion and crises of Ruskin's mental life, the art of drawing served as a means of declaring his passionate feelings for nature and the physical world, in the presence of which, as he recalled in his account of mountain scenery experienced as a child, he felt a delight "no more explicable or definable than the feeling of love itself."[31] As a young man he believed that looking at and observing nature served as a reminder of the immanence of a divine power, as he distinguished in the second volume of *Modern Painters* between "the mere animal consciousness of the pleasantness I call Æsthesis; but the exulting, reverent, and grateful perception of it I call Theoria. For this, and this only, is the full comprehension and contemplation of the Beautiful as a gift of God."[32] Later in his life, he adopted a position whereby he understood the purpose of drawing as being simply to see and record what lay before him, as honestly and objectively as was possible to do, and thus to learn simple truths about the world transmitted to human consciousness through the faculty of sight. "The perception of solid Form is entirely a matter of experience," he wrote; "The whole technical power of painting depends on our recovery of what may be called the *innocence of the eye*; that is to say, of a sort of childish perception of these flat stains of colour, merely as such, without consciousness of what they signify."[33] He knew, however, that keen observation and the authentic representation of things and places was a serious and important undertaking because he perceived the physical world as a sacred inheritance that, in the very process of its replication, might be better understood and perhaps in part preserved.

So, the question remains, what is it that makes these drawings so fascinating and compelling? Why do they speak so powerfully of Ruskin's state of mind and how can they be so infused with feelings of love? In intellectual terms, he was a man of vast erudition and boundless appetite for knowledge and ideas, with a range of interests that was unexampled among the luminaries of the nineteenth century. Yet he was also on occasions almost childlike in his ingenuousness of response and in his delight and spontaneous enthusiasm for simple things. His drawings stem from this latter most personal and almost unconscious side of his personality and thus truly offer a "window into his soul." Each one is coloured by the emotional engagement he felt with the natural world and for buildings and works made by man, his responses to what he saw ranging from ecstatic delight and infantile thrill through to utter despondency and the foreboding of death. Drawing was for him both the expression of his tortured soul and a recourse from the frailty of his mental equanimity (in 1874 in *Fors Clavigera* he asked, "Does it never occur to me ... that I may be mad myself?," then answering his sad self-interrogation with the words: "Well, I am so alone now in my thoughts and ways, that if I am not mad, I should soon become so, from mere solitude, but for my *work*. But it must be manual work. Whenever I succeed in a drawing, I am happy, in spite of all that surrounds me of sorrow").[34] Ruskin could instil into a drawing of a single rock or broken river bank, or of an isolated capital, or of a cloud formation or a view across water at dawn, an intensity of feeling, matched with utter indifference to the conventions of art, which transforms an inanimate object or fragment of landscape into something the contemplation of which seems to explore the mysteries of the universe but which also speaks of the profound loneliness and eventual despair of one man's experience of the world.

NOTES

1 May 1857; reported in the *Journal des Goncourt* I (1988), p. 182.
2 Dearden 1999, pp. 5–6.
3 Ruskin 1956, vol. 3, p. 1128. The "Old man" was of course the mountain known as the Old Man of Coniston, visible across Coniston Water from Brantwood.
4 Ruskin 1903–12, vol. 35, *Præterita and Dilecta*, p. 619.
5 Ruskin 1903–12, vol. 25, *Love's Meinie and Proserpina*, p. xxx.
6 Ruskin 1903–12, vol. 15, *The Elements of Drawing, The Elements of Perspective, and The Laws of Fésole*, p. 13.
7 Ruskin 1903–12, vol. 35, p. 305. The dinner, which was held on 23 June, was described in more sober terms in Ruskin 1956, vol. 1, pp. 82–83.
8 Ruskin 1903–12, vol. 13, *Turner, The Harbours of England, Catalogues and Notes*, p. 237.
9 Ruskin 1903–12, vol. 35, p. 310.
10 Ruskin 1903–12, vol. 36, *The Letters of John Ruskin, 1827–1869*, p. 131.
11 Ruskin 1903–12, vol. 35, p. 311.
12 Ibid., p. 314.
13 Ruskin 1903–12, vol. 3, *Modern Painters I*, p. 624.
14 Ibid., pp. 200–201, note.
15 Ruskin 1903–12, vol. 34, *The Storm-cloud of the Nineteenth Century, On the Old Road, Arrows of the Chace, Ruskiniana*, p. 107.
16 *Academy Notes* consists of mostly quite short commentaries on works of art on display in the London summer exhibitions and was published each year at about the time of the opening of the Royal Academy exhibition, from 1855 to 1859, and once more in 1875. *Fors Clavigera* took the form of open letters published between 1871 and 1884 and addressed to "the workmen and labourers of Great Britain," in which Ruskin explored a multiplicity of topics but in which he occasionally strayed into art criticism – perhaps most notably in his account of the first summer exhibition at the Grosvenor Gallery in 1877, when he launched his attack on the works of James McNeill Whistler.
17 Ruskin 1903–12, vol. 15, *The Elements of Drawing, The Elements of Perspective, and The Laws of Fésole*, p. 354.
18 Letter dated 2 June 1852, quoted in Cook 1911, vol. 1, p. 263.
19 Fuller 1988, p. 47. The concluding quotation from Ruskin is from Ruskin 1903–12, vol. 4, *Modern Painters II*, p. 91.
20 Ruskin 1903–12, vol. 35, p. 368.
21 Ibid., p. 21.
22 Clark 1964, p. 351.
23 Ruskin 1903–12, vol. 16, *"A Joy Forever" and The Two Paths with Letters on the Oxford Museum and Various Addresses 1856–1860*, p. 182.
24 Ruskin 1903–12, vol. 37, *The Letters of John Ruskin, 1870–1889*, p. 566.
25 Ruskin 1903–12, vol. 15, p. 18.
26 Norton 1913, vol. 1, p. 430.
27 Ibid., vol. 2, p. 46.
28 Ruskin Norton 1987, p. 424 (also Ruskin 1903–12, vol. 37, pp. 275–276).
29 Ruskin 1903–12, vol. 13, p. 583.
30 John Ruskin, quoted in New Haven Oxford 2004, p. 24.
31 Ruskin 1903–12, vol. 5, *Modern Painters III*, p. 365.
32 Ruskin 1903–12, vol. 4, p. 47.
33 Ruskin 1903–12, vol. 15, p. 27, note.
34 Ruskin 1903–12, vol. 28, *Fors Clavigera, Letters 37–72*, p. 206.

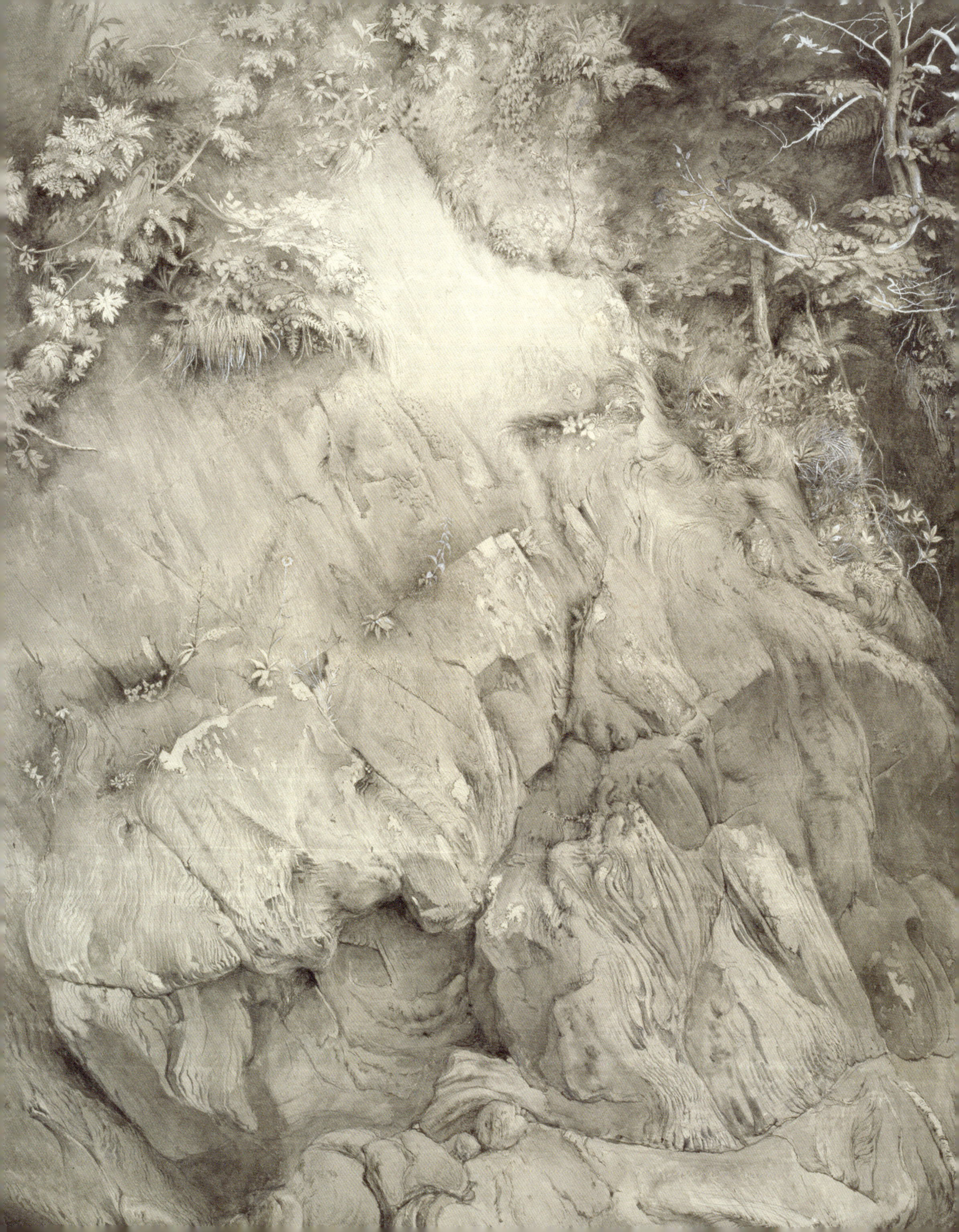

Ruskin and Scotland: The Intimacy of Landscape Art

CHRISTOPHER BAKER

JOHN RUSKIN'S WORK as an artist was shaped and informed by powerful enthusiasms and prejudices that he developed throughout his life. These included a passion for particular places: Venice, the Alps, certain French cities, Scotland and the Lake District all had prominent roles in his career and outlook. Ruskin was never a casual or uninformed traveller and he used the urban scenes, landscapes and cultures he was fascinated by to enrich his intellectual life and develop and refine his extraordinary skills as a draftsman and watercolour painter.

Scotland had a distinctive and curious status in these trajectories: it provided family connections and the context for one of the most traumatic episodes in Ruskin's private life, and visually was a land of variety and wonder, which both stimulated his scientific interest in the marvels of geology and offered delight through the sheer richness and beauty of its landscapes and literary heritage. Ruskin's relationship with the country forms a revealing case study through which to appreciate some of the key developments in his evolving artistic strategies as well as the striking manner in which his work represents the intersection of a rich web of public ambitions and private sensibilities.

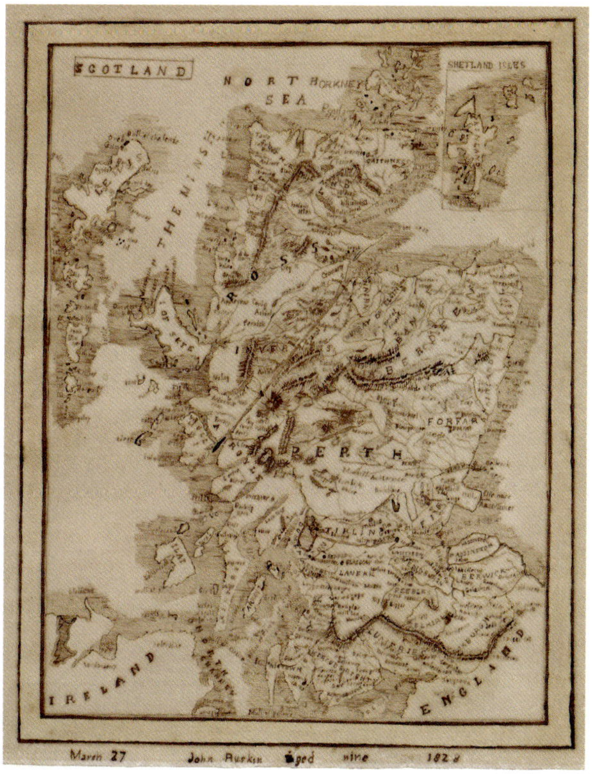

FIG. 2.1
John Ruskin
Map of Scotland, 1828
Ink and watercolour on paper
Ruskin Foundation (Ruskin Library, Lancaster University) (RF 951)

Among Ruskin's childhood drawings are copies of maps, including one of Scotland dating from March 1828 (fig. 2.1). Created at the age of nine, such a study illustrates the young Ruskin's notable precocity and interest in recording intricate, graphic detail; it is also though a testament to the connections with the country that had been forged since his birth. By that date he had already visited it three times; his recollections of his earliest experiences included

Cat. 76, detail

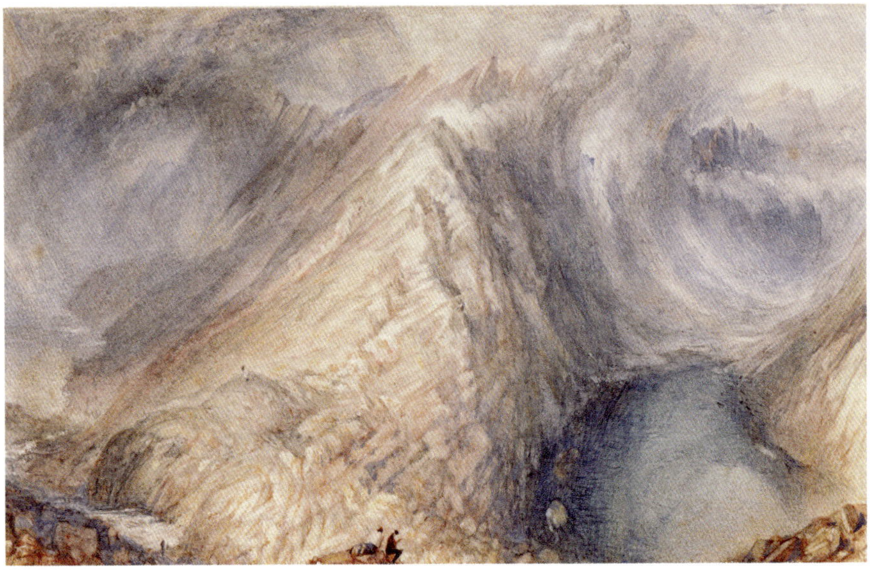

FIG. 2.2
J.M.W. Turner
Loch Coruisk, Skye, 1831
Watercolour with scraping out on paper
Scottish National Gallery, Edinburgh (D NG 861)

"going through Glenfarg, near Kinross, in a winter's morning, when the rocks were hung with icicles,"[1] and he was constantly reminded of his Scottish heritage by his parents in their comfortable London home as he was growing up. The artist's father, John James Ruskin, had been raised in Edinburgh, where he had briefly received instruction from the distinguished landscape painter Alexander Nasmyth, and he spoke with a gentle Scottish accent, which was inherited by his son. This characteristic was complemented from an early age by a diet of literature featuring the regular reading of that most potent of expressions of Scottish and European romanticism – Sir Walter Scott's novels and poems. This enthusiasm was always to remain with Ruskin and was noted in his autobiography *Præterita* (1885–89) as a "chief source of delight."[2] It later became woven with his emotional life, as, in 1847, he courted Charlotte Lockhart, Scott's granddaughter, who had inherited the writer's home, Abbotsford. Furthermore, Scott became almost a source of idolatry as Ruskin built a collection of his manuscripts and letters and stated that he planned to write a seven-volume biography of the writer, which was never realized.

In addition to such inherited enthusiasms, Ruskin was to find that Scotland provided inspiration through other routes, most especially because his first artistic hero, J.M.W. Turner, profitably drew on its landscapes and literature. Turner made six visits from London north of the border between 1797 and 1834, was especially appreciative of the "sublime" qualities of the mountainous landscapes to be experienced there, and came to collaborate directly with Scott, producing watercolours that were engraved to illustrate various works by the author, including his *Provincial Antiquities of Scotland* (1819–26). Ruskin first encountered Turner's work in 1832, met him in 1840, and famously expended vast effort on championing, collecting and interpreting his work.

One example illustrates the complexity of Ruskin's analysis of Turner's Scottish studies. In 1831 Turner made a tour to the most remote parts of the country, resulting in a tiny but spectacular watercolour of Loch Coruisk on the Isle of Skye (fig. 2.2). A wild and turbulent image in which the mountains and stormy skies seem to melt into each other, it was engraved and used to illustrate Scott's *The Lord of the Isles* (1815). Ruskin did not comment on its appropriateness in such a literary context, but twice in the first volume of *Modern Painters* (1843) discussed it in descriptive detail, praising its "geological truth" and marvelling at the artist's recording of the evaporation of rain,

FIG. 2.3
John Ruskin
Trinity College Chapel, Edinburgh, 1838
Graphite on paper
Birmingham Museums and Art Gallery (1907P147)

while comparing the composition with a landscape he believed to be by Salvator Rosa.[3] Ruskin's love of Turner's art was many-faceted; as well as using it as a vehicle for forging such scientific and art historical connections, he employed it to elucidate numerous practical artistic lessons, along with matters of poetic and emotional interpretation. It became for him a prompt to profound insights, which would undoubtedly never have occurred to the ever-practical Turner himself. Intimate engagement

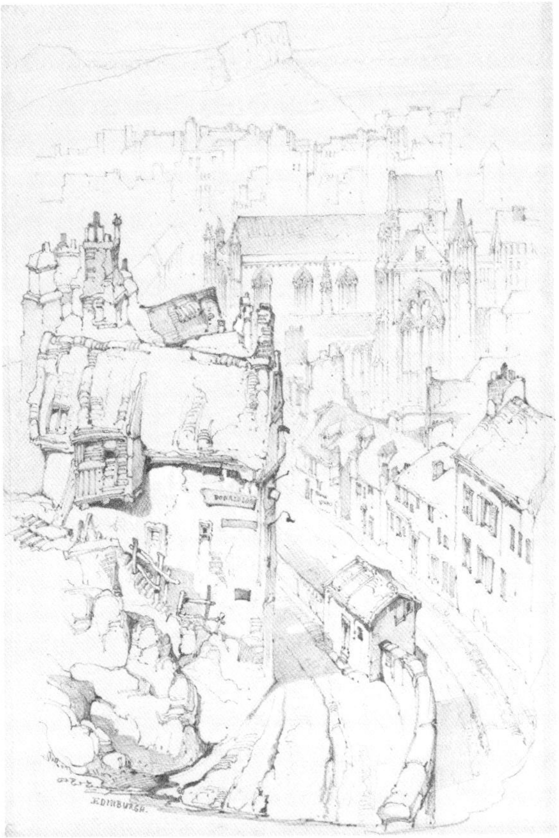

with Turner's Scottish art comprised a key strand of Ruskin's evolving curiosity about the country, but it did not at first directly impact on his own painted and drawn responses, which initially took altogether different forms.

Among the most attractive and early drawn studies of a Scottish scene created by Ruskin is his view of Edinburgh made in 1838, when he was undertaking a tour with his parents (fig. 2.3), which involved visiting Abbotsford and various other sites associated with Scott. It illustrates a sophisticated eye for compositional interest and a somewhat unconventional view of the city. The artist's vantage point was on Calton Hill, looking south toward Trinity Chapel and Edinburgh's old town, with Salisbury Crags in the distance. The contrast between the picturesque crumbling buildings in the foreground and the impressive gothic architecture of the chapel (which was soon to be destroyed), along with the busyness and intensity of detail, attest to various influences, most importantly the work of artist Samuel Prout, who had become a friend of the Ruskin family, and the Edinburgh-born topographer and printmaker David Roberts. Ruskin's evolution as an artist involved the absorption of a variety of sources of inspiration, which also included the work of fashionable tutors such as Anthony Vandyke Copley Fielding and James Duffield Harding, as well as watercolours by a wide range of other artists seen in public exhibitions and private collections.[4] In the 1830s he had not yet found his own language of draftsmanship but was certainly displaying great confidence and an ability to mimic the characteristic features of works that passed before him.

FIG. 2.4
John Ruskin
Dumbarton Castle, 1838
Watercolour over graphite on paper
Birmingham Museums and Art Gallery (1907P167)

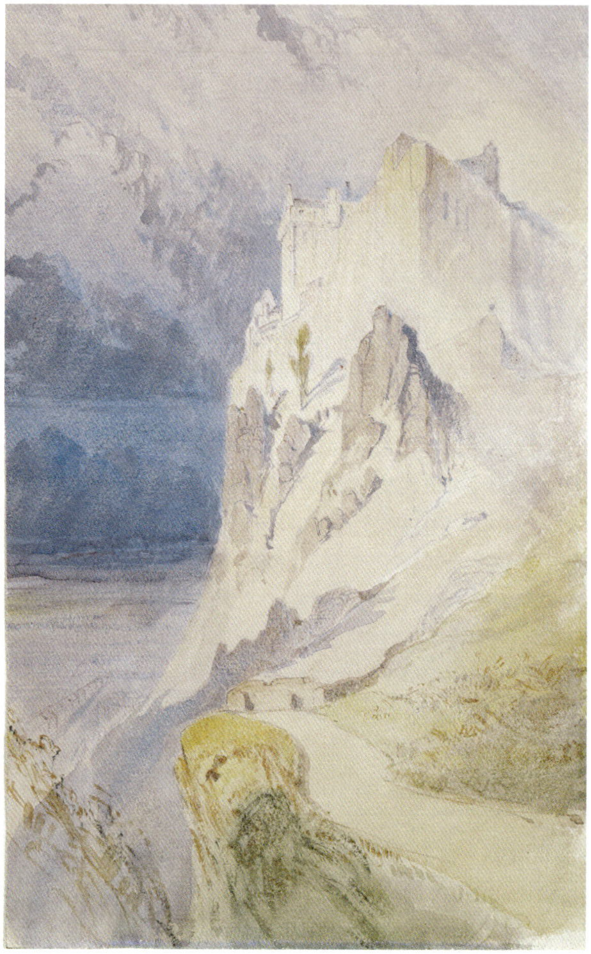

Ruskin's deepening love of Turner's work essentially provided him with a new licence, which meant he could break free from the conventions of drawing masters and gentlemanly amateur practice that Prout in particular represented and seek and depict images of greater drama and richer colouring. A good example of what this meant in practice is his watercolour of Dumbarton Castle of the late 1830s (fig. 2.4). Here Ruskin, adopting a low viewpoint, depicted the venerable fortress by the Clyde towering over him and employed a palette of deep blues and rich yellows, which finds affinities with the work of Harding and Turner. It seems highly likely that Ruskin would have known that Turner had made sketches at the site at the beginning of the decade and that these had been used as the basis for an engraving of Dumbarton that illustrated a collected edition of Scott's prose works (1834–37).

This new sense of liberation was perhaps most brilliantly explored by Ruskin in outstanding Alpine and Venetian watercolour studies throughout the 1840s. It also, however, came to be applied specifically once again to his Scottish experiences in 1847; it was in that year that he displayed a remarkable technical range in his drawn and painted work, the emotional background to which needs to be appreciated.

Charlotte Lockhart was superseded as the focus of Ruskin's affections by Euphemia (Effie) Gray, who was the daughter of a lawyer from Perth. Her father, George, was a family friend and business contact of John James Ruskin, and in 1829 the Grays moved into Bowerswell, which had been the Scottish family home of the Ruskins. Effie first met her future husband, John, at the age of twelve, and they eventually married in 1848 at Bowerswell. The build up to his proposal proved to be a time of turmoil and uncertainty for the artist, during which he created works both of great serenity and wild agitation.

Ruskin travelled to Scotland in 1847 to stay on the Perthshire estate of a family friend, William Macdonald, and on the way stopped for a few days at Dunbar. One of the most impressive results of this interlude was a confident watercolour that depicts a view from rock pools on the south coast of the Firth of Forth, looking along cliffs and across the sea to Fife in the distance (cat. 69). The weather was dull and the Scottish setting calmed Ruskin, leading him to recall in his diary having "a happy day, drawing by the sea shore."[5] He studied the rocks draped in seaweed, and geology and botany were to provide the focus for other works from this trip, created in a quite different aesthetic and emotional vein. These notably include *Crossmount, Perthshire; Study of Crag, Tree and Thistle* (cat. 71), which employs a muted palette of brown ink and wash flecked with touches of white to create an image of grandeur and animation, in which the fierce wind bends the vegetation and clouds scud across the sky above the clefts in the rock. Stylistically, Ruskin has replicated here the rich range of brown tones found in Turner's *Liber Studiorum* prints, while also evoking studies he had made earlier under the guidance of the theologian and geologist William Buckland. What is especially evident is that he was able to work in such different manners at Dunbar and Crossmount within a relatively brief period, shifting his methods to suit his mood and preoccupations.

On the afternoon of the 10th of April the following year, Ruskin and Effie were married and their wedding night was spent at Blair Atholl. This is not the place to revisit the complexities and tragedy of their relationship, but its break up five years later, which was also to be played out in Scotland, was the setting for the next fundamental shift in Ruskin's artistic evolution.

One of the key precursors to this development was the death in 1851 of Turner. Ruskin's devotion to Turner did not decline following this blow; in fact he continued to enthusiastically interpret and promote the work of his hero and sort out the vast quantity of paintings and watercolours that formed the artist's bequest to the nation. But during the same period Ruskin was also searching for new allegiances and causes and these he conveniently found in the work of the Pre-Raphaelite Brotherhood, which had been founded in 1848 by a disparate group of young, reforming artists, who among various ambitions sought to represent directly the beauty and specificity of the natural world. This chimed with Ruskin's own principle of "truth to nature,"[6] which he had articulated at the end of the first volume of *Modern Painters*. In 1851 he studied works by Pre-Raphaelites John Everett Millais and William Holman Hunt at the Royal Academy and defended them in the face of a wave of hostile criticism in letters he sent to *The Times*. This was a flamboyant gesture: in the second letter, Ruskin predicted that they might form "the foundations of a school of art nobler than the world has seen for three hundred years."[7]

Ruskin's support for the Pre-Raphaelites' aims was not merely a piece of public posturing but became a personal crusade and brought him, and his wife Effie, into close contact with these new lions of the art world as they welcomed his endorsement. In 1853 Effie posed as the key protagonist in Millais' dramatic painting *The Order of Release 1746* (1852–53, Tate, London), a powerful history picture that depicts the wife of a wounded Scottish soldier securing his freedom from the English following the 1745 Jacobite rising. She described it as "quite Jacobite and after my own heart,"[8] and soon the Ruskins and Millais were closely allied.

By choosing such a Scottish subject, Millais was contributing to a new-found interest in the highlands and their history in London, which was fed by various developments, including the passion that the Royal Family developed for Scotland and the improved physical access to it for tourists, especially through the spread of the rail network.[9] However, although

FIG. 2.5
John Everett Millais
John Ruskin, 1854
Oil on canvas
Ashmolean Museum, University of Oxford (WA2013.67)

Millais was tackling such themes, he had never visited the country, and so, during the summer of 1853, at Ruskin's instigation, he travelled with his brother and the Ruskins north, and they spent four months in each other's company. They were based at Brig o' Turk in the Trossachs, an area of outstanding natural beauty in the heart of Scotland, and a plan was developed by Millais to create two portraits – one of each of his new friends. The chief results of this period of feverish work were Millais' magisterial portrait of Ruskin at Glen Finglas[10] (fig. 2.5), some brilliant nature studies by Ruskin himself, and the break-up of his marriage, as Millais and Effie became attached. They in turn were married two years later.

Millais' portrait of Ruskin took seventeen months to complete and was essentially a commission for Ruskin's father. It is a key document in his career and a seminal example of mid-nineteenth-century British portraiture. In the context of a study of Ruskin's relationship with and scrutiny of the natural world, however, it remains something of a curiosity. Ruskin is shown in the landscape he loved, but as a dapper, urbane figure adopting a statuesque pose and imperiously surveying and contemplating nature, rather than intimately engaging with it, which is what his own studies and writings suggest he was most passionate about. This sense of dislocation, in part explained because the portrait itself was completed in the studio, was something Ruskin himself was sensitive to; he later wrote that he "looked rather uninterested in the world."[11] The setting Millais chose, with rocks, plants and gushing waters around his subject, was meticulously rendered in the Pre-Raphaelite manner, which means that it does not seem to be merely recorded but presented as a form of heightened, intoxicating reality. One of the consequences of this is that Ruskin appears to almost hover before, rather than be truly integrated into, his environment.

Millais had to complete the picture in the fraught period leading up to the annulment of the Ruskins' marriage, when his love for Effie was growing. It was a laborious process. The challenges he faced in the open air before he retreated to his London studio provide an insight into some of those of Ruskin, who was attempting to learn from his achievement. Ruskin's portrait required Millais to build a temporary platform on the slippery rocks so he had a stable vantage point from which to scrutinize the scene over many hours a day. Both men also had to contend with the annual curse of midges, which became the subject of one of Millais' deliciously farcical contemporary drawings (fig. 2.6). On one level, such an image is a comic commentary, but on another it underlines the staggering dedication and physical discomfort required to pursue the approach to studying nature directly that Millais and Ruskin were championing.

As Millais sat meticulously recording the background to his portrait, Ruskin was only a few feet away, making his own outstanding study of the gneiss rock face with water eddying below (cat. 76). His intense scrutiny of this subject may have been in part prompted by the remarkable small oil study Millais made slightly earlier of a nearby waterfall, which celebrates the visual rhythms of the rocks and shows Effie at the water's edge (fig. 2.7). Ruskin's curiosity about such subjects was so stirred that he was later to write that he was tempted to "devote half a volume to

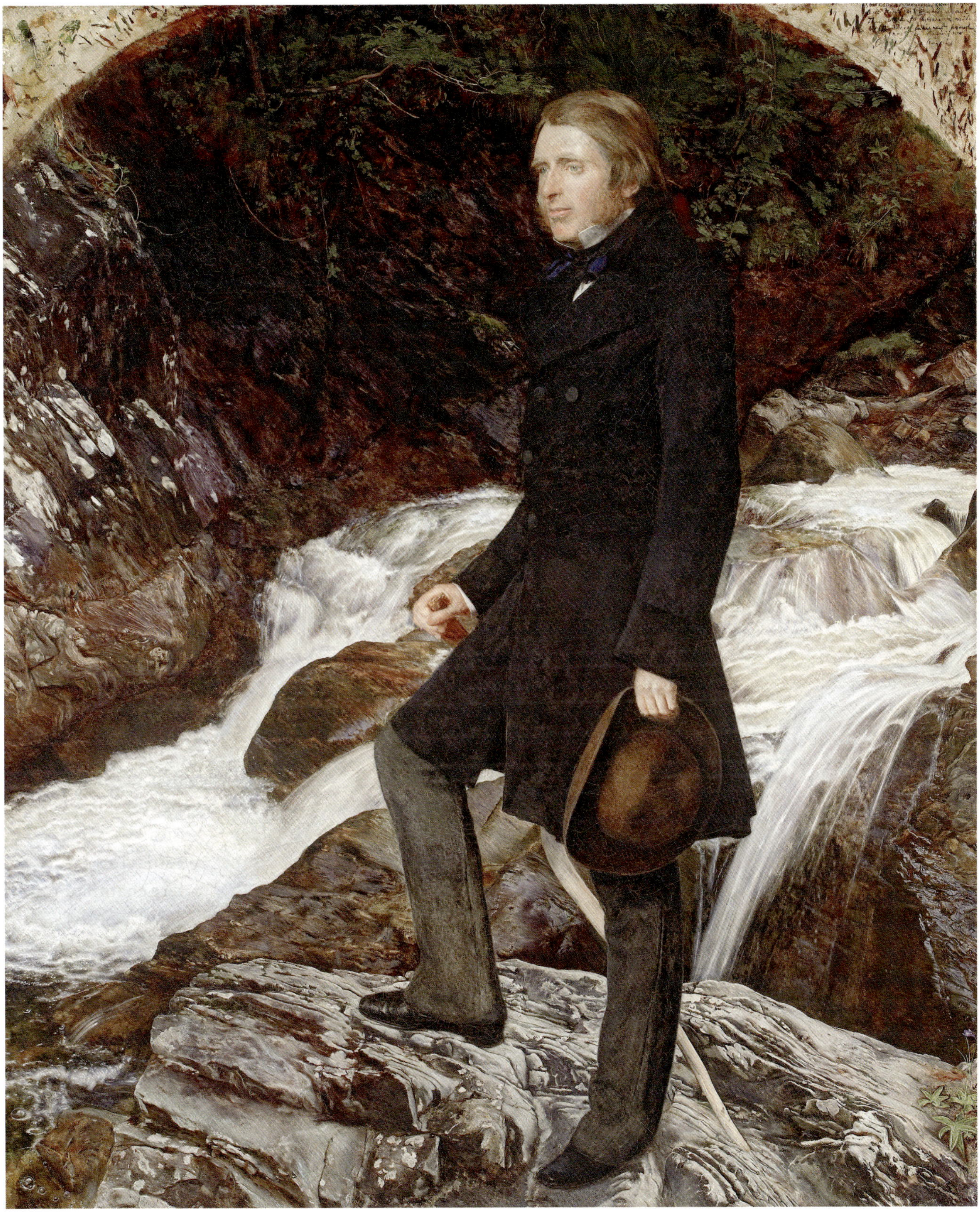

FIG. 2.6
John Everett Millais
Awful Protection against Midges, 1853
Pen and brown ink on medium, smooth, laid paper
Yale Center for British Art, Paul Mellon Fund (B1996.9.2)

a description of the fantastic and incomprehensible arrangements of these rocks."[12] On this occasion, however, drawing rather than writing triumphed, and following Millais' example Ruskin put into practice his new-found belief in the Pre-Raphaelite credo to paint "to the last touch, in the open air, from the thing itself."[13] This formulation of their ambitions was written by him just at the period he was sketching the rock and being portrayed and was part of his

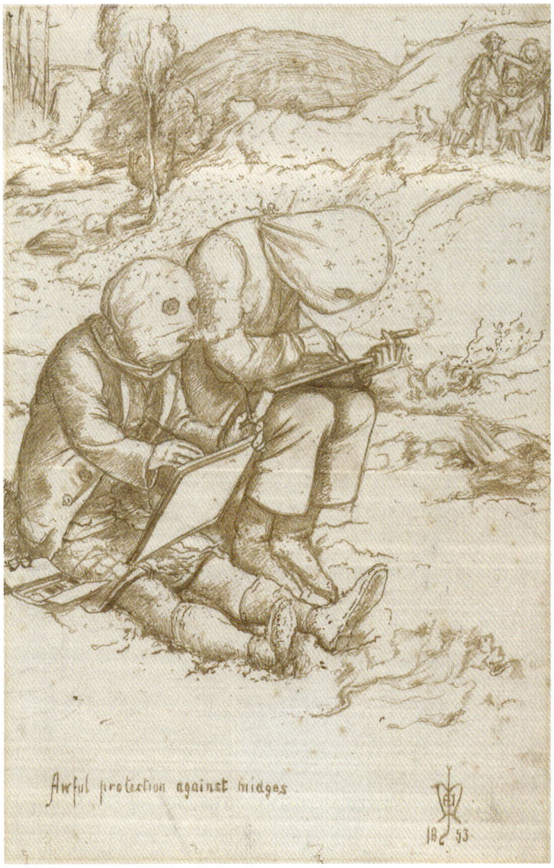

preparation for an important series of lectures that was to be delivered in Edinburgh.

The guidance of Millais and the deep affinity Ruskin felt for the Scottish setting were undoubtedly the immediate sources of inspiration for this tactic; however, it also needs to be seen as a consequence of other strands of artistic and technical innovation. Although the Pre-Raphaelites can be with good reason described as revolutionary, their approach did not spring from nowhere. There was a strong tradition in British art of directly observing and depicting natural phenomena, which extended back into the eighteenth century and earlier. It tended to emerge from two strands of activity. The first was scientific illustration, founded on the belief that empiricism was necessary to record, categorize and understand nature. Alongside this was a more casual but nonetheless significant development, which can be described as the work of artists who derived profound pleasure from pursuing naturalism through the study of the minutiae of landscape, both as an end in itself and as a means of informing their broader topographical work.[14] Notable examples of this type include some of the watercolours of artists such as John Downman, James Ward, John Constable and Cornelius Varley.

In addition to these strands of precedents, Ruskin and Millais were of course working at Glen Finglas only fourteen years after the birth of photography, the potential and snares of which they were entirely familiar with. This new medium seemed to many to miraculously offer an ability to mirror or capture nature. Ruskin's view of its uses are especially complex and relevant here; in essence he considered photography a valuable tool but a mechanical one,

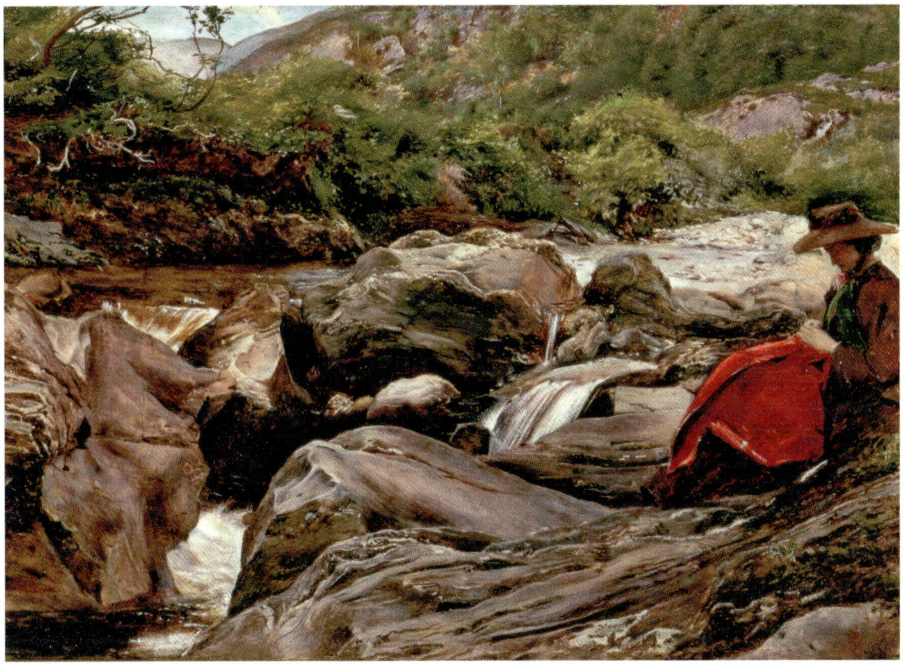

FIG. 2.7
John Everett Millais
The Waterfall, 1853
Oil on panel
Delaware Art Museum, Wilmington. Samuel and Mary R. Bancroft Memorial, 1935 (DAM 1935-53)

and a means of creating records rather than art.[15] In *The Pencil of Nature* (1844–46) the pioneer photographer William Henry Fox Talbot had stated that one of the advantages of photography was that "it will enable us to introduce into our pictures a multitude of minute details which add to the truths and reality of the representation, but which no artist would take the trouble to copy faithfully from nature."[16] So along with all the other motivations that lie behind Ruskin's meticulous work made during this seminal 1853 trip, it should perhaps be seen as an attempt on his part to meet the challenge that such a statement posed. He was being faithful to the subjects before him and creating a passionately felt and scrupulously observed response to the intricacies and beauty of natural phenomena, not merely selecting them.

Works of this type were to become one of the hallmarks of Ruskin's later practice as a draftsman and watercolour painter. At this moment, however, it seems that such obsessive, tight control of draftsmanship paralleled in an uncanny manner the claustrophobic atmosphere of this momentous sketching trip, which resulted in the collapse of his marriage. It might be imagined that such a painful episode would have terminated Ruskin's desire to visit Scotland, where his ex-wife and her new husband had now settled, but this was far from being the case. His bonds with the country, especially through his parents, were too strong. During the summer of 1857, Ruskin spent almost four months with his father and mother journeying up to the highlands. They travelled to Inverness, and then during the return trip to Edinburgh he worked on an outstanding watercolour of the Pass of Killiecrankie (cat. 81), which he recorded took a week, working six hours a day, to paint. The site remains one of great natural interest as well as being remembered for its historical associations, as it was here that a Jacobite victory over government forces was secured in 1689. By Ruskin's day it was the charm and drama of the setting that chiefly delighted visitors: during her visit in 1844 Queen Victoria wrote "how beautiful it is. Albert was in perfect ecstasies."[17] Ruskin certainly shared the royal couple's enthusiasm and created a highly finished – perhaps in fact obsessively laboured – work, which represents a return to the type of studies he had made four years earlier at Glen Finglas. Such images and the experiences they recalled haunted him later in life: in 1873 he was to write of the sound of Scottish streams and how "no other waters [can] be compared with them," in part because of "the pure crystal of the Scottish pebbles, giving the stream its gradations of amber to the edge, and the sound ... mak[ing] the Scottish fords the happiest pieces of all one's day's walk."[18] In this instance he was particularly taking pleasure in the structure and variety of the rock formations, which appear almost overlaid with a celebratory, decorative film, as this section of the pass flickers and glows with opalescent colours.

The watercolour was evidently highly regarded by its creator because he sent it off for public exhibition in 1878 and had it photographed so prints could be supplied to anyone who requested them. This desire for display was a relatively rare occurrence, as the functions of Ruskin's drawings were not those of a professional artist. He was a wealthy gentleman and amateur who never had to draw (or indeed write) for a living. His work was above all the result of a passionately held series of incremental vocations, explored as a means of discovering, interpreting and taking pleasure in the world. His drawings were a personal source of enjoyment, and a support to his writings, as they were often engraved as illustrations and used as a tool for teaching. Only occasionally did he dip into the precarious arena of public exhibitions, where they might become subject to issues of competition and the critical scrutiny of others.

Few who saw his watercolours in such a context would have been fully aware of the emotional and intellectual investment he made in them. Simply put, this is because landscape of this sort was for Ruskin never merely to be admired and celebrated: it was also to be read. Scanning and analyzing it could bring lessons about geology, botany, history, society, self-knowledge, faith and numerous other subjects; in this way, looking at such a phenomenon was for him purposeful, informative and elevating. He had articulated many of these insights through his eloquent, poetic, written commentaries on nature – but with his drawings and watercolours, textual analysis and the creation of images fused – and became a conduit for determining what was both beautiful and instructive.

His passion for geology in particular was profound and certainly not that of a dilettante.[19] Ruskin had been attracted to the subject as a child (when he had with characteristic precocity attempted to write a dictionary of minerals); this led him to study it as an undergraduate and become a Fellow of the Geological Society, where he delivered a number of papers. Although he was comfortable operating in such a formal, scientific context, for Ruskin the formation of the earth and the awesome forces that had shaped it were never explained by rational analysis alone: like many contemporaries he saw the natural world as an expression of divine purpose and a glorious form of revelation that could be interpreted. He had been particularly influenced by the writings of William Buckland, who sought through his theories to form a consistent bridge between Biblical authority and modern earth sciences. Ruskin's religious convictions were later to be undermined, like those of so many in the wake of Darwinism, but at this moment, in 1857, they remained firm.

In addition to all these overlapping layers of meaning, Ruskin felt that the study of landscape

FIG. 2.8
Frederick Hollyer
John Ruskin (1819–1900), c. 1894
Platinotype
Victoria and Albert Museum,
London (7603-1938)

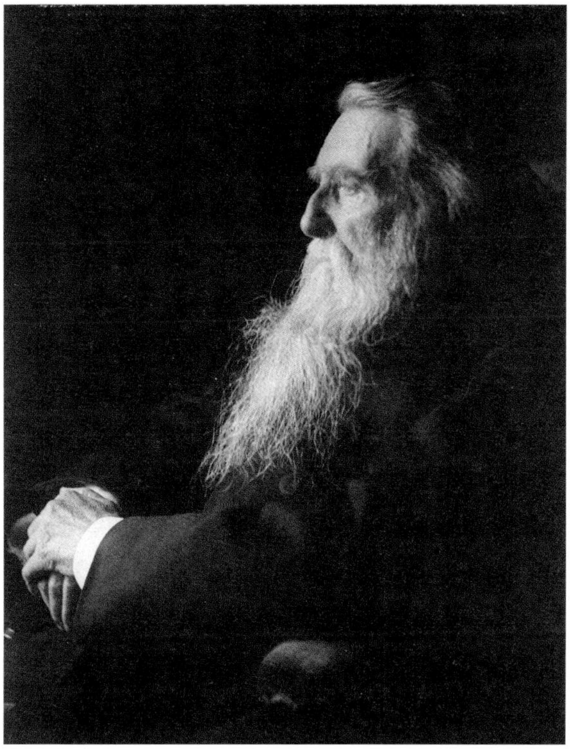

and geology could be used to understand the forging of human history. In this respect he was following other recent writers: for example, Charles Lyell, who noted in his *Principles of Geology* of 1830: "we find inseparably connected the geographical boundaries of a great state, the language now spoken by the inhabitants, their peculiar manners, laws and religious opinions."[20] Ruskin applied such analysis to his reading of Scottish landscapes in particular, and saw them as a key to the country's formation and identity, and therefore at least partially a means of explaining his own. He wrote: "The essential character of Scotland is that of a wild and thinly inhabited rocky country, not sublimely mountainous, but beautiful in low rock and light streamlet everywhere ... This wild land ... has an infinitely tragic feudal, pastoral, and civic history. And in the events of that history a deep tenderness of sentiment is mingled with a cruel and barren rigidity of habitual character, accurately corresponding to the conditions of climate and earth."[21]

Here Ruskin viewed the land through a heartfelt but simplistic prism, hinting at his love of heroism and romance, as well as his profound conservatism. The inevitable consequence of such a worldview was that he did not want Scotland to alter, or for what he perceived as its essential characteristics to be lost. This concern for preservation took different forms. It was expressed through his fears that industrialization was eroding rural life, craft traditions were being forgotten, traditional music was disappearing, and tourists were changing the character of favourite haunts, such as Loch Katrine (which had been sanctified by Scott's narrative poem *Lady of the Lake*).[22] Ruskin did not seem to recognize any irony in the fact that he was one of the most assiduous cultural travellers of the nineteenth century when damning others for their intrusion.

This yearning for conserving the values and fabric of historic societies was paralleled by Ruskin's views of other parts of Europe and its decadence – perhaps most especially, Venice. They also echoed the views expressed by Thomas Carlyle, the distinguished Scottish historian and essayist who settled in London and who, among the complex skein of ideas he developed, espoused social responsibility and condemned the onslaught of materialism. Ruskin and Carlyle enjoyed mutual respect, although they did not always agree,[23] as Carlyle, although he valued portraits, did not consider art a worthy subject for serious discourse. They may not have been allies over aesthetic matters, but were linked by their affection for Scotland, which was especially intense as the country was viewed and remembered by both men from afar.

The Killiecrankie watercolour was to be the last of Ruskin's major Scottish studies and, somewhat sadly, his late, highly expressive forms of drawing were not applied to Scotland's landscapes. By contrast, Millais produced a series of grand painted essays exploring the Scottish scenes that Ruskin had introduced him to. Although Ruskin did not depict Scotland again, he visited one last time, in the autumn of 1883,[24] and this prompted affectionate reminiscences: "I can never hear the whispering and sighing of the [River] Tweed among his pebbles, but it brings back to me the song of my nurse."[25] On this occasion he travelled from the home he had established at Brantwood, by Coniston Water in the Lake District. The latter part of his life was acted out there in some respects as though he was the head of a Scottish household in exile.[26] The reading of Scott's works once again became a regular activity; it provided a route through which Ruskin could return privately and imaginatively to his cosseted early years and be reminded of his heritage. Such reassurance was probably especially welcome as he became increasingly troubled by physical frailty and mental illness.

All of the different overlapping aspects of Ruskin's immersion in Scottish life and landscapes are a potent example of the modern discipline of "cultural geography," which seeks to define and study the consequences of human relationships developed with particular places. Ruskin would never have used such terminology, but he clearly cherished his Scottish connections and utilized them in a sophisticated, layered way to explore both scientific enquiries into the land itself and highly emotive views of its history and culture. Drawing and painting in watercolour were key means for him to define both.

In September 1894, six years before the end of his life, Ruskin was portrayed in a mesmeric photograph by Frederick Hollyer (fig. 2.8). He appears as a prophet or seer with a steady stare, fixed upon the world beyond the window. The photograph was titled *Datur hora quieti* (An hour given to quiet) – a reference to a poem by Scott that opens with the line "The sun upon the lake is low, The wild birds hush their song." The image acts as a haunting emblem that refers both to the artist's enduring appreciation of Scottish culture and his intense scrutiny of the mysteries of nature.

NOTES

1 Ruskin 1903–12, vol. 5, *Modern Painters III*, p. 365.
2 Ruskin 1903–12, vol. 35, *Præterita and Dilecta*, p. 39.
3 Ruskin 1903–12, vol. 3, *Modern Painters I*, pp. 402–405 and pp. 453–455. See also Baker 2011, pp. 355–356.
4 For the various formative influences on Ruskin as a draftsman, see Walton 1972, pp. 5–45.
5 Ruskin 1956, vol. 1, p. 362.
6 Ruskin 1903–12, vol. 3, *Modern Painters I*, p. 617.
7 "Exhibition of the Royal Academy," *The Times*, London, 3, 13 and 26 May 1851.
8 Effie Gray, quoted in Lutyens 1967, p. 37.
9 For the opening up of Scotland to artistic curiosity in the nineteenth century, see Edinburgh 1978.
10 For the creation of the portrait and this entire episode, see Grieve 1996, republished in Hewison 2000.
11 John Ruskin, quoted in Lutyens 1967, p. 247.
12 Ruskin 1903–12, vol. 6, *Modern Painters IV*, p. 150.
13 Ruskin 1903–12, vol. 12, *Lectures on Architecture and Painting, Etc.*, pp. 157–158.
14 See London Washington 1993, pp. 131–138.
15 Hilton 1985b, pp. 196–198.
16 Fox Talbot 1844, p. 33. See also Houston Canberra London 1989, pp. 12–14.
17 September 1844, www.queenvictoriasjournals.org.
18 Ruskin 1903–12, vol. 27, *Fors Clavigera, Letters 1–36*, pp. 594–595.
19 For a recent discussion of this, see Cambridge New Haven 2009, pp. 68–70.
20 Lyell 1847, p. 1.
21 Ruskin 1903–12, vol. 22, *Lectures on Landscape, Michael Angelo & Tintoret, The Eagle's Nest, Ariadne Florentina, with Notes for Other Oxford Lectures*, p. 38.
22 Walton 2000, pp. 70–71, and note 13.
23 For the nature of the relationship between the two men, see Hilton 2000, pp. 32–37.
24 Ibid. pp. 475–476.
25 Ruskin 1903–12, vol. 29, *Fors Clavigera, Letters 73–96*, p. 449.
26 Hilton 2000, p. 426.

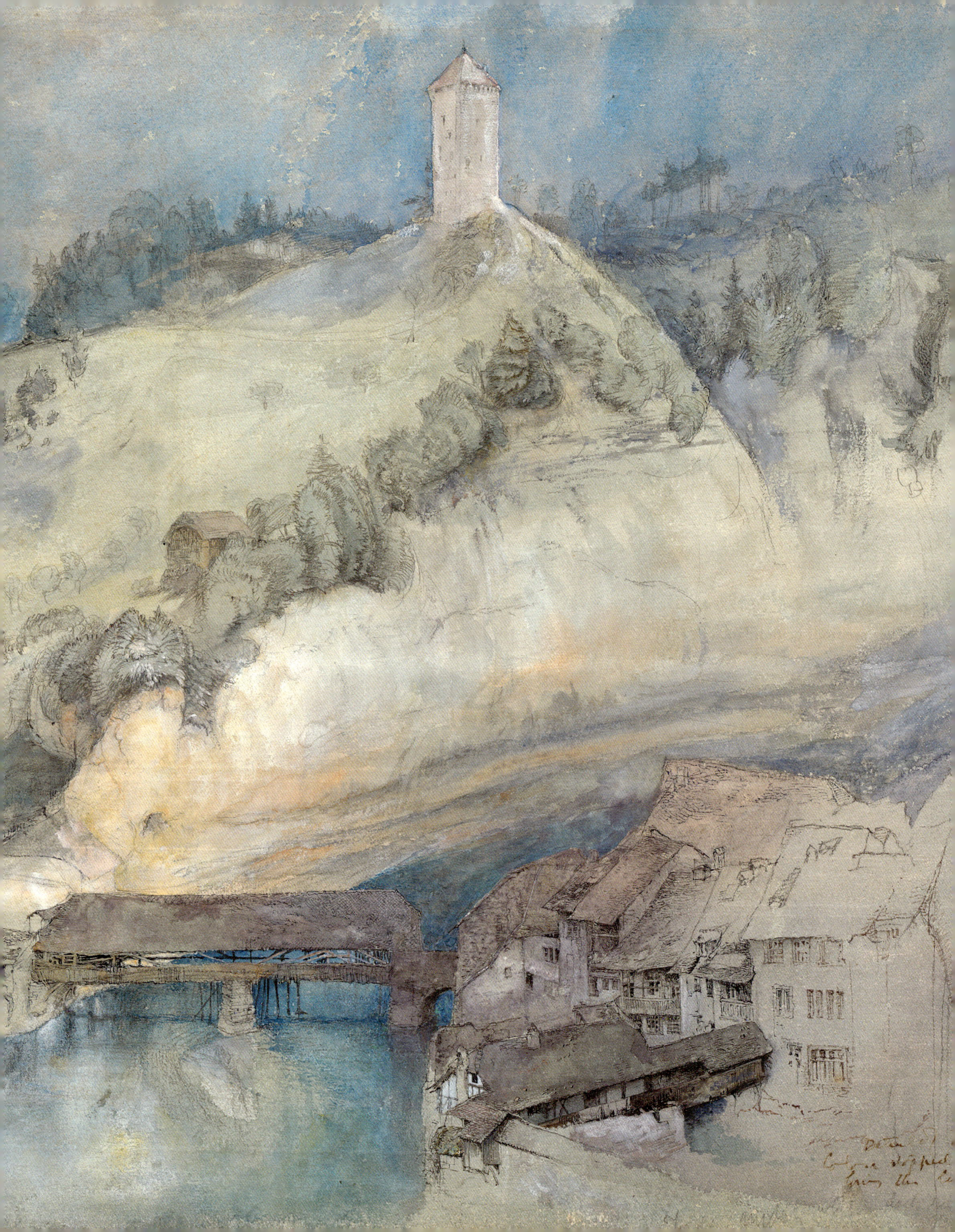

Ruskin as Artist: Seeing and Feeling

CONAL SHIELDS

"The whole function of the artist in the world is to be a seeing and feeling creature; to be an instrument of such tenderness and sensitiveness, that no shadow, no hue, no line, no instantaneous and evanescent expression of the visible things around him, nor any of the emotions which they are capable of conveying to the spirit which has been given him, shall either be left unrecorded, or fade from the book of record." (*The Stones of Venice III*, Ruskin 1903–12, vol. II, p. 49)

ON 22 OCTOBER 1866 John Ruskin wrote to his friend the Reverend Daniel Moore: "I have made no drawings at any time but for notes of fact: never for pleasure of sketching – so that I have had great difficulty in finding one that seemed the least fit for presentation to you. Nor can I ever conceive any one's taking pleasure in my imperfect work." The letter, though, did accompany the gift of a large watercolour of Belinzona, and Ruskin continued, "however the sketch I send looks pretty well at a distance, and it is of an interesting scene enough – in its own way."[1]

This playing down of purpose and the mix of diffidence about his abilities with a claim to some degree of artistic virtue is entirely typical of Ruskin. Moreover, while modesty sometimes became downright self-denigration he could, on occasion, assert his superiority as a draftsman. Indeed, Ruskin knew that the making of visual images lay at the very centre of his existence. Where we would expect him to write "understand" or "grasp' or "think," we often find the word "see."[2] It was first and foremost by means of the eye that Ruskin studied the world around him, and there is good reason to say that it was in the act of drawing that most, perhaps all, of his ideas became truly tangible to him.

Today the common notion of Ruskin is rather unattractive. He is supposed to have been not just intellectually transgressive but dogmatic, authoritarian and preachy, mentally disturbed, a sentimentalist in public and emotionally constrained, even terminally costive, in private. He has appeared in television plays as a dour spoilsport, with the mien of a Victorian funeral director and the manners of a bailiff. There was much in Ruskin's character and in his behaviour at home and at large to support such a view. But, on abundant evidence, he was also a man of huge spiritual and practical generosity, ready to change his mind when given reason to do so, and no less preoccupied with what he took to be the welfare of his fellows on this earth than with the satisfaction of his own wishes and needs.

To put it mildly, Ruskin was a complex creature. He had a breadth and depth of thought that seemed to those of his contemporaries who venerated him and also to those who contemned him wholly extraordinary. And a vast literary output, together with his correspondence, also on a grand scale, and his diaries, testify to the emotional extremes with which he was both blessed and cursed. Though much of Ruskin's artwork was intended for publication, he was not in the contemporary view a professional artist. He drew what he wished to draw. Virtually every day of his long life Ruskin sat down to draw and paint. His private needs no less than his public purposes were his motivation, and we may legitimately look to his

Cat. 45, detail

biography for clues to the sorts of satisfaction art enabled him to achieve.

Ruskin's first biographer, W.G. Collingwood, insisted on the crucial importance of Ruskin's upbringing, which was both curious and bizarre.[3] He was kept for several years in almost cloistral seclusion: he had few playfellows and few play things. Punishment for childish mistakes and minor misdemeanours was prompt and harsh. And yet almost from the beginning Ruskin was treated by his parents as a phenomenon, encouraged to write and made to declaim of an evening, and often it seems exhibited to admiring adult visitors.

Ruskin was educated almost entirely at home. His parents were fervent evangelicals and for a while intended their son to become a Church dignitary, a mainstay of the evangelical branch of Protestantism. At a time when religious beliefs of every kind were under close critical scrutiny, they were strict adherents to a rather narrow set of biblical doctrines. Bible reading was the central feature of each day and the turn of the Bible's last page meant a return to the first. He was soon composing sermons. The exhortation "People, be good," with which he concluded one childish sermon, now as an aesthetic principle, now a political goal or a social imperative, pops up again and again in Ruskin's career. Yet there were also daily readings from Byron. This is surprising, for to most contemporaries the poet's way of life was the stuff of scandal and his poetry a challenge to establishment values. Sir Walter Scott, too, figured largely on the book list. Along with the Bible, these authors remained important to Ruskin for the rest of his life, and there are many signs of their contribution to his thought. From the Bible Ruskin derived much of his language, his prophetic tone, his hope of epiphany and his dread of apocalypse. From Byron came a good deal of his sardonic humour and, perhaps, some part of his readiness to run counter to received opinion and accepted views of intellectual decorum. Scott was probably the principal source of his historical sensibility, while from Homer, Dante and Shakespeare Ruskin learnt most of what he knew about human psychology.

If there was relief from the pressures of his family, the rigours of the Christian regimen and a thoroughgoing programme of mathematics, Greek and Latin, it seems that this came from versifying and drawing and the pursuit of what was then designated natural philosophy, the earth sciences, and especially geology. Ruskin realized in his thirties that he was no poet, but drawing, and eventually painting in watercolour, became a prime medium for expression and intellectual development. Throughout his life, the making of visual constructs was a major part of a hectic public career as a teacher and critic and as often as not assumed a leading role in his presentation of himself to friends and acquaintances.

Ruskin's father John James' cultural aspirations included fine art – he had been a pupil of the landscape painter Alexander Nasmyth – and he was already a picture collector of note by the time of his son's birth. In particular he bought works by J.M.W. Turner, whom Ruskin came to venerate for most of his own artistic career: the reasons for his veneration were prone to significant change but always remained powerful. In addition, some rather less controversial masters of art were available to him, all of them represented on the walls of the family homes, and several of them were actually called in to instruct the young tyro.

The list of Ruskin's early mentors and models is not long but the influence of these was deep and never entirely abated. Some of his first efforts were derived from book illustrations by George Cruikshank, and when Ruskin himself undertook the instruction of neophytes he unhesitatingly commended the illustrator as an example of economical and right draftsmanship, even calling him the equal of Rembrandt. Ruskin's enthusiasm is worth noting because graphic spontaneity and wit, often displayed in his lectures and a striking element of his correspondence, are never sought in his art and certainly ought to be.

Under the influence of Samuel Prout, principally, Ruskin took on the mindset of the Picturesque movement, with its taste for asymmetry, irregularity and rough surfaces, its fondness for "humble" subject matter, and its willingness to deal in the specifics of plants and buildings rather than to tendentiously idealize. The Picturesque is usually treated merely as a chapter in the story of style, but it arose in particular historical circumstances – the industrialization of town and country – that were increasingly meaningful to Ruskin. The movement is better regarded as a celebration of pre-industrial values and an assertion of common humanity. Prout's elaborately detailed treatments of landscape and architecture, his acceptance of the signs of time and the accidents of place, and not least his peculiar dot and carry (or dot and dash) pencil and crayon manner were comprehensively adopted by Ruskin.

From David Roberts, Ruskin tells us, he learnt "the use of the fine point instead of the blunt one; attention and indefatigable correctness of detail; and the simplest means of expressing ordinary light and shade on grey ground, flat wash for the full shadows, and heightening of the gradated lights by warm white."[4] The intricacies of contemporary watercolour technique were passed on by Anthony Vandyke Copley Fielding of the Society of Painters in Water Colours, and doubtless it was from this gentleman's teaching that Ruskin familiarized himself with the extensive repertory of nineteenth-century landscape composition. John Duffield Harding, an accomplished draftsman and the author of influential instructional texts, refined Ruskin's understanding of tree forms, especially foliage. More importantly, Harding may well have helped to crystallize many of Ruskin's views about the relationship between visual art and the world it purported to represent.

Ruskin was taught by several artists in person, ranging from the mechanically proficient to the truly gifted. Charles Runciman versed him in perspective, though Ruskin was often cavalier about formal perspective systems. Prout became an acquaintance and advisor, was copied by his protégé and, once at least, returned the compliment (Prout's *Palazzo Contarini Fasan on the Grand Canal, Venice* [1841, fig. 3.1], was his version of a drawing lent by Ruskin). Copley Fielding and Harding, who were professional teachers, each had Ruskin as a pupil.

However, the most consequential of Ruskin's mentors, without a doubt, was Turner. Ruskin regarded this not-so-old master as supremely knowledgeable and surpassingly clever. From the

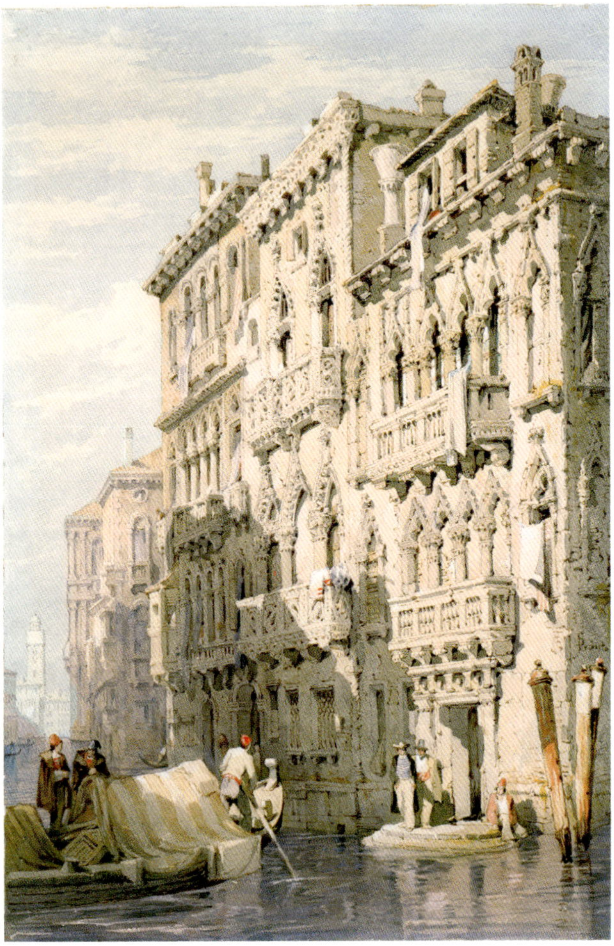

FIG. 3.1
Samuel Prout
Palazzo Contarini Fasan on the Grand Canal, Venice, early 19th century
Watercolour
Victoria and Albert Museum, London. Ashbee Bequest (1732–1900)

moment funds were available to him, Ruskin became a major collector of Turner's work in all media, and expended much time and effort on its examination and analysis. Turner was the great constant, revelatory and mystifying in equal measure. At whatever stage he had reached in his artistic development Ruskin was prone to set his performances against Turner's, usually finding himself more or less inadequate, but somehow finding the will to continue.

It is of crucial significance that during his formative years Ruskin did not come into direct contact with the Renaissance and post-Renaissance mainstream tradition of Western European picture-making and, especially, draftsmanship. His conceptual apparatus and his pictorial methodology never really came to terms with the ideals of balance, formal continuity and general coherence that are commonplace in that tradition. Eventually Ruskin did discover a handful of painters quite outside his original frame of reference, foremost among them Tintoretto and Titian, who were of value to him largely for the affective power of their colour. Albrecht Dürer, a Renaissance outsider, with his devotion to the quirkily distinctive in his art, was also an admired exemplar.

Although indications of Ruskin's artistic sources are usually clear throughout his career, particularly Ruskinian attributes can be found from the start, and quite soon there appeared in his work remarkable qualities that are of compelling interest. For instance, a drawing of 1832 inscribed by Ruskin "My First tree from nature" (fig. 3.2) already shows a marked attention to outline, to the boundaries of things, as peculiarly informative about their character. Such attention is to be found to some degree in most of his visual imagery but is strikingly present during the first decades of his career.

Ruskin's pencil drawing of Roslin[5] Chapel (1838, cat. 1) was made when he was just nineteen-years old. Already certain distinctive characteristics of the artist are evident. The perspective of the scene is fairly systematically laid out, with a couple of anomalies, but this is a relatively marginal aspect, and supposed position in space does not affect the degree of attention paid to details. What really concerned Ruskin here was the intricacy of the sculptural decoration and the condition of the architecture. Every part, starting with the conjoined capitals on the left, has been examined and represented with intense care for its individuality. The movements of the artist's hand lovingly echoed

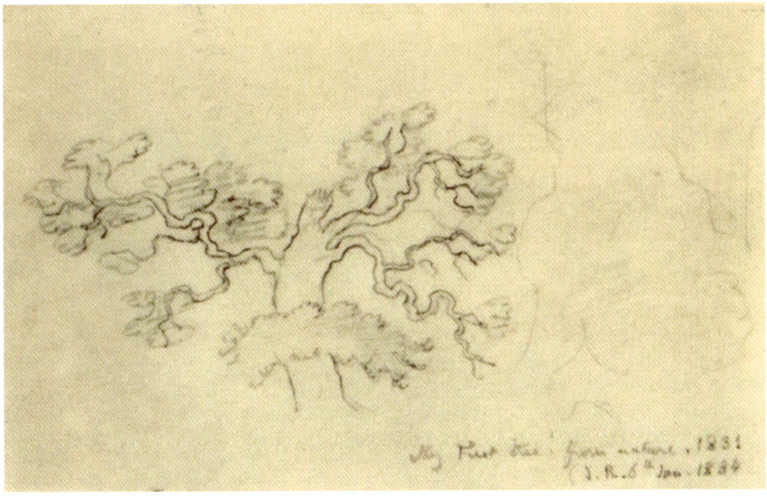

FIG. 3.2
John Ruskin
My First Tree from Nature, 1831
Graphite on paper
Private collection

the gestures of the masons as they revealed within the stone a wealth of plant and animal forms, so that this is very much an account of real people in action rather than a dispassionate report on a piece of historical wreckage. The differences between the architectural members are painstakingly laid down, and wear and tear, the effects of time and use, are patently of prime significance.

The drawing was made in a piecemeal, episodic manner, one element taken as far as the artist could take it before another was tackled. Such a picaresque sequence of events remained Ruskin's procedure virtually to the end.[6] Prout, whom Ruskin had admired since viewing his volume of lithographs *Facsimiles of Sketches Made in Flanders and Germany* in 1833, is obviously the model, but an extreme sensitivity to edge, to the boundaries of things, is very much Ruskin's own. For many years it was by the tracing of contour that Ruskin was in the first instance able to seize what he saw as the essentials of an object or scene, consideration of other aspects then following on. Long after making his drawing of Roslin Chapel, Ruskin acquired a drawing that he labelled "Early sketch by Turner at Chester. From my own collection."[7] This was made in just the same additive mode as the Roslin work, and it is easy to imagine Ruskin inspecting Turner's handiwork here and identifying his own preoccupations and skills with those of the youthful virtuoso.

Ruskin's own accumulation of experience and development of skills was impressive. He was, it seems, ever ready to examine and cross-examine his motives and purposes in art and to consider minutely the means available to him. He continuously placed what he believed he should be doing and his grasp of how it could be done in the context of other artists' behaviour. Before long, Turner – the artist who had, indeed, been an exponent of the Picturesque but had eventually taken on what Ruskin believed to be the most momentous themes and topics that art could accommodate – attracted him hugely.

For his thirteenth birthday Ruskin was presented by a business partner of his father with a copy of Samuel Rogers' lengthy poem *Italy*, illustrated by Turner, among others. It was probably the moment when his engagement with the most comprehensively talented of all English artists began. If the beginning was a small one it quickly grew. Ruskin found the engravings after Turner's richly filled watercolour vignettes enchanting and made his own vignettes in the Turnerian manner. But he soon felt himself obliged to take a broader view when an attack on Turner was mounted in *Blackwood's Magazine*, and he wrote, though was not allowed to publish, an angry essay on the great man's virtues. From this moment, Ruskin placed Turner at the centre of the art world. He met his idol in 1841 and from then on had several

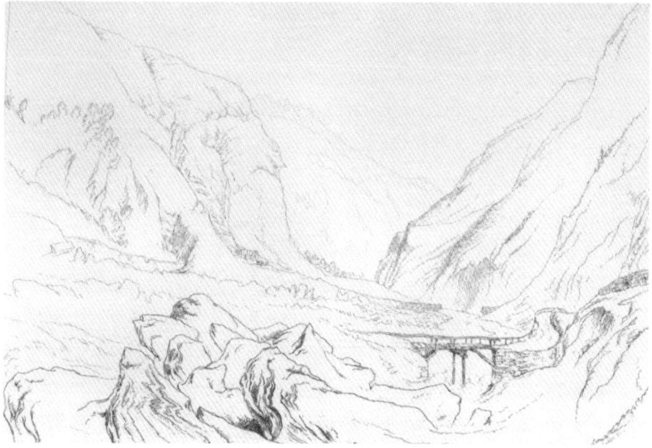

FIG. 3.3
John Ruskin
The Pass of Faido: Simple Topography
From *Modern Painters*, vol. 4,
Library Edition, plate 20

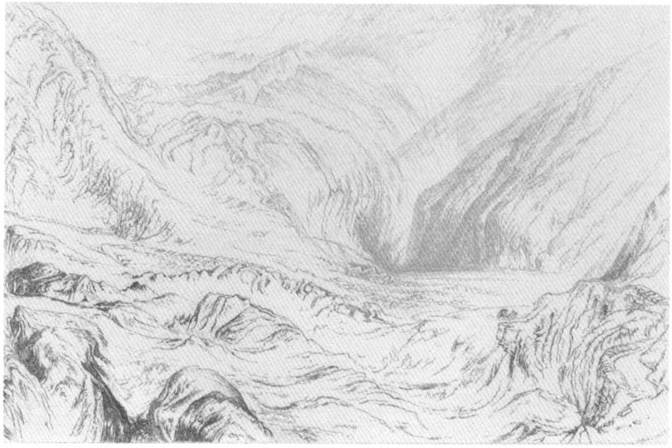

FIG. 3.4
after J.M.W. Turner
The Pass of Faido: Turnerian Topography
From *Modern Painters*, vol. 4,
Library Edition, plate 21

opportunities to discuss, or at any rate, talk about, Turner's work with the man himself.

Between 1843 and 1860 the five volumes of *Modern Painters* – Ruskin's apologia for Turner – appeared. These elaborately argued texts amount to what is in many respects the most thoroughgoing investigation any painter had undergone (and, some of us would say, it has yet to be equalled). Ruskin began by claiming that Turner was, in his landscapes, more true to nature than any of his predecessors or contemporaries. And he went on, with frequent excursions into biblical exegesis, sociology and politics, to explain how, via a distinctive personal philosophy and an imaginative appropriation of history, mythology and science-like speculation, Turner had made art a vehicle for the understanding of some of the most difficult problems – right and wrong as embodied by the visual world, awareness of the past, and personal identity.

In the course of his argument Ruskin looked with considerable critical acumen into the mechanisms of image-making, the manner in which external reality is perceived and the ways in which it might be purposefully depicted. He knew that pencil or pen marks and brushstrokes could never exactly match what artists supposed they saw – the most brilliant of modern pigments were drab when held up to, for instance, a sunlit sky. Thus, in a sense, all art was symbolic. It was a matter of finding, or inventing, equivalents for things "seen" and not of mere reproduction. And, as Turner believed, the traffic between the artist and his subject was two-way: external reality fed an internal nature shaped by thought and feeling. In a key section of the fourth volume of *Modern Painters* Ruskin explained that Turner in his *Pass of Faido* had altered the topography to take account of the viewer's expectations and to inscribe on the landscape an appropriate emotional state (see figs. 3.3 and 3.4).[8]

By following what he supposed was Turner's procedure Ruskin on a number of occasions tried to invoke and inhabit Turner's mental processes. To compare Ruskin's *Amalfi* of 1841 (fig. 3.5) with his version of 1844 (fig. 3.6) is to witness Ruskin reversing his normal practice. Instead of accumulating finely tuned responses to particular stimuli, he laid down a sequence of broad statements in the hope that the salient points of the scene would emerge, spontaneously, from the depths of memory and that something akin to Turner's evocation of atmosphere would become possible. But it never worked like this for Ruskin. He required, as he had to admit more than once, specific prompts to his eye and mind, and only

FIG. 3.5
John Ruskin
Amalfi, 1841
Watercolour on paper
Ruskin Foundation (Ruskin Library, Lancaster University) (RF 856)

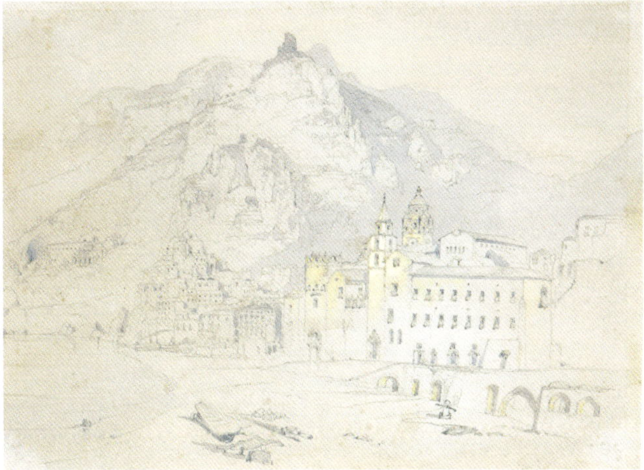

actual objects could supply these. It is one of the great ironies of art history that the most devoted, and most intelligent, of Turner's admirers could never quite tease out from the closest investigation of his works the processes that had produced them. The later *Amalfi* is still a good deal tidier than a typical Turnerian lay-in.

Ruskin was familiar with the description of Turner creating his watercolour of *A First Rate Taking in Stores* (1818), saturating the paper with paint in a confusion of blobs and blots and only gradually resolving these into recognizable forms. But this was not how Ruskin's mind worked. At least once, with his transcript of part of a sky, *Study of Clouds in Turner's "Campo Santo, Venice"* (cat. 103), Ruskin attempted to adopt Turner's actual handling: but, again, the movement of Turner's hand was an awkward fit for Ruskin's trains of thought.

Increasingly, as he sifted through Turner's immense output, Ruskin became aware of a dichotomy in himself, which his great predecessor had, he recognized, risen above – sensitivity to the particular interfered with or even stymied the wish to grasp things, to incorporate the bits and pieces of everyday experience into powerful generalizations. The struggle to reconcile his most acute sensibilities and sophisticated skills with a desire to pontificate largely is reflected in a letter of 1843 to his former tutor at Oxford, William Brown. Here he considered at length the contrasting attitudes and literary strategies of William Wordsworth and Samuel Taylor Coleridge. While the two poets agreed that poetry must eschew flummery and speak out as simply and directly as possible, Coleridge, as Ruskin said, let "the fine brains which God gave him work themselves irregularly

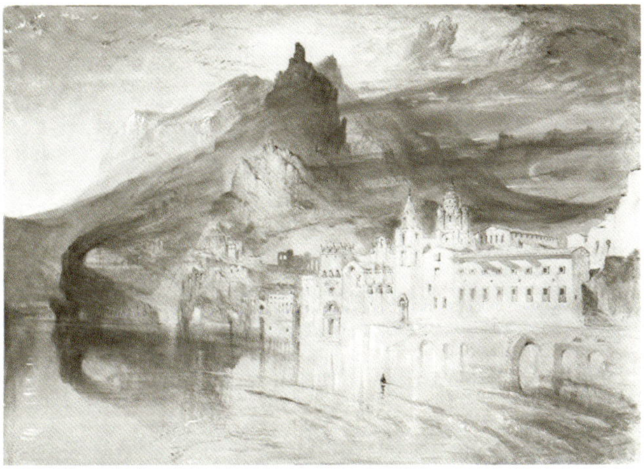

Fig. 3.6
John Ruskin
View of Amalfi, 1844
Watercolour and gouache over graphite on brown wove paper
Harvard Art Museums/Fogg Museum. Gift of Mr. and Mrs. Philip Hofer (1959.113)

and without end or object – and carry him whither they will," and Wordsworth had "a grand – consistent – perfectly disciplined – all grasping intellect for which nothing is too small – nothing too great – arranging everything in due relations."[9] Ruskin was Coleridgean by inclination but hoped ultimately to be of Wordsworth's party.

But the methods that were manageable to Ruskin did yield extraordinary results. And since Ruskin's art has been, in the main, ignored or treated casually – despite the discernible references to his precedents – these results are utterly distinctive. Harding was respected for his mastery of arboreal articulation, but Ruskin's trees have a kind and degree of mastery that leaves the former in the shade. Compare *Stone Pines at Sestri, Gulf of Genoa* (1845, cat. 113) with any of the tree specimens from the treatises of Harding that Ruskin knew. Where Harding invariably moves toward generic types, Ruskin starts and finishes with a sense of extreme individuality. The overlays of pen and wash indicate that the central pine was done first, its minute shifts of angle and its varying textures taken together. Only then did the artist, in episodic fashion, assemble its context, subtly altering his touch, with very visible nervous excitement, so as to capture the special character of each element. By the standards of the day this is hardly a composition. Working alongside Harding in Italy during 1845 Ruskin noted that his companion produced "pictures" whereas he drew "bits." But Ruskin's drawing does have a narrative – it is the story of how he perceived and felt about a sequence of events in physical nature. And there is, too, rhythmic unity as the curves of branch and rock interact across the sheet. To borrow a phrase from Cardinal Newman, the image is "directly tentative and of an empirical character,"[10] but it is certainly not naïve.

Harding's *Principles and Practices of Art* (1845) suggests, somewhat like William Hogarth with his serpentine line, that in a curve of unequal quantities and varying directions lies fundamental beauty, and Ruskin seems to have accepted the notion both for the depiction of detail and for the linkage of parts to the whole. Indeed, rhythmic relationships, rather than relationships of mass, are frequently the binding element in Ruskin's visual art.

Throughout the period of his early maturity Ruskin's experience grew steadily and his skills developed to accommodate it. That sensitivity to shape as the chief indicator of character was joined, somewhat fitfully, by an awareness of substance and a concern with structure, and eventually the ways in which light helps to define form began to fascinate him. The niceties of picture-making were of little relevance and, indeed, he regarded the customary representational devices, assumptions about what marks were appropriate to the depiction of a given subject, as usually obstructing the vital business of the artist, which was to see clearly, to understand what was being looked at, and to pass on understanding effectively. The visible world contained a wealth of "facts," no doubt, but it also enshrined the history of mankind's intellect, was filled with emotional associations and could, if shrewdly investigated, contribute at the highest level to a grasp of the major forces shaping man's fate and, moreover, provide a route into meaningful self-analysis.

Crossmount, Perthshire: Study of Crag, Tree and Thistle (cat. 71 and fig. 3.7) is a strikingly clear

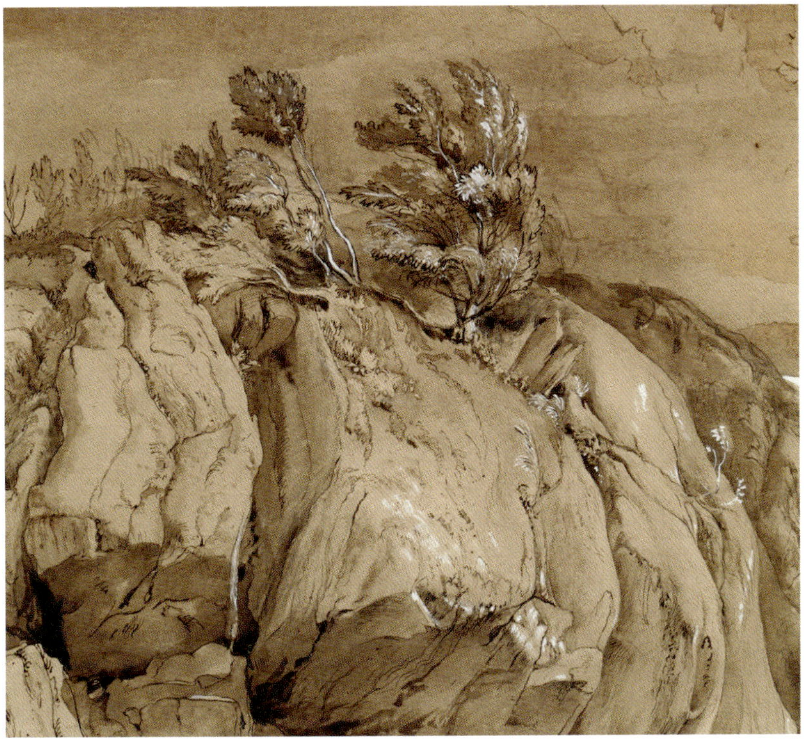

FIG. 3.7
John Ruskin
Crossmount, Perthshire; Study of Crag, Tree and Thistle, 1847
(cat. 71, detail)

example of Ruskin's fluent draftsmanship, but its emotional purport may be a little harder to discern. The succession of marks shows that the artist began by touching in the portion of rock at the top centre of the sheet and outlining the plants emerging from it. As his hand moved down and sideways from these, pencil was exchanged for pen and then brush. After the application of washes of fluctuating intensity there were localized bouts of further activity with the pen, and a white watercolour-laden brush was brought on to define the brightest of the features. It is almost an account of Ruskin's technical evolution: he proceeded from boundary-demarcation, through textural play, to indices of substance and spatial position. Ruskin's appetite for differentiation is unmissable. No aspect of the rock-pile is quite the same as another. The drawing, nonetheless, manages to convey simultaneously a vast quantity of highly specific information and an impression of mass and weight. The sky, added toward the end of the process, patently rehearses the procedure of the principal components.

According to his father, Ruskin was a geologist before he was anything else. Geology was an area of expertise in which his parents could not challenge him and, in adult life, it became one f the principal testing grounds of Ruskin's ability to make sense of his physical environment and a vehicle for the expression of intense feeling. He had probably turned to geology at first for assurance about the essential stability of natural phenomena: a search for stability – for the balancing-out of contrary conditions and the reconciling of mutually destructive pressures – was one of his lifelong goals. But scientists were increasingly discovering evidence of change on the most momentous scale. Ruskin was well aware of this. A member of the Geological Society and an enthusiastic reader of Charles Lyell, the artist was familiar with the major theories in the field including the established theory of metamorphism and the newer theory of glacial movement, which sought to explain the present appearance of mountains and valleys as the result of immense natural forces over a lengthy period.

Crossmount is an entirely appropriate embodiment of such a view.

The mood of *Crossmount* is sombre overall, though, on close inspection, imbued with nervous energy. It has been suggested that the personal circumstances in which the image was made are discernible as a subtext.[11] The drawing was made by Ruskin while en route to the home of the Gray family and considering a marriage proposal to the eldest daughter Euphemia (Effie). He had recently been attracted to Charlotte Lockhart, Sir Walter Scott's granddaughter, and was still prone to recollect his old longing for Adèle Domecq, the child of his father's business partner. In short, girls were on his mind, and, possibly, both the frustration of desire and the possible satisfaction of it figured strongly. Could there be an anthropomorphic aspect to the drawing, the rock forms subtly referring to the spread-eagled female body? That Ruskin could, whether or not deliberately, envisage human content within organic or inorganic nature is certain enough. In his fairy tale *The King of the Golden River* (1841), written for Effie Gray, some of the dramatis personae are transformed into rocks. And it was Ruskin who, in *Modern Painters*, coined the term "pathetic fallacy," but he was against the casual and inapt ascription of sentiment to natural phenomena rather than opposed to the identification of such phenomena with emotions and states of mind.[12] Despite his repeated claims to the contrary, any notion of Ruskin the artist as a dispassionate reporter is contradicted by virtually the entire corpus of his writings on art.

Ruskin is so frequently assumed to be a super "eye," a draftsman of high but somewhat anaesthetic mechanical excellence, a dispassionate observer, that it is proper to point out that the kinds of visualization with which he was preoccupied could not have evolved without imaginative effort and would not have been possible in the absence of powerful emotional impulses. For instance, it is improbable that Ruskin was in a straightforwardly objective state of mind when he made his breathtaking *Study of Gneiss Rock, Glenfinas* (cat. 76) while on a visit to Scotland in 1853. It was drawn as he sat on the stream's bank with the youthful John Everett Millais nearby, who was painting the background to his now famous portrait of Ruskin (fig. 2.5). Millais, as Ruskin must have been aware, was fascinated by Effie, who had married Ruskin in 1848. Far from enamoured in his turn, Ruskin may have welcomed the young man's attentions to his wife, and is anyway likely to have wanted to show that he knew his geology and could give the knowledge a compelling visual.

The very way in which Ruskin touched the paper provides a key to his emotionality. In the case of *Southwest Porch of St. Wulfran's, Abbeville* (cat. 4 and fig. 3.8), it seems at first sight brusquely assured. But careful examination reveals a tentativeness, an acceptance of the possibility of modification that goes to the heart of Ruskin's approach to art and, indeed, his reading of the world. Ruskin's dogmatism is constantly qualified and frequently dissolved. Gothic architecture is strongly patterned and recognition of this allowed Ruskin to seek out endless if tiny variants of form. Here in microcosm, perhaps, we can see why the medieval period so attracted him. It was, as far as he could tell, emphatically circumscribed by moral rules and regulations, yet permitted a significantly

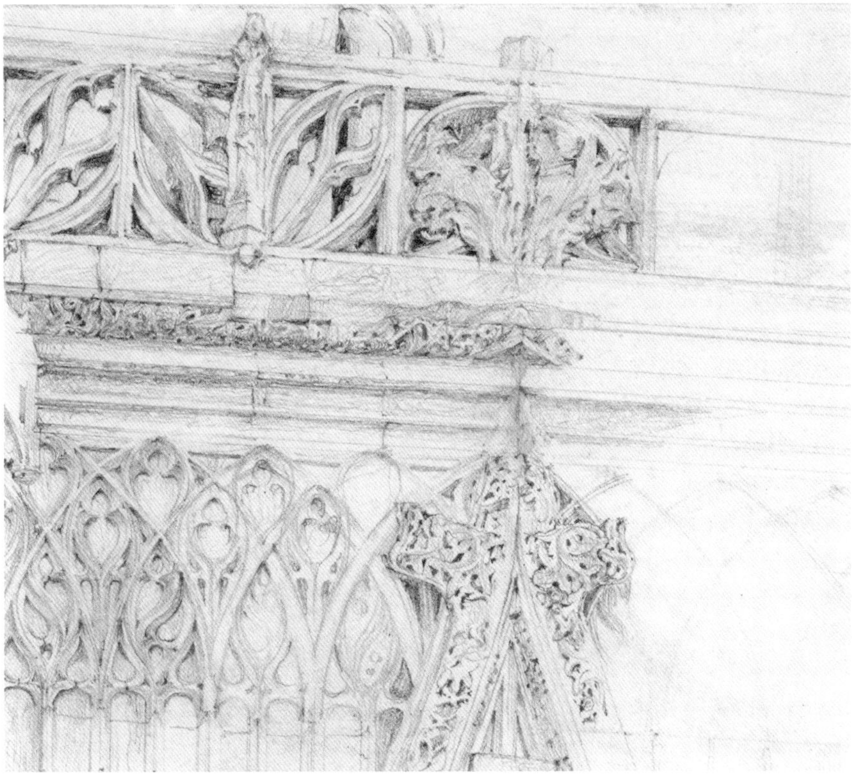

FIG. 3.8
John Ruskin
Southwest Porch of St. Wulfran's, Abbeville, 1848 (cat. 4, detail)

wide range of manoeuvre. Medieval artists/craftsmen were able to express their individuality just because they knew their limits. Comparison with the illustrations in the book from which Ruskin derived his basic knowledge of Gothic style, Robert Willis' *Remarks on the Architecture of the Middle Ages, Especially of Italy* (1835) shows how finely tuned were Ruskin's responses to every sign of the human hand in the supposedly anonymous edifices of Christianity.

Abbeville, where Ruskin drew the church of St. Wulfran, and where he first fully perceived the vital union of individual and community, was forever important to him. Other towns and cities in France, Germany, Switzerland and Italy stirred him, though England's cathedrals were excluded from his canon on the grounds, interestingly, of "discordant civility, or jarring vergerism."[13] It was Venice, however, that became the site of his most extensive and systematic examination of the medieval condition. Ruskin first visited the city of the Lagoon in 1835 and he returned repeatedly over the next forty years. Relatively few historical texts were available, but for Ruskin the buildings and their sculpted and painted decorations constituted the most meaningful evidence of how people in the past had thought, felt and behaved. His attention was concentrated by the dereliction of the Venetian palazzi and churches and what to him were ill-advised or utterly misconceived attempts at restoration. Ruskin said that his Venice was the Venice of Byron and Turner, the wreck of a once resplendent city republic, but while they were content to celebrate past glory and enjoy present decadence, Ruskin was filled with regret for a monumental fall from grace and angered by the failure of contemporaries to learn from history. The drawings he copiously produced during repeated visits run the gamut of his technical abilities and modes of perception.

Detailed, diagrammatic notes in pencil and pen were the basis of his Venetian researches. But brush in hand, he could imaginatively engage to the full with the rich detritus. His watercolour of the

Ca' d'Oro, Venice (cat. 22), for example, lifts off from the familiar architectural grillage into the sheerest visual poetry, where assonantal arches and rhyming medallions sing the joy of discovery, all features in mutual acknowledgment yet subtly individuated. The usual double-take is appropriate, since the tremulous touches of a brush now heavily loaded and now carrying little or no pigment, which embody acts of fresh perception by the dozen, only register on close reading. Here, though, separate studies of capitals show how far Ruskin had gone by the end of the 1840s toward a grasp of structure, as opposed to surface modulation. *Capital 36 of the Ducal Palace, Venice* (cat. 8) uses cast shadow to establish solidity. At last Ruskin could see in his mind's eye the back and front of an object simultaneously. Ruskin's procedure was usually an accumulation of specifics, but from around this date each item in a sequence had a notional connection with its fellows before marks were made.

It was while recording Venetian architectural detail in 1845 that Ruskin became interested in daguerreotypes. Although Ruskin claimed to have come across them early on in Oxford, it was in the Piazza San Marco, Venice, that he actually involved himself with the medium. Urgently recording with pencil and brush the capitals of the Ducal Palace, as masons knocked them around or replaced them with what he regarded as utterly misconceived restorative zeal, Ruskin noticed daguerreotypes on sale to tourists. From this moment on mechanical images were a constituent of Ruskin's worldview. Firstly in Venice and then elsewhere on his travels, daguerreotypes were produced for his own purposes, his valets being trained to use the unwieldy equipment.

By his own admission, Ruskin, who so rarely approached his subject matter within a mental framework of regular perspective constructions, had difficulty with estimating scale, the relative size of objects in space. But the daguerreotype short-circuited this problem for him. A letter written a few years later is relevant. "I am surprised to find," wrote Ruskin, "the terrible difficulty of putting things in their place, even approximately. Surely painters have not enough explained yet to their pupils the infinite way in which everything alters everything else: how what looked too short in outline will look too long in shade, and how a line which seems to slope too much on Wednesday, will slope too little on Thursday, merely because a greater slope has been put beside it. Quite three quarters of my work is in placing and in altering things placed."[14]

There were other advantages to photography, of course, though these were probably of lesser importance. The extensively represented detail of the medium must have seemed to endorse, and doubtless stimulated, Ruskin's fascination with the minutiae of what he looked at and must have been helpful, by its suppression of middle tones, when tonal range was being established. Ultimately, Ruskin came to believe that photography could not fully embody the sensations of the artist or allow the manipulation of motif when this was required. He continued, nevertheless, to derive information from daguerreotypes and its fellow types of photograph.

Ruskin was stimulated by the tools and materials he employed: pencils of different hardness allowed a degree of tentativeness in exploration; the pen answered a need for extreme precision; brushes, finely tipped or bushy, promoted a taste for textural play and gestural variety. It was during the 1850s that Ruskin reached his full artistic maturity, and a greater grasp of structure – the three-dimensionality of things – was accompanied by an enhanced appetite for varieties of surface and, at last, a willingness to try colour as more than a mere attribute of form.

The Elements of Drawing, which appeared in 1857, was ostensibly Ruskin's textbook for neophytes in art, and moreover was designed to sensitize the eye to natural fact rather than to produce artists. But the writing of this entailed a comprehensive review by the artist of his own technical equipment and of the purposes that he wished it to serve. This little volume shows his fascination with the tools and physical materials of art practice and with the processes, intellectual and emotional, of image-making. It amounts to a carefully assembled basic visual vocabulary and grammar. And his exemplifications of usage are imbued with feeling. Thus he advised his readers to study nature in its minutiae, looking for instance at a twig or a branching bough and analyzing its structure. He reminds us that these are living presences and the draftsman must detect their "leading lines,"[15] those that reveal a subject's development, its existence in time.

There are many pointers to Ruskin's own practice in *The Elements of Drawing*, and it seems that his discussions of handling, of decisive yet expressive touch, much affected his own art. The small watercolour of *Prunus Persica* (cat. 117), a flowering peach twig, is set down with full knowledge of its structure and in direct response to its tactility. Every glance at the twig and its blossom seems to have found a quick mix of pigments and a movement of the brush exquisitely expressive. Ruskin is usually missing from histories of botanical art. Yet for understanding of the complexities of plant form and sensitivity to colour and texture he is very nearly without peer. There are indications here of preparation for a semi-public role – the blue background was extended and signed and a mount with a cut-out to reveal the signature was made. And, in fact, the piece was given to Peter Bayne, a fierce advocate of the notion that modern science and biblical revelation could be reconciled, an acolyte of the Scottish geologist Hugh Miller.

Among the most thought through and complete of the drawings produced by Ruskin when mulling over the content of *The Elements of Drawing* is *In the Pass of Killiecrankie* (cat. 81). By contemporary standards this is hardly art: it has no discernible start or finish and is quite without pictorial decorum. But it perfectly embodies the mind of its maker. Wherever the eye alights it is directed, by marks of the brush that hint rather than state in any narrowly literalistic fashion, to adjacent areas, awareness of the quantity and quality of the whole emerging from continual scanning. Ruskin typically preferred to encourage the viewer to engage with his subject, and not to suppose that its hash had been settled by the artist.

In *The Elements of Drawing*, Ruskin touches on what was to him the quandary of composition, arrangement and order in a visual image. A large drawing that arose from his attempts to articulate the problematical in his art while he laid down rules for his readers, *The Bridge at Rheinfelden* (cat. 47 and fig. 3.9) is the adaptation of a Turnerian compositional scheme to his very individual needs. Turner's view of the bridge

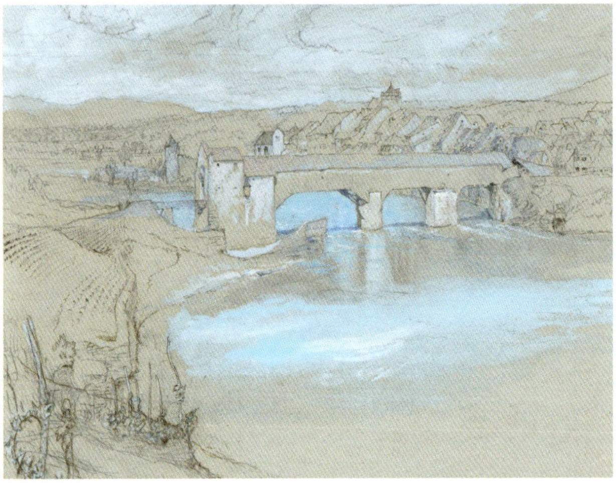

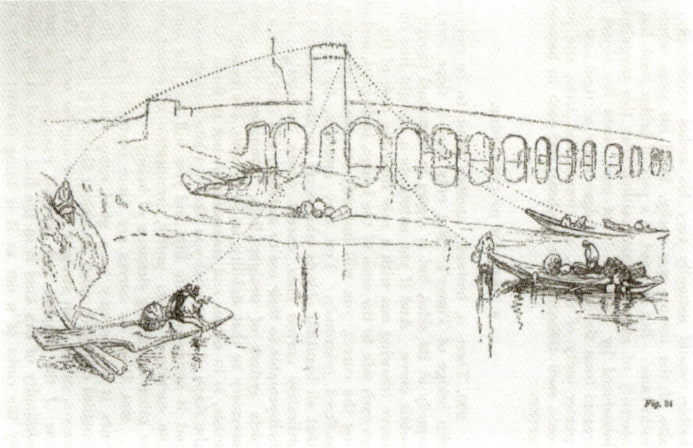

FIG. 3.9
John Ruskin
The Bridge at Rheinfelden, 1858
(cat. 47, detail)

FIG. 3.10
after J.M.W. Turner
The Law of Curvature, Illustrated from the Bridge in Turner's "Coblentz"
From *The Elements of Drawing*, Library Edition, plate 34

at Koblenz (fig. 3.10), we are told by Ruskin, focuses on the tower at the bridge's left side. And every major feature of the scene is related to this by a series of curves.[16]

Ruskin had come across Turner's "Coblentz" bridge and a group of drawings of Rheinfelden when sorting through the nearly 30,000 items of Turner's Bequest to the nation. Finding himself on the spot in 1858, Ruskin sought to test his reading of such a compositional scheme against Turner and the place itself. It is probable that Ruskin began with the tower – which in the Coblentz he had designated "the leading or master feature"[17]: but he seems then to have lightly indicated all the main lines of the scene rather than, as was his wont, adding one comprehensively detailed element after another. From time to time after this Ruskin tried to look and think holistically, to hold together in his mind as he drew the micro and the macro: it was, however, only in special circumstances that such a procedure was anything but effortful. How ready Ruskin was to concentrate on the specific and the minutely characteristic is indicated by a diary entry written just after his work in Rheinfelden: "Purple orchis gathered on hills on Baden side of Rhine last night. Stalk solid, round; small purple leaves springing from it, *a* disclose a twisted fleshy tube, *b* which inserts itself into the flower behind the spur, *c*...,"[18] and so on. It is worth noting that *The Bridge at Rheinfelden* was drawn with a fine line brush, an instrument that Ruskin often used for its expression of the artist's tremors of intent as well as for the sheer skill required. The process was invariably episodic, even when Ruskin tried to keep in mind the connectivity of all elements of his subject.

From the period of *The Elements of Drawing* on, Ruskin's art had a fluency and control as well as an emotional capacity that sets him among the greatest of English painters and draftsmen. Ruskin's full artistic maturity, indeed, has so fascinated his admirers that the relative neglect of his achievement is simply bewildering. During his forties and fifties Ruskin generated a series of works that were spectacularly accomplished and could have come from nobody else. The quest for Turner's secrets continued, and Turner was always the touchstone when self-criticism was in play, but Ruskin now apparently accepted that he must settle for his peculiar wants and his special competencies. When examining and organizing the items of the Turner Bequest in 1857 and 1858, Ruskin discovered new kinds of imagery, notably generalized statements that subsumed an abundance of information. He came to believe that what are today called "abstractions" were the most powerful of all accounts of natural phenomena, summarizing a wealth of observed fact. Confirming Turner's pre-eminence, these discoveries yet released Ruskin from thraldom and, not so paradoxically, encouraged him to go along a novel route.

Many of Ruskin's visual works that emerged from this period depart radically from conventional pictorial procedure. But there is a peculiar logic to them, and once their premises have been accepted they have compelling narrative force and reveal numerous incidental beauties. Always the subjects chosen arise from and minister to the preoccupations of Ruskin's everyday existence. The large watercolours of Fribourg (cats. 41, 43 and 45) were part of his attempt to imagine himself as an inhabitant of the mountainous regions that had since 1835 engaged his affection, while, to an extent, they also satisfied his curiosity about the ways in which large and small aspects of the natural world and human artefacts interconnected. There are in these no signposted starting points, there is no pre-determined clutch of visual priorities. Alight where it will, the eye is momentarily caught by the extreme nicety of the brushwork, the preciousness of perception and handling, with no feature routinely seen – notice how every window differs slightly from its neighbour – and when a certain reticence in the description of a part is noticed the eye moves on, seeking confirmation of what has turned out to be a matter of hints rather than completist reportage, and delighting in the constantly varying signs of the artist's hand and indications of his perceptual liveliness.

Daguerreotypes were used in the assemblage of these images, and here it is easy to grasp why Ruskin came to believe that their value was limited. Ruskin's comment on the pictures of James Tissot as "unhappily, mere coloured photographs"[19] suggests that Ruskin feared that over-reliance on mechanical aids might restrict an artist's awareness. Only the intimate conjunction of sensitive eye, experienced hand, and an elaborately manoeuvrable instrument could register the shifts and stretches of a continuously inquiring mind. These watercolours contain no more than the slightest pencil pointers to what should go where. Almost at once Ruskin began to brush in tone and colour, subtly differentiating greens and greys, and refining each area with a delicate linearity. It was a high-risk strategy, each mark must sit convincingly with the mark beside it, but Ruskin's control of hue and tonality and his aptitude in the précis of structure were now highly evolved. By the standards of the day, however, this is so careless of pictorial decorum, a schematically prioritized order of events, that it would surely have entirely failed to meet the expectations of the contemporary spectator.

For all the apparent attention to the actuality of the moment, these views of Fribourg are the embodiments of a dream. Ruskin was studying the history of Switzerland and intended to write his own, wherein the architecture of the region would be understood as deriving from the rocky environment and at the service of a social equanimity that reflected the necessary interdependence of mountain folk. He bought a plot of land and hoped to erect a retreat. Alas, he soon decided the Swiss were as boorish as anybody else, and the notion of an Alpine home was abandoned.

In his sky paintings Ruskin's analytical skills, his ability to discern structural coherence in relatively amorphous and continuously altering natural phenomena, is masterly. And a grasp of the patterns within cloudscapes allowed him to note an extensive repertory of colouristic, tonal and textural effects, a repertory that takes him beyond any of his predecessors in art. Although Ruskin coined the term "pathetic fallacy," the specious or downright inappropriate attribution of mental or emotional states to natural appearances provoked his scorn: he was, indeed, prone to identify his hopes and fears with landscape generally and with meteorological events most directly.

"A July Thunder-cloud in the Val d'Aosta" (cat. 102) is a well-documented case. In a letter to his father the day after the depiction of this he wrote that the storm came on him "like an army in detached columns" and reaching the mountains "began to play … first it broke up against them, and great foaming thunderclouds dashed up here and there just like the spray of tremendous waves broken on the ridge. Then the Alps broke through these spray clouds and laid them this way and that on their sides, and made necklaces of them, and threw them out in long sheets far over the plain, shadowing it into deep blue, while the sun traversing over the peaks, sent long red rays over the sheets of foam through every gap of the rocks, pieces of pure and perfect blue sky set here and there so calmly in the midst of anger."[20] More than the analogies that aided Ruskin in his search for effective pictorial counterparts to every feature of the scene, one is conscious here of the topic uniting a sequence of perceptions – conflict, the struggle of light against dark, war in the heavens. It is no accident that Ruskin later used this image to illustrate his reading of weather as a portent of disaster in world affairs.

The art of Ruskin's full maturity is astoundingly diverse in its subject matter. He continued to draw and paint architecture, of course, with extreme sensitivity to the revelation in stone of the maker's humanity, always alive to the individual character of a building or a bit of a building, statuary or fragments of carved decoration. And as he got older he drew with increasing frequency and great affection a medley of flora and fauna.

Ruskin was usually at the top of his game when in an instructional role, and the works that followed his election to the new Slade Professorship in 1869 and the establishment of the Ruskin School of Drawing in 1871 show Ruskin at his inventive and manually dextrous best. The watercolours that were intended to serve as models for those who wished, or according to Ruskin desperately needed, to have their eyes opened to the world by means of visual investigation are time and again comprehensive in their evocation of the subjects chosen and yet minutely expressive of the artist's feelings. *Study of a Kingfisher, with Dominant Reference to Colour* (cat. 122) is probably the only widely familiar Ruskin image, but familiarity may have occluded the close reading it deserves. A monochrome drawing of the bird first settled its substance in the artist's mind, and then with a sensuous mix of graphite and brilliant modern pigments Ruskin went for broke. Every movement of his hand simultaneously determined the surface play of the plumage and insinuated the underlying configuration of flesh and bone. Just notice how chalky dry and silky wet paint shade off

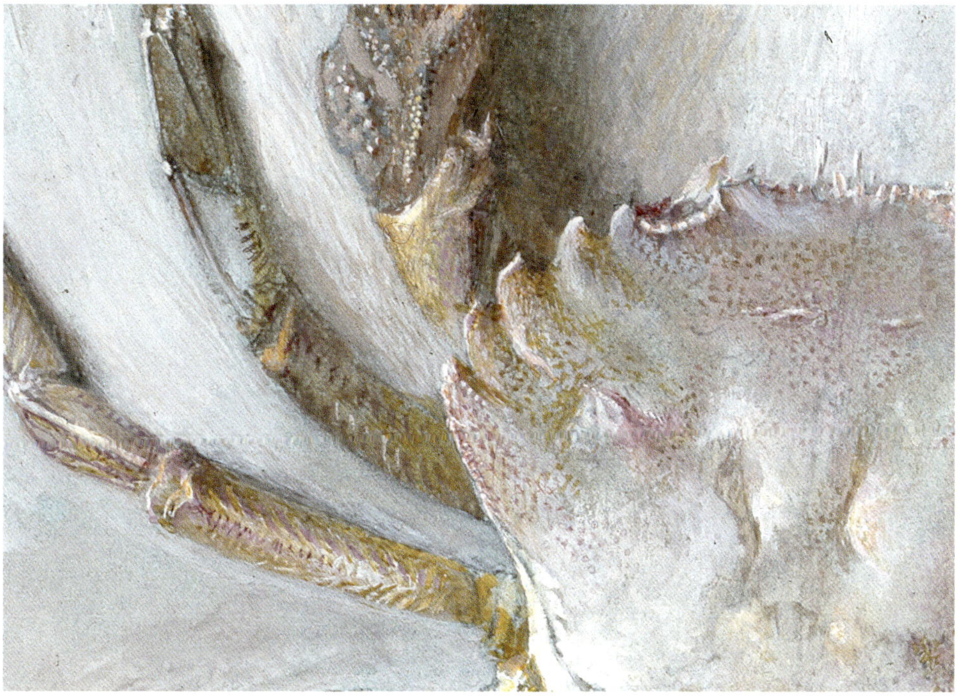

FIG. 3.11
John Ruskin
Study for a Velvet Crab, 1870 (?)
(cat. 121, detail)

into the knowing graphite strokes under the creature's tail.

For *Study of a Velvet Crab* (cat. 121 and fig. 3.11) Ruskin devised a mini lexicon of degrees of hardness, represented by changing consistency in the pigments used and almost infinitely variable speed of application. The brush dances over some sections of the image and elsewhere drags its heavy loaded paint mixes into the nooks and crannies of the carapace. Luminosity and light resisting sculptural solidity tease the eye. It is iridescent with refracted and reflected light. A compound of gorgeous hues and intricately detailed but never costive draftsmanship, prompting the spectator to slip and slide over certain parts, to linger upon others, and to chase down detail that comes close to vanishing on the closest inspection, this is genuine visual wit.

There is much sheer enjoyment in the creation of Ruskin's images of the 1870s but also signs of strain. In 1876–77 Ruskin spent nine months in Venice. Before leaving home he wrote that he was more depressed than he had ever been, and for most of his Venetian stay he was semi- or entirely delusional. Rose La Touche, thirty years his junior, with whom Ruskin had gone through a tortuous and tortured romance, had recently died, and he came to believe that he was in touch with her spirit, one that he associated with Saint Ursula. At Ruskin's request Carpaccio's painting of *The Dream of Saint Ursula* was taken down from its public place in the Accademia and made available for him to copy. The watercolour version manufactured by Ruskin (cat. 132) was relatively small, but he worked and reworked it in an unprecedentedly obsessive manner – it is very nearly choked by the amount of scraping out and repainting it underwent.

Away from the Carpaccio and in the vaporous, sun-diffusing atmosphere of the Serene Republic, Ruskin tried to gather his thoughts about a place that had long stirred his imagination, exercised his analytical expertise, and stimulated his artistry. Seeking an inclusive and coherent vision of a Venice that had largely been to him an assemblage of spectacular bits and pieces, he composed a number of sizeable cityscapes: *The Grand Canal, from the Palazzo Bernardo to the Palazzo Dolphin-Manin* (cat. 61) is the largest

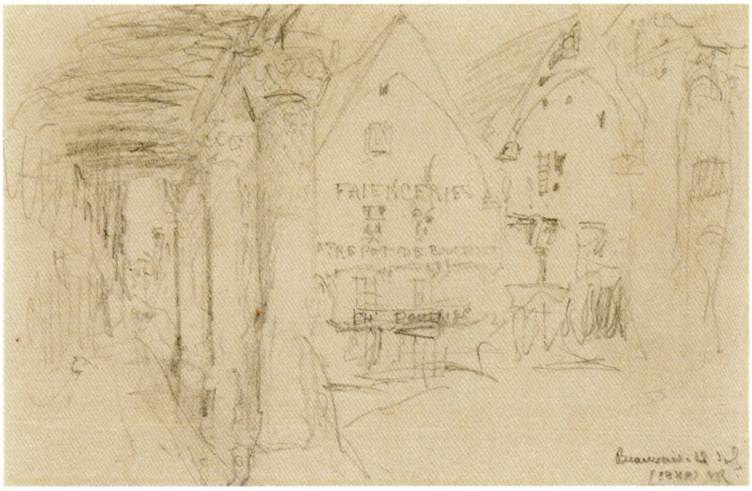

FIG. 3.12
John Ruskin
A Corner of the Market Place, Beauvais, 1888
Graphite on buff paper
Private collection

and most complete of them. At a glance painstakingly literal, it dissolves on closer examination into a flurry of precisely perceived but systematically understated elements. The fabric of the palaces consists of a host of tiny, tentative marks, which only add up if related to their fellows – constant scanning and the linkage of all elements across the picture plane are required if the image is to become more than the sum of its parts. The degree of connectivity, the interdependence of all marks, is extraordinary in Ruskin: it is what he had so often sought and not so often achieved. Something of the graphic fluidity and swell of the water in which the buildings stand is carried into the architecture, and that Byronic and Turnerian notion of a culture sinking under its own weighty history is discernible.

The effort entailed by such projects was immense, and Ruskin could hardly keep it up. "Left off tired" is the inscription on another, unfinished, or barely begun, large canal scene (cat. 60). And several sheets of sketches, loose and awkward, suggest a loss of interest in the specific character of the Venetian *mise en scène*. A depiction of San Michele, Venice (cat. 64) from the same visit indicates that the sustained control of the large drawings was not Ruskin's sole strategy. He could also identify the dreamier aspects of this Italian episode, when his physical situation was infiltrated and transformed by a sense of the noumenal and (so he wrote) the ghost of his dead amour was present, with the near hallucinatory atmospheric effects of the Lagoon. This work is radically unlike the large canal drawings in every respect. Starting off from a few loosely positioned pencil marks, Ruskin moves immediately to washes of intense colour. With this and a couple of others Ruskin seems to be remembering his pleasure in the paintings of the late fifteenth and early sixteenth-century Venetians, Tintoretto and Titian, which had overwhelmed him in 1845, and which at odd moments had affected him to a degree he could acknowledge but not explain.

The polarities of Ruskin's art, minutely particular and subtle in its equations of optical discovery and inventive mark-making, or, less frequently, non-linear and impulsively gestural, point to extremes in his intellectual and emotional constitution. Ruskin was aware of the extremes and engrossed in their management.

The story of Ruskin's later years is sad, and in the end tragic. Increasingly prone to depression and to episodes of what he himself called madness, unable to recapture the Christian faith of his youth, convinced that there was no life after death, and doubting that a beneficent deity and the world's wickedness could co-exist, Ruskin moved toward silence and immobility. Neurologists have a physical explanation for Ruskin's depressive behaviour, but the claim that he suffered from relapsing encephalopathy is unconvincing.[21]

Beset by dreams in which he was the victim and sometimes victimizer too, Ruskin seems eventually to have sunk into a sort of stupefaction. The company of females, children, teenagers and young women could rouse him at least momentarily, but correspondence with the "girlettes" (as he called them) often sounds a note of desperation. There are during Ruskin's later years flashes of brilliance, but the breakdown of self-confidence, the reduction of ambition and a decline in artistic skills are obvious. Compare any of the masterly townscapes of the 1850s and *A Corner of the Market Place, Beauvais* (fig. 3.12).

For the whole of his career as an artist, as in his voluminous writings, Ruskin sought coherence, tried to establish links between disparate areas of thought and practice, and attempted to extract from finely focused investigations of the seen world an essential kinship between individual elements and the main features of their larger context. It was a struggle that yielded magnificently innovative results that were however, in the artist's mind, no more than steps toward an unattainable goal. Like the aged Leonardo da Vinci, the aged Ruskin asked what had been achieved and decided that the labour and wounds were in vain and the struggle had come to naught. To adopt an ancient apophthegm, Ruskin was a fox who wanted to be a hedgehog. Despite the sense of failure that dogged him always though latterly becoming deeply oppressive, Ruskin was responsible for some of the most acute acts of visualization ever and radically revised the vocabulary and grammar of art in order to accommodate them.

NOTES

1 Letter from John Ruskin to the Reverend Daniel Moore, 22 October 1866, transcribed from the original, private collection.
2 See Landow 1985.
3 See Collingwood 1893.
4 Ruskin 1903–12, vol. 35, *Præterita and Dilecta*, p. 262.
5 Ruskin's spelling of Rosslyn.
6 I am no supporter of glib comparisons across the arts, but there seems to be an intriguing parallel to Ruskin's episodic mode of picture-making in the music of his contemporary Franz Liszt. The formation of intricate narratives from small units, with piecemeal motivic development by means of constant cross reference and incremental alteration of shape and rhythm is very similar. However, it is unlikely that Ruskin was familiar with the Hungarian's public performances and certain that he lacked the musical nous to appreciate their departures from tradition.
7 J.M.W. Turner, *Number 10 Watergate Street, Chester* (1793, private collection).
8 See Chapter II, "Of Turnerian Topography," in Ruskin 1903–12, vol. 6, *Modern Painters IV*, pp. 27–47.
9 Letter from John Ruskin to William Brown, 20 December 1843, transcribed from the original, private collection.
10 Newman 1875, p. 66.
11 The suggestion comes from Helen Walton, though she now has doubts about it.
12 See "Of the Pathetic Fallacy," chapter 12, in Ruskin 1903–12, vol. 5, *Modern Painters III*, pp. 201–220.
13 Ruskin 1903–12, vol. 15, *The Elements of Drawing, The Elements of Perspective, and The Laws of Fésole*, p. 110.
14 Ruskin to J.L. Lewis, 26 August 1858. See Hayman 1982, p. 187.
15 Ruskin 1903–12, vol. 15, p. 91.
16 Ibid., pp. 167–178.
17 Ibid., p. 167.
18 Ruskin 1958, vol. 2, p. 535.
19 Ruskin 1903–12, vol. 29, *Fors Clavigera, Letters 73–96*, p. 161.
20 31 July 1858. See Hayman 1982, p. 109.
21 See Kempster Alty 2008.

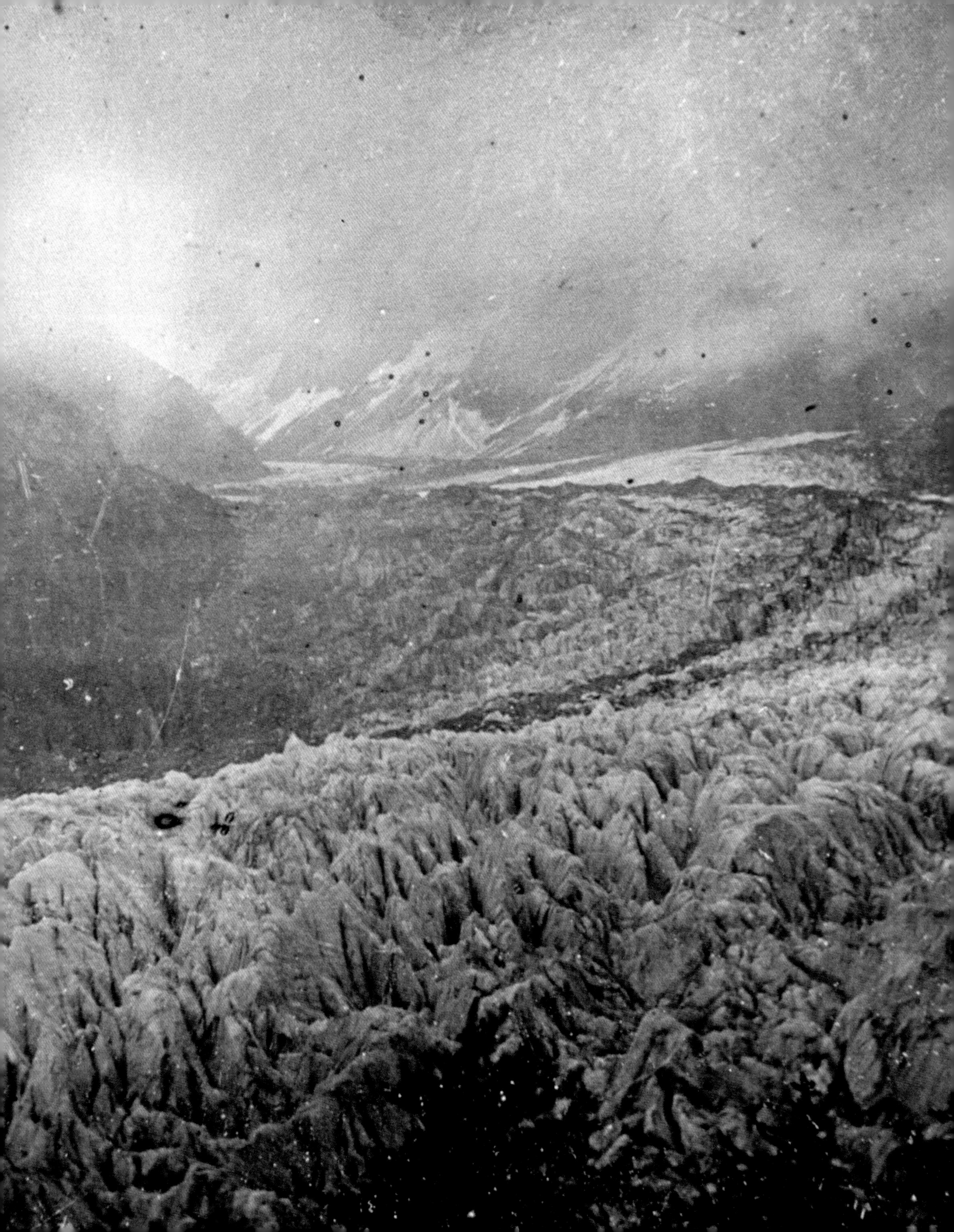

Fatal Praise: John Ruskin and the Daguerreotype

IAN JEFFREY

BETWEEN 1845 AND 1858 John Ruskin put together a collection of more than 320 daguerreotypes, mostly of architectural subjects in Italy, Switzerland and France. Also included in this collection were some landscapes showing mountains, glaciers and boulders in the Alps. A few of the pictures were bought from local photographers, but most were taken by assistants working in collaboration with Ruskin – John Hobbs (known as "George" to distinguish him from John Ruskin and his father John James) and Frederick Crawley, who replaced Hobbs in 1852. Ruskin probably acquired his daguerreotype camera in 1846, and pictures were taken sporadically throughout the 1840s and 1850s. In 1858 he travelled to Rheinfelden and Bellinzona in Switzerland and then Arona and Turin in Italy – his last tour on which photographs were taken. Thereafter the camera seems to have been put away, and nothing further added to the collection.

It is not clear why Ruskin desisted after 1858, for the daguerreotype process was still viable, even though it was beginning to become outmoded. Nor do we know why he carried on for so long as he did. Daguerreotypes were certainly useful as a basis for the engravings in his publications, such as *Modern Painters* (1843–60) and *The Stones of Venice* (1851–53). Some may have been intended for ventures that were never realized, for Ruskin always thought ahead. Others may have been taken because he found the process interesting in itself, capable of unexpected disclosures. In the 1840s photography was a new medium and, although much admired by Ruskin's contemporaries, not much was expected of it apart from mere fidelity to appearances. No one at that time ever seems to have thought of looking into a photograph for the sake of any underlying significance, or if they did they kept quiet. One of the most intriguing problems in early photography involves the reading of pictures by William Henry Fox Talbot, inventor of the negative-positive process. Did he take pictures simply to see how things looked when they were photographed, or did he have undeclared intentions that might be uncovered by research?[1]

In the 1840s photography was disconcerting because of its dispassionate eye for incidentals. Even in a site photographed for its historic interest certain elements might try to tell other stories both compelling and beside the point. In 1843, for instance, Talbot took a picture of the Place du Carrousel in Paris (fig. 4.1) as it was being cleared to make way for an extension to the Louvre. The square derived its name from an equestrian ball given there by Louis XIV in 1662. Talbot's picture, however, insists on current interests signaled by a handcart and ladders as well as by many large-scale posters advertising printers' inks and, in one case, a dogs' hospital.[2] It is likely that Ruskin, a very careful observer, appreciated the appearance of such details in photography.

Ruskin was, by his own admission, attentive to the natural scene. In a typically engrossing letter written to his father on 25 August 1845 he described the death of a guide on an Alpine glacier. The guide, he wrote, could not have known that the smooth part of a glacier would be "cut by cross crevices." Ruskin himself, who had been on the same glacier, had seen the lines of these crevices "marked as if with the trace of a camels hair pencil by the light indentation of the fresh snow."[3] This particular sharp-eyed remark may have been made to reassure his parents that he could

Cat. 96, detail

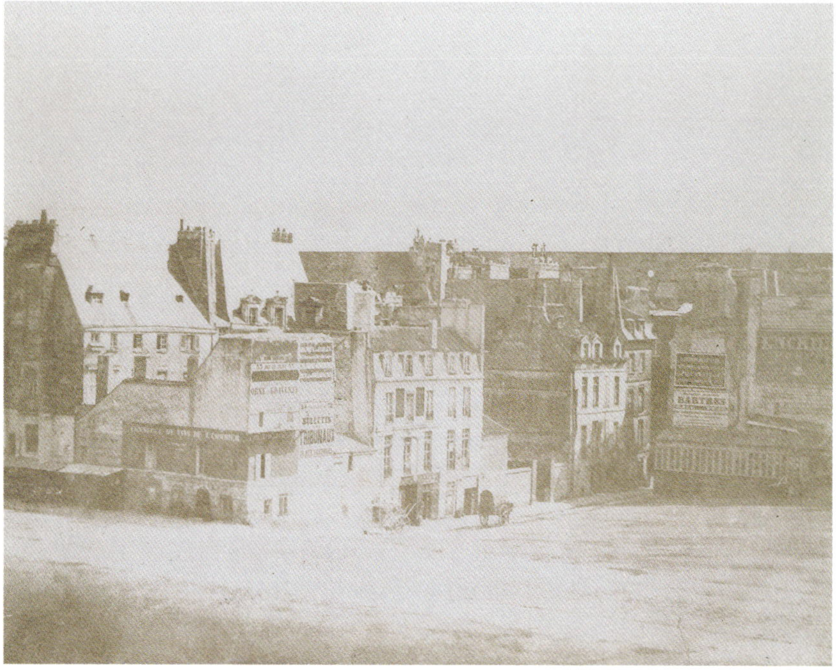

FIG. 4.1
William Henry Fox Talbot
Place du Carrousel, Paris, 1843
Daguerreotype
National Media Museum,
Bradford / Science & Society
Picture Library

look after himself, but there are other perceptions of this quality in his texts of the 1840s and 1850s. It is likely, given his taste and capacity for close observation, that some of the daguerreotypes were taken for pure love of discernment. Daguerreotypes were ultra-sensitive to nuances of light. In one of several pictures of the façade of San Zeno in Verona (fig. 4.2) the wall shows a series of pale smudges where passersby had made brief contact with the stone – just the sort of naturally occurring decoration that Ruskin approved of. On 14 September 1845 he wrote to his father deploring the loss of "all the glorious old weather stains" that had characterized the walls of St. Mark's in Venice.[4]

Architecture, with its symmetries and comparable modules, invites scrutiny and discloses irregularities and differences, which interested Ruskin. In the summer of 1846, during another extended tour in Italy, this time with his parents, he acquired a daguerreotype of the façade of Filippo Brunelleschi's late church the Badia, in Fiesole, near Florence (fig. 4.3). The building is notable for its strict, classical symmetries, which, at first sight, look as if they can be taken in at a glance; but it is soon clear that weather has damaged the structure, blurring the outlines. The picture also shows that whoever decorated the blank arcading to either side of the main door had had trouble with proportions and intervals.[5]

In 1841, aged 22, Ruskin visited Venice for the first time, and in 1845 and 1846 he returned for prolonged visits. He spent the winter of 1850–51 studying Venetian architecture on site and later on, in 1851, began to write *The Stones of Venice,* which he eventually completed in the winter of 1853. In 1845 Ruskin was an enthusiast. His letters home have a tremendous verve, only matched by the indignation he felt for the vandalism he encountered almost everywhere. By 1853, though, his opinions had consolidated after years of intense fieldwork and prolonged exposure to the kind of materials presented in his picture of the Badia. He had developed a substantial interest in patterning and repetition in building, forcefully theorized on in *The Stones of Venice.* His idea was that in worthwhile architecture no two modules, panels or carved ornaments should ever be the same. If they are slightly dissimilar it is

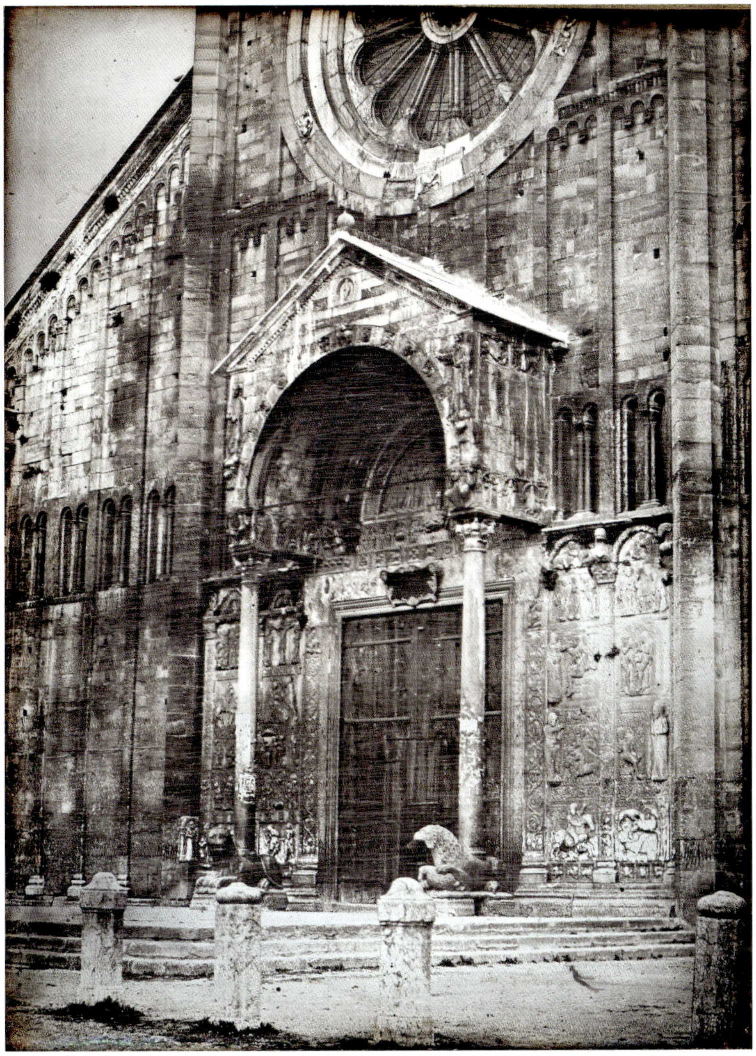

FIG. 4.2
John Ruskin and John Hobbs
San Zeno, Verona: Main Door from Side
Daguerreotype
Ruskin Foundation (Ruskin Library, Lancaster University)
(RF Dag 32)

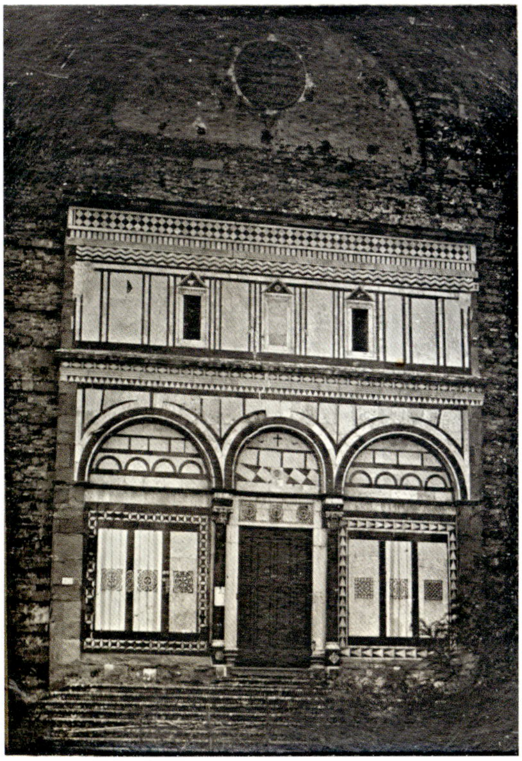

FIG. 4.3
Unknown photographer
Badia, Florence (Fiesole)
Daguerreotype
Ruskin Foundation (Ruskin Library, Lancaster University)
(RF Dag 53)

a sign that they have been made by hand and not by machine, which is a good thing and acknowledges the workman as a creator. Irregularity also implies change, which Ruskin valued above stasis; and perfection destroys expression, checks exertion and paralyzes vitality.[6]

In his letters to his parents in 1845 Ruskin was forthcoming, in part because he was justifying an expensive excursion. He had set off for the Continent in April and at first concentrated on drawing until, in Venice that autumn, he came across a "poor Frenchm[an] ... said to be in distress," from whom he bought "some most beautiful, though small, Daguerreotypes of the palaces I have been trying to draw."[7] The first mention of the "poor Frenchman" is on 7 October, and Ruskin left the city on 14 October on his journey home. In that one week he spent twenty napoleons on daguerreotypes, a large sum at a time when a napoleon was worth twenty francs. In Venice in 1845 a gondola could be hired for a day's work for five francs, and Joseph Couttet, Ruskin's companion and guide, was paid four francs per day.[8] Looking back in *Præterita,* Ruskin recalled paying a napoleon each for the "exquisitely bright small plates" and buying "the Grand Canal from the Salute to the Rialto" for two hundred francs.[9]

Ruskin may have been thinking about the virtues of daguerreotypes before he found his French supplier in early October. In a letter from Venice to his father, dated 1 October, he wrote about the trouble he had had in making records of the Palazzo Foscari. He was successful with "measures & mouldings" but had no time to make a general view because of his painstaking drawing style. What had happened, he explained, was that he had been "studying architecture carefully," by implication more carefully than before, and this resulted in him seeing "things about five times as beautiful as I used to do, and as I can't draw much better, I am reduced to knocking my fists together and moaning." He was reluctant to commit himself to general views. Not only did they take an inordinately long time to complete but he was not especially interested in them. What really attracted him to buildings were "the cracks & the stains."[10]

His justification for buying daguerreotypes was that they would take care of general views of buildings, but what he seems to have found is that they too were responsive to "every chip of stone & stain." In theory he was still interested in general views as a necessary part of any survey, and in his letter of 7 October extolling daguerreotypes to his father, he remarked on how accurate they were with regard to "*proportions*" – but it was something of an afterthought.[11] At that time he was beginning to recognize a new aesthetic inclination that marked him out and set him apart. He found himself resistant to contemporary taste, including that of his father. In his letter of 1 October to his father he had dismissed taking an outline as "what has been done a thousand times."[12] In the second volume of *Præterita*, signed off in 1887, Ruskin recalled his father's acute sense of loss in 1846 at "my now constant habit of making little patches and scratches of the sections and fractions of things in a notebook which used to live in my waistcoat pocket, instead of the former Proutesque or Robertsian outline of grand buildings and sublime scenes. And I was the more viciously stubborn in taking my own way, just because everybody was with him in these opinions."[13]

In 1845 and 1846 Ruskin found himself in a quandary. He was committed to a punctilious style of draftsmanship that was very much admired by some of those around him. Couttet was astonished by Ruskin's lifelike drawings, and another travelling companion, the artist James Duffield Harding, said of one of Ruskin's studies of the Palazzo Foscari (see cat. 3) that it "should frighten the Daguerreotype into fits."[14] One consequence of this painstaking style was that drawings took a discouragingly long time to complete. In *Præterita,* remembering his visit to Macugnaga in July 1845, Ruskin wrote that his "Florentine studies had not taught me how to draw clouds or stones any better; that the stream under my window was no more imitable than the Rhone itself, and that any single boulder in it would take all the month, or it might be, six weeks, to paint the least to my mind."[15]

Early on, in October 1845, Ruskin wrote enthusiastically of daguerreotypes: they were "beautiful, though small;" they were "glorious things." In the same letter he went on to say that the daguerreotype was "a noble invention, say what they will of it."[16] Photography, in other words, was admired but not altogether esteemed, which left him in a difficult position, for he was, according to Harding, a daguerreian artist. Ruskin never lost his admiration for the process; in *Præterita* he remembered the daguerreotypes that he had bought in Venice.[17] Even so, photography was no more than a means to an end, a way of keeping the scene for future reference. Harding's praise must have been hard to take, for in the first volume of *Modern Painters,* written in the winter of 1842–43, Ruskin had decried Canaletto: "He professes nothing but coloured daguerreotypeism." He disliked Canaletto, accusing him of "the most servile and mindless imitation," but at the same time his accusations were thoughtful. He added at the end of his diatribe that he had "seen daguerreotypes in which every figure and rosette, and crack and stain, and fissure is given on a scale of an inch to Canaletto's three feet."[18] It was, it appears, lack of proportion that mattered to him rather than the mere naturalism of the process.

In 1845, when Ruskin undertook his first independent tour in Italy, he was 26 years old and still in formation, even if he had already written the first volume of *Modern Painters.* He had, for instance, great ideas for the future of painting, one of which involved "the reconciliation of true aerial perspective and chiaroscuro with the splendour and dignity obtained by the real gilding and elaborate detail." This was to be achieved with "the help of the daguerreotype, and the lessons of colour given by the later Venetians."[19] One of the Venetians especially admired by Ruskin was Tintoretto, and the picture he had in mind was *The Presentation of the Virgin* in the Madonna dell'Orto. When Ruskin wrote the first volume of *Modern Painters* during the winter of 1842–43 he still had to learn that his bias was really toward cracks and stains and other significant minutiae.[20] Even then, though, there were straws in the wind. He liked the art of the great topographer Samuel Prout and took from it "that feeling which results from the influence, among the noble lines of architecture, of the rent and the rust, the fissure, the lichen, and the weed, and from the writing

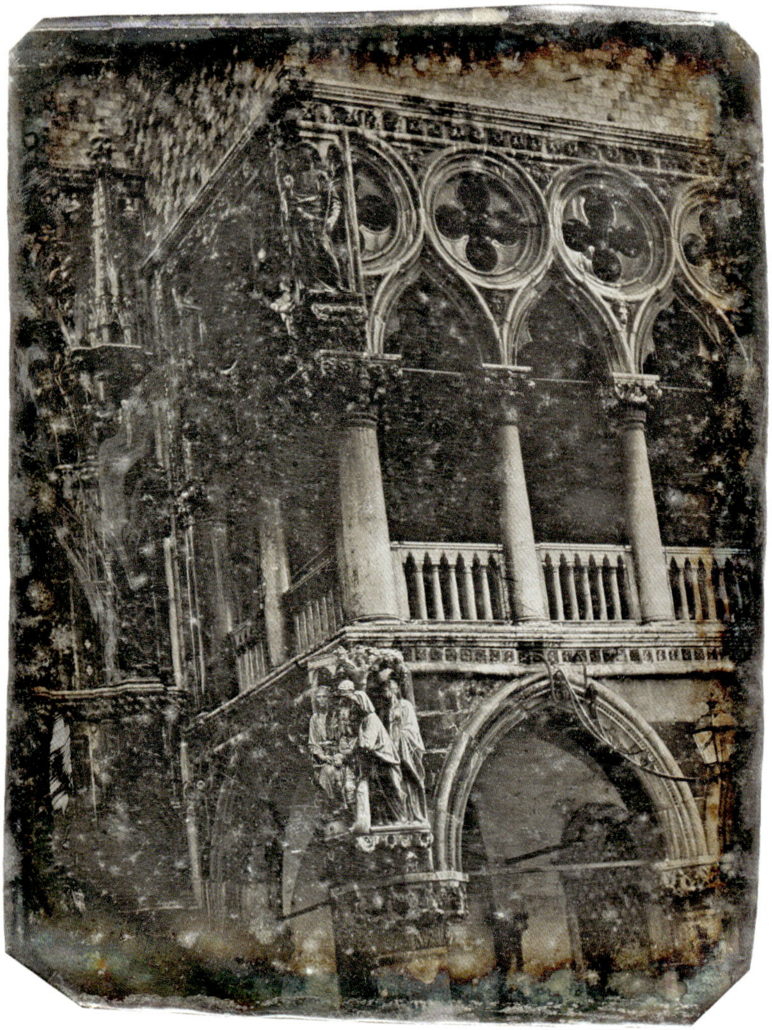

FIG. 4.4
Unknown photographer
Ducal Palace: Judgment of Solomon, Northwest Angle
Daguerreotype
Ruskin Foundation (Ruskin Library, Lancaster University)
(RF Dag 28)

upon the pages of ancient walls of the confused hieroglyphics of human history."[21]

By 1846 it was becoming clear, to Ruskin's father at least, that fragments were taking up an increasing amount of Ruskin's attention. On 25 May 1846 his father wrote from Venice to William Henry Harrison, a Scottish friend:

> He is cultivating art at present, searching for real knowledge, but to you and me this is at present a sealed book. It will neither take the shape of picture nor poetry. It is gathered in scraps hardly wrought, for he is drawing perpetually, but no drawing such as in former days you or I might compliment in the usual way by saying it deserved a frame; but fragments of everything from a Cupola to a Cart-wheel, but in such bits that it is to the common eye a mass of Hieroglyphics – all true – truth itself, but Truth in mosaic.[22]

Daguerreotypes contributed to this mosaic for they fixed traces that would otherwise have been overlooked. On 15 October 1845, writing to his father from Padua, Ruskin noted that he had been looking at pictures of St. Mark's "and found a lot of things in the Daguerreotype that I never had noticed in the place itself."[23] What these things were can only be guessed (see fig. 4.4), but daguerreotypes were unsparing of details, including the new gas lighting and its tubing that writhed through the balustrades of the increasingly disfigured city.

Eventually it seems that survey work sickened Ruskin of Venice. He had spent the winters of 1849–50 and 1851–52 in the city researching *The Stones of Venice*, and in a letter of May 1859 to his friend Charles Eliot Norton he recalled the work with distaste: "I went through so much hard, dry, mechanical toil there, that I quite lost, before I left it, the charm of the place: Analysis is an abominable business: I am quite sure that people who work out subjects thoroughly are disagreeable wretches – One only feels as one should when one doesn't know much about the matter."[24] The city of Venice itself was also a disappointment, for in the 1840s it was being defaced and upgraded at a great rate. Ruskin's letters home in September 1845 teem with bad news about brutal cleaning programs, demolitions and rebuildings. Once upon a time Venice had been a great city, home to major builders and painters, whose spirit had vanished almost completely. Ruskin's diatribes are entertaining and they contribute to his picture of Venice as a montage of beautiful seascapes, gas lighting, garish stucco, bow windows, brick buildings and billowing smoke from a manufactory on the Rialto. In this conflict between ill-considered development and under-funded conservation there could be no happy outcome – and according to Ruskin's accounts the damage had already been done. As Venice was an insoluble civic problem, Ruskin turned his attention elsewhere – to Switzerland, which he was beginning to think of as the birthplace of democracy.

Ruskin's Swiss venture resulted in a number of impressive general views, large coloured drawings of Thun and Fribourg, for example. Crawley also made daguerreotypes of Fribourg and Rheinfelden. W.G. Collingwood, in his early biography of Ruskin, wrote of a projected "study of Swiss history: to tell the tale of six chief towns – Geneva, Fribourg, Basle, Thun, Baden and Schaffhausen, to which in 1858 he added Rheinfelden and Bellinzona."[25] The project began in the summer of 1854 and ended in 1858, following pressure from Ruskin's father, who wanted to see the completion of *Modern Painters*. In a memoir of 1903, Collingwood noted that Ruskin, who collected maps, had an "old Keller's 'Switzerland' of 1844, which he used forty years later, saying that he did not want the railways, and no new map showed the road better."[26] In the collection there was also "Beck's raised map of Switzerland (1853) ... often in use." On Ruskin's shelves Collingwood identified "a splendid tome, lettered on the back 'SWISSE HISTOR.,' evidently bound abroad, which on opening you find to be Gaullieur's 'La Suisse Historique,' much used for intended work on Swiss towns."[27] On the centre of the mantelpiece at Brantwood, Ruskin's Lake District home, there was a woodcarving of a Swiss maid holding a pruning-hook, which, according to Collingwood, had belonged to Ruskin's mother.[28] Ruskin's connection with Switzerland had many aspects.

Ruskin later discussed the Swiss project in *Præterita* in a section entitled "The Grande Chartreuse." In retrospect he was dissatisfied: "The events of the ten years 1850–1860, for the most part wasted in useless work." His intention was to engrave a series of drawings of Swiss towns. The first of the drawings, of Thun, took up "the whole of the summer, and is only half done then." Things were little better in 1856 when "two drawings at Fribourg took up the working summer." In 1858, accompanied by Couttet, he spent the spring at Rheinfelden and the summer at Bellinzona: "But Couttet being of opinion that these town views will come to no good, and that the time I spend on the roof of 'cette baraque' at Bellinzona is wholly wasted, I give the town views all up, and take to Vandyke and Paul Veronese again in the gallery of Turin."[29] Later in the same chapter he returned to the problem of 1858 and put his failure down to "a too ambitious attempt at the cliffs of the Bay of Uri, which crushed the strength down in me; and next, a persistently furious one to draw the entire town, three fortresses, and surrounding mountains of Bellinzona, gradually taming and contracting itself into a meekly obstinate resolve that at least I would draw every stone of the roof right in *one* tower of the vineyards, – 'cette baraque,' as Couttet called it."[30]

The attempt to deal with Swiss history turned out to be unmanageable.[31] In Venice in 1845 Ruskin had had trouble with general views, which had taken up too much of his time. Things were no different in 1854, 1856 and 1858. By 1858 they may even have been worse. Writing in 1893, Collingwood described the drawings of 1858 as being "in the style of fine pen-etching combined with broadly gradated and harmonious tints of colour; or, when they were simply pen or pencil outlines, they were much more refined than those of ten years earlier."[32] Couttet seems to have recognized that the project would take too long to complete, and even that there was something else amiss. It is possible that Ruskin realized that he was no historian. In *Præterita*, for instance, he included several uninspiring pages on Swiss history drawn from E.H. Gaullieur's book *La Suisse Historique* (1855). His prose only revives when he recalls that he had rented a chalet from Gaullieur's widow and that it was near to the "pleasure villa" of "old Dr. Gosse of Geneva," whose mountain garden was situated in the ruins of the old Castle of Savoy.[33]

Ruskin was in two minds about Switzerland. He knew from Gaullieur's book that there had been an exemplary democratic land near Lake Lucerne. This land measured about forty miles from east to west and as many from north to south, and it had been peopled by "another race of men" who led "an entirely pastoral life."[34] These Helvetii had remained changeless and unconquered even though they had placed themselves under the protection of the House of Hapsburg. In the fourth and fifth volumes of *Modern Painters* Ruskin went to some lengths to explain himself regarding the Swiss. He adduced environmental theories. The Swiss heartland was too exposed to bad weather to allow vine growing, and the population had been forced to become pastoralists, which Ruskin suggested was a precondition of good government. Elsewhere in Switzerland conditions were not so favourable, especially in the mountains where the struggle to survive took up all the attention of the inhabitants. Ruskin's idea was that a poorer landscape "contracts the conceptions, and hardens the temperament of both mind and body."[35]

Ruskin's diatribes in *Modern Painters* are worth waiting for. Although they begin mildly enough, they soon gather force. One of his finest is devoted to

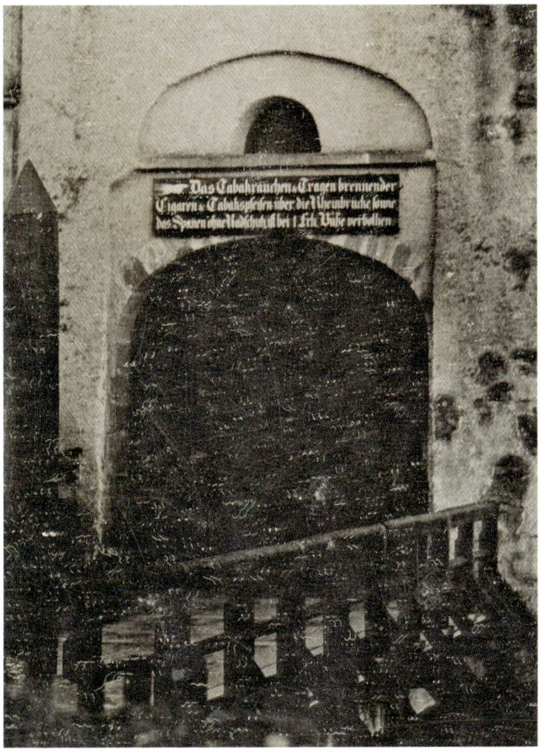

FIG. 4.5
John Ruskin and Frederick Crawley
View of the Bridge at Rheinfelden, 1858
(cat. 48b, detail)

the Swiss town of Sion, a ruined and neglected spot, marred by improvized repairs where "a dull smell of mortar, mixed with that of stale foulness of every kind, rises with the dust, and defiles every current of air; the corners are filled with accumulations of stones, partly broken, with crusts of cement sticking to them, and blotches of nitre oozing out of their pores." The long account of Sion reaches a visionary conclusion where the writer imagines the great mountains seceding into supremacy "through rosy depths of burning air." On the crescents of snow that gleam "over their dim summits," he envisages "a line of waning moons might be set for lamps along the sides of some sepulchral chamber in the Infinite."[36]

The description of Sion repays attention. Its rocky sub-structure is "curiously traversed by stairs and walls and half-cut paths that disappear below starkly black arches, and cannot be followed, or rise in windings round the angles, and in unfenced slopes along the fronts, of the two masses of rock which bear, one the dark castle, the other the old church and convent of Sion." Sion appears to have been a labyrinth. Ruskin also remarked on "the Episcopal palace, a half-deserted, barrack-like building" that overlooked "a *neglected vineyard*."[37] Barracks crop up in Ruskin's texts where they signify a bleak regimented future: "I do not say that it may not be desirable that one city, or one country, sacrificed for the good of the rest, should become a mass of barracks or factories."[38] Monasteries, too, belong in the same iconographic company.

The Swiss project may have been intended as a worthwhile exercise. It should ideally have drawn attention to the heartland with all its virtues, but in the event it seems that the converse became the obverse – that despised Sion took centre stage precisely because of its shortcomings. Bathos came readily to Ruskin. Elsewhere in "The Mountain Gloom," for instance, he contrasted the bleakness of real Alpine life with the "simulacra of peasants, in gay ribands and white bodices, singing sweet songs" among the "gauze flowers and crackling tinsel of theatres" in London and Paris.[39] He noted that on one of the old covered bridges at Lucerne the pictures painted within the covered walkway were of a *Dance of Death* – an example of noble gloom,[40] which he compared with what might be found on "a new 'promenade' in some flourishing modern town" in Britain or France. These covered bridges were significant as places of public resort. The other covered bridge in Lucerne had pictures representing "all the important Swiss battles and victories."[41] At Rheinfelden on the Rhine, where Ruskin made drawings in 1858, Crawley took daguerreotypes of another of these covered bridges (cat. 48, fig. 4.5). What caught Crawley's eye, and possibly Ruskin's too, was an inscription on the entry tower warning against the dangers of smoking pipes and cigars. Old wooden bridges burned easily, which is probably why the authorities wanted to get rid of them. This is just the kind of practical aside that photography picked up on: the trivial aspect of commonsense intruding into a high-toned context of Swiss ethics and the legacy of J.M.W. Turner, who had also made drawings at Rheinfelden.

Daguerreotypes captured disinterested impressions from whatever came their way, whether of no smoking signs on an old covered bridge across the Rhine, gas piping and stains on walls in Venice, or builders' scaffolding on the towers of ancient French cathedrals. Ruskin, who could almost outdo the daguerreotype for accuracy, according to James Duffield Harding, must have been downcast. It was not simply that Ruskin was no better than an automaton, but that in striving for accuracy he came up with the unexpected. The town views in Switzerland, which took up so much of his time, were intended to show settlements in their context of plains, mountains and rivers – and in some cases they did just that. At times, though, his focus shifted and he began, possibly despite himself, to experiment. Fribourg, which he visited in 1856, had towers, spires and monuments, but he also represented it as a labyrinth. What fascinated him were its covered walkways edging their way through the buildings. It too had canopied bridges as well as a prison-like Augustinian convent – a reminder of the barrack-like Episcopal palace in decrepit Sion.

In Switzerland Ruskin found himself in strange territory, albeit quite familiar to him. Ancient Fribourg with its winding passageways and ducts turned out to be a secretive and intimate place – and eerily uninhabited. Fribourg may have been known for its originating role in constitutional government, but in Ruskin's drawings it looks like the setting for an elaborate folk tale. The twenty or so daguerreotypes taken there by Crawley supplement this enticing aspect of a place with many nooks and crannies, gables and towers, huddled among rocks and waters. It is probably that Ruskin hoped that his fastidious drawing style could be controlled and that it would serve him well. This is implied in his recollection in *Præterita* of having resolved at Bellinzona, during the excursion of 1858, "that at least I would draw every stone of the roof right in *one* tower of the vineyards." His sense of duty and notions of rightness made certain demands, especially that he should be accurate, but his temperament took him in unexpected and contrary directions, into the picturesque and moralized ruins of Sion, for example, and onto the tinseled stages of London and Paris. It took him, too, into the entrails of Fribourg when he had imagined that he was really in search of insight into the origins of constitutional government. Eventually it took him, more prosaically, into the "luxury of the Hotel de l'Europe" in Turin,[42] where he found relief from the exigencies of the severe style and of daguerreian seeing in general.

NOTES

1 For an ambitious and vivid reading of early photographs, see Mike Weaver's classic text, *The Photographic Art: Pictorial Traditions in Britain and America* (Weaver 1986), especially the opening section, "A Photographic Artist, W.H.F. Talbot," pp. 10–15.
2 See Lassam 1979, for this and comparable photographs.
3 Ruskin 1972, p. 188.
4 Ibid., p. 201.
5 In the summer of 1845 Ruskin sometimes walked out to Fiesole from Florence, for the exercise and to escape from the city. His right-hand man, Joseph Couttet, made a collection of plants from the hills around Fiesole that Ruskin thought would be useful "as many of them are the originals of flowers in the old pictures" (Ruskin 1972, p. 130).
6 Ruskin is at his most ethical in chapter VI, "The Nature of Gothic," of the second volume of *The Stones of Venice*. In this chapter he proposes "that imperfection is in some sort essential to all that we know of life" (Ruskin 1903–12, vol. 10, *The Stones of Venice II*, p. 203).
7 Ruskin 1972, p. 220.
8 Ruskin, who was accountable to his father in 1845, often mentioned his travel costs in his letters home.
9 Ruskin 1903–12, vol. 35, *Præterita and Dilecta*, p. 373.
10 Ruskin 1972, p. 218.
11 Ibid., p. 220.
12 Ibid., p. 218.
13 Ruskin 1903–12, vol. 35, p. 419.
14 Ruskin 1972, p. 218.
15 Ruskin 1903–12, vol. 35, p. 366.
16 Ruskin 1972, p. 220.
17 Ruskin 1903–12, vol. 35, p. 373.
18 Ruskin 1903–12, vol. 3, *Modern Painters I*, p. 215. The paragraph is given over largely to the shortcomings of Canaletto.
19 Ibid., p. 210.
20 At the time he wrote the first volume of *Modern Painters* he had not seen Tintoretto's paintings in the Scuola di San Rocco. These made a great impression on him when he first saw them in the company of Harding in September 1845.
21 Ruskin 1903–12, vol. 3, p. 217.
22 This extract is quoted by John Dixon Hunt in his article *Ut pictura poesis, the Picturesque, and John Ruskin,* in Bloom 1986, p. 68.
23 Ruskin 1972, p. 225.
24 Ruskin Norton 1987, p. 34.
25 Collingwood 1893, vol. 1, pp. 178–179. W.G. Collingwood wrote a biography in 1889, followed by *The Life and Work of John Ruskin* in 1893.
26 Collingwood 1903, p. 115
27 Ibid., 184.
28 Illustrated in ibid., p. 185.
29 Ruskin 1903–12, vol. 35, *Præterita and Dilecta*, pp. 483–485. Ruskin here gives a year-by-year account of the decade.
30 Ibid., p. 494.
31 The Swiss venture is not usually given much attention in Ruskin's accounts. It looks, at first sight, and by his own admission, like a failure. However, the story is admirably told by Jeanne Clegg in a chapter called "Swiss Life in the Olden Times" in Sheffield 1983, pp. 33–36.
32 Collingwood 1893, vol. 1, p. 217.
33 Ruskin 1903–12, vol. 35, p. 516. Dr. Gosse had converted one of the towers of the castle into a reservoir. On first meeting Ruskin, he exclaimed, "Voyez. C'était une tour de guerre. J'en ai fait une bouteille!" (pp. 516–517).
34 Ruskin 1903–12, vol. 7, *Modern Painters V*, p. 111.
35 Ruskin 1903–12, vol. 6, *Modern Painters IV*, p. 171. Ruskin's opinions on Switzerland feature in the fourth volume of *Modern Painters*, mainly in part V, chapter XIX, "The Mountain Gloom." His misgivings regarding beautiful landscapes and their impact on character surface toward the beginning of chapter XI in part V, "The Materials of Mountains." In the eighth section of that chapter he considers the landscape surrounding Fribourg, an important settlement in the Swiss heartland. For a résumé on the Swiss question, see the concluding paragraphs in chapter IX in part VI of the fifth volume of *Modern Painters*, a chapter entitled "The Leaf Shadows." In this summing up he is hard on the people of the Valais: "Beneath the glaciers of Zermatt and Evolena, and on the scorching slopes of the Valais, the peasants remained in aimless torpor, unheard of but as the obedient vassals of the great Bishopric of Sion" (Ruskin 1903–12, vol. 7, p. 111).
36 Ruskin 1903–12, vol. 6, pp. 413–414.
37 Ibid.
38 Ruskin 1903–12, vol. 7, pp. 424–425.
39 Ruskin 1903–12, vol. 6, p. 390.
40 Ibid. p. 395.
41 Ibid., p. 394.
42 Ruskin 1903–12, vol. 35, p. 494. Ruskin gives a charming account of his retreat from Bellinzona in *Præterita* toward the end of the section called "The Grande Chartreuse."

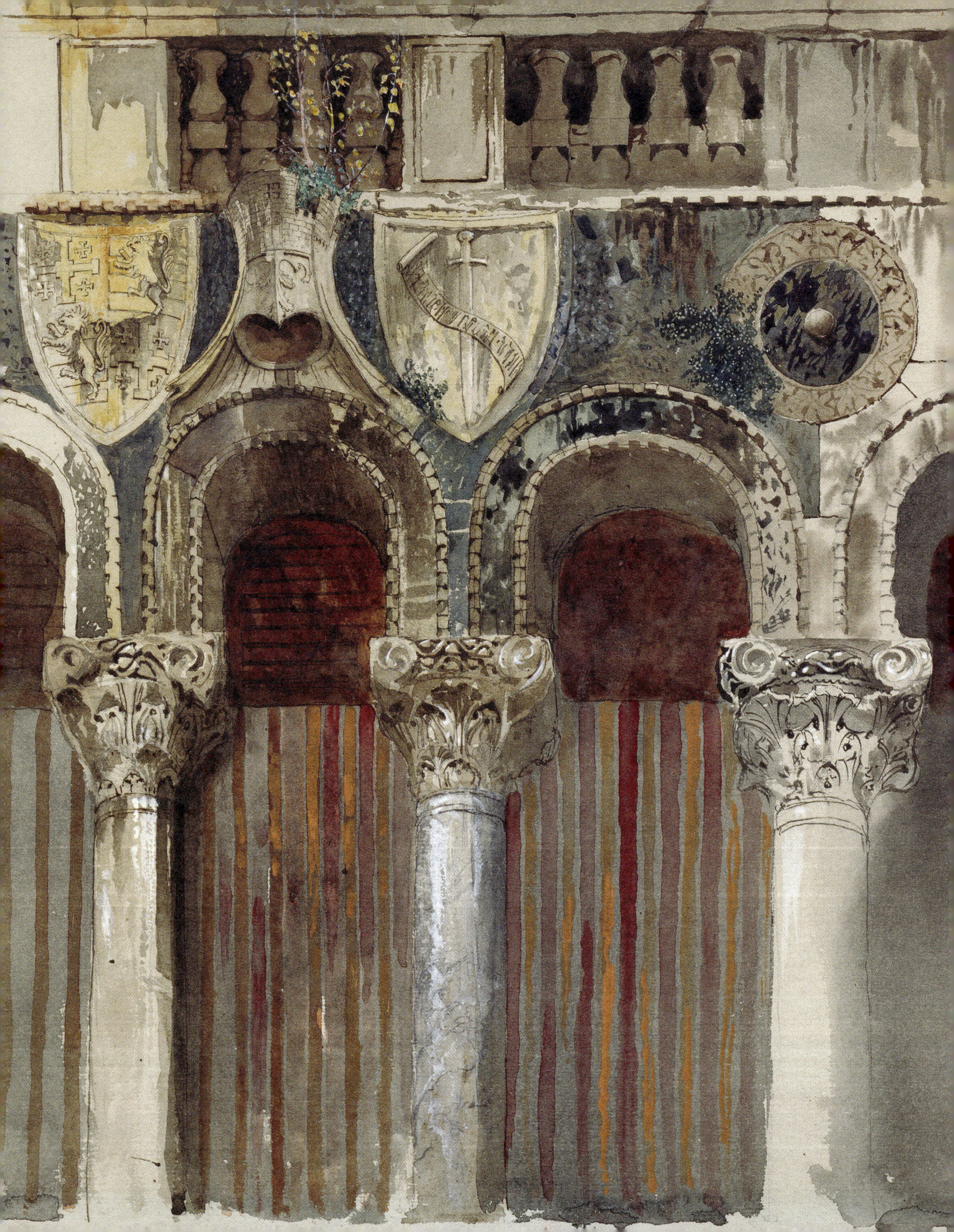

Architectural Detail & Ornament

1

Rosslyn Chapel 1838

Graphite on buff paper; 52.8 × 36.6 cm
Ruskin Foundation (Ruskin Library, Lancaster University) (RF 987)
Inscriptions: graphite, *ROSLIN CHAPEL Aug 3 38*, ink, *by J. Ruskin (given to A.D.O. Wedderburn.)*

Ruskin and his family stayed in Edinburgh at the end of July 1838 in the course of the long Scottish tour they made that summer, and from there visited the mid-fifteenth-century Rosslyn Chapel, close to the castle that is the ancestral home of the earls of Rosslyn. Ruskin was just nineteen years old, but was already engaged in writing a series of articles on the theme of "Poetry in Architecture" for Loudon's *Architectural Magazine*. Submitted under the pseudonym "Kataphusin," the texts were the immediate incentive for seeking out such historical buildings.

Although the chapel was never finished according to the intended cruciform plan, the choir and eastern walls of what would have been the transept if the edifice had been carried forward to completion are richly decorated with carved stone figures and other embellishments on every surface, from floor level into the barrel vaults of the roof. The present view shows the central nave of the choir, looking toward the altar.

The chapel was described in Walter Scott's *The Lay of the Last Minstrel*, a narrative poem in which the character Rosabelle evokes a scene in which the building is flooded with a supernatural evening light: "Blazed battlement and pinnet high, / Blazed every rose-carved buttress fair – / So still they blaze when fate is nigh / The lordly line of high St. Clair."[1] Ruskin remembered the place all his life, naming a chapter in his autobiography *Præterita* for it and associating it in his memory with the death of girls he had known in his youth. He concluded his chapter with an account of Rosslyn and its landscape setting, ending by quoting from Scott's poem: "the blue of the mountains became deep to me with the purple of mourning, – the clouds that gather round the setting sun, not subdued, but raised in awe as the harmonies of a Miserere, – and all the strength and framework of my mind, lurid, like the vaults of Roslyn, when weird fire gleamed on its pillars, foliage-bound, and far in the depth of twilight, 'blazed every rose-carved buttress fair.'"[2]

This large drawing shows extraordinary technical virtuosity; Ruskin has used the soft line of the pencil to describe the richly decorated stone surfaces of the chapel interior. It is one of a set of three interior views at Rosslyn (the others are titled *Rosslyn Chapel, Interior, with Prentice Pillar* and *Rosslyn Chapel, Entrance Porch*). In later life, he decried what he had come to see as the mannered and meretricious character of these drawings: "when I got a subject that suited my trick of style, the practised ease of it told," and this despite acknowledging that "one or two of those Scottish sketches have been extremely popular among the public of my friends."[3]

NOTES

1 Scott 1805, p. 184. St. Clair [-Erskine] was the family name of the earls of Rosslyn.
2 Ruskin 1903–12, vol. 35, *Præterita and Dilecta*, p. 233.
3 Ibid., vol. 35, p. 612.

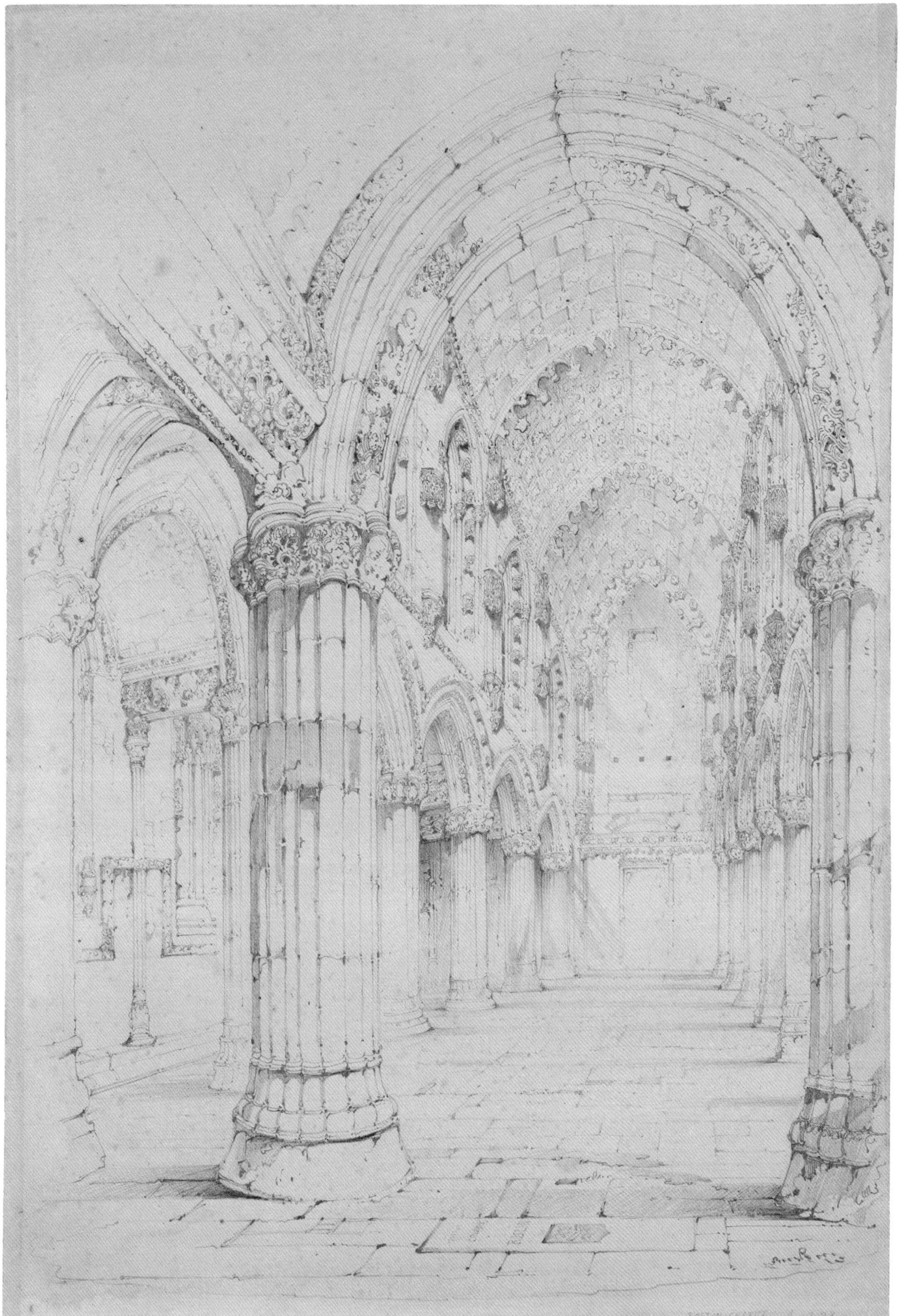
ROSLIN CHAPEL

2

Study of the Marble Inlaying on the Front of the Casa Loredan, Venice 1845

Watercolour, bodycolour and pen and ink over graphite on pale grey wove paper; 34.2 × 29.7 cm
The Ashmolean Museum, Oxford. Presented by John Ruskin to the Ruskin Drawing School (University of Oxford), 1875 (WA.RS.RUD.022)
Inscriptions: ink, *Casa Loredan.*

The Casa Loredan stands on the Grand Canal in Venice on the San Marco side, on the reach that runs between the Rialto and Accademia bridges. Ruskin later made frequent references to it in the chapter "Byzantine Palaces" in the second volume of *The Stones of Venice.* In the appendix to that volume, he drew attention to it as a building that "though not conspicuous, and often passed with neglect, will, I believe, be felt at last, by all who examine it carefully, to be the most beautiful palace in the whole extent of the Grand Canal."[1] When Ruskin gave the drawing to Oxford University in 1875, he described it thus: "The building is of three dates: its capitals, and the arches they bear, are Byzantine; the shields and casque, inlaid with modifications of the earlier work, presumably in the fifteenth century; the balustrade above, barbarous seventeenth. But nothing could surpass the beauty of the whole when I made this sketch in 1845."[2]

This drawing shows four of the thirteen archways of the arcade that runs across the entire width of the palace on the first floor, or *piano nobile* (the central arch is the one above which was placed in the fifteenth century the sculpted casque of Peter Lusignan, King of Cyprus, who lived at the palace with the Correr family in the previous century). Restorations had already occurred to the palace when Ruskin drew it, but the original fabric of the building was largely intact. However, in 1881, after the Loredan family had vacated and the building had become a municipal office, the façade was ruinously reconstructed and all the colour and variation of surface that Ruskin had admired was swept away.

In the description of the Loredan capitals in the manuscript notes added to *The Stones of Venice*, Ruskin expressed the view that they were "excessively rude in cutting, blunt and imperfect."[3] But as he explained in the context of the capitals of the Doge's Palace, if a piece of stonework is viewed at a distance, the mason's efforts to make it finer might be regarded as redundant. The drawing depends upon a diagrammatic placing of the architectural elements foursquare on the sheet without any attempt at the perspectival closing of the spaces, which would be expected given the angle at which the arcade would be seen from a gondola moored on the Grand Canal.

That the drawing was intended as a working record is further made clear in Ruskin's 1878 account of it: "Although I did not in 1845 know how to paint, the extreme fault of this and other drawings of mine at the time are owing to the fact that I was always working, not for the sake of the drawing, but to get accurate knowledge of some point in the building – which knowledge I always expressed securely first with the pen, however hard or bad the effect might be afterwards."[4] This description of his method is interesting and is borne out by a close study of the drawing. Ruled graphite lines may be detected beneath a pen and ink grid to lay out the main elements of the composition – the

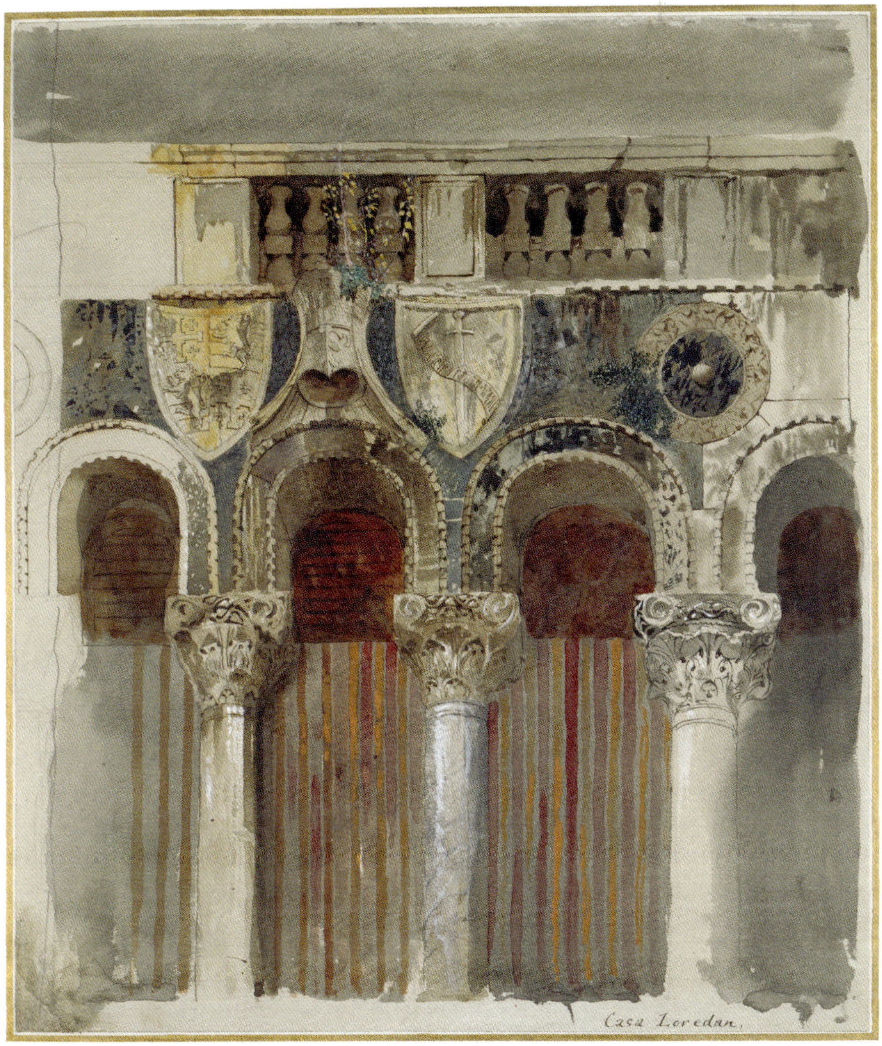

columns and capitals, the stilted arcade and the wall surface and decoration above. Parts of the structure that Ruskin regarded as particularly precious, most obviously the Corinthian capitals but also the projecting dentil bands (mouldings of alternating faceted oblongs of stone that rise in parallel lines from the capitals and that describe the semi-circular shape of the arches), have been carefully drawn in ink and with skill in the rendering of a consistent fall of light. Ink washes have then been applied to make the whole volumetric and massive in its feel, while lastly, gorgeous colours, richly applied as opaque bodycolour, have been used to convey the building's sumptuous and oriental character. Ruskin was a brilliant natural colourist with a particular love of greys and blues and greens, here allowed to coalesce and overlap. These tones simulate the actuality of a building made up of a patchwork of injuries and repairs, with blotched and smeared surfaces. In the spaces of the arcade hangs an awning patterned with orange and magenta vertical stripes. These colours are distinct in parts and in other areas suffuse into the beautiful duck-egg-blue wash of the background.

NOTES

1 Ruskin 1903–12, vol. 10, *The Stones of Venice II*, p. 454.
2 Ruskin 1903–12, vol. 21, *The Ruskin Art Collection at Oxford: Catalogues, Notes, and Instructions*, p. 175.
3 Ruskin 1903–12, vol. 10, p. 149.
4 Ruskin 1903–12, vol. 21, p. 175.

3

Window at the Ca' Foscari, Venice 1845

Graphite and watercolour on paper; 46.6 × 31.6 cm
Victoria and Albert Museum, London (D.1726-1908)
Inscriptions: *Ca' Foscari No. 4. September 1845*

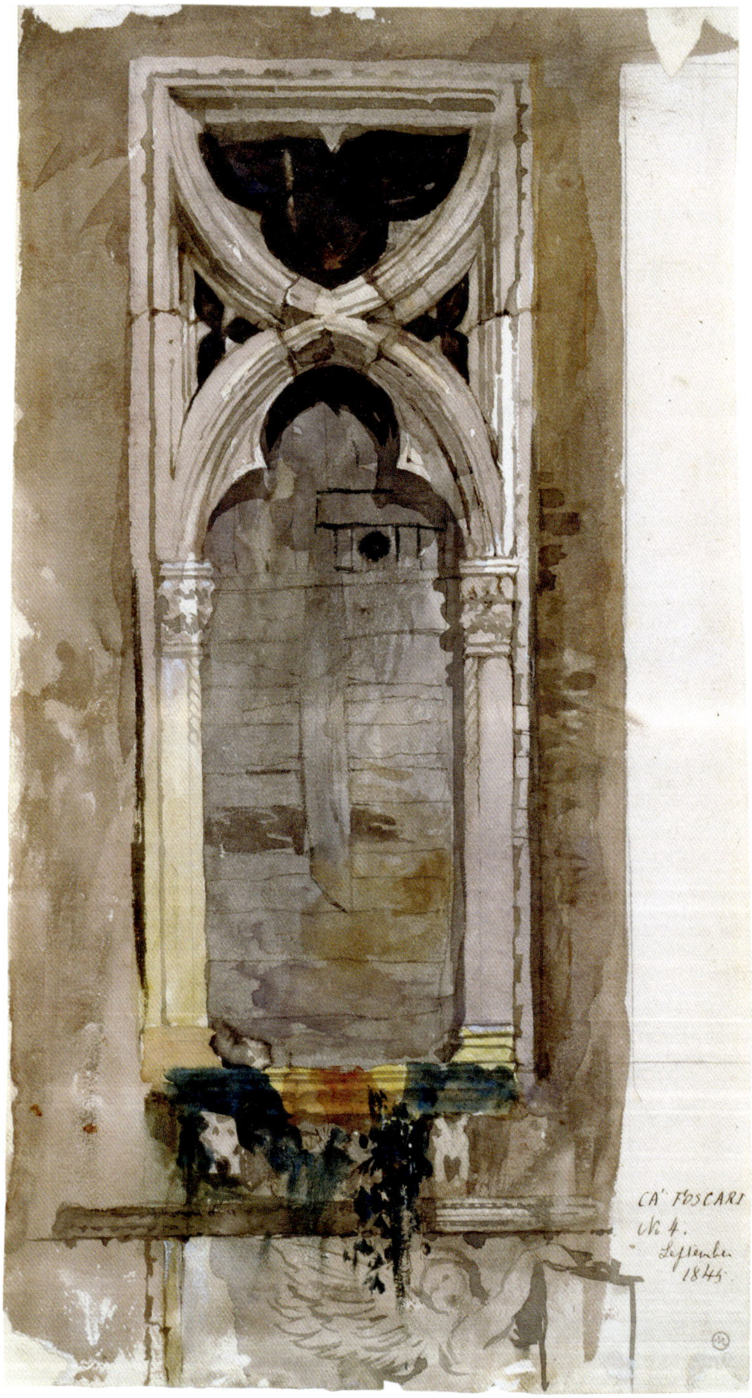

The Ca' Foscari was one of the buildings in Venice to which Ruskin paid particular attention during his stay in the city in September and October 1845. Standing on the Dorsoduro side of the Grand Canal close to San Samuele, its position on the bend of the canal allows it to be seen from the entire reach running up to the Rialto. Built by Doge Francesco Foscari in 1453, it was described by Ruskin as "the noblest example in Venice of the fifteenth-century Gothic."[1] In a letter of 17 September, Ruskin reported on the progress that he and Harding were making in providing a record of the building: "Harding & and I shall do the Foscari pretty well between us. I have got the architecture – mouldings, capitals & all. I began it small."[2] A fortnight later, again in a letter to his father, he talked of the difficulty he was having with a general view: "I am thoroughly thrown on my back with the Palazzo Foscari – [and] don't know what the deuce to do with it. I have all its measures & mouldings, & that is something, but I can't get on with the general view." He seems at this time to have been comparing his own capacity to record the minute details of buildings with that which might be conveyed in a daguerreotype. In the case of the general view of the Ca' Foscari, he "began," as he told his father, "as it *should* be done, taking plenty of time," and apparently achieved such completeness that it was J.D. Harding's opinion that the drawing would "'frighten the Daguerreotype into fits,' and [that] Cout[t]et [had] said on being asked if it was like – "Ça ne lui *ressemble pas* – c'est la meme [*sic*] chose."[3]

The present drawing shows the window that stands on the left side of the central group of four combined lights on the building's upper storey as it faces onto the Grand Canal. It is identified by the short section of raised moulding ascending from the lower left corner of the sheet, forming the frame of a sculpted marble panel showing winged putti that runs across the central compartment of the façade (a glimpse of a wing and the head and raised right arm of one of the figures appears at the bottom edge of the drawing). Now glazed, in 1845 the window was closed with an improvised shutter. In *The Seven Lamps of Architecture*, published in 1849, Ruskin gave a detailed analysis of the geometry of the mouldings of the palace windows, illustrated with an etching after a drawing of his of one of the side windows of the *piano nobile* (which are similar to those of the upper storey except that the pattern of the mouldings has been turned through 90 degrees).[4]

Ruskin was appalled by the destruction that was being wrought upon Venice, and his letters home are a litany of accusations against the Venetian authorities for the desecration of the fabric of the city through neglect or restoration. In a state of emotional frenzy, he alternated between a lament that buildings might be about to collapse – "The Foscari palace is all *but* a total ruin," he wrote, "the rents in its walls are half a foot wide"[5] – and a despair that he might not be able to draw them to his satisfaction and to take account of their timeworn decrepitude: "I should have taken a month to do it & now I can find no expedient nor mode of getting at it that will give me what I want. To ta[ke t]he outline is what has been done a thousand times – the bea[uty] of it is in the cracks & the stains, and to draw these out is impossible and I am in despair."[6] In the Index that was attached to later editions of *The Stones of Venice*, Ruskin reminisced that "the restoration [of the Palazzo Foscari] was necessary, however: for when I was in Venice in 1845, this palace was a foul ruin; its great hall a mass of mud, used as the back receptacle of a stonemason's yard; and its rooms whitewashed, and scribbled over with indecent caricatures."[7]

NOTES

1 Ruskin 1903–12, vol. 11, *The Stones of Venice III and Examples of the Architecture of Venice*, p. 378.
2 Ruskin 1972, p. 205.
3 Ibid., p. 218. Joseph Couttet, a valued friend and companion, was on frequent occasions Ruskin's mountain guide in France and Switzerland and sometimes travelled with him in Italy.
4 See Ruskin 1903–12, vol. 8, *The Seven Lamps of Architecture*, p. 94 and plate VIII, opposite p. 132.
5 Ruskin 1972, p. 199. The building was restored in 1867 when it became the Faculty of Commerce and Economics of Venice University, with further adaptations being made in the twentieth century (see Touring Club Italiano 1985, p. 444).
6 Ibid., p. 218.
7 Ruskin 1903–12, vol. 11, p. 378.

4

Southwest Porch of St. Wulfran's, Abbeville 1848

Graphite on white paper; 32.6 × 15 cm
Private collection

Ruskin visited northern France several times as a child. In later life, he stayed often in Normandy and Picardy, where he studied Gothic buildings and explored medieval towns in the course of his journeys to and from Italy or Switzerland. In the summer of 1848, shortly after his marriage to Effie Gray, he made a tour of that part of France, the departure for which was laconically recorded by his father: "saw my son and his wife off by rail to Abbeville," with the further observation that this was a place "where he is in his element among cathedrals and tumble-down houses."[1] Ruskin presumably thought of Abbeville as an auspicious place to take his bride because he had himself loved its buildings and way of life when he had been there at the age of sixteen.

The couple stayed in Abbeville from the 8th to the 15th August, and it was probably in the course of these few days that the present drawing of the town's collegiate church was made. The beauty of its west front induced a declaration of ecstatic thrill: "Much as I admired Abbeville porch before," Ruskin told his parents on the day of their arrival, "it comes upon me now in such *luscious* richness, – so full, so fantastic, – so exquisitely picturesque that I seem never to have seen it before."[3] The drawing shows the most southerly of the three portals that form the church's façade and was made from a vantage point just outside the main west door. Ruskin paid very close attention to the flamboyant Gothic mouldings that form such a fantastic shape within the triangular gable that rises from the pointed archway of the door below and to the blind arcade of lancets with interwoven traceries on each side. Already at this stage he had devised a manner of drawing that allowed immaculately detailed observation of particular parts of the building, but with other parts left blank or just blocked in with carefully plotted lines. Beautiful though it may be, a drawing of this type was not intended as a complete and pictorial composition, but instead as a means of record-making and as something to which he might return for information while writing.

When preparing the proofs of chapter nine of *Præterita*, Ruskin added a passage in which he described a particular aesthetic predisposition he felt for "all sorts of filigree and embroidery, from hoarfrost to the high clouds. The intricacies of virgin silver, of arborescent gold, the weaving of birds'-nests, the netting of lace, the basket capitals of Byzantium, and most of all the tabernacle work of the French flamboyant school."[4] This love of a complex and rhythmical surface pattern, within which there might be both consistency and variation, commenced, as he remembered, with his "first sight of Rouen." At the same time, Abbeville was for him "the preface and interpretation of Rouen,"[5] and a place where he reflected upon and digested the beauty of abstract decorative pattern in architecture.

NOTES

1 John James Ruskin, quoted in Ruskin 1903–12, vol. 8, *The Seven Lamps of Architecture*, p. xxix.
2 Ruskin 1903–12, vol. 35, *Præterita and Dilecta*, p. 156.
3 Ruskin 1903–12, vol. 8, p. 188, note 3.
4 Ruskin 1903–12, vol. 35, p. 157, note 3.
5 Ibid., pp. 156–157.

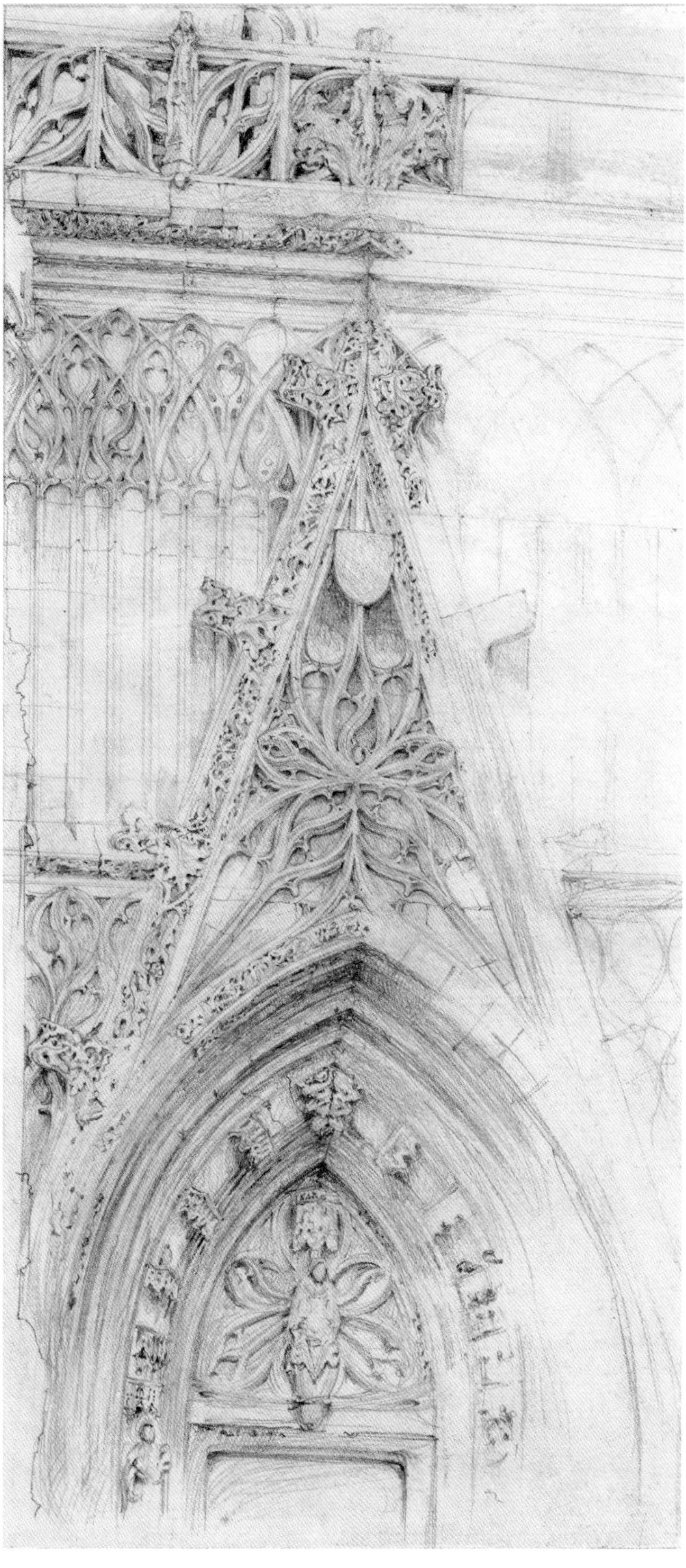

5

End View of the Pulpit in the Church of San Ambrogio, Milan 1849 (?)

Graphite with light washes of colour on buff paper; 43.8 × 33 cm
Victoria and Albert Museum, London (226-1887)

The pulpit of the great Lombard Romanesque basilica of Sant'Ambrogio in Milan stands in the central nave of the church and was reconstructed in 1196 by Guglielmo da Pomo. An arcade of columns supports an entablature decorated with human and animal forms and lively spirals of vegetable stems and leaves. At the corners are, on the left side, an eagle with its wings open to form the shape of the pendentive of the arch and, on the right, a draped telamon supporting the cornice upon his shoulders and upraised arms. Within the arcade is the paleochristian sarcophagus of the Roman general Flavius Stilicho, decorated on its front side with a sculpted relief of Jesus and the Apostles.

Ruskin passed through Milan twice in the summer of 1845, and the suggestion has been made that the present drawing was done then.[1] There are frequent references to the church, and even to the pulpit, in the first volume of *The Stones of Venice*, published in 1851. However, Ruskin's most detailed description of the pulpit occurs in the lecture that he gave at the Architectural Museum in London in 1858 entitled "The Two Paths."[2] The question of when the drawing was made, therefore, remains open; subsequent visits to Milan took place in 1846 and 1849, and then again in 1851. He returned to Milan in 1862 with Edward and Georgiana Burne-Jones. The only evidence of his having worked in the church on a particular occasion is the date of 27 October 1849 inscribed on a drawing entitled *St. Ambrogio: Capital and Base*, listed in the catalogue of Ruskin's drawings in the Library Edition.[3]

NOTES

1 London Washington 1993, p. 308, cat. 244.
2 The lecture was published in 1859 with an illustration showing "the Serpent beguiling Eve" from the sculpted decoration, which Ruskin described as more interesting than Michelangelo's "Temptation of Eve" in the Sistine Chapel because in it is seen "the birth of Italian art." Ruskin 1903–12, vol. 16, *The Two Paths*, p. 276.
3 Ruskin 1903–12, vol. 38, *Bibliography, Catalogue of Ruskin's Drawings, Addenda et Corrigenda*, p. 267.

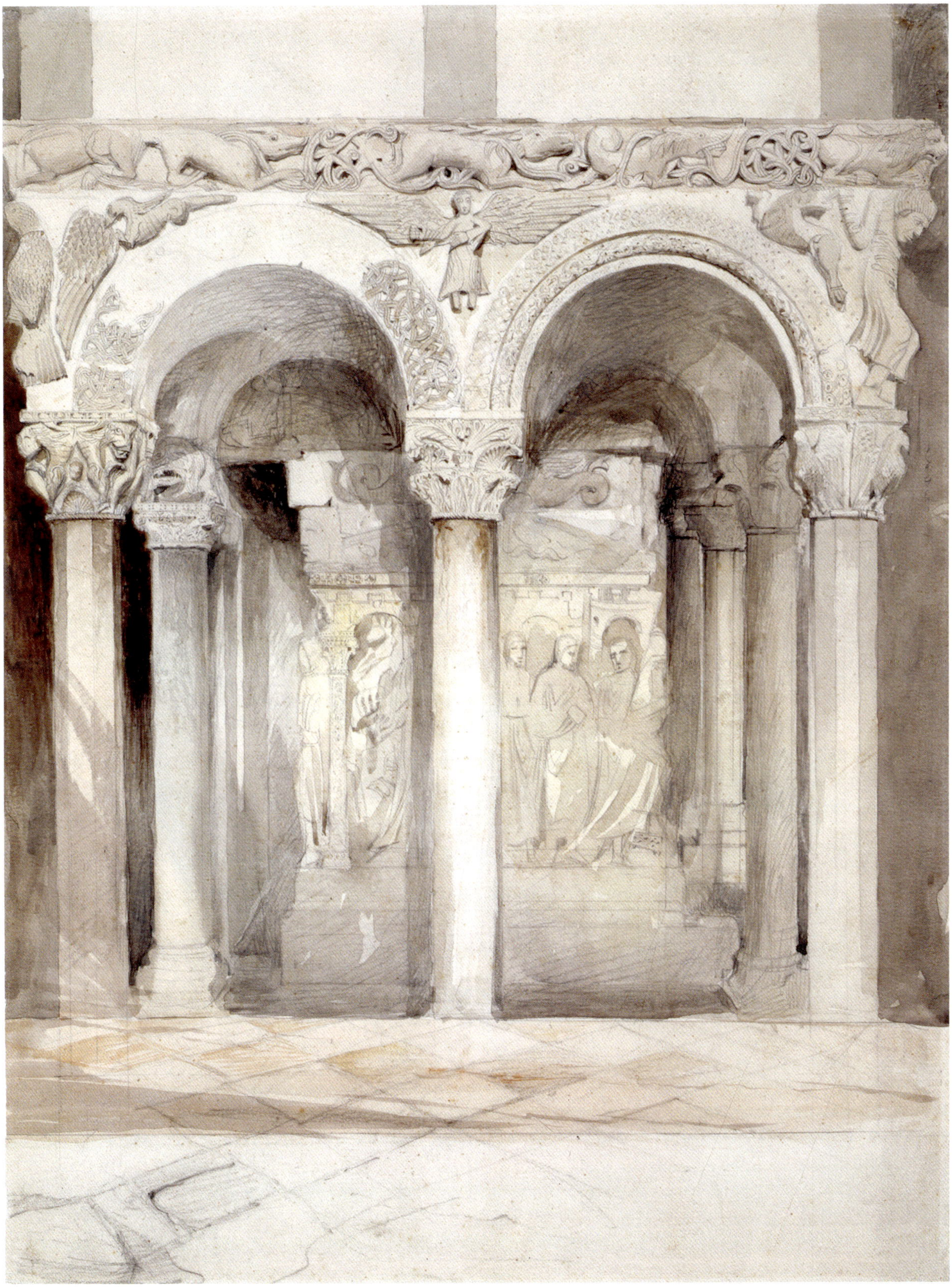

6

Byzantine Capitals, Convex Group, for "The Stones of Venice" c. 1851–53

Graphite, black ink and ink wash on two joined sheets of white paper; 18.4 × 13.5 cm (overall)
Ruskin Foundation (Ruskin Library, Lancaster University) (RF 1582)

This beautiful collection of studies of twelve Venetian capitals was made in preparation for plate VIII, engraved by John Henry Le Keux, in the second volume of *The Stones of Venice* (as it appears there, one further register of capitals of a very simple type is given, but all of the others are immediately recognizable as having been engraved from this drawing).[1] The plate serves as an illustration to a passage of text in which Ruskin described "the two great orders of capitals in the world," one of which is "convex in its contour, the other concave." Of the former, "all freedom of fancy" is found, while he described the concave group as marked by "severity of ornament" and as an order that is "longest-lived, and extends itself into the Gothic times." Both groups, Ruskin believed, were "formed upon the types of flowers, – [the concave] upon that of the water-lily, [the convex] upon that of the convolvulus. There was no intention in the Byzantine architects to imitate either one or other of these flowers; but, as I have already so often repeated, all beautiful works of art must either intentionally imitate or accidentally resemble natural forms."[2]

Ruskin understood the vital role that Venice had performed in transmitting into the West the architectural practices and traditions of the Greek city of Byzantium (the capital of the Roman Empire from AD 330). The sack of Constantinople by the Venetians in 1204 during the Fourth Crusade and the wholesale import of vast masses of precious building materials set a pattern of building in Venice that was both historicist and independent.

Of the capitals shown in the drawing, the first and second in the upper register are Corinthian in type and were taken from the ground floor arcade of the Casa Loredan (slightly faint in the present drawing but more clearly seen in the engraving). They prompted Ruskin to write that he had "never [seen] one of these Venetian capitals in all respects like another." The third capital, of a similar type to the previous two, comes from the Fondaco dei Turchi. The fourth is again from the Casa Loredan, but from the upper arcade. Capitals five and six were drawn from St. Mark's Basilica, the latter of a "favourite early Lombardic form,"[3] while the seventh was taken from what Ruskin called "The Braided House,"[4] now known as Palazzo Donà (on the Grand Canal on the San Polo side, between San Silvestro and San Tomà). The eighth in the sequence, which is of the "lily capital" type as seen in the north and south porticoes of St. Mark's (see cat. 7), is another Byzantine trophy incorporated into the Casa Loredan. The ninth and tenth capitals are from St. Mark's, the former identified by John Unrau as the second from the corner facing westward on the upper storey of the northwest portico, while the latter is that placed closest to the door on its left side on the most southerly porch of the basilica's west front. The eleventh capital, with windswept acanthus leaves, was observed on the upper arcade of the

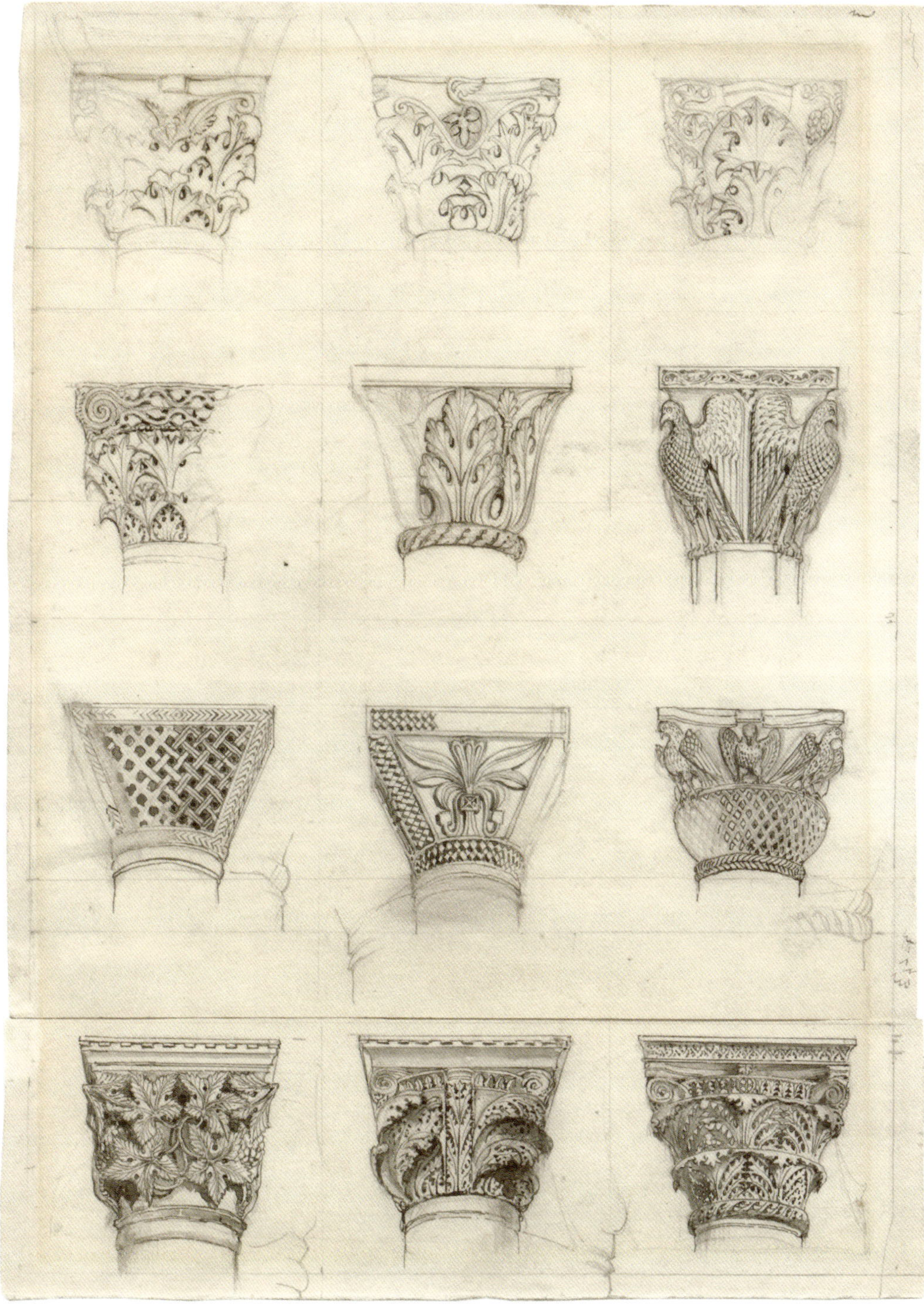

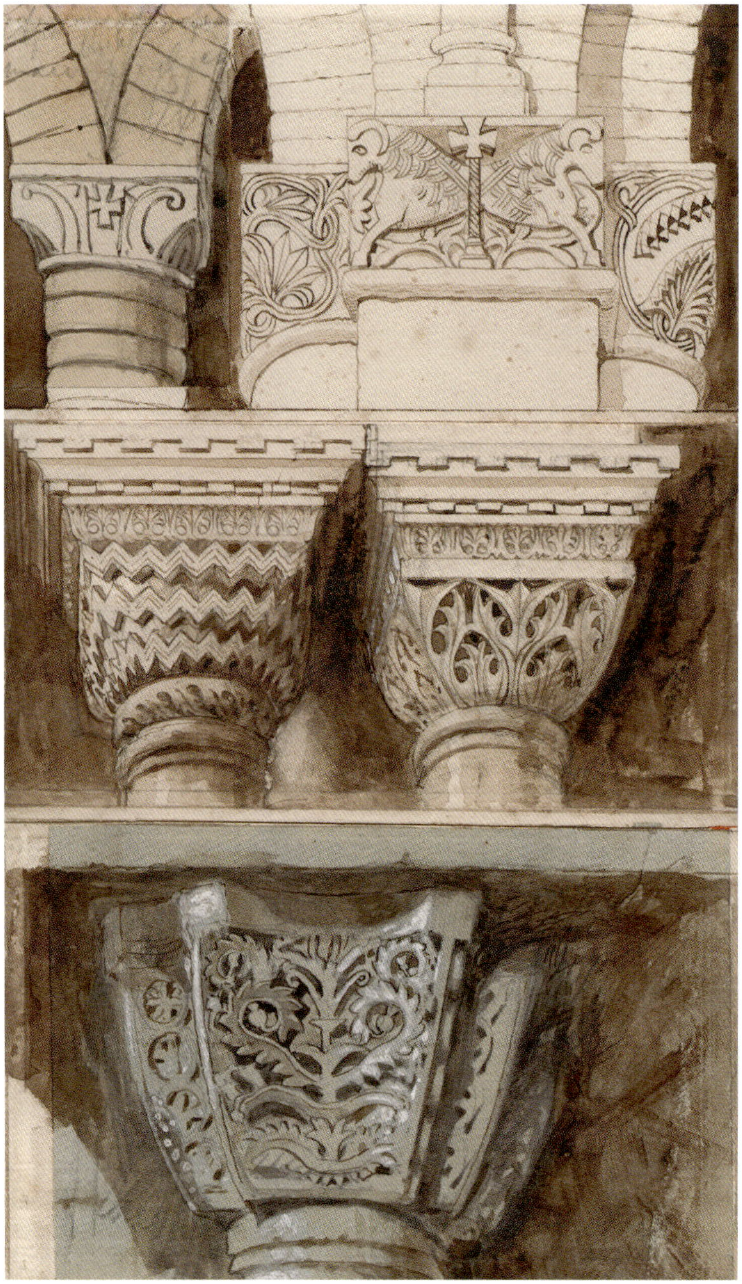

FIG. 5.1
John Ruskin
Capitals, Convex Group, for "The Stones of Venice," c. 1851
Graphite, black and brown ink, ink wash, watercolour and bodycolour on four joined sheets of white paper laid onto card
Ruskin Foundation (Ruskin Library, Lancaster University) (RF 1031)

Fondaco dei Turchi. The twelfth capital, with an unruffled acanthus pattern, was identified by Ruskin as showing "one of the most delicate of the varieties occurring in St. Mark's ... remarkable for the cutting of the sharp thistle-like leaves into open relief, so that the light sometimes shines through them from behind, and for the beautiful curling of the extremities of the leaves outwards, joining each other at the top, as in an undivided flower."[5] Unrau has located it in the transept of the basilica.[6]

The drawing is also especially interesting as an example of how Ruskin planned the illustrations for the three volumes of *The Stones of Venice* (see also fig. 5.1). The engraver John Henry Le Keux was provided with the sheet and others showing single capitals but with even closer attention to the detail of their decoration (two drawings of this type for the ninth and twelfth capitals are in the collection of the Ruskin Foundation at Lancaster University).[7] An unpublished letter from Ruskin to Le Keux from the time when the second volume of *The Stones of Venice* was being prepared explains how Ruskin wanted the plates to appear, with instructions to the engraver in relation to architectural details that he had left incomplete but wished to have worked up to a consistent whole. Ruskin warned Le Keux that he was particularly concerned that the projecting mouldings at the tops of the shafts should not "look like iron rings," and peremptorily told him to "mind what he is about," as Ruskin himself had "only taken real pains with two[8] ... which are of the finest time of Venetian Gothic [while] no 8 is also a great favourite of mine."[9] Lastly, he asked Le Keux to introduce the "squaring lines that divide the plate into compartments."[10]

NOTES

1 In my discussion of the capitals shown, I have numbered them from one to twelve, working from top left to bottom right. Ruskin's discussion of the fifteen capitals in the engraving uses a different numerical to take account of the further register of three capitals at the top.
2 Ruskin 1903–12, vol. 10, *The Stones of Venice II*, pp. 155–156.
3 Ibid., pp. 159–160.
4 Ibid., p. 453.
5 Ibid., p. 157.
6 Unrau 1984, p. 158.
7 Ibid., pp. 83, 58; figs. 49, 112.
8 The sixth and ninth capitals in the sequence, each from St. Mark's.
9 "No 8" was of course the fifth drawing as seen here, again from St. Mark's.
10 Letter from John Ruskin to John Henry Le Keux, private collection.

7

Basket and Lily Capital, St. Mark's 1849–52

Graphite with grey and brown washes heightened with touches of white bodycolour on paper; 22.4 × 15.1 cm (sight)
Private collection

The drawings that Ruskin made in the course of his two long stays in Venice, from 1849 to 1850 and 1851 to 1852, served as records to have to hand as he worked on the three volumes of *The Stones of Venice.* His purpose was to make detailed and accurate records of whatever it was he was studying, without invention or elaboration. At St. Mark's, he particularly admired the Byzantine capitals of the west façade and of the two porticoes of the basilica, believing them especially to be valued as parts of the surviving fabric of the thirteenth-century building (although themselves older even than that, having been brought to Venice as booty following the sack of Constantinople in 1204 during the Fourth Crusade).

Discussion of the capitals occurs in chapter five of the second volume of *The Stones of Venice*, entitled "Byzantine Palaces." Speaking specifically of the four so-called by him "lily capitals," which are seen at the head of the pairs of single columns supporting clusters of four and form the outside part of the arched structures that stand as buttresses at each end of the west façade, he refuted the claim that they were in some way primitive or unsophisticated: "These capitals, called barbarous by our architects, are without exception the most subtle pieces of composition in broad contour which I have ever met with in architecture."[1] He went on to describe in rhapsodic terms the marble fretwork that forms a honeycomb-like pattern over the concave surface of the capitals of the northwest and southwest porticoes: "No amount of illustration or eulogium would be enough to make the reader understand the perfect beauty of the thing itself, as the sun steals from interstice to interstice of its marble veil, and touches with the white lustre of its rays at midday the pointed leaves of its thirsty lilies."[2] In *The Stones of Venice*, a line engraving after another drawing by Ruskin of the same capital – that which supports the northwest portico (although shown from a position 90 degrees further to the right) – was reproduced (fig. 5.2).

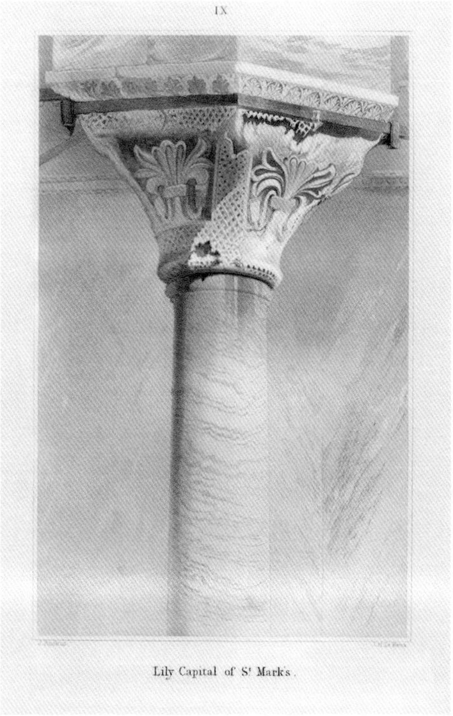

FIG. 5.2
John Ruskin, engraved by John Henry Le Keux
Lily Capital of St. Mark's, 1853
From *The Stones of Venice II*, Library Edition, plate IX

NOTES

1 Ruskin 1903–12, vol. 10, *The Stones of Venice II*, p. 156.
2 Ibid., pp. 164–165.

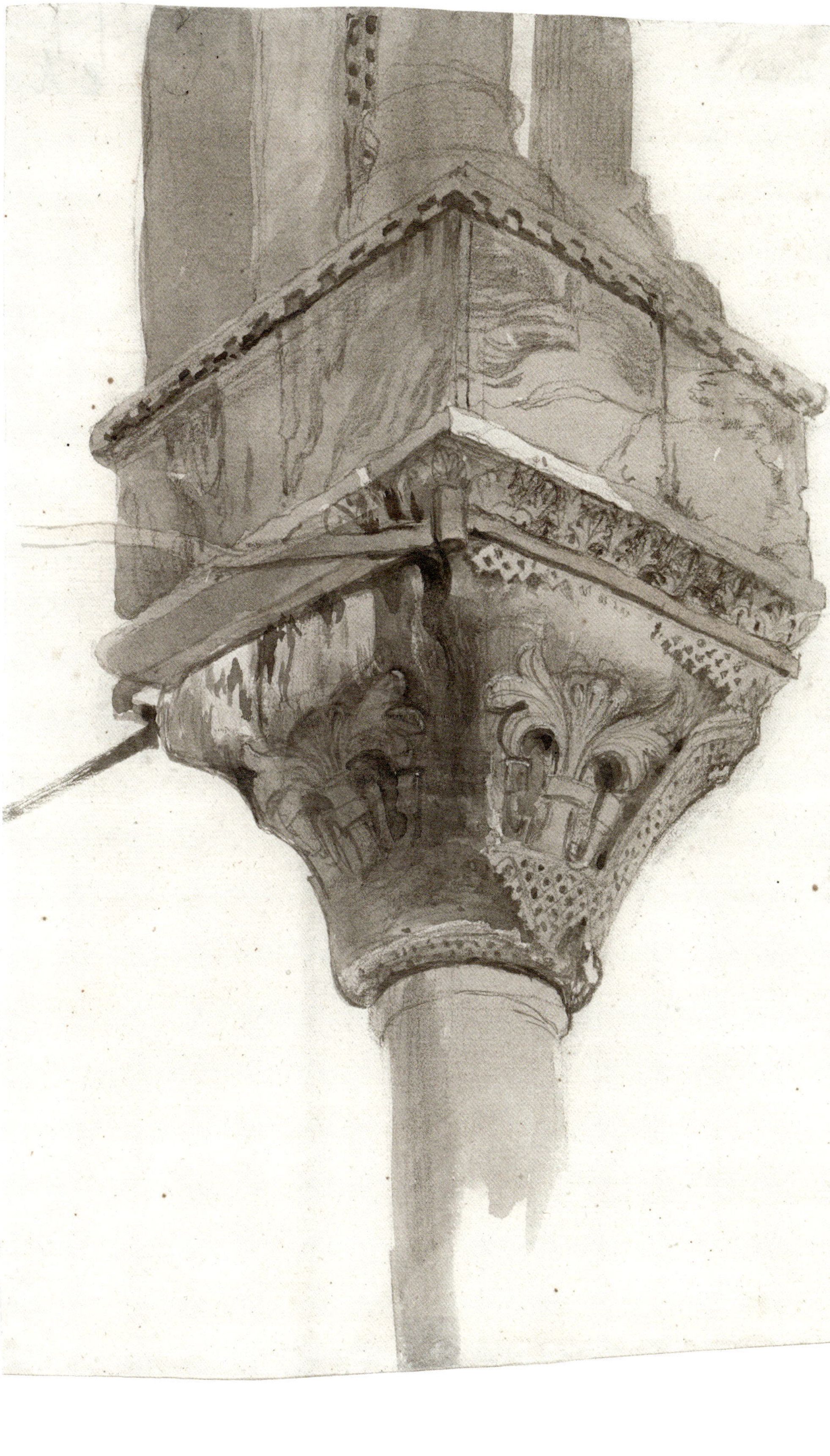

8

Capital 36 of the Ducal Palace, Venice 1849–52

Graphite and wash on white laid paper; 22.3 × 23.5 cm
Ruskin Foundation (Ruskin Library, Lancaster University) (RF 1601)
Inscriptions: *IUSTITIA and ARISTOTLE – CHE – DIE – LEGE*

As he began to prepare his thoughts for what was to become *The Stones of Venice*, Ruskin came to realize that there was very little reliable information about the fabric of Venice. It was his purpose, therefore, to create a methodology by which building styles and techniques could be placed into chronological sequence, dependent on careful measurement of mouldings and analysis of curves and shapes, and upon the stylistic characteristics of sculpted decoration. In the case of the Doge's Palace, he was thus able to draw the conclusion that the building "has two principal façades; one towards the sea, the other towards the Piazzetta. The seaward side, and, as far as its seventh main arch inclusive, the Piazzetta side, is the work of the early part of the fourteenth century, some of it perhaps even earlier; while the rest of the Piazzetta side is of the fifteenth." Taking a dig at those in Venice who he had attempted to consult, he further explained that this "difference in age has been gravely disputed by the Venetian antiquaries, who have examined many documents on the subject, and quoted some which they never examined." However, Ruskin was confident of his own account of the building, "for not only the masonry, but the sculpture, changes at the ninth lower shaft, and that in the capitals of the shafts both of the upper and lower arcade: the costumes of the figures introduced in the sea façade being purely Giottesque ... while the costume on the other capitals is Renaissance-Classic."[1]

He made a very careful study of all the capitals of the lower arcade of the Doge's Palace, describing them in detail in chapter eight of the second volume of *The Stones of Venice*. Capital 36 stands at the far end of the Piazzetta front of the building toward the basilica and in the section of the palace's arcade that was built in the fifteenth century, and beneath the sculpted angle showing the Judgment of Solomon. It corresponds to the subject of the sculpture as it also shows the figure of Justice enthroned and "on the seven other sides examples of acts of justice or good government, or figures of lawgivers."[2] Ruskin saw this, along with the Judgment of Solomon above, as "an assertion by that government [of Venice] of its belief that Justice only could be the foundation of its stability, as these stones of Justice and Judgment are the foundation of its halls of council."[3] On the whole, he was inclined – at least in *The Stones of Venice* – to accept this as a legitimate claim, and this despite his view that as a society Venice was increasingly given to hubris and self-satisfaction. Furthermore, and notwithstanding Ruskin's notorious aversion to the "pestilent art of the Renaissance,"[4] he believed that it would always be regarded as "the most beautiful of the whole series: and indeed it is very noble; its groups of figures most carefully studied, very graceful, and much more pleasing than those of the earlier work, though with less real power in them."[5]

NOTES

1 Ruskin 1903–12, vol. 9, *The Stones of Venice I*, pp. 52–53.
2 Ruskin 1903–12, vol. 10, *The Stones of Venice II*, p. 425.
3 Ibid., p. 427.
4 Ruskin 1903–12, vol. 9, p. 47.
5 Ruskin 1903–12, vol. 10, p. 425.

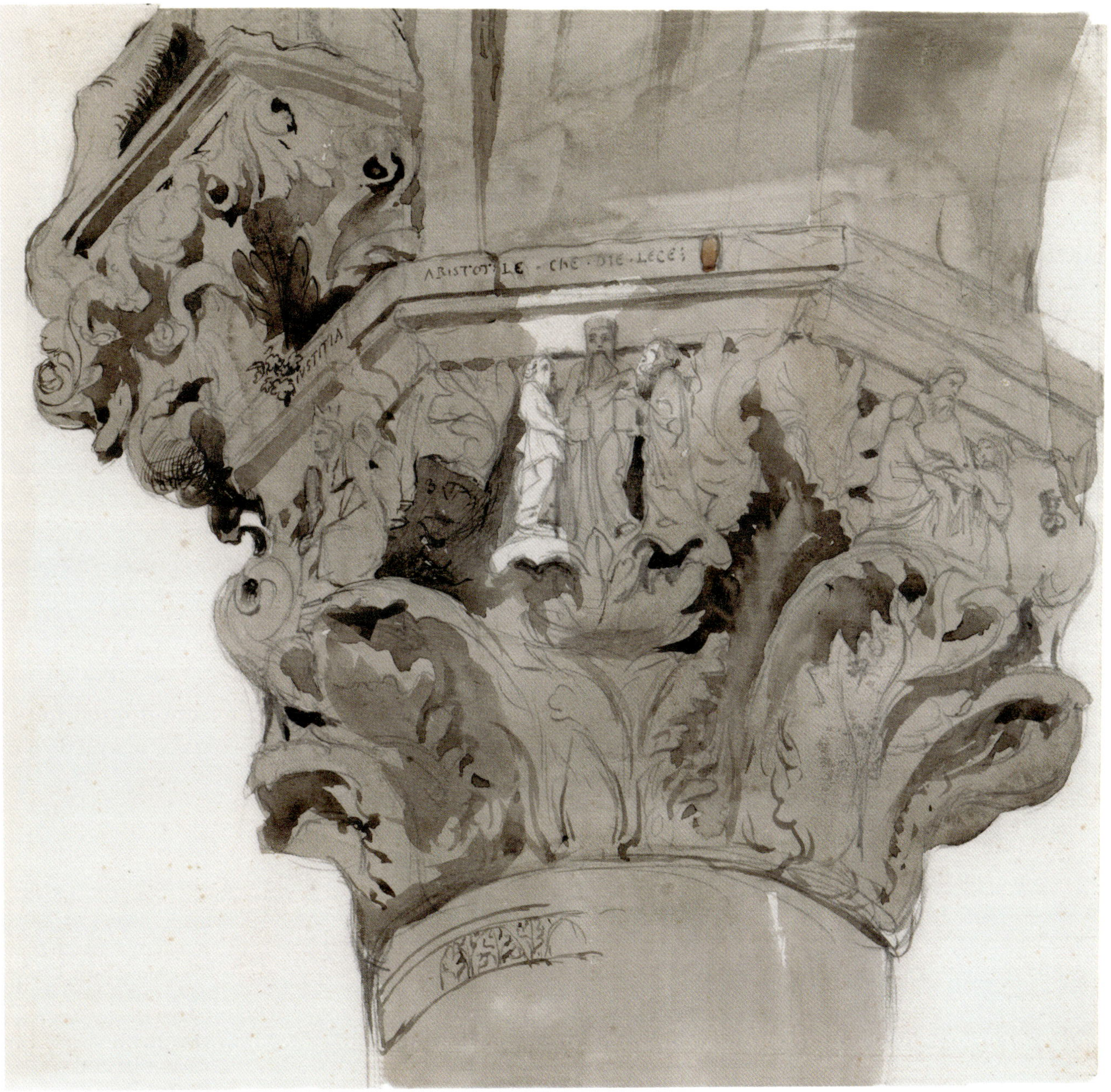
CHE · DIE · LEGE

9

Cornice Decoration – for "The Stones of Venice" c. 1851

Graphite, brown ink and ink wash on white paper; 24 × 16.2 cm
Ruskin Foundation (Ruskin Library, Lancaster University) (RF 1036)
Inscriptions: inscribed with letters and titled in brown ink, *XVI / J. Ruskin Thos. Lupton / CORNICE DECORATION*

Whereas on previous visits to Venice Ruskin had focused his attention on whole buildings, and usually the more familiar Venetian landmarks, in 1849 and 1850 he frequently moved closer to his subjects – indeed on many occasions he made studies of small details of their decoration, often packing these together in confusing arabesques upon the sheet. It was Ruskin's insight that the apparently unconscious shaping of cornices and mouldings, as well as arch profiles and the shape of window apertures, and any other part of a building if found in its original condition, might give some clue as to the larger state of mind of the men who created them. Thus that winter and the following spring he made an exhaustive search for authentic fragments of the city's original structure. Ten years later he was inclined to denigrate the importance of this campaign of close observation, writing to Charles Eliot Norton, who was then also in Venice: "I went through so much hard, dry, mechanical toil there, that I quite lost, before I left it, the charm of the place ... Venice presented itself to me merely as so many 'mouldings,' and I had few associations with any building but those of more or less pain and puzzle and provocation."[1] However, in 1849 Ruskin knew the vital importance of making careful measured drawings of architectural detail, so as to be able to construct typologies of the main elements that could be used to chart the evolution of style and allow specific buildings to be placed within chronological sequences. *Studies of Foliage Reliefs, Scaliger Tombs, Verona* (fig. 5.3) is an example of the type of working sheet he made in situ, and in this instance includes mouldings seen in the Scaliger tombs in Verona, which correspond with the lowest of the five mouldings on the present sheet.

The drawing was reproduced by Thomas Lupton as a mezzotint and appeared as plate XVI in the first volume of *The Stones of Venice.*[2]

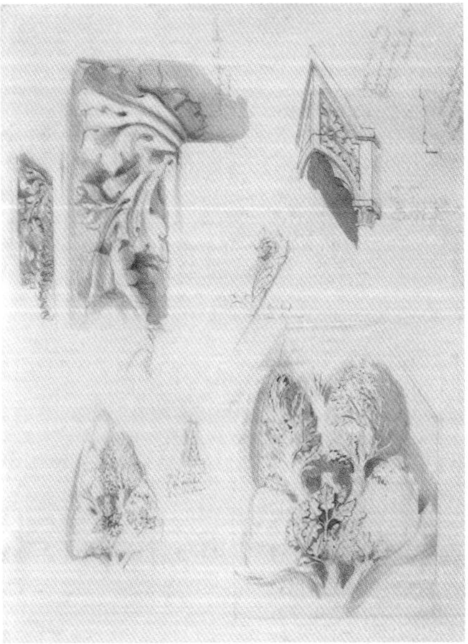

FIG. 5.3
John Ruskin
Studies of Foliage Reliefs, Scaliger Tombs ("Stones of Venice" Worksheet No. 179), 9–18 March 1850
Graphite, pen and black ink with grey wash laid down on wove paper
Private collection

NOTES

1 Ruskin 1903–12, vol. 9, *The Stones of Venice I*, pp. xxvii–xxviii.
2 The mezzotint appeared opposite p. 302 in the first edition of *The Stones of Venice I.* In the Library Edition, the original mezzotint was reproduced as a photogravure made by George Allen, which appears in ibid, opposite p. 365.

XVI

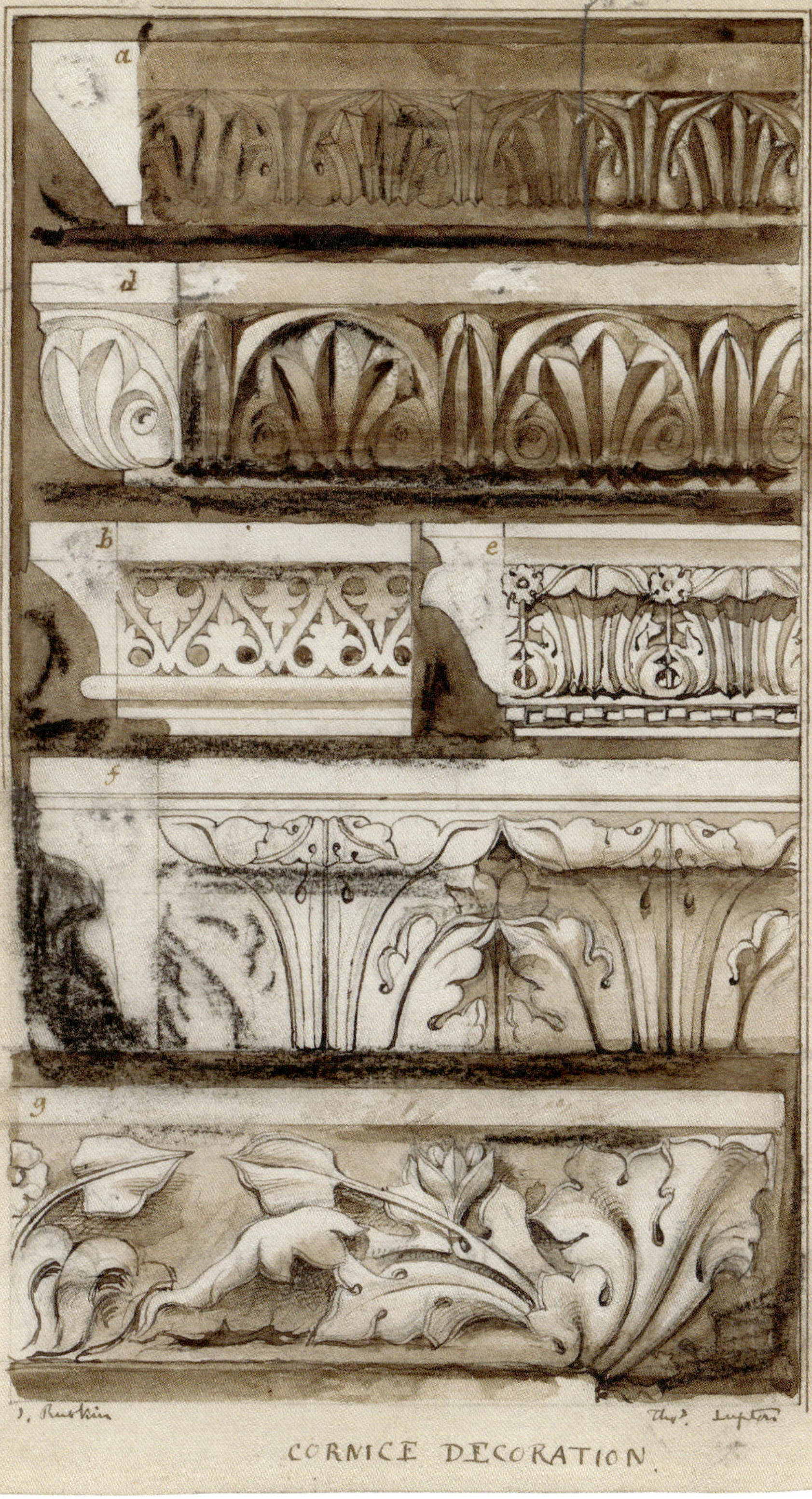

J. Ruskin Thos. Lupton

CORNICE DECORATION.

10

The Gryphon Bearing the North Shaft of the West Entrance of the Duomo, Verona 1869

Watercolour and bodycolour over graphite on wove paper; 22.1 × 35.9 cm
The Ashmolean Museum, Oxford. Presented by John Ruskin to the Ruskin Drawing School (University of Oxford), 1875 (WA.RS.ED.082)

Ruskin loved Verona almost as much as he loved Venice. During his early visits there he studied its buildings and recommended the city to fellow travellers. The Verona cathedral, dedicated to Santa Maria Matricolare, was commenced after the earthquake of 1117, and its façade and spiral-decorated marble columns are of Romanesque style. In a diary entry for 12 May 1846, Ruskin gave a graphic account of the two griffins that support spiral-patterned columns and upon which stands the portal of the cathedral's west front. In the third volume of *Modern Painters*, published in 1856, he explained how the principle of "truth to nature" might even be applied to the representation of a mythic beast, comparing the Verona griffin with a "false grotesque from classical (Roman) architecture,"[1] supporting his argument with an etching after his own drawing of the head of the griffin. On 22 June 1869, he wrote to his mother from Verona to tell her how he was getting "'quite round' my favourite Griffin. I am painting him on the other side from that I engraved in *Modern Painters*, and the marble of him comes all into beautiful orange and grey, and I'm continually finding out new feathers and sinews in him that I did not know of."[2] In his 1870 lectures on sculpture, *Aratra Pentelici*, he explained that the "Griffin representing Christian life is restraining the dragon in its claws."[3]

Ruskin displayed the present drawing with illustrations of Italian Gothic art in the Educational series of his drawings at the Oxford Drawing School. In the appendix to *The Stones of Venice*, he told how, even despite their being "the noblest pieces of mediæval sculpture in North Italy, the two griffins at the central (west) door of the cathedral at Verona, were daily permitted to be brought into service, when I was there in the autumn of 1849, by a washer-woman living in the Piazza, who tied her clothes-line to their beaks."[4]

NOTES

1 Ruskin 1903–12, vol. 5, *Modern Painters III*, p. 140.
2 Ruskin 1903–12, vol. 19, *The Cestus of Aglaia and The Queen of the Air with Other Papers and Lectures on Art and Literature, 1860–1870*, p. li.
3 Ruskin 1903–12, vol. 20, *Lectures on Art and Aratra Pentelici with Lectures and Notes on Greek Art and Mythology 1870*, p. 362.
4 Ruskin 1903–12, vol. 9, *The Stones of Venice I*, p. 439.

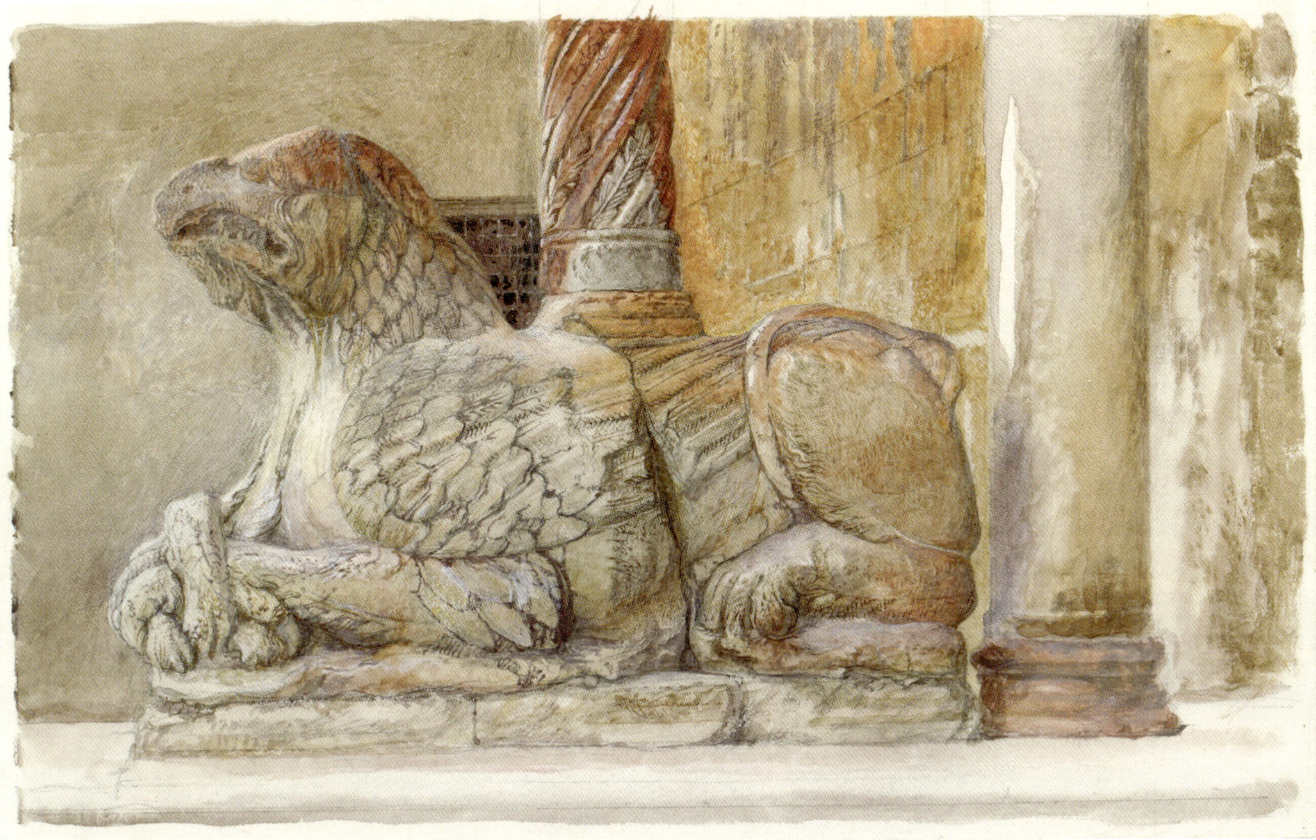

11

JOHN RUSKIN AND JOHN HOBBS

View of the West Front of the Duomo, Verona, Showing the Gryphon Sculpture 1852 (?)

Daguerreotype (half plate; image laterally reversed); 15.5 × 11.5 cm (sight)
Ruskin Foundation (Ruskin Library, Lancaster University) (RF Dag 30)

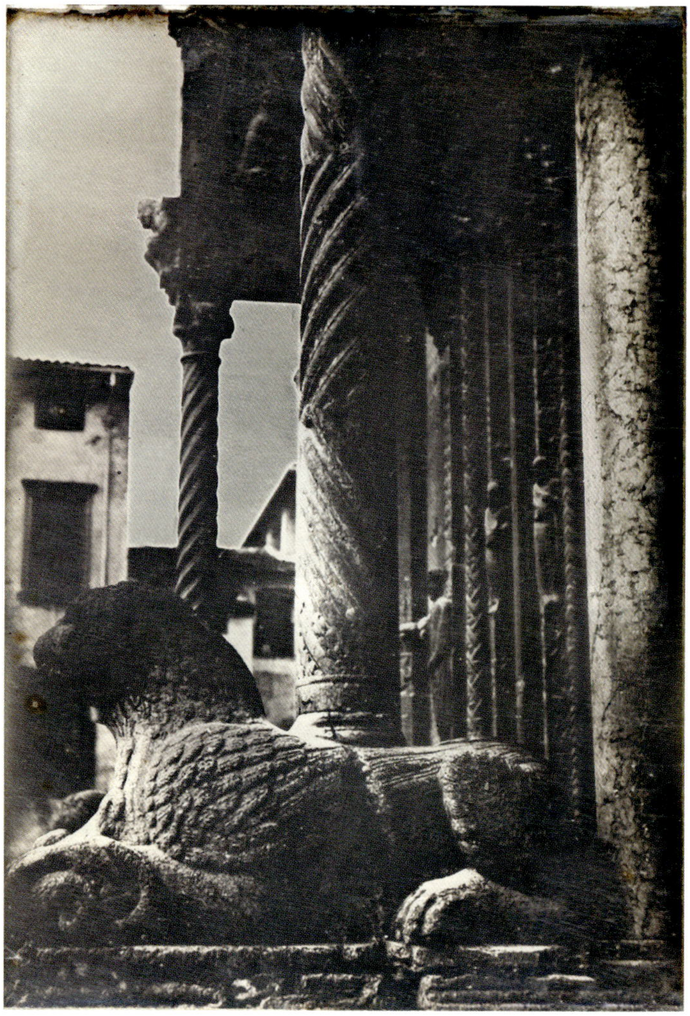

Ruskin seems first to have acquired equipment for making daguerreotypes in 1845, and at about that time trained his servant John Hobbs in the practical business of photography. Daguerreotypes record his travels in Italy that summer – notably his time in Pisa (see cat. 28). Ruskin was in Verona in 1845 and 1846, and again for short periods during each of his long stays in Venice with his wife Effie, from 1849 to 1850 and 1851 to 1852, which led to the three volumes of *The Stones of Venice*. Therefore, when he might have commissioned or taken the group of photographs of the Scaliger Tombs, the churches of Sant'Anastasia and San Zeno, and of the west front of the Duomo is an open question. One clue to a possible date, pointed out by Stephen Wildman,[1] may be deduced from the list of illustrations for Ruskin's 1869 lecture "The Flamboyant Architecture of the Valley of the Somme," in which a pencil study of one of the tombs is described as having been copied "from daguerreotype, and pencil drawings taken in 1852."[2]

The question also arises whether the present image can be regarded as Ruskin's own work or should be regarded just as something that he initiated or controlled. Certainly Hobbs played an important part in the whole undertaking, organizing the equipment and developing the plates. On the other hand, we have Effie's vivid account of her husband "with a black cloth over his head taking Daguerreotypes or climbing about the capitals covered with

NOTES

1 Lancaster 2006, p. 11, note 22.
2 Ruskin 1903–12, vol. 19, *The Cestus of Aglaia and The Queen of the Air with Other Papers and Lectures on Art and Literature, 1860–1870*, p. 270.
3 Lutyens 1965, p. 146.

dust,"[3] so Ruskin's involvement does seem to have been quite direct. There appears to be something of a stylistic divide between those daguerreotypes where careful attention has been paid to the rectilinear framing of the composition to achieve legible and pictorial effect and those in which the photographer has pressed forward to observe the particular object of attention as closely as possible, ignoring the peripheries and careless of the larger perspective and context. This second approach to photography, where all sense of relative scale and practical cognizance of three-dimensional space has been abandoned, and of which this is perhaps an example, may be recognized as exemplifying Ruskin's own work on the basis of analogy with at least some of his drawings.

12

Design Studies for Capitals for the University Museum, Oxford c. 1855–58

Watercolour over graphite with touches of white bodycolour on white paper; 26.2 × 36.7 cm
The Ashmolean Museum, Oxford. Bequeathed by Theodore Dyke Acland, 1931 (WA1931.50)

In both *The Seven Lamps of Architecture* and the three volumes of *The Stones of Venice*, Ruskin had insisted that architectural decoration should be meaningful and relevant to the lives of people and that it should be expressive of the craftsman's own creative personality. This was an artistic philosophy further explored in the lecture series given at the Philosophical Institution in Edinburgh in November 1853, in which Ruskin railed against stylized ornament. During the period that Ruskin and John Everett Millais spent together at Brig o' Turk in the Scottish Highlands earlier that same year, the latter made a series of illustrations – sometimes using Effie Ruskin as a model – for costumes and pieces of furniture that were to incorporate what Ruskin called "natural ornament," by which was meant recognizable and carefully observed botanical or animal specimens, sometimes with punning references to the wearer or intended use of an object.

There was at this time a movement afoot to provide a museum building and facilities for the teaching of the natural sciences at Oxford, a project headed by Ruskin's friend and one-time fellow undergraduate Henry Acland. A competition for the appointment of an architect was held in October 1854. The winning firm was the Dublin-based company Deane and Woodward, of which Benjamin Woodward was a committed Gothicist profoundly influenced by Ruskin's texts. The remarkable building that came about, standing on Parks Road in Oxford, is eclectic in its parts. The street front is modelled on a Flemish cloth hall, while behind is a quadrangle with a glazed roof supported on cast-iron columns and with sinuous wrought-iron traceries and spandrels above. The internal arcades are supported on colonettes cut from varieties of marble indigenous to the British Isles, and the capitals were carved by the sculptors Woodward had brought with him from Ireland – the brothers James and John O'Shea, of Ballyhooly, and their nephew Edward Whelan. The three were gifted with the most extraordinary technical skill; their stone replications of the forms of plants and animals throughout the museum were intended to inspire and instruct those drawn to the study of nature and the physical environment.

In a practical sense, Ruskin remained a bystander during the process of Woodward's appointment as architect for the Oxford museum. However, by the end of 1854 he was seized by the importance of the project and saw it as an opportunity to apply the principles of art and decoration that he had espoused. The situation was auspicious because, as Ruskin wrote to Acland, "Mr. Woodward is evidently a person who will allow of suggestion and is glad of help,"[1] while in a letter to Pauline Trevelyan he expressed boyish excitement at the prospect of getting involved in the project: "Acland has got his museum – Gothic – the architect is a friend of mine – I can do whatever I like with it ... I shall get all the Pre-Raphaelites to design me – each an archivolt and some capitals – & we will have all the plants in England and all the monsters in the museum."[2]

In the event, the Pre-Raphaelites generally kept out of it: John Everett Millais and Ruskin were no longer on good terms as Effie had left Ruskin in April 1854, and it had become general knowledge that she and Millais had fallen in love, while William Holman Hunt was painting in the Middle East. Dante Gabriel Rossetti was therefore the only Pre-Raphaelite available for the project, but nothing from him was forthcoming.

Ruskin himself made beautiful drawings such as the present in which he sketched out possible schemes of decoration that the masons might follow and in which he carried forward the principle of careful incorporation of the forms of animal and plant specimens into the architecture. On the right side is a tiny sketch of a spray of strawberry leaves against a dark background so as to show the brightness of the foliage. At the centre, and in a subsidiary line drawing placed higher on the sheet, is a scheme for linked capitals to stand above paired colonettes of the kind used on some of the windows of the building's main façade, and in which the stems were intended to overlap and intermingle, with leaves and fruit clustered in the interstices. Organic, symmetrical and compellingly decorative, and yet originating so clearly in the direct observation of an actual specimen, the drawing serves as an exemplar of the applications of Pre-Raphaelite artistic principles to architecture, nudging forward to the art nouveau.

NOTES

1 John Ruskin, quoted in Blau 1982, p. 66.
2 Ruskin 1979, pp. 94–95.

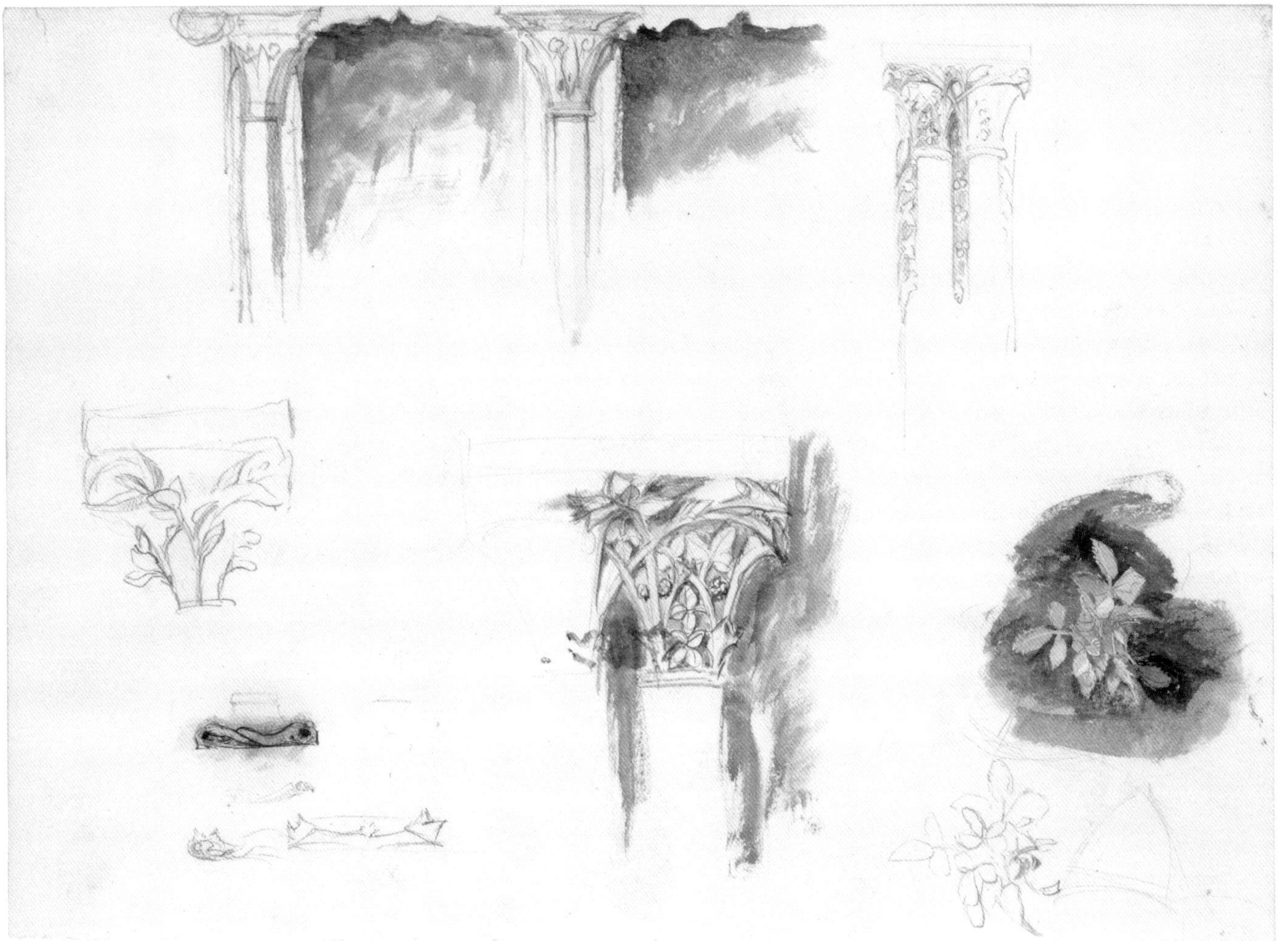

13

Design for a Window at the University Museum, Oxford c. 1855–58

Watercolour and gouache over graphite on white paper; 36.8 × 25.8 cm
The Ashmolean Museum, Oxford. Bequeathed by Theodore Dyke Acland, 1931 (WA1931.48)

In a letter to Jane Welsh Carlyle of about 1855, in which Ruskin listed the range of activities into which he was pouring his prodigious energy, he told her: "I have also designed and drawn a window for the Museum at Oxford; and have every now and then had to look over a parcel of five or six new designs for fronts and backs to the said museum."[1] Which particular window he was referring to is not clear, but it was perhaps the one immediately to the left of the main entrance, referred to in the nineteenth century as the "Ruskin Window."[2]

As construction commenced, Ruskin was burning with enthusiasm, reassuring Acland that he would help carve and inlay the windows, if need be with his own hands, and that money should not be a problem: "I will pay for a good deal myself, and I doubt not to find funds."[3] However, as time went by, his commitment to the project slackened as he was increasingly disappointed that a building he had believed might come to define a Gothic style with modern relevance – and that he had pioneered most notably in the chapter "The Nature of Gothic" in the second volume of *The Stones of Venice* as morally edifying, emotionally uplifting, and serving to educate and delight – had fallen short.

The present drawing does not appear to correspond precisely to any particular window of the lower story of the façade, which in any case show variations from one to another and exist in differing degrees of finish (as the decoration of this part of the building was never completed because of a shortage of funds). Some of the windows have paired central colonettes (as Ruskin was contemplating in his drawings of capitals (cat.12)), but here there is just a single shaft. The stone carving that the drawing was intended to inspire, in the capitals and in the wonderful form of the lizard or salamander that clings to the wall with outstretched claws on the left side, were never carved in the form seen here, but exemplify the principle of "natural ornament" that Ruskin had discussed with Henry Acland and John Everett Millais at Brig o' Turk in 1853.

NOTES

1 Ruskin 1903–12, vol. 5, *Modern Painters III*, pp. xlix–l.
2 Brooks 1989, p. 126.
3 Ruskin 1903–12, vol. 16, *"A Joy Forever" and The Two Paths with Letters on the Oxford Museum and Various Addresses 1856–1860*, p. xlv.

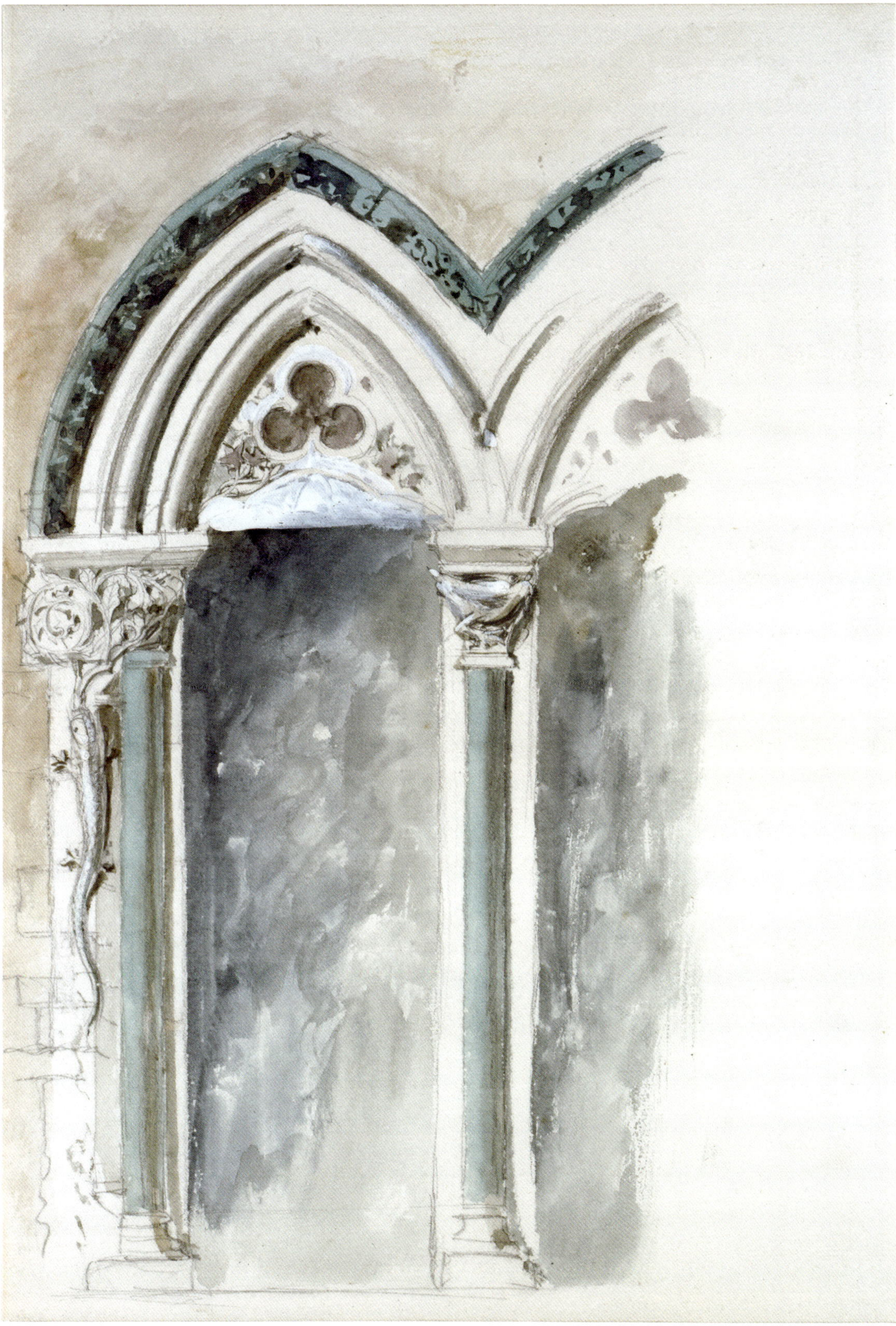

14

The Tomb of Frederick II in the Cathedral of Palermo 1874

Watercolour and bodycolour over graphite on paper; 49.5 × 32.9 cm
The Ashmolean Museum, Oxford. Presumably presented by John Ruskin to the Ruskin Drawing School (University of Oxford), where it was first recorded in 1906 (WA.RS.REF.084)

English friends invited Ruskin to stay with them in Palermo, Sicily, in the spring of 1874. His first impression was discouraging, finding it "a town built of large stones of the colour of mud, with an iron *curled* balcony to every window and everybody's shirts, chemises, petticoats, and bedclothes hung out over them to dry." However, on 22 April he recorded the things that had made a positive impression upon him, writing: "Fifthly, I've seen the tomb of Frederic II and knelt at it! and am going to draw it to-morrow – God willing."[1] The tomb, of "Corinthian porphyry and gold,"[2] was for Ruskin the "perfect type of Greek-Christian form ... temple over sarcophagus."[3] Ruskin had thought of writing a biography of Frederick, who until his death in 1250 was both King of Sicily and Holy Roman Emperor, and in his 1873 lecture *Val d'Arno* discussed his protracted contest with the papacy.

The tombs of the Norman and Hohenstaufen kings of Sicily were originally placed in the choir of Palermo cathedral, but were moved into two communicating chapels off the south aisle by Ferdinando Fuga in the last years of the eighteenth century. Frederick II's tomb – almost certainly one of the two that his grandfather Roger II had commissioned for himself but which Frederick stole from the cathedral in Cefalù in 1213 (leading to his excommunication) – is shown on the left. Roger rests in the one behind, also made of porphyry over a carved marble base and with a marble baldachino.

The chilly neoclassical interior of Palermo cathedral – the consequence of Fuga's wholesale reconstruction of the Norman church in 1781 – was exactly what Ruskin most disliked. Curiously, he appears not to have commented on the loss of what must have been the most astonishing church – Archbishop Walter Offamilio's defensive citadel in the heart of Palermo, built in the 1180s in competition with William II's Benedictine foundation, Monreale – though he had presumably seen engravings of it as it once stood.

NOTES

1 Ruskin 1903–12, vol. 23, *Val d'Arno, The Schools of Florence, Mornings in Florence, The Shepherd's Tower*, pp. xxxii–xxxiii.
2 Ruskin 1903–12, vol. 31, Ruskin 1903–12, vol. 31, *Bibliotheca Pastorum: The Economist of Xenophon, Rock Honeycomb, The Elements of Prosody and A Knight's Faith*, p. 26.
3 Ruskin 1903–12, vol. 33, *The Bible of Amiens, Valle Crucis, The Art of England, The Pleasures of England*, p. 477.

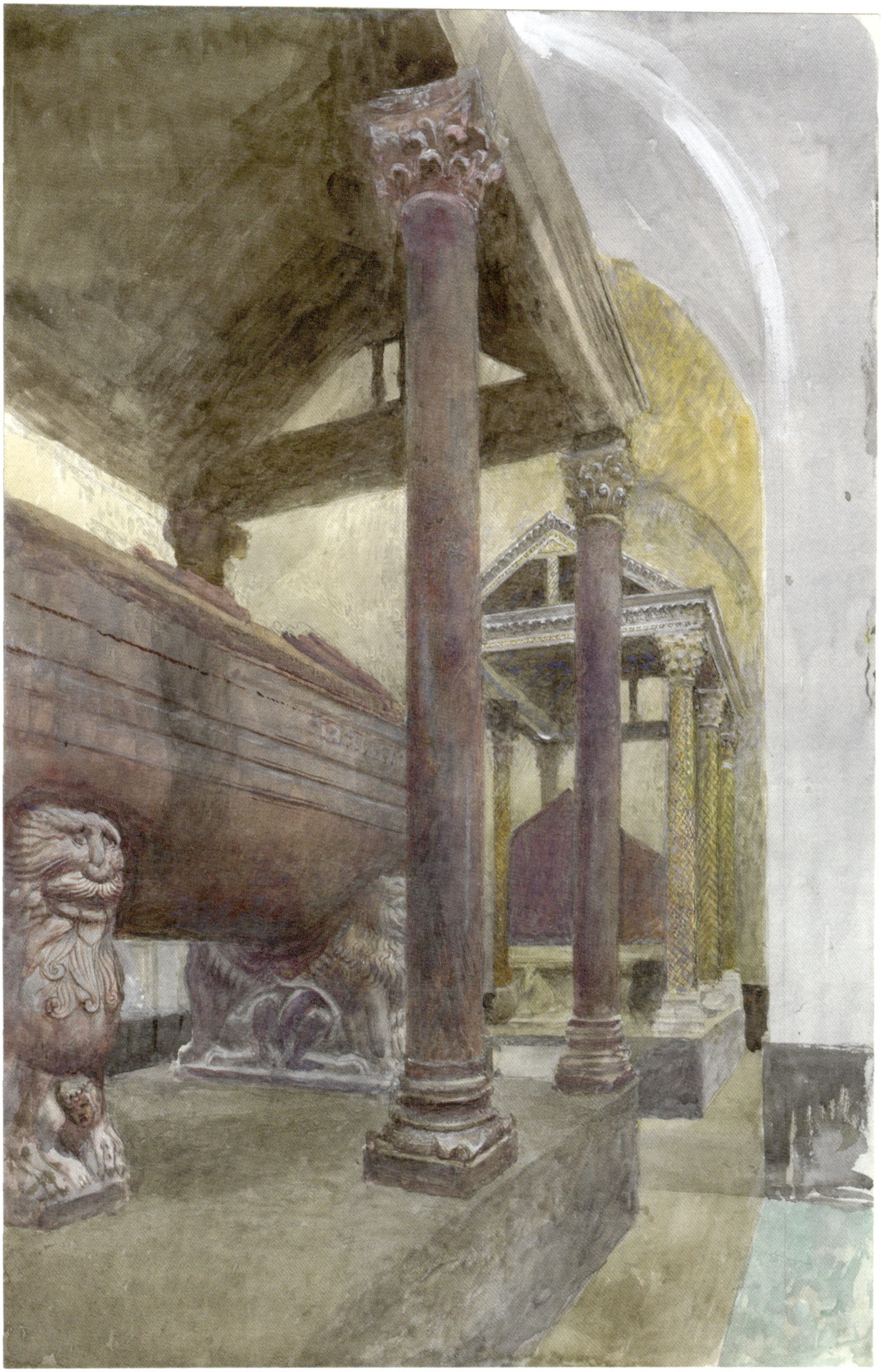

15

The Tomb of Ilaria del Carretto in the Duomo, Lucca 1874

Watercolour and bodycolour over graphite on paper, some lines ruled; 21.7 × 48.8 cm
The Ashmolean Museum, Oxford. Presumably presented by John Ruskin to the Ruskin Drawing School (University of Oxford), where it was first recorded in 1906 (WA.RS.REF.079)

Ruskin's first account of the tomb of Ilaria del Carretto was in a letter to his father of 6 May 1845. Having described its different parts, he concluded: "It is impossible to tell you the perfect sweetness of the lips and closed eyes, nor the solemnity of the seal of death which is set upon the whole figure. The sculpture – as art – is in every way perfect: truth itself, but truth selected with inconceivable refinement of feeling."[1] In the 1883 epilogue to the second volume of *Modern Painters*, he stated categorically (having equivocated in 1846) that Jacopo della Quercia's statue of Ilaria was his "ideal of Christian sculpture."[2]

This drawing is one of three made in the summer of 1874 showing the tomb. Ruskin's meditation upon the death of a beautiful young woman brought a cruel sense of his own loneliness and personal failure. As he explained in *Fors Clavigera*, studying it had once turned him "from the study of landscape to that of life." In 1874, however, he informed his readers: "I feel the separation between me and the people round me, so bitterly, in the world of my own which they cannot enter; and I see their entrance to it now barred so absolutely by their own resolves."[3] Still later, in 1878, with thoughts of the loss of Rose La Touche – the young woman with whom he had fallen in love and had hoped to marry, but who had died in 1875, and whom he obsessively associated with Ilaria del Carretto – racking his consciousness, he meditated on the transition between life and death: "And through and in the marble we may see that the damsel is not dead, but sleepeth: yet as visibly a sleep that shall know no ending until the last day break, and the last shadow flee away; until then, she 'shall not return.'"[4]

NOTES

1 Ruskin 1903–12, vol. 4, *Modern Painters II*, p. 122, note 1.
2 Ibid., p. 347.
3 Ruskin 1903–12, vol. 28, *Fors Clavigera, Letters 37–72*, p. 146.
4 Ruskin 1903–12, vol. 34, *The Storm-cloud of the Nineteenth Century, On the Old Road, Arrows of the Chace, Ruskiniana*, p. 171.

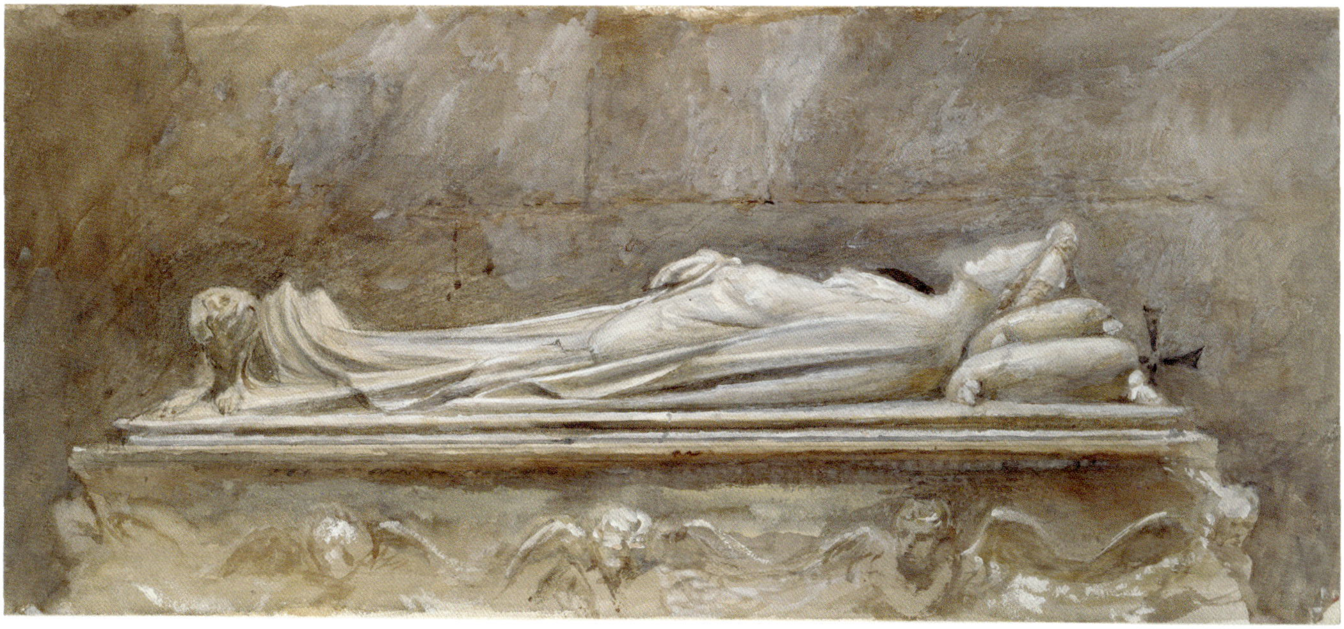

16

Study of an Acanthus Boss, Archivolt of the Central Door, San Marco, Venice 1877

Graphite and bodycolour on paper; 14 × 12.3 cm
Collection of the Guild of St. George, Museums Sheffield (CGSG00050)

This study of a sculpted whorl of acanthus leaves, with a bird from whose wings more leaves seem to grow, was drawn from one of the projecting bosses of the outer archivolt of the central porch of St. Mark's Basilica in Venice.[1] Ruskin referred briefly to this sculpted decoration in *The Stones of Venice*, writing of it in an appendix entitled "The Northern Energy": "If the great outer archivolt of St. Mark's is Byzantine, the law is somewhat broken by its busy domesticity; figures engaged in every trade ... interleaved (literally) by the superb balls of leafage, unique in sculpture."[2] He wrote further about these thirteenth-century sculpted decorations in his book *St. Mark's Rest*, published in 1877 following the traumatic winter of 1876–77 that he had spent in the city. The drawing has a frenzied quality that may be regarded as symptomatic of that agonizing period of fluctuating moods of excitement and despondency. It is treated in a style of draftsmanship of feathered and compacted strokes of graphite, touched with sparkling points of white gouache, which was a newly devised method for him, adapted to his increasing sense that time was too short to devote hours to single drawings.

Ruskin seized upon the archivolt, as if transfixed, and regarded it as the epitome of delicacy and richness of decoration. He saw that the "outer foliage is all of one kind – pure Greek Acanthus, – not in the least transforming itself into ivy, or kale, or rose: trusting wholly for its beauty to the varied play of its own narrow and pointed lobes" and following with a contrast with the "Northern spiral [which] is always elastic – like that of a watch-spring" and the "Greek [by which he meant Byzantine or Venetian] spiral, drifted like that of a whirlpool, or whirlwind ... [and which] is always an eddy or vortex – not a living rod, like the point of a young fern."[3]

NOTES

1 The sculpted boss that is here represented is the second up on the left side of the outer carved archivolt of the central or third porch of St. Mark's. See Unrau 1984 (fig. 70, p. 100) and Quill 2000 (p. 57) (in this last can be found an invaluable comparison between the drawing and the actual carving). The same winter that Ruskin created the present drawing, he had a plaster cast made of another of the bosses for the Guild of St. George collection, now in Sheffield.
2 Ruskin 1903–12, vol. 9, *The Stones of Venice I*, p. 428.
3 Ruskin 1903–12, vol. 24, *Giotto and his Works in Padua, The Cavalli Monuments, Verona, Guide to the Academy, Venice, St. Mark's Rest*, p. 287.

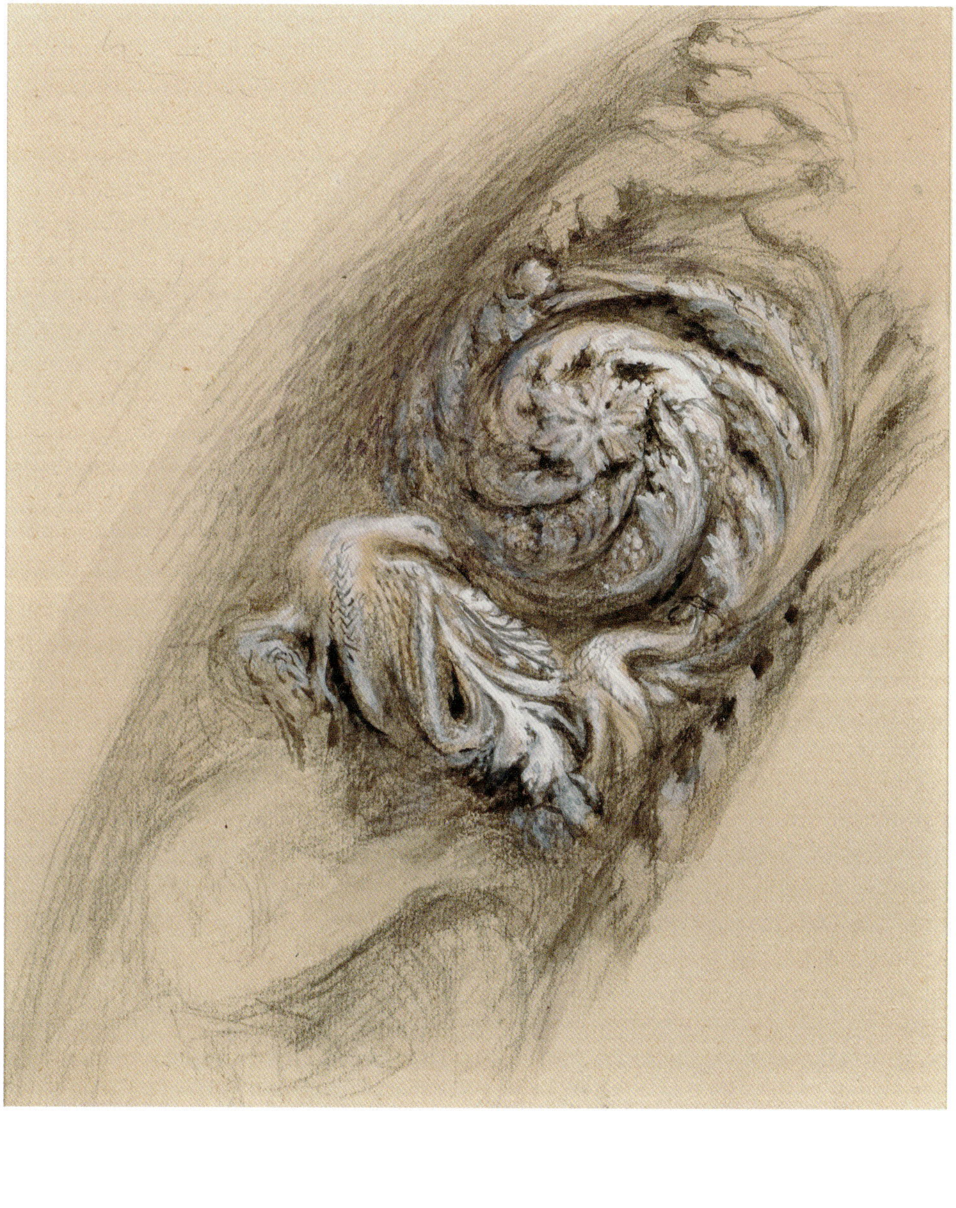

17

Spiral Relief from the North Transept Door, Rouen Cathedral 1882

Graphite, watercolour and bodycolour on white paper; 21.3 × 17.2 cm
Ruskin Foundation (Ruskin Library, Lancaster University) (RF 1197)
Inscriptions: graphite, *Feb. 1882*

Ruskin had long been interested in the so-called Booksellers' door, or "*Portail des Libraires*," of the north transept of Rouen Cathedral, describing its sculpted decorations in *The Seven Lamps of Architecture*. In 1880 he made his last visit to Rouen, a town that had been – as he was to write in *Præterita* – along with Pisa and Geneva, one of the "three centres of my life's thought."[1] Because so much damage had been done to the places he loved through insensitive restoration or neglect, he was on this occasion delighted to find his "old favourite porch and pinnacle bit at Rouen, all safe."[2] Seeking to preserve record of the building for posterity, he commissioned a photograph of the doorway from his assistant Arthur Burgess (fig. 5.4), and had a plaster cast of the relief made for the museum of the Guild of St. George. As may be seen by comparison of the drawing with the photograph, the particular spiral that is shown in Ruskin's drawing is that which is placed fourth up on the left-hand side of the door. This and another less finished drawing are each dated February 1882, and so it may be assumed that they were done from the plaster copy rather than in situ in Rouen.

One can only imagine the delight that Ruskin found in the ten sculpted spiral patterns at Rouen. He had a particular fascination with patterns with repeated elements, as in the stones of a necklace or the petals of an oxalis or daisy, but in which – upon closer observation – small variations, whether of shape or size or even of imperfections or blemishes, were apparent, and which Ruskin read like a genetic code of the infinite variety of nature. The fact that the spirals appeared each superficially alike but were in reality all different must have appealed to his sense of connection with the personalities and creative instincts of the individual masons who made them. Furthermore, a love of forms that imply dynamic motion and intrinsic energy, even when carved in stone or occurring naturally in the petrified thrusts and enclosing coils of igneous rocks, was something that remained with Ruskin all his life. Here he observed patterns that originated in the medieval mason's "peculiar fondness for the forms of Vegetation,"[3] as he explained in the chapter "The Nature of Gothic" in *The Stones of Venice*, but he has also instilled in his drawing a menacing sense of mutual aggression between the parts, as if two reptiles or birds were circling one another in preparation for battle, with each taunting the other to make the first lunge.

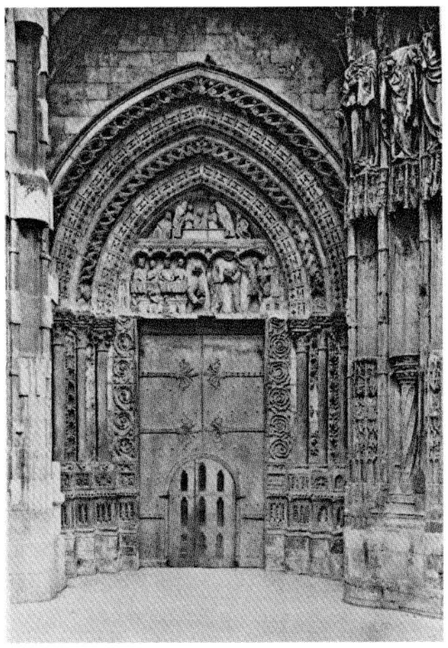

FIG. 5.4
Arthur Burgess
The North Door, Rouen Cathedral
From *The Guild and Museum of St. George*, Library Edition, plate IX

NOTES

1 Ruskin 1903–12, vol. 35, *Præterita and Dilecta*, p. 156.
2 Ruskin 1956, vol. 3, p. 986.
3 Ruskin 1903–12, vol. 10, *The Stones of Venice II*, p. 235.

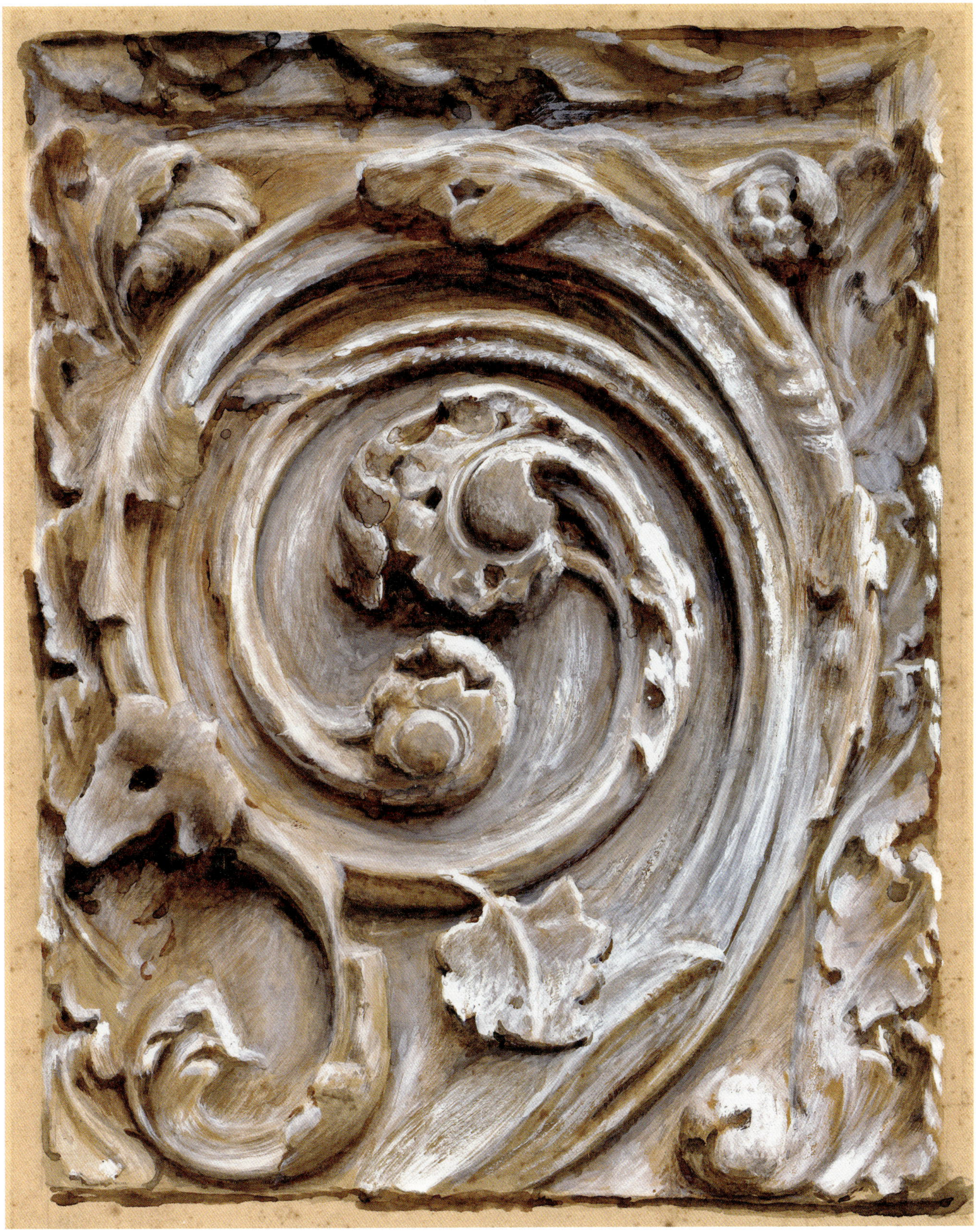

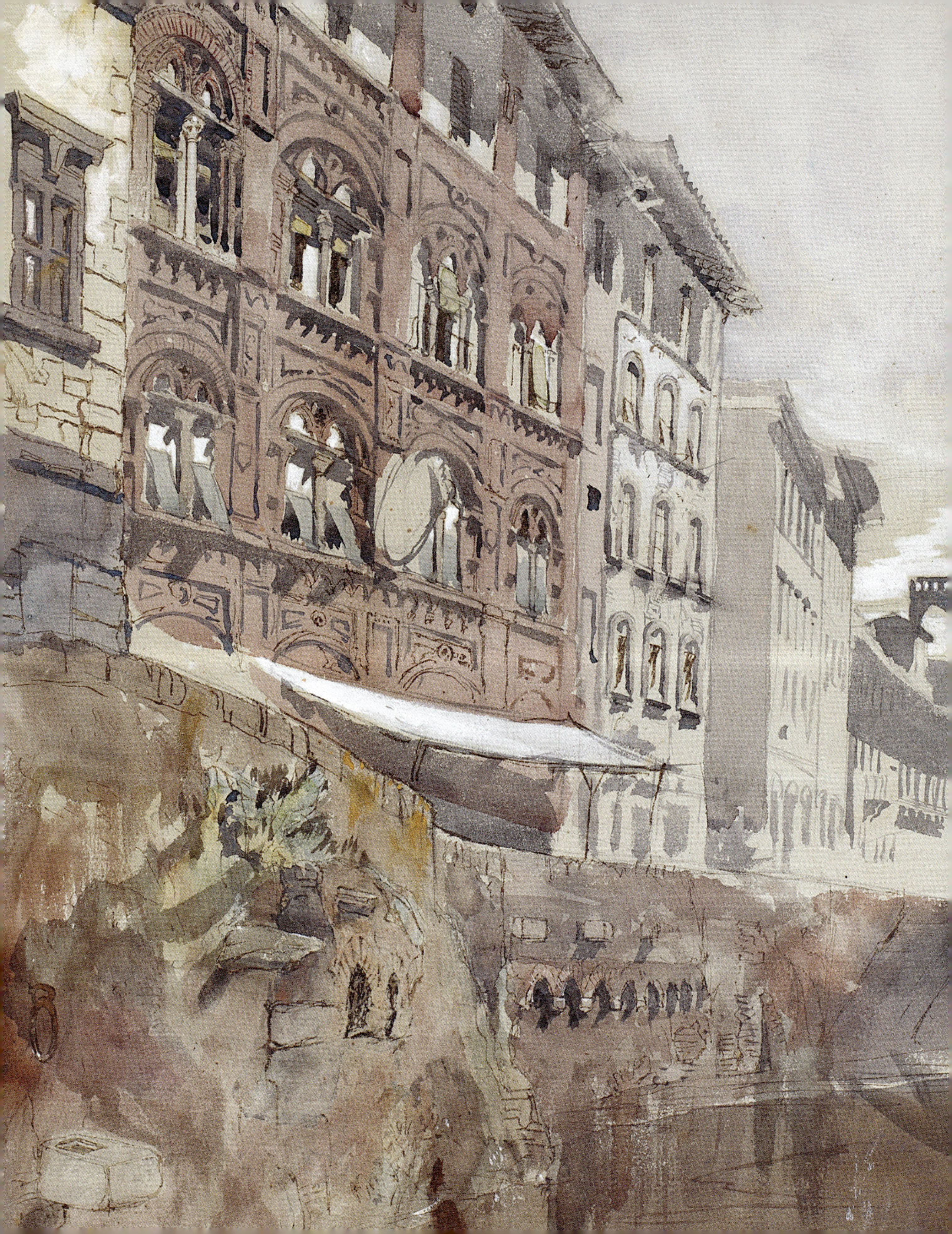

Buildings

18

The Piazzetta and St. Mark's, Venice 1835

Graphite and black ink on white paper; 24 × 33 cm
Ruskin Foundation (Ruskin Library, Lancaster University) (RF 1055)
Inscriptions: black ink, *Part of St Mark's Church, and entrance to Doges Palace, / VENICE.*

This drawing of the façade and southern flank of St. Mark's Basilica, the Porta della Carta and the northwestern angle of the Doge's Palace was made during Ruskin's first visit to Venice, which formed the conclusion of the long Continental tour that he and his parents undertook in the summer and autumn of 1835. Rome had been their intended final destination, but they abandoned this when news reached them of cholera and plague in the south of Italy. Instead, they went to Venice, arriving there on 6 October, and although they stayed in the city for only a week, the immediate impression that it made upon Ruskin remained with him all his life.

Ruskin had by this time started drawing lessons with Anthony Vandyke Copley Fielding – in the course of which he learned how to wash translucent layers of colour onto a sheet so as to create a rich and glowing effect. For the present drawing, however, he persisted with the pen and ink method that he had acquired by imitation of the architectural drawings of Samuel Prout. In *Præterita*, Ruskin recalled his work on another drawing, a view of the Doge's Palace and Riva,[1] which is analogous to the present drawing in technique. Although he had "meant to make such a drawing of the Ducal Palace as never had been made before ... [done] by collecting some hasty memoranda on the spot, and finishing my design elaborately out of my head in Treviso," he came to criticize this view as being "out of perspective, which I had now got too conceited to follow the rules of, – and with the diaper pattern of the red and white marbles represented as a bold patterning in relief."[2] The clumsiness of these 1835 architectural drawings is in part due to their having been worked up away from the motif and in a crude ink line, as if in imitation of engravings.

NOTES

1 *The Ducal Palace, Venice*, 1835, reproduced in Ruskin 1903–12, vol. 35, *Præterita and Dilecta*, plate VIII, opposite p. 182.
2 Ruskin 1903–12, vol. 35, *Præterita and Dilecta*, p. 182.

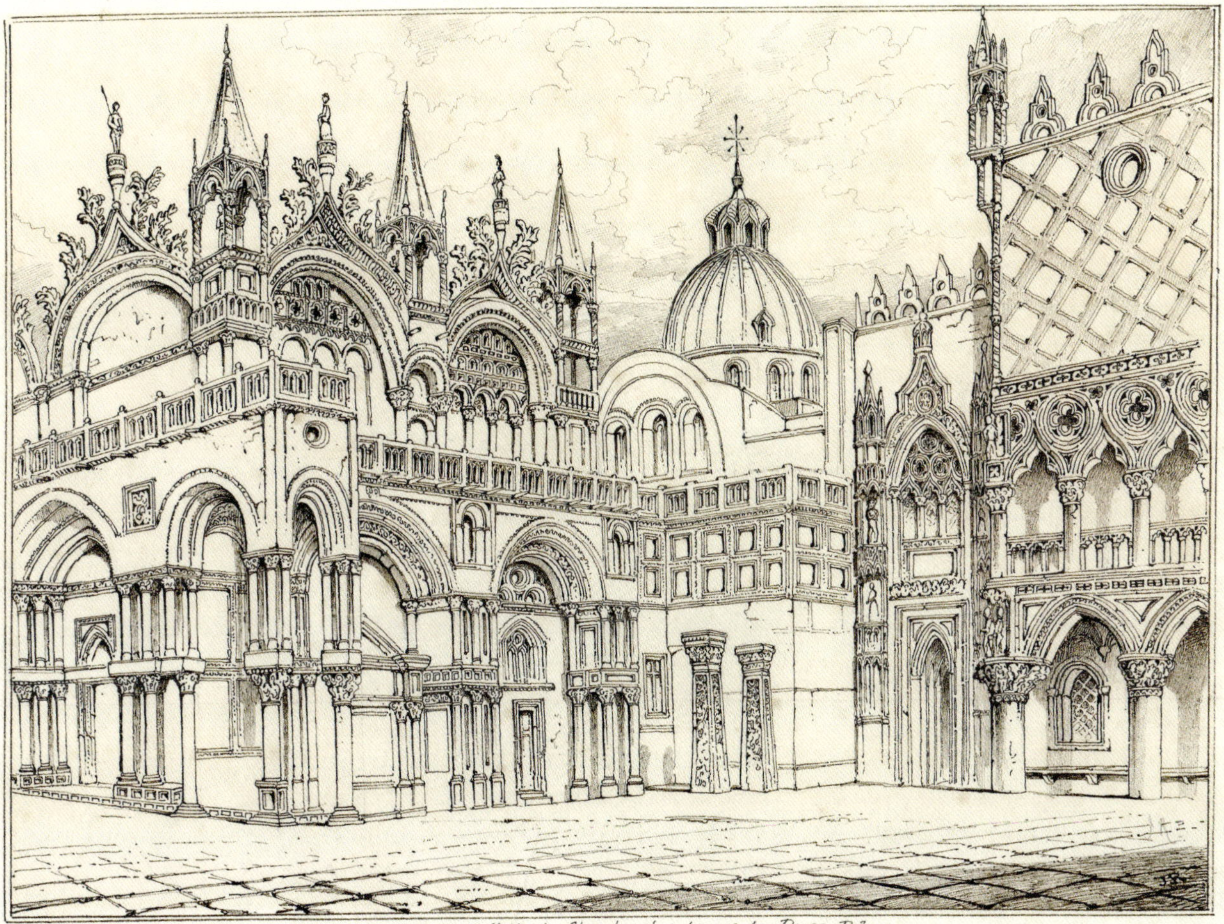

Part of St Marks Church, and entrance to Doges Palace,
VENICE.

19

The Palazzo Contarini-Fasan, Venice 1841

Graphite, watercolour and bodycolour, with some scratching out, on grey paper; 42.8 × 31.5 cm
The Ashmolean Museum, Oxford. Presented by John Ruskin to the Ruskin Drawing School (University of Oxford), 1875 (WA.RS.REF.065)

On 6 May 1841 Ruskin returned to Venice for the first time since his brief visit in 1835. Having previously travelled as far south as Rome and Naples, he marked his arrival with the heartfelt exclamation, "Thank God I am here! It is the Paradise of cities." Two days into his stay, however, he described himself as "excessively sulky and bored about my drawing today – could not get on; drew like a child, and did not like the general effects of the narrow canals; disappointed in the ordinary houses." Later he rationalized his dissatisfaction with the vernacular architecture of Venice, thinking that "the exquisite grace and finish of pieces of ordinary-life architecture about Rome spoiled one for the *common* houses here ... On the other hand, I think a single passage of the grand canal or the Piazzetta worth all Rome and Naples together."[1]

As he tired of the type of picturesque street scene that he had drawn in the south, he turned instead to the representation of architecturally significant buildings about which he might gain closer knowledge by the detailed inspection that went with drawing. He was increasingly aware of the limitations of his two erstwhile masters, Samuel Prout and David Roberts. The former's calligraphic exaggeration of the ornateness of decoration and the latter's reliance on bland tinting seemed inadequate as methods in which to achieve veracity of form and effect. In a letter to his Christ Church friend Edward Clayton, written on 16 May, the day of his departure from Venice, Ruskin summarized his own crisis of confidence: "After a thorough spell of drawing, I have put up my pencils – rather sulkily, by-the-bye: for this place is quite beyond everybody but Turner."[2]

The present drawing, which despite Ruskin's misgivings about his capability as a draftsman is one of his earliest and most extraordinary *tours de force*, was begun it seems on 12 May. Occupying Ruskin for perhaps two or three days, it was by his account, "almost the only thing I have got in Venice worthy of Venice."[3] Taken from a gondola, the view shows the façades of five neighbouring palaces on the San Marco side of the Grand Canal. Robert Hewison has identified them as, from right to left, Contarini-Pisani, Contarini-Fasan, Manolesso-Ferro, Fini and (on the bend as the canal turns to the right) Gritti – each with its Gothic decoration carefully specified and elaborated.[4] After his return to London, Ruskin lent the drawing to Samuel Prout, who used it as the basis of his own watercolour (fig. 3.1), although omitting the fourth palace from the right as shown in Ruskin's drawing.

NOTES

1 Ruskin 1956, vol. 1, pp. 183–185.
2 Ruskin 1903–12, vol. 1, *Early Prose Writings*, p. 447.
3 Ruskin 1956, vol. 1, p. 187.
4 Hewison 1978, p. 42.

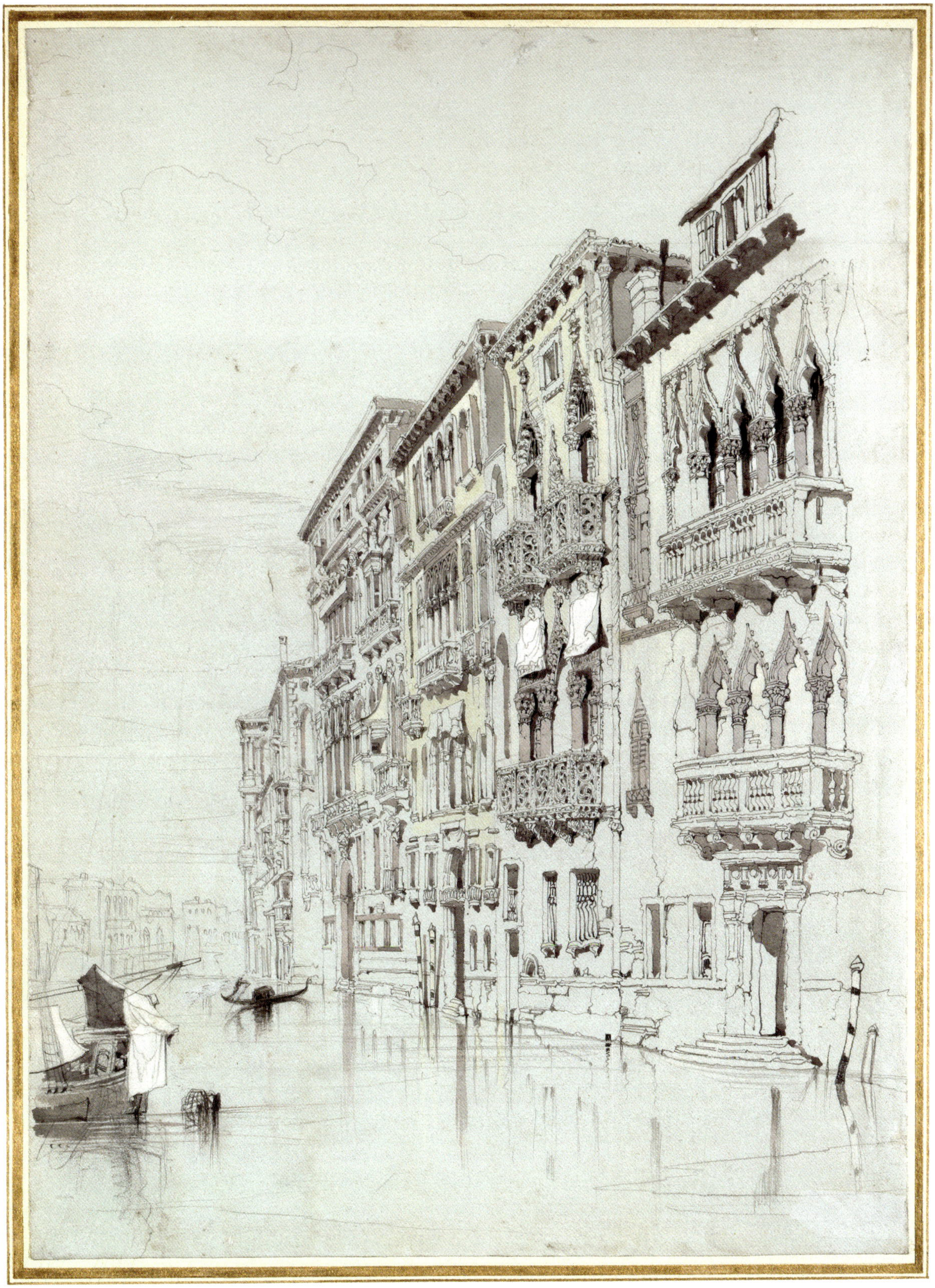

20

Part of the Façade of the Destroyed Church of San Michele in Foro, Lucca, as it Appeared in 1845 1845

Watercolour and bodycolour over graphite on grey wove paper; 33 × 23.3 cm
The Ashmolean Museum, Oxford. Presented by John Ruskin to the Ruskin Drawing School (University of Oxford), 1875 (WA.RS.ED.083)
Inscriptions: below the left-hand detail of a column, graphite, *[...] / [...] / across*, just below both inscriptions, graphite, *bottom [...] I like f[...]*, graphite, *Five arches below / small one at each / 4 middle [...] / pairs & one in / middle_all [...] / only*, labelled down the left-hand side of the main image, graphite, *P* and *P*, labelled down the right-hand side of the main image, graphite, *P, A, C, S, B* and *P*, bottom right, ink, *San Michele. Lucca / 1845. JR.*

Ruskin's earlier architectural drawings, such as those he made in Rome and Naples in 1840 and 1841, show decrepit buildings but without apparent awareness that their condition was inflicted upon them by human agency. As time went by, however, he was seized with a sense of bewildered outrage that so much damage should be wrought upon an architectural heritage as a result of ignorance and indifference. In May 1845, writing to his father from Lucca, he listed the threats – both natural and the result of feckless administration – that seemed to place that city's Romanesque churches in such peril: "Eaten away by the salt winds from the sea, splintered by frost getting under the mosaics, rent open by the roots of weeds ... fallen down from the rusting of the iron bolts that hold them, cut open to make room for brick vaultings and modern chapels, plastered over in restorations, fired at by the French, [so that] nothing but wrecks remaining."[1]

Here, for the first time, he set about drawing particular buildings, not for the sake of producing pleasing sketches that might be admired by friends and family, but to provide a systematic record of their historic fabric. Again to his father, he described the working routine that he had adopted in Lucca: the mornings were spent drawing the interiors of San Frediano, "for the people hardly frequent this (owing to its age & gloom I suppose) & therefore I can draw there, without disturbing anyone even during the mass hours." Later in the day he would visit San Romano and the Duomo, "writing as I go, all I can learn about the history of the churches, and all my picture criticism." After lunch, he was "ready to set to work ... [sitting] in the open warm afternoon air, drawing the rich ornaments on the facade of St. Michele. It is white marble, *inlaid* with figures cut an inch deep in green porphyry, and framed with carved, rich, hollow marble tracery."[2]

In *Præterita* he recalled the impact that the study of the Romanesque churches of Lucca had made upon him:

> Hitherto, all architecture, except fairy-finished Milan, had depended with me for its delight on being partly in decay. I revered the sentiment of its age, and I was accustomed to look for the signs of age in the mouldering of its traceries, and in the interstices deepening between the stones of its masonry ... Here in Lucca [however] I found myself suddenly in the presence of twelfth-century buildings, originally set in such balance of masonry that they could all stand without mortar; and in material so incorruptible, that after six hundred years of sunshine and rain, a

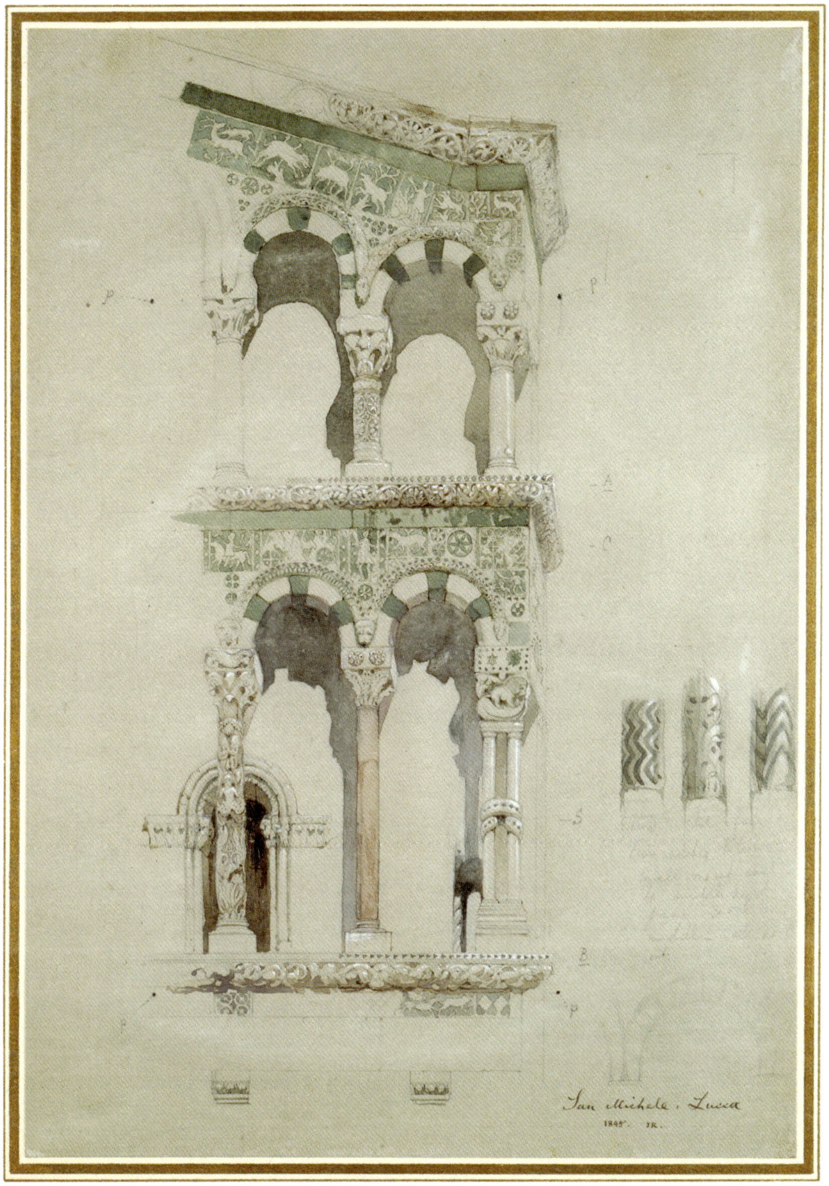

lancet could not now be put between their joints. Absolutely for the first time I now saw what mediæval builders were, and what they meant.[3]

San Michele is of the twelfth-century Pisan-Lucchese type, with four tiers of columned arcades running across the width of the façade and on the third register subtly lessening in height toward the sides to accommodate the slanting roofline of the aisles. Construction began in 1143 (the date is carved on a column of the central archway), while the façade was completed early in the thirteenth century. Each of the columns is different: some loop back upon themselves in knots, others are doubled, some twist into solomonic (or "barley-sugar") shapes. Many are inlaid with Cosmati mosaics, while others are plain marble. Thus the arcades of the church's exterior are of the Romanesque type that Ruskin most admired and that he would regard subsequently in *The Stones of Venice* as a form of architectural decoration in which the inventive imaginations and skills of medieval craftsmen – anonymous in every other respect – were memorialized.

The name of the church refers to the ancient Roman forum on the site of which it stands. Ruskin's title for the drawing, established by the time he gave it to Oxford in 1875, makes the sad inference that in the thirty years that had passed since he drew the building, it had been desecrated by vile restoration.

NOTES

1 Ruskin 1972, p. 52.
2 Ibid., pp. 53–54.
3 Ruskin 1903–12, vol. 35, *Præterita and Dilecta*, p. 350.

21

Palazzo Agostini, Pisa 1845

Ink and watercolour on paper; 47.8 × 33.8 cm
The Fitzwilliam Museum, Cambridge (1590)

Ruskin moved on from Lucca to Pisa on 12 May 1845, travelling as he explained in a letter to his father by "voiturin … [which was] to take me for 25 paoli in 2 hours & a half. Half price of posting, & saves all bother with blackguards of postillions." Anticipating that "the Campo Santo will keep me at work for a fortnight,"[1] he embarked on a series of beautiful and starkly linear drawings in which he paid careful attention to the drapery folds and distribution of the figures of frescoes by Benozzo Gozzoli and others that he believed to be by Giotto (in fact by Taddeo Gaddi). The mural decorations of the Campo Santo, which although famous throughout Europe through the plates of Carlo Lasinio (first published in 1812), were suffering chronic neglect. Ruskin described them as "much injured even *since* I was here … while for want of glass, and a good roof, these wonderful monuments are rotting every day."[2]

From the Tre Donzelle hotel, which stood on the Lungarno and where he and his two servants stayed in comfort, Ruskin explored Pisa thoroughly, buying guidebooks[3] and prints to allow him to identify buildings and to serve as *aides-mémoire*. A particular cause of concern to him was the restoration of the Palazzo Agostini, on the north bank of the Arno between the Ponte di Mezzo and the Ponte Solferino. Writing to his father on 21 May, he enquired:

> You know the fine old brick palace here, on the quay[?] It is very nearly all over with it. They have knocked a great hole in the middle to put up a shield with a red lion and yellow cock upon it for a sign of a consul, and they have knocked another at the bottom to put up a sign of a soldier riding a horse on two legs, with inscription All–Ussero–Cafè–&c, and they have knocked down the top storey altogether, & put [up] a whitewashed wall instead, and they have filled up one of the windows with bricks, and as the necessary result of all these operations the whole building has given way and is full of fearful rents and curves and broken arches. It can't possibly stand much longer … and I want to get a study of it.[4]

Four days later he wrote again to say that he had postponed his onward journey to Pistoia, "merely to draw this brick palace, because I expect it to be destroyed when I return, and there is nothing precisely like it in Italy that I know of," and carping that the "guide book never even notices it, though it tells me all about the 'uffizio dei *fossi*' – *sewer* offices next door."[5] The weather was bad, but he managed finally to settle to the task of drawing the palace:

> I had a nice piece of work to get my old house yesterday – luckily the weather was *warm* enough for the first time here, but everything else against me except temperature – and that indeed, the other way. First instead of getting to work early in the morning, it rained till 8, and then I had to wait for the quay wall to dry. Then out came a sun which even

NOTES

1 Ruskin 1972, p. 59.
2 Ibid., p. 61.
3 Jeanne Clegg and Paul Tucker in *Ruskin and Tuscany* established that the guidebook upon which Ruskin depended was the *Nuova Guida di Pisa*, published in 1845. See London Sheffield Lucca 1993.
4 Ruskin 1972, p. 71.
5 Ibid., p. 79.

Cout[t]et[6] (who held the umbrella) could hardly bear – a *rain* sun of the hottest. Presently that went in and up came half an hour of strong west wind that was like to blow all my brushes into the river – books & umbrella & all. Then it began to rain again, and in the middle of the rain came half a dozen boats towed by men on the top of the wall so that I had to jump up every two minutes. Then sun again & so on, but I have got it in spite of all – a dashing sketch of its shadows, and architectural ones from which I could build, of its details – the *lowest* I have down to the smallest rosettes, and the uppermost I should have had if I could have got a ladder, but I hunted all over the town and couldn't get one![7]

In a further observation, Ruskin told his father: "I'm never satisfied now with my architectural sketches unless I have measures & details,"[8] a clue to the purpose appointed to these drawings, which was to store precise documentary information about the places seen.

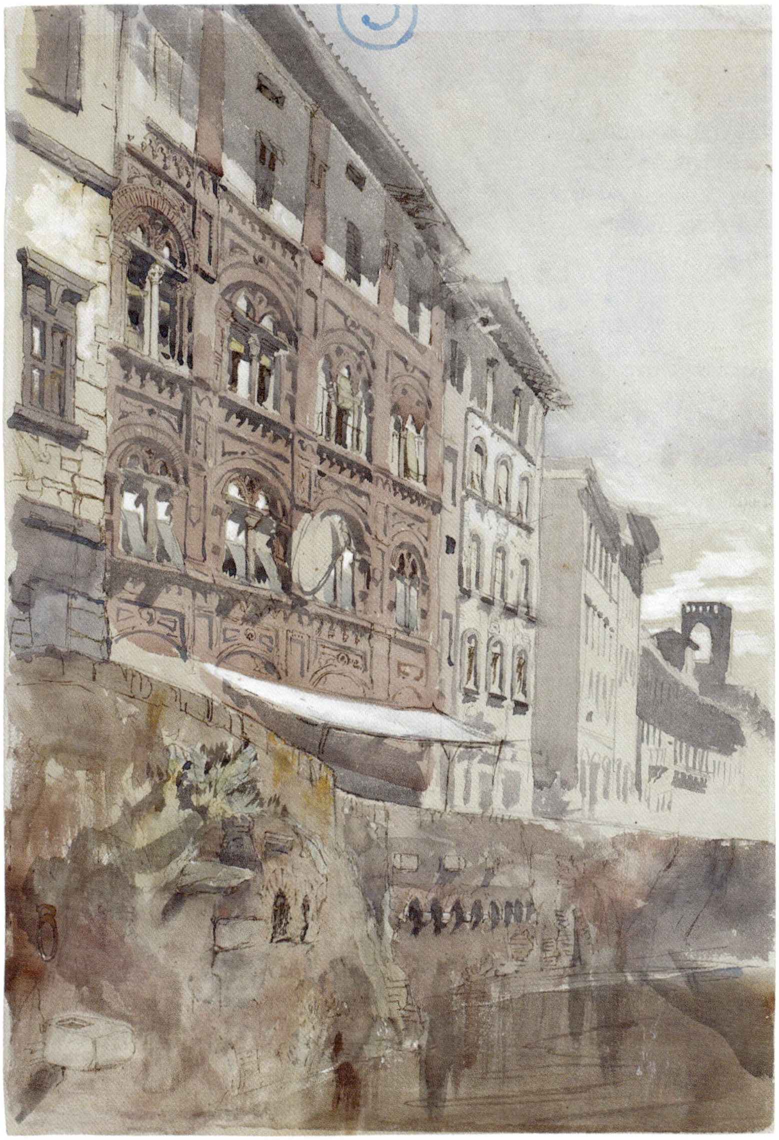

6 Ruskin's manservant.
7 Ruskin 1972, p. 84.
8 Ibid.

22

Ca' d'Oro, Venice 1845

Graphite, watercolour and bodycolour on toned paper; 33 × 47.6 cm
Ruskin Foundation (Ruskin Library, Lancaster University) (RF 1590)
Inscriptions: graphite, *Casa d'Oro*, brown ink, *Ca d'Oro / J. Ruskin. 1845.*

Writing from Florence in June 1845, Ruskin expressed the sorrow he felt at "seeing a whole nation employed in destroying the most precious of its heritages, and sinking deeper & deeper every day into apathy, ignorance, & sensuality."[1] Acting upon this feeling and the anxiety it aroused in him, he drew buildings so as to provide a record of them as they stood, always paying close attention to their timeworn character as evidence of their history.

He reached Venice on 10 September, hoping to savour the atmosphere of the city as he had known it on the occasions of earlier visits with his parents (this was the first Italian tour that he had undertaken without them – but instead with two manservants, John Hobbs (familiarly known as "George" to avoid confusion within the Ruskin family) and Joseph Couttet. Nonetheless, he wrote to his father almost every day describing the places and things he saw. Much had changed as the Austrian administrators sought to modernize the fabric of the city. The causeway connecting Venice to the mainland was virtually complete, and although Ruskin crossed from Mestre by gondola, for him the view across the lagoon was forever spoiled. Gas lighting had been introduced, with what he regarded as hideous iron lampstands sprouting in the Piazza and calli. Worse still, programmes of restoration were underway on the city's principal building, so that Ruskin had cause to tell his father that, "after whitewashing the Doges palace, and daubing it with the Austrian national distillation of coffins & jaundice,[2] they are *scraping* St. Mark's clean. Off go all the glorious old weather stains, [and] the rich hues of the marble which nature, mighty as she is, has taken ten centuries to bestow."[3] Many of the palaces of the Grand Canal were likewise being titivated or in some cases reconstructed, often in an attempt to make them appear more thoroughly Byzantine or Gothic, according to nineteenth-century perceptions of those architectural styles.

Ruskin was transfixed by the importance of his task of drawing buildings that he perceived to be at risk, explaining to his father the necessity of extending his stay, even though what he was witnessing caused him such distress: "be assured it is misery for me to stop here, but every hour is destructive of what I most value, and I must do what I can to save a little." He went on to describe his purpose in drawing the façade of the Ca' d'Oro, which was, he thought, "the noblest Palace of the grand Canal [and where] the stonemasons are hard at work, and of all its once noble cornice there remains one fragment only."[4]

The beauty of colour and line of Ruskin's drawing was achieved despite the most difficult working conditions. As he wrote to his father:

> You cannot imagine what an unhappy day I spent yesterday before the Casa d'Oro, vainly attempting to draw it while

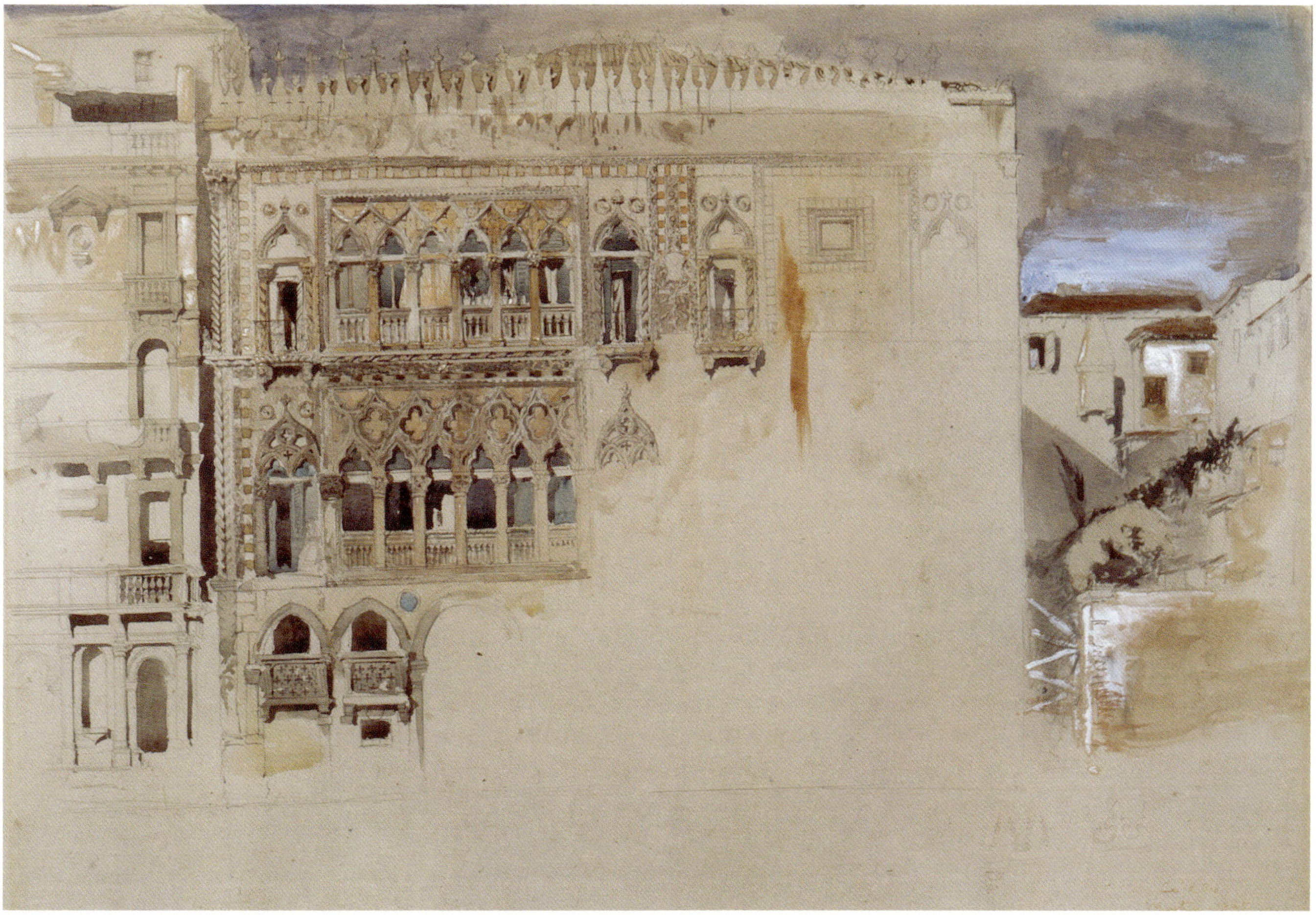

the workmen were hammering it down before my face. It would have put me to my hardest possible shifts at any rate, for it is intolerably difficult, & the intricacy of it as a study of colour inconceivable ... but fancy trying to work while one s[ees] the cursed plasterers hauling up beams & dashing i[n the] old walls & shattering the mouldings, & pulling b[arge]s across your gondola bows & driving you here & there, up & down & across, and all the while with the sense that *now* one's art is not enough to be of the slightest service, but that in ten years more one might have done such glorious things.[5]

Treating the subject foursquare to the sheet, Ruskin gave careful attention to the Gothic arcade of the piano nobile and upper storey, but also left blank a large area on the right side of the building, presumably because it would have served no useful purpose merely to extend the representation of the decoration over a wider surface, particularly when the time available for records of this kind appeared so desperately short.

NOTES

1 Ruskin 1972, p. 128.
2 The sentry boxes that were placed within the building's lower arcade were painted black and yellow, in itself an affront to sensibilities of Venetians who resented the occupation of their city.
3 Ruskin 1972, p. 201.
4 Ibid., p. 208.
5 Ibid., p. 209.

23

Palazzo Dario, Venice 1845

Graphite, black ink, ink wash, watercolour and bodycolour on white paper; 23.7 × 13.6 cm
Ruskin Foundation (Ruskin Library, Lancaster University) (RF 1035)

In Venice, Ruskin took delight in places that maintained Byzantine traditions of decoration – whereby coloured marble facings in square and circular patterns were applied to the exteriors of buildings. He had noticed ornament of this kind on palaces of the Grand Canal in the course of his early visits (as is witnessed by his diatribe against the eighteenth-century painter Canaletto in the first volume of *Modern Painters* for not having recorded "the magnificent coloured marbles, many of whose greens and purples are still undimmed upon the Casa Dario, Casa Trevisan, and multitudes besides"[1]). Schemes of decoration made up of marble disks gave a plethoric richness of colour and pattern – his word to describe this style of decoration regardless of the period was "incrustation"[2] – and exemplified what Ruskin called the Byzantine Renaissance. Superb examples of this style were the Palazzo Dario, for which construction commenced in 1487, along with contemporary buildings such as Santa Maria dei Miracoli and the Scuola Grande di San Marco. In an appendix to the first volume of *The Stones of Venice*, Ruskin divided the Renaissance "into three correspondent families: Renaissance engrafted on Byzantine, which is earliest and best; Renaissance engrafted on Gothic, which is second, and second best; Renaissance on Renaissance, which is double darkness, and worst of all."[3] The Palazzos Dario and Trevisan represented this "earliest and best" style.

Ruskin's view of the Palazzo Dario has a delicious freshness of colour and a loose almost impressionistic touch that seems to simulate the effect of seeing the building across the surface of the Grand Canal, with sparkling light reflected from the water and an apparent rocking motion that recalls the sensation of being seated in a moored gondola. The view of the façade, which, as with the Ca' d'Oro (cat. 22), is shown foursquare to sheet, allows the three storeys of arcading, decorated walls, windows and doors to be appreciated in terms of an abstract pattern, but also as diagrammatically informative of the structure itself and with no diversion into picturesque peripheries. Ruskin's interest in the building, which stands on the Grand Canal on the Dorsoduro side, was heightened when in 1849 he made friends with Rawdon Brown, an English antiquarian who had settled in Venice and who lived in the palazzo.

NOTES

1 Ruskin 1903–12, vol. 3, *Modern Painters I*, p. 215.
2 For his account of the decoration of St. Mark's Basilica see Ruskin 1903–12, vol. 10, *The Stones of Venice II*, pp. 93–94.
3 Ruskin 1903–12, vol. 9, *The Stones of Venice I*, p. 425.

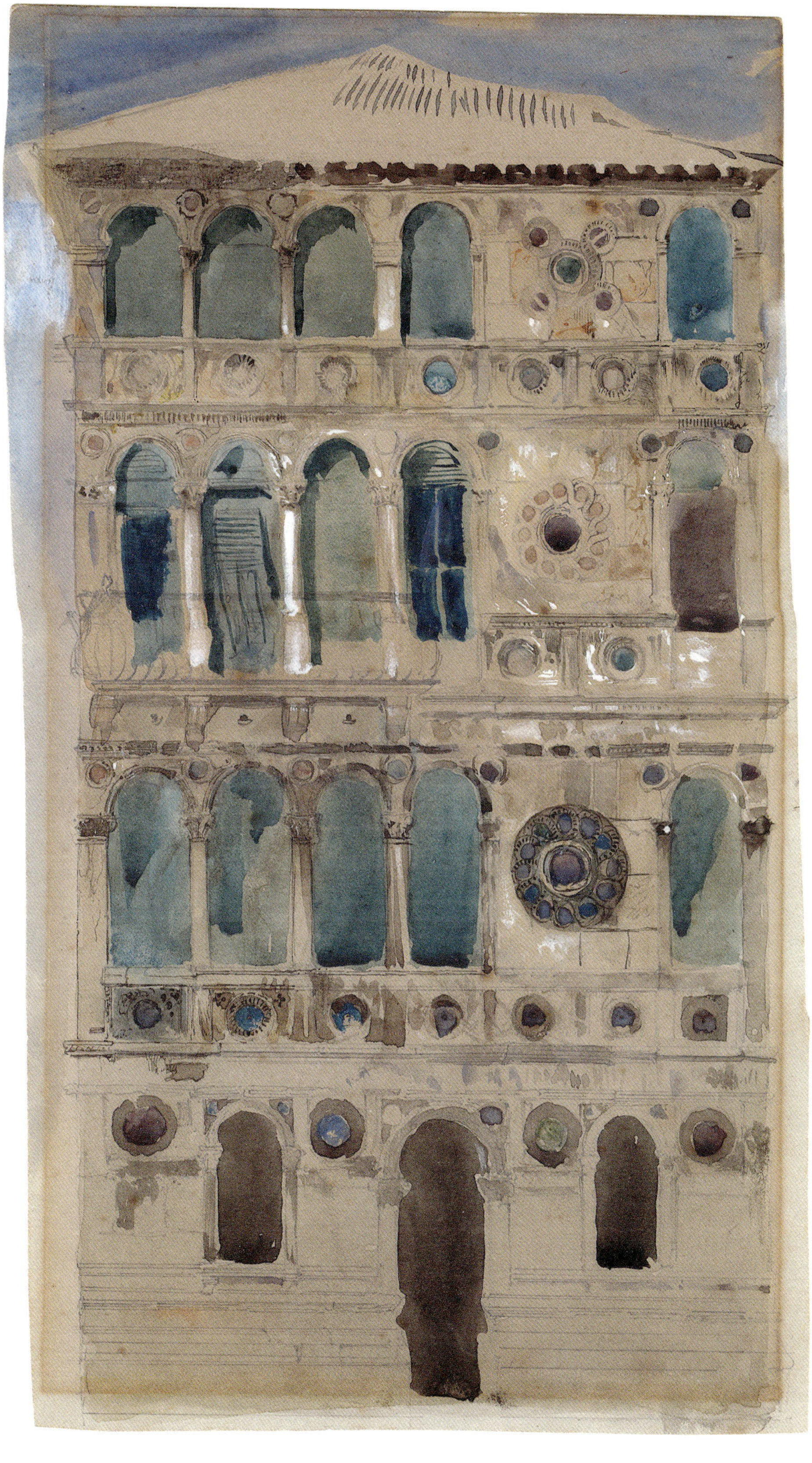

24

Part of St. Mark's Basilica, Venice: Sketch after Rain 1846

Watercolour and bodycolour and ink over graphite on grey wove paper; 42.1 × 28.6 cm
The Ashmolean Museum, Oxford. Presented by John Ruskin to the Ruskin Drawing School (University of Oxford), 1875 (WA.RS.ED.209)
Inscriptions: graphite, *27th May. 1846*, with numbers *1–5* marked as a code on various pieces of architectural detail and corresponding to a written description in Ruskin's diary entry for 27 May 1846

Ruskin returned to Venice on 14 May 1846, on this occasion with his parents in tow. The visit was intended as an opportunity to show John James and Margaret Ruskin the places and things that had made such a vast impression on him in 1845. The family remained in Venice for a fortnight, during which time they endured a heat wave followed by spectacular storms.

Having taken with him to Venice a copy of Robert Willis' *Remarks on the Architecture of the Middle Ages, especially of Italy* (1835), in which there is a detailed account of St. Mark's Basilica, Ruskin himself made a careful survey of the building. In his diary entry of 27 May – the very day that, according to its inscription, he completed the present drawing – he recorded measurements and made notes about its exterior in a spirit that anticipates the scrupulous observation of architectural forms large and small that led to *The Stones of Venice*. The drawing shows the archivolt, window and doorway (now closed) on the building's south side, forming the façade of the baptistery. Ranks of columns with Byzantine carved capitals flank the bay, while disks of multi-coloured marble against a dark background fill the lunette above. A Gothic window, with stone traceries and twin quatrefoils, is shown above the door. In front, standing in the Piazzetta, is one of the square pillars brought by the Venetians from St. Jean d'Acre in the thirteenth century, while on the right, sketched in pencil, is a single column of the western arcade of the Doge's Palace.

Ruskin's purpose was to make a visual record of a building the vast importance and complexity of which was becoming ever more apparent to him. He achieved this by fluency of watercolour technique and a willingness to combine different media as well as to alternate between areas of detail and other parts that are treated to the broadest and most abstract evocation. A sense of *plein-air* freshness is given as the late-morning sun blazes down following what must have been a torrential rainstorm, casting deep shadows within the interstices of the columns and across the upper arch. Furthermore, the wet marble pavement reflects the forms of the pillar and the light and dark shapes of the fabric of the basilica. In *The Stones of Venice* Ruskin celebrated the sheer beauty of the building in language that anticipates the playful capriciousness of aestheticism:

> Like other beautiful things in this world, its end is to *be* beautiful; and, in proportion to its beauty, it receives permission to be otherwise useless ... [At St. Mark's] we must be constantly prepared to see, and to see with admiration, shafts of great size and importance set in places where their real service is little more than nominal, and where the chief end of their existence is to catch the sunshine upon their polished sides, and lead the eye into delighted wandering among the mazes of their azure veins.[1]

NOTE

1 Ruskin 1903–12, vol. 10, *The Stones of Venice II*, pp. 102–103.

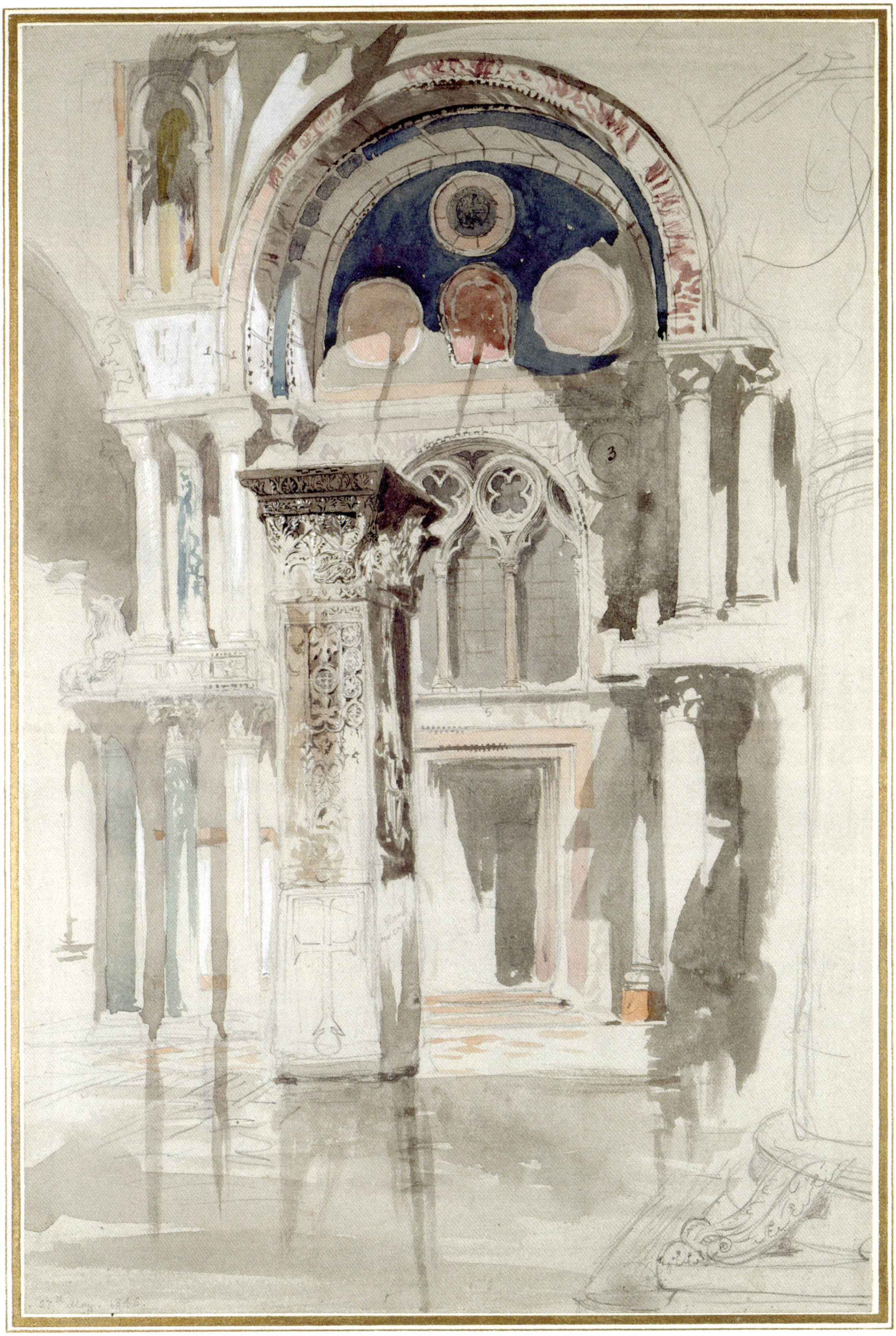
27th May. 1846.

25

Part of the Façade of the Destroyed Church of San Michele in Foro, Lucca, Sketched in Colour 1846

Watercolour over graphite on wove paper; 40.7 × 24.6 cm
The Ashmolean Museum, Oxford. Presented by John Ruskin to the Ruskin Drawing School (University of Oxford), 1875 (WA.RS.ED.084)

It is usually assumed that this drawing of the front of San Michele was made during Ruskin's return visit to Lucca in the summer of 1846. A brilliant effect of sunlight has been achieved, with a glimpse of azure sky on the left and the variegated colours of the marbles of the structure showing brightly. Particularly noticeable is the treatment of deep shadow cast onto the inner wall of the façade by the projecting arcade, with the outline of colonettes, capitals and archway seen as a carefully delineated edge of darkness against the ochre of the lit wall. In treating the boundary between shadowed and illuminated areas with such strong definition, Ruskin may have had in mind the effect of contrast that occurs in daguerreotypes. It was probably during the same visit to Lucca that Ruskin purchased a daguerreotype of San Michele (cat. 27), or he may have commissioned Fortunato Lasagna, a professional photographer, to take it for him. The daguerreotype, also of the left side of the façade of the church (reversed in the image), includes the three principal tiers of the arcade, with a glimpse of the lowest of the tiers that form the upper gable.

26

Lateral View of the Façade of San Michele in Foro, Lucca 1846

Watercolour and pen and ink over graphite on wove paper; 45.7 × 23.9 cm
The Ashmolean Museum, Oxford. Presented by John Ruskin to the Ruskin Drawing School (University of Oxford), 1875 (WA.RS.ED.085)

Travelling with his parents, Ruskin passed briefly through Lucca at the end of June 1846, en route for Bologna. Although he wanted to share with his father the sense of excitement that he felt for the places he had seen in Italy the previous year, the 1846 trip was not wholly a success, for John James Ruskin seems to have been irritated by his son's unbridled enthusiasm for things that he himself did not understand or appreciate, and by his especially regrettable tendency to skim from one thing to another without appearing to carry forward his researches to any formal conclusion.

The same utilitarian attitude that determined that efforts expended should have a positive outcome, and thus perhaps

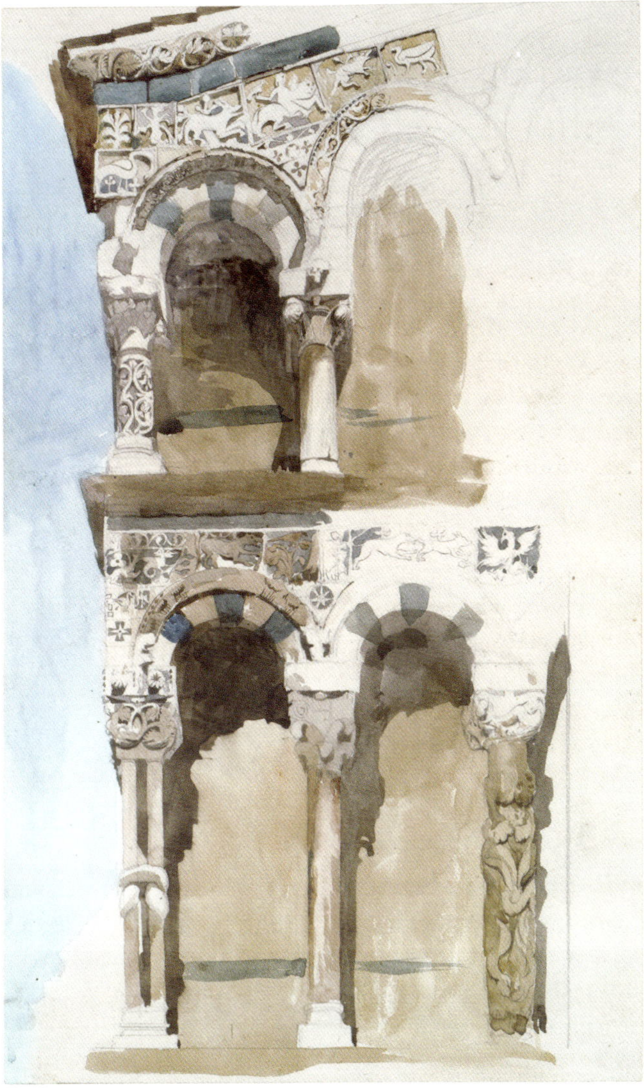

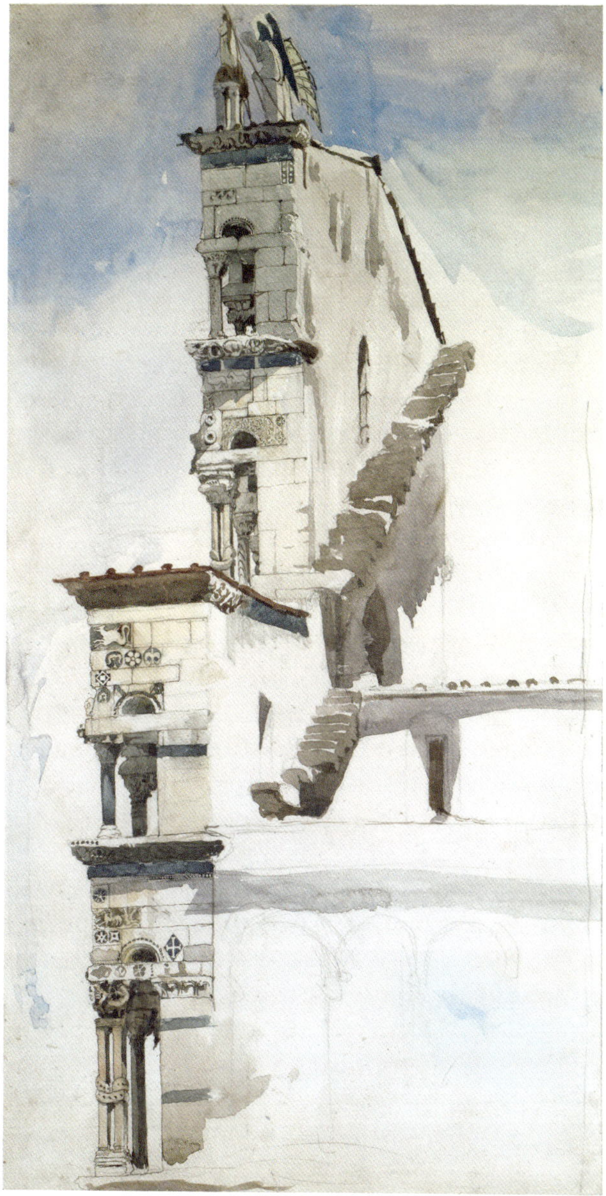

lead to professional advancement, caused John James to judge that his son's style of drawing was one that lacked focus and direction. As he explained in a letter to a friend written in May: "he is drawing perpetually, but no drawing such as in former days you or I might compliment in the usual way by saying it deserved a frame; but fragments of everything from a Cupola to a Cart-wheel, but in such bits that it is to the common eye a mass of Hieroglyphics – all true – truth itself, but Truth in mosaic."[1]

The present drawing, made a few weeks later, may be regarded as representing the type that Ruskin's father objected to: careless of conventional expectations of finish and formed of a constellation of areas of focused attention that only loosely coalesce into a coherent whole. And yet it expresses a soaring sense of exhilaration as Ruskin stood beneath the towering façade, which rises like a great theatre drop, and evokes the brightness of a Tuscan morning (the shadows indicate a sun still low in the eastern sky), showing its form in extraordinary three-dimensional perspective.

The west front of San Michele – out of view from this vantage point but familiar from other drawings of 1845 and 1846 (cats. 20 and 25) and a daguerreotype (cat. 27) – was built in the second half of the twelfth century and completed early in the thirteenth. It was raised to a greater height than the roof level of the nave required because there was an intention to rebuild the main body of the church on a larger scale that would then meet the façade, a project that was, however, never carried out.[2] At the apex of the pedimented central part of the fourth tier of arcades stands a colossal marble figure of the archangel Michael destroying a dragon and flanked by angels, seen here from the side.

NOTE

1 Ruskin 1903–12, vol. 8, *The Seven Lamps of Architecture*, p. xxiii.
2 Touring Club Italiano 1974, p. 240.

27

FORTUNATO LASAGNA

Lower Portion of the Façade of San Michele, Lucca 1846

Daguerreotype (quarter plate, image laterally reversed); 10 × 7.5 cm (sight)
Ruskin Foundation (Ruskin Library, Lancaster University) (RF Dag 69)
Inscriptions: incised into plate, *F. Lasagna 1846*

Although by the mid-1840s Ruskin was making daguerreotypes of his own (or at least supervising his servant John Hobbs to make them), he was also acquiring them from professional photographers, and in fact spending large sums of money for their purchase. The signature etched into the right-hand side of this plate is presumably that of Fortunato Lasagna, younger brother of Deogratias, both painter-photographers living in Parma. The implication is that Ruskin must have commissioned this plate from him, and probably for other subjects in Tuscany previously assumed to have been made by John Hobbs.

In 1848–49 Ruskin made a soft-ground etching of the outermost arch on the arcade of the façade's third tier on the south side (its equivalent at the northern end of the arcade is visible on the right side in the present photograph, which shows the front of the church in reversed image) that appeared as an illustration to *The Seven Lamps of Architecture* (fig. 1.7).[1]

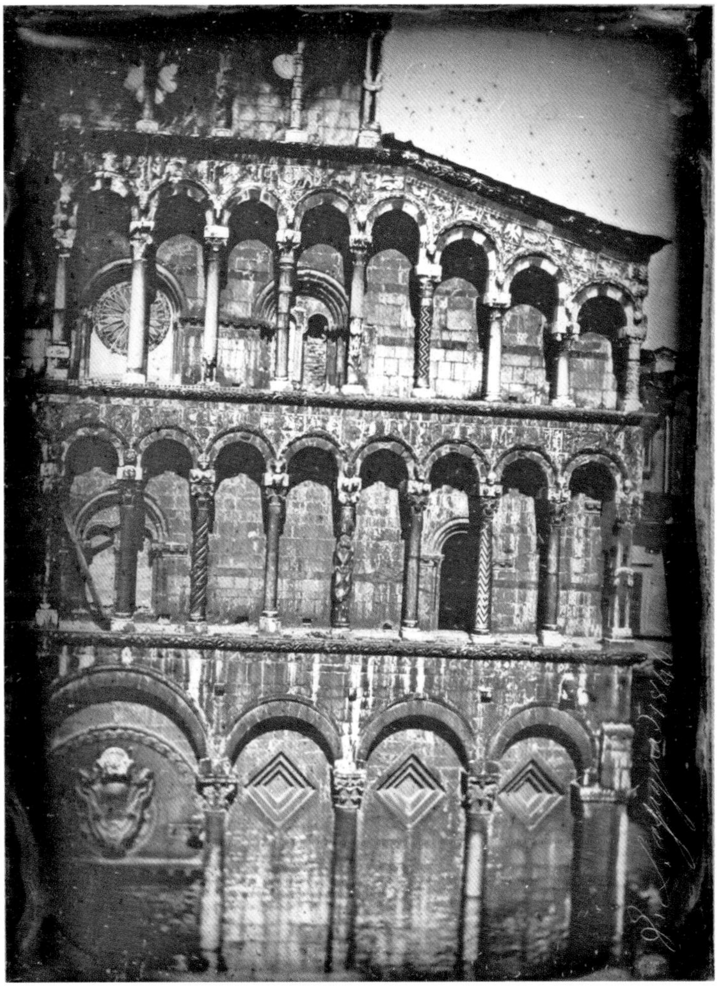

NOTES

1 Ruskin 1903–12, vol. 8, *The Seven Lamps of Architecture*, plate VI, opposite p. 125.

28

UNKNOWN PHOTOGRAPHER

Santa Maria della Spina, Pisa (South Side Towards East End) c. 1846

Daguerreotype (half plate); 15.5 × 11.5 cm (sight)
Ruskin Foundation (Ruskin Library, Lancaster University) (RF Dag 62)

Ruskin seems to have first begun to acquire photographs in 1845, as he wrote to his father from Venice on 7 October that year:

> I have been lucky enough to get from a poor Frenchm[an] here, said to be in distress, some most beautiful, though small, Daguerreotypes of the palaces I have been trying to draw – and certainly Daguerreotypes taken by this vivid sunlight are glorious things. It is very nearly the same thing as carrying off the palace itself – every chip of stone & stain is there – and of course, there is no mistake about *proportions*. I am very much delighted with these and am going to have some more made of pet bits.[1]

As by the time of this letter Ruskin had already departed from Pisa, it may be assumed that the present daguerreotype came into his possession the following season, when he returned to Tuscany with his parents.[2] Who made it is an open question, but most probably it and another of the building's west side were purchased from a professional photographer (and as such it makes a useful basis of comparison with the less pictorially coherent but more idiosyncratically personal shots that Ruskin or his servants made).[3]

From the first, Ruskin used daguerreotypes both as *aides-mémoire* and to test his observation of buildings against what was seen in the photographic record. As he explained a week later: "Among all the mechanical poison that this terrible 19th century has poured upon men, it has given us at any rate *one* antidote, the Daguerreotype. It's a most blessed invention, that's what it is. I have been walking all over St. Mark's place today, and found a lot of things in the Daguerreotype that I had never noticed in the place itself."[4]

The watercolour drawing that Ruskin made of Santa Maria della Spina (cat. 29) was copied from the photograph, probably soon after his return to London in September 1846, and follows it in every particular, including the fall of light within the niches and the shadowing on the building's southeast corner as morning sunshine casts across the structure. His motive for making such a meticulous copy from the photograph was to be able to study the complexities of the building as if standing in front of it and – as he explained years later – so "that people might not be plagued in looking [at the daguerreotype], by the lustre."[5] Jeanne Clegg and Paul Tucker have suggested that he may also have copied the daguerreotype for the purpose of exhibiting it and the resulting drawing at a meeting of the Graphic Society in London in February 1847. A display of architectural images was staged then, in which, according to a press report, drawings by Ruskin of San Michele in Lucca were shown "in juxtaposition with [a] series of daguerreotype views of many of the Italian ecclesiastical buildings."[6]

NOTES

1 Ruskin 1972, p. 220.
2 And this is despite its having been described as having been "taken … on the spot, 1845" (Ruskin 1903–12, vol. 30, *The Guild and Museum of St. George*, p. 210).
3 Ruskin wrote in 1872 that he himself had "daguerreotyped the eastern end of [Santa Maria della Spina] … and copied the daguerreotype" (Ruskin 1903–12, vol. 27, *Fors Clavigera Letters 1–36*, p. 349), but he may not have been thinking of this particular photograph, or he may have been mistaken in thinking that he made it himself.
4 Ruskin 1972, p. 225.
5 Ruskin 1903–12, vol. 27, p. 349.
6 London Sheffield Lucca 1993, p. 54.

29

Santa Maria della Spina, Pisa; East End 1846–47

Watercolour, ink and graphite on paper; 50 × 36.7 cm
Collection of the Guild of St. George, Museums Sheffield (CGSG00740)
Inscriptions: *Not to be [...?]*

As has been seen, the present view of the church of Santa Maria della Spina was made as a copy of a daguerreotype (cat. 28) that Ruskin was likely to have acquired in Pisa in 1846. He had been interested in the church, which stands on the Lungarno on the south side of the river, since 1840, when he had first drawn it. Five years later, he heard of intentions to injure "Poor little Santa Maria della Spina – they want to pull it *down* to *widen the quay*."[1] In letters to his father in 1845, Ruskin explained that he had been given permission to climb onto the roof of the church, "to draw the details before they throw them into the river."[2] His sense of alarm was repeated the following year in the second volume of *Modern Painters*, where the church was included in a list of buildings from all across Europe that were, he feared, in jeopardy.[3] In 1872, after a further stay in Pisa, he gave an account in *Fors Clavigera* of how when he had first seen Santa Maria della Spina it had been "as perfect as when it was built," as "six hundred and ten years had only given the marble of it a tempered glow, or touched its sculpture here and there with softer shade," but how "the last quarter of a century [had] brought changes," and how the authorities, finding "a troublesome pair of human arms out of employ ... [had] set them to break up the Spina Chapel."[4]

A photogravure plate of the present drawing was used as a frontispiece to Letter 20 of *Fors Clavigera*, and Ruskin subsequently asked the draftsmen among his readers to see whether they could match the degree of detail that he had achieved: "copy a bit of it; – try merely the bead moulding with its dentils, in the flat arch over the three small ones, lowest on the left," to discover "the quantity of manual labour" involved in making such a drawing.[5]

NOTES

1 Ruskin 1972, pp. 62–63.
2 Ibid., p. 65.
3 Ruskin 1903–12, vol. 4, *Modern Painters II*, p. 39.
4 Ruskin 1903–12, vol. 27, *Fors Clavigera Letters 1–36*, p. 349. In fact, it was realized in 1871 that the fabric of the church, which stood close to the river, was becoming unstable, and so a decision was made to reconstruct on a new foundation at a higher level.
5 Ruskin 1903–12, vol. 28, *Fors Clavigera Letters 37–72*, p. 408.

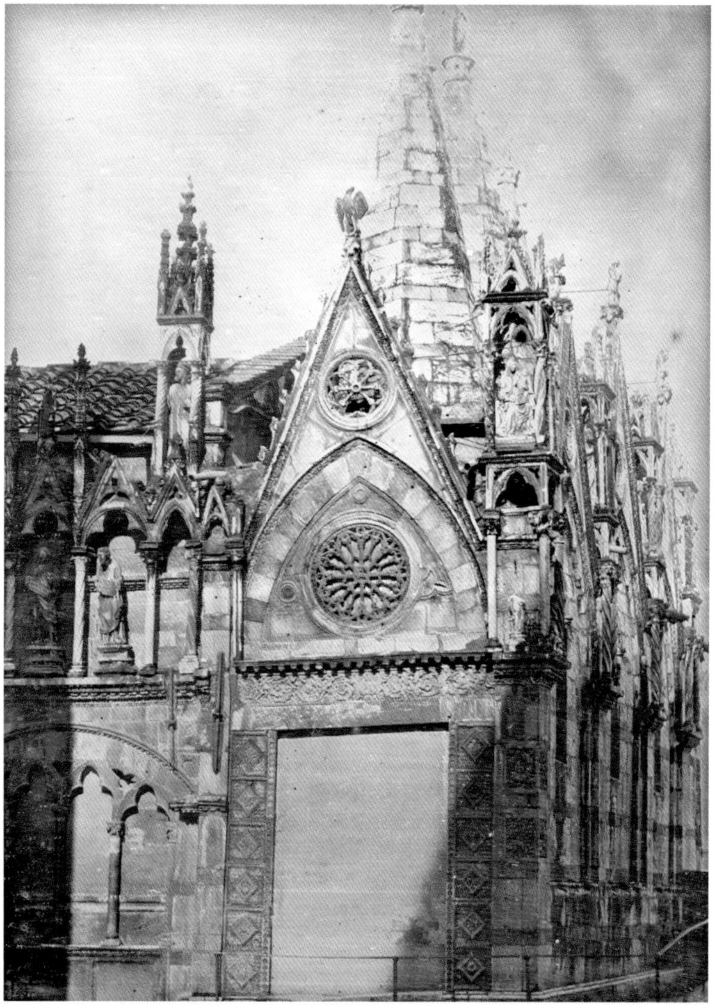

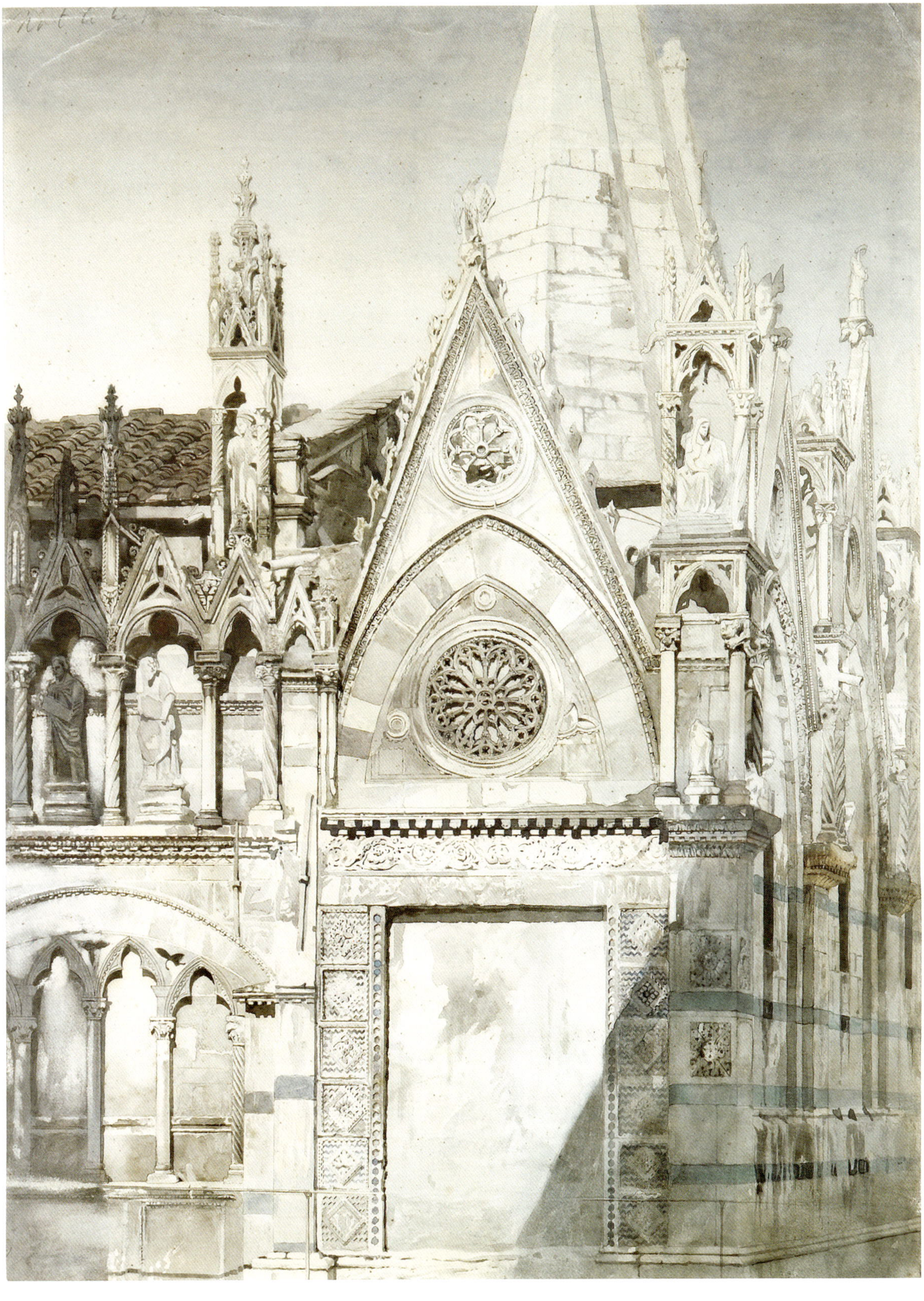

30

Stilted Archivolts, from a Byzantine Ruin in the Rio di Cà Foscari, Venice 1849

Graphite, watercolour and bodycolour on two sheets of white paper; 24.2 × 48.2 cm
Ruskin Foundation (Ruskin Library, Lancaster University) (RF 1583)

Ruskin's great project of compiling a history of Venice on the basis of the city's surviving buildings and their decorations – which became the three-volume *Stones of Venice* (1851–53) – was already in his mind in the late 1840s. However, he was prevented from returning to Venice during the 1848 revolution against the Austrians, who had had territorial control of the city and much of the north of Italy since the Congress of Vienna of 1815, and the devastating siege that followed. Ruskin expressed no sympathy for the cause of liberty for the Venetians or the self-determination of their government, but feared for the physical safety of the city for, as he wrote to his wife Effie in April 1849, "if the blockheads [the Venetians who were resisting the Austrian siege] stand out, it may be all destroyed. Brescia I am sorry enough for,[1] though it was one of the Italian towns I could best spare: if they knock down Venice, I shall give up all architectural studies: and keep to the Alps: they can't knock down the Matterhorn."[2]

From October 1849 to March 1850 and from August 1851 to June 1852, Ruskin, accompanied and assisted by Effie, engaged in two exhaustive research tours in Venice in preparation for *The Stones*, and from which masses of drawings derived. The present study was made directly from the motif in the Rio di Cà Foscari, from the canal below but involving a degree of improvisation. As Ruskin explained in the text that accompanied a plate made from the drawing in *The Stones of Venice*, it was, "a curious instance ... of the difficulty of being absolutely faithful, however we may desire it" as "there was no way of drawing this arch but out of a gondola immediately underneath, in a position from which it was quite impossible to see the upper portion of the archivolt distinctly."[3]

The light of the sky reflected in the window and the weed that has rooted itself into the architrave are observed with delight. What remained there, Ruskin thought, was "a beautifully picturesque fragment; the archivolt sculptures being executed in marble, which seemed, in some parts, rather to have gained rather than lost in whiteness by its age, and set off by the dark and delicate leaves of the Erba della Madonna [ivy-leaved toadflax – the weed growing on the entablature], the only pure piece of modern addition to the old design, all else being foul plaster and withering wood."[4]

NOTES

1 Brescia had been retaken by the Austrians in March.
2 John Ruskin, quoted in Lutyens 1972, p. 184.
3 Ruskin 1903–12, vol. 11, *The Stones of Venice III and Examples of the Architecture of Venice*, pp. 336–337.
4 Ibid., p. 336.

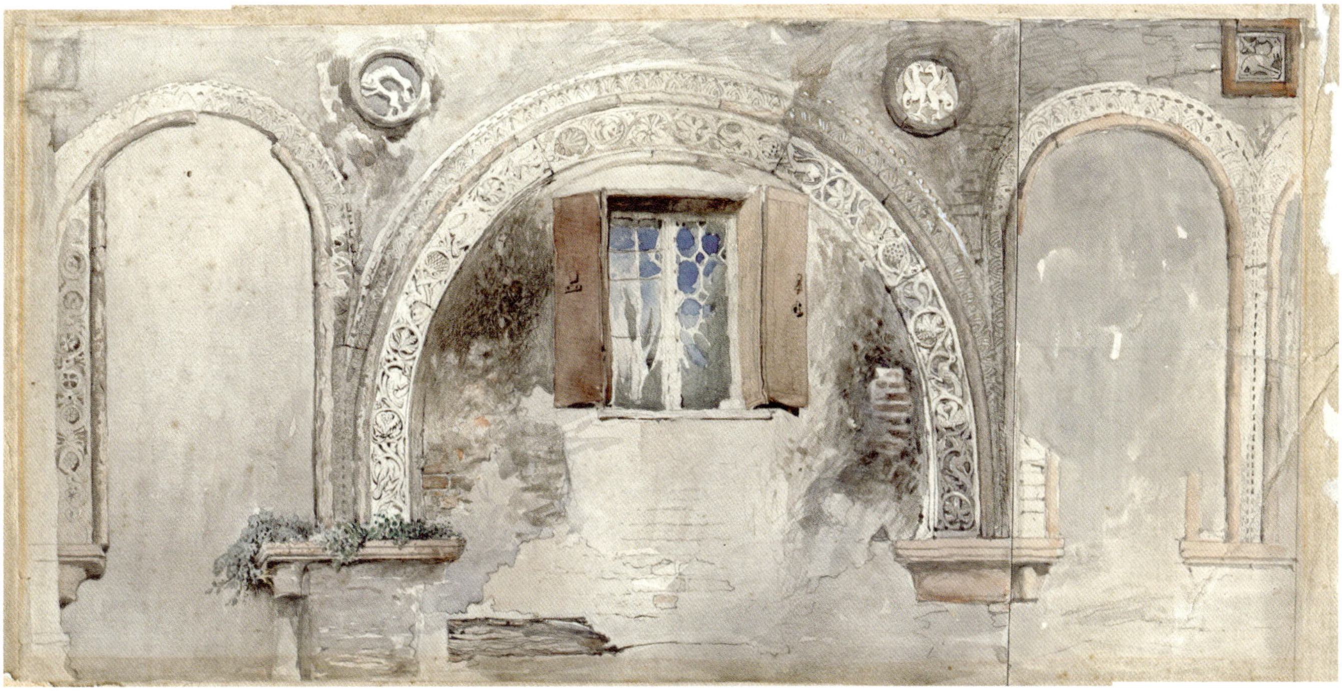

31

Byzantine Ruin, Rio di Cà Foscari, Venice c. 1851

Graphite, ink and wash on toned paper; 30 × 43.5 cm
Ruskin Foundation (Ruskin Library, Lancaster University) (RF 1584)

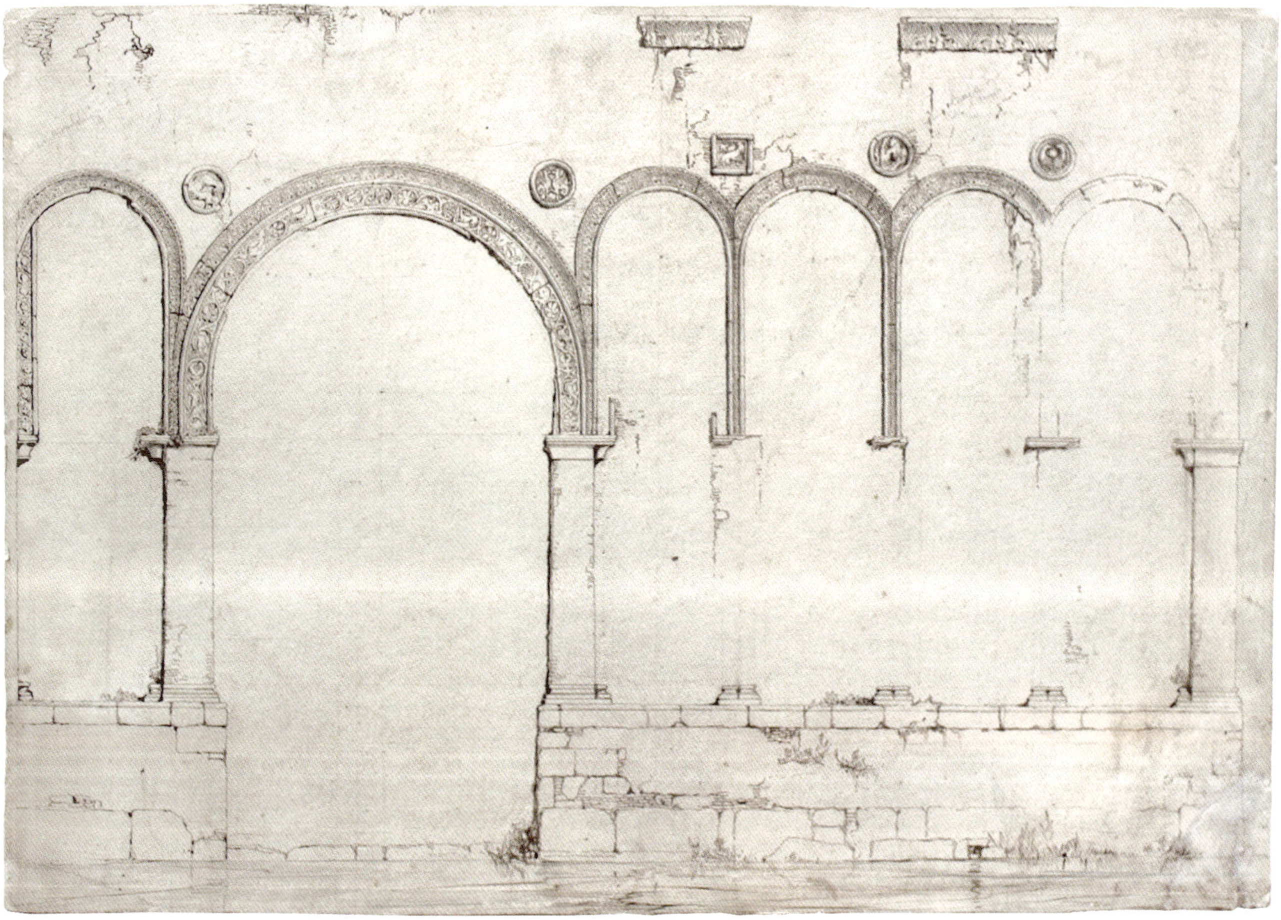

Incidental detail of the kind seen in Ruskin's 1849 watercolour of the same building in the Rio di Cà Foscari (cat. 30) is eliminated in this carefully ruled and measured line drawing, which was in turn reproduced by Thomas Shotter Boys as part of the set of plates that accompanied the first volume of *The Stones of Venice*. Ruskin identified it as showing "the wreck of one of the most ancient and interesting palaces in Venice [which] has been abandoned to utter neglect, and hitherto unnoticed even by the native antiquary, much more by the careless traveller."[1]

NOTES

1 Ruskin 1903–12, vol. 11, *The Stones of Venice III and Examples of the Architecture of Venice*, p. 334.

32

JOHN RUSKIN AND JOHN HOBBS

Southwest Portico of St. Mark's, Venice c. 1849–50

Daguerreotype (half plate); 15.5 × 11.5 (sight)
Ruskin Foundation (Ruskin Library, Lancaster University) (RF Dag 4)

Taken under Ruskin's direction by his servant John Hobbs during the first of the two *Stones of Venice* research tours, from October 1849 to March 1850, this daguerreotype shows the portico at the southern end of the basilica's west façade, supported on columns upon which rest what Ruskin called the "lily capitals" (see cat. 7), above which stand sets of four columns. This was the image that Ruskin copied to make the large drawing of the southwest portico (cat. 33). Also shown here, but omitted from the watercolour copy that focuses just on the portico, is the pedimented marble wall that was constructed in 1501 to close the Porta da Mar and thus create the space occupied by the Zen Chapel. The placing of this wall was sometimes taken as a symbol of rising indifference on the part of Venice's government to the city's links with the sea – the Porta da Mar (literally, the "sea door") was by custom the entrance to the basilica used by mariners to give thanks for their safe homecoming.

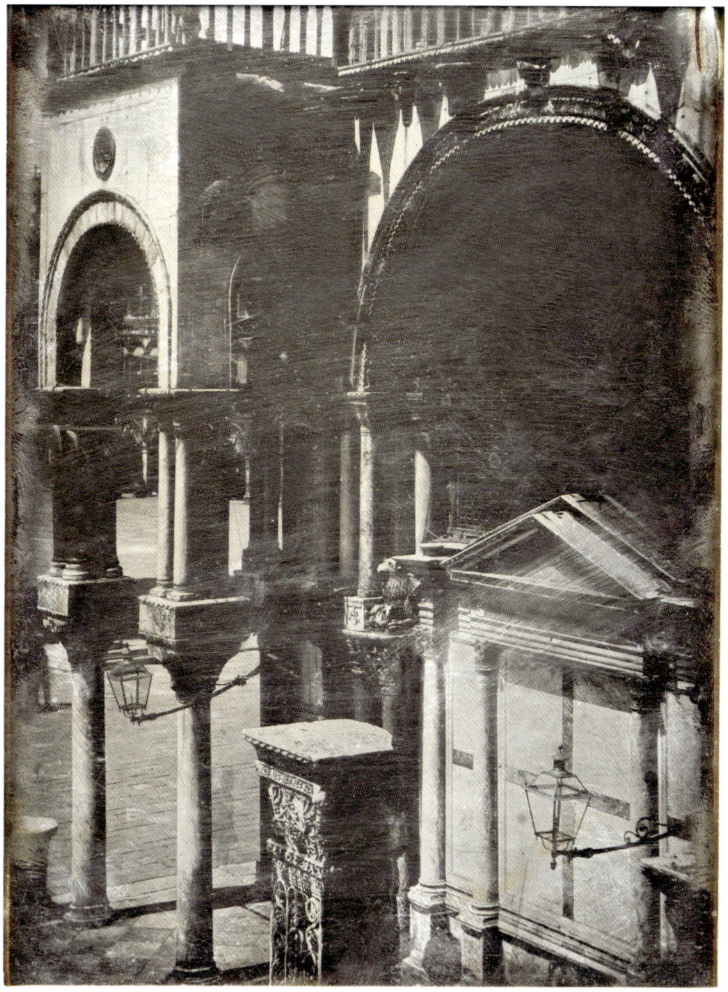

33

The South Side of the Basilica of St. Mark's, Venice, from the Loggia of the Doge's Palace c. 1851

Graphite and watercolour heightened with white on three joined pieces of paper; 95.9 × 45.4 cm
Private collection

This large and impressive drawing was scaled up from the daguerreotype made by Ruskin's servant John Hobbs during the first of the two *Stones of Venice* research tours in 1849–50 (cat. 32). The plate was corrected so that the image appeared the right way around, allowing Ruskin in his drawn replica of the photograph to show the forms of architecture clearly and with emphasis on the clusters of columns and Byzantine capitals and the sculpted relief decorations, all within a pronouncedly upright composition but without any allowance for perspectival recession. The drawing was apparently intended as the basis for a lithographic plate for *Examples of the Architecture of Venice* (published in three parts in 1851), but was never finished.

Ruskin knew that the loggia of the Doge's Palace offered a good vantage point from which to inspect the basilica's south flank and the southern portico. In 1854 he recommended the watercolourist George Price Boyce to draw from "one point, as far as I know, never done" (a statement that may be taken as demonstrating that Ruskin's own drawing really was copied from the photograph rather than done in situ). Boyce was "to make friends with the old porter of the Ducal Palace – and get into the upper loggia at the corner. [From there] St. Marks portico comes in somehow so [Ruskin gives a sketch] – with the top of the broken square capital of the St. Jean d'Acre pillar underneath – and St. Marks place behind most beautifully."[1]

NOTES

1 Boyce 1980, p. 120.

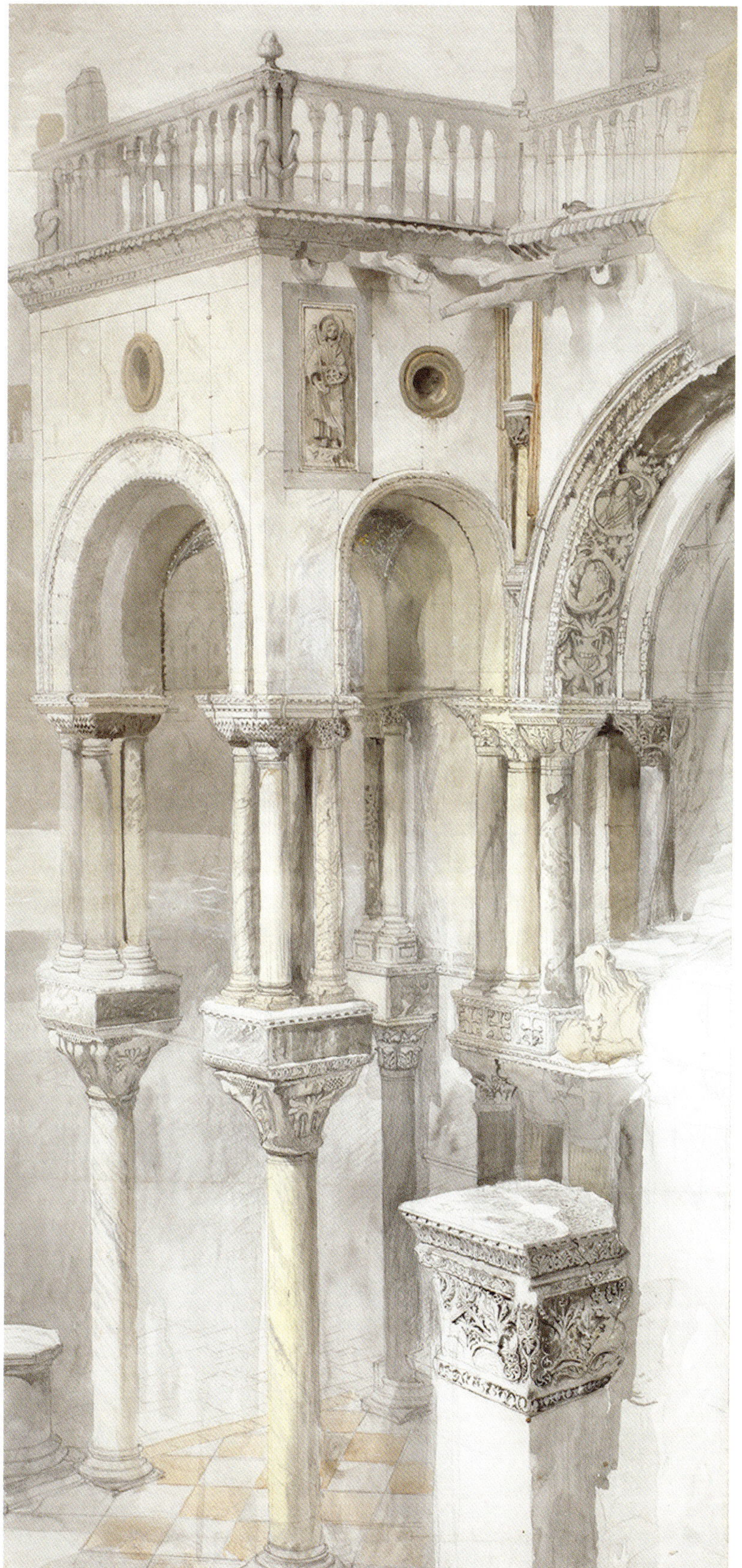

34

Study for the General Chiaroscuro of the Sarcophagus and Canopy of the Tomb of Mastino II della Scala at Verona c. 1869

Graphite on paper; 50.7 × 33.3 cm
The Ashmolean Museum, Oxford. Presented by John Ruskin to the Ruskin Drawing School (University of Oxford), 1875 (WA.RS.REF.058)

Ruskin visited Verona several times between 1851 and 1852, when he was working in Venice on the second and third volumes of *The Stones of Venice*. He was fascinated by the Scaliger tombs there, analyzing them in similar terms to those he used to describe the tombs of the doges in the Dominican basilica of Santi Giovanni e Paolo in Venice – seeing in them clues to a progression from something that was sincere and pious, and appropriate to a funerary monument, toward styles of building and ornamentation that he took to be symptoms of hubris on the part of the rulers of each city. He frequently recommended the Scaliger tombs to artists who were travelling in Italy and who sought his advice as to where they should go and what to paint or draw, for example to George Price Boyce in 1854, to whom he wrote: "the little group of the Scala Monuments is altogether unrivalled *in the world* for sweet colour & light and shade; and in these times there is no knowing how long it may stand."[1]

The present drawing was probably made during Ruskin's stay of about four months in Verona in 1869. Although he was then contemplating writing at length about the Romanesque and Gothic architecture of the city, the principal outcome of his study there was his lecture "Verona, and its Rivers," given at the Royal Institution on 4 February 1870, on which occasion an exhibition of his Verona drawings was staged. In his drawing of the tomb of Mastino II – the ruler of Verona who died in 1351, shown lying upon his sarcophagus, with an angel with extended wings at each corner and with scenes from the Passion of Christ on each side – Ruskin fulfills one of the essential principles of his own architectural draftsmanship. This was to approach closely to the subject and allow the forms of the building represented to fill the sheet, while avoiding all peripheral or incidental detail. The drawing, achieved by sweeping strokes of graphite, emphasizes the contrast of tone between the lit parts and the shadowed underside of the Gothic canopy and its trefoil-shaped archways. Ruskin was interested in the way dramatic effects of irradiating light cause the projecting features of a structure to be seen in stark relief, or conversely how suffused shadows might allow buildings to appear soft and mellow. In the case of the Scaliger tombs, he noticed that they were seen in half-light because the direct light of the sun was blocked by surrounding buildings. To his perception, this was a determining factor in the aesthetic impact of the cemetery, and one that he feared might be disrupted by any changes to the larger setting.

NOTES

1 Boyce 1980, p. 119.

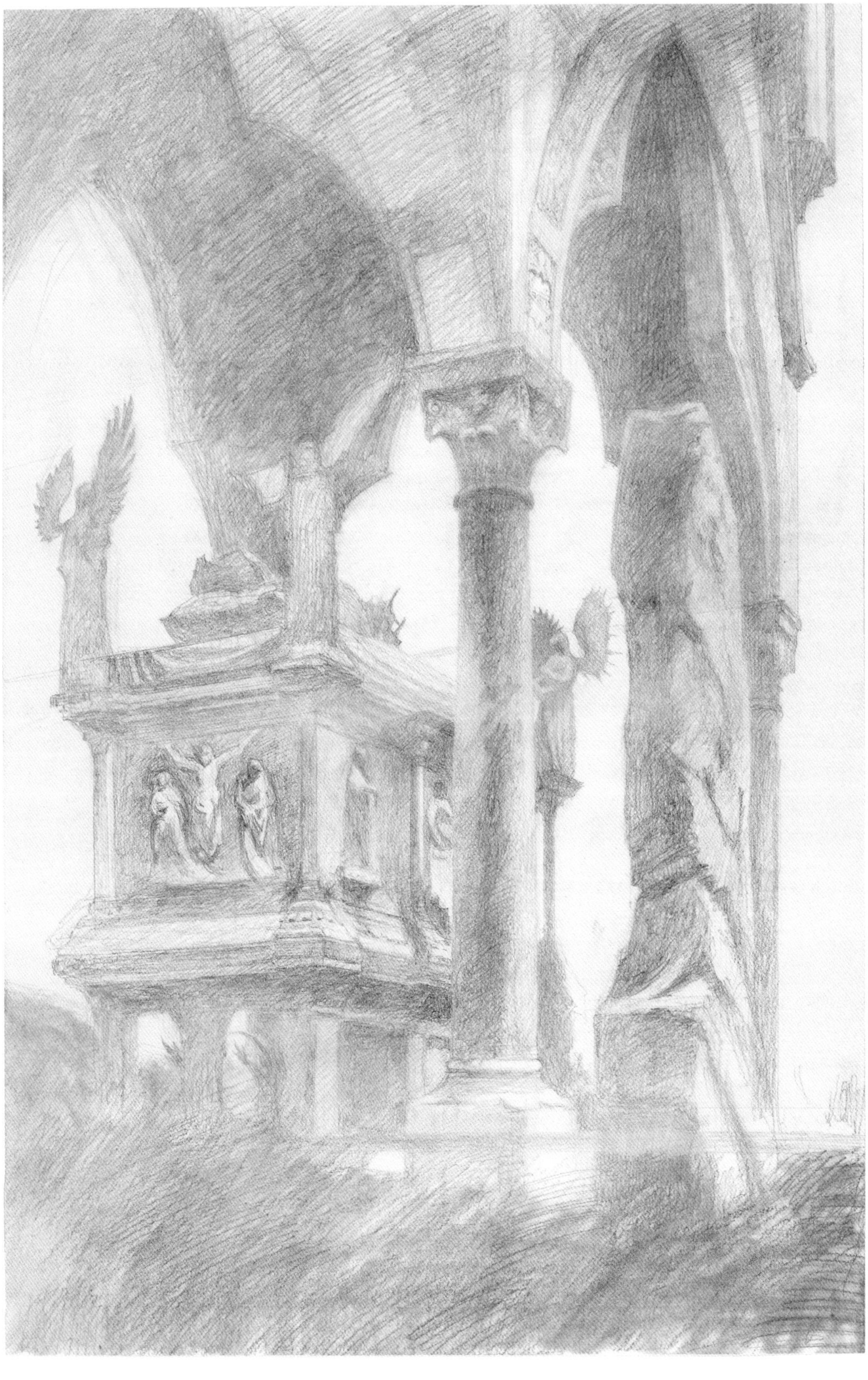

35

The Baptistery, Florence: Study of the Upper Part of the Right-hand Compartment on the Southwest Façade 1872

Watercolour and bodycolour over graphite on wove paper; 52 × 34.6 cm
The Ashmolean Museum, Oxford. Presumably presented by John Ruskin to the Ruskin Drawing School (University of Oxford), where it was first recorded in 1906 (WA.RS.REF.120)

In March 1872 Ruskin explained in *Fors Clavigera* that he intended to go to Florence to draw the Baptistery in connection with the lecture series on architecture that he was preparing to give at Oxford. It was, he believed, a building of great importance; indeed it was his stated opinion that the "whole history of *Christian* architecture and painting begins with [the] Baptistery of Florence,"[1] and that it might be regarded as the consummation of an ancient Greek tradition of architecture as "the last building raised on the earth by the descendants of the workmen taught by Dædalus."[2]

Ruskin was instinctively drawn to geometric surface decoration in buildings. Here he paid close attention to the patterning of the marble facings, which he described as "white substance, cut into, and filled with black, and dark green,"[3] and celebrated the Baptistery as something "on the surface of which the eye and intellect are to be interested by the relations of dimension and curve between pieces of encrusting marble of different colours, which have no more to do with the real make of the building than the diaper of a Harlequin's jacket has to do with his bones."[4]

The present drawing shows the upper part of the right-hand bay of the southwest face of the Baptistery looking onto the Piazza San Giovanni. Although each of the six side flanks of the building are apparently alike, with a blind arcade of white and green marble (from the quarries of Luni and Prato respectively) forming the central register, Ruskin had noticed that in fact "there wasn't a single space in all the octagon and all the panelling, that matched another."[5] By his own account, Ruskin paid close attention to the exact pattern and distribution of the architectural elements: "I painted ... one compartment of it with the best care I could – [and] never took more pains with a drawing."[6] Only those on the southwest and northwest flanks have such narrow window spaces, and only that facing the southwest has square patterns in the upper part that meet but do not overlap with the semicircular band that runs around the inside of the blind arch. Looking even more closely, it may be observed that the cracks and joint marks in the marble facings as shown in the drawing remain visible in the building today, even including the small square repair marks in the white panel on the right of the window. However, two of the three rectangular sheets of marble with half disk tops in the lower part (those on each side, but not that in the centre), as well as parts of the green marble, including the pediment of the window, have been replaced since Ruskin drew there.

NOTES

1 Ruskin 1903–12, vol. 22, *Lectures on Landscape, Michael Angelo & Tintoret, The Eagle's Nest, Ariadne Florentina, with Notes for Other Oxford Lectures*, p. 343.
2 Ruskin 1903–12, vol. 23, *Val d'Arno, The Schools of Florence, Mornings in Florence, The Shepherd's Tower*, p. 413.
3 Ruskin 1903–12, vol. 22, p. 344.
4 Ruskin 1903–12, vol. 20, *Lectures on Art and Aratra Pentelici with Lectures and Notes on Greek Art and Mythology 1870*, p. 217.
5 Ruskin 1903–12, vol. 37, *The Letters of John Ruskin, 1870–1889*, p. 414.
6 Ruskin 1903–12, vol. 23, p. 241.

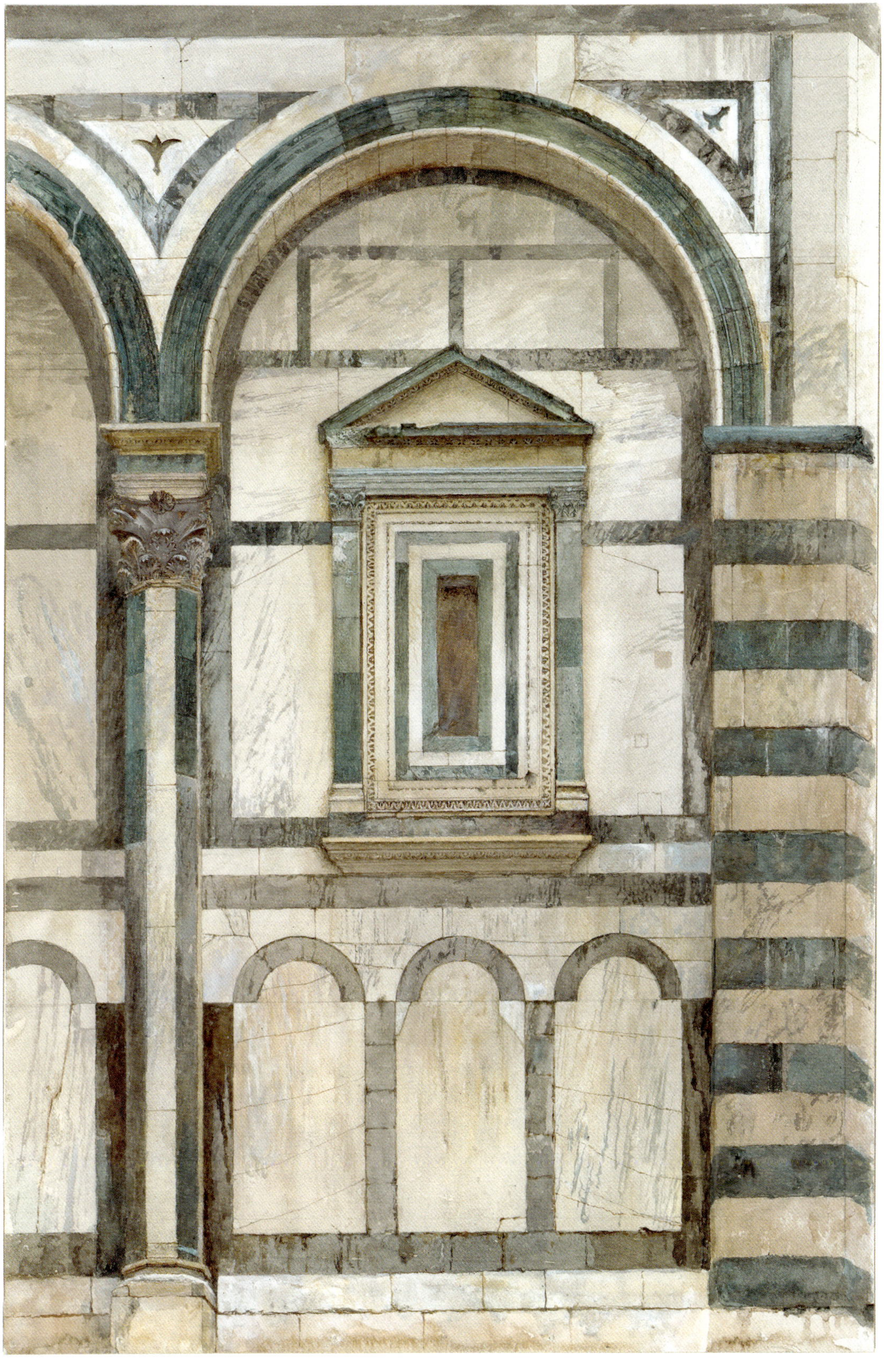

36

Northwest Porch of St. Mark's, Venice 1877

Graphite, watercolour and bodycolour on white paper; 64.8 × 77 cm
Ruskin Foundation (Ruskin Library, Lancaster University) (RF 1633)

It was only toward the end of his long stay in Venice in the winter of 1876–77 that Ruskin embarked on this challenging and exhaustive study of the northern section of the west façade of St. Mark's Basilica. During the preceding months he had vacillated between different projects, so the adoption of the present subject, which amounted to a determined attempt to study and observe with fresh eyes a building he knew intimately, appears to have been so that he would have at least one really substantial drawing to take back to England. A diary entry for 29 March seems to indicate that he gained comfort from the task that he had set himself: "But this a better morning after prosperous beginning of St. Mark's in divine morning yesterday."[1]

In the second volume of *The Stones of Venice*, a resonant and beautiful sentence describes the basilica's façade and exemplifies the kind of symbolic listing of qualities in sensuous and exotic terms, and in which plethoric multiplicity may be seen to be contained within an organic and integral whole. Hugely influential, the description was to inspire later authors such as Marcel Proust in their own accounts of Venice:

> ... a multitude of pillars and white domes, clustered into a long low pyramid of coloured light; a treasure-heap, it seems, partly of gold, and partly of opal and mother-of-pearl, hollowed beneath into five great vaulted porches, ceiled with fair mosaic, and beset with sculpture of alabaster, clear as amber and delicate as ivory, – sculpture fantastic and involved, of palm leaves and lilies, and grapes and pomegranates, and birds clinging and fluttering among the branches, all twined together into an endless network of buds and plumes; and in the midst of it, the solemn form of angels.[2]

Ruskin's perspective in this drawing is upward, so as to focus on the ranks of Byzantine capitals of the first and second tiers of columns both of the northwest portico and the most northerly of the basilica's five western portals. On the left, supporting a heavy abacus from which rise porphyry columns, is one of the church's four "lily" capitals (see cat. 7). Above, within the west-facing blind arch of the portico, is the sculpted relief of peacocks eating from a date palm and drinking at a fountain. In the half-vault of the portal is the St. Alypius mosaic, made in the 1260s and showing the body of St. Mark being brought to the church (and especially valuable as a record of the building following the incorporation of materials from Constantinople in 1204). Even this part, as Ruskin explained in *St. Mark's Rest*, was only "*nearly* intact [as] the three figures on the extreme right are restorations; and if the reader will carefully study the difference between these and the rest; and note how all the faults of the old work are caricatured, and every one of its beauties lost – so that the faces which in the older figures are grave

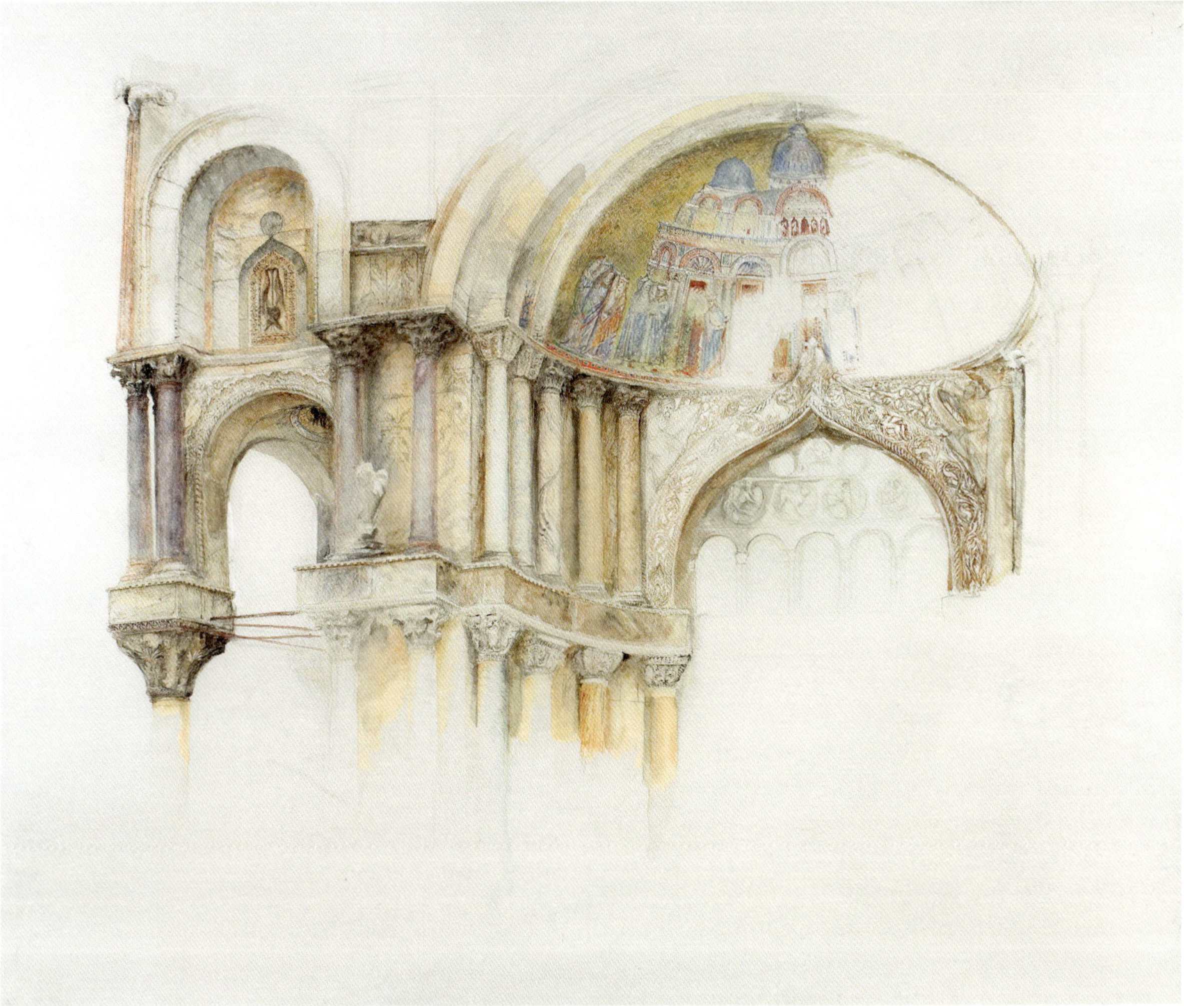

or sweet, are in these three new ones as of staring dolls."[3] Ruskin accordingly omitted this part of the mosaic from his drawing.

Since his first visits to Venice, Ruskin had been concerned by the periodic attempts made to clean and restore St. Mark's. In the winter of 1876–77, he became aware of a plan devised by the architect Giambattista Meduna and apparently approved by the city administration to reconstruct the church's west front, which was to involve reordering the columns and destroying the old mosaic. Ruskin immediately protested against the scheme, using his influence as a recently appointed member of the Venice Historical Society; and after his return to England he involved himself in the international campaign to preserve the building led by William Morris and Mary Gladstone through the agency of the Society for the Protection of Ancient Buildings. Two years later, but still in connection with Ruskin's wish to draw attention to the danger that the building was in and also to raise funds to pay for copies to be made of mosaics at St. Mark's and elsewhere in Venice, he allowed this drawing to be shown at the Society of Painters in Water Colours' 1879–80 winter exhibition.

NOTES

1 Ruskin 1956, vol. 3, p. 945.
2 Ruskin 1903–12, vol. 10, *The Stones of Venice II*, p. 82.
3 Ruskin 1903–12, vol. 24, *Giotto and his Works in Padua, The Cavalli Monuments, Verona, Guide to the Academy, Venice, St. Mark's Rest*, p. 286.

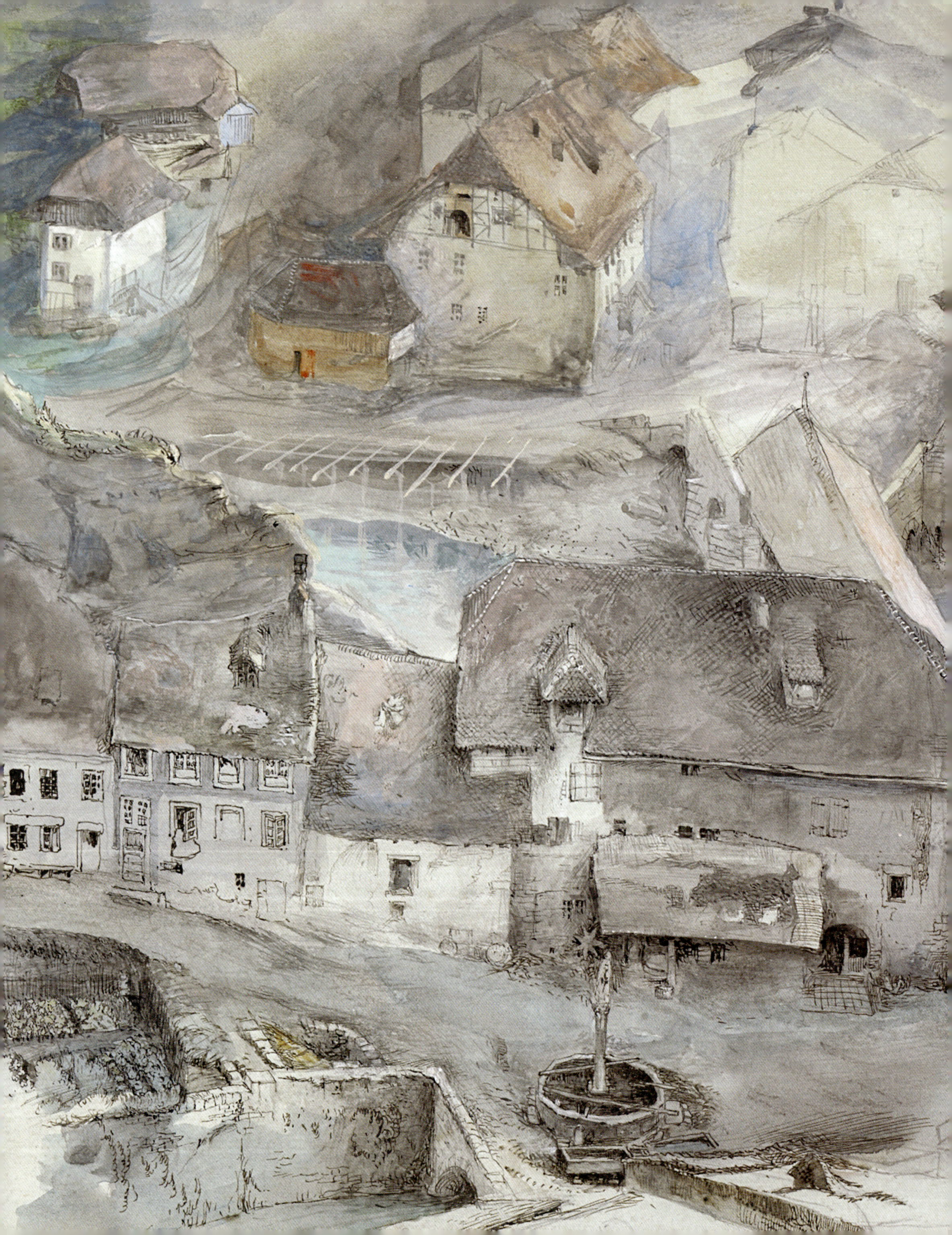

Towns & Topography

37

Fisher Street, Carlisle 1837

Graphite on white paper; 27.2 × 18.3 cm
Ruskin Foundation (Ruskin Library, Lancaster University) (RF 1194)
Inscriptions: graphite, *JR* [monogram], brown ink, *J Ruskin / Signed Jan 7th / 1880*

From early childhood, Ruskin was taken on long tours of Scotland and the north of England, travelling with his father or both parents in an antiquated post-chaise pulled by hired horses and loaded with guidebooks and drawing materials. The city of Perth, where the Ruskins had many relatives, was frequently their ultimate destination, but they would travel via parts of England and Scotland where Ruskin's father, John James, might visit clients to take orders for the sherry that he imported.

Both father and son enthusiastically inspected the medieval buildings of the towns and villages they visited and took every opportunity to see country houses and their picture collections. They were both entranced by the sublime scenery of the North, responding to the places they visited in the spirit of Romanticism, but at the same time searching the landscape for evidence of its geological past and attempting to understand it in the light of scientific theory. The delight that Ruskin experienced in these tours lessened as he got older, and in *Præterita* he described his 1837 journey to the English Lakes and Cumberland, in the course of which the present drawing of a street in Carlisle was made, as the last occasion when he felt "the pure childish love of nature which Wordsworth so idly takes for an intimation of immortality."[1] Nonetheless, he grew up with a close familiarity with parts of the British Isles far distant from his childhood home in Herne Hill, London, and thus he developed an appreciation of the variety and richness of the topography and architecture of England and Scotland.

Ruskin's drawing style remained at a formative stage in the late 1830s. Charles Runciman, from whom he had earlier received lessons, had taught him how to use a sharply defined pencil line to imitate the linear quality of engravings. Similarly, Ruskin's familiarity with Samuel Prout's architectural drawings and the lithographic plates that were made from them (for example, those published in 1833 as *Facsimiles of Sketches Made in Flanders and Germany*) inspired his own soft pencil drawings of picturesque architectural subjects.

In his view of the medieval Guildhall building in Carlisle, standing on the junction of Fisher Street and the Greenmarket,[2] Ruskin paid close attention to the decrepit plasterwork, allowing glimpses of diaper-laid brick beneath. A single chimney pipe, emerging at ground level, snakes upward with its shadow casting on the wall, and the upper floors, supported on jutting beams, overhang the building's lower storey.

NOTES

1 Ruskin 1903–12, vol. 35, *Præterita and Dilecta*, p. 218.
2 The location was identified by Stephen Wildman in Lancaster 2003, pp. 10–11.

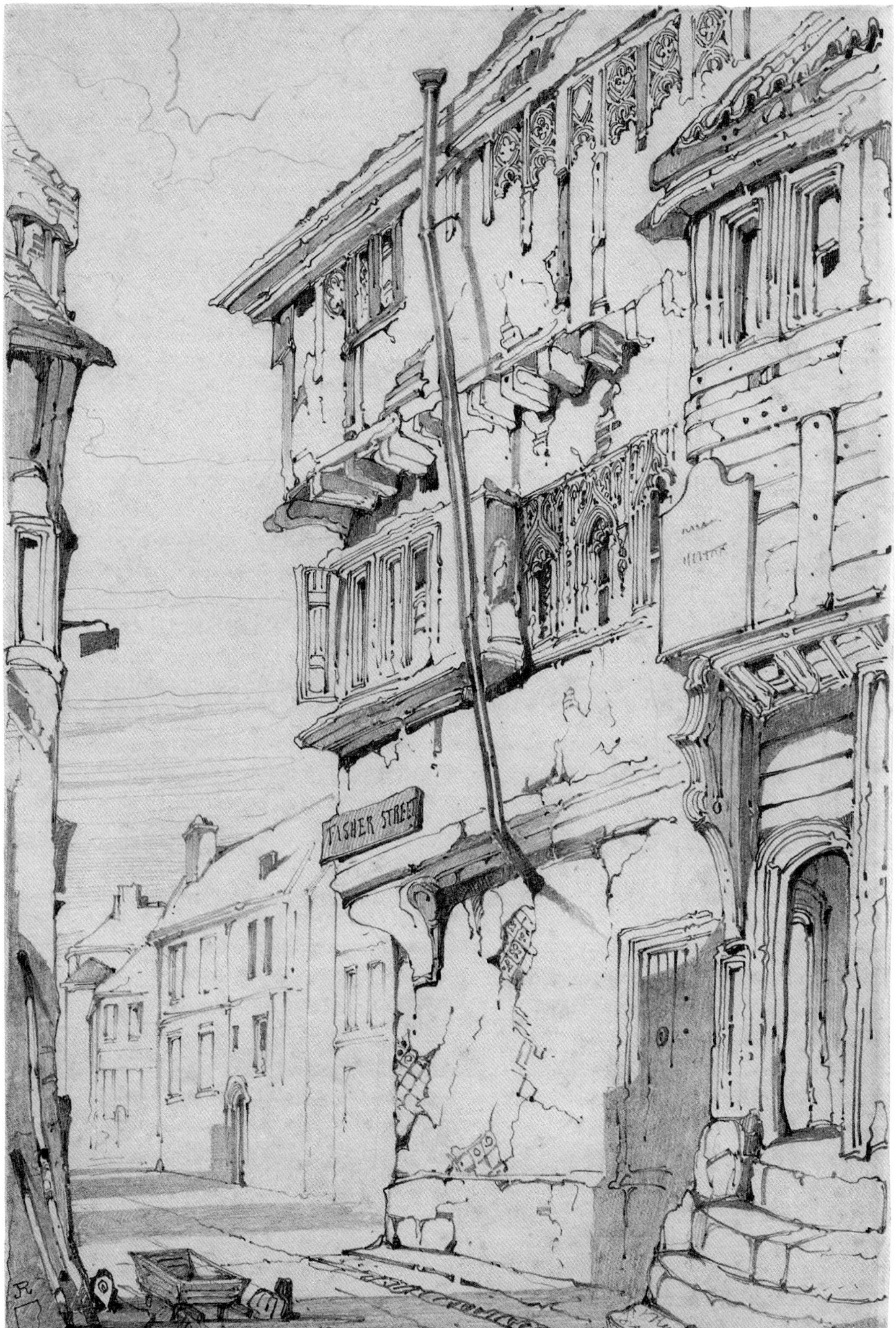
FISHER STREET
1830

38

Merton College and Magpie Lane, Oxford 1838

Graphite heightened with bodycolour on white paper; 45.8 × 27.5 cm
Ruskin Foundation (Ruskin Library, Lancaster University) (RF 967)

Ruskin went up to Oxford University in 1837, his college being the prestigious Christ Church, where his status was that of a gentleman-commoner (a rank that brought special comforts and privileges such as not having to take entrance examinations, and that was available for purchase). His mother, Margaret, accompanied him to Oxford, occupying rooms close by at 90 High Street so that she could keep a watchful eye on her emotionally fragile son with whom she spent the evenings (her husband, John James, travelled down from London each weekend). Ruskin's academic career was unremarkable – his greatest success being the winning of the Newdigate Prize for Poetry, at his third attempt, in 1839. In the spring of 1840 his studies were interrupted because of a nervous breakdown; when finally he took his degree, two years later, he gained a double fourth.

At Christ Church, Ruskin was conspicuous for his independence of mind, also because he was a published poet and geologist, and a skilled draftsman. Henry George Liddell, later Dean of the College, mentioned in a letter of 1837 that he was "going to ... see the drawings of a very wonderful gentleman-commoner here who draws wonderfully."[1] Liddell went on to give a pen portrait of Ruskin as "a very strange fellow, always dressing in a greatcoat with a brown velvet collar, and a large neckcloth tied over his mouth, and living quite in his own way among the odd set of hunting and sporting men that gentlemen-commoners usually are ... [He] tells them that they like their own way of living and he likes his; and so they go on, and I am glad to say they do not bully him, as I should have been afraid they would."[2]

Ruskin's artistic reputation led to his being asked to make drawings for members of his college, in the first instance by Charles Newton, who required a view of a Norman archway to illustrate a talk he was to give at the Oxford Society for Promoting the Study of Gothic Architecture. But, as Ruskin recalled, Newton was dissatisfied with the result: "When I got to work on it, he had to point out to me that my black dots and Proutesque breaks were no manner of use to him, and that I must be content to draw steady lines in their exact place and proportion. I fulfilled his direction with more difficulty than I had expected [but then] went back to my dots and breaks for three years more. Yet the lesson stayed with me."[3]

Ruskin here shows the view of the tower of Merton College Chapel as seen from Magpie Lane, with the back of Oriel College on the right. The choir of Merton Chapel was built in the last decade of the thirteenth century, but the tower – in the English Perpendicular style and with an embattled parapet and eight pinnacles – was not completed until 1450. This was a familiar topography to Ruskin, within minutes' walk of his rooms in Christ Church's Peckwater Quad.

NOTES

1 Henry George Liddell, quoted in Hilton 1985, p. 48.
2 Ibid.
3 Ruskin 1903–12, vol. 35, *Præterita and Dilecta*, pp. 611–612.

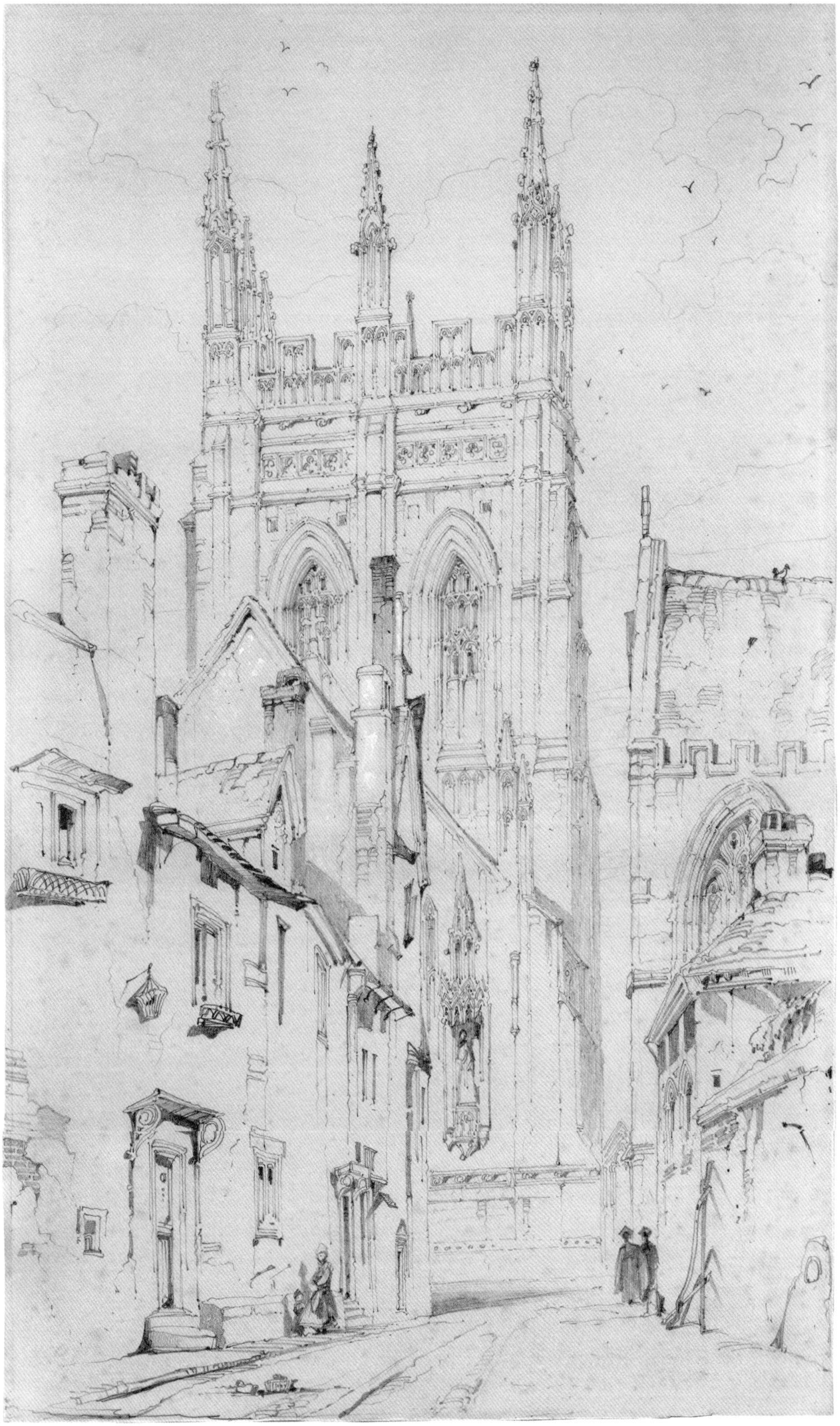

39
Piazza Sta Maria del Pianto, Rome 1840

Graphite heightened with touches of white bodycolour on grey-green paper; 26.5 × 37.3 cm
Private collection

In April 1840 Ruskin's studies at Christ Church were temporarily broken off as he left Oxford following a physical and psychological breakdown, brought on it seems by the disappointment he felt on hearing the news that Adèle Domecq, his father's business partner's daughter, was engaged to be married. In September he set out with his parents on a journey of recuperation that was to last nine months. They stayed for periods in the Auvergne and then travelled to Liguria and Tuscany, finally spending most of December in Rome and moving on to Naples early in the new year.

According to Ruskin's account in *Præterita*, in both these last places he avoided or dismissed many things that he might have been expected to admire. A determined prejudice against the Roman Catholic Church, fostered and enforced in him by his mother who was an evangelical Protestant, led him to castigate St. Peter's. He objected to the classical art that he saw in the Vatican museum and was appalled by the products of the Renaissance and Baroque periods, so much to the fore in Rome. In a febrile frame of mind, and having decided that "the sentiment of Raphael and tints of Titian were alike beyond me, if not wholly out of my way; and that the sculpture galleries of the Vatican were mere bewilderment and worry," he "took the bit in my teeth, and proceeded to sketch what I could find in Rome to represent in my own way, bringing in primarily, – by way of defiance to Raphael, Titian, and the Apollo Belv[e]dere all in one, – a careful study of old clothes hanging out of old windows in the Jews' quarter."[1]

The beauty of Ruskin's early street drawings derives from their crowded surfaces and rich textures and for the delight that Ruskin took in observing incidental detail. The picturesque character of Rome depended, he wrote in his diary:

> ... not on any important lines or real beauty of object, but upon the little bits of contrasted feeling – the old clothes hanging out of a marble architrave, that architrave smashed at one side and built into a piece of Roman frieze, which moulders away the next instant into a patch of broken brickwork – projecting over a mouldering wooden window, supported in its turn on a piece of grey entablature, with a vestige of inscription; but all to be studied closely before it can be felt or even seen; and I am persuaded, quite lost to the eyes of all but a few artists.[2]

The church of Santa Maria del Pianto stands next to the Palazzo Cenci and within the angle formed by the Via del Portico d'Ottavia and the Via del Progresso, but is embedded within the fabric of surrounding buildings and therefore has no façade.

NOTES

1 Ruskin 1903–12, vol. 35, *Præterita and Dilecta*, p. 276.
2 Ruskin 1956, vol. 1, p. 118.

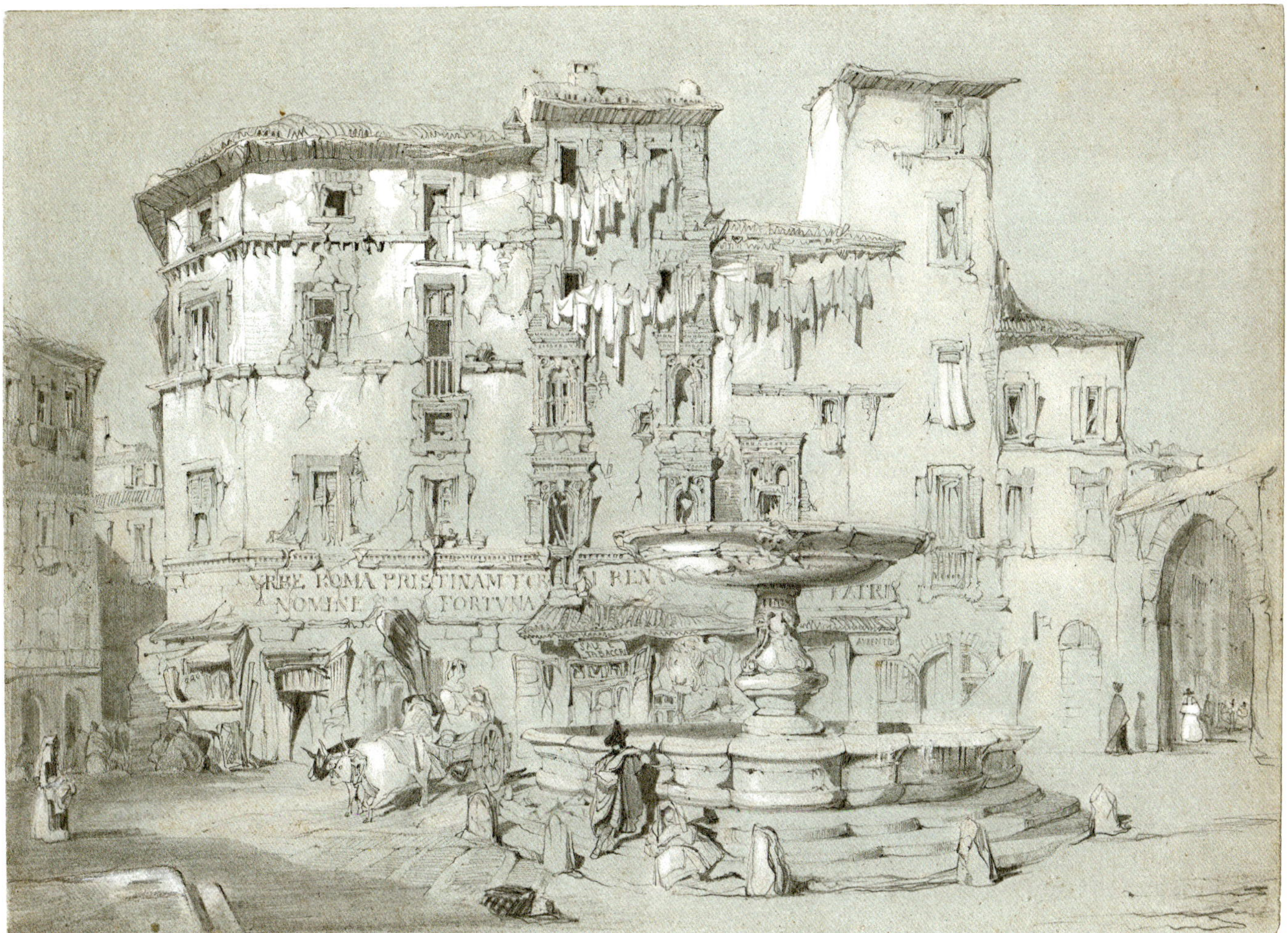
ROMA PRISTINAM
NOMINE
FORTVNA

40

Street Scene, Naples 1840–41

Graphite, ink wash and watercolour on white paper; 34.3 × 47.4 cm
Ruskin Foundation (Ruskin Library, Lancaster University) (RF 1409)
Inscriptions: graphite, *Naples*

The Ruskins travelled southward from Rome in the new year of 1841, arriving in Naples on 9 January. Ruskin's first response was one of disappointment, finding "a slight degree of gloom" about the city, but "Vesuvius certainly a far nobler thing than I had ever supposed it to be."[1] They departed on 16 March, having made a number of trips in the area, as far south as Paestum, to the west to Pozzuoli, and into the Sorrento peninsula. In Naples itself, Ruskin thoroughly inspected the churches and historical monuments, as recorded in his diary and in a series of topographical drawings. The squalor of the place was impossible to ignore; on 22 February he described walking along "the quay and among some abominable streets behind, just enough to get an idea of their populous misery ... Still, there are curious arched bits about the courts by which they enter their churches, and bright flashes of white far above, half way to the sky, and always a characteristic, though often disgusting population."[2]

The precise location of this wonderful drawing, in which Ruskin relishes the abstract pattern of a typical Neapolitan rookery, with cantilevered balconies and wrought-iron railings and washing strewn across every surface, is not known. Its manner of treatment represents an amalgam of the drawing styles of his masters, Samuel Prout – in the use of ornate pencil line – and David Roberts – in its dependence on tints of lemon-yellow and grey-pink to give volume to the buildings represented.

NOTES

1 Ruskin 1956, vol. 1, p. 141.
2 Ibid., p. 157.

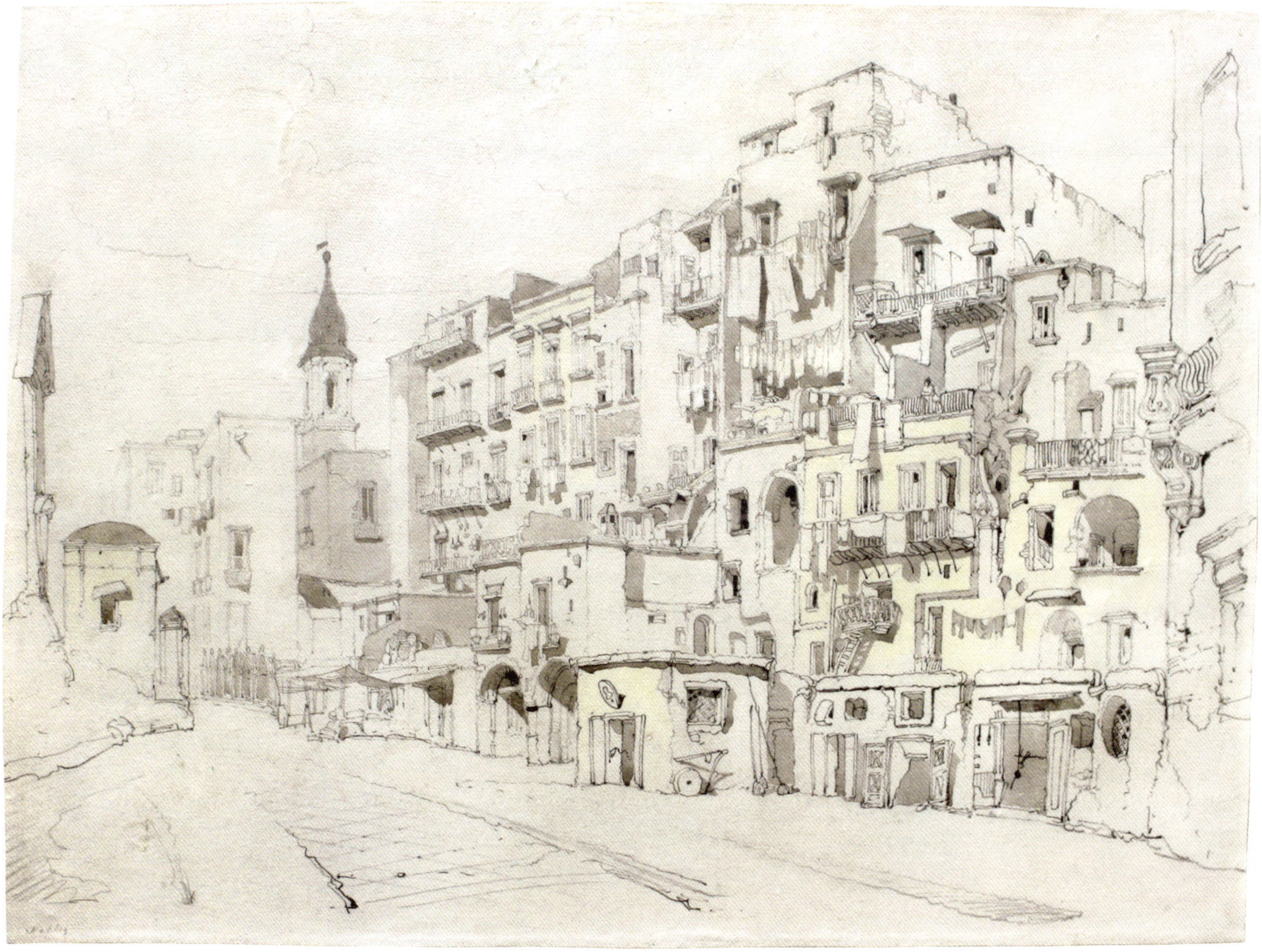

41

Fribourg, Switzerland 1856 (?), dated 1859 by Ruskin in a later inscription

Pen and ink and watercolour with touches of bodycolour on blue-grey paper; 22.5 × 28.8 cm
The British Museum, London (1901.0516.4)
Inscriptions: *Fribourg. / Sketch for / etchings of Swiss / towns. 1859 / Signed (1879) J Ruskin*

In the 1850s, following the publication of *The Stones of Venice*, Ruskin turned his attention to the vernacular architecture of Switzerland. He intended to write another book in which buildings were used as historical evidence, showing how people had lived in past centuries. The venture was never completed, but is usually referred to as the Swiss towns project.

The present drawing is one of a number of views of Fribourg that Ruskin made, in this particular instance in preparation for an intended etched illustration for the projected book.[1] Part of the old town, which stands on either side of the Sarine river as it makes a tight bend and beneath steep sandstone cliffs, is seen in a view looking toward the southwest, and taken from the galleried defensive wall that meets the Tour des Chats on the higher ground that encloses the town. The gabled building with two dormer windows at the drawing's centre is La Maison Mooses, while the buildings to its left, as shown by Ruskin – now all gone – were constructed with their back walls formed by a spur of rock, through which is a gaping hole. The street that runs in front of the line of houses is the rue de la Palme, and the basin with sculpted figure that appears close to the composition's lower edge is the Fontaine de la Fidélité, carved by Hans Gieng between 1552 and 1557. Running horizontally across the composition is the river, with the characteristic tile-roofed Pont de Berne seen at an angle that shows the structure almost end on. On the river's far right side, just blocked in in the drawing, is the Auberge du Cygne, while out of view to the right stands the Augustinian convent (see cat. 43). Other drawings of Fribourg are of a similarly vertiginous type, including one that was made from a position on the far side of the river and out of view to the right, so that part of the Pont de Berne and the northwestern gable end and riverfront of the Maison Mooses are seen (cat. 45). Ruskin also instructed his valet Frederick Crawley to make daguerreotypes showing the town from above (cat. 44).

Particularly delicious is the muted and yet intense range of colours – principally blues, greys and greens – that Ruskin used in the drawing, and once again is found the fusion of forms into shifting masses animated by areas of carefully observed detail, but with other parts reduced to abstraction and indefiniteness. By these means, he simulated the very process of seeing, as the eye shifts from one salient detail to another with a constant variety of intensity and fluctuating focus forming a random pattern of shapes, textures and colour. As Lindsay Stainton has written, the drawing depends upon a technique that combines "Turnerian impressionism and Pre-Raphaelite detail."[2]

NOTES

1 In the *Catalogue of Ruskin's Drawings* that forms part of Ruskin 1903–12, vol. 38, the drawing is simply described as "Study for Etching (1856)" (p. 253).
2 London 1985, p. 76.

42

JOHN RUSKIN AND FREDERICK CRAWLEY

Fribourg. Rue de la Palme and Houses Beyond Pont de Berne c. 1854 or 1856

Daguerreotype (half plate); 11.5 × 15.1–15.2 cm
Courtesy of K. & J. Jacobson (132)

The present daguerreotype, presumably made by Frederick Crawley and Ruskin together, corresponds closely to the view taken in the British Museum watercolour (cat. 41), with La Maison Mooses and neighbouring houses at the centre of the composition. The rue de la Palme runs across the width of the subject in the foreground, with the Fontaine de la Fidelité at the centre. The photograph must surely have been taken from the city wall on the northeastern side of the old town of Fribourg and from a position just a few steps to the right of that which led to the watercolour (as may be judged from the angle of alignment of the tiled roof of the Pont de Berne).

Which came first – the daguerreotype or the drawing – is not clear, nor whether there may have been some degree of interdependence between the two in the process of observation of the topography. Ruskin was interested in how images in various media might offer different degrees of information and divergent impressions of a place. In a passage in the fourth volume of *Modern Painters*, he described how he had both drawn and photographed Fribourg, and how the latter "unexaggerated statement, with its details properly painted [sic], would not only be the more right, but infinitely the grander of the two." However, in Ruskin's view, a "first sketch nevertheless conveys, in some respects, a truer idea of Fribourg."[1]

NOTES

1 Ruskin 1903–12, vol. 6, *Modern Painters IV*, p. 46.

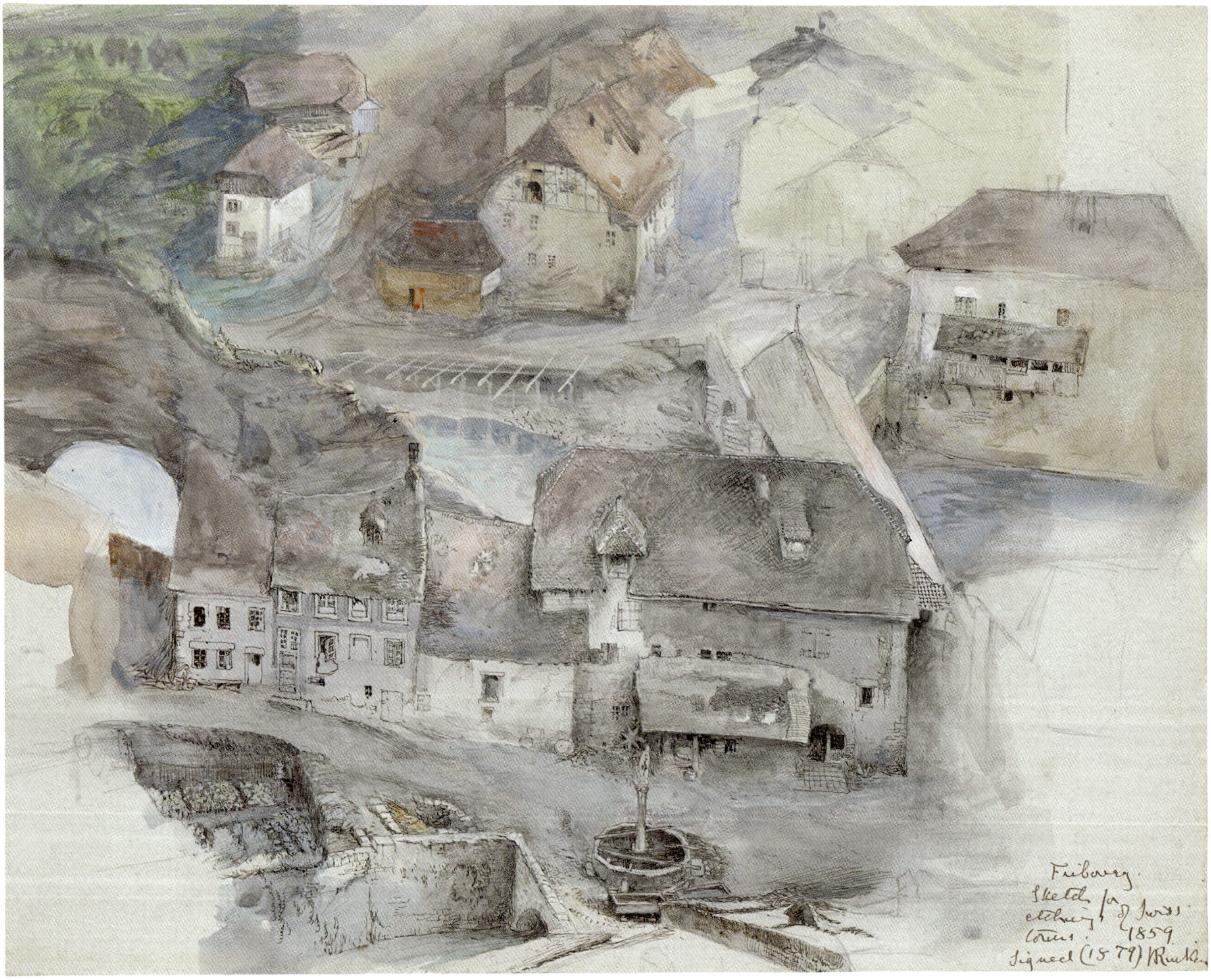
Fribourg.
Sketch for
1859
Signed (1879)

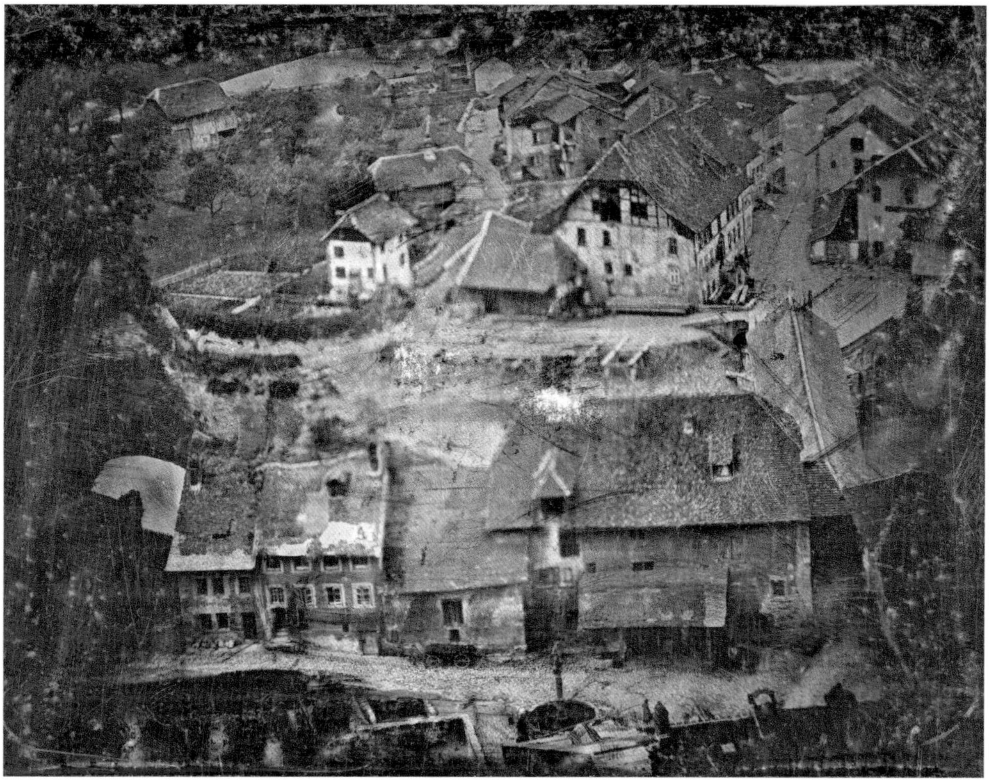

43

The Augustinian Convent, Fribourg 1854 or 1856

Graphite, pen and brown ink, watercolour and bodycolour on blue paper; 30 × 47.3 cm
Private collection
Inscriptions: *Fribourg*

Ruskin's view here is from the northeast, his vantage point being on the higher ground on the Route de Bourguillon on the northern side of the old town of Fribourg, looking steeply downward toward and across the Sarine river, with the Pont de Berne out of view on the left. The monastery is the massive four-storeyed building, its structure dating in part to the thirteenth century, seen at the centre, while immediately beside it is the Augustinian church of St. Maurice, with a Gothic exterior and containing rich Baroque interior decorations.

Travelling in Switzerland with his father in the summer of 1854, Ruskin began pondering various ideas that found expression in the penultimate chapter of the fourth volume of *Modern Painters*, entitled "The Mountain Gloom." A disdain for Roman Catholicism had been implanted in his mind by his parents, and he was interested in looking for ways in which Catholic and Protestant cantons differed in the condition and demeanour of the local population, a comparison that usually reflected favourably on the latter.[1] However, in the mid-1850s this prejudiced conviction was beginning to slacken. His interest in Fribourg – a bastion of Catholicism and the seat of the Catholic bishoprics of Lausanne, Geneva and Fribourg itself, and a place where numerous religious orders had monastic houses – was thus perhaps a sign of greater open-mindedness on his part.

NOTES

1 Ruskin 1903–12, vol. 7, *Modern Painters V*, p. xlii.

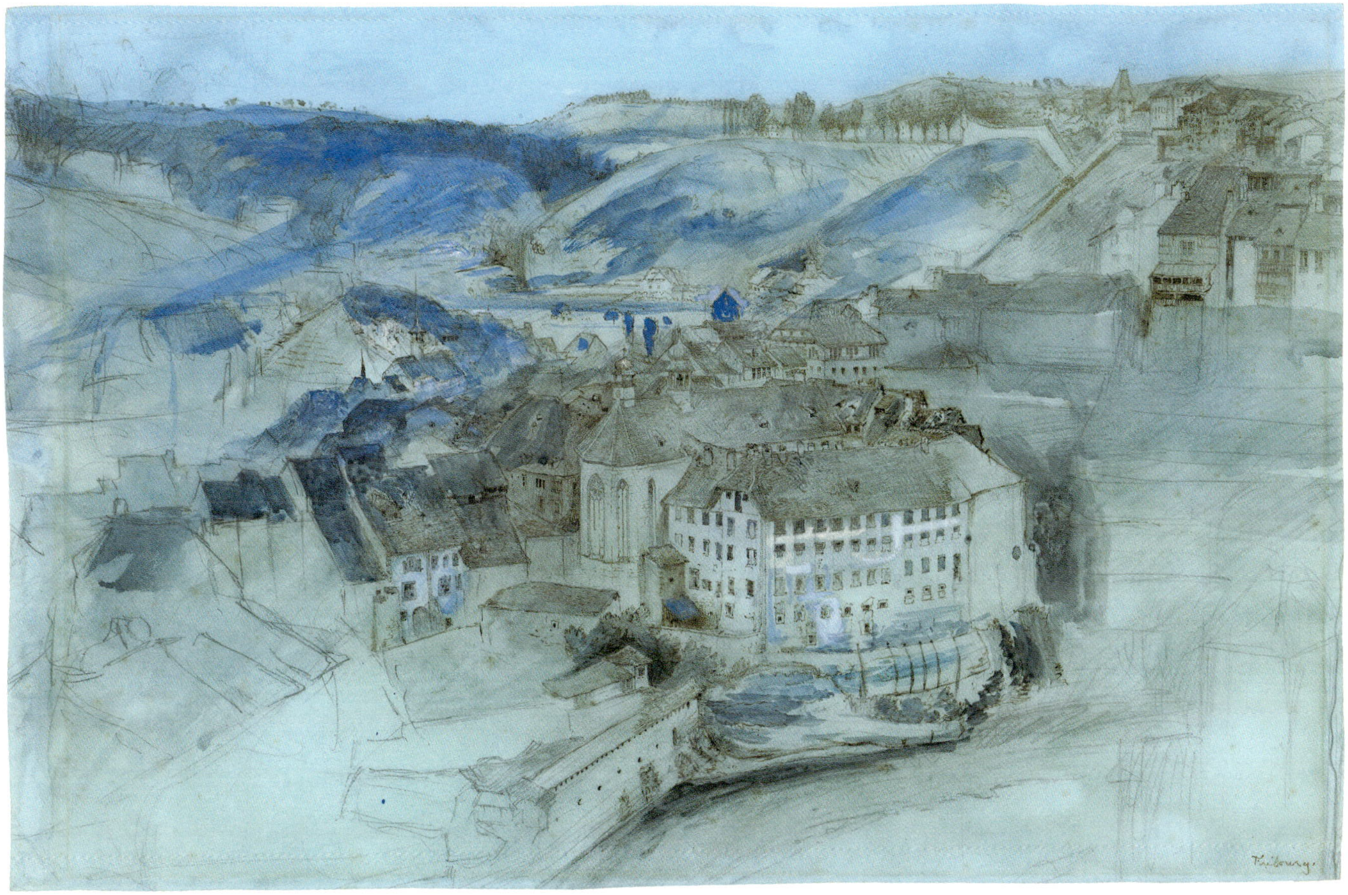
Fribourg.

44

JOHN RUSKIN AND FREDERICK CRAWLEY

Fribourg. The Augustinian Convent. Distant View c. 1854 or 1856

Daguerreotype (half plate); 10.9–11 × 14.4–14.5 cm
Courtesy of K. & J. Jacobson (123)

As with the corresponding views of the rue de la Palme and the Pont de Berne in watercolour (cat. 41) and daguerreotype (cat. 42), the present photograph of the Augustinian Convent at Fribourg bears a close relation to the matching drawing (cat. 43) and was presumably taken by Frederick Crawley and Ruskin together from the same vantage point on the Route de Bourguillon. The convent building appears to be seen at a greater distance in the photograph than in the watercolour (the daguerreotype method did not allow for the increase in scale of elements, whereas in his drawings Ruskin seems to have been willing to enlarge the scene represented). However, the building's structure, with the pattern of its white walls and registers of dark-framed windows on two flanks, is shown with absolute clarity.

Possibly the result of accidental damage to the plate, the foreground is indefinite with the only clues to the larger topography being a gleaming expanse on the right and a dark triangular shape indicating the Sarine river and buildings on its northern bank. Beyond are clusters of buildings and vegetation, but as they lie outside the photographic depth of field they show as mottled patches rather than legible architectural forms. Thus the convent itself appears as the composition's principle motif, looming from a surrounding miasma of atmospheric but uninformative visual texture.

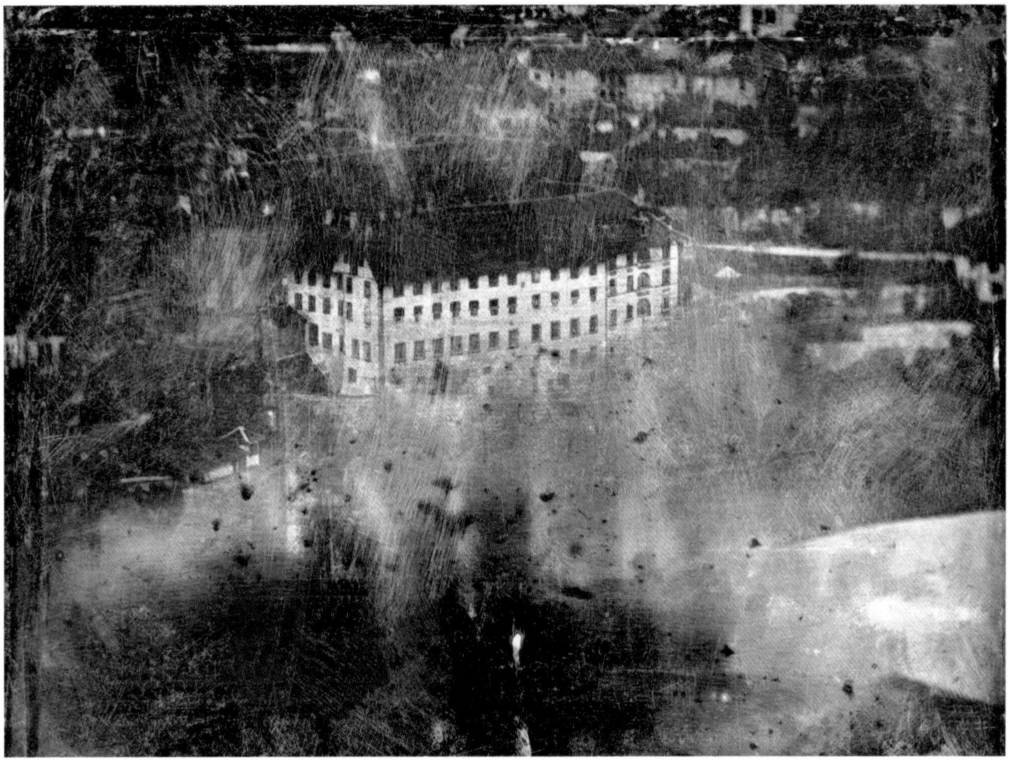

45

Fribourg 1856

Pen and ink and watercolour on heavyweight cream wove watercolour paper;
36.7 × 48.3 cm (edges irregularly cut)
Private collection
Inscriptions: ink, *Drawn Detail of Fribourg. 1856 / Colour stopped for fear of / losing the lines / J Ruskin Brantwood / 1879*, ink, *Fribourg*, graphite, *Tower inside …*

This spectacular and beautifully coloured drawing shows a group of historic buildings in the medieval centre of Fribourg, and was likewise connected with Ruskin's determination to gather information about the town for inclusion in his projected history of Switzerland on the basis of its vernacular architecture. At the centre of the work is the medieval structure of the Pont de Berne, seen from the northwest. The perspective is steeply downward to the Sarine river as it flows out of the tight bend enclosed by an almost vertical cliff, with the main part of the old town on the right side on the peninsula formed by the river's loop. The buildings close to the left-hand end of the bridge are the Auberge de l'Ange and beside it the watergate where the Gottéron joins the Sarine. A little further back, with the outline of its roof and a spire shown against a dark mass of coniferous trees, is a small chapel dedicated to St. Béat, while the Dürrenbühl Tower stands against the horizon at the crest of the hillside. At the extreme right, Ruskin has squeezed into the panoramic composition the bell-tower of St. Maurice, while in the foreground almost abutting the river is a wooden gallery that stands at the far end of the garden of the neighbouring Augustinian monastery.

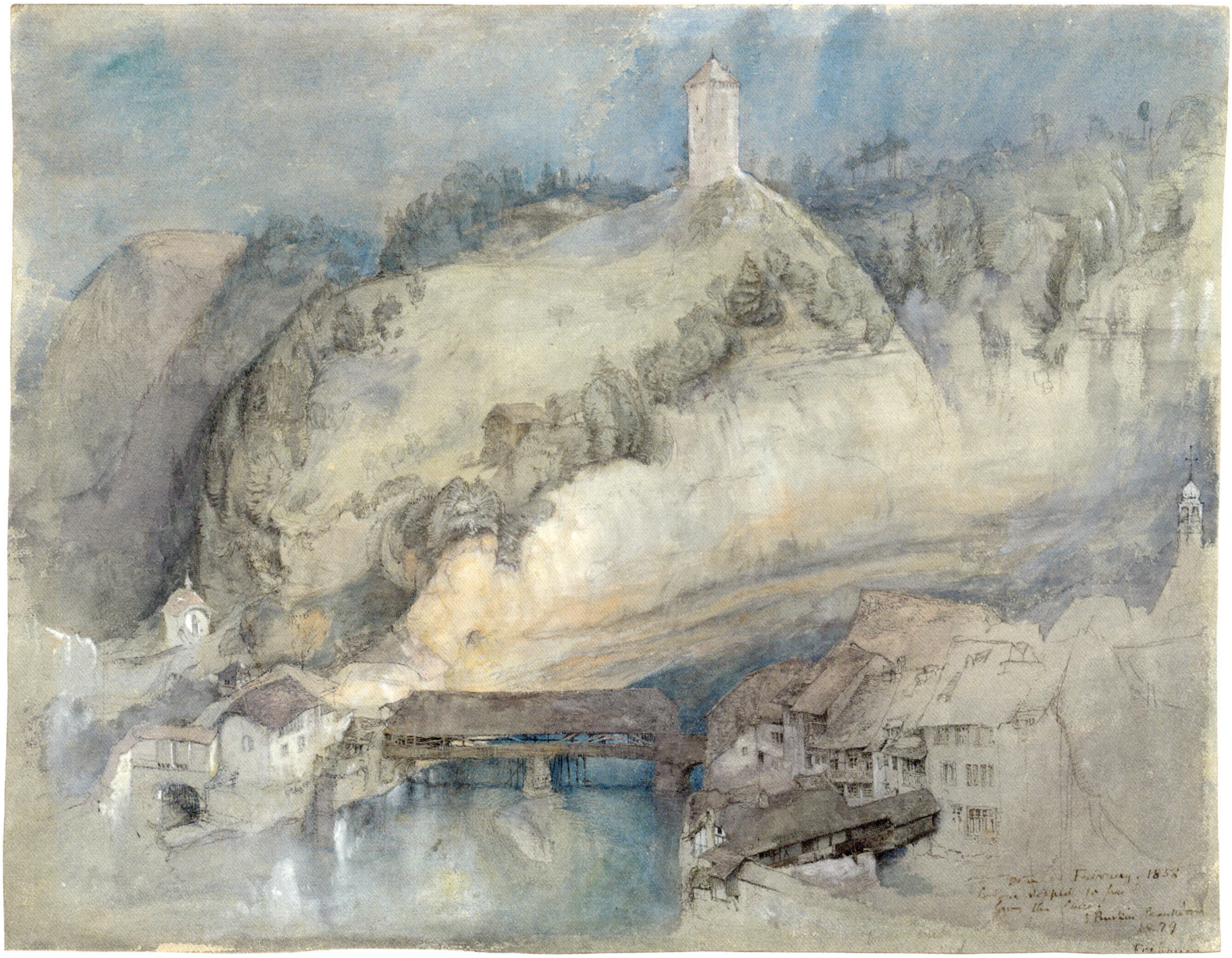
February, 1858
1879

46

Farm Buildings in Switzerland c. 1856–59

Graphite and watercolour with touches of bodycolour on blue paper; 10.7 × 20.6 cm
Private collection

This study of farm buildings was likely to have been done in Switzerland in the late 1850s. Completely without artifice or self-consciousness, the draftsman's eye wanders over the forms of barns, walls and gardens – flooded with bright Alpine sunlight or immersed in mauve-tinged shadow so that the viewer peers into the dark spaces of stables and byres. The ranges of buildings may be judged to have evolved through a long process of additions and reconstructions, while other parts seem to have fallen into a state of near abandonment. The rooflines, buttresses and walls create intriguing angularities and asymmetries, which make this a drawing that is deceptively simple and yet extraordinarily pictorially rich, with the beauty of a musical notation.

Observed from a hillside or bank in the immediate vicinity, which offers a perspective on the whole rambling confusion of a similar kind to the series of views that Ruskin made of Fribourg in the mid-1850s, the drawing offers some evidence of the life that was led in this farmstead. An animal is held in a stall standing in the grassy yard, and sheets hang to bleach in the sun; but despite these indications of human activity, no figures are seen. Ruskin sought to document such habitations and the people who lived there, but did so by observing the daily setting rather than giving a prosaic account of working routines or agricultural methods.

Ruskin was in this period increasingly absorbed by Alpine life – observing on the one hand the poverty and hardship that the mountain peasants endured, but also admiring those people for their self-reliance and determined independence. He was interested in their economic circumstances and concluded that this could be regarded as a model society of mutual cooperation and pooled resources. The link with the land and the variety of work that farming involved – quite different to the mindless repetition and unhealthy working environment that industry seemed inevitably to inflict upon its labour force – was seen to be good for people. A decade or so later, when Ruskin founded the Guild of St. George, it was thus his intention that a community should be established in which field work and the care of livestock were an integral part of people's daily routines.

Two of the Pre-Raphaelite landscape artists whose early careers owed so much to Ruskin's written works and personal exchange with him – John William Inchbold and John Brett – were encouraged by Ruskin to make careful studies of Alpine chalets. The former drew a series of such structures for him in 1856 or 1857,[1] while Brett incorporated into his painting *Val d'Aosta* (Lord Lloyd Webber Collection) a cluster of cottages, viewed from high above, and apparently depending on Ruskin's own specification of the essential elements of the mountain landscape in the fourth volume of *Modern Painters*.[2]

NOTES

1 See Leeds 1993, pp. 52–53, cat. 8.
2 See Ruskin 1903–12, vol. 6, *Modern Painters IV*, p. 388. For an expanded discussion of Brett's response to Ruskin's landscape teaching, see Newall 2007.

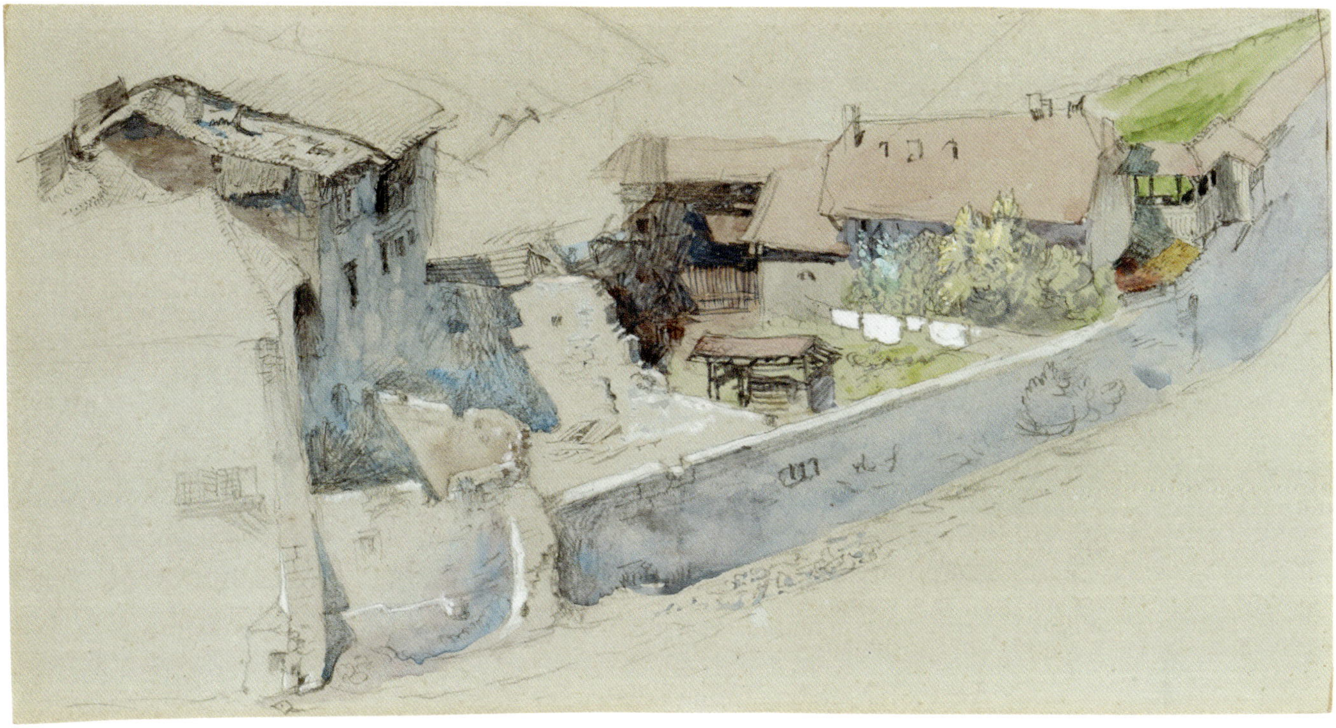

47

The Bridge at Rheinfelden 1858

Graphite, pen and brown ink and watercolour heightened with bodycolour on blue paper; 31.4 × 47.6 cm
Private collection

Ruskin's summer tour of 1858 commenced at Rheinfelden, on the Swiss-German border and straddling the Rhine. His visit was prompted by the sketches that J.M.W. Turner had made there in 1844 and that Ruskin had studied in the *Rheinfelden Sketchbook,* which was part of the Turner Bequest. In the fifth volume of *Modern Painters*, Ruskin used two of these Turner drawings, each showing the Holzbrücke[1] from the riverbank on the northern or German side and looking from the northwest, as illustrations.[2] A footnote chronicled Ruskin's interest in Turner's Rheinfelden work and how this sparked his own preoccupation with the place:

> A scratched word on the back of one of them, "Rheinfels," which I knew could not apply to the Rheinfels near Bingen, gave me the clue to the place; – an old Swiss town, seventeen miles above Basle, celebrated in Swiss history as the main fortress defending the frontier toward the Black Forest. I went there the moment I had got Turner's sketches arranged in 1858, and drew it with the pen (or point of brush, more difficult to manage, but a better instrument) on every side on which Turner had drawn it, giving every detail with servile accuracy, so as to show the exact modifications he made as he composed his subjects.[3]

The calm and loving attention to detail expressed in Ruskin's drawing of the old town of Rheinfelden speaks of personal resolution and a feeling of delight at seeing new places. As he wrote of the trip in *Præterita*, he found "great joy, and stayed to draw the town and bridges completely." Sadly, however, confusion and frustration gradually overtook him, with "the real new fact in existence for me [being] that my drawings did not prosper that year, and, in deepest sense, never prospered again." Ruskin described the drawings that he made of the Rheinfelden bridge as "really pretty colour-vignettes, which, had I only gone on doing the like of, the journey would have been visibly successful in everybody's sight. Whereas, what actually followed those vignettes at Rheinfelden was a too ambitious attempt at the cliffs of the Bay of Uri [(cat. 100)], which crushed the strength down in me."[4]

NOTES

1 The bridge was destroyed by fire in 1897.
2 Ruskin 1903–12, vol. 7, *Modern Painters V*, plate 82, between pp. 436 and 437.
3 Ibid., p. 436.
4 Ruskin 1903–12, vol. 35, *Præterita and Dilecta*, pp. 493–494.

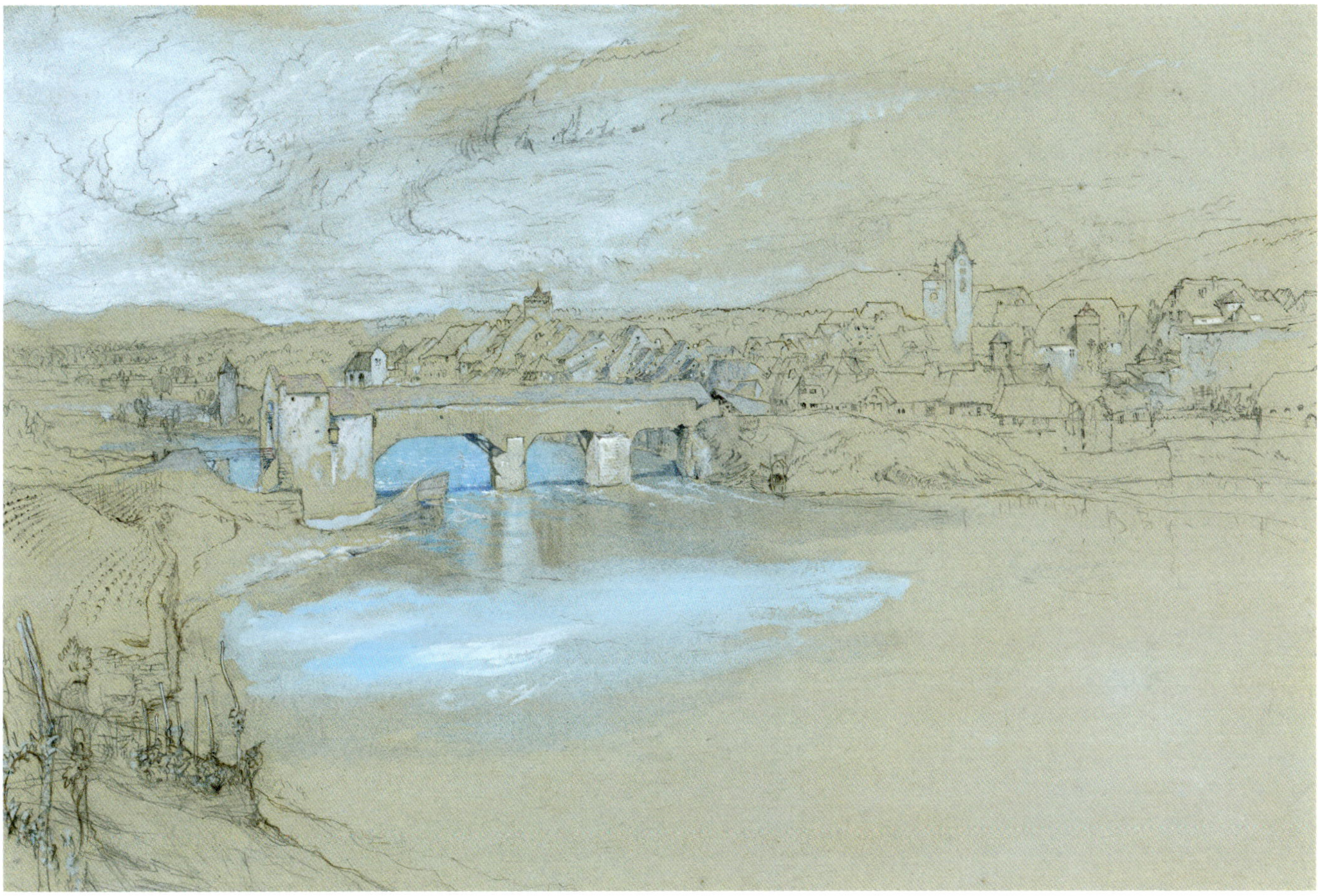

48

JOHN RUSKIN AND FREDERICK CRAWLEY

a. *General View at Rheinfelden* 1858

Daguerreotype (half plate); 11.5 × 15.5 cm (sight)
Ruskin Foundation (Ruskin Library, Lancaster University) (RF Dag. 113)

b. *View of the Bridge at Rheinfelden* 1858

Daguerreotype (half plate); 15.5 × 11.5 cm (sight)
Ruskin Foundation (Ruskin Library, Lancaster University) (RF Dag. 120)

c. *View of the Entry Post on the Bridge at Rheinfelden* 1858

Daguerreotype (half plate); 11.5 × 15.5 cm (sight)
Ruskin Foundation (Ruskin Library, Lancaster University) (RF Dag. 119)

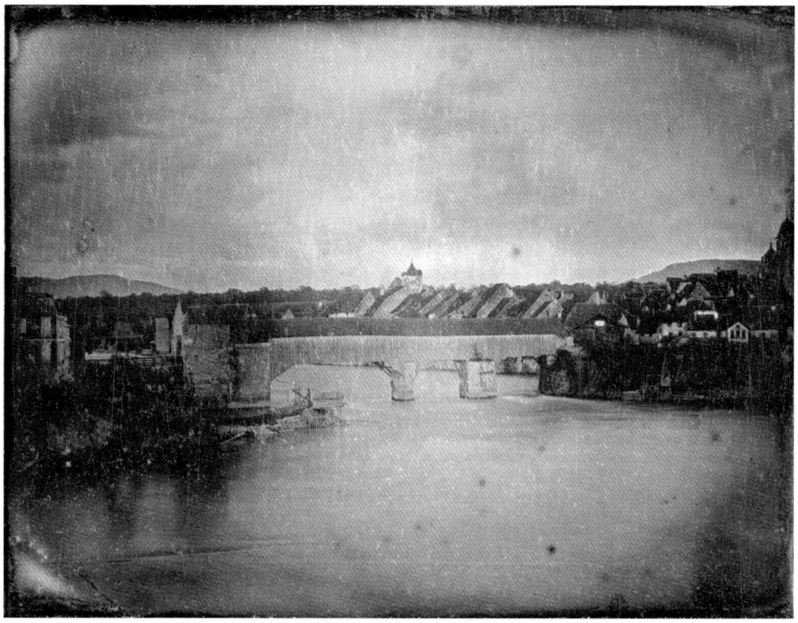

As with his drawings, Ruskin seems to have deliberately placed photographic images in series so that each informs others in the set about the wider topography. These three daguerreotypes must surely have been made by Ruskin, or under his supervision, in 1858 during his stay in Rheinfelden that spring. The first (a) includes a general view of the river, bridge and town that corresponds quite closely to his drawing *The Bridge of Rheinfelden* (cat. 47), although with the bridge at the centre of the composition and with a section on the right, as seen in the drawing, omitted. The other two photographs show the entry post of the bridge – viewed from the front and the side (each seen at right angles to the other). An open walkway resting on a tall pier meets a doorway in the entry post, through which all traffic would travel, with the shape of its gable outlined against the sky.

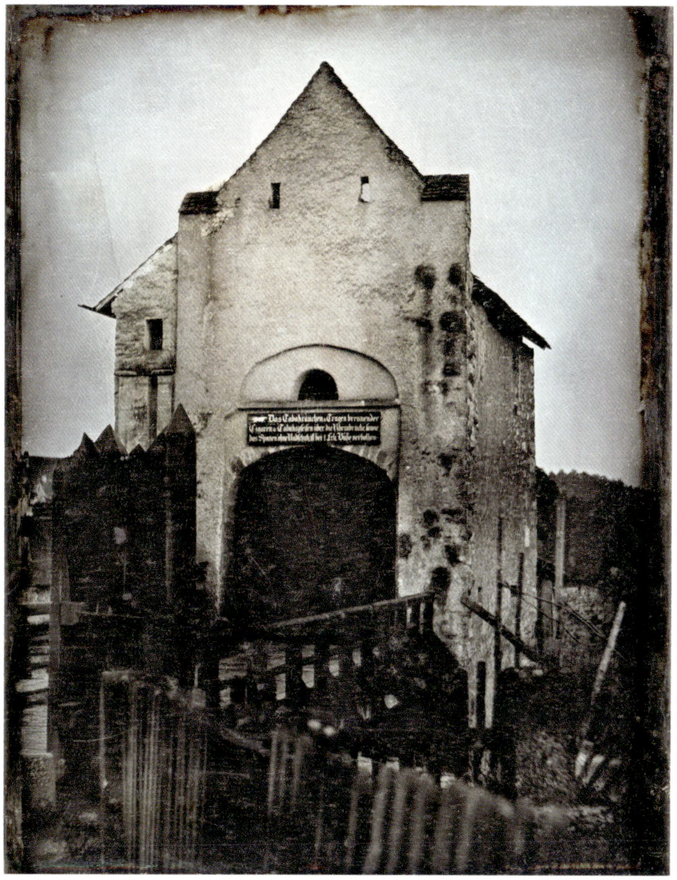

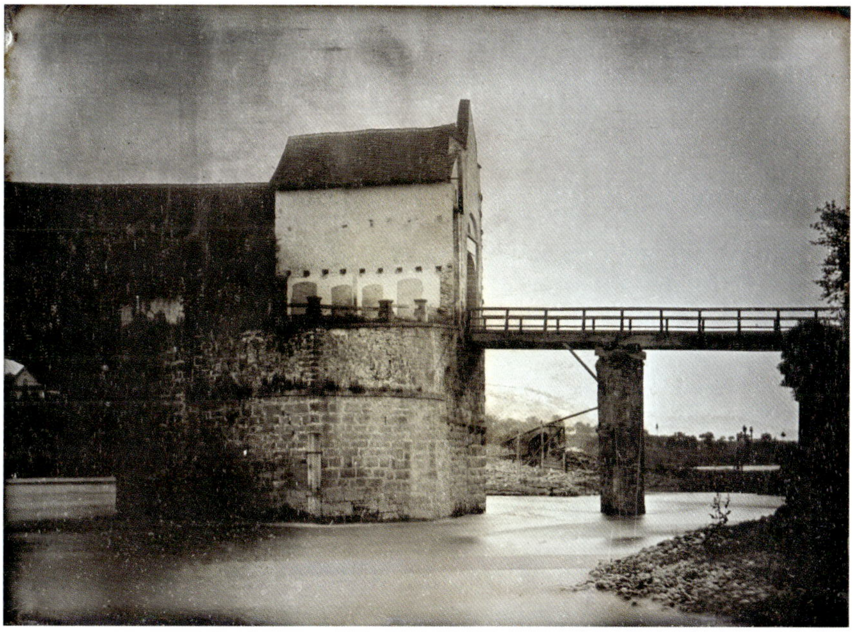

49

The Kapellbrücke at Lucerne 1861

Watercolour and bodycolour over graphite on wove paper; 29.7 × 39.3 cm
The Ashmolean Museum, Oxford. Presented by John Ruskin to the Ruskin Drawing School (University of Oxford), 1875 (WA.RS.ED.116)

The present drawing, which was said to have been made in 1862 in the catalogue of the first Educational Series of drawings given to Oxford, was in fact probably done during Ruskin's long stay in Lucerne in the autumn of 1861. Diary entries for 17, 18 and 19 October appear to chart his progress on the watercolour, with the laconic comments "Paint bit of Lucerne Bridge. Determine to stay," "Painting Bridge. Get on badly," and finally, "Paint Bridge; get on well, but stopped by cold,"[1] giving some idea of how much time was involved in a drawing of this scale and degree of elaboration.

The view is taken from the quay on the south bank of the Reuss and looks northeast, therefore showing the shorter southerly section of the famous covered bridge that crosses the river as it broadens out to meet the lake. On the right side is the octagonal Wasserturm, a defensive tower subsequently used as a prison and torture chamber and that even pre-dates the bridge itself, which was completed in 1333. The spire that appears from behind the bridge is an eighteenth-century addition to the ancient chapel of St. Peter, which stands on the far bank of the Reuss and from which the bridge takes its name.

Ruskin worked hard to distinguish the contrasting colours and textures of the vertically placed slats that form the side walls of the bridge and has likewise carefully studied the stone blocks that are its foundations. The outlines of the bridge and tower are softly reflected in the water surface of greens, blues and greys. The drawing's dramatic perspective and the way in which the composition is cropped as if the forms resist containment within the confines of the sheet make it dynamic and exciting to look at.

NOTES

1 Ruskin 1956, vol. 2, p. 554.

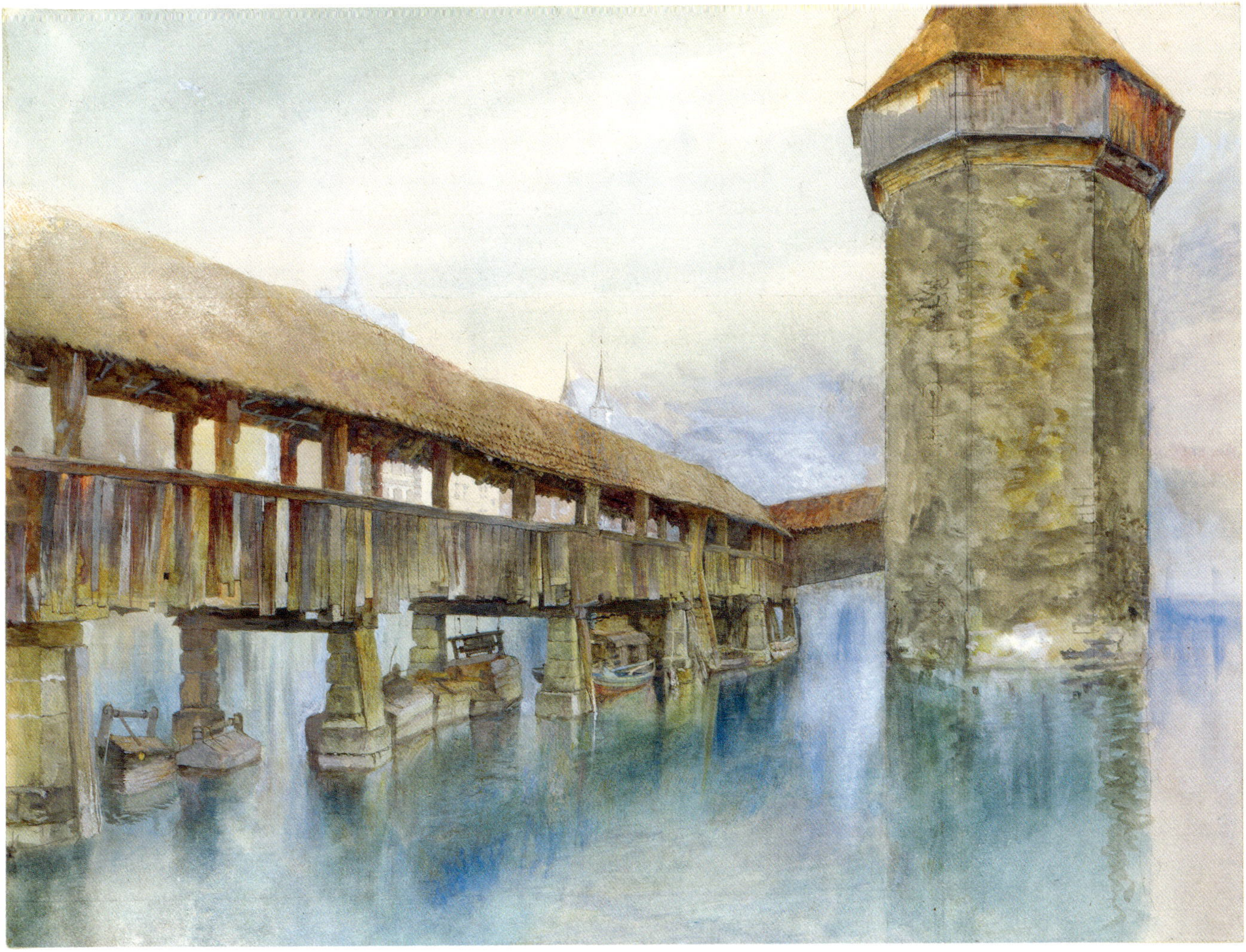

50

Lucerne 1861 (?), dated 1863 by Ruskin in a later inscription

Graphite and watercolour heightened with white bodycolour on paper; 14.3 × 22.2 cm
Private collection
Inscriptions: *J.Ruskin / 1863*

Ruskin's view shows Lucerne from above, looking down onto the Reuss river as it flows through the town and with the wide expanse of Lake Lucerne beyond, and with the glowing pink outline of the Rigi in the distance to the left and the Bürgenstock to the right. Within the town itself, the two covered bridges – the Spreuerbrücke (in the foreground) and the Kapellbrücke (close to where the Reuss flows from the lake), each built in the fourteenth or early fifteenth centuries – may be seen. On the left bank of the Reuss stands the circular tower, the Nöllithor, which was the last of the series of turrets connected by walls that formed the town's fortifications, the Museggmauer. Other buildings are less easily recognized, but in the middle distance on the south quay of the Reuss a jumble of forms stands for the Franciscan and Jesuit churches.

Ruskin was a neurotic man given to extremes of ecstatic emotion and bleak despair. This pattern of bipolarity can be read in his drawings, which are on occasions exhilarating and joyous and on others marked by ominous forebodings. This panorama of the town and lake of Lucerne, loosely sketched but delicious for its sunlit colour, speaks of his simple pleasure in being in a place where he felt secure, the experience of which reassured him that his work was worthwhile. The autumn of 1861, when the watercolour seems likely to have been made,[1] was a period when Ruskin found himself especially responsive to the beauty of the physical world and believed that he was appreciating the landscape with a particular intensity as a result of having trained his eye by the study of Venetian painting: "I cannot imagine how it is," he wrote from Lucerne that autumn, "that I feel, or see, everything so much more beautiful than even when I was in Switzerland only last year."[2]

The long shadows and glowing effect of purple-tinted light certainly suggest fine autumnal weather, and it happened that Ruskin was lucky to enjoy a succession of clear days while there, described in diary entries and letters to his parents. For example, on 12 November he wrote to his mother and father: "You had all much better come to Lucerne. I had never before seen autumn. Yesterday I had such a ruby sunset on Alps as I have not seen these ten years: the day was entirely cloudless, the afternoon all purple and gold."[3]

J.M.W. Turner remained a source of inspiration and was constantly in Ruskin's thoughts as he visited places where the late artist had painted. He had in his own collection several of Turner's views of Lucerne, including one entitled *Lucerne from the Walls* (National Museums, Liverpool), made in 1842 on the basis of sketches done in Switzerland the previous autumn. Although taken from further back and a greater height, and therefore offering a wider panorama than in Ruskin's view, it nonetheless contains many of the same topographical features. Writing of the original sketch

NOTES

1 As Paul Walton has observed (Walton 2000, p. 113), there is no record of Ruskin having been in Lucerne in 1863 – the year to which the present drawing has been dated. It seems likely therefore that this was an error introduced by Ruskin himself when attaching dates to drawings decades later. The suggestion that the drawing may in fact have been made in 1861, in which year he spent a period from mid-October until the end of November in the town, is explored in depth by Walton.
2 Ibid., p. xxxvi, note.
3 Ruskin 1903–12, vol. 17, *Unto this Last, Munera Pulveris, Time and Tide, with Other Writings on Political Economy, 1860–1873*, p. xliii.

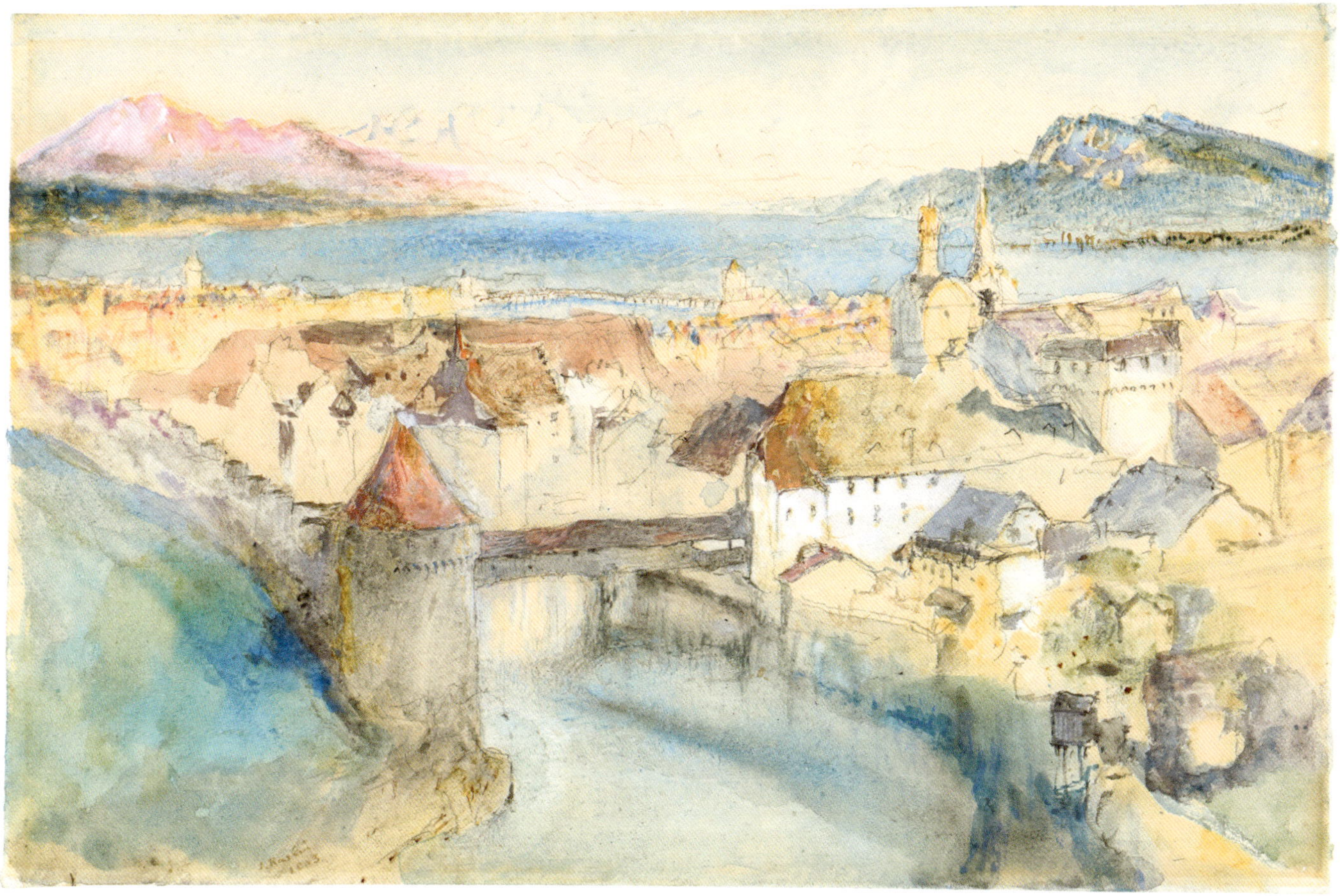

– from which Turner had worked up the watercolour of Lucerne – when it was exhibited as part of the Turner Bequest in 1857, Ruskin described the very experience of "Arriving at Lucerne": "we immediately climb the hill above the Reuss to try if we can see the Alps. No Alps to be seen, the day being grey and misty and disagreeably hot besides. The form of the Rigi is however, dimly visible beyond the first branch of the lake; and the old town delights us, especially the wall and towers bent like a bow over the hill behind it, which defended it in the old times of Austrian spears from any attack on the land side."[4]

This was, Ruskin thought, "an elaborate and most precious drawing, all the more valuable, as the characteristic features of Lucerne are now being rapidly destroyed."[5]

4 Ruskin 1903–12, vol. 13, *Turner, The Harbours of England, Catalogues and Notes*, p. 200.
5 Ibid.

51

Baden, Switzerland 1863

Graphite and watercolour heightened with white on five sheets of buff paper and with further slips making up the complete format; 51.7 × 38 cm (irregularly shaped)
Private collection

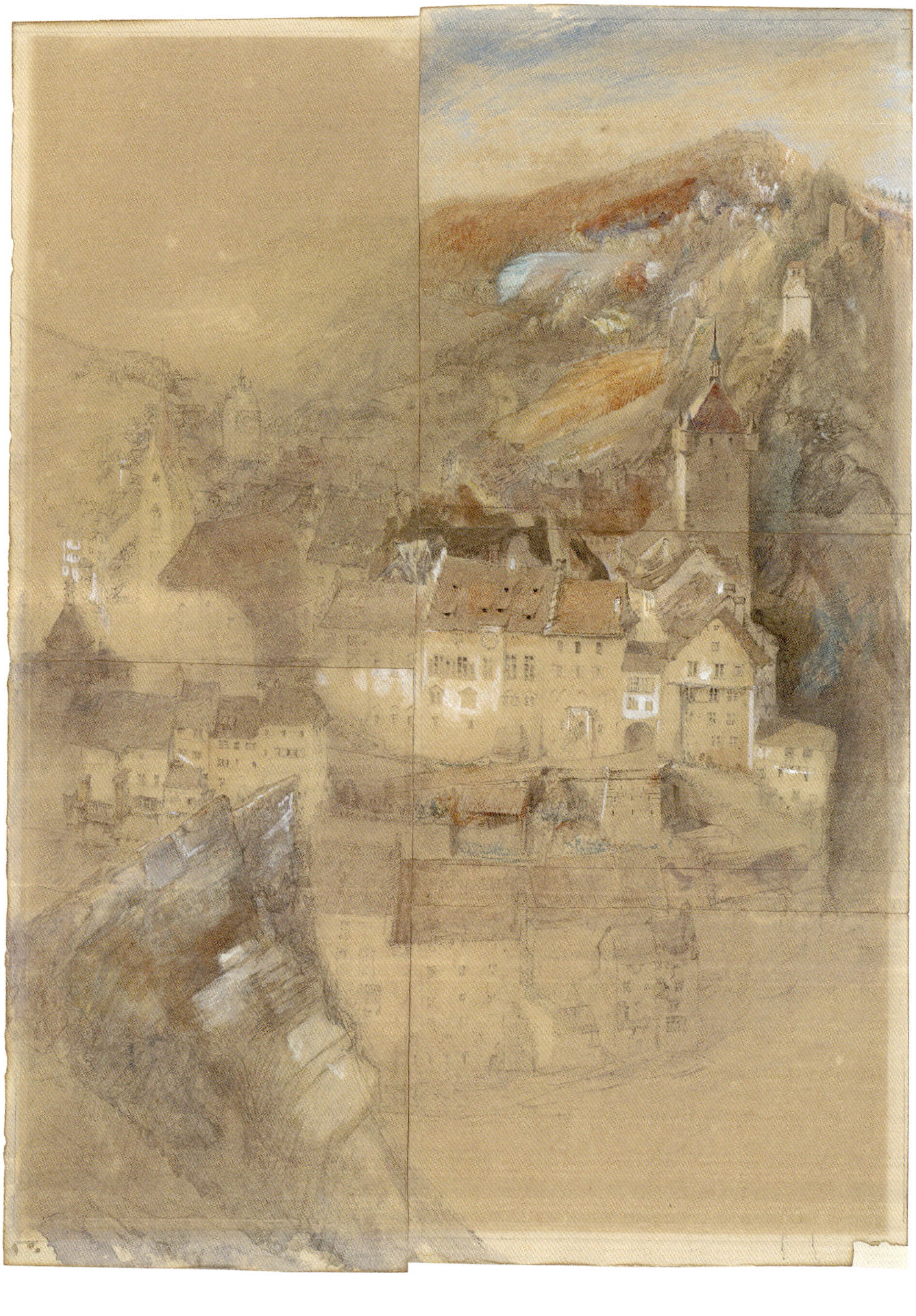

This stupendous view of Baden was made in the course of Ruskin's Alpine tour in 1863, during which he lodged in the Swiss town for about two weeks in the latter part of October. Diary entries from this period are cursory, but glimpses are given of day trips by train to Laufenburg and Brugg, and on foot to neighbouring towns and villages, and of fine autumnal weather interspersed with bitter northerly winds. Frequent references are made to his work on drawings and the difficulty he found in completing them.

As early as 1835 Ruskin had visited Baden with his mother and father and had made an elaborate drawing of the town and its principal buildings (now in the South London Gallery). His return there must therefore have kindled memories of the delight he had once experienced in seeing places that appealed so strongly to his Romantic imagination. Ruskin later invited readers "to compare my boy's drawing of the Swiss Baden ... made when I was sixteen, with the hard effort to get it right, in [the present drawing] – coloured only in a quarter of it before the autumn leaves fell – then given up – cut into four – [and] now pasted together again to show how it was meant to be." This was to be an exercise that might "amuse the reader," but one that "will also make him a little sorrowful for me."[1]

This view of Baden, taken from a vantage-point high on the bank of the Limmat river and looking west, shows, on the left side and only loosely sketched in, the town's principal Catholic parish church, while on the right is the Stadtturm – a defensive tower with distinctive corner turrets that forms the first part of a fortification – which is seen rising up into the distance and following the contour of the hillside above. Once again, Ruskin took a position from which to draw the city that allowed a downward view and in which the tiled and dormered roofs form a complex pattern of multi-faceted surfaces, across which the soft light of an October afternoon casts. In the distance is a rust-coloured woodland and a meadow, the shadowed surface of which in the lea of the trees Ruskin has treated to a vivid touch of blue. In the foreground appears an outcrop of rock, introduced as a repoussoir and to give scale to the composition. He treated virtually the same view on two occasions; a more summary version, on a single sheet, and with the inscription "first try," is in the collection of the Ruskin Foundation at Lancaster University.

The question remains, what was the working process that led to a drawing that extends over five principal sheets, crudely abutted together and with two further slips of paper inserted to make up an irregular rectangle? The explanation must surely be that Ruskin commenced the drawing on a single sheet – probably either that which forms the central right-hand compartment or that at the upper right – and without any clear idea of what its eventual scale and scope might be, but then as his attention wandered more widely across the panorama that lay before him more space was needed that could only be provided by tacking on further sheets. There is a noticeable difference in degree of finish in the left-hand and lower parts of the whole, suggesting that these were the sheets attached at a later stage, and that received less-focused attention.

NOTES

1 Ruskin 1903–12, vol. 13, *Turner, The Harbours of England, Catalogues and Notes*, p. 522.

52

The Walls of Lucerne c. 1866

Graphite, watercolour and bodycolour on blue paper; 34 × 48 cm
Ruskin Foundation (Ruskin Library, Lancaster University) (RF 1376)

Ruskin's editors E.T. Cook and Alexander Wedderburn suggested that the present view of Lucerne was probably done during the week's stay that Ruskin made there in June 1866.[1] If correct, diary references for 18 and 19 June may refer to it, as Ruskin described an early morning exploration of the town and the relief he felt when he "found my great view of Lucerne safe"; and then on the following day, he recorded that he "drew towers in forenoon."[2] The walls, called the Museggmauer, enclose the old town on the north side, commencing at a point close to the Reuss river at one end, rising up over a summit, and terminating at the east near the lakeshore. Nine large towers survive from the once more extensive fortifications, constructed between 1370 and 1442. The present view – which is one of Ruskin's most celebrated works – shows a section of the wall at its eastern end, from a vantage point close to the lake. The tower at the extreme left of the sheet, up to which the line of the wall itself makes a steep ascent, is the Allenwindturm, while the square-shaped tower with a pyramidal roof supported on protruding corners at the centre of the composition is the Dachliturm – in fact the lowest of all the Lucerne towers but most striking as it is seen in abrupt perspective at the top of the steep bank that rises above the town.

The drawing has a dramatic and transitory quality, as a momentary blaze of sunlight falls on the central tower and on a section of the wall to its right. The sky against which the structure is seen is purple, and it is clear that a spectacular Alpine storm is about to break. Urgency and imminence are thus conveyed, with the effect that one looks at the drawing with a sense that what one is seeing will moments later be subsumed in torrential rain and clouded darkness.

Kenneth Clark gave a memorable account of the drawing, finding in it clues to the "bias of taste which led [Ruskin] to look for detail rather than mass":

> Combined with his love of inscape, it meant that he could seldom grasp an object in its totality ... [I]n the beautiful drawing of the walls of Lucerne where his eye, starting soberly enough with the left hand tower, skips down the battlements, pausing at cracks and crannies with a rapturous suggestion of bonfires beyond them, is almost blinded by the light on the central tower, and passes with relief to the little gazebo in half shadow, where for a minute the irregular form of an iron railing is irresistible; is off again in raptures along the sunny wall with its espalier fruit trees, and finally drops rather sadly to the potting shed in the bottom corner.[3]

The drawing exemplifies Ruskin's way of seeing, with areas of close and scrupulous observation, for example in the crenellation of the turret on the left side and with other parts that are abstractly but suggestively marked by mere washes of dilute colour. All is held together and linked by an

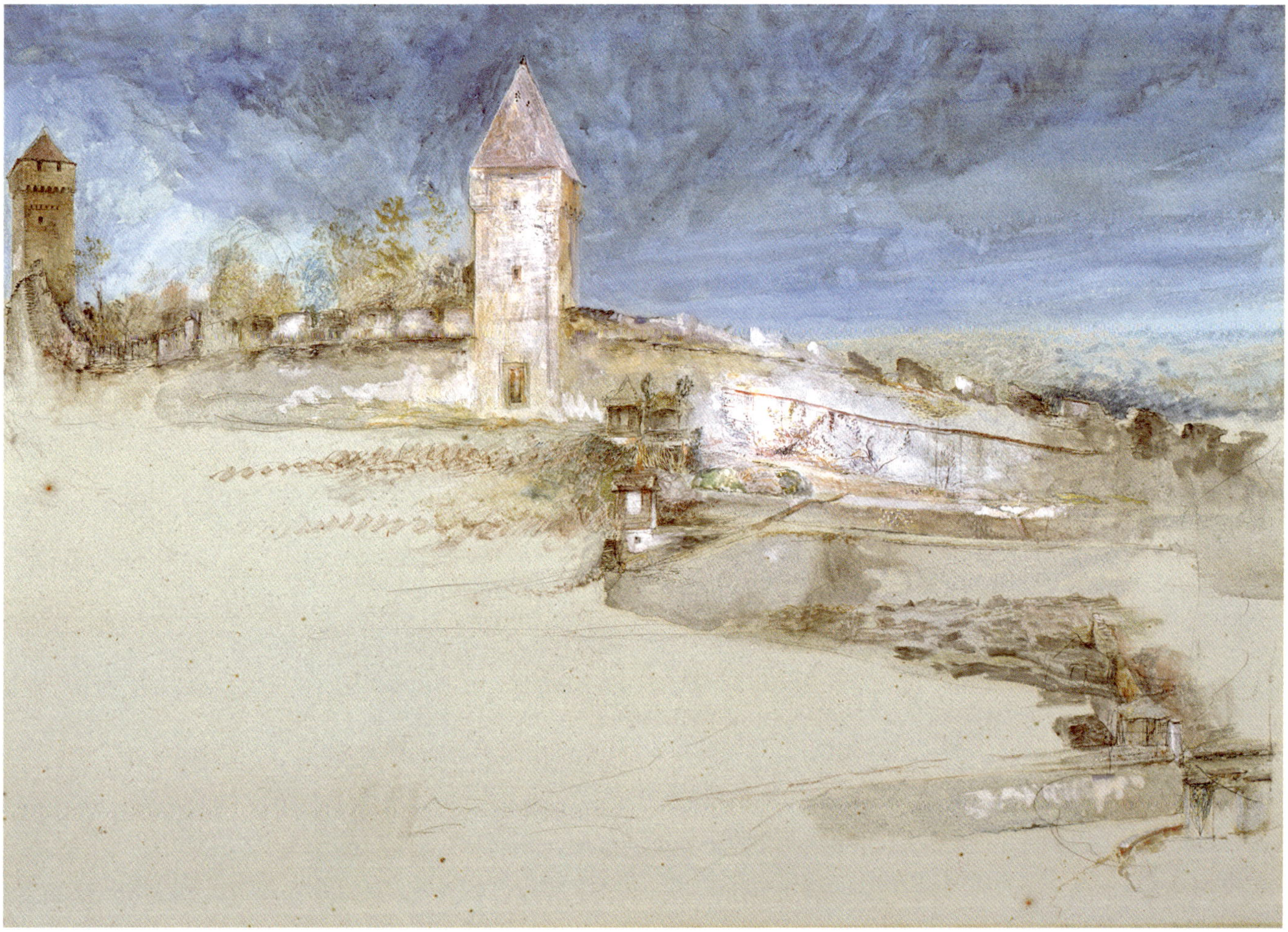

encompassing zigzag pattern that sweeps across the width of the paper. Thus he seems to echo the motion of an excited eye as it searches for structure in the landscape and ranges from side to side across the breadth of a panoramic view. Colubrine patterns emerge, with elements assuming apparent importance and then expiring or withdrawing into obscurity, and other parts commencing as careful replications of forms but gradually translating into mere *vibrato* notations. Here we witness Ruskin transcending his self-appointed duty of record-making to explore and achieve aesthetic delight from line, pattern and colour, and investing his view with an overpowering emotional charge.

NOTES

1 Ruskin 1903–12, vol. 38, *Bibliography, Catalogue of Ruskin's Drawings, Addenda et Corrigenda*, p. 265.
2 Ruskin 1956, vol. 2, p. 591.
3 London 1960, pp. 6–7.

53

St. Wulfran, Abbeville, Seen from the River 1868

Graphite, ink, watercolour and bodycolour on white paper; 34.3 × 50.2 cm
Ruskin Foundation (Ruskin Library, Lancaster University) (RF 1100)

This was the most finished and ambitious of several large drawings of the collegiate church of St. Wulfran that Ruskin made during a stay in Abbeville from 25 August to 21 October 1868. A diary entry for 16 September records his having "finished houses of great cathedral view,"[1] which seems likely to be a reference to the present drawing, showing the church from the east with a glimpse of the river Somme as it flows through the medieval town and a picturesque grouping of steep-roofed and dormered houses, one of which stands on a bridge over the river. The size of these last buildings contrasts dramatically with the soaring outline of the church's north transept, so that they seem almost to have the appearance of models in their charming diminutiveness. In addition to the effect of looming scale that Ruskin gave to the church, he also chose to represent the building at a time of day when there was no direct sunlight upon it, so that all the colours of the stone from which it was made, and the tiles of its roof, are suffused into a soft and muted range of warm greys and mauves.

Even in 1848 Ruskin had lamented the damage that was being done to Abbeville, telling his father that "there is not a street without fatal marks of restoration,"[2] and indeed much destruction had occurred in the revolutionary uprising and its violent suppression earlier that same year. By 1868 further injury had been wrought upon the town and, as Ruskin told his mother, "too many [remnants] are already gone for ever."[3] The following year, in the course of his lecture "The Flamboyant Architecture of the Valley of the Somme," given at the Royal Institution, he thought Abbeville had come to look like London, with "rows of houses, all alike, with an heap of brickbats at the end of it." The only consolation for such wholesale destruction was that "St. Vulfran is still left," but only just, and it was, Ruskin thought, "the last of [its] race."[4]

So appalled was Ruskin by all of this destruction that he contemplated a volume that might serve as a "Stones of Abbeville,"[5] and into which he thought of incorporating the drawings and data that he had collected and that would serve as a memorial to a place that had in effect been sacrificed by neglect and carelessness. The distress that came upon him in Abbeville in 1868, perhaps combined with physical ill health and certainly exacerbated by Rose La Touche's refusal of his marriage proposal earlier in the year, sapped his energy and made him despondent. On occasions, even the act of drawing became a chore, although he drove himself on, and neurotic symptoms may be detected in diary entries, anticipating the mania he suffered in later years, for example on 12 October: "to-day I am better, but very strangely languid. What a terrible thing illness is! Wall papers all turning into faces – consider this sign of weakness."[6]

NOTES

1 Ruskin 1956, vol. 2, p. 655.
2 Ruskin 1903–12, vol. 8, *The Seven Lamps of Architecture*, p. xxix.
3 John Ruskin, quoted in Lancaster 2002, p. 9.
4 Ruskin 1903–12, vol. 19, *The Cestus of Aglaia and The Queen of the Air with Other Papers and Lectures on Art and Literature, 1860–1870*, p. 245.
5 He wrote to his mother on 9 September: "I think I shall be able to write a little Stones of Abbeville when I have done, as I shall know every remnant of interest in the town" (ibid., p. xli).
6 Ruskin 1956, vol. 2, p. 659.

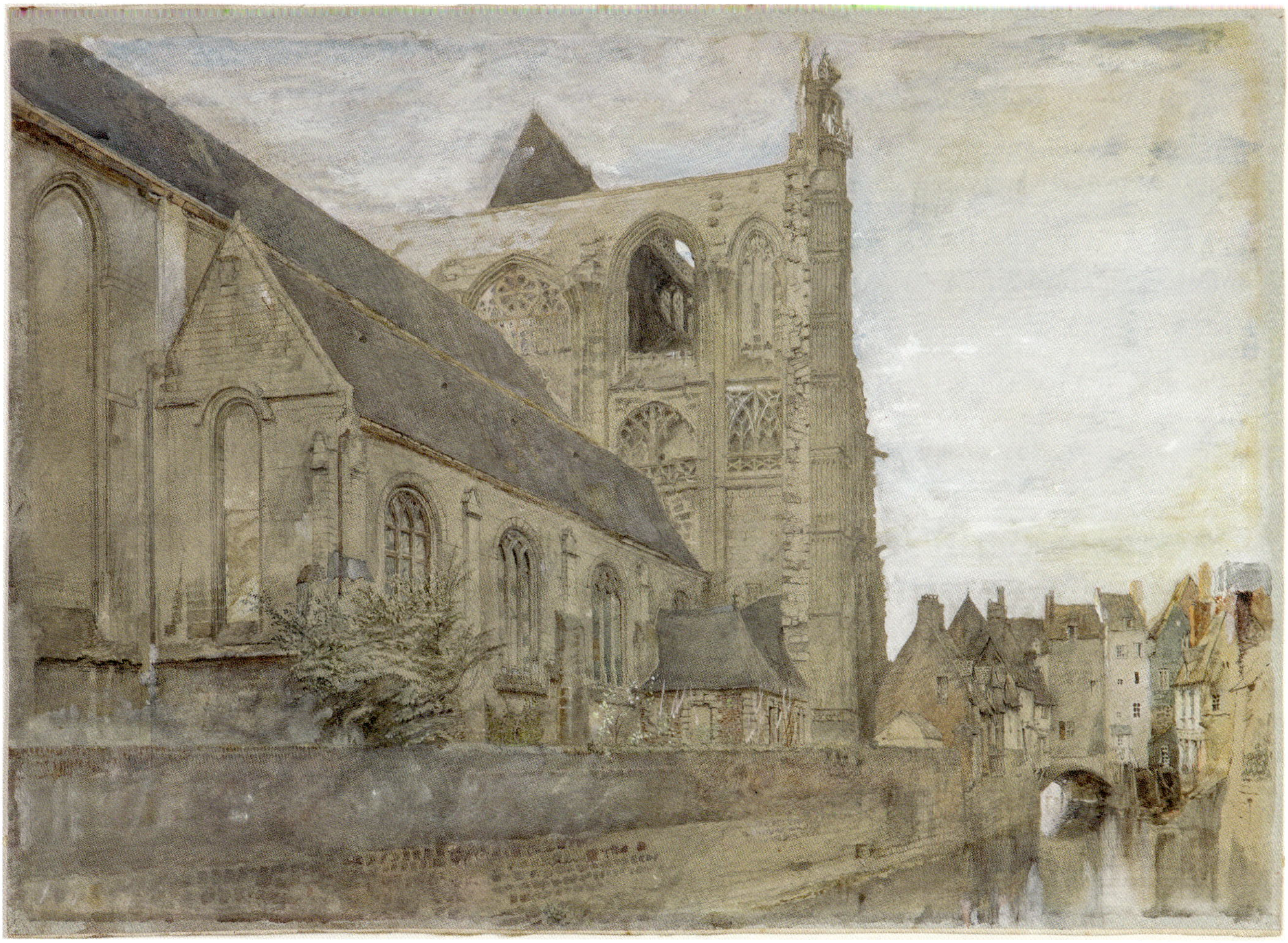

54
Church of St. Wulfran, Abbeville 1868

Graphite on paper; 36.6 × 53 cm
Private collection
Inscriptions: *Abbeville. J Ruskin 1868*

This more distant view of St. Wulfran was taken from the town's ramparts to the northeast, with a middleground of trees growing along the banks of the Somme and a blocked-in area on the right standing for the rows of medieval houses by the marketplace on the north side of the church. It may be the drawing Ruskin referred to in his diary entry for 25 September 1868, when he worked in the "afternoon on distant cathedral from hill," and, as he thought, "successfully."[1]

In a discursive note on a drawing of the church by Samuel Prout, Ruskin explained that "of the central St. Wulfran, never completed, there remain only the colossal nave, the ruined transept walls, and the lordly towers and porches of the west front."[2] The building dates for the most part from the fifteenth century, with that part that was completed built in the style that Ruskin called "Flamboyant," and that he attempted to compare and place within the development of building types in Flanders, Italy and England, in the lecture "The Flamboyant Architecture of the Valley of the Somme," given at the Royal Institution in January 1869. Ruskin characterized this late Gothic style as "black and white sketching against perfect form," by which he meant the deep cutting of calcareous stone to provide dramatic outline and rich and fantastic patterning, even leading to a "final corruption: – that it becomes a design of lace in white on a black ground."[3]

Paul Walton has associated the present drawing with the condemnatory crescendo of the "Flamboyant Architecture" lecture,[4] in which the spiritual truth of the northern Gothic style, which had once "breathed in affectionate faith and childish obedience," was seen to give way to a "strange fear and melancholy," "so that the very threads of the now thin and nervous stone work catch the ague of mixed wantonness and terror, and – weak with unwholesome and ominous fire – flamboyant with a fatal glow – tremble in their ascent as if they were seen through troubled and heated air, over a desert horizon."[5]

Some kind of analogy between the moulded traceries and spandrels, buttresses and pinnacles, and the trees that stand beneath seems to have been in Ruskin's mind, a point that he made explicit in 1872 when he stated that the craft skills that were seen in the buildings of Abbeville "could only have risen in a richly-wooded chalk country, where the sapling trees beside the brooks gave example to the workmen of the most intimate tracery, and the white cliffs above the meadows furnished docile materials to his hand."[6] The present drawing was included in the display of works by Ruskin and others that accompanied his 1869 lecture, and was then described as "showing general effect of towers and ruined wall of transept."[7]

NOTES

1 Ruskin 1956, vol. 2, p. 656.
2 Ruskin 1903–12, vol. 14, *Academy Notes, Notes on Prout and Hunt, and Other Art Criticisms, 1855–1888*, p. 395.
3 Ruskin 1903–12, vol. 19, *The Cestus of Aglaia and The Queen of the Air with Other Papers and Lectures on Art and Literature, 1860–1870*, pp. 251–252.
4 Walton 2000, pp. 142–147.
5 Ruskin 1903–12, vol. 19, pp. 260–261.
6 Ruskin 1903–12, vol. 22, *Lectures on Landscape, Michael Angelo & Tintoret, The Eagle's Nest, Ariadne Florentina, with Notes for Other Oxford Lectures*, p. 188.
7 Ruskin 1903–12, vol. 19, p. 276.

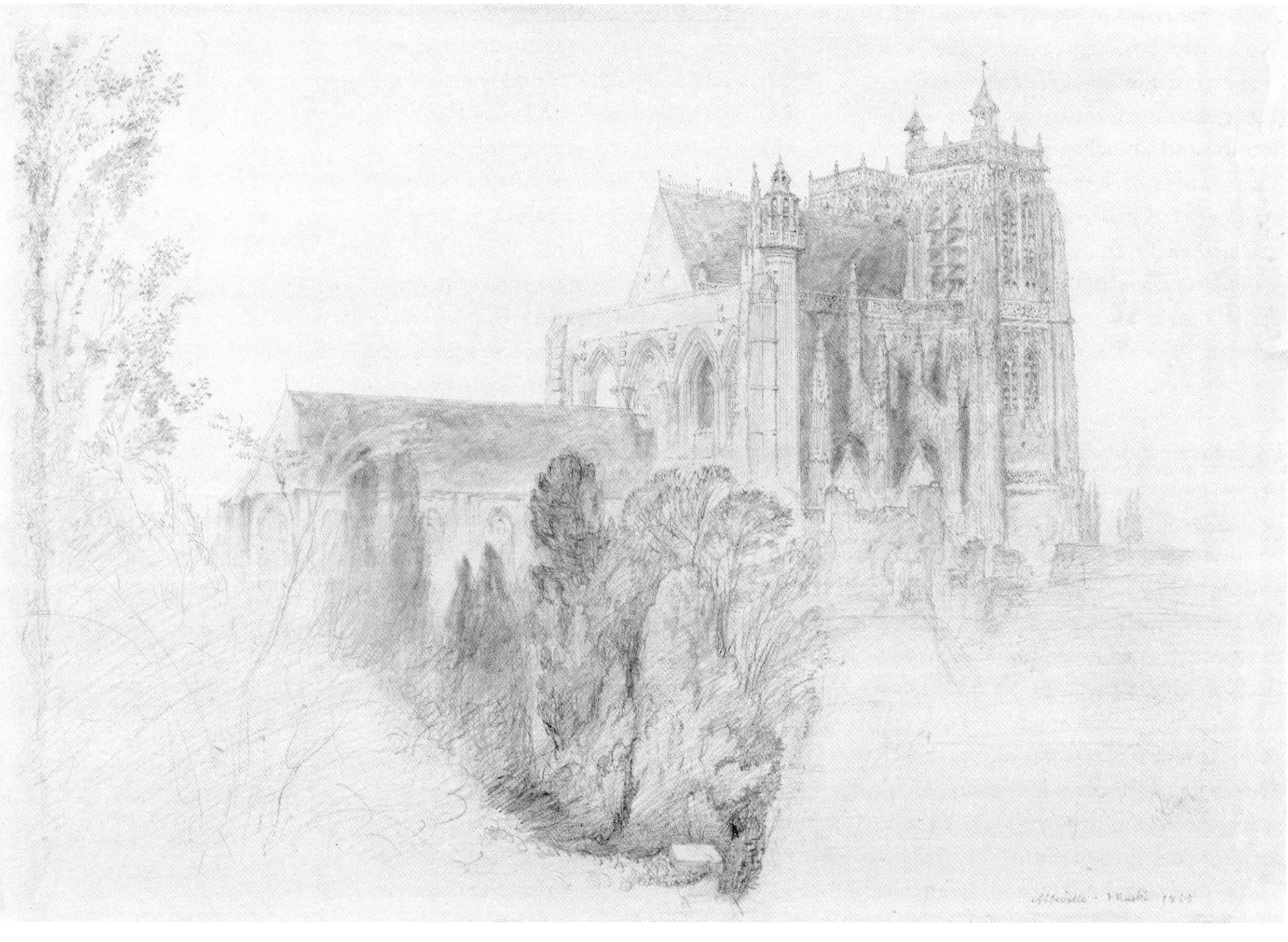

55

Ponte della Pietra, Verona 1869–72

Graphite and brown wash heightened with white bodycolour on brown paper; 17.5 × 25.6 cm
Private collection
Inscriptions: *Ponte della Pietra, Verona / – Sunset Adige in rather a temper! / My best sort of sketching but of course – incomplete – wanting shutting off the light on left / and some river under / the arch*

Ruskin returned to Verona in 1869, the year in which he also revisited Venice after a long period of what seems to have been almost a deliberate avoidance of a place that had once been so important to him. There was some thought of a project on the lines of "The Stones of Verona," but in the event his intensive study of the city led only to a lecture, given the following year at the Royal Institution in London, entitled "Verona and its Rivers." Whether the present drawing of the famous Roman bridge that crosses the Adige river was made in the course of his 1869 stay or on the occasion of various shorter sojourns in Verona that he made in the 1870s is unknown. The view is from the east bank of the river close to the site of the Roman theatre, looking northwest and with the dome and towers of the church of San Giorgio in Braida in the distance, and on the left, the Bishop's Palace and east end of the Duomo. The two bridge arches that Ruskin has shown in the drawing are those that survive from the original structure, dating from the 1st Century BC and with square piers and openings in the spandrels of the arches.

The drawing exemplifies Ruskin's increasingly frenzied and impatient approach to architectural and topographical subjects at times when seized with a sense of urgency and the need to capture the essence of places visited and things seen. He seems to have believed that more truth might be instilled in a sketch of this kind, which conveys a feeling of amazement at the energy of the river and the beauty of shape and extraordinary resilience of the bridge itself, than in a laborious and time-consuming exercise in meticulous observation. Pencil lines course across the width of the composition, capturing the breadth and curvature of the arches and parapet of the bridge, and elsewhere collapsing into feverish eddies and whorls, signifying the foliage and foundation at the river's bank. Smears of white bodycolour have been introduced to indicate the evening sky and its light reflected in the surface of the surging river, but otherwise the devices that have led to a drawing of such power, and yet may have been the work of just half an hour, are minimal. Ruskin's own inscription – "My best sort of sketching" – tells of the satisfaction that such a drawing brought him, at least on occasions.

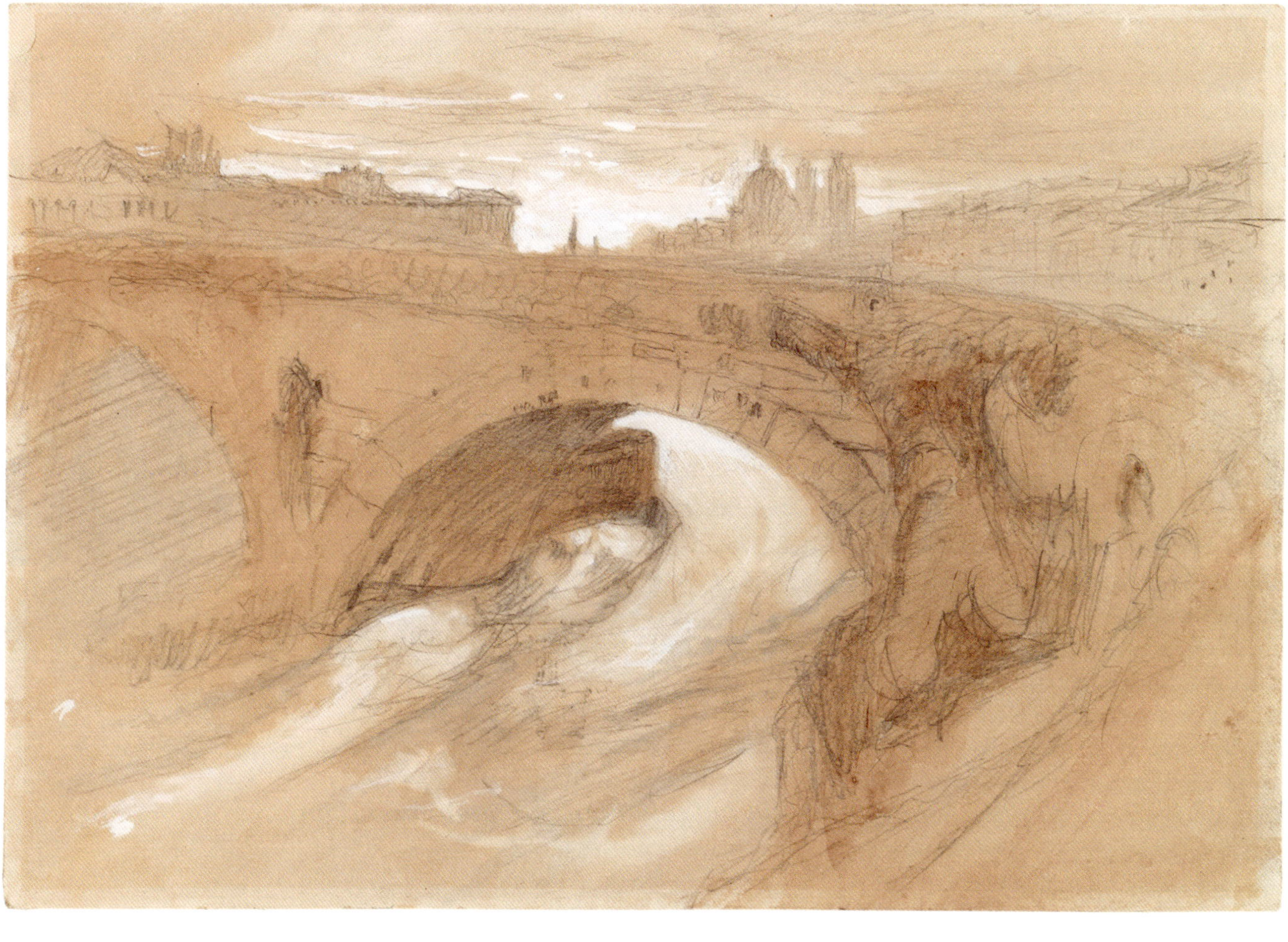

56

Riva degli Schiavoni, the Ducal Palace and the Campanile of St. Mark's 1870

Graphite and watercolour on paper; 24.8 × 37 cm
The Fitzwilliam Museum, University of Cambridge (1154)
Inscriptions: old mount, *Now your little Ducal Palace / is really the best colour study / I made in Venice and I should / by obliged if you would lend it to me for three weeks, / Ever affectionately yours, John Ruskin*

Ruskin returned to Venice in the summer of 1869, seventeen years after his departure from the city in June 1852 on completion of the research for the second and third volumes of *The Stones of Venice*. In this period he seems deliberately to have kept away from a place that had once been so important to him, an avoidance that must in part have been a consequence of his association of the city with the humiliating failure of his marriage to Effie Gray. Ruskin made a further short stay in Venice in May and June 1870, travelling with his cousin Joan Severn and others, during which the present study as well as the first of his broad perspectival views of buildings on the Grand Canal (cat. 57) were made.

Venice – recently liberated from Austrian political control – was once again an ideal to Ruskin and a place of refuge, where he had even thought of going to live. In his teaching at Oxford he placed Venice higher than other Italian cities in terms of artistic achievement – as on the occasion, for example, of his controversial lecture "The Relation between Michael Angelo and Tintoret,"[1] in which the Venetian painter is seen as one who benefited from the honest and democratic conduct of the arts in his native city. The drawing may therefore be seen as an emphatic, if coded, expression of approval of a place that was regaining importance in Ruskin's mind.

A familiar Venetian topography is shown; at the composition's centre appears the Doge's Palace, as Canaletto (an artist whom Ruskin despised) might have represented it. Beyond, on the left side, are the twin columns of St. Mark and St. Theodore, standing in front of the Marciana library. On the right of the Doge's Palace stand the state prisons. There follows the site of a house demolished by order of the state in 1172 because it had belonged to the assassin of Doge Vitale Michiel II, and then beyond that is the nineteenth-century façade of the Hotel Danieli (closest to Ruskin's vantage point, which must have been at the extreme edge of the Riva degli Schiavoni or perhaps in a gondola moored in St. Mark's Basin). Behind all of this rises St. Mark's Campanile. On this occasion, Ruskin made no judgment on architectural quality, but simply represented the line of buildings in receding perspective.

NOTES

1 Given in Oxford in June 1871. Ruskin 1903–12, vol. 22, *Lectures on Landscape, Michael Angelo & Tintoret, The Eagle's Nest, Ariadne Florentina, with Notes for Other Oxford Lectures.*

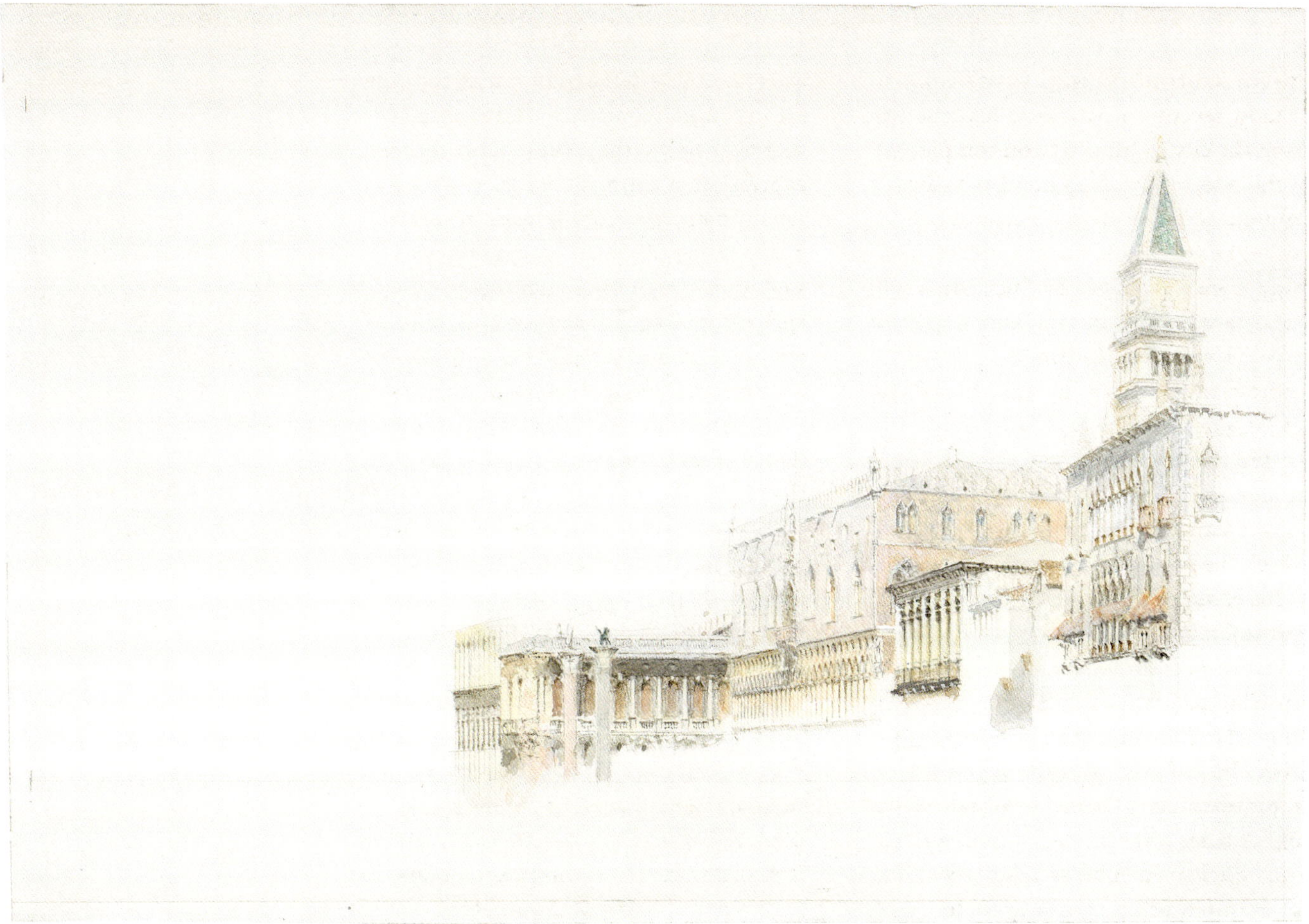

57

View from the Palazzo Bembo to the Palazzo Grimani, Venice 1870

Graphite and watercolour on paper; 35.3 × 50.8 cm
The Ashmolean Museum, Oxford. Presented by John Ruskin to the Ruskin Drawing School (University of Oxford), 1875 (WA.RS.REF.066)

This is one of the pencil views of ranges of buildings on the Grand Canal that Ruskin occasionally made in the course of his later visits to Venice. Drawn from a moored gondola close to what is now the Rialto vaporetto stop and looking toward the southwest, down the central reach of the canal, the drawing shows the Palazzo Bembo – a late Gothic reconstruction of a Byzantine structure – on the immediate left; in front runs the Riva del Carbon, against which barges are moored and onto which faces the Palazzo Loredan and the Ca' Farsetti; further down, and with a façade the height of which stands above its neighbours, is the Renaissance Palazzo Grimani, built to the design of Michele Sanmicheli.

Although this type of drawing may be seen to have originated in the Venice palace views that Ruskin had made in 1841 in imitation of the work of Samuel Prout, by the 1870s he increasingly employed a calligraphic shorthand that led to a degree of generalization, particularly in the more distant parts of the composition. In this, Ruskin was in tune with a broader evolution of taste. Artists such as John William Inchbold, who worked in Venice in the early 1860s, had pioneered a way of representing cities and their wider settings as entire topographies with all their architectural elements melded into an organic whole, and gradually Ruskin's own response to the depiction of Venice became more concerned with ambience and atmosphere than the itemization of particular buildings. In the course of the 1870s, his method of painting in watercolour and draftsmanship in pencil and chalk adapted extraordinarily to the evocation of places by qualities of texture and colour – and, incidentally, in a method akin to the impressionism of James Whistler (who himself made a series of drawings and prints of Venice after the debacle of the court case that he brought against Ruskin in 1878).

The date given to the drawing here is that proposed in the catalogue of the Drawings Collection at Oxford, to which Ruskin presented the work in 1875. The work has had various alternative titles: in the Reference Series catalogue it was called *Casa Manin and Casa Grimani, Venice* (which is odd, because the Casa Manin is out of view on the left of the actual composition).[1] When exhibited as part of the Ruskin Collection at Oxford in 1878 the drawing was described as a "*View of the Upper Reach of the Grand Canal, Venice, looking north* [again a confusion] *and, – (given up in despair)*."[2]

NOTES

1 Ruskin 1903–12, vol. 21, *The Ruskin Art Collection at Oxford: Catalogues, Notes, and Instructions*, p. 31.
2 Ruskin 1903–12, vol. 13, *Turner, The Harbours of England, Catalogues and Notes*, p. 500.

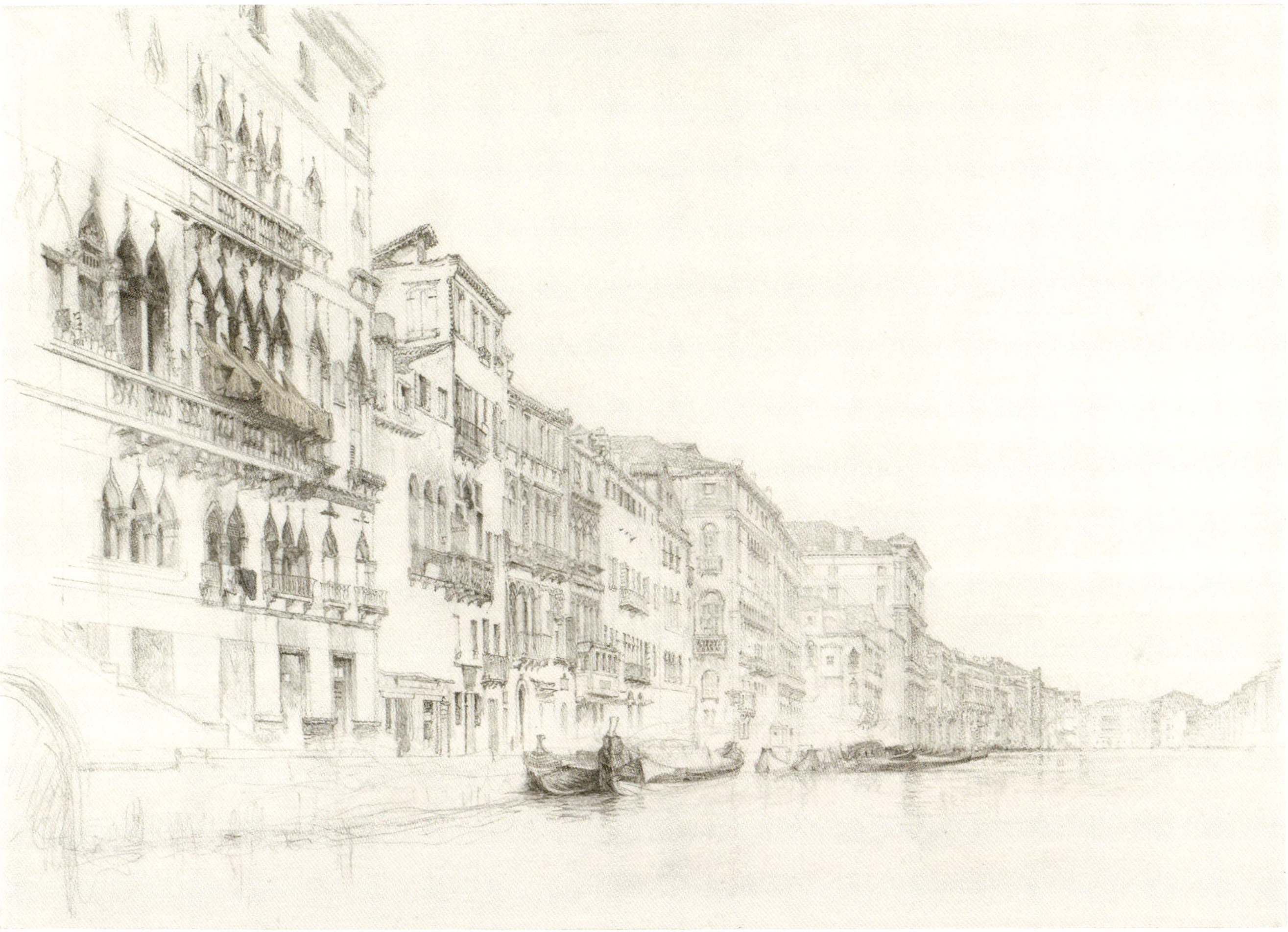

58

Vineyard Walk, Lucca 1874

Graphite, watercolour and bodycolour on white paper; 35.6 × 48 cm
Ruskin Foundation (Ruskin Library, Lancaster University) (RF 1369)

This extraordinary and powerful drawing has a dynamic quality instilled by the sense of claustrophobic enclosure between a stone wall and a bank, and evokes the walker's longing for the crest of the path and the view of open countryside and sunlit air that will be achieved. Ruskin drew it while staying in Lucca in August or September 1874,[1] finding the precise spot at a hamlet called Pozzuolo, which lies a short distance to the southwest of the town.[2] He was in a disturbed state of mind and had left England in March to attempt to distract himself from anxieties about the deteriorating health of Rose La Touche (she had been admitted to a nursing home and was to die on 26 May the following year).

E.T. Cook and Alexander Wedderburn gave the work the title *"A Vineyard Walk: lower stone-work of tower, 12th cent"*, and it was exhibited as such at the Royal Watercolour Society in 1901, the year after Ruskin's death.

NOTES

1 He interrupted his stay in Lucca by visiting Florence on 19 August, but returned to Lucca on 22 September. There is no specific reference in his diary to his having worked on the present drawing, but two entries seem to describe the location: the first, on 18 August, when he writes of walking "up to village with old masonry in tower, beyond the marble ravine" (Ruskin 1956, vol. 3, p. 805); the second, on 24 September: "Up to country church, and drew well; then to highest top of hill, but tired" (ibid., p. 812).

2 The twelfth-century campanile at the centre and the church of which only the upper part of the façade is visible were identified by Jeanne Clegg and Paul Tucker in London Sheffield Lucca 1993, pp. 98–99.

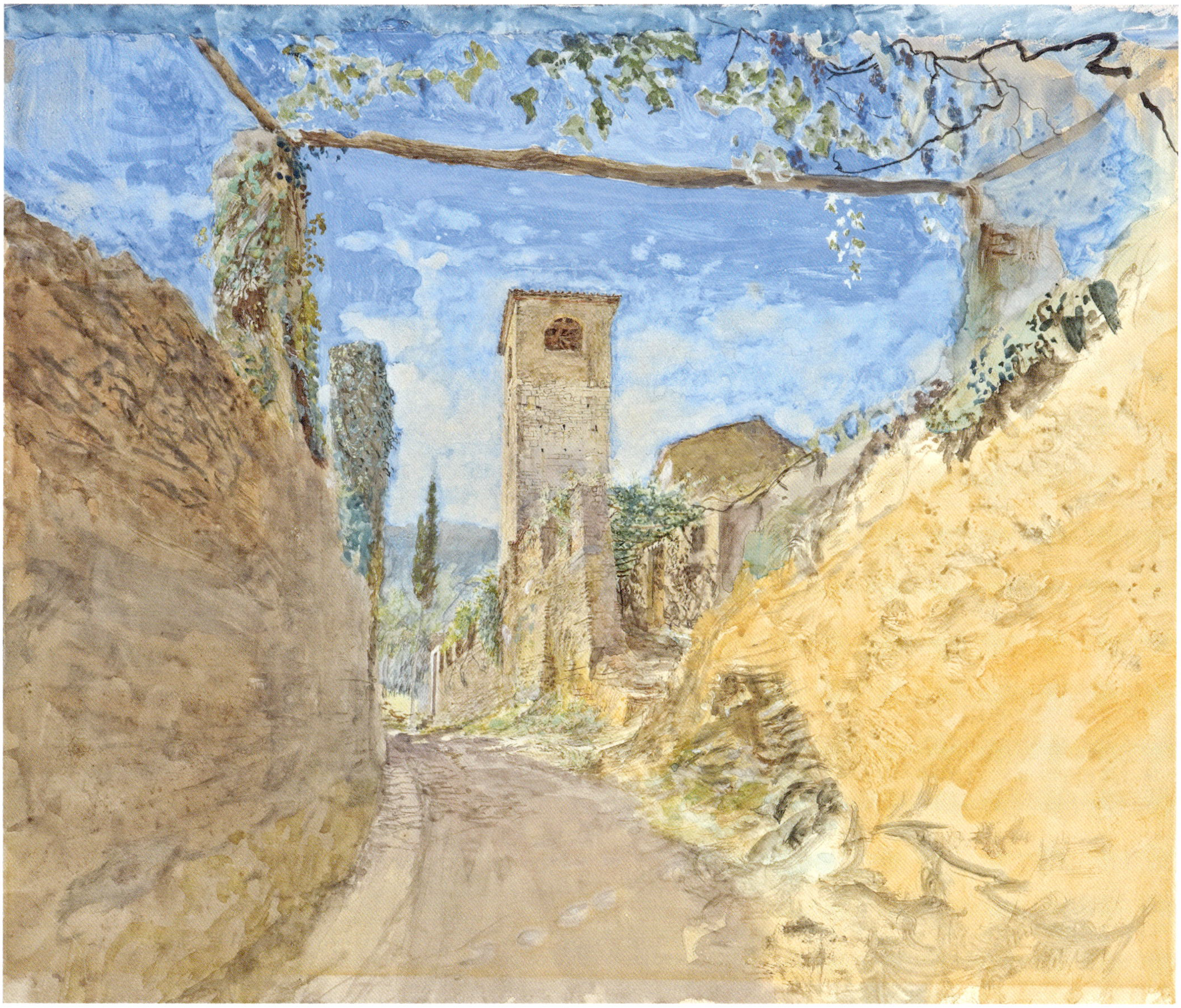

59

a. *Rialto Bridge, Venice* 1876

Graphite on toned paper; 13.7 × 7.7 cm
Ruskin Foundation (Ruskin Library, Lancaster University) (RF 1052)
Inscriptions: brown ink, *Rialto / J. Ruskin Dec. 1876*

b. *San Niccolo de Tolentini, Venice* 1876

Graphite on toned paper; 7.7 × 13.7 cm
Ruskin Foundation (Ruskin Library, Lancaster University) (RF 1061)
Inscriptions: graphite, *S.N. de' Tolentini 31 Dec 76*, brown ink, *J. Ruskin*

c. *Rialto Bridge, Venice* 1877

Graphite on toned paper; 7.7 × 13.7 cm
Ruskin Foundation (Ruskin Library, Lancaster University) (RF 1053)
Inscriptions: brown ink, *Rialto / January 77 / J Ruskin*

d. *Cannaregio, Venice* 1877

Graphite on toned paper; 7.7 × 13.7 cm
Ruskin Foundation (Ruskin Library, Lancaster University) (RF 1029)
Inscriptions: brown ink, *Cannareggio* [sic], *Venice / January. 77. J Ruskin*

e. *Canal, Venice* 1877

Graphite on toned paper; 7.7 × 13.7 cm
Ruskin Foundation (Ruskin Library, Lancaster University) (RF 1030)
Inscriptions: brown ink, *Venice Feb. 77 / J Ruskin*

Ruskin was in Venice from early September 1876 until 23 May the following year. He stayed at the Grand Hotel until mid-February 1877, when he transferred to rooms on the Zattere. His ostensible purpose in being in the city for such an extended period, and the excuse given to the university authorities in Oxford for his long absence, was to produce a new edition of *The Stones of Venice*, which was to "have all the 'eloquent' bits in the second and third volume served up like pickled walnuts, in sauce of a very different flavour – [or] perhaps brandy cherries would be a better symbol of what I hope the book will be."[1]

In a letter to Charles Eliot Norton of 5 October 1876, he described his routine: rising at six; punctually at his writing table by seven; reading the *Laws* of Plato for half an hour, and then off by gondola "to the bridge before St. John and Paul, where I give an hour of my very best day's work to painting the school of Mark and vista of Canal to Murano." The day was then occupied with sessions of work on *Stones* and on his copy of the *Dream of Saint Ursula* (cat. 132); dinner at three,

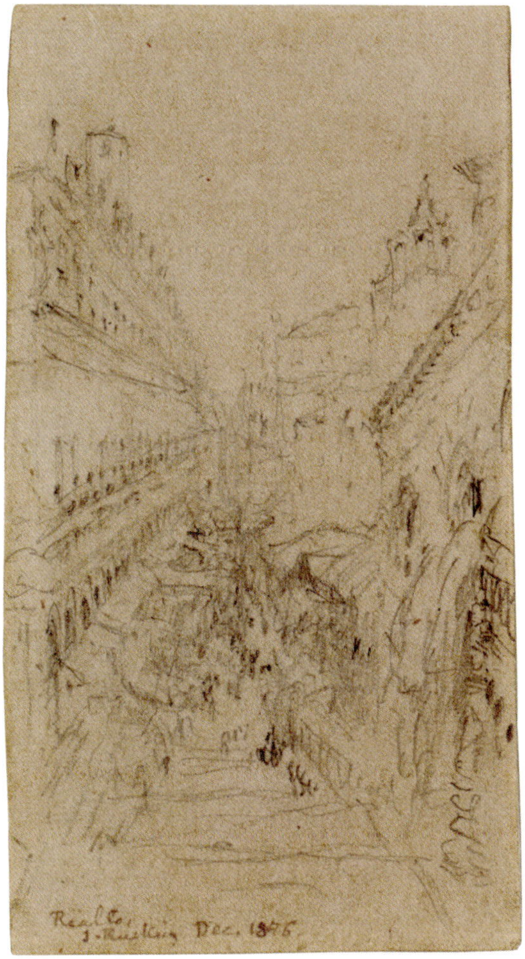
J. Ruskin Dec. 1876

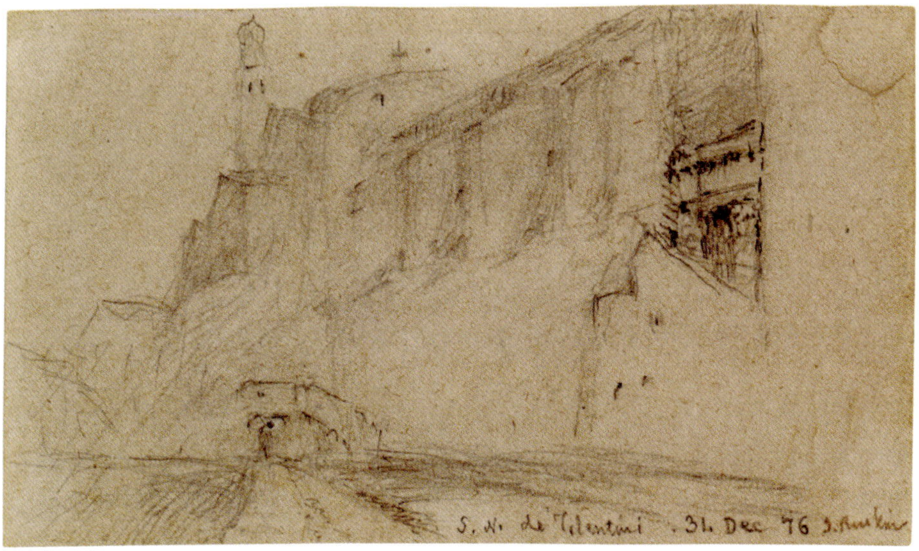
31 Dec 76 J. Ruskin

and after that, a period of relaxation when he would "lie on sofa and read any vicious book I can find to amuse me – to prevent St. Ursula having it all her own way. Am greatly amused with the life of Casanova at present." Then more floating through the back canals of Venice, or across the lagoon to Murano or further afield, and more sketching. Letters and reading occupied the evenings, "and to bed at ten."[2] Ruskin was in a fragile frame of mind, beset by thoughts of Rose La Touche, and was finding it difficult to decide to what task to apply himself.

Two books did materialize from this Venetian sojourn: *Guide to the Principal Pictures in the Academy of Fine Arts at Venice* (1877) and *St. Mark's Rest* (1877–84). The intended secondary title for the latter was to be *The History of Venice, Written for the Guidance of English Travellers While they Visit her Ruins*, but this was substituted with *The History of Venice, Written for the Help of the Few Travellers Who Still Care for her Monuments*. He had come to despise what he saw as the commercialization of Venice as a tourist destination and the unconcern that he perceived on the part of the mass of visitors for the obscure and hidden parts of the city. Anticipating twenty-first century proposals for controlling the flood of people wanting to see the place, he believed that a fee should be charged "for leave to come to Venice,"[3] as he wrote in his guide to the paintings of the Accademia, so that only those who really cared about the city would trouble to go there. In *St. Mark's Rest* he offered a litany of recommendations as to where precisely the visitor should stand to appreciate buildings and street vistas that might otherwise be missed, and what to see in the obscure calli and back canals.

Ruskin made a large number of pencil sketches of Venice's streets and canals in the course of his stay, ranging from summary notations to very careful studies. Using soft pencil or chalk, he captured the dark and ominous character of the city, which matched his own mood of mounting despair as the winter wore on, while on other occasions colour – inspired by the sunrises and sunsets that he observed each day almost as a self-appointed act of sacrament – burst across the sheet. Some sense of the loneliness and isolation that he endured – in a place that he loved but that also was the setting of his most intense unhappiness – can be read in the frenzied and seething surfaces of such studies.

NOTES

1 Ruskin 1903–12, vol. 37, *The Letters of John Ruskin, 1870–1889*, p. 208.
2 Ibid., pp. 210–211.
3 Ruskin 1903–12, vol. 24, *Giotto and his Works in Padua, The Cavalli Monuments, Verona, Guide to the Academy, Venice, St. Mark's Rest*, p. 150.

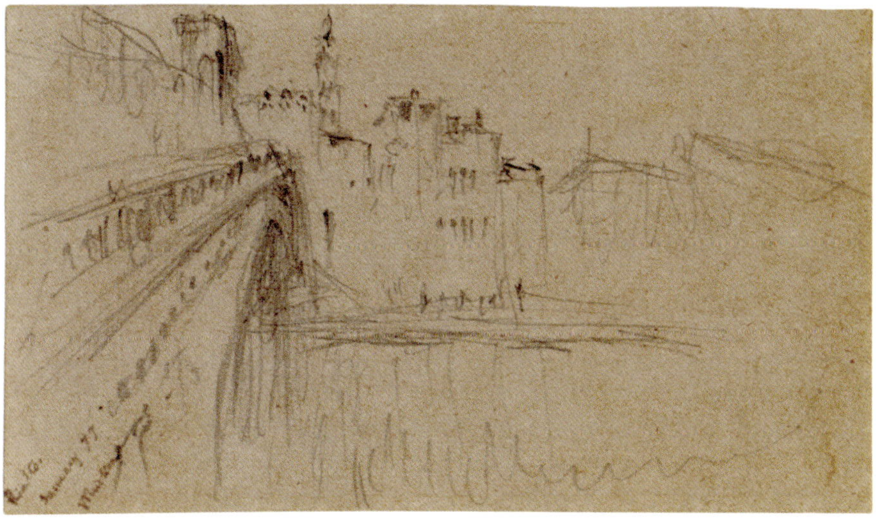

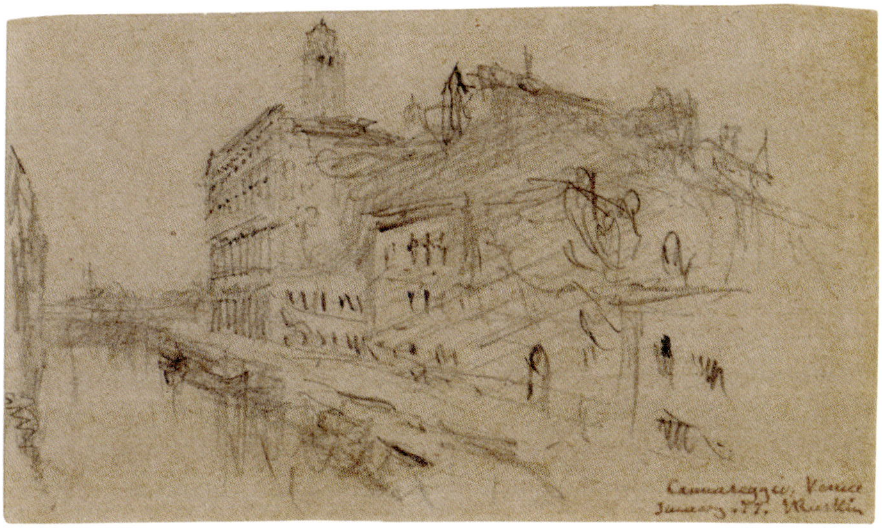

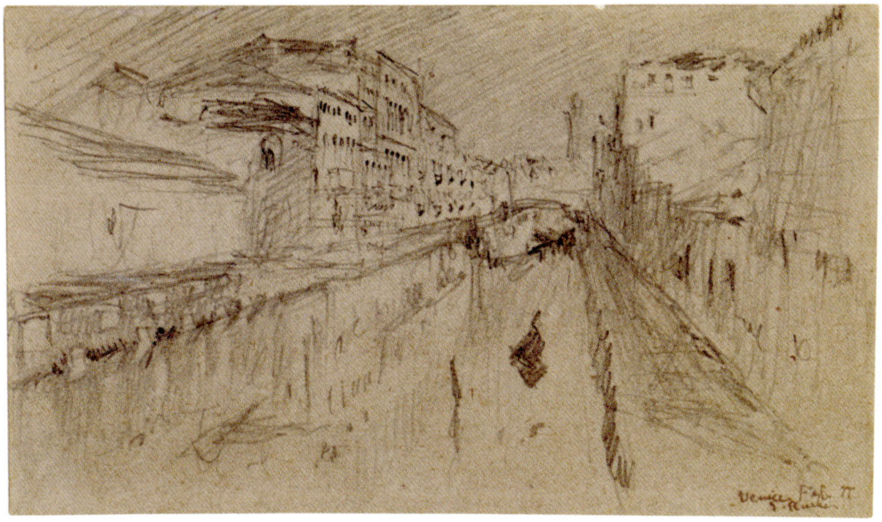

60

The Grand Canal, from the Ca' Tron to the Ca' d'Oro 1876

Graphite on white paper; 33.2 × 40.5 cm
Private collection
Inscriptions: ink, *Left off tired. Venice 1876 / J Ruskin*

This tentative outline, drawn with tremulous strokes of a soft pencil, suggests Ruskin's equivocation as to whether Venice should be drawn as an entity or in terms of its individual parts. The artist's sense of the importance of each and every architectural element had lessened, with instead a new feeling overtaking him of the value of the city itself as a refuge from the antagonism that he had experienced in Oxford and as a place where he might collect his thoughts and dwell upon the past.

The view is taken on the upper reach of the Grand Canal from a vantage point close to the Fondaco dei Turchi, with the sixteenth-century Ca' Tron on the immediate right and the late Gothic Palazzo Duodo, with its curious pedimented upper floor, beyond on the Santa Croce side of the canal. In the distance, on the canal's Cannaregio side, are the façades of the Ca' d'Oro (almost entirely reconstructed since Ruskin had drawn it in detail in 1845) and neighbouring palaces.

Ruskin's inscription gives some indication of the mental and physical energy that went into these meticulous accounts of the city, as well as his fluctuating level of energy and commitment (and, as he said in a letter to Joan Severn, architectural drawings of this kind "take such a time to do well, and the houses have got *so* many windows in them!").[1]

NOTES

1 Ruskin 1903–12, vol. 24, *Giotto and his Works in Padua, The Cavalli Monuments, Verona, Guide to the Academy, Venice, St. Mark's Rest*, p. xxxvii.

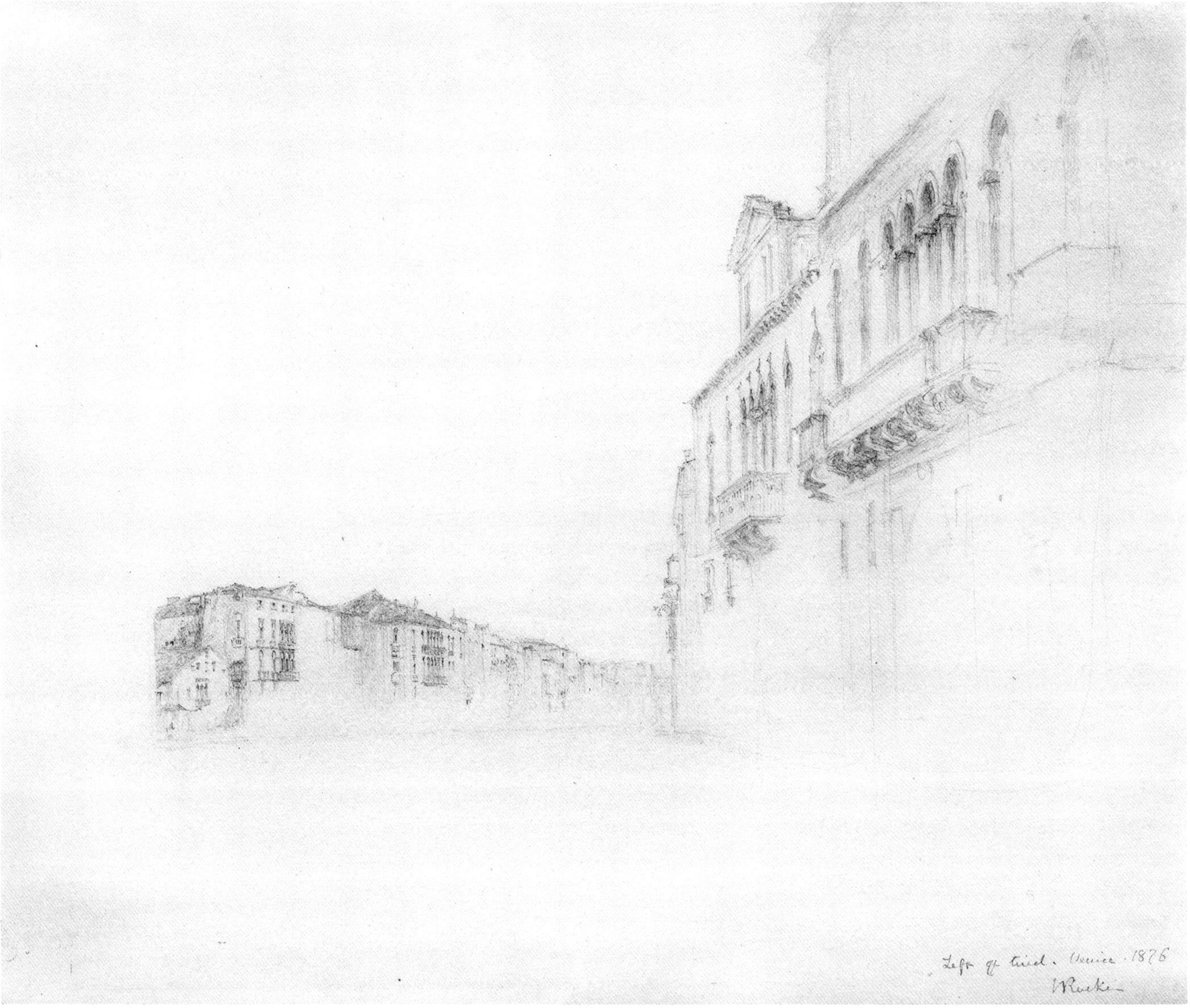
Venice · 1876

61

The Grand Canal, from the Palazzo Bernardo to the Palazzo Dolfin-Manin 1876

Graphite heightened with white and black bodycolour on paper; 36.5 × 53 cm
Private collection

Despite all the sadness and sense of loss that Ruskin felt in Venice in 1876–77, in moments of more positive mood he thought about how the years that remained to him should be put to useful purpose. Writing to Charles Eliot Norton, he confided how strange it was "to feel all my life become a thing of the past, and to be now merely like a wrecked sailor, picking up pieces of his ship on the beach [for] this is the real state of things with me, of course, in a double sense – People gone – and things. My Father and Mother, and Rosie,[1] and Venice, and Rouen – all gone; but I can gather bits up of the places for other people."[2]

On his arrival in the city, he embarked on the present view of the Grand Canal, numbering the sessions spent on it in his diary over five successive days from 9 to 13 September.[3] To get the view, Ruskin's gondola must have been moored at the entrance of the Rio di San Polo to the Grand Canal, thus offering an eastward vista along the length of the canal's central reach. Immediately on the left is the late Gothic façade of the Palazzo Bernardo. Beyond, further along the San Polo side, is the Palazzo Papadopoli, marked by twin obelisks standing on its parapet. The principal building on the far side of the canal is the Palazzo Grimani, with the Corner Contarini dei Cavalli, Ca' Tron and Martinengo palaces on its right, and the Ca' Loredan and Ca' Farsetti on its left. In the far distance, just before the canal turns left, and with the Rialto bridge just out of sight, is the Palazzo Dolfin-Manin. The baroque campanile of San Bartolomeo stands beyond.

The Renaissance Palazzo Grimani, built to the design of Michele Sanmicheli between 1556 and 1575 and towering as it does above its neighbours, had received a perhaps surprising plaudit in the third volume of *The Stones of Venice* as "at once simple, delicate, and sublime,"[4] and the noblest of all buildings in Venice after the final additions to the Doge's Palace. Ruskin may have felt comfortable with a building that had been the subject of a painting by Turner that had belonged to his father.[5]

This was a style of drawing that Ruskin had previously explored in his *View from the Palazzo Bembo to the Palazzo Grimani, Venice* (cat. 57) of 1870 (the two drawings show the same central reach of the Grand Canal, but seen from opposite directions). Although the present drawing was referred to as a "sketch" in diary notes, it shows extraordinary draftsmanship. He described the fourth session of work on the drawing as "a fatiguing day, the Ca' Grimani too hard to do in the size of a visiting card, and sense of failing eyes always oppressing me."[6] The most complete of all Ruskin's late Venice drawings, and perhaps intended for publication in the projected revision of *Stones*, it was in the event used as a frontispiece in the Library Edition.[7]

NOTES

1 Ruskin's father and mother died in 1864 and 1871 respectively; Rose La Touche died in 1875.
2 Ruskin 1903–12, vol. 37, *The Letters of John Ruskin, 1870–1889*, p. 183.
3 Ruskin 1956, vol. 3, pp. 906–907.
4 Ruskin 1903–12, vol. 11, *The Stones of Venice III and Examples of the Architecture of Venice*, p. 43.
5 As pointed out in Walton 2000, pp. 164–166. The painting, entitled *The Grand Canal, Venice*, is now in The Huntington Library, Art Collections and Botanical Gardens, San Marino, California.
6 Ruskin 1956, vol. 3, pp. 906–907.
7 Ruskin 1903–12, vol. 9, *The Stones of Venice I.*

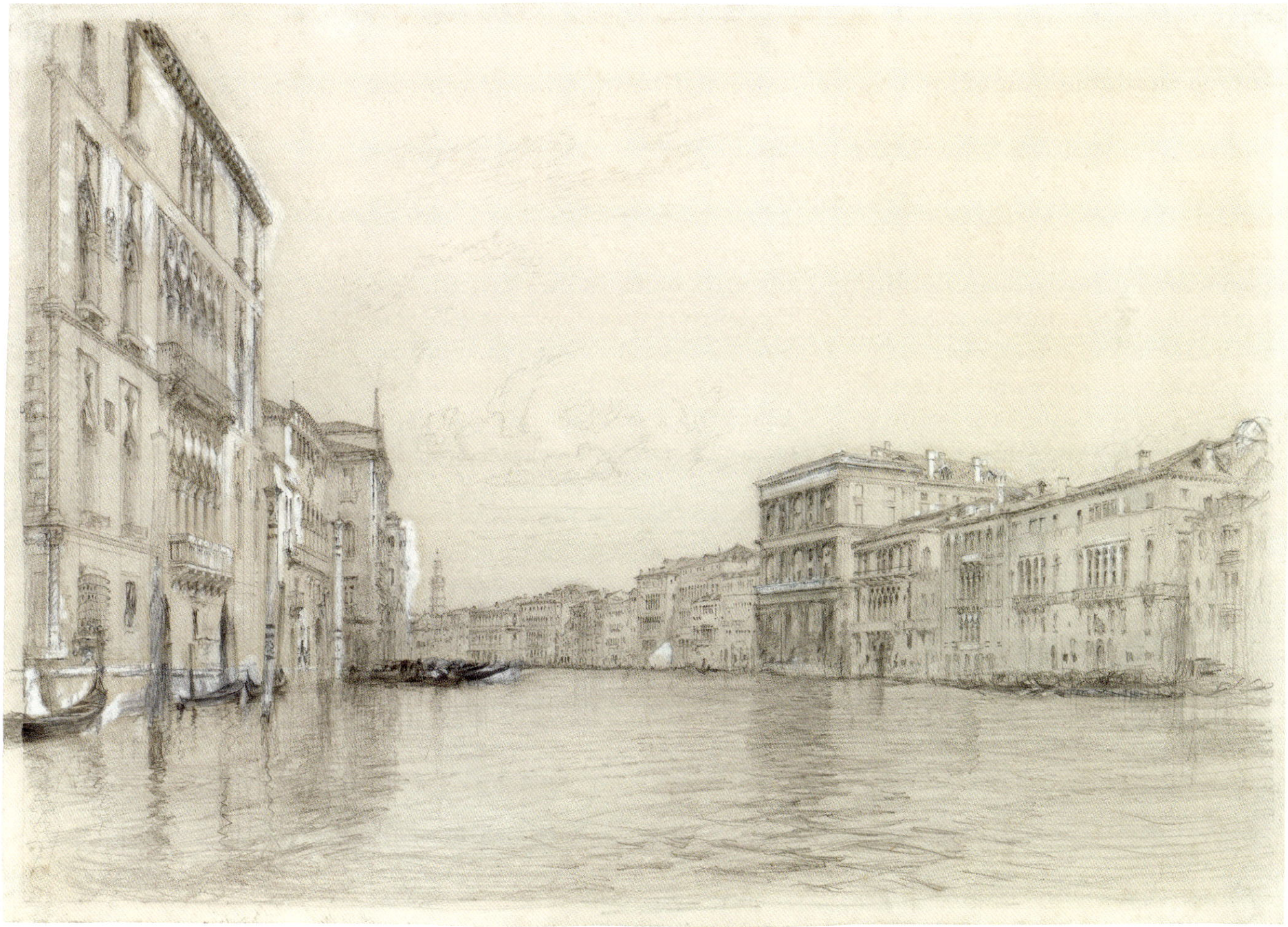

62

View on the Upper Reach of the Grand Canal, Venice 1876–77

Graphite, wash and bodycolour on white paper; 36.2 × 52.1 cm
Ruskin Foundation (Ruskin Library, Lancaster University) (RF 1612)

In his panoramic pencil views of the buildings of the Grand Canal, Ruskin employed varying degrees of strength of line and hardness of point to achieve depths of shadow and three dimensionality of architectural form. His vantage point in making this drawing was somewhere close to the entrance of the Rio dei Santi Apostoli above the Rialto bridge on the Cannaregio side. His view was toward the northwest, with the Grand Canal turning to the left in the distance and the imposing façades of the Ca' Pesaro (the construction of which was begun by Baldassare Longhena in 1628) and the mid-eighteenth century Ca' Corner della Regina, the two principal buildings on the canal's far side (the Ca' Pesaro is on the right and separated from the Ca' Corner by two lesser eighteenth-century palaces). On the right side, but seen in such oblique perspective so as to make it unrecognizable, is the Ca' d'Oro. That Ruskin was here interested in the first place in the overall ambience of the city rather than any didactic representation of architectural elements is demonstrated by the fact that the most conspicuous parts of the composition – although beautifully blended into the atmospheric whole – are from a period and of an architectural type that he had previously despised.

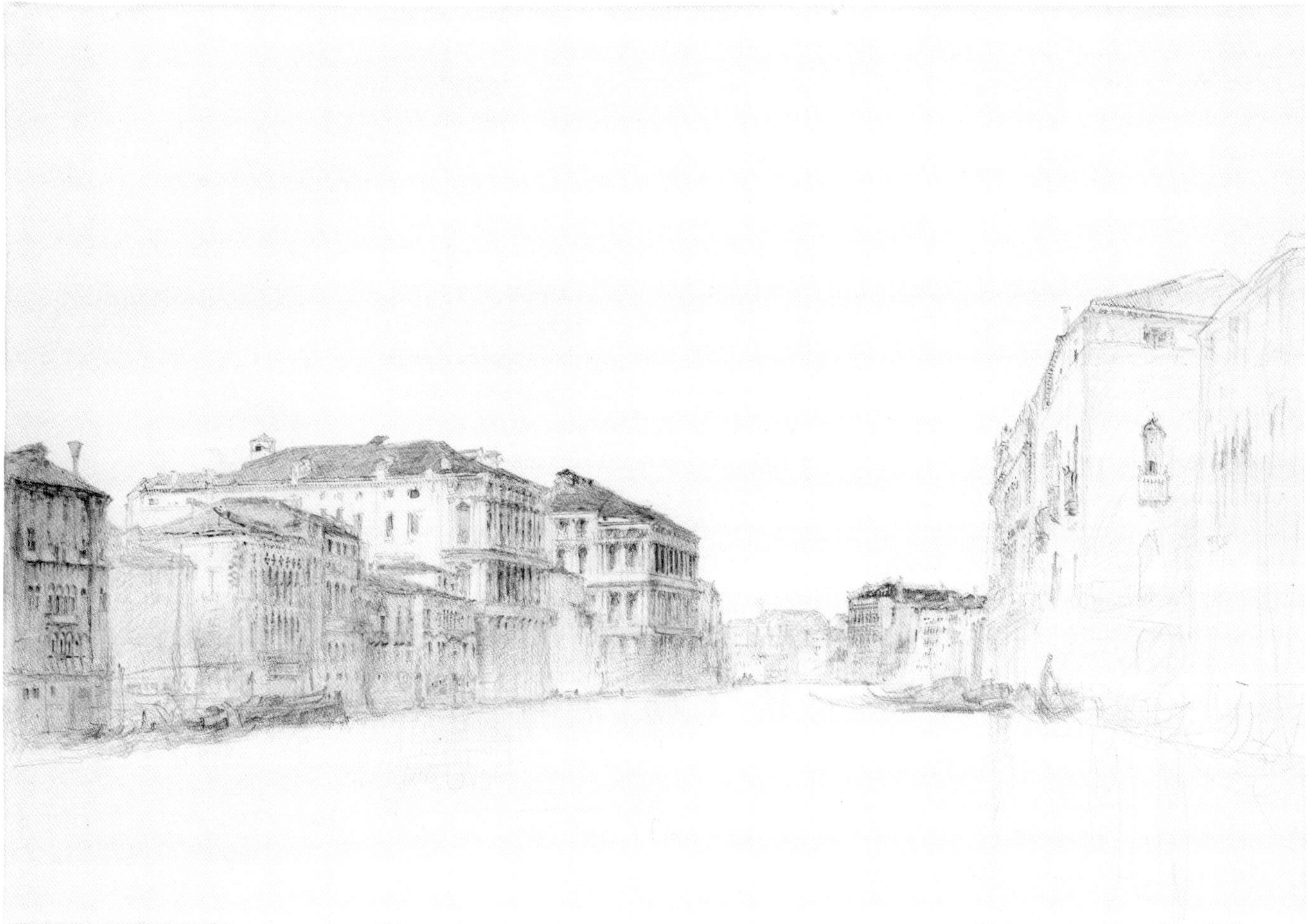

63

Casa Falier, Venice 1877

Graphite on paper; 14 × 8 cm
Private collection
Inscriptions: *Ca' Falier / 1st Jan 77 / JRuskin*

The present view, made by Ruskin on New Year's Day 1877, was taken from the Ponte dei Santi Apostoli, looking eastward along the Rio dei Santi Apostoli. The thirteenth-century Veneto-Byzantine Palazzo Falier is immediately on the right with a passageway running along the canal's edge and interconnecting with the neighbouring building. Doge Marin Falier, executed on 16 April 1355 and condemned to *damnatio memoriae* for attempting to establish his family as dynastic rulers of Venice, lived in this house. In *Præterita*, Ruskin recalled that it was his early reading of Lord Byron's poetic drama *Marino Faliero* (1821) that had prompted him when in Venice as a boy to find the "ruined homes of Foscari and Falier."[1] In his description of the typology of the window arches of Gothic palaces in the second volume of *The Stones of Venice*, following an account of the difficulty of finding the Palazzo Falier, he identified the windows of the *piano nobile* as being of the second order[2] – a hybrid of a Byzantine semicircular arch on stilts inspired by Arab architecture.

Drawn in quite a different manner to the Grand Canal views of the same winter, and representing the type that Ruskin called his "diary sketches," the forms of the buildings are shown in patterns of dark and fleshy chalk, the volume of which scours and indents the sheet. Motifs such as the palace balconies and a group of moored gondolas are achieved by a frenzied scribble of jagged strokes. In other areas – for example the surface of the canal below or the stucco palace walls – a gauze-like effect is given by rapid brushing of the chalk's soft edge. As compared to the serene but emotionally detached perspective views on the Grand Canal (cats. 60, 61 and 62), Ruskin's draftsmanship here speaks of frustration and impatience. The sense of purpose that he had felt at the time of his arrival in Venice in September of the previous year had diminished in the course of the autumn and winter, with ever more ominous indications of his mental instability, leading in the last days of 1876 to what seems to have been a bout of outright insanity. The wide stylistic spectrum of his works from this period, from calm deliberation and meditative observation of open and airy spaces to wild and visceral annotation of obscure and enclosed aspects of the city, may be seen as indicative of alternating states of mind.

NOTES

1 Ruskin 1903–12, vol. 35, *Præterita and Dilecta*, p. 150.
2 Ruskin 1903–12, vol. 10, *The Stones of Venice II*, pp. 296–297.

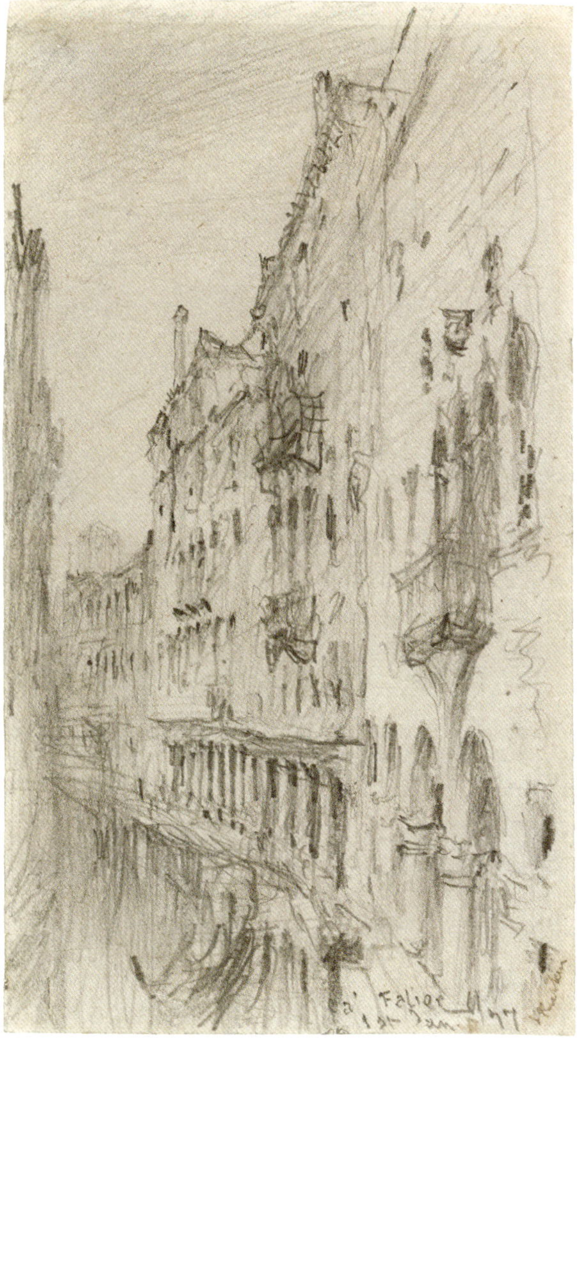

64

Sunset on San Michele, Venice 1877

Watercolour over graphite heightened with touches of bodycolour on paper; 12.9 × 21 cm
Private collection
Inscriptions: *17th Jan. 77*

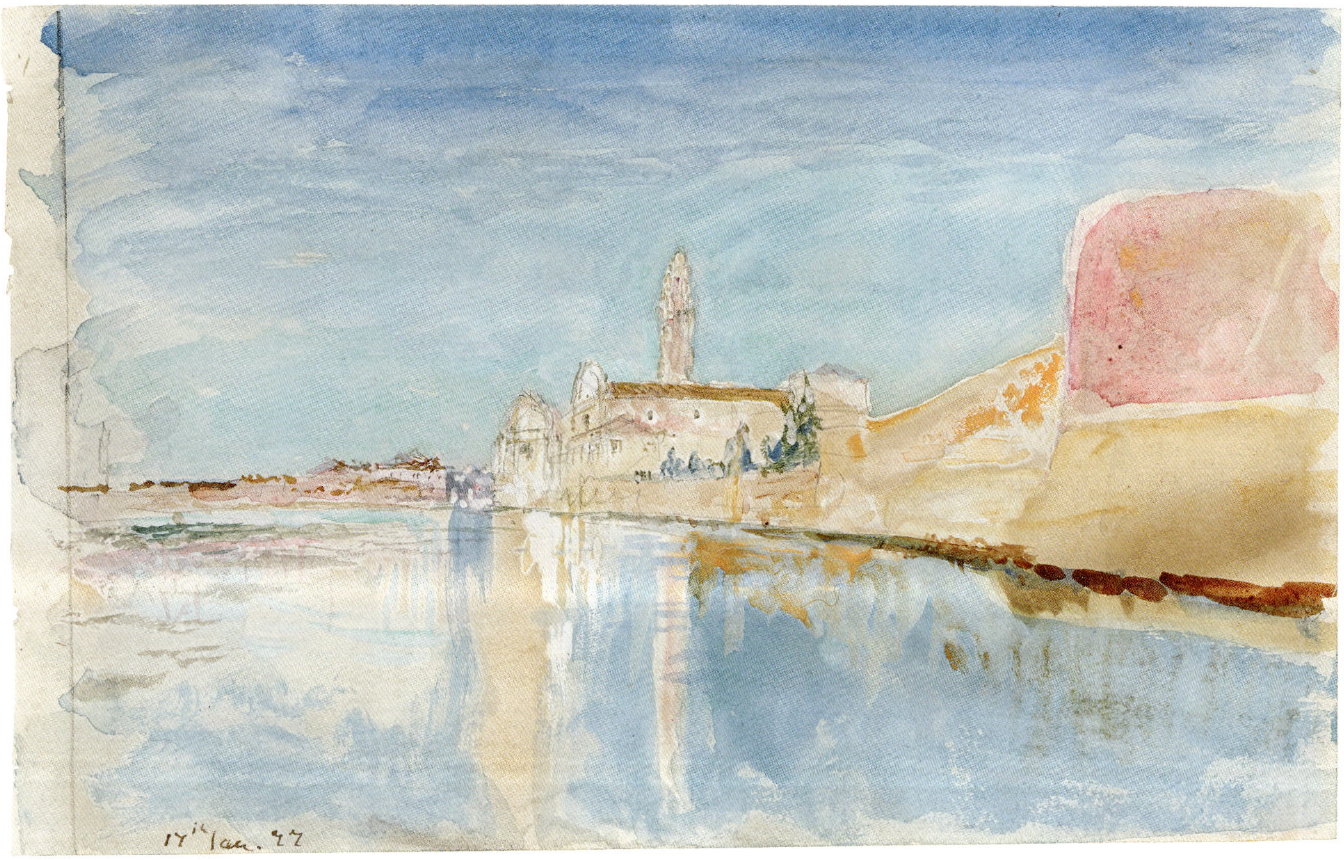

Ruskin described in his diary how on 17 January 1877, after a long day spent working at the Correr Museum and Accademia and visits to churches and other buildings all over Venice, and besides "my hour and a half writing in the morning," he had ended the day by drawing "the sunset on St. Michele di Murano." Two days later, "after entirely dazzling day of pure lustre, [and] moon-light sun," he returned "to rosy sunset on San Michele," giving it a "second day's work."[1] An essay in intense but ethereal colour, applied in broad wet strokes that are allowed to blend and coalesce on the sheet, this drawing shows Ruskin responding in the most direct and empirical way to the extraordinary atmospheric effects that are characteristic of Venetian winters, when the air is clear and the light cold and brilliant. The deep turquoise-blue of the sky reflects in the glassy surface of the lagoon, so that all is drawn together as a harmonious colour study. To achieve this view of San Michele, Ruskin had his gondolier row him close to the brick enclosing wall of the cemetery island, with the church of San Michele in Isola – built by Mauro Codussi between 1469 and 1478 – at the centre. Murano itself lies in the distance on the left.

Ruskin believed that the appreciation and use of colour depended on the physical and moral equanimity of the artist. As he had explained twenty years earlier to readers of *The Elements of Drawing*: "Your power of colouring depend[s] much on your state of health and right balance of mind; when you are fatigued or ill you will not see colours well, and when you are ill-tempered you will not choose them well."[2] Clearly, drawings of this type – aimed to capture a sense of shifting luminosity and atmospheric effect – owe much to the example of J.M.W. Turner. Ruskin especially had in mind the series of drawings that Turner had made in Venice in 1840 (of which he was in possession of a number of examples) and that – according to Ruskin's perception – preceded the deterioration in quality of Turner's work that was linked with the mental frailty of old age.

The sense of euphoria expressed in Ruskin's *Sunset on San Michele* may itself be seen as a summit of excitement in an alternating pattern of high and low moods that accelerated through the winter and spring of 1876–77. Beset with feelings of loss and isolation, he found that he could only achieve an ecstatic pitch when momentarily relieved from the doubts and anxieties that haunted him. In turn, however, brief interludes of delight would, almost as if in self-punishment for his momentary escape from his own demons, bring on further mental agony. So, having enjoyed such pleasure in observing and drawing the effects of sunset on the Venetian lagoon and island of San Michele, the following week Ruskin reverted to a state of dementia, disturbed by weird dreams and insomnia and given to what he had called during a previous bout of mania "egotistical wandering of thought."[3] Ruskin's friend and assistant in the project of recording Venice, J.W. Bunney, had told him that in his view "it was most probably the sunset air at S. Michele [that] put me wrong."[4] Thus the rapture that Ruskin felt in witnessing such wonderful sights as he had drawn on this occasion seems to have prompted a further period of confusion and despair.

NOTES

1 Ruskin 1956, vol. 3, p. 931.
2 Ruskin 1903–12, vol. 15, *The Elements of Drawing, The Elements of Perspective, and The Laws of Fésole*, p. 156.
3 Ruskin 1956, vol. 3, p. 930.
4 Ibid., p. 933.

65

The Fondamenta Nuove, Venice 1877

Graphite, watercolour and bodycolour on paper; 9 × 26.5 cm
Private collection
Inscriptions: *by JR*

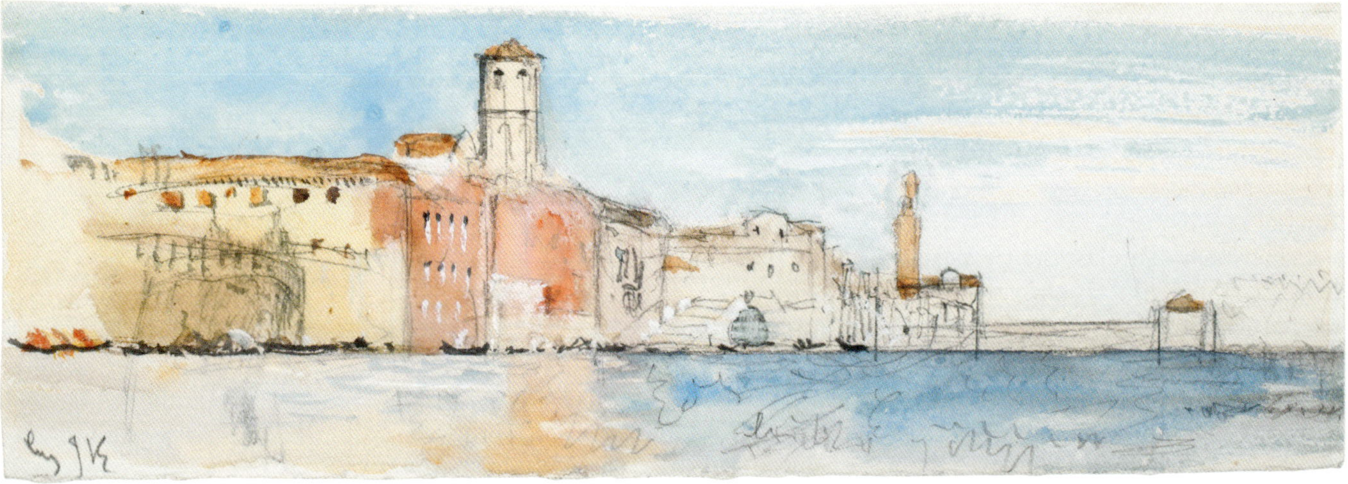

This view of the northern flank of Venice was almost certainly made on one of the two afternoons of the 17 and 19 January, when Ruskin went out by gondola toward the cemetery island of San Michele to observe and draw the effects of light at sunset. Taken from approximately the same vantage point as *Sunset on San Michele, Venice* (cat. 64), but here facing the city, the drawing shows the flanks of buildings on the Fondamenta Nuove with the campaniles of the Gesuiti and the Madonna dell'Orto (the latter the more distant of the two) on the right side. The structure that extends outward toward the right is the quay on the far side of the Sacca della Misericordia. What is usually thought as a melancholy part of the city here glows with colour as rays of winter sunshine flush the fabric, and the buildings and sky are reflected in the water.

While in Venice in 1876–77 Ruskin gravitated toward the more obscure and peripheral parts of the city, perhaps to escape the madding crowds of San Marco. Early on in his stay he transferred his lodgings from a hotel on the Grand Canal to much simpler rooms on the Zattere. The outdoor drawings that he made, as well as his diary entries, give some indication of how he ranged about looking at out-of-the-way parts, and it can only be imagined how these aspects of the city must have heightened his sense of loneliness and futility.

Ruskin continued to meditate on the way in which the rise to power of a people or a city and the inevitable process of vainglorious distraction from civic virtues seem inevitably to lead to corruption and decay. The third chapter of the second volume of *The Stones of Venice*, principally an account of the church of Santa Maria e San Donato on Murano, commences with a description of the Fondamenta as a place seized by "the frost of death" and where "the grasp of mortal disease is marked daily by the increasing breadth of its belt of ruin."[1] These opening words, although written more than two decades earlier, must have been in Ruskin's mind those January evenings. His text continues with a plea for the beauty of a world untouched by human agency:

> Yet the power of Nature cannot be shortened by the folly, nor her beauty altogether saddened by the misery, of man. The broad tides still ebb and flow brightly about the island of the dead, and the linked conclave of the Alps know no decline from their old pre-eminence, nor stoop from their golden thrones in the circle of the horizon. So lovely is the scene still, in spite of all its injuries, that we shall find ourselves drawn there again and again at evening out of the narrow canals and streets of the city, to watch the wreaths of the sea-mist weaving themselves like mourning veils around the mountains far away, and listen to the green waves as they fret and sigh along the cemetery shore.[2]

NOTES

1 Ruskin 1903–12, vol. 10, *The Stones of Venice II*, p. 36.
2 Ibid., pp. 37–38.

66

The Ponte Vecchio and Lung'Arno, Florence, Looking Toward the Southeast 1882 (?)

Graphite and watercolour heightened with white bodycolour on paper; 12.1 × 20.1 cm
Private collection

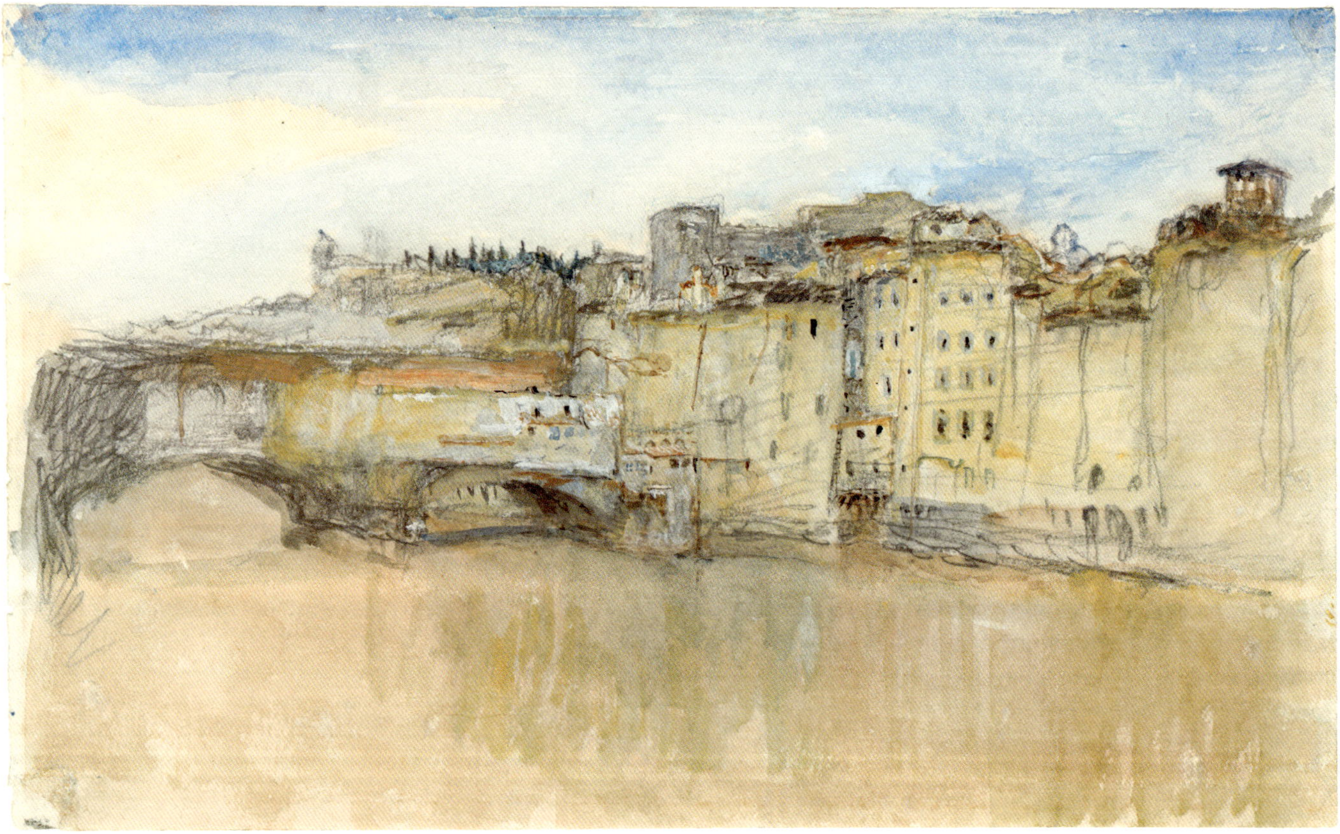

By its freedom of handling, this drawing is to be recognized as the product of Ruskin's later years as a draftsman. The forms of the buildings that make up the central register of the composition consist of washes of colour of varying intensity of tint and gradated texture, with intermittent points of opaque bodycolour giving depth and three-dimensional structure to the mass. These are laid over soft and broadly applied strokes of soft pencil or BB pencil with areas where scribbles of graphite remain unconcealed. Patches of blue show in the sky, while the brown waters of the Arno lie sluggishly; undisturbed by wind or current, the surface of the river seems to absorb rather than reflect light from the eastern sky.

The view is from a building – most likely the Hotel Grande Bretagne, where

Ruskin was staying in 1882 with his travelling companion William Gershom Collingwood – on the Lungarno just to the west of the point where the Via de' Tornabuoni meets the Ponte Santa Trìnita. Ruskin was looking southeast and included, on the left, the Ponte Vecchio – Florence's famous medieval covered bridge – and, on the right, the flank of buildings that backs onto the south side of the river, lit by the morning sun. Against the skyline are seen, on the right, a tower close to or part of the Palazzo Pitti and, at the centre, the outline of the Forte di Belvedere, while in the distance on the left is glimpsed the church of San Miniato al Monte. In taking this view, Ruskin will have remembered the watercolour that John Brett had made in 1862 from his lodgings on the Piazza Santa Trìnita, which shows essentially the same view out onto the river and bridge, and which his father had bought from Brett, probably on Ruskin's recommendation, in 1863.[1]

By the time of his last visit to Tuscany in 1882, Ruskin had been overtaken by three mental breakdowns and was travelling on his doctor's recommendation in search of rest and recuperation. His arrival with Collingwood on 5 October was recorded in his diary: "In Gran Bretagna once more; very well and very comfortable. Sun just glinting along sides of yellow houses beyond Arno; which, if it's bad weather, I shall perhaps draw." The next day, however, his mood had sunk: "Everywhere paviours, masons, ruin – degradation, folly, and noise; and the wretched Germans, English, and Yankees busy upon it like dung-flies."[2]

The present drawing is related to a series of three pencil studies in the collection of the Ruskin Foundation at Lancaster University showing the Ponte Vecchio, all apparently made from this vantage point, and therefore assumed to have been done in 1882. That Ruskin drew the river from the rooms that he occupied at the Grande Bretagne, of which intention he had announced on arrival, is further corroborated by mention in a letter to Joan Severn of 28 October that he had "done a pretty chiaroscuro of Ponte Vecchio this morning ... Usually, the sun shines in at the windows so that one can't draw in the morning, but it has been most usefully grey till now – 1/2 past ten."[3] Ruskin had begun work on a series of connected histories of different European towns under the title *Our Fathers Have Told Us*, of which only one, *The Bible of Amiens*, was ever completed; the projected fifth volume was to be of Florence and titled *Ponte Vecchio*. He thus had that project and the need for suitable illustrations in mind when making drawings in the city.

NOTES

1 See Oxford 2010, p. 103, cat. 54.
2 Ruskin 1903–12, vol. 33, *The Bible of Amiens, Valle Crucis, The Art of England, The Pleasures of England*, pp. xl–xli.
3 John Ruskin, quoted in London Sheffield Lucca 1993, p. 134.

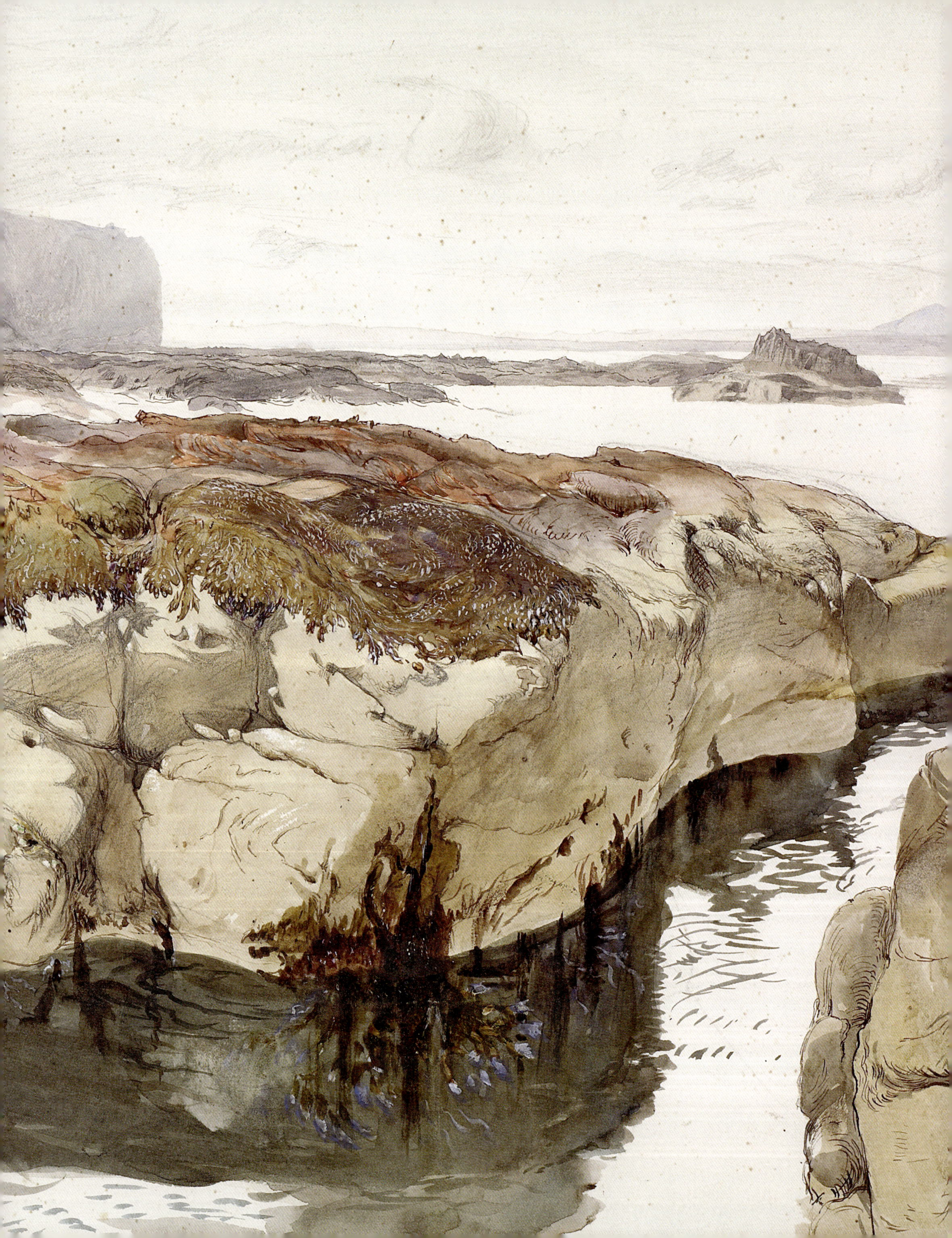

Geology & Foregrounds

67

Geological Diary 1835 (open at pp. 50–51)

Black ink on white paper; 18 × 11.5 × 1.5 cm (open)
Ruskin Foundation (Ruskin Library, Lancaster University) (RF MS 1)
Inscriptions: inside cover, ink, *J. Ruskin / 1835*

From the age of about ten, Ruskin adopted the habit of carrying a sketchbook with him whenever he travelled. The first of these books records a visit to Derbyshire in 1829 as well as explorations of southern England made over the next three years. The drawings that are contained within his early sketchbooks serve as a kind of travelogue of the places visited and provide evidence of his particular enthusiasms as a boy for medieval architecture, landscape and geology.

Ruskin's obsessive fascination with geology and the construction of the landscape commenced with his father's purchase of a collection of rock specimens during a visit to the Lake District. The acquisition led Ruskin later to proclaim that "no subsequent possession has had so much influence on my life."[1] The family mineral collection expanded, while Ruskin began a mineralogical dictionary on the basis of drawings he made of examples in the British Museum. In later years he seems occasionally to have regretted that he did not devote himself entirely to the science of geology, instead allowing himself to be distracted into the realm of art.

The present notebook was used during a tour of France and Switzerland (with an onward journey to Venice) in the summer and autumn of 1835. The Alpine exploration that occupied the Ruskins for at least two months was inspired by Horace-Bénédict de Saussure's book *Voyages dans les Alpes* (1779–96), which Ruskin had been given as a birthday present in February 1834. The pages of Ruskin's notebook are filled with detailed and enthusiastic accounts of places seen and natural phenomena. Particular attention was paid to rock formations and types, with constant reference to the directions and shaping of strata in the Alpine sedimentary rocks and the contours of the mountains according to their geological composition, with verdicts volunteered as to which were the most pleasing to look at (generally concluding that "mountains wholly composed of limestone ... are always beautiful. Their outline is varied and their colouring magnificent"[2]).

In addition, Ruskin commented on the flora and fauna (principally snakes) and the climatic conditions (including frequent measurements of the intensity of blue of the sky with an instrument called a cyanometer). Vivid descriptions were offered of landscape formations, for example in the valley that runs between Saint-Maurice and Martigny, where he wrote of the limestone cliffs as telling "every traveller a wonderful tale of ancient convulsions. Such coiled crags I never saw; whole mountains twisted like macaroni, as if they had been tortured on the rack and broken on the wheel of the world for ages. I sketched three dispositions, and could have had a hundred."[3] Careful ink drawings of landscapes and geological formations – from expansive and panoramic vistas of entire mountain ranges to diagrammatic observations of strata – are inset into the texts.

NOTES

1 Ruskin 1903–12, vol. 26, *Deucalion and Other Studies in Rocks and Stones*, p. 294, note.
2 Ruskin 1956, vol. 1, p. 62.
3 Ibid., p. 22.

but these are sufficient for illustration. Fig 9. is a crag just above St Maurice. remarkable for the immense scale of its contortions, since ~~from St~~ the height of this crag is not less than 2000 feet perpendicular; The curve of this crag is rendered conspicuous at a glance by the disposition of the pines, which grow in belts; upon the ledges formed by the projection of the strata from beneath one another.

(10)

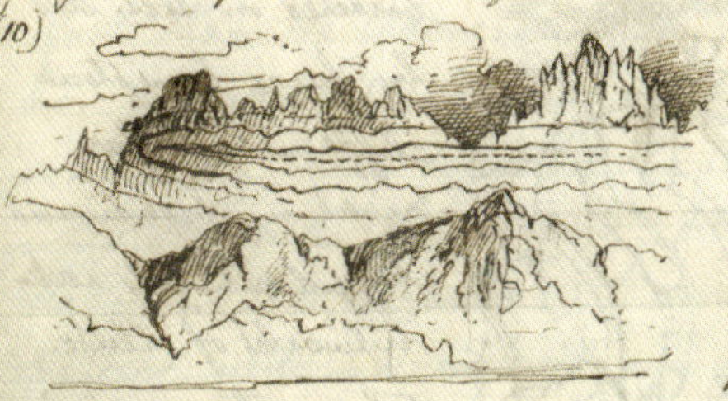

Fig 10 is a still more remarkable instance. It is a chain of calcareous peaks which you come in sight of on the right half away between St Maurice and Martigny. I was at first struck by their beautiful outline, which exactly resembles that of a granite mountain. which indeed I should have been mistaken them for, had it not been for their finely marked strata. These, it will be observed are not only curved but bent completely round upon themselves.

ata.

being perfectly straight both before and after this singular bend, and the rest of the mountain bearing no traces of contortion. Below these

(11)

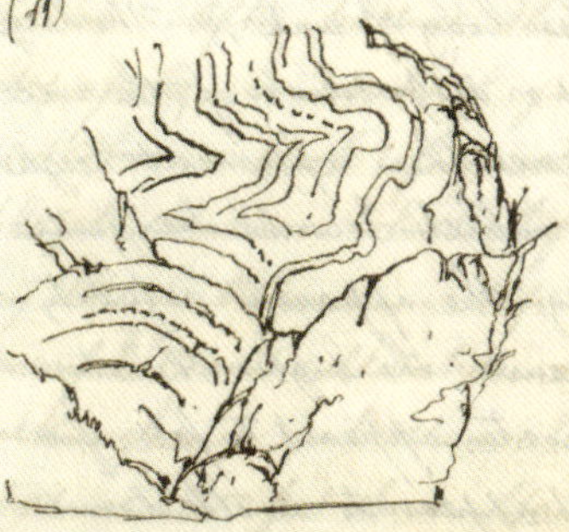

peaks, rather nearer St Maurice, is a more isolated rock whose beds are most singularly twisted. fig 11. These sketches are all taken from the rocks on the east side of the valley. those on the opposite one are much distorted. but not on so large a scale.

The cascade of the Pissevache near Martigny is a sort of split the difference between the immense body of water and small height of the cataract of the Rhine, and the enormous height and dribbling stream of the Nant D'Arpenaz. It is, I think, one of the finest falls in Switzerland, with its head buried in spray, and its feet planted on the rainbow. These high cascades fall like reversed

68

Study of a River Bank, Beauvais 1846

Pen and ink over graphite heightened with white bodycolour and with sepia, yellow and green washes on grey paper; 12.8 × 17.4 cm
Private collection
Inscriptions: *Beauvais April 10. J Ruskin / 1846*

This drawing was made in the course of the Ruskins' journey to Italy in 1846. Although there is no diary entry describing the Ruskins' stay in Beauvais, accounts were given a few days later of their onward journey to Switzerland. The sketches on the verso of the drawing of a flooded meadow and trees at Pont-sur-Yonne, close to Sens and to the southeast of Paris, made on 14 April, and of a classically formed dormer window at Chanceaux, northwest of Dijon, from 17 April, chart their progress.

In the present drawing we see a wooden construction, presumably serving as landing stages or loading platforms, and bits of ladder and embanked quay, beyond a surface of water. Much of this is overgrown with weeds; herbage, ferns and thistles cling to the surface of the wood and earth, and the stems of invasive trees and shrubs emerge between the posts and against the brick and plaster wall of a building that stands behind. This is one of the first of Ruskin's drawings to explore the potential of nature to overwhelm and negate human efforts to harness the landscape. There is no sense of despair or feeling that this was a process of corruption, but rather a delight in nature's elemental power.

In the second letter of Ruskin's instruction manual *The Elements of Drawing* (1857) one specification seems to have been inspired by the memory of working on the present drawing a decade earlier. It was Ruskin's view that "in general, all banks are beautiful things, and will reward work better than large landscapes. If you live in a lowland country, you must look for places where the ground is broken to the river's edges, with decayed posts, or roots of trees; or, if by great good luck there should be such things within your reach, for remnants of stone quays or steps, mossy mill-dams, etc."[1] The essential principle of *The Elements of Drawing* and of Ruskin's art teaching at the Working Men's College in London, from which the book derived, was one of utter simplicity and ingenuousness. Thus by engaging with the complexity of unremarkable but authentic aspects of the countryside at close range and with an appreciation of the incidental and timeworn beauty of places, his followers might make drawings that were truthful and personal rather than attempt to conform to artistic conventions or theory, or worse learn the easy techniques and pictorial trickeries that many other drawing manuals advocated. Ruskin's desire for a form of art based simply on the observation of natural shapes – the inspiration for drawings such as the present – was expressed with complete sincerity in a footnote to *The Elements of Drawing*: "The whole technical power of painting depends on our recovery of what may be called the *innocence of the eye*; that is to say, of a sort of childish perception of these flat stains of colour, merely as such, without consciousness of what they signify, – as a blind man would see them if suddenly gifted with sight."[2]

NOTES

1 Ruskin 1903–12, vol. 15, *The Elements of Drawing, The Elements of Perspective, and The Laws of Fésole*, p. 109.
2 Ibid., p. 27, note.

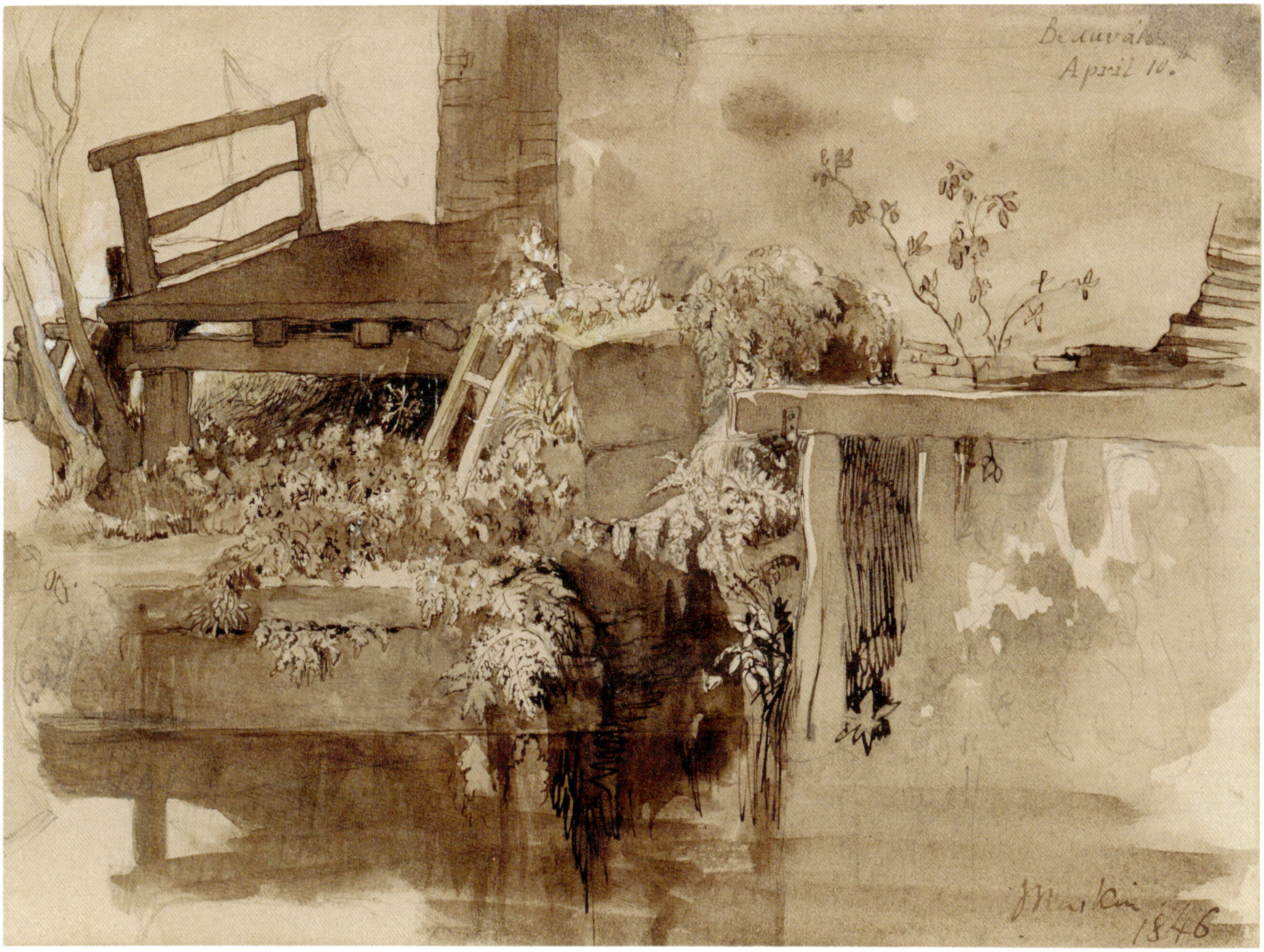
Beauvais
April 10th
1846

69

Coast Scene near Dunbar 1847

Watercolour over graphite on paper; 32.5 × 47.5 cm
Birmingham Museums and Art Gallery (1907P139)

Ruskin spent a few days in Dunbar, to the east of Edinburgh on the North Sea coast, in August 1847, interrupting a journey to Perthshire where he was to stay with family friends. He was in a morose state of mind – disturbed in the earlier part of the year by an unhappy relationship with Charlotte, the daughter of Sir Walter Scott's biographer John Gibson Lockhart, and then by uncertainty about what might come of his feelings for Effie Gray. Disconsolately moving about and finding it hard to apply himself to work, he had spent periods in Ambleside in the spring and then, in the summer, had taken a cure at Leamington Spa. The very experience of finding himself back in Scotland seemed to raise his spirits, as he wrote in his diary on 18 August: "I entered Scotland about four hours ago (at six) under happy auspices. Gloomy sky all the way over Northumberland; a dark curtain of cloud rolled off the sea at Berwick and when we crossed the Tweed, all was bright and heavenly. I never was more touched in my life than by the look of the heathery knolls and wild happy streams ... God grant I may gain in mind and health of body from being here." Three days later he noted that he had spent "a happy day, drawing by the sea shore,"[1] working, presumably, on the present view.

Ruskin's drawing shows a low-lying rock close to the shore at Dunbar, part of the limestone reef that emerges below the steep sandstone cliffs that are seen in the distance. The stone has been smoothed by the action of waves and tide and is crested with seaweed, while water laps gently in the surrounding channel. The view is toward the northwest, with the Bass Rock on the horizon to the right. If 21 August saw clement weather and calm sea, the following day brought a stupendous storm: "Far as the eye could reach the sea was one white, quavering, vaporous field, more like a desert of white sand than sea ... [then] it began to rain and remained black until sunset."[2]

NOTES

1 Ruskin 1956, vol. 1, p. 362.
2 Ibid., p. 363.

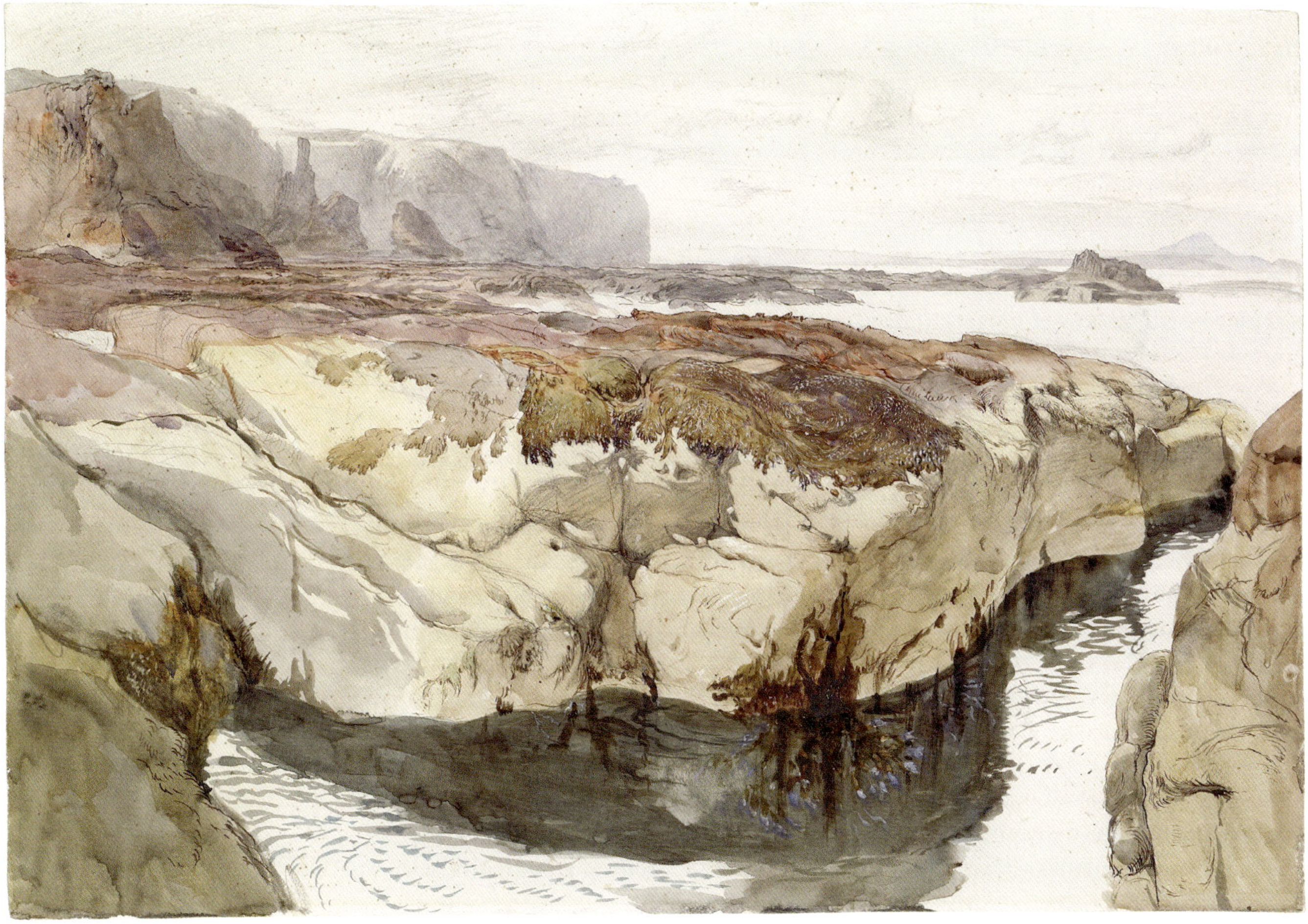

70

Diary Notebook or *Crossmount Sketchbook* (open at page of studies of funnels and sails, 1847) 1846–49

Black ink, ink wash, graphite and watercolour on paper; 26.5 × 21 × 4 cm (closed)
Ruskin Foundation (Ruskin Library, Lancaster University) (RF MS 5C)
Inscriptions: paper label on spine, ink, *6 / 1846 / 1847*

This sketchbook is named for Ruskin's stay at William Macdonald's estate at Crossmount on Kinloch Rannoch in the summer of 1847, but was in use from the previous year until 1849. In addition to landscape and geological studies there are pages devoted to architectural drawings and diagrams (with drawings generally appearing on the left-hand page) as well as sheets of careful handwriting, including notes on Homer, religion and church teaching, Salisbury cathedral, perspective, plants, and "the truth of wheels." Ruskin also used the sketchbook as a diary in 1846, when travelling in the Alps and Italy with his parents, and again sporadically in Perthshire in 1847. On this last occasion, his mood was bleak, as he described feelings akin to there being "a strange deadly shadow over everything – such as I hardly could comprehend,"[1] symptoms of what would now be diagnosed as clinical depression.

The drawing of funnels and masts was presumably made in Scotland and is a personal and idiosyncratic demonstration of the interest Ruskin took in his surroundings. It was perhaps done for no larger purpose than to give visual expression to a pattern of shapes and textures that he found beautiful. Sometime later, possibly reflecting on the little drawing, he made a further note in the sketchbook in which he gave a brief discourse on the abstract beauty of stripes: "Compare this coloured stripe with the brick or stone courses, as at the treasury. Consider the appearance of stripes in steps. On ship sides. In bold quaint draperies. Giotto in Sta Croce. Veronese. Patterns & c. Stripes on shells & stones. On zebra. Rare in flowers, and why? In agates."[2] This listing of disparate things, linked only by their stripyness, recalls in its surreal and incidental succession the Walrus' speech to the Carpenter in Lewis Carroll's *Through the Looking-Glass* and is a clue to the workings of Ruskin's mind and his peculiar capacity to make connections between unrelated objects and see consistency in things that would otherwise appear miscellaneous.

The question remains, was Ruskin here, in combining and contrasting a group of pristine and smartly painted funnels and the masts of sailing ships with forlornly limp and dirty coloured sails, dwelling upon the impact of technological progress? The 1840s witnessed an extraordinary expansion in the merchant fleet of steam-powered ships, with Isambard Kingdom Brunel's SS *Great Britain* – launched in 1843 and featuring an iron hull and screw propulsion – regarded as one of the marvels of the age (although in fact the greatest achievements of sailing ships was still to come in the form of the clippers that carried tea and other freight between China and Britain in the 1860s). In making this study, Ruskin must surely have been thinking of J.M.W. Turner's paintings of steamships and the effects of smoke rising from their funnels. The critical reception of one such work, Turner's

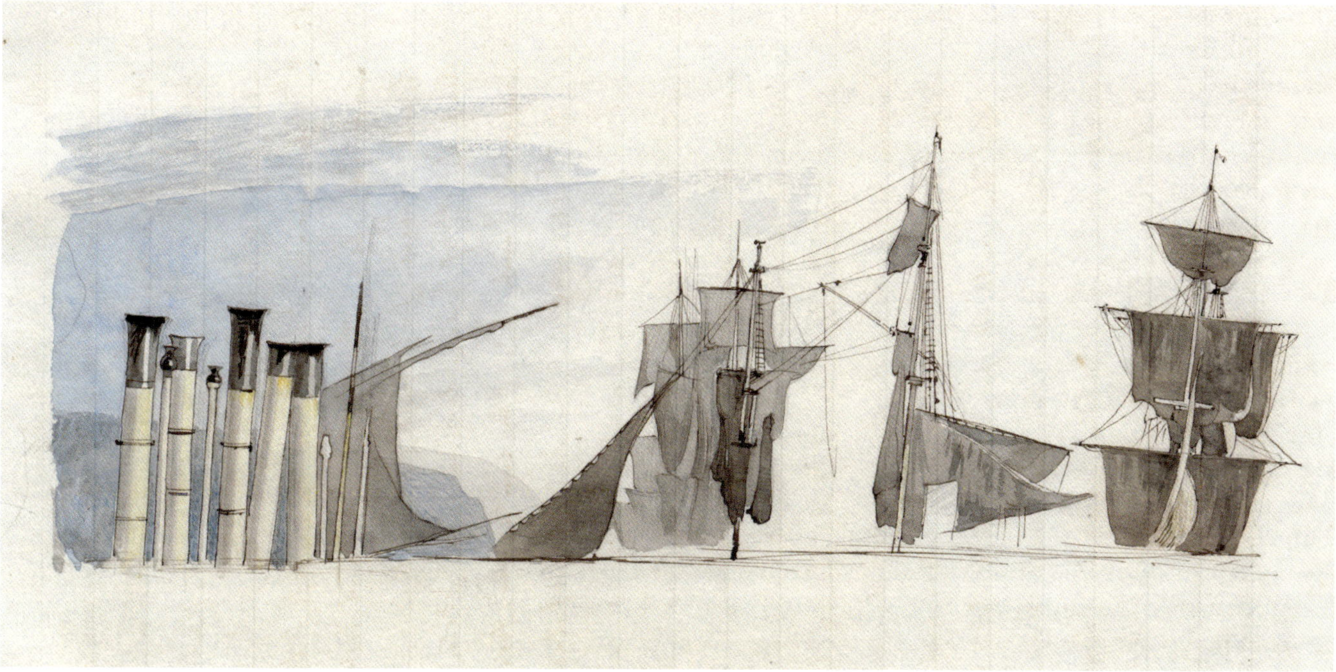

Peace – Burial at Sea (1842, Tate, London), when exhibited at the Royal Academy in 1842, had provoked Ruskin to write *Modern Painters* in defence of one he believed to be England's greatest painter. Turner's *The Fighting Temeraire* (1839, National Gallery, London) also famously shows steam and sailing ships together, and was referred to by Ruskin in the first volume of *Modern Painters* in 1843 as a work "incapable … of any improvement conceivable by human mind."[3]

NOTES

1 Ruskin 1956, vol. 1, p. 364.
2 Ibid.
3 Ruskin 1903–12, vol. 3, *Modern Painters I*, p. 248.

71

Crossmount, Perthshire; Study of Crag, Tree and Thistle 1847

Graphite, pen and brown ink and brown wash heightened with white bodycolour on buff paper; 47.5 × 60 cm
Private collection

In the present drawing, made at William Macdonald's estate at Crossmount on Kinloch Rannoch, Ruskin observed an outcrop of exposed rocks, their outer forms smoothed by ancient glaciers but also undercut by the plucking action of the ice as it has swept over the projecting masses. In a further process of erosion, the blocks have been riven by freeze-thaw action, with gash-like clefts opened in the surface and fragments fractured from the bedrock and littered on the ground below. Wiry shrubs cling to the crevices, contorted by the driving wind and their forms moulded and beaten by ceaseless buffeting. Thistles – also referred to in the drawing's original title – are seen growing in the immediate foreground, with leaves spreading out like spiny flames.

All the elements of this momentous composition are drawn together by a pattern of curved and twisted line suggestive of and echoing the natural forms themselves and that make a volumetric and massive whole. On this occasion Ruskin treated the entire composition in a neutral monochrome, the tones of which range from a deep cuttlefish sepia through to cream washes hardly darker than the surface of the paper below. By this device, he further emphasized the harmonious cohesion of the composition, making all parts of the landscape appear unified and organic, subject to the relentless forces of weather. Ruskin saw the physical world as a living entity – fluctuating in its mood and disposition and seething with energy. His engagement with the landscape, as a geologist and draftsman and as a walker and mountaineer, was visceral in the way he allowed himself to be emotionally involved with particular places and climatic conditions – whether expressing emotions of delight or feelings of oppression.

The types of landscape to which Ruskin was attracted at any given moment may offer clues to his larger mental equanimity. Here we see rock formations that are strangely marked, with swelling protuberances and cracks and creases that bear analogy to human anatomy. That he did recognize in natural forms echoes of bodies or physiognomy – and there is a succession of drawings that suggest he was prompted by what he saw in the landscape to think about anatomical form – is borne out by a passage in the first volume of *Modern Painters*. Ostensibly a discussion of cloud formations, he commented on "such accidental resemblances" as something that gives "to the scenery of the sky a force and variety no less delightful than that of the changes of mountain outline in a hill district," but "that there is added to this a spirit-like feeling, a capricious mocking imagery of passion and life, totally different from any effects of inanimate form that the earth can show."[1]

NOTES

1 Ruskin 1903–12, vol. 3, *Modern Painters I*, p. 373.

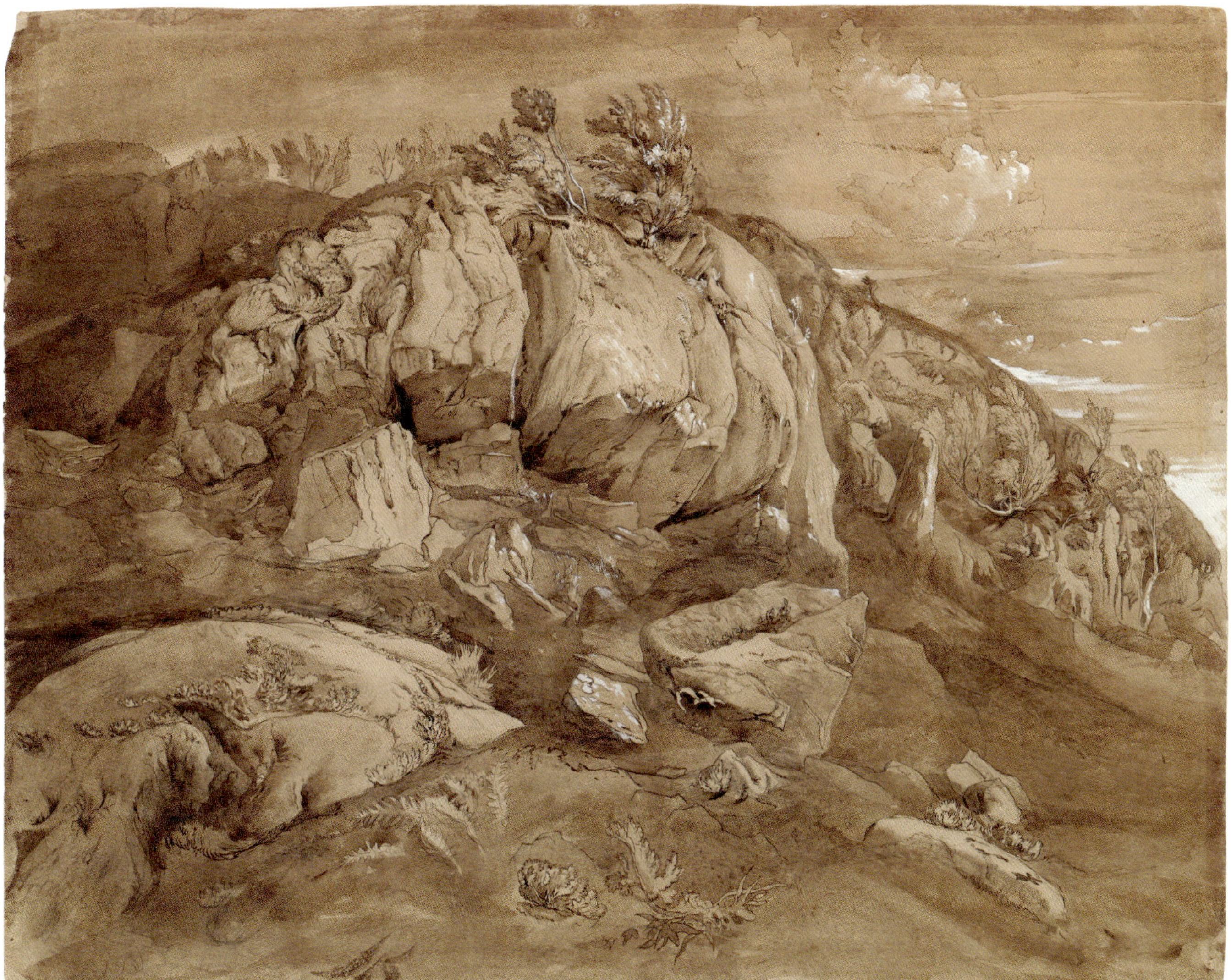

72

Rocks and Ferns in a Wood at Crossmount, Perthshire 1847

Pen and ink and watercolour over graphite on paper; 32.3 × 46.5 cm
Courtesy of Abbot Hall Art Gallery, Lakeland Arts Trust, Kendal, Cumbria, UK (AH1134/73)
Inscriptions: verso, ink, *Crossmount Perthshire 1847 / original drawing by John Ruskin / purchased from Mr. and Mrs. Severn / Robert E. Cunliffe*

By contrast with Ruskin's drawing *Crossmount, Perthshire* (cat. 71), done during the same stay at Crossmount, *Rocks and Ferns* is richly coloured with a particularly lovely use of soft greens and greys to suggest the grass of a woodland glade. Where the soil is exposed, it is inky black, moist and peaty. Half-buried boulders, their upper surfaces covered with yellow-green moss and lichen, form a complex structure at the centre. In the foreground, fronds of ferns weave and gyrate like flames, while on the right an ungainly thistle appears to keel over under the weight of its own stem and leaves (earlier in the summer, while still in Leamington, Ruskin had gathered thistles and made careful studies of their forms). Most beautiful is the way in which he has captured in colour the softly gleaming whiteness of the trunk of a silver birch, with a second tree beside it, the bark of which is less smooth and marked with distinctive dark flecks and bands. As ever, Ruskin shows each botanical specimen in a way that allows it to be recognized and to leave no doubt at all in the mind of the spectator that these particular plants were growing in the very spot where he drew them.

Once again, the spectator is left to speculate as to the scale of the piece of ground represented and to notice Ruskin's unwillingness to include any peripheral vista. All attention is focused on what lies immediately before one's eyes, which can be studied and relished as a microcosm of the larger landscape. Its authenticity as a representation of real and living nature as opposed to something cultivated or arranged by humans is corroborated, both by the sense of being witness to a process of disintegration – with the bank and the meadow beyond broken up by the mechanisms of physical geography, revealing boulders and bedrock beneath – and with the force of nature allowing new plants to establish and thrive. As Ruskin recalled of this period when writing the chapter "Crossmount" in *Præterita*: "On fine days, when the grass was dry, I used to lie down on it and draw the blades as they grew, with the ground herbage of buttercup or hawkweed mixed among them, until every square foot of meadow, or mossy bank, became an infinite picture and possession to me."[1]

Although Ruskin had grown up in suburban London, his true allegiance was to wild and elemental landscapes into which he might lose himself and escape all anxieties and associations. In the chapter entitled "The Moral of Landscape," in the third volume of *Modern Painters*, he described "the intense joy mingled with awe" that he had felt in childhood at Friar's Crag on Derwent Water "in looking through the hollows in the mossy roots, over the crag, into the dark lake."[2] This fascination with enclosed and enclosing forms of landscape, into which he might glimpse the epic struggle of conflicting mechanisms of growth and corruption, remained with him all his life.

NOTES

1 Ruskin 1903–12, vol. 35, *Præterita and Dilecta*, p. 429.
2 Ruskin 1903–12, vol. 5, *Modern Painters III*, p. 365.

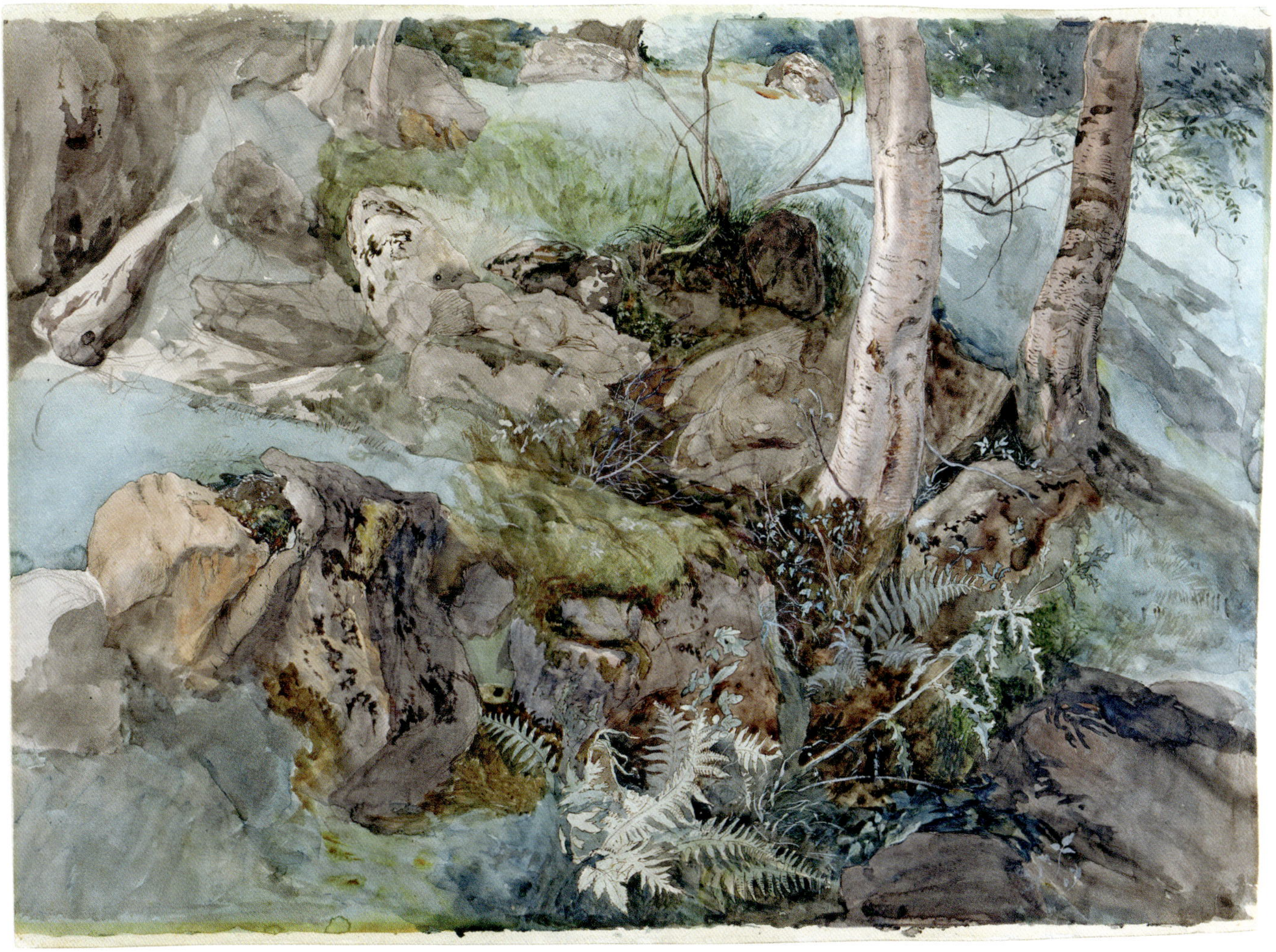

73

Mountain Rock and Alpine Rose 1844–49

Black ink, chalk, watercolour and bodycolour on white paper; 29.8 × 41.4 cm
Ruskin Foundation (Ruskin Library, University of Lancaster) (RF 1395)

The present celebrated drawing has been associated with an entry in Ruskin's diary for 28 June 1849 in which he described a climb made the previous day up the Cascade des Pèlerins to the south of Chamonix and into the gorge that contains the Glacier des Bossons, which is a mountainside littered with glacial debris.[1] On that occasion, Ruskin was delighted by what he saw, "the Alpine rose clinging to its warm and tiger striped crags, the pines above stretching their arms over one's head like nets and [out of view in the drawing, but the object of careful study from the valley below in cat. 91] the ridge of the glacier, so warm, so strange, so rent and broken, so wild and fair and fantastic."[2]

Ruskin's guide and companion Joseph Couttet had a house somewhere on this mountainside overlooking Chamonix, and indeed the evidence in this drawing of stacked firewood and lengths of timber leaning against the boulder may suggest that there were homesteads close by. An alternative possible indication of the location and circumstances of the drawing may be deduced from a diary entry written on 15 June – the third day of Ruskin's 1849 sojourn in Chamonix – when, in the course of an evening walk to the foot of the Montenvers, he "noticed a few blocks of stone worth looking at, as I thought, among the pines; on approaching them, I found they were all one – the vastest granite block (of moraine) I have ever seen, whole body guard of pines about it."[3] It must be said, however, that there are boulders of this type strewn across the Arve valley, and of course elsewhere throughout the Alps, so any attempt to locate the setting of the drawing must be regarded as speculative.

The accounts that Ruskin gave of the Alpine landscape in diary entries from the 1840s and 1850s are peppered with references to individual rocks for which he felt affection or association. Among those that lie in the woods above Chamonix on the northwest side, on the flanks of the Brévent, there was one especially that was for Ruskin an object of pilgrimage,[4] as he indicated in a diary entry for 10 July 1854; having returned to Chamonix that day – he recorded that he had "been up to my stone upon the Bréven," and had found "all unchanged, and happy."[5] Isolated boulders perhaps struck him as emblematic of his own loneliness and the difficulty he found in connecting with others in love or lasting friendship.

The present drawing shows a stupendous block of stone, with sunlight casting over its exposed surfaces and revealing seams and fissures and places where lichen or moss had established. Its undercut sides and roughly spherical shape indicate that this is not part of the bedrock and that it may be recognized as a so-called erratic boulder, i.e. one that has been transported from its place of geological origin by the movement of a glacier at a time when the ice cover on the north flank of Mont Blanc was more extensive. By contrast, the brown rock in the left foreground, upon which is found

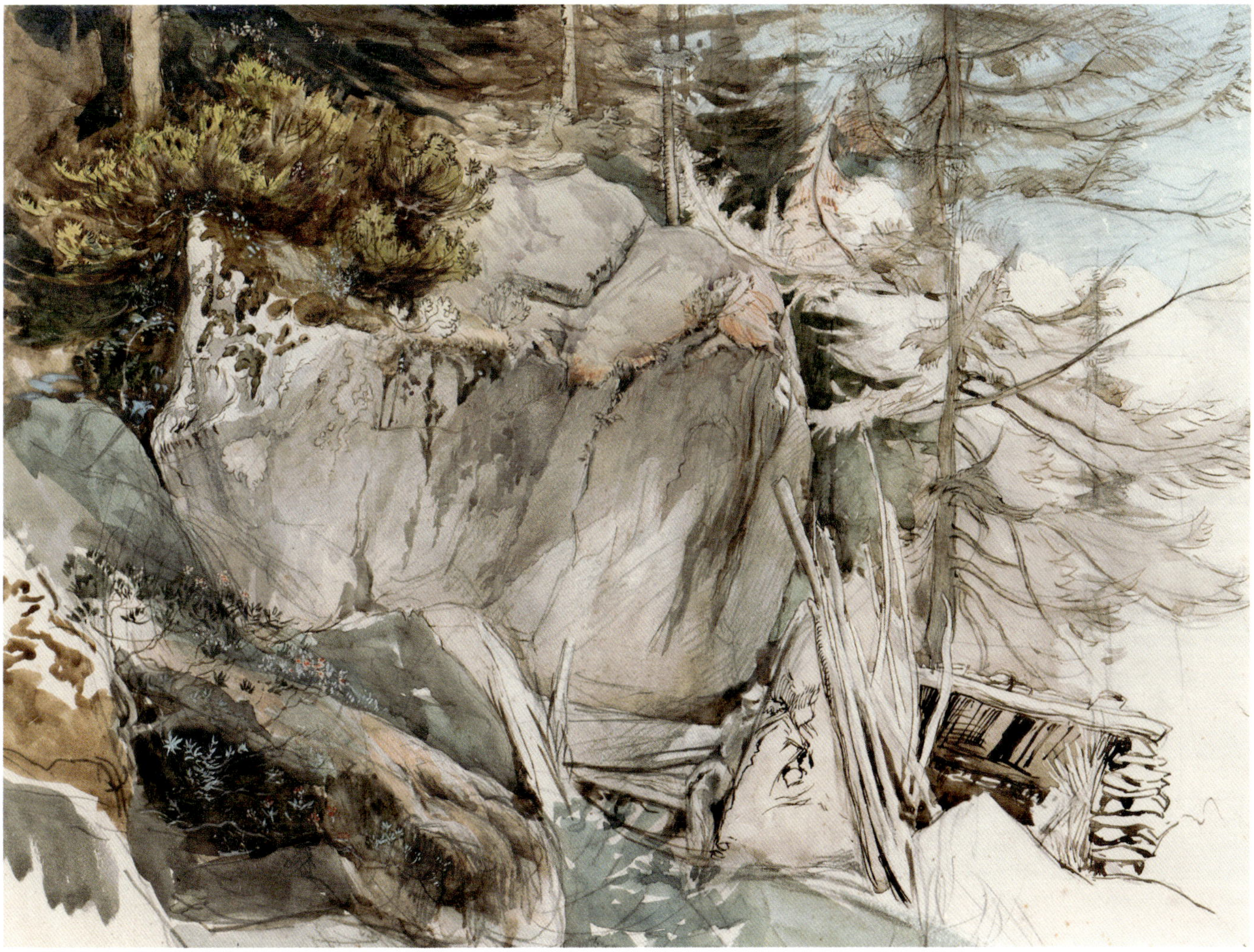

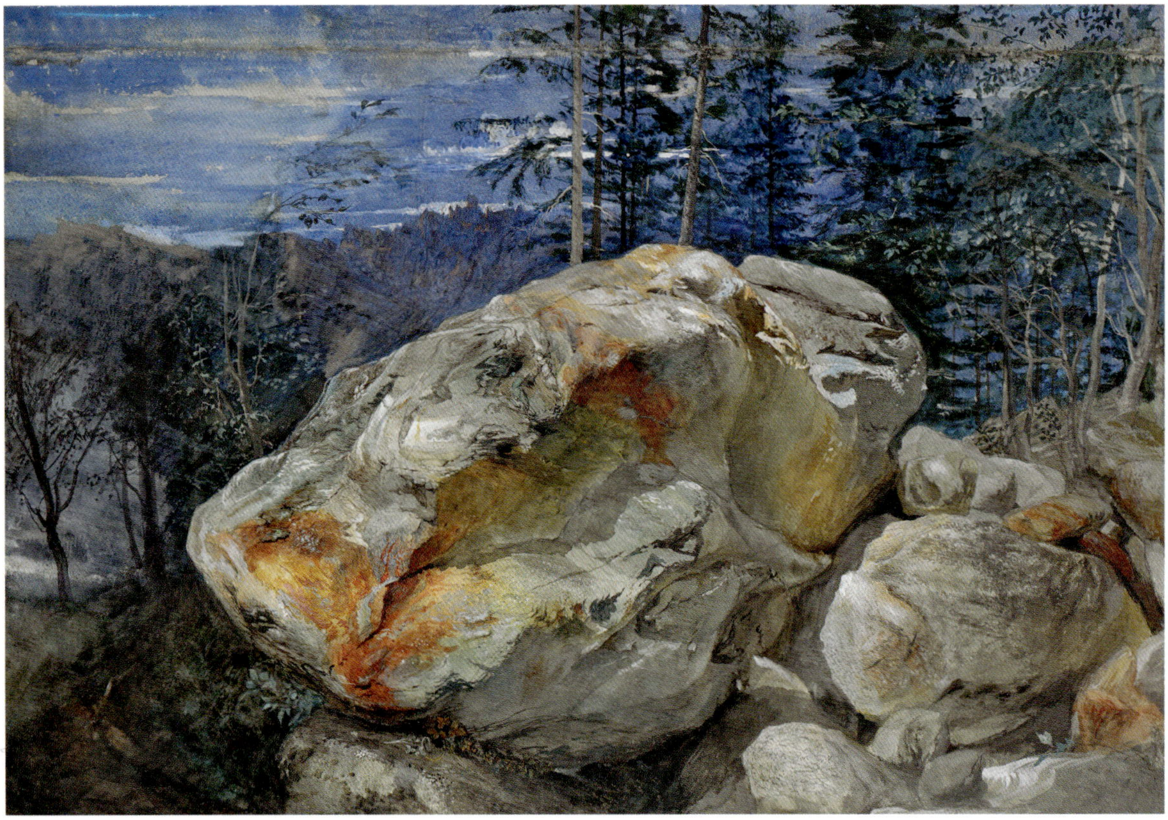

FIG. 6.1
John Ruskin
Study of a Block of Gneiss, Valley of Chamouni, Switzerland [sic] (now known as *Fragment of the Alps*), c. 1854–56
Watercolour and gouache over graphite on cream wove paper
Harvard Art Museums / Fogg Museum, Cambridge, Mass.
Gift of Samuel Sachs (1919.506)

the alpine rose of the drawing's title, has a profile that suggests that it is an indigenous variety of stone, having been swept and smoothed into a shape that has been determined by the downward flow of ice.

Ruskin's particular interest in erratic boulders commenced in the 1840s when he made a close study of the available geological textbooks and contributed himself to the debate about the mechanisms of glaciation. Charles Lyell's *Principles of Geology* (1830–33), Louis Agassiz's *Études sur les Glaciers* (1840) and James David Forbes' *Travels through the Alps of Savoy* (1843) encouraged travellers to look at mountains with a new comprehension of how such landscapes had been created. Ruskin's frequent visits to the Alps allowed him both to expand his knowledge of physical geography and to test received theories. In 1849, in the course of his month-long stay in Chamonix that summer, he was reading newly published texts, researching by close observation, and making drawings that might serve as evidence of his own ideas about how the landscape was formed.

Although Ruskin was a reluctant exhibitor of his own drawings, he made an exception when he allowed a work to be included in what was called the American Exhibition of British Art, which travelled successively to New York, Philadelphia and Boston in 1857 and 1858. The drawing that he exhibited was entitled *Study of a Block of Gneiss, Valley of Chamouni, Switzerland* [sic] (fig. 6.1; now known as *Fragment of the Alps*) and shows a boulder with ferrous staining perched upon a confused mass of other rocks before a backdrop of pine trees and undergrowth. A comparison of that drawing with the present demonstrates Ruskin's adherence to a purpose of naturalistic documentation when he made *Mountain Rock and Alpine Rose*, as opposed to the iconographic simplification and self-consciousness of statement that characterizes *Study of a Block of Gneiss*.

NOTES

1 See London 2000, cat. 130, p. 151.
2 Ruskin 1956, vol. 2, p. 397.
3 Ibid., p. 387.
4 Probably identical to the boulder that is known as the "*Pierre à Ruskin*," upon which in 1925 a bronze relief portrait of Ruskin was placed.
5 Ruskin 1956, vol. 2, p. 498.

74

a. *Ravine at Maglans* 1849 (?)

Graphite, brown ink and ink wash heightened with bodycolour on white paper;
28 × 21.2 cm (sheet trimmed at right and bottom edges)
Ruskin Foundation (Ruskin Library, Lancaster University) (RF 946)
Inscriptions: verso (in a later hand), graphite, *Ravine at Maglans, Valley of Cluses / by John Ruskin*

b. *Ravine at Maglans* 1849 (?)

Black and brown ink and ink wash heightened with bodycolour and scratching-out
over etched outline on white paper; 22.4 × 14 cm
Ruskin Foundation (Ruskin Library, Lancaster University) (RF 854)
Inscriptions: plate below image, *The Base Aquafort* (inscription trimmed laterally)

After a stay of about a month at Chamonix in the summer of 1849, on 10 July Ruskin and his mother and father decided to move on – the parents to Geneva, he to Zermatt. They travelled together for the first leg of the journey as far as the village of Saint-Martin-sur-Arve, close to Sallanches, where they stayed at the Hôtel du Mont Blanc. Ruskin's spirits were depressed by being away from the high mountains, and he wrote: "What a strange contrast there is between these lower valleys, with their over wrought richness mixed with signs of waste and disease, and their wild noon-winds shaking their leaves into palsy and their black clouds and dark storms folding themselves about their steep mural precipices; and the pastoral green and ice, and pure aiguilles and white fleecy rainclouds of Chamouni."[1]

The ravine represented in the present pair of drawings is about four kilometres north of Saint-Martin, toward a place named Magland, on the west-facing hillsides of the Arve valley. Ruskin had first discovered it on his 1835 journey with his parents, when he had described it in a diary entry on 6 July as "one of the most superb vallies [sic] or rather ravines of the Alps ... bordered by enormous precipices of limestone, ... veiled with pine forests of enormous extent."[2] Fourteen years later, on 12 July 1849, once again wanting to inspect the mountain cascades of the Arve valley, he revealed how he had gone down "after breakfast to Maglans, and found my torrent bed entirely dried up. Much vexed but did what I could." He continued that morning on foot past the Cascade d'Arpenaz, which was similarly "reduced to a thread," but then went on to notice that there was a series of "horizontal cleavages or steps," and also "an overhanging ledge near the bottom of the great leap, right across the rocks, making a great fault or fissure there."[3] Ruskin here appears to be describing the very landscape observed in the present two drawings: strips of quartz rest like ribbons across the left-hand foreground and the rock forms seem to take the shape of steps and a ledge overlooking a gaping void.

Ruskin had a particular love of ravines and clefts, cut by the action of mountain torrents and incising themselves upon a larger landscape softened and smoothed externally by the motion of ancient glaciers. It was his instinct to peer downward into the shadowy depths of these naturally occurring vessels to search for water flowing within and to study the textures of the chamber walls. In the darker of the two drawings, just a glimpse of daylight, casting from the east through a fringe of shrubs, appears at the top of the composition. In its pair – which shows the same location but from slightly further back, as may be judged from the identical bars of quartz running at right angles to the cleft (and which in the second drawing may be understood to have once formed a continuum with another section on the right side, since broken by the carving of the ravine by the cascade) – the darkness of the ravine shows strongly against the sunlit surfaces of the surrounding rock.

Is it absurd to suggest that Ruskin, who had no experience of shared physical love, found himself subliminally attracted to the forms of rocks and ravines, which may have been in some way suggestive to him? Was his instinct to look deeply into and explore and have knowledge of these cavities a reflex led by anxieties and desires connected with his unconsummated marriage? He had married Effie Gray in April 1848, but for reasons in part to do with her irritation at the interference in their relationship by his parents, it had been agreed that she would spend the summer of 1849 with her family in Scotland and not travel to the Alps with the Ruskins. In her absence, and with undoubted feelings of romantic affection, Ruskin wrote letters that make clear that he desired her physically and that he hoped that they would consummate their marriage on his return.[4] These two drawings may provide clues to the pattern of his thoughts in her absence. In October of that year Ruskin and Effie went to Venice together, but still without achieving a complete sexual relationship.

This was a time in Ruskin's life when his neurotic symptoms and feelings of isolation might still be reconciled or propitiated by the simple pleasures that he took from the study of nature. At the same time, however, so deep was his engagement with the physical world that he came to count upon the emotional stimulus rewarded him from what he saw and often found himself overtaken by despondency if a place did not meet his expectations, or if his own responsiveness to it was less than intense. Thus, in a letter written to his father from Venice in 1851, he continued to dwell upon his experiences in Savoy two years previously, finding analogy with "the land of Uz, in which Job lived," and which he believed might be "exactly that which would occur to a man living in such a place as the valley of St. Martin's." He went on to stress that he was "disappointed in the autumn when I went to look for my favourite spring at Maglans, that comes out of the limestone strong enough to turn a mill, and there was nothing but the dry stones;" for the waters that had flowed there with energy and force and that had been exhilarating to Ruskin were in fact "snow waters"[5] rather than something constant and integral to the mechanisms of the landscape.

As Stephen Wildman has recently determined,[6] the larger of the two present drawings was presumably made before the motif, while the smaller, which is worked in ink and wash over an etched line, seems likely to have been made after Ruskin's return to London. This conclusion is reinforced by the degree of pictorial dramatization in the latter work – as in for example the cast of light through the group of pine trees at the upper centre of the composition – and darkening for effect. Whether he had in mind to use the subject as an illustration to a written text or was simply experimenting with the reinterpretation and transfer of what he had seen into an alternative medium is not clear. The complexity of technique and the intensity of the resulting image are extraordinary and a testament to Ruskin's inventiveness in the handling of materials.

NOTES

1 Ruskin 1956, vol. 2, p. 408.
2 Ibid., vol. 1, p. 11.
3 Ibid., pp. 408–409.
4 Ruskin and Effie's relationship from the time of their marriage to their departure for Venice is described in detail by Mary Lutyens in the chapter "Prelude to Venice" in Lutyens 1965, pp. 3–40.
5 Ruskin 1903–12, vol. 12, *Lectures on Architecture and Painting, Etc.*, p. 105, note 2.
6 Conversation with the author.

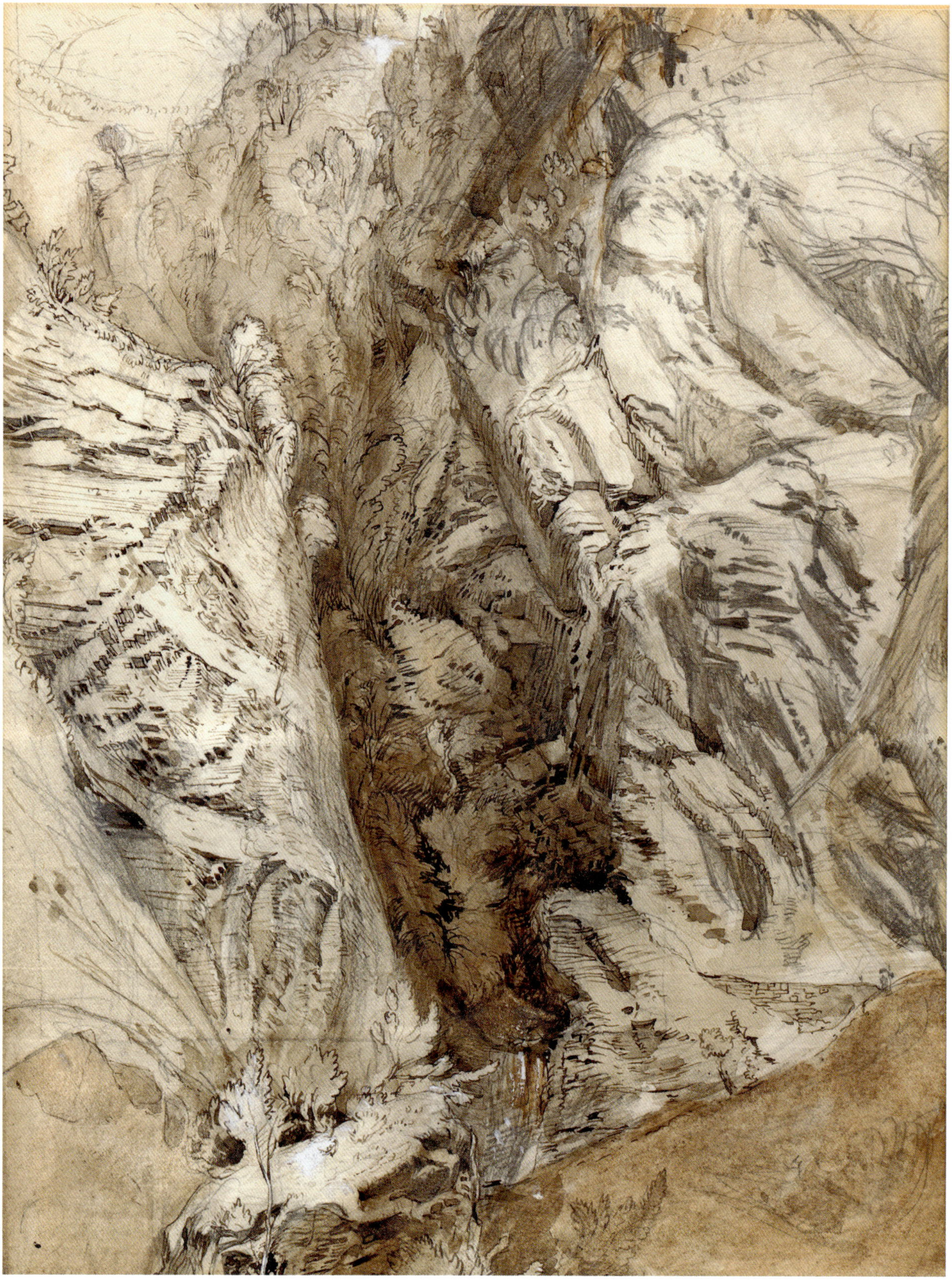

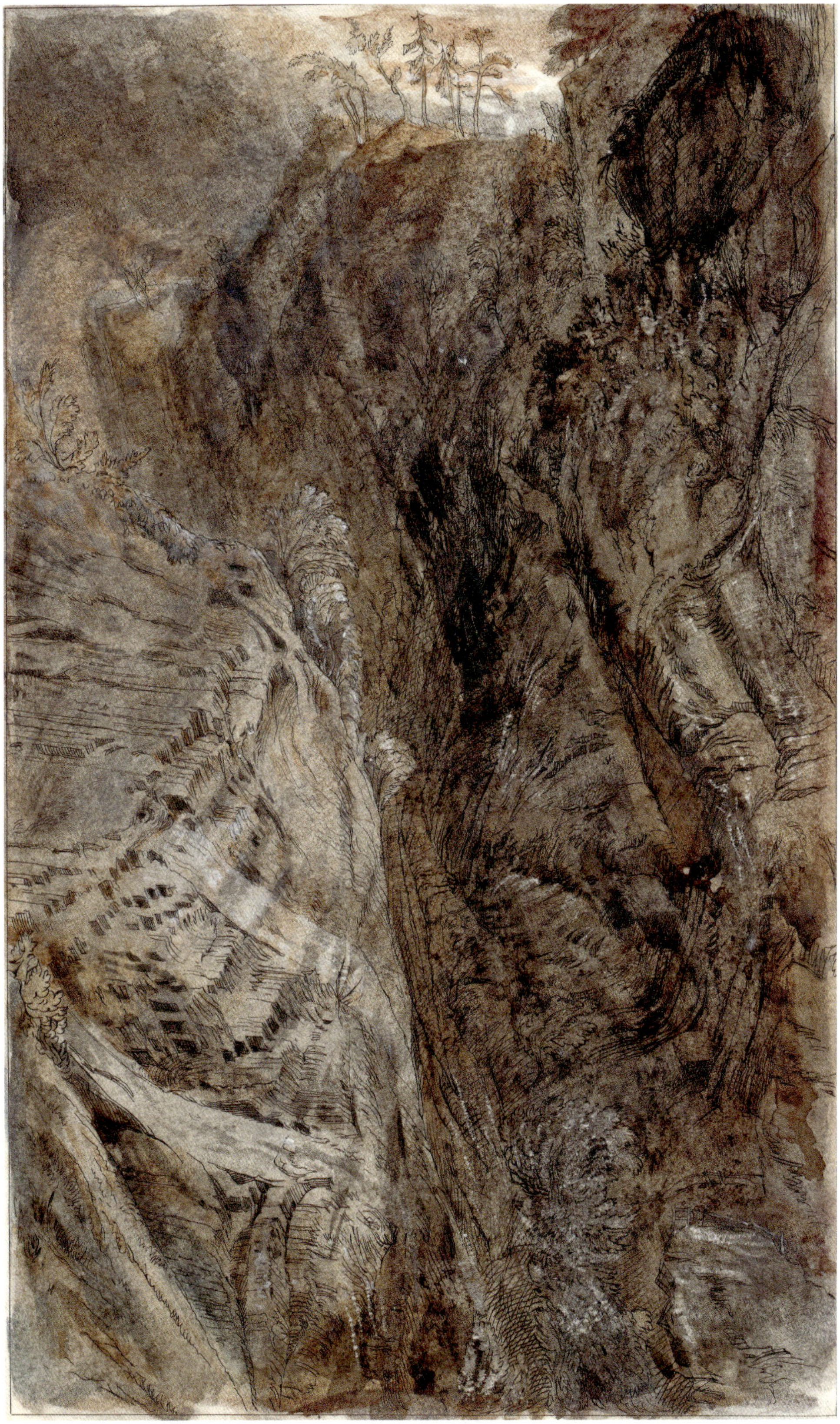

75

Study of Boulders 1850s

Watercolour on paper; 13.6 × 20.3 cm
Private collection

The extraordinary sense of volume of the boulders that are strewn across this sheet and the reduction of the wider landscape in which they stand to a mere calligraphy of stylized pen-work indicating foliage and tree stems at the upper right suggest a date in the 1850s, but whether this is a setting found in Scotland or the Alps is impossible to determine.

Ruskin was fascinated by the consistency of natural materials regardless of their size. In his early text *The Poetry of Architecture*, issued in 1838, he described seeing the same "character of outline" in a "piece of stone 3 in. in diameter" and "a mountain of the same material 6000 ft. high,"[1] while in a famous passage in the chapter "Resulting Forms: – Fifthly, Stones" in the fourth volume of *Modern Painters* he sought to focus the reader's attention upon "the stone under his foot," on the grounds that "there are no natural objects out of which more can be ... learned than out of stones," and to which the reader was recommended to give "some reverence and watchfulness, [as] there is bread of thought in it, more than any other lowly feature of all the landscape." This was because, he believed, "a stone, when it is examined, will be found a mountain in miniature," into which nature "can compress as many changes of form and structure, on a small scale, as she needs for her mountains on a large one."[2] In the case of the present drawing, because there is almost no yardstick of relative size offered, the viewer is left with no clear sense of whether these rocks are mere pebbles lying in a stream bed and observed at a range of a few feet or instead massive volumes of stone.

Ruskin's inspection of the physical world, which had once brought him joy and delight, started to cause him distress in the course of the 1850s. Instead of viewing the processes of physical geography as evidence of a benign and ordered providence, he came to fear that they signalled corruption and desolation. In the penultimate chapter of the fourth volume of *Modern Painters*, entitled "The Mountain Gloom," he unleashed a baleful warning to the effect that the physical world was ungoverned by any divinity and that it was only incidentally the home of man. In 1875 he ended a letter to Susan Beever with the sad account of the "crushing and depressing effect on me, of what I learn day by day as I work on, of the cruelty and ghastliness of the *Nature* I used to think so divine."[3]

NOTES

1 Ruskin 1903–12, vol. 1, *Early Prose Writings*, p. 48.
2 Ruskin 1903–12, vol. 6, *Modern Painters IV*, p. 368.
3 Ruskin 1903–12, vol. 37, *The Letters of John Ruskin, 1870–1889*, p. 154.

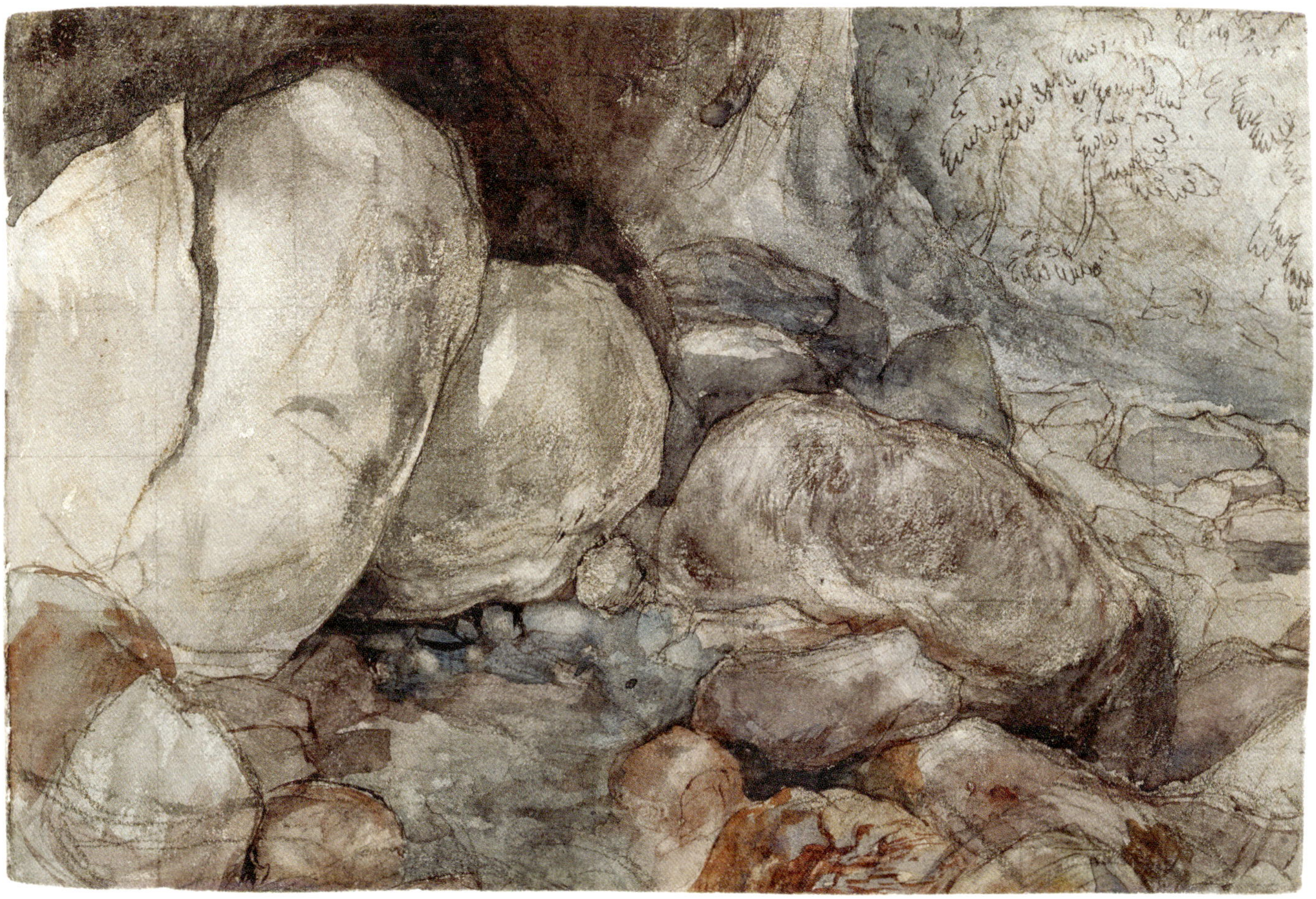

76

Study of Gneiss Rock, Glenfinlas 1853–54

Lampblack, bodycolour and pen and ink over graphite on wove paper with some scratching out; 47.8 × 32.7 cm
The Ashmolean Museum, Oxford. Presumably presented by John Ruskin to the Ruskin Drawing School (University of Oxford), where it was first recorded in 1906 (WA.RS.REF.089)

One of Ruskin's most famous and admired drawings, *Study of Gneiss Rock, Glenfinlas* shows a view of exposed rock surfaces within the ravine in which flows the Finglas Water in the Trossachs in the Scottish Highlands. It was made during the period when he and a party of friends, including the Pre-Raphaelite painter John Everett Millais, stayed at Brig o' Turk in the summer and autumn of 1853, which led to Millais' portrait of Ruskin (fig. 2.5). Both the portrait and the present drawing show a spot about a kilometre north of the village where the burn turns in its course, with a steep bank of exposed stone on the west side (see fig. 6.2).[1] The two works were under way in early August, as Ruskin explained in a letter to his father written on the fourth of the month: "We had a glorious day to-day, quite quiet and fine – and I think the picture will be peculiarly beautiful because there is no *sun* in it; all dark rocks with plants hanging down over them and the foaming water below – [while] I am drawing part of the rocks close to him and Effie [Ruskin's wife Euphemia, later to be married to Millais] reads to us, or draws separate plants and flowers."[2]

A month later, in a letter to Pauline Trevelyan, Ruskin described both the place and the working routine that he and Millais had adopted. The mornings were spent in writing and sketching, "until about 12 oclock when the sun is right for his picture ... we all go out to the place where he is painting – a beautiful piece of Torrent bed overhung by honeysuckle & mountain ash – and he sets to work on one jutting bit of rock – and I go on with mine."[3] Although Ruskin informed Lady Trevelyan that he intended to use his drawing as an illustration for the projected third volume of *Modern Painters*,[4] it is tempting to suppose that an ulterior purpose in making it was to demonstrate to Millais the careful attention to geological fact that he wished to be incorporated into the background of the portrait; Ruskin's drawing corresponds to an area of the oil painting at the far left side and in which is found a matching pattern of undulating veins. That Ruskin felt that he had to set a standard of pictorial minuteness to Millais is indicated by his remark in a letter to his friend Frederick J. Furnivall, written on 16 October: "I have stopped all this time to keep Millais company – to keep him up to the Pre-Raphaelite degree of finish – which I have done with a vengeance, as he has taken three months to do half a background two feet over, and perhaps won't finish it now. But I have got maps of all the lichens on the rocks, and the *bubbles* painted in the foam."[5]

The rock face that Ruskin drew is still clearly recognizable in the landscape, and a comparison of the drawing and the actual spot allows one to evaluate his intentions in giving absolute verisimilitude in his representation of a geological type. Furthermore, and although it was observed at a range of just a couple of yards, a sense is given of the larger environment.

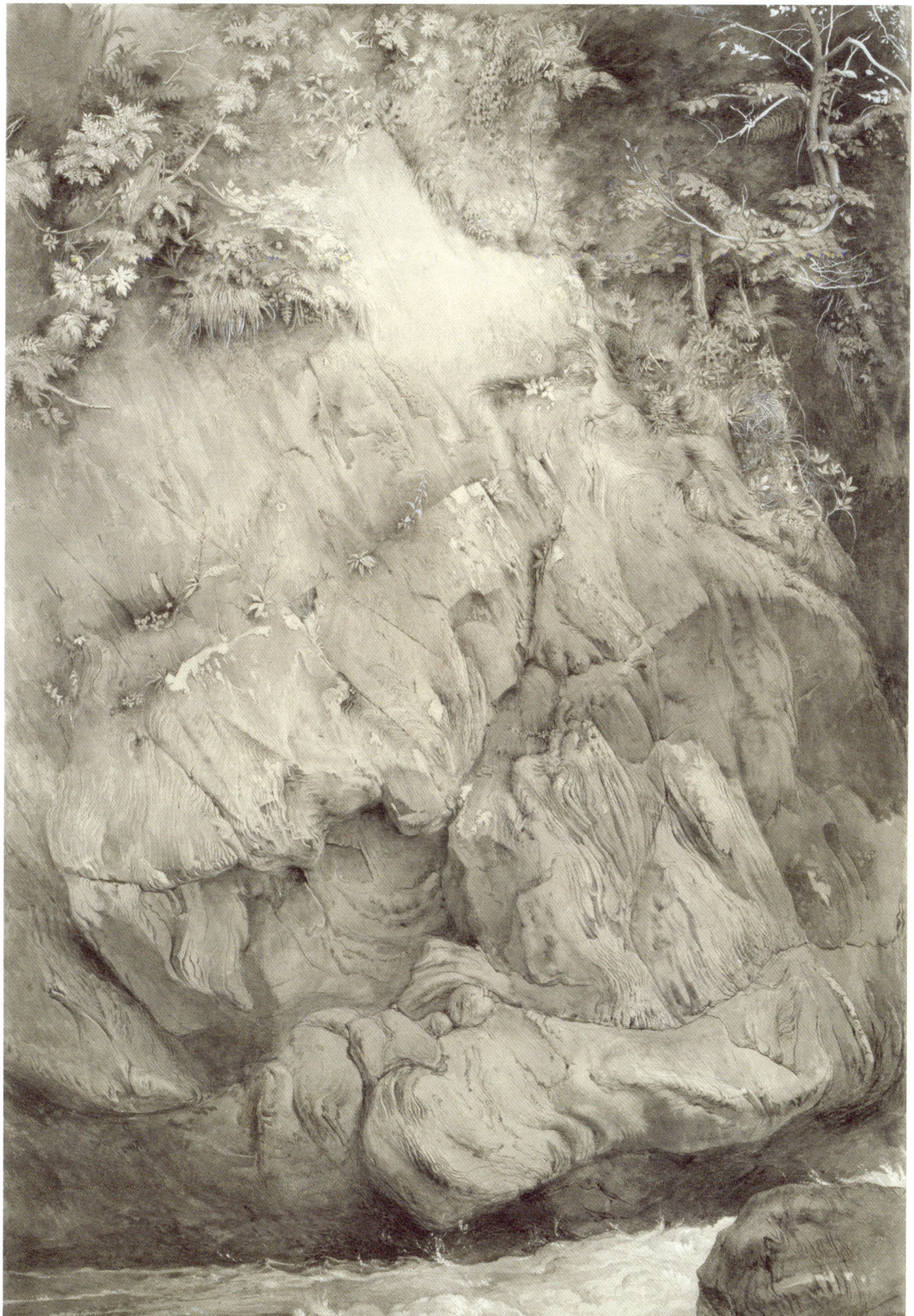

FIG. 6.2
View of Rock Formation on the Glen Finglas, March 2013
Photograph by Christopher Newall

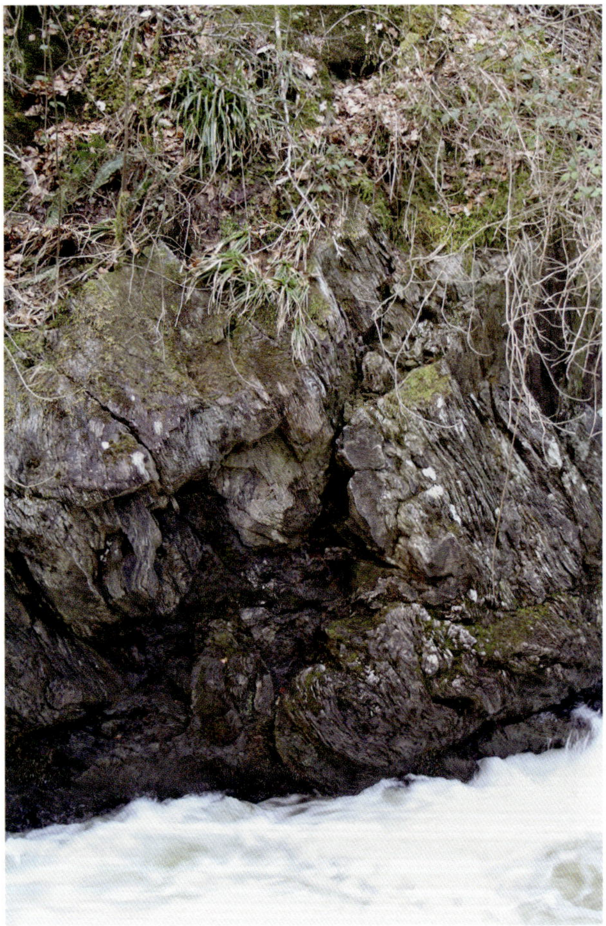

In fact, the drawing may be seen as a landscape in microcosm rather than some kind of diagrammatic representation of a geological specimen undertaken for scientific record. In Ruskin's mind, any element of the physical world – however closely observed – was part of an infinitely larger setting and should be seen as organically related to all else.

Although Millais' portrait and Ruskin's drawing were both determinedly dependent on an exact location, each was in fact completed away from the motif – thus in some sense contradicting the essential principle of Pre-Raphaelitism, stated by Ruskin in his Edinburgh lecture of 18 November 1853, which was one "of absolute, uncompromising truth in all that it does, obtained by working everything, down to the most minute detail, from nature, and from nature only."[6] Bad weather and shortening days in the autumn of 1853 prevented Millais from finishing the portrait that season, and so the canvas was taken back to London. The following spring, the watercolourist and Pre-Raphaelite associate George Price Boyce suggested that Millais might find similar rock formations from which to paint the background at Capel Curig in North Wales. Ruskin was not having this, however, and as Millais quoted him in a letter to Furnivall, Ruskin insisted that the rocks were "of quite a different Strata there."[7] The painter was therefore forced to make the long journey back to Scotland the following May, spending a further month on the background. Ruskin expected Millais to paint the setting of the portrait directly from the motif and in an absolutely literal way, even if the figure might be permitted simply to be blocked into the composition and then added in his London studio. As Ruskin wrote in the fourth volume of *Modern Painters*, "not a line is to be altered, not a stick nor stone removed, not a colour deepened, not a form improved; the picture is to be, as far as possible, the reflection of a place in a mirror; and the artist to consider himself only as a sensitive and skilful reflector."[8]

As regards Ruskin's own drawing, it was – according to a diary entry of 8 February 1854 – finished in London, so that many years later, in his description of it when exhibited at the Fine Art Society, he considered that it had "had a chance of being finished, but the weather broke," and for this reason "the stems in the upper righthand corner had to be rudely struck in with body-colour."[9] Nonetheless, Ruskin's Glen Finglas drawing, even though by his own admission completed away from the motif, has within it such an extraordinary degree of exactitude that it may be regarded as the defining achievement of the principle of "truth to nature."

Frequent references in Ruskin's writings as well as a number of drawings give evidence of the particular fascination he felt for the way in which the strata of gneiss rock tends to describe a swirling pattern, seeing in such shapes indications of the very processes by which the physical world was created and evidence of universal laws of nature. In the chapter "Slaty Crystallines" in the fourth volume of *Modern Painters*, he warned the reader that he was tempted to "devote half a volume to a description of the fantastic and incomprehensible arrangements."[10] The geomorphic rocks – ancient igneous materials that had been transformed chemically and physically by intense heat and pressure – revealed their extraordinary histories, it seemed to him, by the contorted shapes that they assumed and that were visible in places where erosion had exposed their strata. He understood that the geological processes that any specific part of the landscape had undergone were unique and that the patterns and textures that were to be observed in natural forms were particular to that precise environment and should be regarded as a kind of coded system of identification of that place.

Of all rocks, gneiss was Ruskin's favourite and that which to him most clearly – in the texture of the quartz and feldspar and the patterning of bands of mica and amphibole – suggested the nature of the transformation that it had undergone. His fascination with the differences between superficially similar rock types led him to compare examples from location to location, so that for instance he might point the contrast between "the gneissitic schists of Chamouni [which] are all rectilinear; [while] those of Val d'Aoste and the Black Forest are coiled like knots of passionate snakes."[11] Ruskin found a seething vitality in the inorganic elements of nature, which seemed to be energized by the fission that had formed the landscape, and which were for him fearsome as well as thrilling.

NOTES

1 The most useful and complete account of the circumstances that led to Millais' portrait, and the first published identification of the exact spot in Glen Finglas where the portrait was made, is in Alastair Grieve's article "Ruskin and Millais at Glenfinlas" (Grieve 1996, pp. 228–234).
2 Lutyens 1967, p. 77.
3 Ruskin 1979, p. 57.
4 Ibid.
5 Ruskin 1903–12, vol. 12, *Lectures on Architecture and Painting, Etc.*, p. xxiv.
6 Ibid., p. 157.
7 John Everett Millais, quoted in Lutyens 1967, p. 215.
8 Ruskin 1903–12, vol. 6, *Modern Painters IV*, p. 31.
9 Ruskin 1903–12, vol. 13, *Turner, The Harbours of England, Catalogues and Notes*, p. 524.
10 Ruskin 1903–12, vol. 6, p. 150.
11 Ruskin 1903–12, vol. 26, *Deucalion and Other Studies in Rocks and Stones*, p. 30.

77

The Rocky Bank of a River 1853 (?)

Pen and black ink, grey wash, graphite and white gouache on cream wove paper; 32.5 × 47.3 cm
Yale Center for British Art, New Haven. Paul Mellon Fund (B1984.13)

Neither the date nor the location represented in the present drawing of eroded rock and vegetation at the edge of an upland stream is securely established. The principal elements of the subject and its angle and range of vision are however entirely characteristic of Ruskin's approach to landscape in the late 1840s and 1850s. The volumetric treatment of the stone is analogous to that seen in his Crossmount drawings of 1847 (cats. 71 and 72), and there is an obvious common interest in the boundary between rock and water, as demonstrated in the two Scottish tours of 1853 and 1857. Robert Hewison has noticed that the sheet is the same size as that used for *Study of Gneiss Rock, Glenfinlas* (cat. 76).[1] A closer comparison of the types of paper of each drawing might therefore show whether the sheets came from the same batch, and might further support a dating of 1853 for the present work.

Ruskin's method of drawing here is in fact entirely personal and of his own devising. The forms of the landscape are built up from a laminate of washes placed over rapidly drawn pen lines, achieving the flux of detailed observation and looming indefiniteness that is so characteristic of his draftsmanship. Paul Walton has described drawings of this type, which may be regarded as "essentially 'foreground studies,' where tree trunks and branches form flowing arabesques interwoven with the contours of rock and cloud, nervously outlined by the pen in flat patterns of considerable decorative elegance. Yet the effect is not simply decorative, for there is a flame-like agitation in the rhythm of pen and brush stroke that conveys intense emotional excitement."[2]

NOTES

1 London 2000, p. 163.
2 Walton 1972, pp. 58–60.

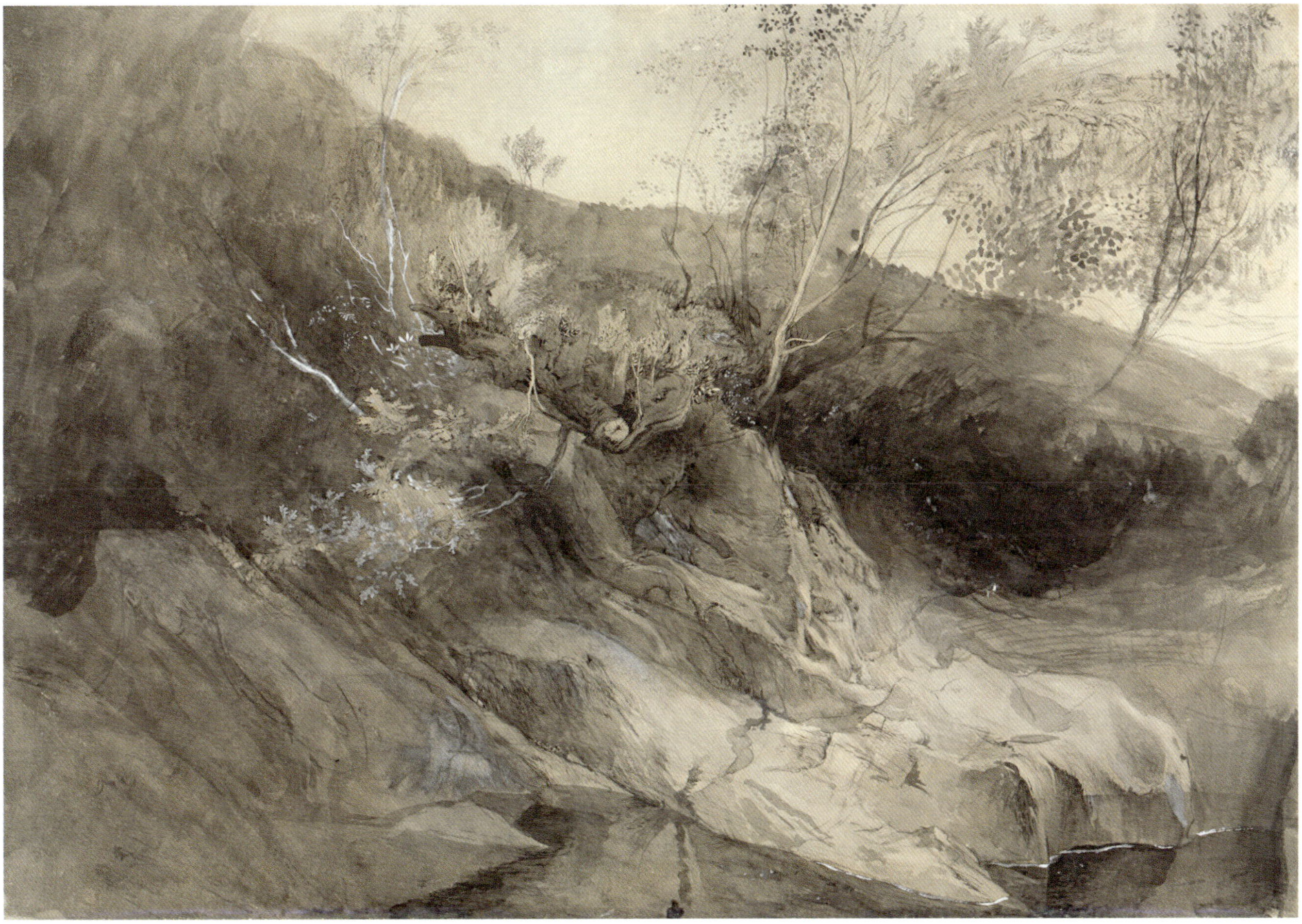

78

Gorge at Ardon 1854

Graphite and watercolour on white paper; 18 × 22 cm
Ruskin Foundation (Ruskin Library, Lancaster University) (RF 863)
Inscriptions: brown ink, *Ardon 1854 / Notebook 15, p 54*

Ardon is a village just to the north of Champagnole on the western flank of the Jura Mountains. Ruskin was there at the beginning of June 1854, and again in September, on the outward and return journeys of an expedition to the Alps with his parents. In this period he was contemplating new ventures and objects of research – notably the Swiss towns project – but also found himself in a despondent mood, the inevitable consequence at least in part of the failure of his marriage and the humiliation of its annulment, which was granted on 15 July. Diary entries from that season alternate between meditations on Biblical texts, the usefulness or otherwise of art, and occasional assaults on the practices of the Roman Catholic Church.

He also made frequent notations on the geological character of the places he was passing through and drew the landscape in an attempt to understand it. From Martigny, on 12 September 1854, he wrote of his frustration in trying to draw in a way that would serve as a geological record: "I never felt the ineffable difficulty of drawing hill outline so much ... The whole upper surface of these rocks is rounded by the glaciers, traversed by magnificent sweeps of striae ... The whole of the limestone above the ravine at Ardon is striated also, showing that the glaciers have poured over these shoulders of the hills into the valley of the Rhône itself one vast torrent of ice."[1] The present drawing seems to show the smoothed surfaces of the exposed rock, but scoured across by the action of boulders lodged in the under surfaces of the ice and deeply cut by the torrential flow of mountain cascades.

Ruskin was at this time a man of Christian faith, but also one who was devoted to science. The study of geology had made rapid advances since about 1820, and with this came an understanding of the landscape in terms of processes of uplift, erosion and deposition, as well as the establishment of an order for rock forms. By the middle of the nineteenth century there was a general acceptance that the earth's history was enormously long, even on the part of Protestant churchmen who had come to understand the Creation as a metaphor rather than a factual account. Three years earlier, anticipating the religious doubts that would assail him in the second half of the 1850s, leading to his "un-conversion" in 1859, Ruskin had answered his friend Henry Acland: "You speak of the Flimsiness of your own faith. Mine, which was never strong, is being beaten into mere gold leaf, and flutters in weak rags from the letter of its old forms ... If only the Geologists would let me alone, I could do very well, but those dreadful Hammers! I hear the clink of them at the end of every cadence of the Bible verses."[2]

NOTES

1 Ruskin 1956, vol. 2, pp. 509–510.
2 Ruskin 1903–12, vol. 36, *The Letters of John Ruskin, 1827–1869*, p. 115.

79

JOHN RUSKIN AND FREDERICK CRAWLEY

a. *Gorge at Ardon* 1854

Daguerreotype (half plate); 11.5 × 15.5 cm (sight)
Ruskin Foundation (Ruskin Library, Lancaster University) (RF Dag 76)

b. *Gorge at Ardon* 1854

Daguerreotype (half plate); 11.5 × 15.5 cm (sight)
Ruskin Foundation (Ruskin Library, Lancaster University) (RF Dag 78)

These two daguerreotypes are part of a series made for or by Ruskin, almost certainly in the course of his 1854 Alpine tour, and have been recognized as views of the exposed limestone cliffs at Ardon. The photographs that he brought back at the end of the trip are complementary to the drawings he made of the mountains and rock formations (see, for instance, cat. 78) and were regarded as especially valuable as records of geological type.

Although in the paragraph in his diary headed "Notes on Ravine at Ardon," he described the landscapes in the two photographs and opined, "looking down from the ridge on which I stood to the valley, a plunge of at least three thousand feet ... the magnitude of the landscape soon ceases to be impressive,"[1] the clarity and yet strangeness of the photographed landscape nonetheless makes them compelling. Each shows a bulbous headland of limestone with a vertical or overhanging cliff dropping down into a deep hollow. Bright sunshine irradiates over the rock surfaces causing deep shadows to reveal the crevices and contours of the eroded stone, while a bar of differently coloured sedimentary rock, or perhaps an extrusion of quartz running through the bedrock, may clearly be seen.

NOTES

1 Ruskin 1956, vol. 2, p. 507.

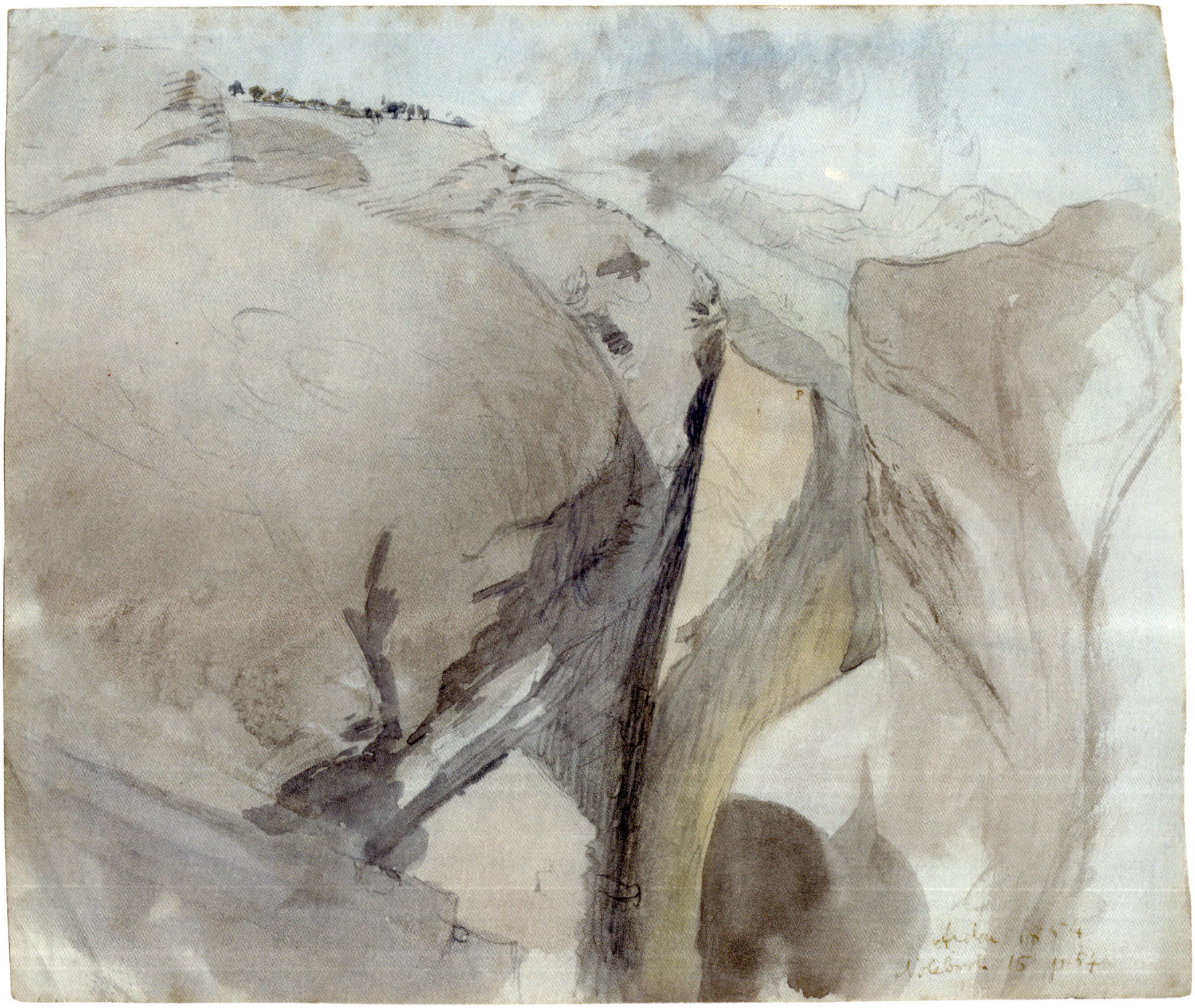

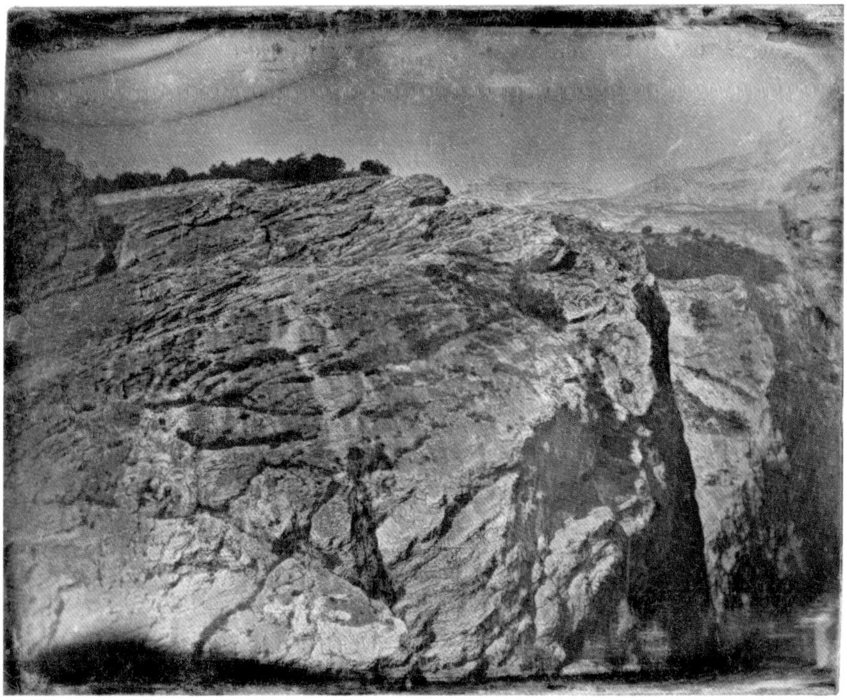

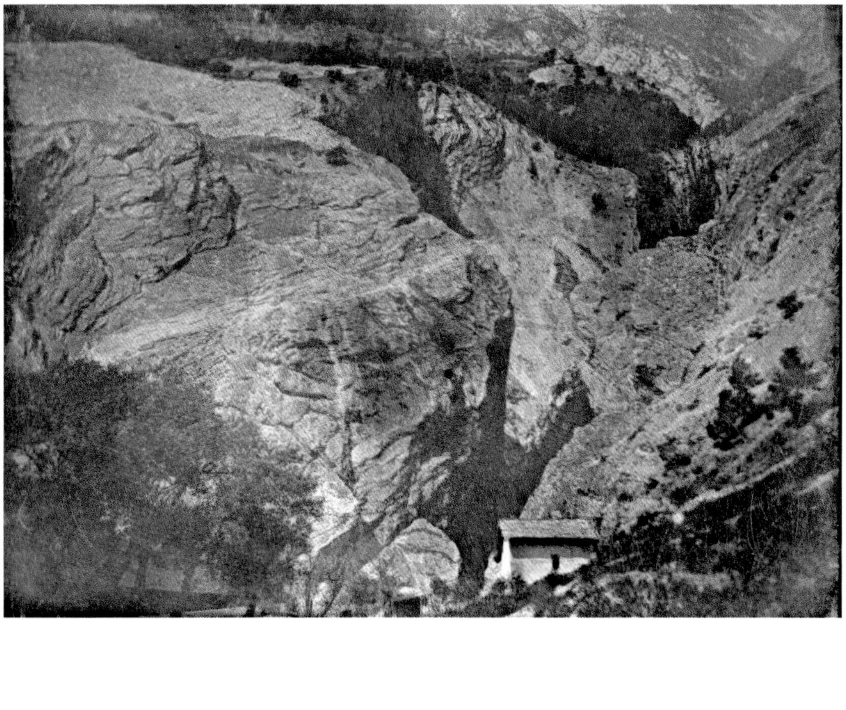

80

Chamouni: Rocks and Vegetation 1854

Watercolour, graphite and bodycolour on paper; 25.2 × 26.7 cm
Courtesy of Abbot Hall Art Gallery, Lakeland Arts Trust, Kendal, Cumbria, UK (AH1133/73)

This drawing of a boulder, with a mere glimpse of sky and foreground grass to suggest the wider landscape, is possibly identical to the study that Ruskin exhibited at the Fine Art Society in 1878 as *Old Sketch of Gneiss, with its Weeds, in Colour (Chamouni)*. If so, it may be more precisely dated to the fortnight he spent in Savoy in July 1854 and serves as a reminder of the special place that Chamonix had in his intellectual and emotional life. In a diary entry of 10 July, Ruskin recorded his return there: "Thank God, here once more; and feeling it more deeply than ever. I have been up to my stone on the Bréven, all unchanged and happy."[1] On 25 July, prior to his departure, a longer description serves to demonstrate the parallel mechanisms of observation and poetic metaphor with which he responded to the landscape:

> My farewell evening for this time. It is a soft starlight night, Mont Blanc lying just like a white vapour, with a film of cloud on it; the whole heavens shaking with sheet lightning, and the stars quivering as if every flash shook them like magnetic needles, and they could not get quiet again before the last one; the light for the most part filling the heavens from side to side as with a liquid wave, but now and then flowing out in distinct flame from behind a fish-shaped cloud in the south west, the snow seen by it indistinctly opposite, like answering flashes.[2]

The present watercolour is confusing to look at, and there has been uncertainty as to which way up it should be placed. If the area of blue bodycolour that stands for the sky goes at the upper right, the boulder may be recognized as of the type referred to by geologists as *roche moutonnée* – i.e. with an upper surface smoothed by the flow of ice and a rougher undercut flank made irregular by the plucking action of the ice flow.

NOTES

1 Ruskin 1956, vol. 2, p. 498.
2 Ibid., p. 499.

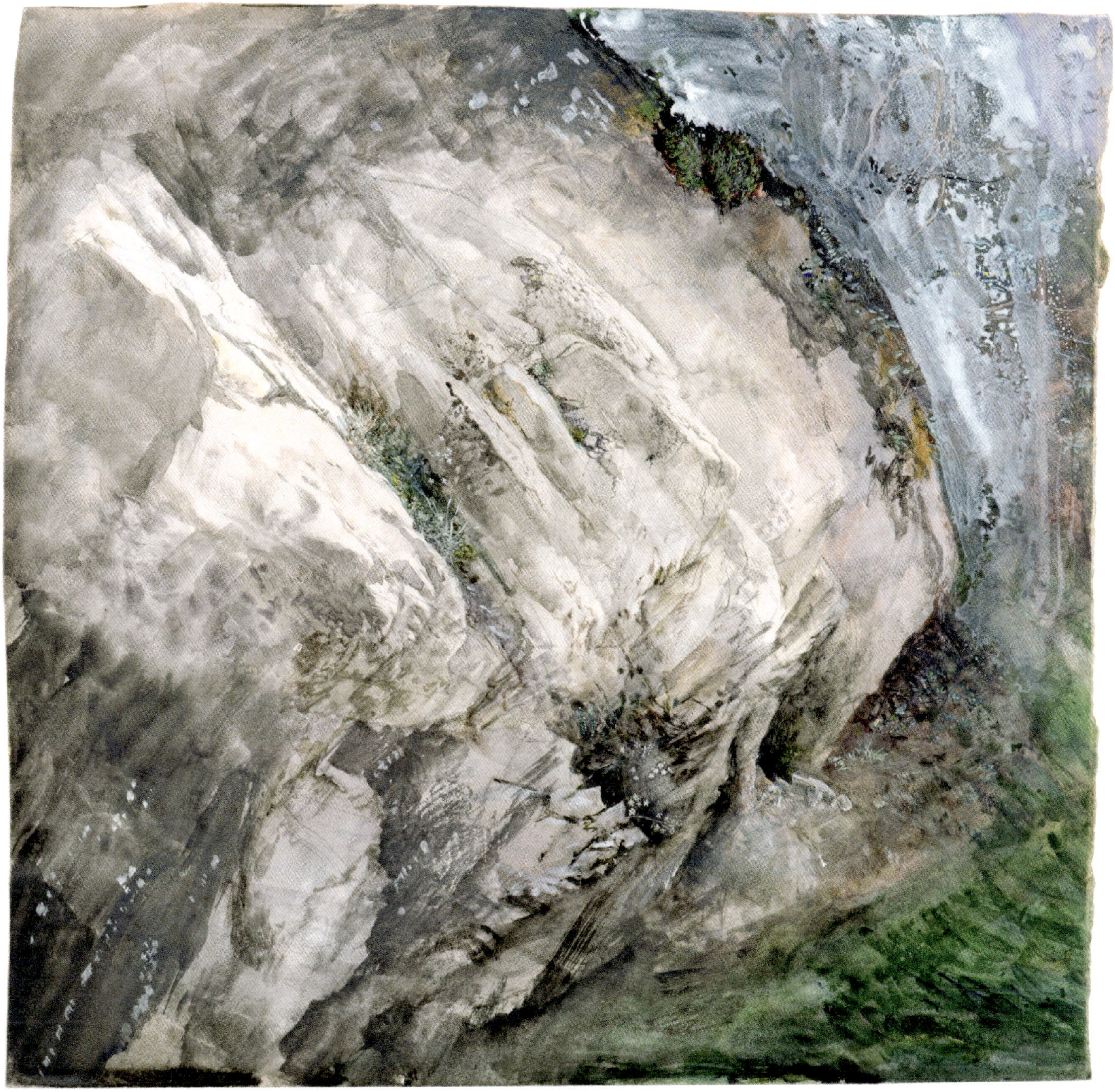

81

In the Pass of Killiecrankie 1857

Watercolour and bodycolour on board; 28.7 × 24.7 cm
The Fitzwilliam Museum, Cambridge (1589)
Inscriptions: old back-board, label, ink with brush, *In Pass of Killiecrankie / J.R. 1857*
(Scotland venue only)

Among the most celebrated and best known of Ruskin's drawings, *In the Pass of Killiecrankie* stands as a whole, and artistically committed, work of art. The composition is complete to its edges, with its upper and lower right corners offering glimpses through woodland toward distant mountains and a surface of water reflecting the blue of the sky. As Allen Staley has written, "detailed observation is incorporated into a pictorial whole, [as drawings of this kind] show considerably more ambition in the use of colour and in the treatment of space [and as such] ... represent the height of Ruskin's pictorial ambitions."[1] Completeness of this kind is most unusual in Ruskin's work, causing him to confess in *Præterita* his "childish delight in beginning a drawing; and usually acute misery in trying to finish one."[2] The watercolour stands as an example of what might be aimed for by an artist committed to carrying works forward to their logical conclusion, and may be linked with the publication in the same year of the fourth volume of *Modern Painters*, in which Ruskin described different types of mountain landscape as they might be treated by artists. It may also serve to illustrate the main thesis of *The Elements of Drawing*, in which he laid out a course of instruction for would-be painters, imploring students to look for abstract principles of beauty in the forms of nature and to take delight in the infinite variety and constant fluctuation of all aspects of the landscape.

In the Pass of Killiecrankie was drawn during the Scottish tour that Ruskin and his parents made between July and October 1857. The place itself, which lies between Blair Atholl and Pitlochry, was familiar to travellers approaching the main body of the Highlands from Perth and the southeast, and was known for its beauty but also as a formidable obstacle. Although it seems likely that the view was taken at the point where the river Garry narrows between steep and rocky banks – known as the Soldier's Leap (in memory of the escape of Donald MacBean from the pursuing highlanders of the army of James Graham, Viscount of Dundee, after the Battle of Killiecrankie on 27 July 1689, during the first Jacobite uprising) – no indication is given of the wider topographical setting or its historical associations.

Very few of Ruskin's drawings were exhibited in his lifetime, the majority being put away and taken little account of. *In the Pass of Killiecrankie* was, however, shown on two occasions at the Dudley Gallery in London in the early 1880s and again several times after Ruskin's death.

NOTES

1 Staley 2001, p. 209.
2 Ruskin 1903–12, vol. 35, *Præterita and Dilecta*, p. 368.

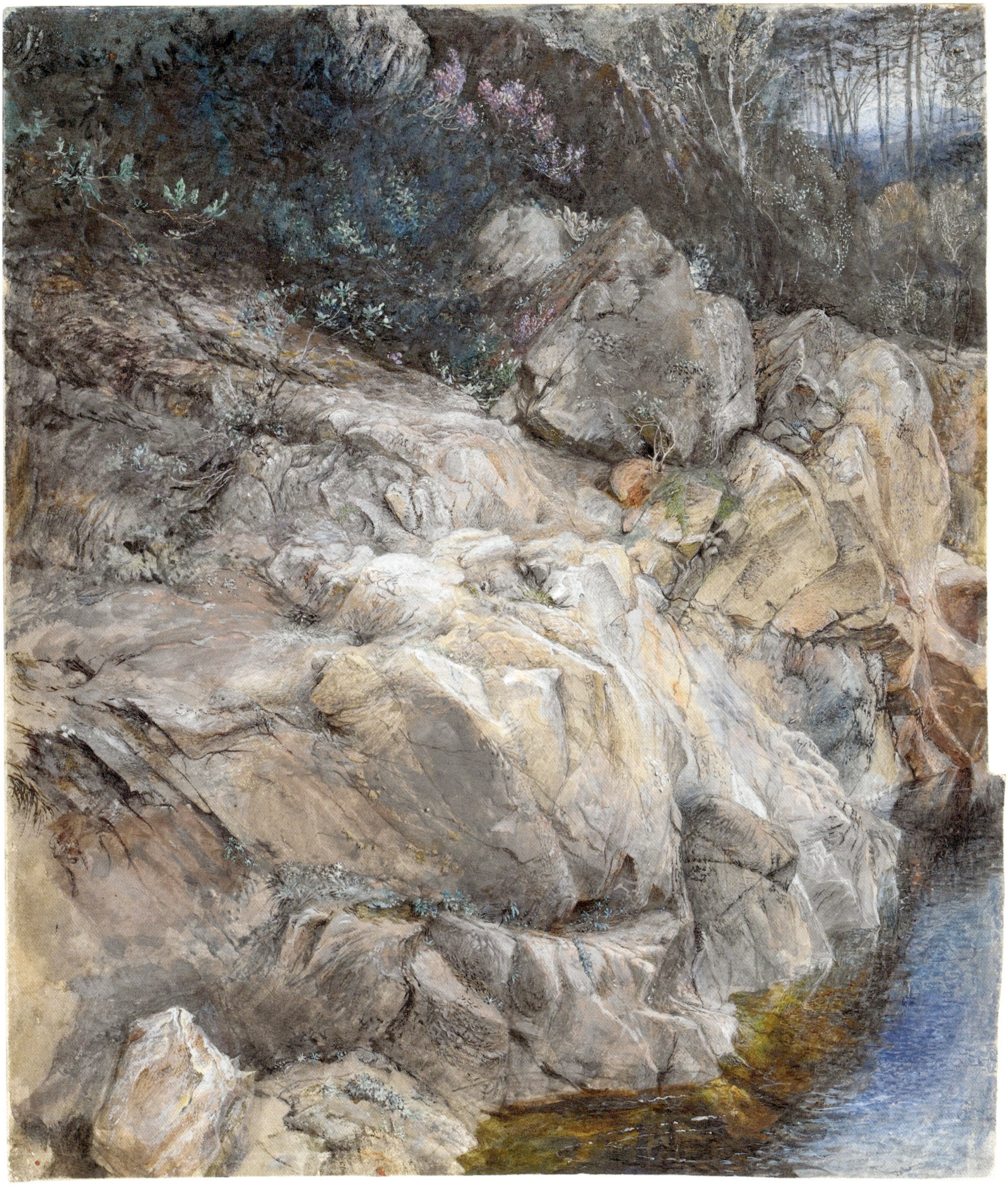

82

View of a Cliff-side with Buildings 1861–63

Watercolour over graphite on paper; 25.7 × 36.2 cm
Private collection
Inscriptions: graphite, *espalier / vines, grand* [?] *many* [?] *rock steps*

Offering an extraordinary instance of how Ruskin perceived the landscape as a mosaic of points of detail – observed with scrupulous attention – but existing within a flux of seething texture and resonant colour, the present drawing is entirely personal to him and offers a glimpse of his mentality as a draftsman and as one who responded impulsively to every aspect of the natural setting in which he found himself.

The larger part of the drawn surface appears to show a wide and deep hollow or pit, whether cut out by human agency or, perhaps more likely, occurring naturally by fluvial erosion. The colour of the exposed surfaces of the embrasure – a rich yellow-brown – suggests that the sub-soil here is friable sand or gravel, and one that would be likely to erode rapidly or be subject to landslips, thus placing neighbouring buildings in jeopardy. Along its upper edge there appears to be a wall (blocks of masonry are evident at the point just beneath the tree that is seen as a green ball almost halfway across the width of the sheet). The horizon was intended to show gardens and vineyards (indicated by the words "espalier," "vine" and "rock steps," written by Ruskin in pencil in areas where he has made drawn annotations over an area of grey wash) and a building, which appears as an ochre outline. At the left side there is a white-fronted house with a gable wall with a mullioned window and a grey-tiled roof and a single dormer window. Beyond, even closer to the sheet's left margin, other structures are indicated, with surfaces suggestive of tiling and masonry, but not lending themselves to easy reconstruction. All of the myriad complexity of landscape form is treated with broad sweeping strokes of translucent colour – greens, yellows, soft warm greys, delicate touches of blue – and with pen-work used to make points of definition.

Where it was done and when can only be a matter of speculation. The building on the left is of a type that especially interested Ruskin during his Swiss tours in the early 1860s, when thinking about how the history of that country might be understood in the light of its vernacular architecture. The rolling undulations of the distant landscape and the fact that they are planted with vines and fruit trees (as indicated by the inscriptions) might again support the theory that the place was somewhere in sub-Alpine France, Germany or Switzerland. Ruskin roamed through Switzerland and Germany in 1859, returned to Savoy and Switzerland in 1860, and was again in Chamonix in 1861, on which occasion he conceived the plan to live in Savoy (see cats. 101 and 105).

Ruskin's ideas about the mechanisms of physical geography as operated on the mountain landscape were evolving in this period, and in his June 1863 lecture "On the Forms of the Stratified Alps of Savoy" and a paper issued in 1865 under the title "Notes on the Shape and Structure of Some Parts of the Alps, with Reference to Denudation," he seems to have departed

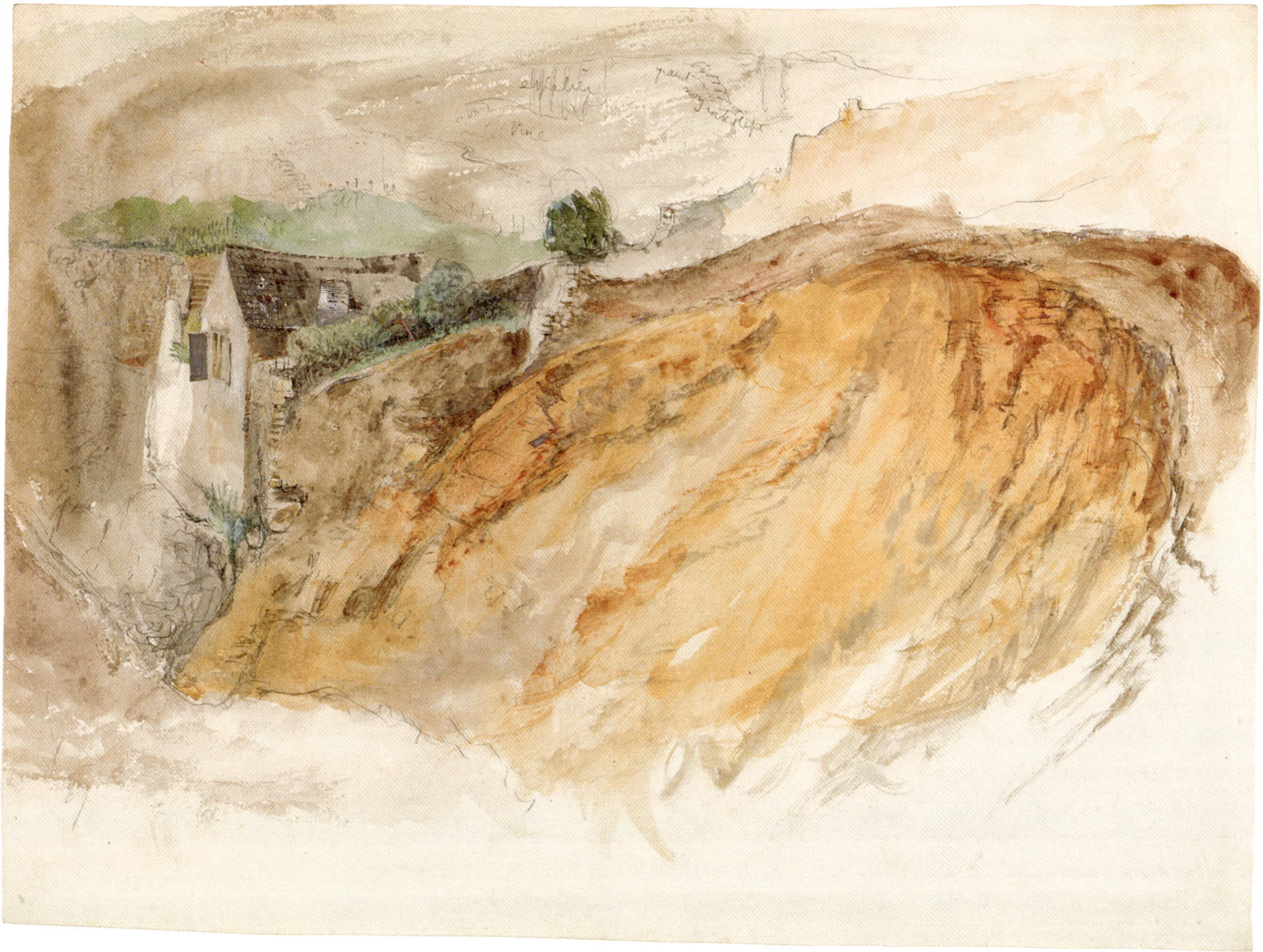

from a belief that the Alpine landscape owed its character principally to the agency of glaciation toward an acceptance that a whole variety of different forces of erosion must be seen to have been constantly in operation. The present drawing, ambiguous and indefinite in its forms though it may be, stands as a witness to Ruskin's mounting sense that all matter was perpetually in a state of physical corruption and facing an inevitable and wholesale disintegration, thus depending upon "accidental circumstances: first on the attractions of the component elements among themselves; secondly, on every change of external temperature and relation. So that mountains are at different periods in different stages of health (so to call it) or disease."[1]

NOTES

1 Ruskin 1903–12, vol. 26, *Deucalion and Other Studies in Rocks and Stones*, p. 4.

83

Study of a Piece of Brick, to Show Cleavage in Burnt Clay c. 1871

Watercolour and bodycolour over graphite on wove paper; 21.9 × 15.4 cm
The Ashmolean Museum, Oxford. Presented by John Ruskin to the Ruskin Drawing School (University of Oxford), 1875 (WA.RS.ED.281)

As Ruskin had on other occasions made careful studies of naturally occurring geological specimens, here he devoted himself to the scrupulous observation of a piece of broken brick. The object of the exercise appears to have been to see how the surfaces of the fired material had gradually become indented and fractured, whether in the course of the destruction of whatever building it might once have been part of or through wear caused by abrasion or exposure to the elements of weather. One surface has been invaded by moss – suggesting that the clay had been penetrated by moisture, leading to its more rapid disintegration. In his inspection of stones or rock formations, or as on this occassion a piece of brick, Ruskin was habitually looking for evidence of how those materials had originated, but also how the processes of erosion operated upon them – with the implication that all matter would eventually fall into formless dust.

The drawing seems to have been done in connection with an extempore discussion that Ruskin made in the course of his February 1871 lecture "Light and Shade," the main theme of which was landscape painting. In a footnote added to the text of the lecture in its published form, Ruskin described how a student had objected to a method of work that depended on meticulous detail and how he had painted the brick to demonstrate how an object or material of any kind might be represented minutely. In addition, he explained that the artistic quality of a drawing was irrelevant to its larger purpose as an exercise in observation. It seems that the present watercolour was itself put on display or passed around within the audience, for the note continues with an instruction: "Here show brick, and note the action of the moss on it and cleavage. The red and brown and green are nothing."[1]

The issue of whether artists should be expected to give closely focused and objective accounts of what lay before them or whether – conversely – it was the painter's prerogative to depart from a supposed reality to achieve an emotionally led evocation of the forms of nature was a game of cat and mouse that Ruskin played with his readers and in his personal relations with artists over many decades. In the fifth volume of *Modern Painters*, he made a distinction between "niggling," by which term of disparagement he meant the "mechanical trick or habit of hand"[2] that led to the working up of textures in drawings so as to suggest close observation of detail and texture but without actual looking, and an objective of truthfulness in finish in which the artist might even with quite broad handling of graphite or colour convey an understanding of the seething actuality of forms in nature.

NOTES

1 Ruskin 1903–12, vol. 22, *Lectures on Landscape, Michael Angelo & Tintoret, The Eagle's Nest, Ariadne Florentina, with Notes for Other Oxford Lectures*, p. 33, note 1.
2 Ruskin 1903–12, vol. 7, *Modern Painters V*, p. 54.

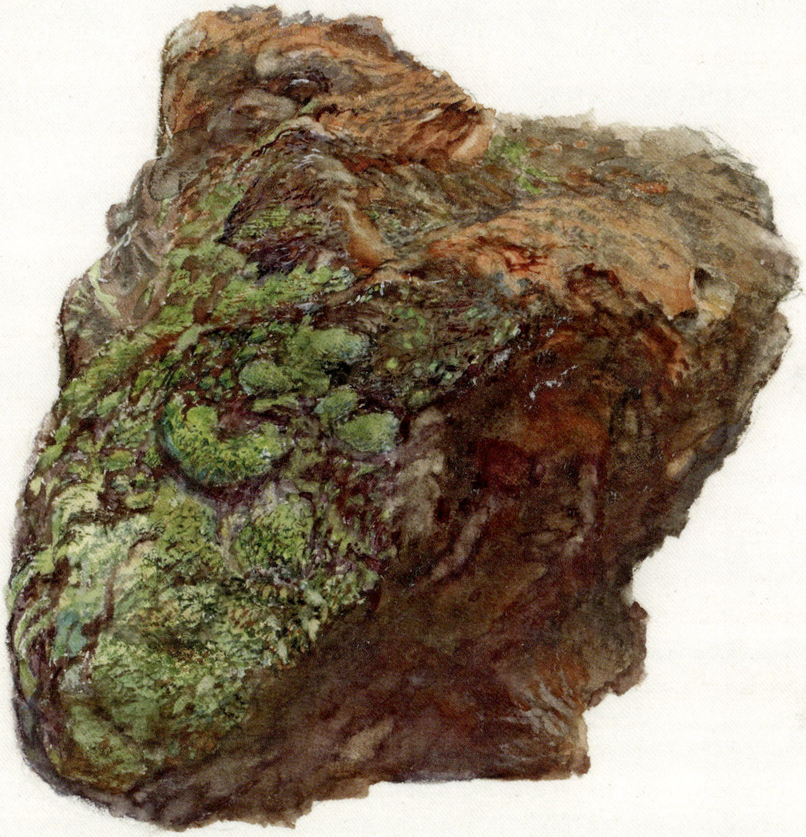

84

Moss and Wild Strawberry 1873 (?)

Graphite and traces of bodycolour on grey-blue paper; 54.1 × 37.6 cm
The Ashmolean Museum, Oxford. Presumably presented by John Ruskin to the Ruskin Drawing School (University of Oxford), where it was first recorded in 1906 (WA.RS.REF.090)

Ruskin had a particular love of wild strawberries, often remarking on them in diary accounts of his Alpine and Scottish rambles and frequently drawing their leaves and observing "the exquisite mode of branching and budding in this flower," as he noted in his commentary on the Educational Series at Oxford. He went on, "I give the strawberry-blossom to Demeter because it is the prettiest type of the uncultured and motherly gifts of the Earth."[1]

The present drawing shows a cleft of rock, from which the delicately shaped leaves of wild strawberry plants peep, their tendrils lying like strands of filigree. Globes of moss grow luxuriantly, while a soft down lies across the triangular surfaces. This drawing exemplifies Ruskin's desire to approach ever more closely to the forms of nature, as if in a desire to embrace the landscape or be subsumed into it. For a man who had no experience of physical love, works of observation of this kind – in which the landscape is seen at a range that suggests that one might extend one's hand to stroke and explore the soft and flowing forms – are both ravishing and beguiling. A drawing that once again seems extraordinarily suggestive of the contours and concealed parts of a woman's body, and one in which the very scent of nature may be savoured, can surely be read as a sublimation of sexual feeling.

Where Ruskin found this particular fissure, which he observed with absolute and loving fidelity, is not known. Other drawings of this type were made in the sloping gardens that lead up to the Coniston Fells above Ruskin's Lakeland home, Brantwood, which was his principal home from 1872 and to the end of his life. There he had a seat placed overlooking a beck running down from the fell, from which the view was of the bank rising up on the far side of the stream, strewn with wild flowers and dense with herbage, and offering him the opportunity for private meditation on the complexity and infinite variety of nature.

NOTES

1 Ruskin 1903–12, vol. 21, *The Ruskin Art Collection at Oxford: Catalogues, Notes, and Instructions*, p. 111.

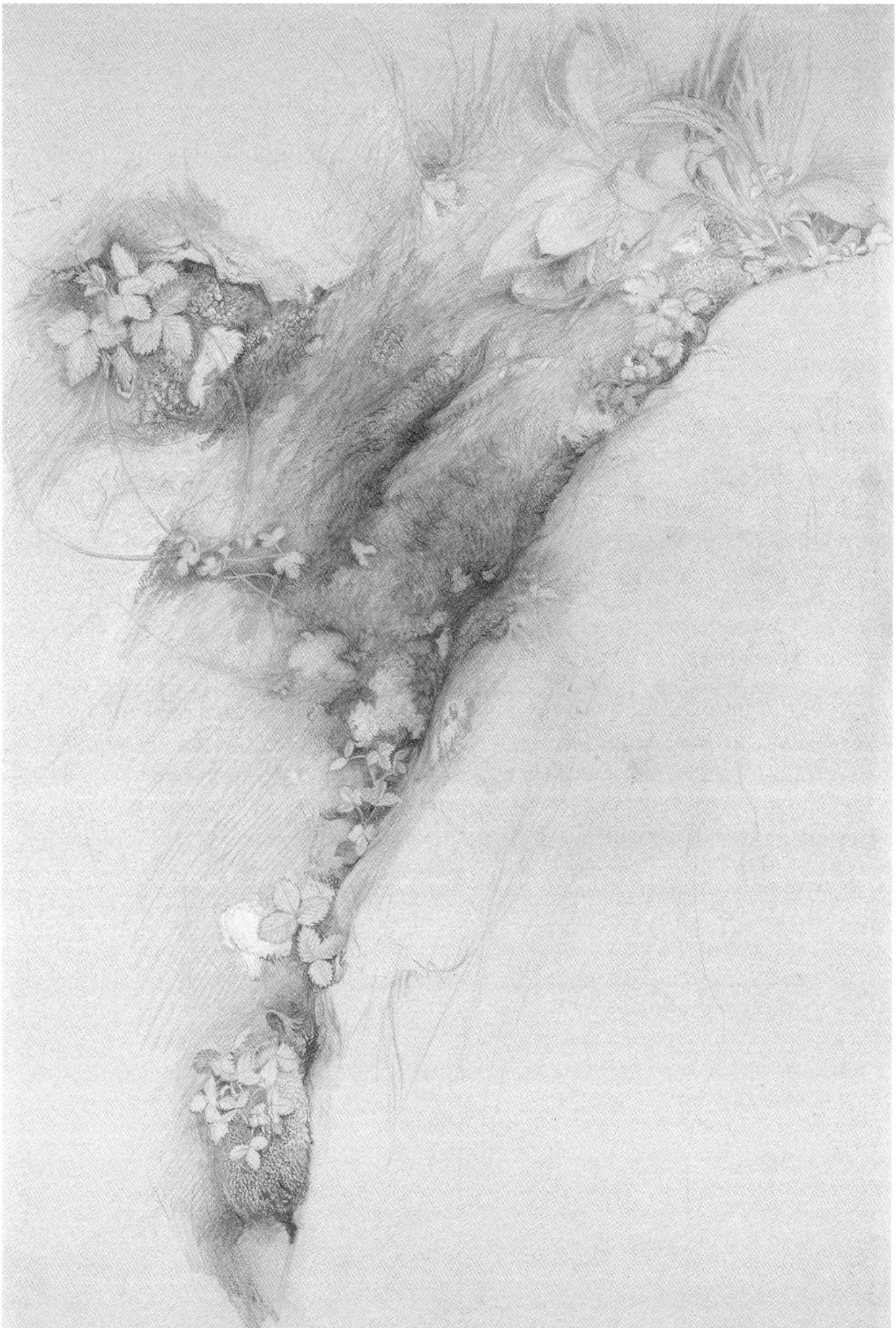

85

Rock Study with Oxalis and Heather mid-1880s (?)

Graphite and watercolour heightened with white bodycolour with scratching out on paper; 19.5 × 28.4 cm
Private collection
Inscriptions: on reverse, *given to J.R. Severn / by John Ruskin – / Painted at Brantwood / from its rock, heather & / oxalis / [Joan] Ruskin Severn, Herne Hill, oxalis & heather*

No precise date can be given to this glorious study of rock and wild flowers; Ruskin first installed himself at Brantwood – the house that he had bought sight unseen and that was positioned on the eastern shore of Coniston Water – in the autumn of 1871, but the drawing, which was made there, may have been done at any time up until the conclusion of his working life following his final mental breakdown in 1889.

The two varieties of plant shown here were both ones of which Ruskin was especially fond. Of heather, the purple-red flowers of which are seen at the left and centre around the base of the boulder, he had written in the fourth volume of *Modern Painters* that as it grew in Scotland it was "wholly without similitude."[1] It was clearly for him a symbol of the country that felt like home, and brought memories of the journeys that he had made there as a child. The oxalis, or wood sorrel – the white, veined Spring flowers of which would have been long since over by the time heather would be in bloom, but of which we see here the trifoliate leaves – was for Ruskin, "a perfect or pure flower ... composed on an unbroken whorl, or corolla, in the form of a disk, cup, bell, or, if it draw together again at the lips, a narrow-necked vase,"[2] but in which all the parts showed variation, and which each May was succeeded by the wild strawberry "in perfect beauty."[3] He had loved the oxalis since the time of the first volume of *Modern Painters*, when he had noticed them in paintings by Fra Angelico. Referring to the acid taste of its leaves, Ruskin had speculated that the Renaissance artist, "in using its leaves mixed with daisies in the foreground of his Crucifixion, was perhaps thinking of its peculiar power of quenching thirst."[4]

In "Of Caprice in Flowers" in his series *Proserpina*, the tenth part of which was issued in 1886, Ruskin again described the plant, believing that "its entire function [was to be] decorative ... and the whole aim of Nature in it is to give the flower an infinite tenderness."[5] The leaves of this shade-loving plant, painted a shadowy blue rather than the vivid green that they display in spring, seem to crowd into the lee of the boulder beneath which they have found root. By the time he wrote these words, Ruskin had long departed from the Darwinian principle that species should conform to type according to the laws of natural selection, preferring to trace "the personal character of plants, as distinguished from their enforced structure,"[6] and instead viewing them as individual organisms with unique predispositions and character traits.

NOTES

1 Ruskin 1903–12, vol. 6, *Modern Painters IV*, p. 422.
2 Ruskin 1903–12, vol. 25, *Love's Meinie and Proserpina*, p. 389.
3 Ibid., pp. 528–529.
4 Ruskin 1903–12, vol. 3, *Modern Painters I*, p. 175, note.
5 Ruskin 1903–12, vol. 25, p. 529.
6 Ibid., p. 526.

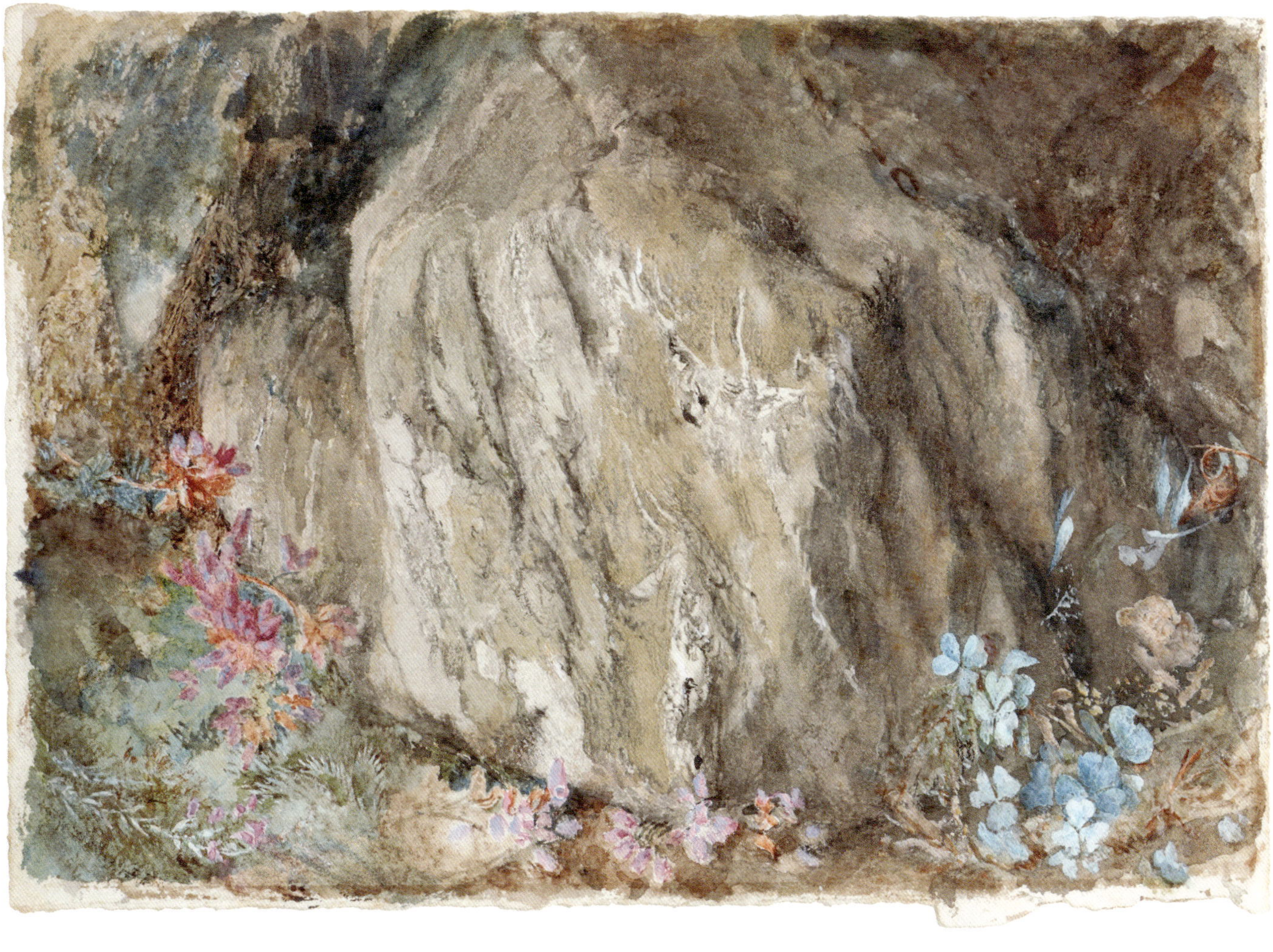

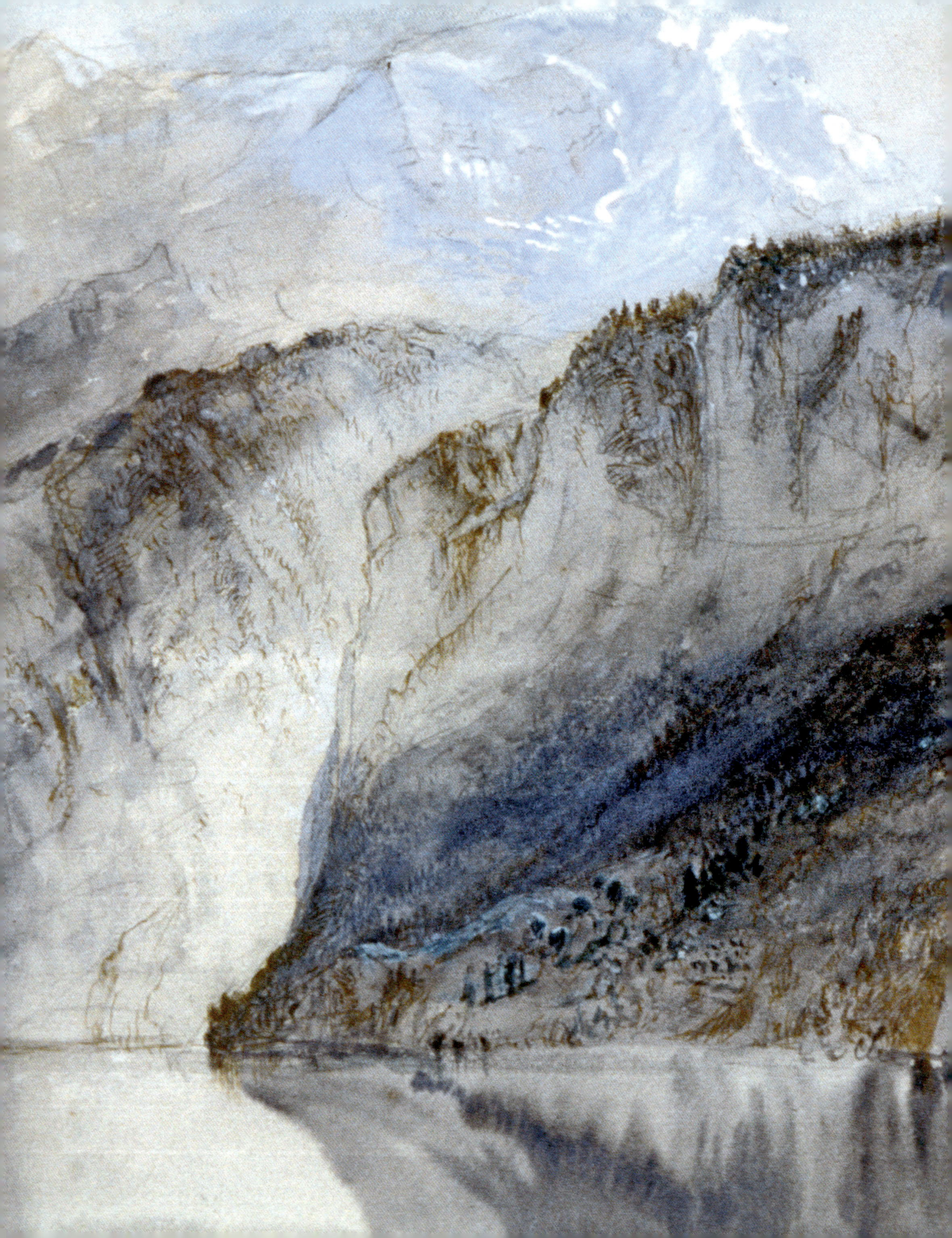

Mountains & Skies

86

Ben Venue and the Trossachs over Achray 1838

Graphite on buff paper; 25.7 × 36.5 cm (corners removed)
Ruskin Foundation (Ruskin Library, Lancaster University) (RF 872)
Inscriptions: graphite, *Benvenue. & Trossachs. over Achray. / July 25th 38.*, brown ink, *J Ruskin. Signed. Dec. 28th / 1879*

Ruskin was deeply conscious of his Scottish ancestry and often felt elated during visits to the country of his father's birth. He had been taken on three expeditions to Scotland in his early childhood – in 1824, 1826 and 1827 – and memories of the place as he had first known it, intensified by their association with his much-loved parents, recurred throughout his life. The northern landscape, especially mountains and upland scenery, seemed to Ruskin to represent a pristine bastion and refuge from the pollution and physical corruption that he believed was being spread throughout the inhabited world. The Ruskins spent two months in Scotland in the summer of 1838, following an itinerary suggested by the novels of Sir Walter Scott and the events of his life as chronicled by John Gibson Lockhart in his biography of the writer published in 1837–38. After staying for a while in Edinburgh in late July, the Ruskins moved on to Linlithgow and then into the Trossachs, the range of hills that stands between Lochs Katrine (to the west) and Achray.

This drawing is one of two made by Ruskin on 25 July 1838, each in the collection of the Ruskin Foundation, showing the mass of Ben Venue beyond a surface of water. It corresponds closely in its main elements to a watercolour by Anthony Vandyke Copley Fielding "of Ben Venue and the Trossachs, with brown cows standing in Loch Achray,"[1] which Ruskin had copied while he was taking drawing lessons from him. This was an area of Scotland to which he had a particular attachment; in 1853 he was to return there with his wife Effie, the painter John Everett Millais and Millais' brother William Henry. It was on that occasion, in the bed of the Glen Finglas river, that Millais painted Ruskin's portrait (fig. 2.5) and Ruskin made the drawing *Study of Gneiss Rock, Glenfinlas* (cat. 76).

NOTES

1 Ruskin 1903–12, vol. 35, *Præterita and Dilecta*, pp. 215–216.

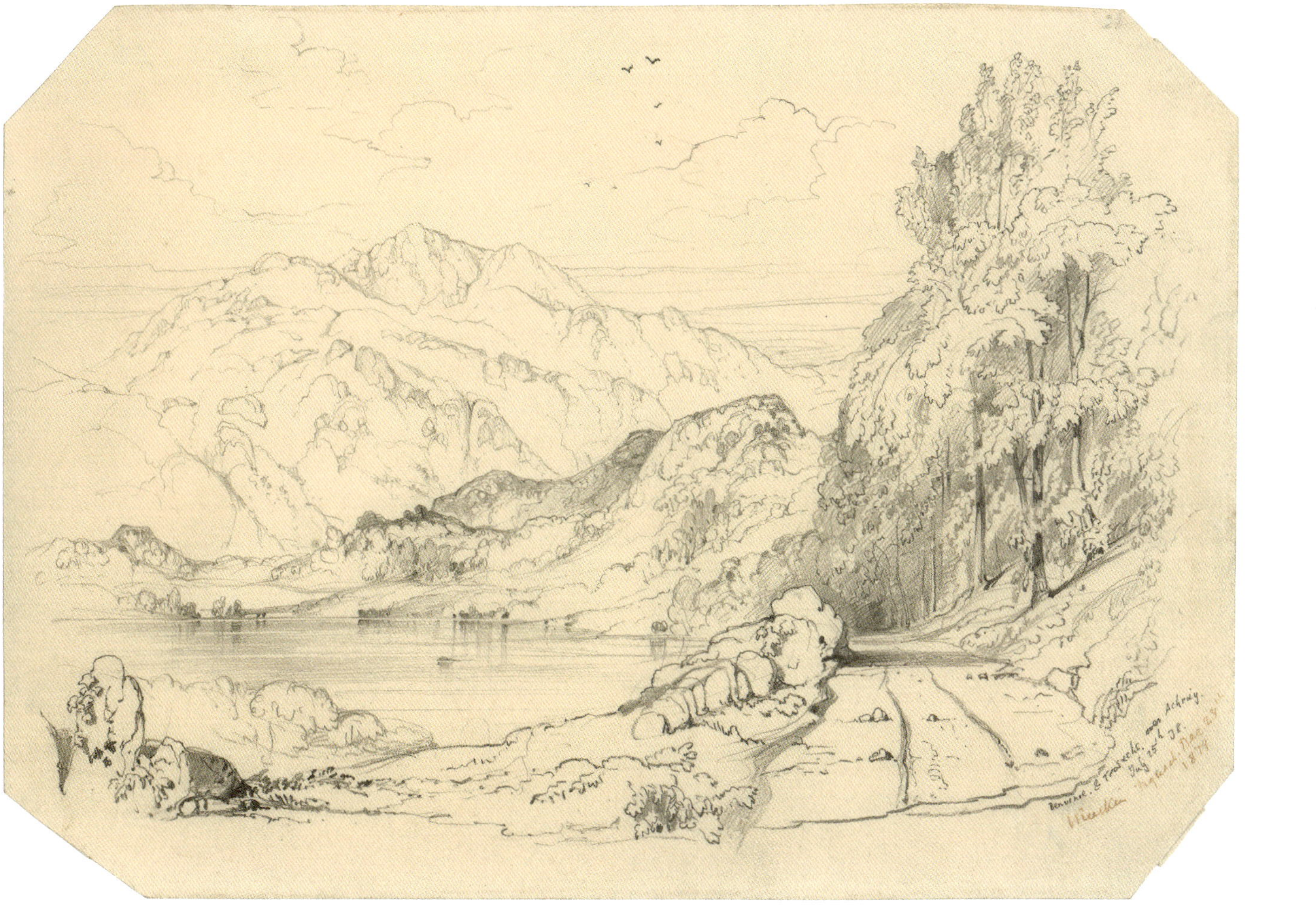
Benvenue. & Trossachs. over Achray.
July 25th 38.

87

The Glacier des Bois c. 1843–44

Black ink, watercolour and bodycolour on white paper; 32 × 21.5 cm
Ruskin Foundation (Ruskin Library, Lancaster University) (RF 893)
Inscriptions: with point of brush, *J.R.*, titled in watercolour, strengthened with ink, *Le Glacier Des Bois*

Since 1833, when Ruskin had had his first sight of the high mountains of Germany, Switzerland, Italy and France, the Alps were a passion and a source of inspiration and consolation to him. In February 1834, as a birthday present from his father, he received a set of Horace-Bénédict de Saussure's *Voyages dans les Alpes* (1779–96), the four quarto volumes of which he read and re-read all his life. De Saussure is regarded as the first person to have attempted to understand mountains in purely scientific terms and on the basis of observation rather than folklore. The parts of the Alps that de Saussure knew best – Chamonix and the Mont Blanc massif – and the mountains that he climbed and described (he made the third ascent of Mont Blanc in 1787) were to become places that Ruskin loved too. Ruskin travelled to the Alps with his parents in May 1844, spending most of June in Chamonix. This was his first opportunity for an extended study of the mountains of Savoy; his diary entries give insight into the way the experience affected him intellectually and emotionally and the feeling of possession he had about the place. For instance, an entry for 6 June states simply, "A lovely day, to light me to my own valley."[1]

The present watercolour, although in a sense a mere caprice when compared to later more searching drawings (which in any case were made directly from the motif, whereas this work represents a dreamlike vision of mountain scenery), contains the two geographical elements that were most striking to the young Ruskin's scientific inclinations as well as his artistic sensibility. The first of these elements, the crests of rock that stand on the uppermost parts of glaciated mountains, sharpened into needle-like shards by erosion on their flanks and known by the French term aiguilles, are shown in the distance on the upper-left side of the circular composition. The second, the glacier itself, appears as a series of serrated ridges occurring longitudinally in the body of ice as it advances toward the vantage point (itself indicated by a loosely defined shape and a spray of foliage in the foreground, intended to represent one of the viewing platforms placed there for tourists). Ruskin's knowledge of Alpine physical geography was as yet undeveloped, as he admitted in *Præterita* when he said that "the month's time set apart for the rocks of Chamouni [Ruskin's usual spelling of the place name] was spent in merely finding out what was to be done, and where."[2]

Although largely abstract in topographical terms, the title inscribed upon the sheet indicates that when Ruskin made the drawing, he had in mind the glacier that is now known as the Mer de Glace. From beneath the glacier close to its snout emerged a cascade of water, the source of the Arveyron river, a location painted by J.M.W. Turner and a spot frequently visited by Ruskin (who was certainly attracted both by its spectacular physical character and its association

NOTES

1 Ruskin 1956, vol. 1, p. 277.
2 Ruskin 1903–12, vol. 35, *Præterita and Dilecta*, p. 315.
3 Published with an engraving of the present drawing by J.C. Armytage in an annual giftbook called *Friendship's Offering* in 1844. For the text of Ruskin's poem, see Ruskin 1903–12, vol. 2, *Poems*, pp. 222–226.

with the painter to whom he was at this time starting to devote his attention). The aiguilles and distant massif in the top left of the oval composition may be recognized as the Aiguille Verte, which stands on the arête or ridge that runs between the Mer de Glace and the Glacier d'Argentière. The glacier, which in the mid-nineteenth century almost reached the village of Les Bois, a short distance along the road to Martigny on the northeast side of Chamonix, has since then steadily retreated and is no longer visible from the valley bottom.

In its vignette format, the drawing of the Glacier des Bois was in fact a deliberate imitation of a type of composition that Turner used on occasions in the 1830s, often for illustrations to accompany verse, such as those in Samuel Rogers' volume of poems entitled *Italy*, which Ruskin had had in his possession since 1832. Ruskin seems to have thought the association of the vignette format with poetry a happy one, and probably himself made the present drawing to accompany his own poem "A Walk in Chamouni" of 1843, which describes the "proud summits" that "rise passionless and pure, but all unblest."[3]

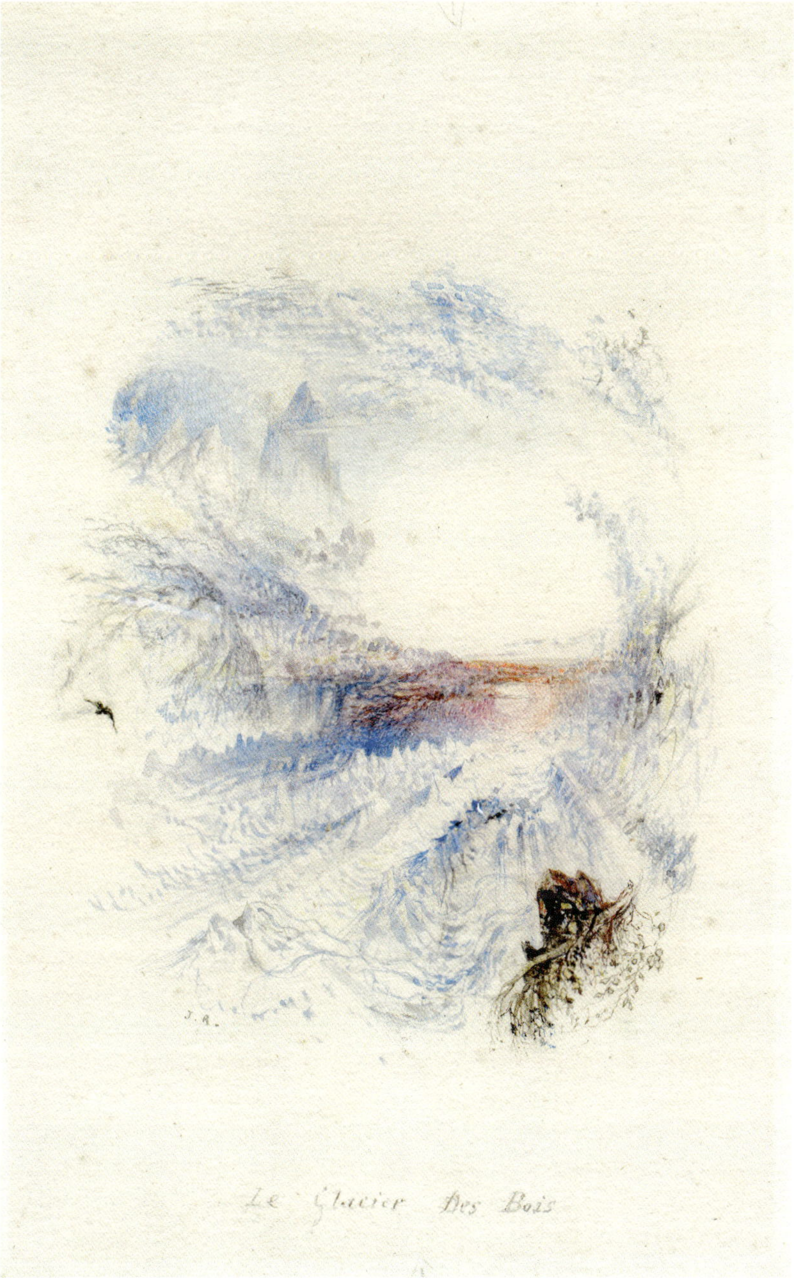

88

Val Anzasca 1845

Graphite and pen and brown ink with brown wash heightened with white bodycolour on paper; 15.6 × 22.2 cm
Private collection
Inscriptions: *Val Anzasca / J. Ruskin 1845. Signed 1879*

In August 1845, in a state of physical and mental exhaustion following months of intensive study of the historic schools of painting in Tuscany, and having told his father that he would not "recover spring of mind until I get on a glacier,"[1] Ruskin withdrew to the Piedmontese Alps for a period of rest and recuperation. He had often looked forward to this mountain sojourn in moments of distress or irritation in the course of his travels (as when, for example, he saw the destruction that was being wrought upon the Romanesque churches of Lucca, and was prompted to say to his father: "I shall have to go back to M[onte] Rosa, I think, or I shall get to hate the human species, [of] our days, worse than any Timon"[2]).

Ruskin stayed in the village of Macugnaga at the foot of Monte Rosa, on the Italian side of the frontier with Switzerland to the east of Zermatt, where he found mountain brooks "tumbling down about my cottage over blocks of granite and [that] sing to me all night." During the day the air was sweet with the smell of hay-making, and in the cold of the Alpine night it was "crisp, clear & delicious."[3] In the mountains he made detailed studies of clouds, vegetation and rock-forms, and carried forward experiments with a drawing technique that was to serve both aesthetic and scientific purposes – learning to represent the landscape by means of richly curving and rhythmic lines and dense vibrant textures.

This drawing shows the valley with the village of Macugnaga resting on the hillside to the right, with the Anza river flowing among meadows below. A smear of white bodycolour indicates the sun as it sinks toward the line of mountains that forms the flank of Monte Rosa to the west (the main body of the mountain, which rises to 4,634 metres, is out of view on the left side). The atmospheric effect of late afternoon is captured by the way in which the stems and foliage of trees standing in the right foreground are shown in stark *contre-jour*, while the open ground in the valley bottom appears bathed in warm light. Another drawing of the same tree-lined pathway leading up to the town (private collection), including the identical arcaded building in the middle ground, is dated 12 August 1845.

NOTES

1 Ruskin 1972, p. 148.
2 Ibid., p. 52.
3 Ibid, p. 160.

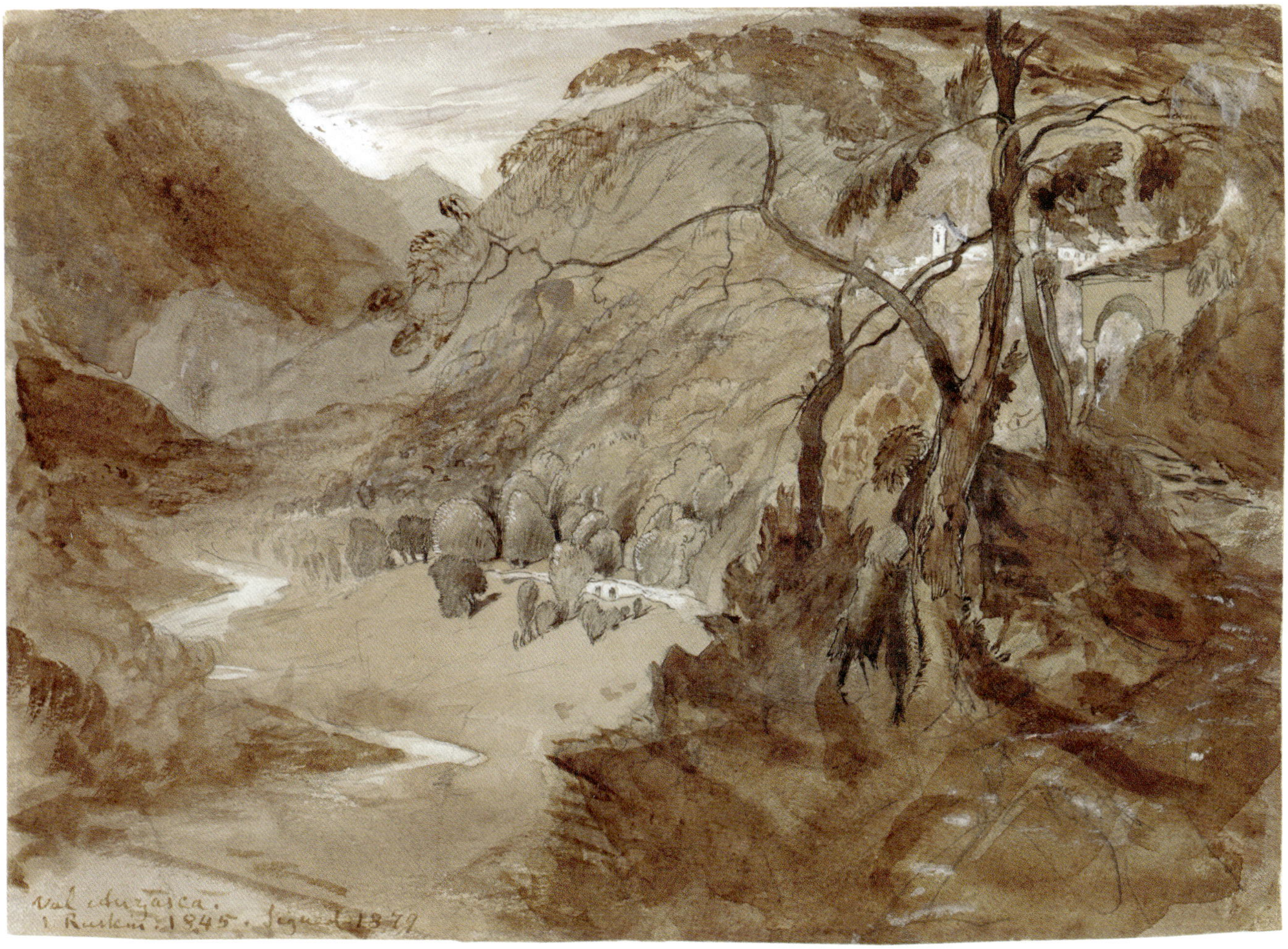
Val Anzasca.
J Ruskin. 1845. Signed 1879

89

Mountain Landscape, Macugnaga 1845

Pen and brown ink, brown wash, graphite and scraping out on thick, smooth, cream wove paper; 29.8 × 40 cm
Yale Center for British Art, New Haven. Paul Mellon Collection (B1975.4.1585)
Inscriptions: brown ink, *MACUGNAGA / J Ruskin – 1845*

J.M.W. Turner was much in Ruskin's thoughts during his late summer mountain sojourn of 1845, following his period of study in Italy in connection with the planned second volume of *Modern Painters*. As Ruskin wrote to his father from Macugnaga on 29 July, with a sense of relief to find himself in the mountains again: "I had got my head perfectly puzzled in Italy with the multitude of new masters & manners and I was getting a little adrift from my own proper beat, & forgetting nature in art – now I am up in the clouds again, I see my way. Titian[']s all very well, but I don't see anything like him here. It is all Turner, and Turner *only*, nobody else."[1]

Ruskin hoped for a while that Turner might be persuaded to join him in the mountains of Piedmont that summer, but the painter was otherwise engaged. James Duffield Harding – intermittently Ruskin's drawing master since 1841 – was however more biddable. In anticipation of his arrival to their agreed rendezvous at Baveno, however, Ruskin confided to his father that he feared that "Harding will not like anything that I have done, for I have entirely left his manner, and have been following Titian and the liber studiorum ... Harding won't understand my drawings of ilex leaves counted, and I am afraid he will think my studies have been very brown."[2]

The present drawing shows the Anzasca Valley from a vantage point close to its westernmost col and at an altitude at which the stream that runs in the valley bottom is little more than a mountain torrent a few metres in width (and this despite the storms and heavy rain that Ruskin suffered while in the mountains that July). The valley runs toward the east, so here we see the bright light of the southern sky cresting the mountains of the valley sides on the right. The village of Macugnaga itself lies out of view beyond the spur that runs down to the boulder-strewn valley bottom on the left.

Because no meeting with Turner took place that summer, Ruskin found an alternative way of communing with the painter who so engaged his thoughts – by travelling to a location where Turner had painted and that had assumed a hallowed status in Ruskin's mind because of its association with him. Thus, in August he travelled on from Macugnaga to Faido, where two years previously Turner had sketched the valley of the Ticino river as it flowed down from the Pass, which he later worked up as the watercolour *The Pass at Faido, St. Gotthard* (Thaw Collection, The Morgan Library and Museum, New York), commissioned by the Ruskins shortly afterwards.

NOTES

1 Ruskin 1972, pp. 164–165.
2 Ibid., p. 181.

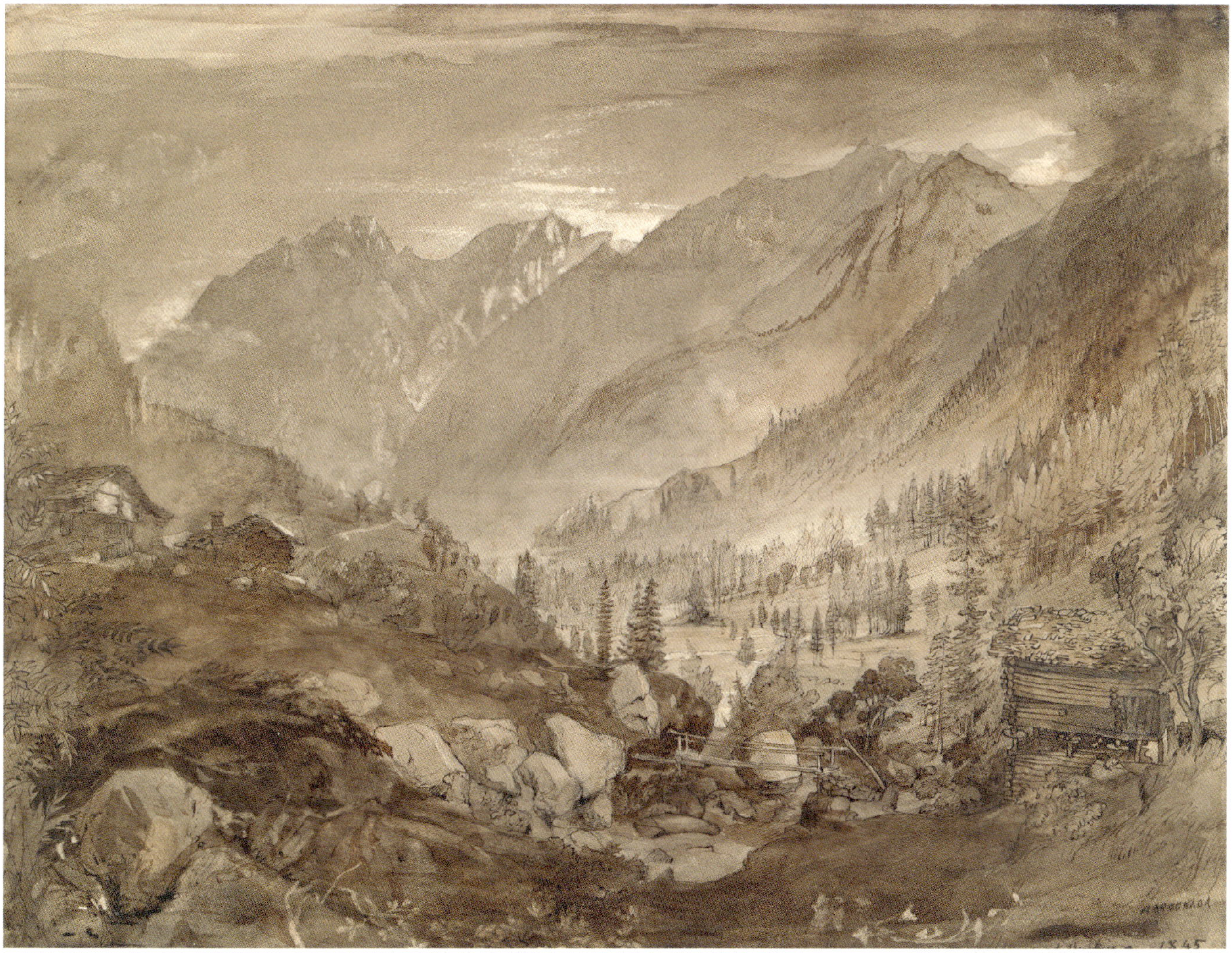
1845

90

Mountains of Villeneuve (Near the Eastern End of the Lake of Geneva) 1846

Graphite, ink and ink wash on white paper; 27.8 × 45.5 cm
Ruskin Foundation (Ruskin Library, Lancaster University) (RF 1673)

This is a view of the mountains at Lake Geneva, looking toward the north or northwest, with the level ground on the lakeshore close to the mouth of the Rhône forming the foreground. Ruskin delighted in the rhythmic pattern of lit and shadowed areas of the sloping surfaces, sweeping downward at a precipitous angle, but with constant variety of clefts and swelling protuberances. A writhing confluence of lines allows the contours and scale of the mountain to be read geographically, but is also powerfully suggestive of its soaring mass and daunting complexity. On the right side, strata protrude at right angles to the surface of the slope; elsewhere the smoothness of the mountain forms bears evidence of ancient glaciation. Pine forests are indicated by a vibrato-like pen technique, and all is treated with freedom, confidence and excitement.

Ruskin thought of mountains as organic and elemental, their parts linked together and balanced by physical forces, but in constant motion and competition. It was as if his knowledge of and the fascination he felt for glaciers and his appreciation of the latent energy of the flow of ice caused him to regard rock as a similar material and subject to analogous laws of science. In descriptions of the mountains in which he likened their forms to "the recoil of a broken wave cast against it from the other side; and yet, as the recoiling water has a sympathy with the under swell of the very wave against which it clashes, the whole mass writhes together in strange unity of mountain passion,"[1] he was speaking with the authority of a geologist, but one whose eye had been trained by the discipline of looking so as to see to draw.

Ruskin and his parents stayed at Vevey, on the lake's north shore, in the course of their return journey from Switzerland in August 1846. On 10 August Ruskin described "a long walk over the hills between [Vevey] and the Dent de Jaman, remarkable for abundant springs and stoneless pastures with splendid pines."[2] The Dent de Jaman stands above Montreux, a mile or two to the north of Villeneuve, so the present drawing may be presumed to have been made in the course of his ramblings during the stay. Ruskin had an engraved plate of the present drawing made to use as an illustration to the fourth volume of *Modern Painters*, which was devoted to the question of how mountains might be represented in art with understanding and in which context he used it to demonstrate the principle that the mountains that are most "striking to the general eye ... almost always have the high crest or wall of cliff on the *top* of their slopes, rising from the plain first in mounds of meadow-land, and bosses of rock, and studded softness of forest ... until just where the deep shade of the pines becomes blue or purple in the haze of height, a red wall of upper precipice rises from the pasture land, and frets the sky with glowing serration."[3]

NOTES

1 Ruskin 1903–12, vol. 6, *Modern Painters IV*, p. 250.
2 Ruskin 1956, vol. 1, p. 344.
3 Ruskin 1903–12, vol. 6, pp. 300–301.

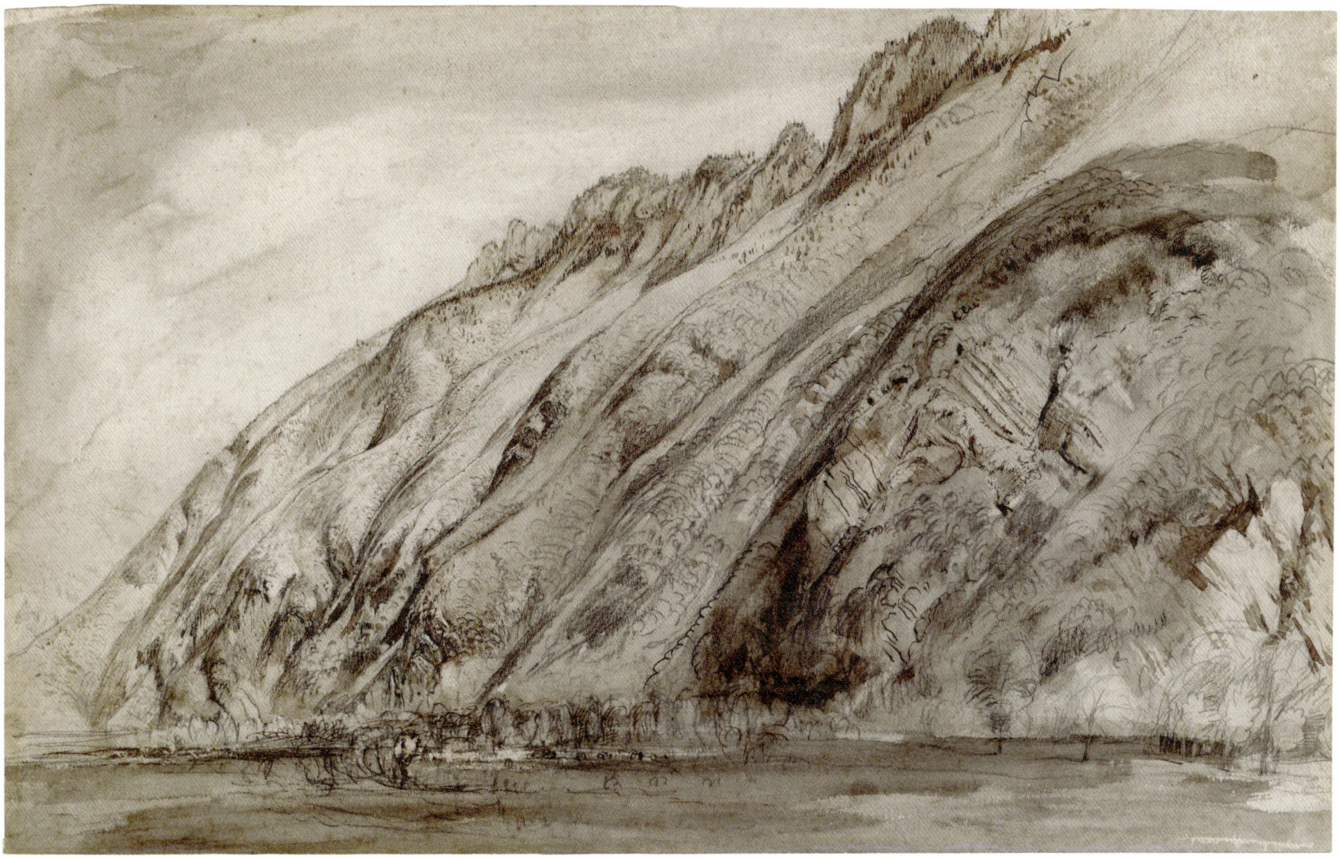

91

The Glacier des Bossons, Chamonix 1849

Pen and wash in sepia ink and bodycolour over graphite on wove paper; 33.8 × 47.7 cm
The Ashmolean Museum, Oxford. Presumably presented by John Ruskin to the Ruskin Drawing School (University of Oxford), where it was first recorded in 1906 (WA.RS.REF.091)

The most elaborate and complete of all of Ruskin's drawings of the glaciers of Chamonix, this work was almost certainly made in the summer of 1849, when he spent a month there with his parents. Each day he explored the surrounding mountains or – as in the present instance – observed the Alpine ranges from the valley below. His particular interest, as witnessed by diary entries, was in the meteorological conditions and the constant change of light on the landscape, along with the physical geography of the mountains and in particular the mechanisms of glaciation. In this he was dependent on the research of the pioneering glaciologist James David Forbes, who had done fieldwork on the Glacier of the Aar and the Mer de Glace in 1840 and 1841, and in whose book *Travels through the Alps of Savoy* (1843) it was stated that "a glacier is an imperfect fluid, or a viscous body, which is urged down slopes of a certain inclination by the mutual pressure of its parts."[1] Ruskin was himself to write of glaciers and the plastic quality of ice that allows it to flow under the momentum of its own mass as being like "a stream of honey ... only to be understood by keeping always clearly in view the great law of its motion as a viscous substance."[2]

The Bossons Glacier lies on the northern slope of Mont Blanc and flows toward the town of Chamonix. It is now about seven kilometres in length, and because of its very steep incline it is extraordinarily fast flowing – moving at a speed of between 250 and 300 metres a year. Ruskin's drawing shows the spectacular ribbon of ice, flexing its mass and breaking into jagged crevasses as it rides over undulations in the bedrock. In the mid-nineteenth century the glacier was approximately 1,200 metres longer than it is now and reached almost to the valley bottom (the glacier's snout now rests at a point directly above the river Arve, as seen in the present drawing, while the mountainside below from which the ice has retreated is a vast hollow of smoothed rock surfaces and glacial debris). The pyramidal mountains beyond are those shown with greater brevity in the drawing *Montagne de la Côte and Glacier des Bossons* (cat. 92). The point from which the drawing was made was the Hotel de l'Union, which was at the centre of Chamonix and was where the Ruskin family stayed, but which no longer stands.

The use of sepia washes and ink is especially effective in this sombre but beautiful drawing, allowing the brightness of the ice to be seen like the blade of a dagger across the width of the composition. Ruskin worked on the drawing intermittently during his stay in Chamonix; in a diary entry for 15 June, the third day that Ruskin was there, he recorded that he had drawn "after dinner from window at glacier des Bossons,"[3] while on the 5 July he "had the most unlucky day ... vainly trying to finish my brown study from the window."[4] That the drawing was important to him as the outcome of a stay when he had produced less than he might have hoped is indicated

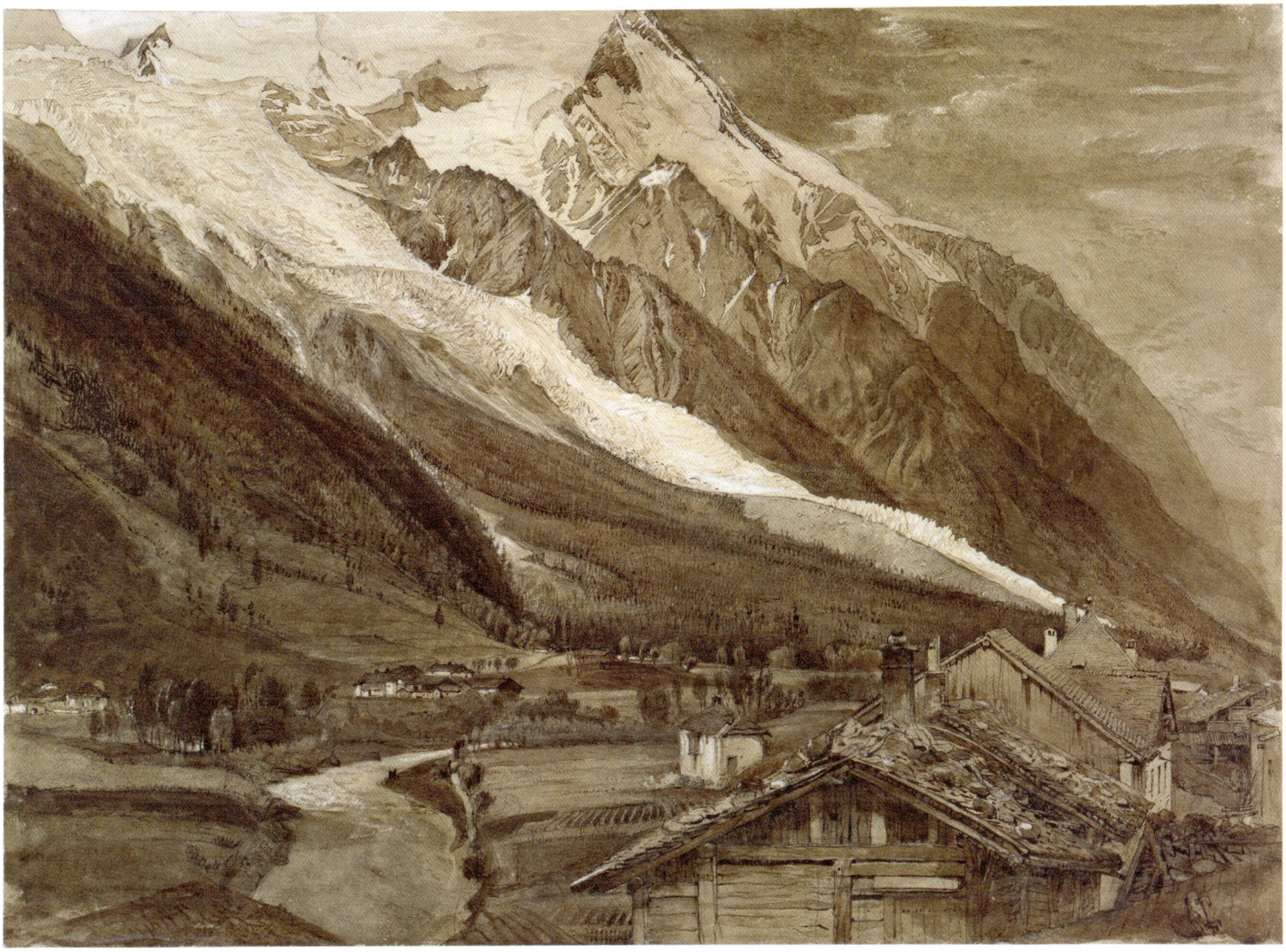

by a memorandum from four days later when prospects for a satisfactory outcome were improving: "I ... have been working since tea time on my brown study, with great pleasure. I hope to conclude it tomorrow; it will at all events be *one* worth coming for."[5]

NOTES

1 Forbes 1900, pp. 365–366.
2 Ruskin 1903–12, vol. 26, *Deucalion*, p. 10.
3 Ruskin 1956, vol. 2, p. 387.
4 Ibid., p. 404.
5 Ibid., p. 406.

92

Montagne de la Côte and Glacier des Bossons c. 1849

Graphite, ink and watercolour on paper; 12.4 × 21 cm
The Alpine Club, London

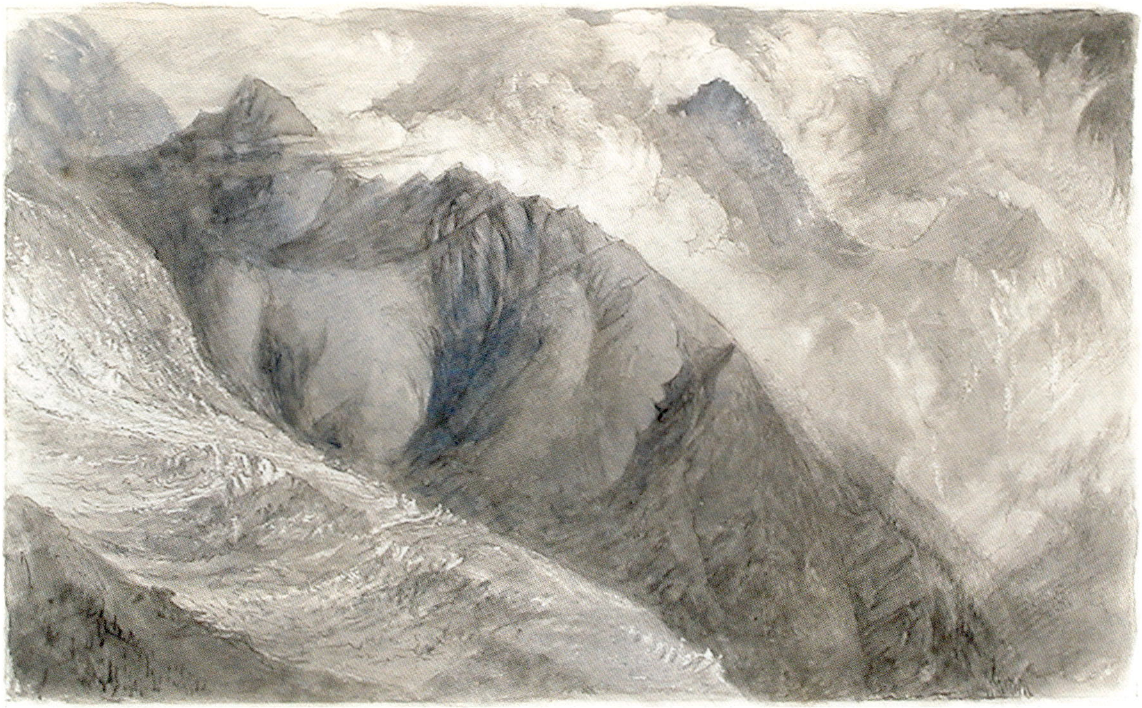

The present drawing is likely to have been made in 1849, during the month-long stay that Ruskin and his parents made in Chamonix between June and July. Successive diary entries describe the atmospheric effects to be observed on the surrounding mountains. On 13 June, for example, Ruskin wrote, "a very strange effect of cloud on Montagne de la Côte. The upper sky, down to top of G[lacier] des Boss[ons], was all of the common grey massy raincloud; but from the top of the ice there formed, as I looked, a filmy veil of vapour, through which the la Côte was plainly seen, which was thrown outward and across the mountain, falling from the glacier, or rather thrown out from it, like jets of seeds from a sower's hand: very beautiful."[1]

With a technique involving tremulous pen-work, translucent washes of monochrome, and cutting and scratching into the surface of the paper, Ruskin captured the surging energy of the moving ice and the massive solidity of the mountains between which the glacier flows.

NOTES

1 Ruskin 1956, vol. 2, p. 386.

93

La Cascade de la Folie, Chamouni 1849 or 1854 (?)

Graphite, ink and watercolour on paper; 46.1 × 37.3 cm
Birmingham Museums and Art Gallery (1905P2)

Ruskin visited Chamonix on many occasions and made countless drawings of the stupendous glaciers that flow down toward the town and into the valley of the Arve river, and of the serrated arête horizons and surrounding massifs, dominated by Mont Blanc to the south. Ruskin was conversant with theories of physical geography and a contributor to the debate about how forces of erosion and uplift form the landscape. His own drawings of Alpine subjects are thus both investigations and records of scenery that was recognized as being in a constant state of flux and subject to the continuous stress of stupendous and elemental geological forces. Nonetheless, as a young man he believed, as his parents had taught him, that the physical world was evidence of and controlled by God.

In the catalogue of Ruskin's drawings compiled by E.T. Cook and Alexander Wedderburn, the present beautiful watercolour was given the title *Cascade de la Folie and its Uplands, as seen from the old Hotel de l'Union*.[1] The drawing shows the arête on the southeastern side of Chamonix with the Glacier des Nantillons visible as the expanse of ice on the horizon at the centre, with the Aiguille du Grépon and Le Bec d'Oiseau on the left of the glacier and the Aiguille de Blaitière on the right. In the dark area that creates the foreground can be seen the ribbon-like form of the Torrent de Blaitière, referred to in the nineteenth century as the Cascade de Fouilly (or Folly), fed with melt-water from the Glacier de Blaitière. The cascade itself flows over relatively level ground to a rock shelf, from which point it descends more steeply toward Chamonix itself (on the outskirts of which, in the nineteenth century, stood a hamlet of chalets called Fouilly), before joining the Arve at Praz Conduit. Showing as a ribbon of white, the stream finds its way from the distant col through dense pinewoods and over a threshold of ground before plunging again into a further steep-sided and tree-lined gorge. The flow of water itself serves as a measure of the different geological zones through which it makes its course, with parts of the mountainside resisting the processes of erosion and others being more readily cut into by the water. Because the shadows cast by the trees fall leftward, it may be determined that the drawing was made at midday or in the early afternoon, before which time even in summer the mountainside is in shade.

A second drawing shows the lower section of the Cascade as seen in the present drawing, with a glimpse only of the more open ground above and with no view at all of the aiguilles on the horizon. Of the type that once again suggests the most intimate part of a woman's body (whether or not consciously so to Ruskin), it was reproduced in the Introduction to the third volume of *Modern Painters* in the Library Edition (see fig. 1.8).[2] Neither drawing, however, is mentioned specifically in Ruskin's diary account of his 1849 visit to Chamonix (where on several occasions he

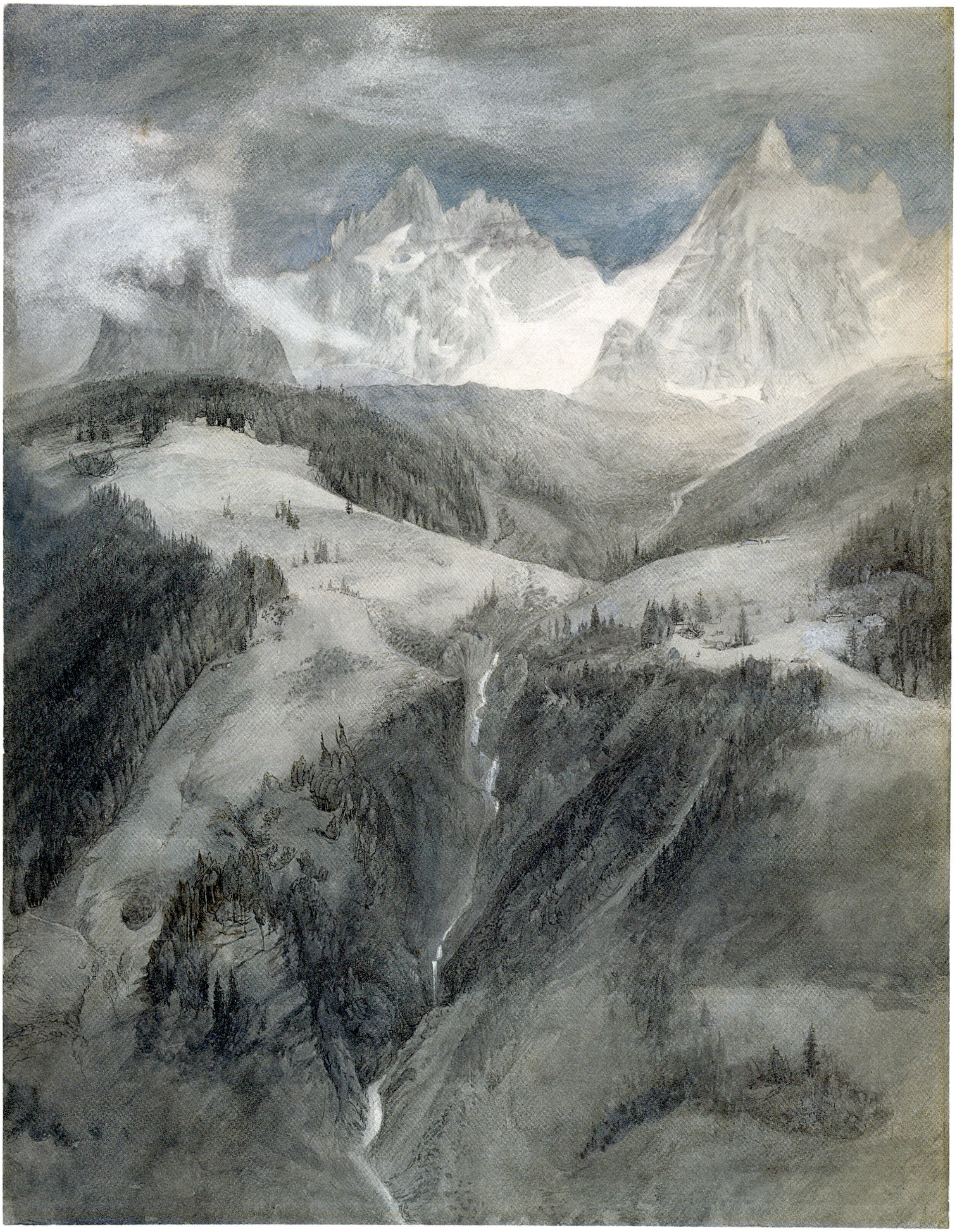

laments the small number of completed drawings that he had made that season),[3] nor do they appear under any immediately recognizable title in the list of drawings done in Chamonix that Ruskin prepared and incorporated into his 1854 diary.[4]

Frederick Crawley, presumably working on Ruskin's instructions, made a daguerreotype of the same mountain flank, with the line of the Cascade just visible (fig. 7.1), and Ruskin may perhaps have consulted this when working on the present drawing. That on certain occasions Ruskin actually copied details or large landscape forms from the daguerreotypes that he was either buying from professional photographers or instructing his servants to make is demonstrated by a diary entry for 21 June 1849, written at Chamonix and following a session attempting to draw the surrounding mountains: "I drew at my beautiful place near les Tines and worked hard for two hours, and did everything wrong; nearly the same in the evening, when I could not draw the aiguilles from my window, and got nervous and uncomfortable. I have this morning put all to rights from Daguerreotype."[5]

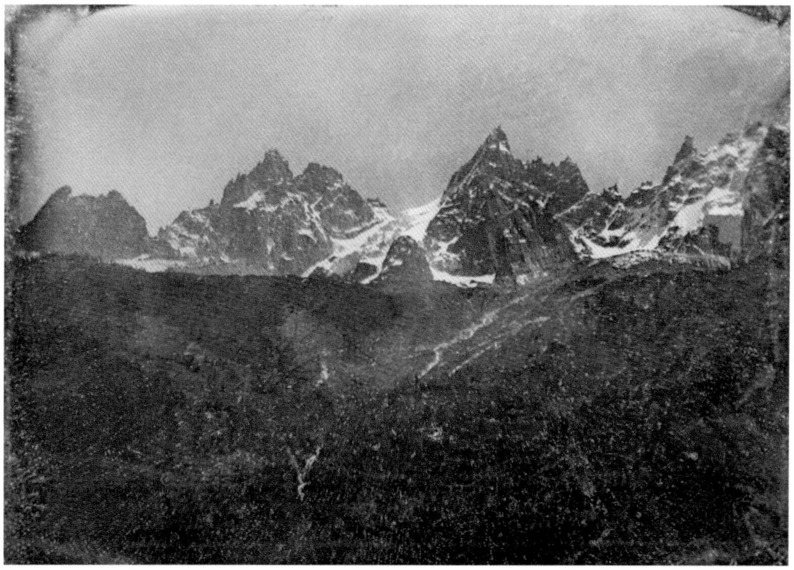

FIG. 7.1
John Ruskin and Frederick Crawley
Aiguilles, Chamonix, 1854
Daguerreotype
Ruskin Foundation (Ruskin Library, Lancaster University)
(RF Dag 73)

NOTES

1 Ruskin 1903–12, vol. 38, *Bibliography, Catalogue of Ruskin's Drawings, Addenda et Corrigenda*, p. 241. Ruskin was presumably staying at the hotel that since 1816 had been considered the best in Chamonix and that was demolished in the 1920s to make way for the town's post office.
2 See Ruskin 1903–12, vol. 5, *Modern Painters III*, opposite p. xxii.
3 As for example on 5 and 6 July, see Ruskin 1956, vol. 2, p. 404.
4 See Ruskin 1903–12, vol. 5, *Modern Painters III*, pp. xxi–xxii.
5 Ruskin 1956, vol. 2, p. 394.

94

Aiguilles de Chamonix 1849

Watercolour over graphite on paper; 34.6 × 47.5 cm
Birmingham Museums and Art Gallery (1907P150)
Inscriptions: encircled, *33*, [... ... ...] *Tines*, *Charmoz*, *Blatiere*, *Plan*

This is a view from the valley bottom close to the course of the Arveyron river, with the hamlet Les Gaudenays forming the foreground. The drawing shows the northwest facing flank of the Arve valley in which Chamonix stands, with pine forests, mountain torrents and open meadows – all of which Ruskin explored in the course of his month-long stay there in the summer of 1849. Chamonix itself is out of view on the right. The Cascade Blaitière, which Ruskin called the Cascade de la Folie, flows in the ravine that runs diagonally across the mountainside on the right, as seen in another drawing from Birmingham (cat. 93). The immediate horizon on the left is the ridge of Montenvers (which Ruskin called Montanvert), beyond which lies the lower section of the Mer de Glace. The ridge that runs above that is called the Frêtes des Charmoz, with the aiguilles of the Grands Charmoz and the Grépon at the composition's centre. Further to the right, showing as an expanse of snow in a saddle is the Glacier de Blaitière and to its right the Aiguille de Blaitière. Beyond, and in fact still higher than those already seen although from this angle it appears lower, is the Aiguille du Plan. Treated with freedom and breadth, and with mountain forms irradiated by afternoon sunlight, the whole seems to seethe and flow with a quality of living animation, in which Ruskin has explored the beauty of organic motion and the cohesion of the physical world as an entity regardless of scale.

These were, to Ruskin's perception, hallowed landmarks and a topography with which he was intimately and emotionally familiar. When asked in 1855 what places he loved best in Chamonix, he distinguished between "the top of the Montanvert and a small rock on the flank of the Breven"; saying, "I have been *happiest* on the Montanvert, but *oftenest* at this rock, where I generally pass my evenings when at Chamouni."[1]

NOTES

1 Ruskin 1903–12, vol. 36, *The Letters of John Ruskin, 1827–1869*, p. 193. The Brévent is the mountain on the northwest side of Chamonix, out of view on the right as it would be in the present drawing. Ruskin had his own preferred forms of spelling for many of these place names. Chamonix was to him "Chamouni"; Le Brévent, "Breven"; and Montenvers, "Montanvert." Ruskin's beloved rock remains in situ, marked on maps as "*Pierre à Ruskin*," and has since 1925 been a memorial to him and his affection for Chamonix and its mountains, with a bronze relief portrait of him attached to its side.

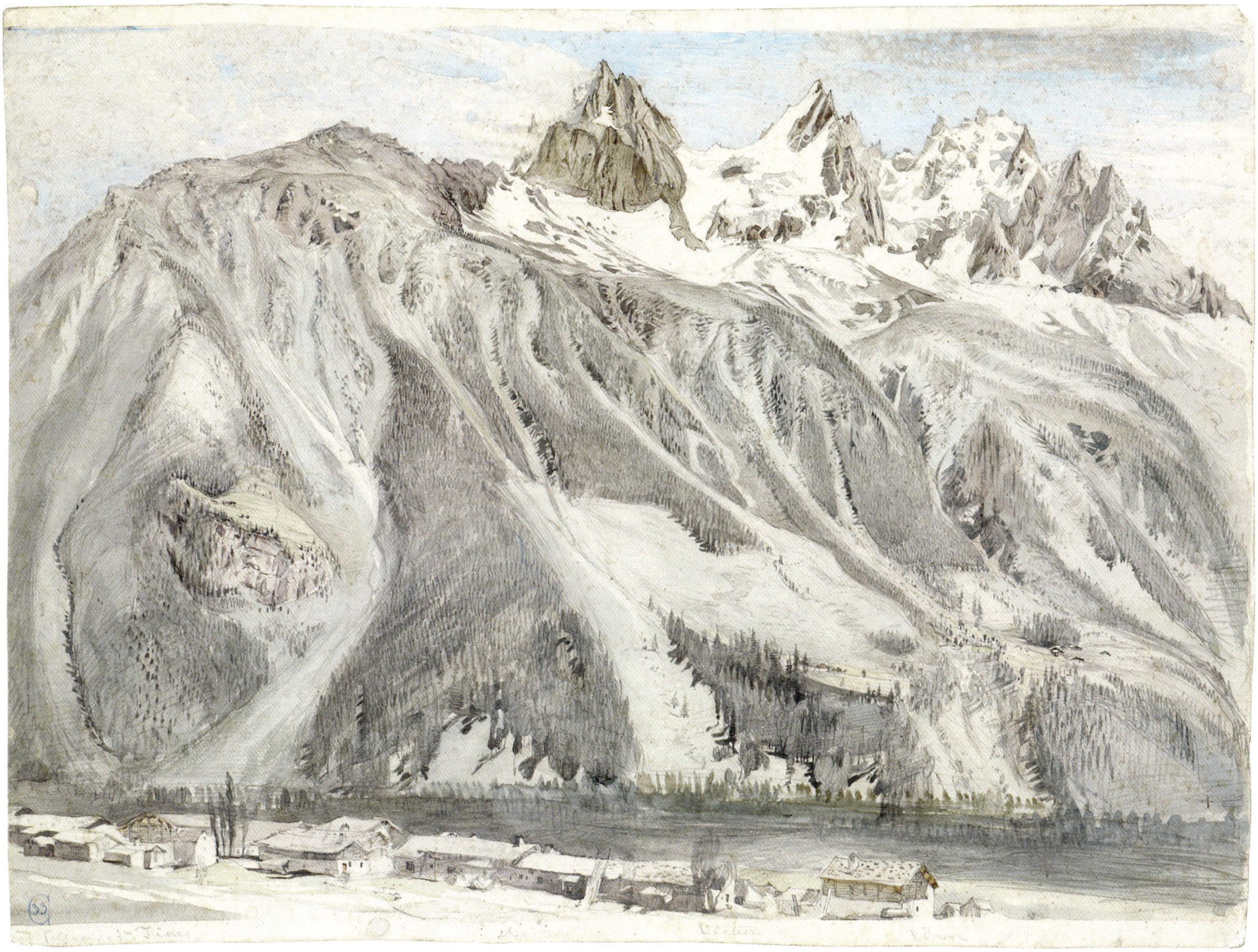

95

Mer de Glace, Chamonix 1849

Graphite, watercolour and bodycolour on white paper; 27.3 × 50 cm
Ruskin Foundation (Ruskin Library, Lancaster University) (Ref 1206)

This drawing, given the title *The Mer de Glace from the Montanvert* when it appeared as a photogravure illustration to Ruskin's collection of writings about geology, *Deucalion*,[1] was done during his month-long stay in Chamonix in the summer of 1849. It may perhaps have been made on the occasion when Ruskin and Joseph Couttet climbed the Montenvers, the arête of which stands above the snout of the Mer de Glace, as the former described in a diary entry on 19 June, and upon which he found "some of the sweetest strawberries I ever tasted on its steep southern rocks; climbed it, and found one of the grandest sweeping views of glacier I have ever seen; gravelly ridge of moraine."[2] The view of the glacier from this position, as depicted in the drawing, offers a glimpse in the far distance of the point where two separate ice flows – the Glacier de Leschaux on the left and the Glacier du Tacul on the right – merge to form the Mer de Glace, and then in the middle distance the great curve that it makes at the foot of the Arête des Flammes de Pierre and Les Drus, which are both seen on the left of the drawing. In addition, clearly visible from this point are the medial moraines – lines of rock debris formed by lateral moraines in the two upper glaciers, which have joined together and form a course down the centre of the main body of ice.

Ruskin was intensely interested in how vast accumulations of snow, gradually compacted into what is called firn, on the upper slopes of the mountains might gather together into rivers of ice flowing at speeds determined by the angle of incline of the glacier's bed and the contrary friction of physical obstructions. Having paid careful attention to the contemporary debates about glaciers and in 1849 not yet confident of regarding himself as an authority, Ruskin made references in his diary to the exchange of ideas – sometimes acrimonious – between scientists at the time. For example, earlier on the same day that he commented on the "sweeping views" of the Mer de Glace, he had been "reading a paper of [Sir Roderick] Murchison's on erratic detritus – ... denying extended glacial action, [but instead] attributing all to a great and unequal elevation sustained by the Alps and Jura." Seeking further information and perhaps alternative opinions on the matter, he turned to James David Forbes' *Travels through the Alps of Savoy* (1843), where he found the "account of it ... most obscure."[3]

The daguerreotype (cat. 96) that Ruskin had made by John Hobbs or Frederick Crawley shows approximately the same view as in the present drawing, but from a vantage point closer to the ice flow.

NOTES

1 See Ruskin 1903–12, vol. 26, *Deucalion and Other Studies in Rocks and Stones*, pl. A, opposite p. xxii.
2 Ruskin 1956, vol. 2, p. 392.
3 Ibid.

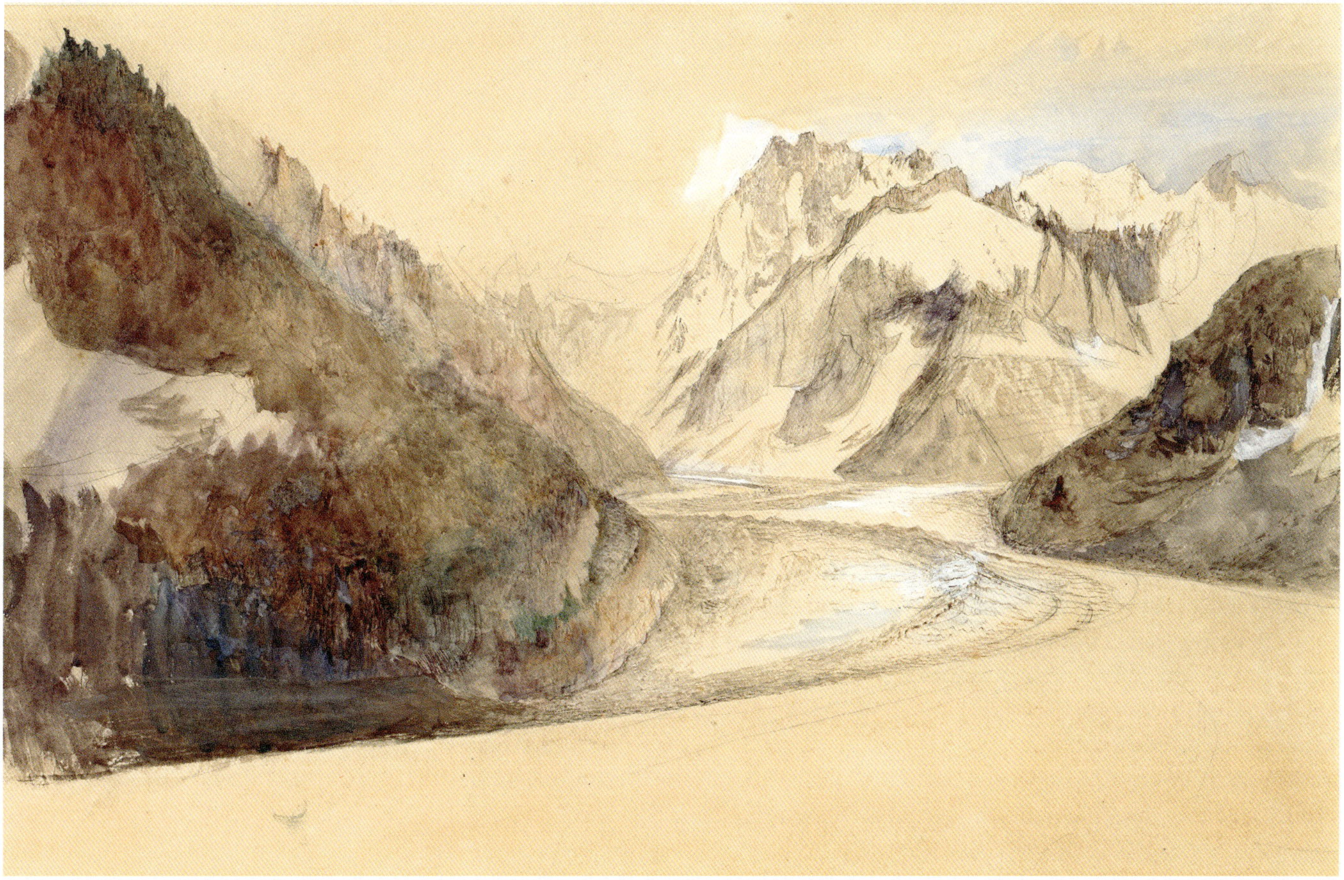

96

JOHN RUSKIN AND JOHN HOBBS OR FREDERICK CRAWLEY

Mer de Glace, Chamonix c. 1849–54

Daguerreotype (half plate); 11 × 15.5 cm (sight)
Ruskin Foundation (Ruskin Library, Lancaster University) (RF Dag. 75)

This daguerreotype, which shows the great Mer de Glace as it flows northward on the flank of the Mont Blanc massif, was likely to have been taken either by John Hobbs or Frederick Crawley, each of whom was with Ruskin at Chamonix at different times and had been instructed in the use of his daguerreotype equipment, purchased some years earlier. The vantage point was close to the surface of the ice at the foot of the eastern side of the Montenvers ridge, from which point the glacier is seen to curve away to the point – about four kilometres distant – where two separate ice flows, the Glacier de Leschaux (on the left) and the Glacier du Tacul, join to form the Mer de Glace. The view corresponds closely to that taken by Ruskin himself in his drawing *Mer de Glace, Chamonix* (cat. 95). The mountainsides and aiguilles are wreathed in mist and cloud, but the forms of the glacier itself can be seen in minute detail in the photograph, with lines of longitudinal moraines and a jagged surface in which pillars of ice stand in serried ranks separated by crevasses. There is expressed here an extraordinary sense of the relentless energy and erosive power of the ice.

Ruskin had embraced photography early on as a means of providing documentary accounts of buildings that were in jeopardy through neglect or destruction. The photographing of landscape forms may have seemed less urgently important to him at first, as he only gradually came to realize that nature was constantly in flux, and perhaps also at risk as a result of human agency. Ultimately the value of photography, he believed, was as a medium of documentation: "Anything more beautiful than the photographs of the Valley of Chamouni, now in your printsellers' windows, cannot be conceived," he stated in a lecture at Oxford in 1872; "For geographical and geological purposes they are worth anything; for art purposes, worth – a good deal less than zero."[1]

NOTES

1 Ruskin 1903–12, vol. 22, *Lectures on Landscape, Michael Angelo & Tintoret, The Eagle's Nest, Ariadne Florentina, with Notes for Other Oxford Lectures*, p. 220.

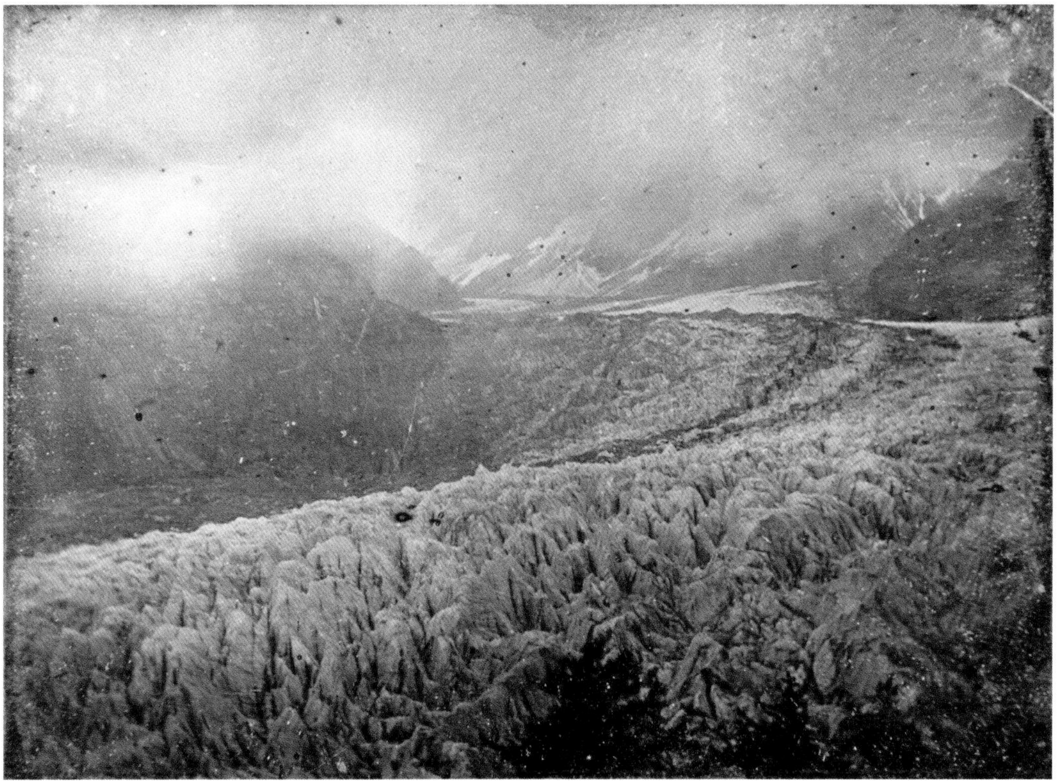

97

Aiguilles de Chamonix c. 1849

Graphite, pen and ink and wash on card; 25 × 35.7 cm
The Fitzwilliam Museum, Cambridge (1453)
Inscriptions: *showing finest conchoidal-riband structure. J.R. on the spot, 1849*
(Scotland venue only)

Ruskin's view of the Aiguille de Blaitière, seen beyond an expanse of snow that forms the Glacier de Blaitière, was taken from the Plan de l'Aiguille. The sun shines on the exposed southern flanks of the pyramidal needle of rock while deep shadows are observed in the area of rock debris and boulders strewn in the foreground. The Aiguille rises to 3,522 metres, and with others such as Le Grépon, the Aiguille du Plan and the Aiguille du Midi makes up the astonishing arête that stands above Chamonix on its southeastern side and forms the confining wall on the western side of the Mer de Glace. Ruskin's inscription on the present drawing indicates that it was made from a vantage point high on the mountain – at thirty he was certainly physically capable of reaching considerable altitudes and was always competently led by Joseph Couttet. The drawing (and one showing the Glacier des Bossons from above [cat. 92]) may therefore be regarded as another example of the type of work made in situ on that mountainside in extreme physical circumstances.

In 1854 Ruskin compiled a list of all the drawings he had made in the vicinity of Chamonix and attached it to his diary of that year as a "Catalogue of Sketches in the Neighbourhood of Mont Blanc."[1] At least six of the Aiguille de Blaitière were specified.

NOTES

1 Ruskin 1903–12, vol. 5, *Modern Painters III*, pp. xxi–xxii.

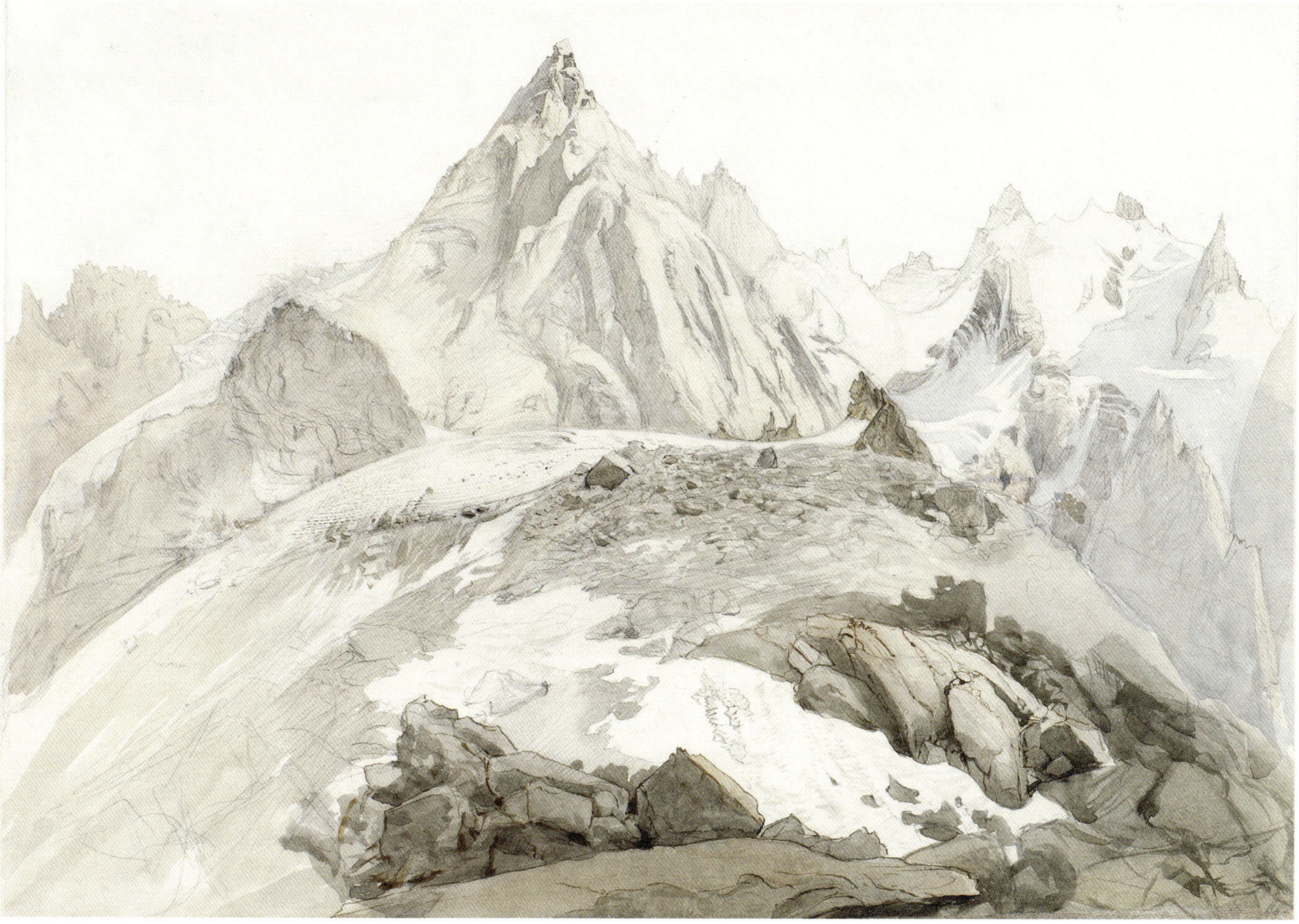

98

Rapid Studies of Effects from the Faulhorn, or *Studies of Alpine Peaks* 1846 or 1854

Watercolour, bodycolour and graphite on three joined sheets of grey-green paper; 16.8 × 25.2 cm
Birmingham Museums and Art Gallery. Presented by an anonymous donor, 1907 (1907P145)
Inscriptions: *Schreckhorn* (twice), *F. Aarhorn* (twice), *Mettenberg*, *Eiger* (twice), *Jungfrau*

Robert Hewison has convincingly proposed that the present drawing is identical to one that Ruskin gave to the Oxford Drawing School but then removed in 1887.[1] Ruskin's own description of that drawing explains that the series of views of the different mountains of which it consisted were made from a single vantage point, as is indicated by its original title – *Rapid Studies of Effects from the Faulhorn*. As he wrote in the catalogue of drawings given to Oxford:

> I had only one bit of paper [in fact several pieces, which had been or were subsequently jointed together] and packed the mountains all over it; but the Schreckhorn and Finsteraarhorn are all right as they first appear behind the brown rocks of the Faulhorn. Then, the summit of the Schreckhorn becoming clear, I sketched it above the Finsteraarhorn. Presently the Finsteraarhorn throwing off its clouds, I saw I had got it too steep, and drew it again below itself. Farther to the right the Eiger and Jungfrau had to be packed in at the left-hand bottom corner, and a final study of the quite clear Schreckhorn filled up what was left. These memoranda recall to me a most lovely scene, and I think the method of their execution is the most serviceable that can be adopted for such rapid work.[2]

E.T. Cook and Alexander Wedderburn believed the drawing was made in 1846, in which year Ruskin and his parents travelled in Europe together. Hewison has questioned this dating, suggesting 1854 as a likely alternative.[3] In June of that year, again with his parents, Ruskin visited the Bernese Oberland, and certainly on that occasion he took particular interest in several of the mountains seen in the present drawing, finding spiritual inspiration in looking at them. For example, as described in a diary entry for 24 June, he climbed early one morning from Thun to a point where "the Jungfrau and the two Eigers were clear and soft in the intense mountain light ... I stood long, *praying that these happy hours and holy sights might be of more use to me than they have been*, and might be remembered by me in hours of temptation or mortification."[4]

Given that Ruskin was working at such a range and was intent upon giving as accurate a representation as possible of each mountain as viewed in the morning light and with the sun casting on their left-hand flanks, it must be assumed that he was on this occasion using binoculars or a telescope. The Faulhorn stands to the east of Interlaken and south of Lake Brienz; from this point the peaks that were the object of his attention are visible to the south and southeast, with the Mättenberg (the closest, seen at a distance of about 10 kilometres), the Schreckhorn and the Lauteraarhorn in near alignment. Further to the south, at a distance of about 18 kilometres, is the Finsteraarhorn, while due south of the Faulhorn stands the Eiger, with the Jungfrau further to its left and at a distance of about 15 kilometres. Ruskin

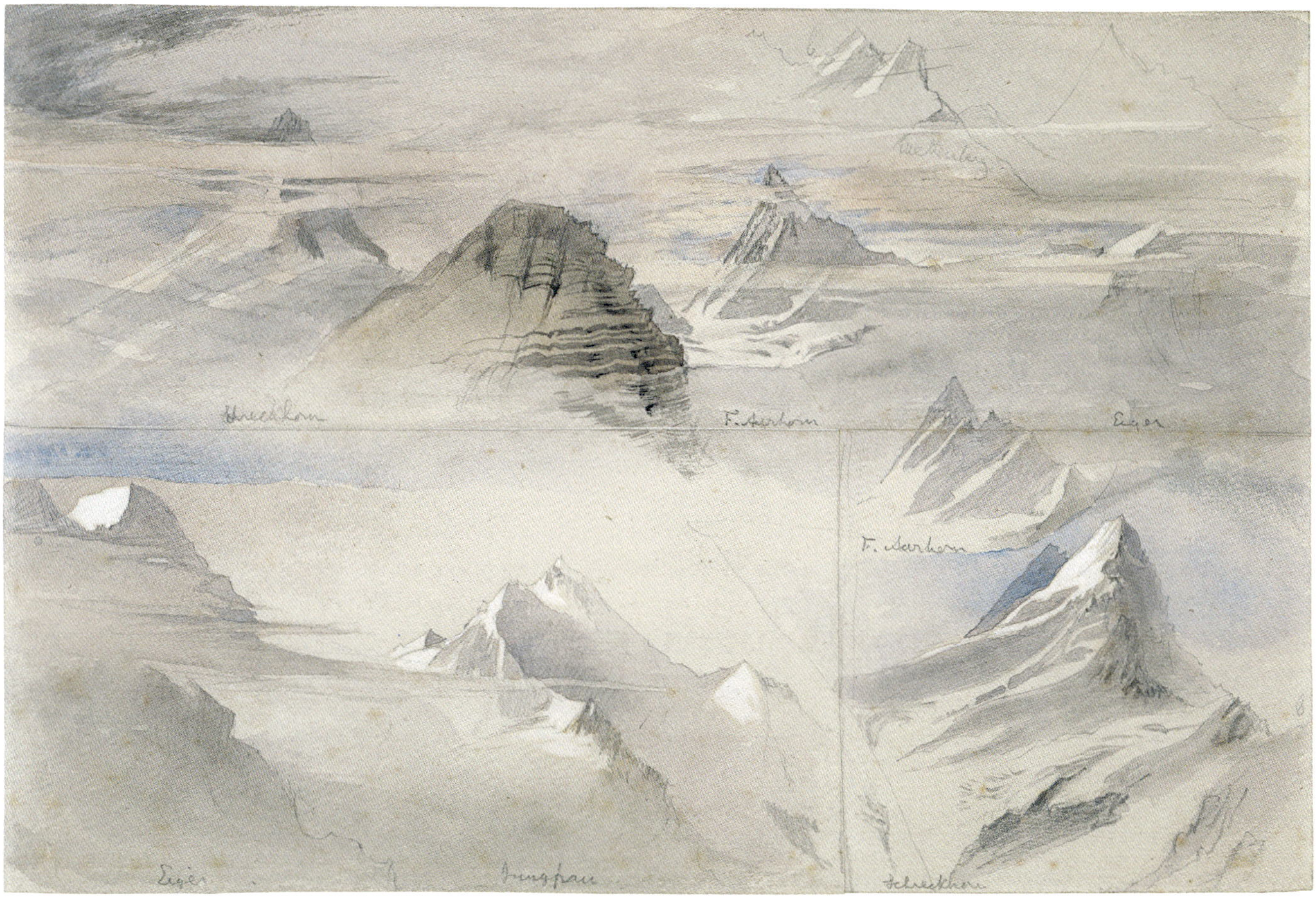

had mentioned several of these peaks in the opening passage of the chapter "Of the Central Mountains" in the first volume of *Modern Painters*,[5] in which he discusses the impression of height – actual and in relation to neighbouring mountains – that each might have, and this text may perhaps have been in his thoughts as he drew.

The peaks are not given in any logical geographical sequence, and therefore one can imagine Ruskin's attention moving from one to the other as he recognized them and as each came in and out of view as clouds drifted over (as he described in his catalogue text). The word "rapid" of the title is perhaps a misnomer, but the purpose of the drawing was to make a visual record of the specific characteristics of each mountain. At the time, Ruskin was beginning to prepare his thoughts for the fifth volume of *Modern Painters*, the gist of which was that landscape painters should only treat mountain subjects on the basis of a close familiarity with the particular peaks and wider ranges that they sought to represent.

NOTES

1 London 2000, p. 150.
2 Ruskin 1903–12, vol. 21, *The Ruskin Art Collection at Oxford: Catalogues, Notes, and Instructions*, pp. 277–278.
3 See London 2000, p. 150.
4 Ruskin 1956, vol. 2, pp. 496–497.
5 Ruskin 1903–12, vol. 3, *Modern Painters I*, p. 431.

99

Pass of the Cenis, above St. Michel, or *Pine Forest on Mont Cenis* 1854 or 1856

Watercolour, bodycolour and pen and ink over graphite on grey wove paper; 49.4 × 33.3 cm
The Ashmolean Museum, Oxford. Presented by John Ruskin to the Ruskin Drawing School (University of Oxford), 1875 (WA.RS.ED.275)

In the summers of 1854 and 1856 Ruskin travelled through France and Switzerland with his parents. On one or other, or both, of these trips the family stayed at San Michele, on the Italian side of the Mont-Cenis Pass close to the town of San Ambrogio, where there was a medieval Benedictine abbey.[1] In the catalogue of the exhibition of J.M.W. Turner watercolours from Ruskin's collection held at the Fine Art Society in 1878, which included a selection of his own drawings, the present view appeared with the first of the two titles given above. However, Ruskin was uncertain as to the date of the drawing.

From 1841 onward Ruskin frequently crossed the Mont-Cenis Pass – which runs between Lanslebourg in Savoy and Susa and forms the western approach toward Turin – and on each occasion was excited by its geological character and spectacular scenery. The French-Italian frontier then ran along the summit of the pass (but in 1947 was redrawn on a line closer to Turin so that the entire Col du Mont-Cenis is now French territory). This was one of the historic routes into Italy through the southern Alps, traversed by Charlemagne in 773 and Napoleon's general Alexandre Dumas in 1794.

In a passage omitted from the final text of *Præterita*, Ruskin recalled the objective and circumstances that led to the present drawing:

> I had long intended to make a careful study of the pine forests, traversed by cascades, on the left bank of the Arc, four miles above St. Michel on the Cenis road. We [Ruskin and his parents] found very pleasant rooms in the little inn of the village of St. Michel, and there papa and mamma settled themselves for ten days or a fortnight, in which time I promised to complete my drawing; and for a wonder, and for once, did so. But of course my subject, with effect of sunshine aslope from the east and south, could only be worked upon in the morning; and I used to drive the four miles up hill to it, work for two or three hours steadily, and get back to the village in time to take papa and mamma for a walk before dinner. On both sides of the valley of St. Michel, the terraced walks from cottage to cottage are of perfect beauty."[2]

On 2 September 1858, in a letter written to his mother on her birthday, Ruskin described the homeward journey he was then making after the six-week stay in Turin that had occupied him that summer and the route that he was taking, which was leading him back through this familiar country: electing to walk the last leg of the distance from Turin to San Michele, he "mistook a bit of the road; so that I was perhaps a little later in passing under the pines of my drawing than you would calculate on my being,"[3] a reference that makes clear that the drawing in question was known to Margaret Ruskin and therefore almost certainly identical with the one done when the family had

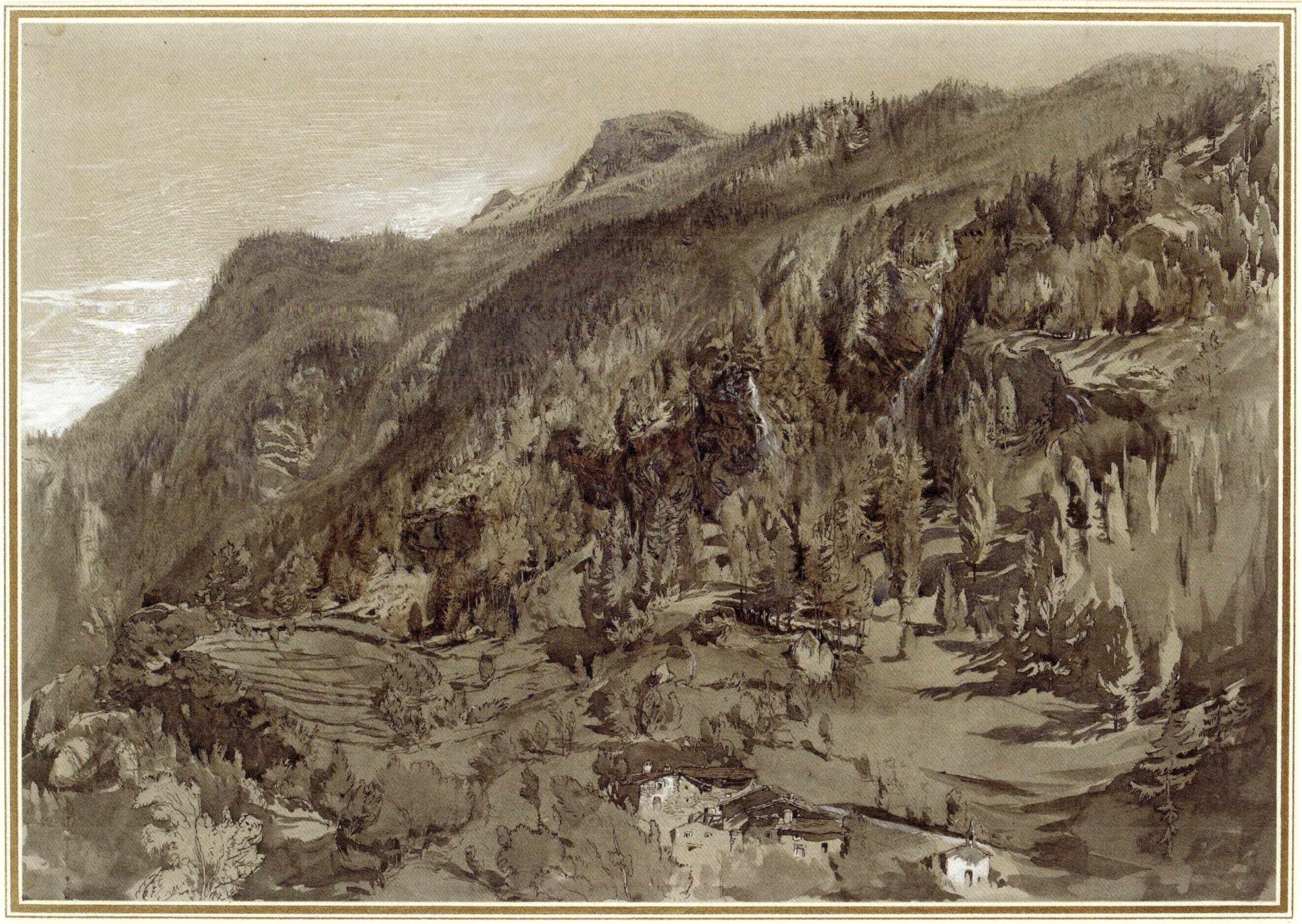

been there together two or four years previously.

In the same 1878 catalogue, Ruskin explained that he believed that Turner had wisely recognized the impossibility of conveying the vastness of Alpine scenery by the detailed rendering of its individual elements. Of his own approach, he said that he "did not understand [Turner's] warning, and went insanely at them at first, thinking to give some notion of them by sheer labour." In conclusion, he said of his attempt at representing the hollows and protuberances of the faceted hills and the morning shadows casting over mountain and trees that "one couldn't draw them with pen and sepia, I found; nor even with one's best pains in softer grey."[4] However, of the place shown, it was, as he recalled, "a glorious piece of Alpine wilderness, radiant with cascades and flowers among the forest glades," and one from which the traveller "derives much benefit, doubtless, from the dews of morning on those wild-wood glens."[5]

NOTES

1 However, no mention is made of their having reached so far south or having penetrated into Italy in Ruskin's diary accounts of the 1854 and 1856 trips.
2 Ruskin 1903–12, vol. 35, *Præterita and Dilecta*, p. 637.
3 Ruskin 1982, p. 161.
4 Ruskin 1903–12, vol. 13, *Turner, The Harbours of England, Catalogues and Notes*, p. 510.
5 Ibid.

100

Grütli, Uri-Rotstock from Lake Lucerne 1858 (?)

Graphite, watercolour and bodycolour on paper; 34.5 × 54 cm
The Alpine Club, London
Inscriptions: *Grutli*

Ruskin's view on this occasion is on the Bay of Uri or Urnersee, which is the most southeasterly of the various reaches of Lake Lucerne. The almost vertical cliffs largely consisting of sheets of sheer bare rock rising up from the lake shore are those at Grütli close to the village of Bauen, while to the south soars the peak of the Uri-Rotstock, a mountain that rises to nearly 3,000 metres, in the ancient Swiss canton of Uri. The drawing is likely to have been made in the summer of 1858, when in June Ruskin travelled to Flüelen, at the most southerly point on the Urnersee, to meet the painter John William Inchbold. Diary entries and letters home give detailed accounts of the formation of the cliffs and shoreline of this part of the lake; the present drawing and the beautiful prose descriptions that were incorporated into the fifth volume of *Modern Painters*, to be published two years later, make clear the impression that the landscape had upon Ruskin.

Grütli was a place hallowed in Ruskin's mind, and so the drawing may be seen as a conscious tribute to what he took to be the particular qualities of resilience and fortitude of the Swiss. It was here that in 1291 the people of the three so-called forest cantons – Schwyz, Unterwalden and Uri – met and swore an oath to found the Swiss Confederation. Ruskin perceived the physical setting as emblematic of the fight for liberty and independence, and that the Swiss character was in some way linked to the ruggedness of landscape and hardships that went with living in the mountains. In the fifth volume of *Modern Painters*, he described what he regarded as "the most sacred spot in Swiss history, the Meadow of the Three Fountains," which was to be reached by bidding "the boatmen row southward a little way by the Bay of Uri." In purely physical terms, the place was stupendously impressive, for "steepest there on its western side, the walls of its rocks ascend to heaven. Far in the blue of the evening, like a great cathedral pavement, lies the lake in its darkness; and you may hear the whisper of innumerable falling waters return from the hollows of the cliff, like the voices of a multitude praying under their breath."[1]

In a letter to his American friend Charles Eliot Norton, written later in the year and after his return to London, Ruskin gave an account of his travels that summer and the malaise of spirit that had overtaken him, explaining that he had been "out of heart ... chiefly owing to the reaction from the intense excitement of the Turner work"[2] (referring to his work on the contents of J.M.W. Turner's studio and the preparation of the 1857 exhibition of Turner drawings). The artist was constantly in Ruskin's thoughts at this time, so that in his letters to his father he explained his whereabouts by reference to drawings by Turner that were familiar to them both, at the same time feeling that his own work was inadequate by comparison. From Rheinfelden he had written on 24 May that, although his drawing was going

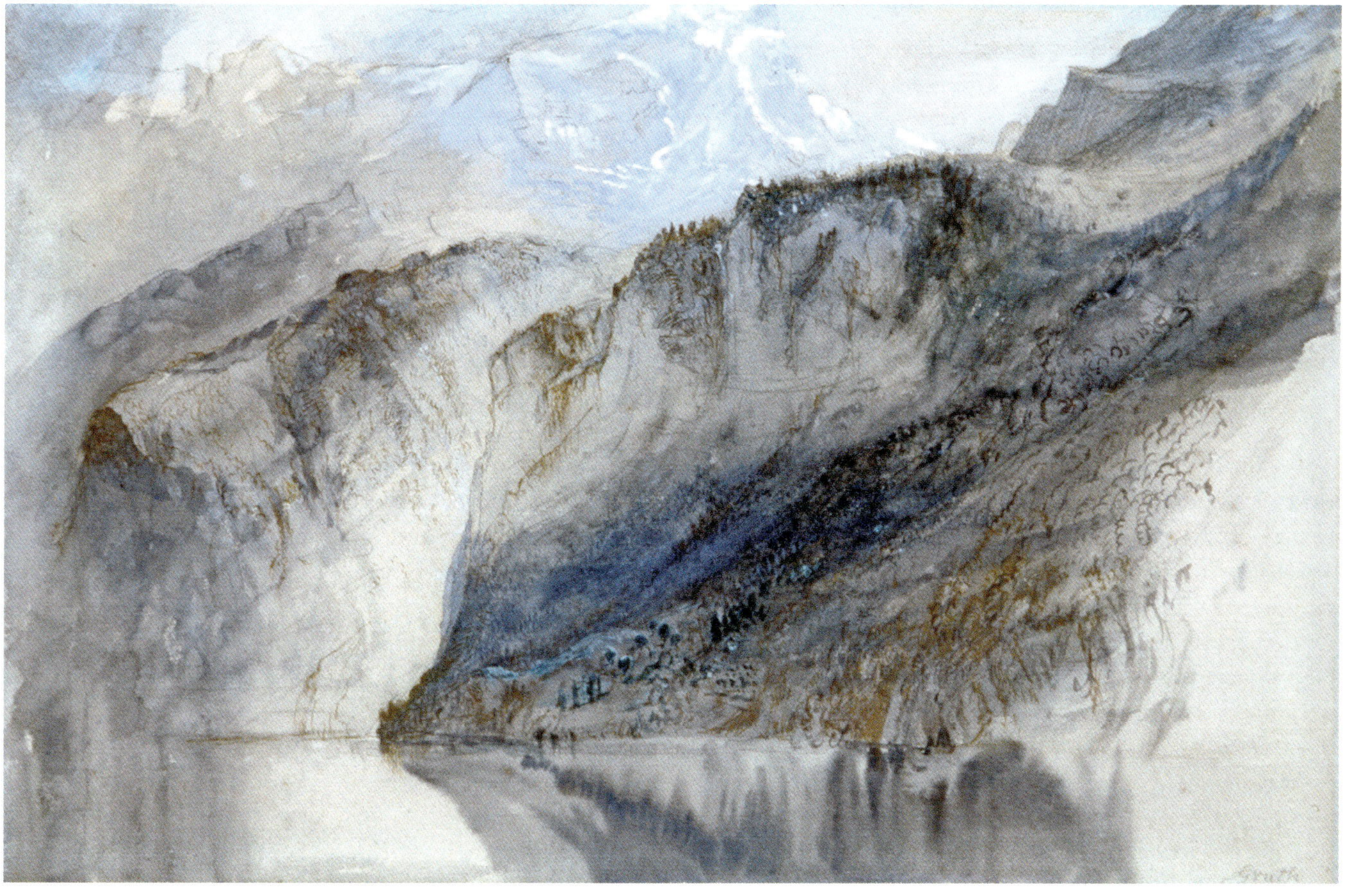

well, "the worst of it is that unless it be as good as Turner, it doesn't please me; so that on the whole I am seldom pleased, and I find it very difficult to sketch after having accustomed myself to finish: but I force myself to it."[3] Then, on 6 June, he wrote again to his father: "I am getting a nice drawing here – though always in a despairing temper from not being able to do as well as Turner so that I don't in the least enjoy my work as I used to do."[4] The fact is, Ruskin was himself adopting an impressionistic breadth in his style of drawing in this period and was impatient with the standard of "finish" of what he was coming to see as niggling or mechanical methods (as was witnessed by his dissatisfaction with Inchbold's work at Fluelen, and again in his exchanges with John Brett later in the summer, when that artist was working on his landscape *Val d'Aosta* [Lord Lloyd Webber collection]).

Ruskin had learned how to instil a fluid and living quality to his landscape studies that was different to Turner's work and that equally represented a departure from Pre-Raphaelite landscape principles. In the present drawing he shows the effect of light flooding in from the west between the vast hull-like projections of rock that form the lakeshore, with pools of shadow on the flanks facing the spectator. An ominous mood is achieved, perhaps fitting to the momentous historical associations of the place, and the stupendous scale and vertiginous slopes of the mountains seem threatening and inhospitable. All appears to be in movement with the treatment of rock faces, forested slopes and the surface of the lake seeming to seethe before one's eyes, while the fluctuating gradation of intensity of semi-transparent washes of colour makes everything appear indefinite and in flux. Even so, when the drawing was exhibited under the title *Cliff of the Bay of Uri* in 1878 it was, Ruskin thought, "the best I could do, but still useless to express the pine beauty."[5]

NOTES

1 Ruskin 1903–12, vol. 7, *Modern Painters V*, pp. 113–114.
2 Ruskin 1903–12, vol. 36, *The Letters of John Ruskin, 1827–1869*, p. 293.
3 Ruskin 1982, p. 41.
4 Ibid., p. 31.
5 Ruskin 1903–12, vol. 13, *Turner, The Harbours of England, Catalogues and Notes*, p. 510.

101

View from my Window at Mornex, Where I Stayed a Year 1861–62

Watercolour and bodycolour on paper; 27.5 × 37.5 cm
Courtesy of Abbot Hall Art Gallery, Lakeland Arts Trust, Kendal, Cumbria, UK (AH284/63)
Inscriptions: *View from my Window – Mornex where I stayed a year*

Ruskin had long contemplated making a home for himself in the Alps – whether in Switzerland or France – dreaming perhaps of a place where he might work without distraction, and with the opportunities of devoting more time to geology and the physical sciences. In addition, the prospect of having his own place and no longer being entirely reliant on his parental household at Denmark Hill must have been attractive to him. In *Præterita*, he described various locations that he contemplated for permanent residence or as an occasional place of refuge: he was, he said, "in treaty again and again for pieces of land near the chain of Mont Blanc on which I thought to establish my life, and round which to direct its best energies."[1]

First, he explained how he had bought a parcel of land above Chamonix, but then "sold it on perceiving what ruin was inevitable in the valley after it became a tourist rendezvous"; he then negotiated to purchase the crest of Mont Brezon above Bonneville, which was, he said, "a waste of barren rock, with pasturage only for a few goats," but gave up when the town council proved impossible to negotiate with. Next he considered a fourteenth-century castle at La Roche, long used for storing fruit and with walls six feet thick, before he "abandoned also the idea of this gloomy magnificence."[2] In August 1862, after travelling in Italy with Edward and Georgiana Burne-Jones, he found accommodation in the village of Mornex – beside his beloved Arve, but conveniently just an hour and a half's walk southeast of Geneva[3] – where he spent most of the remaining part of the year and until the following March.

Ruskin needed to get away and have peace at this time because he was prohibited from seeing Rose La Touche, the Irish girl with whom he had fallen obsessively in love. Furthermore, he was beset by religious doubts and a mounting concern for social conditions and economic disadvantage, all of which gave him a sense that the things that he was coming to believe in and be particularly interested in would alienate him from his mother and father. As he wrote to his American friend Charles Eliot Norton in December of the year: "I've had a weary time of it since last I wrote,[4] and have been quite finally worried & hurt, and the upshot of it is that I've come away here to live among the hills, and get what sober remnant of life I can, in peace, where there are no machines, yet, nor people – nor talk – nor trouble – but of the winds."[5]

In the same letter, Ruskin described his quarters at Mornex, which consisted of the lodgings where he first settled but that he then found cramped and dark so that in addition he rented a large house – 150 yards down the hill but with much better light and views and let to him by the Empress of Russia. He continued to dream of building for himself "a nest, high on the hills, where they are green," but in the "meantime I've a little garden with a spring in it; and a grey rough granite wall; and a vine or two;

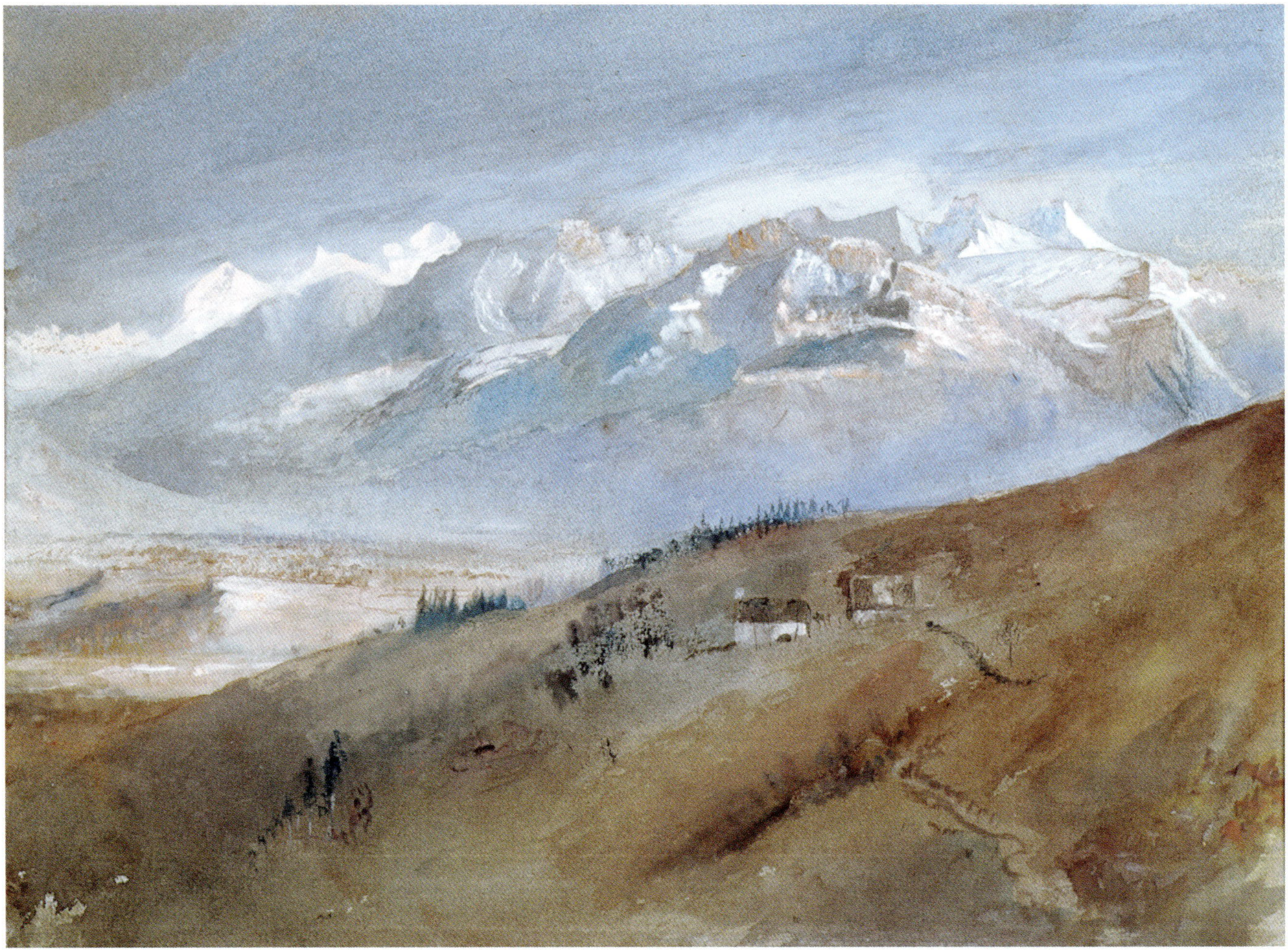

and then a dingle about 300 feet deep – and a sweet chestnut & pine wood opposite, and then Mont du Reposoir – & Mont Blanc, and the aiguilles of Chamouni, which I can see from my pillow, against the dawn."[6] By the following February he was beginning to feel worn down by the extremes of the Alpine winter and seems also to have been restlessly incapable of working, and so he began to realize that the place would not suit him long-term. Looking back on his sojourn in Savoy when writing *Præterita*, he concluded that "the journeying of the year ... gave me the melancholy knowledge of the agricultural condition of the great Alpine chain which was the origin of the design of the St. George's Guild; and ... virtually closed the days of youthful happiness, and began my true work in the world – for what it is worth."[7]

There are few references to work on drawings during the time Ruskin was at Mornex. However, on 10 March 1863 in a letter to Norton, which gives an account of his daily routine, he described how he had gone "to my other house ... which looks up the valley of the Arve and [how there he had worked on] a very careful drawing I'm making of it – very slowly & feebly."[8] This is almost certainly a reference to the pencil drawing that bears the title *The Brezon, and Alps of the Reposoir, seen from Mornex*, which Ruskin described in his catalogue of the Rudimentary Series of drawings given to Oxford as "an example of mountain drawing in pure pencil, which will show what kind of labour I had to go through in gaining my knowledge of mountain-form."[9]

The view taken in the pencil drawing and the present gouache corresponds exactly, both in the middleground of chalets and pinewood and in the representation of the distant Mont Blanc massif. There is, however, a marked contrast of impression between the meticulous pencil work of the Oxford drawing and the *plein-air* freedom and expansiveness of the gouache. In this last, the colours alternate between the russets and greys of the shadowed foreground, achieved by allowing pools of colour to spread and coalesce on the sheet, and the staccato alternation of patches of grey-blue and white in the mountains.

NOTES

1 Ruskin 1903–12, vol. 35, *Præterita and Dilecta*, p. 436.
2 Ibid, pp. 436–437.
3 As he specified in a diary entry for 18 August 1862 (Ruskin 1956, vol. 2, p. 567).
4 Ruskin's previous letter to Norton, among those to survive, had been written on 28 August.
5 Ruskin Norton 1987, p. 74.
6 Ibid.
7 Ruskin 1903–12, vol. 35, p. 437.
8 Ruskin Norton 1987, p. 78.
9 Ruskin 1903–12, vol. 21, *The Ruskin Art Collection at Oxford: Catalogues, Notes, and Instructions*, p. 209.

102

"A July Thunder-cloud in the Val d'Aosta" 1858

Graphite and watercolour heightened with white bodycolour on paper;
24.2 × 53.5 cm (irregularly shaped)
Private collection

The present drawing presumably received its current title when a diagram based on it was used as an illustration to Ruskin's lecture "The Storm-cloud of the Nineteenth Century," given at the London Institution on two occasions, on 4 and 11 February 1884.[1] These colour projections were prepared by Arthur Severn and William Gershom Collingwood and – in the case of the *July Thunder-cloud* – represented a reworking of the left-hand two-thirds of the present drawing. Severn's diagrams were in turn reproduced as woodcuts by J.D. Cooper and used to illustrate an article by Alexander Wedderburn in the 1884 *Art Journal* reporting on Ruskin's lectures.[2]

The original drawing was in fact made in August 1858, near the end of Ruskin's long stay in Turin that summer. Rather than showing the Val d'Aosta, it represents a view from the city looking northwest across the Val di Susa, with L'Iseran and the Grande Aiguille Rousse close to Val d'Isère forming the horizon. On 20 August Ruskin wrote a letter to his father, the concluding paragraph of which described the season and meteorological conditions observed in the drawing: "Autumn is clearly the time for Italy & the distant Alps; I have had them today in far grander power than even that night when the storm got so broken to pieces by them.[3] It has been raining in the night – & snowing on Mont Iseran, and there is a clear south west wind, and the Alps are indulging in this sort of thing" (inserted at the bottom of the sheet is a pen and ink sketch of the Alps as seen from Turin, corresponding both in its perspective on the mountains and treatment of the cloud formations to the present drawing).[4]

The "Storm-cloud" lectures of 1884 represented a return on Ruskin's part to the study of clouds. In 1837, at the age of eighteen, he had read a paper to the august Meteorological Society entitled "On the Formation and Colour of such Clouds as are caused by the Agency of Mountains."[5] In the first volume of *Modern Painters*, three successive chapters were given to the theme "On Truth of Clouds," in which he discussed a typology of cloud formations, the variations and complexities of which, "all unlike each other, except in beauty," were regarded by him – along with everything in nature – as "bearing witness to the unwearied, exhaustless operation of the Infinite Mind."[6] In 1858, however, during his stay in Turin, a crisis of faith that had been incipient for a year or two previously occurred – firstly in reaction to his mother's evangelical Protestantism but also as a prelude to a complete loss of belief in divine providence.

In 1858 Ruskin was gathering material and preparing his thoughts for the fifth and final volume of *Modern Painters*, which was to be published two years later. Outlining an approach to natural phenomena quite different to what had gone before, it represented a departure from the dogmatism and schematic views of earlier volumes. Likewise, drawings

NOTES

1. See Ruskin 1903–12, vol. 34, *The Storm-cloud of the Nineteenth Century, On the Old Road, Arrows of the Chace, Ruskiniana.*
2. "Mr Ruskin on 'The Storm-Cloud'," *Art Journal* (1884), pp. 105–108. The woodcut reproducing the present drawing is shown on p. 107 (and appears again in Ruskin 1903–12, vol. 34, opposite p. 40). A watercolour version or preparatory study for the subject by Arthur Severn is in the collection of the Ruskin Foundation (no. 1217).
3. The night of 30 July 1858, when Ruskin had seen a "wonderful sunset" and "a storm that came up in fragments along the plain" (Ruskin 1982, p. 109).
4. Ruskin 1982, p. 140 (for the text of the letter) and plate 10 (for a facsimile of it).
5. The text has not survived, but the title alone indicates its gist.
6. Ruskin 1903–12, vol. 3, *Modern Painters I*, p. 381.

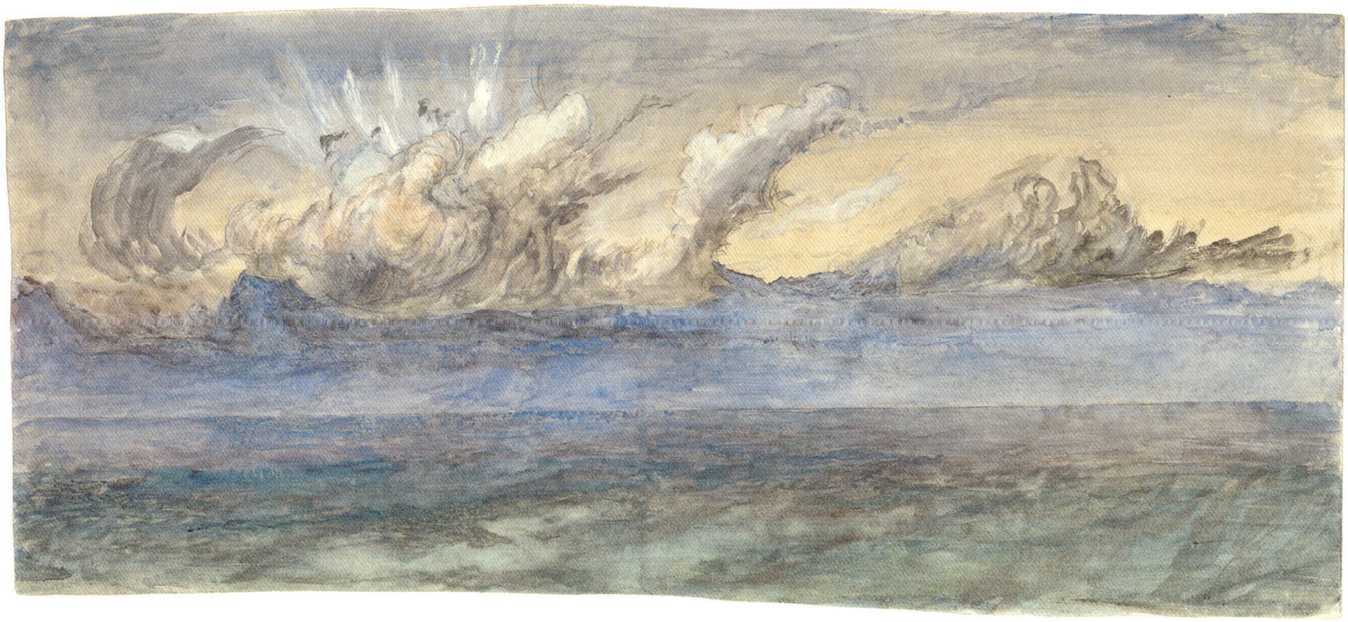

such as the present depict chaotic elemental forces that were potentially devastating and to be feared. In the fifth volume of *Modern Painters*, once again, a whole section comes under the heading "Of Cloud Beauty," but here the tone is for the most part enquiring and tentative, with only occasional passages in which Ruskin invokes awesome and eschatological imagery. One such must surely depend on his memories of the view of the Alps from Turin, describing as it does "war-clouds that gather on the horizon, dragon-crested, tongued with fire; – how is their barbed strength bridled? What bits are these they are champing with their vaporous lips; flinging off flakes of black foam? Leagued leviathans of the Sea of Heaven, out of their nostrils goeth smoke, and their eyes are like the eyelids of the morning."[7]

In the "Storm-cloud" lectures, as has been seen, Ruskin found use for a drawing he had made a quarter of a century earlier and carried forward imagery of a natural world from which no comfort might come, not only because nature was no longer to be regarded as a benign or benevolent entity created by God as a haven for mankind, but instead as an elemental force subject to its own laws, even in addition a mechanism that because of man's abuse of his own environment would be the cause of self-inflicted destruction. On that occasion, the "July Thunder-cloud" was seen as an "example of a good old-fashioned healthy storm,"[8] from a time before the climate was upset and unbalanced by human agency.

7 Ruskin 1903–12, vol. 7, *Modern Painters V*, p. 135.
8 "Mr Ruskin on 'The Storm-Cloud'," *Art Journal* (1884), p. 107.

103

Study of Clouds in Turner's "Campo Santo, Venice" 1859–60

Watercolour and bodycolour on pale grey wove paper; 35.7 × 46.7 cm
The Ashmolean Museum, Oxford. Presumably presented by John Ruskin to the Ruskin Drawing School (University of Oxford), where it was first recorded in 1906 (W.RS.REF.098)

Ruskin studied clouds and their formations and understood them in scientific terms. On frequent occasions in his letters and diary he described particular atmospheric effects, often with sketches attached. This lifelong fascination was given its most complete expression in part seven of the fifth and final volume of *Modern Painters*, entitled "Of Cloud Beauty," for which the present copy of a detail in J.M.W. Turner's painting *Campo Santo, Venice* (fig. 7.2) was made as an illustration. There, Ruskin announced that "Turner stands more absolutely alone in his gift of cloud-drawing than in any other of his great powers," while the painting upon which Ruskin's drawing was based "is exquisite in rounding of the separate fragments and buoyancy of the rising central group, as well as in its expression of the wayward influence of curved lines of breeze on a generally rectilinear system of cloud."[1]

Ruskin's appreciation of the importance of clouds as an integral part of the landscape as represented in art is demonstrated by the present study of cirrus copied from *The Campo Santo, Venice*. This was a painting that he had long admired (it had been lent to him by its owner Elhanan Bicknell and had been the object of close contemplation during the winter of 1842–43, when he was working on the first volume of *Modern Painters*), and had come to his mind in 1851 when he had received a letter in Venice from his father telling him of Turner's death – "every thing in the sunshine and the sky so talks of him. Their great witness lost," he replied.[2]

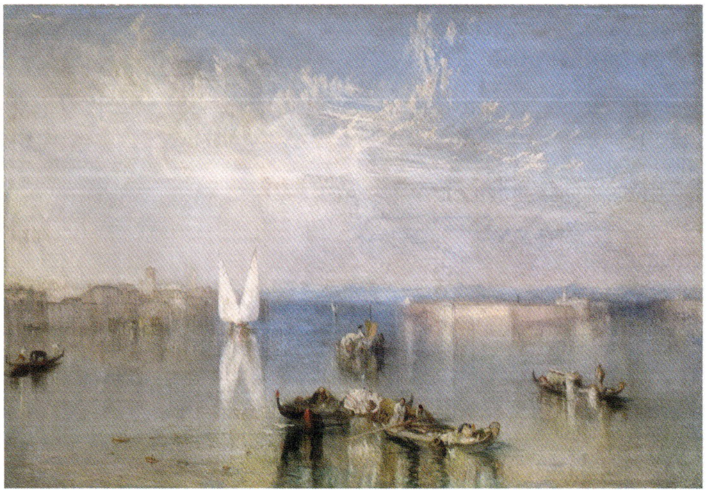

FIG. 7.2
J.M.W. Turner
The Campo Santo, Venice, 1842
Oil on canvas
Toledo Museum of Art (Toledo, Ohio). Gift of Edward Drummond Libbey (1926.63)

NOTES

1 Ruskin 1903–12, vol. 7, *Modern Painters V*, pp. 156–157.
2 Bradley 1955, p. 112.

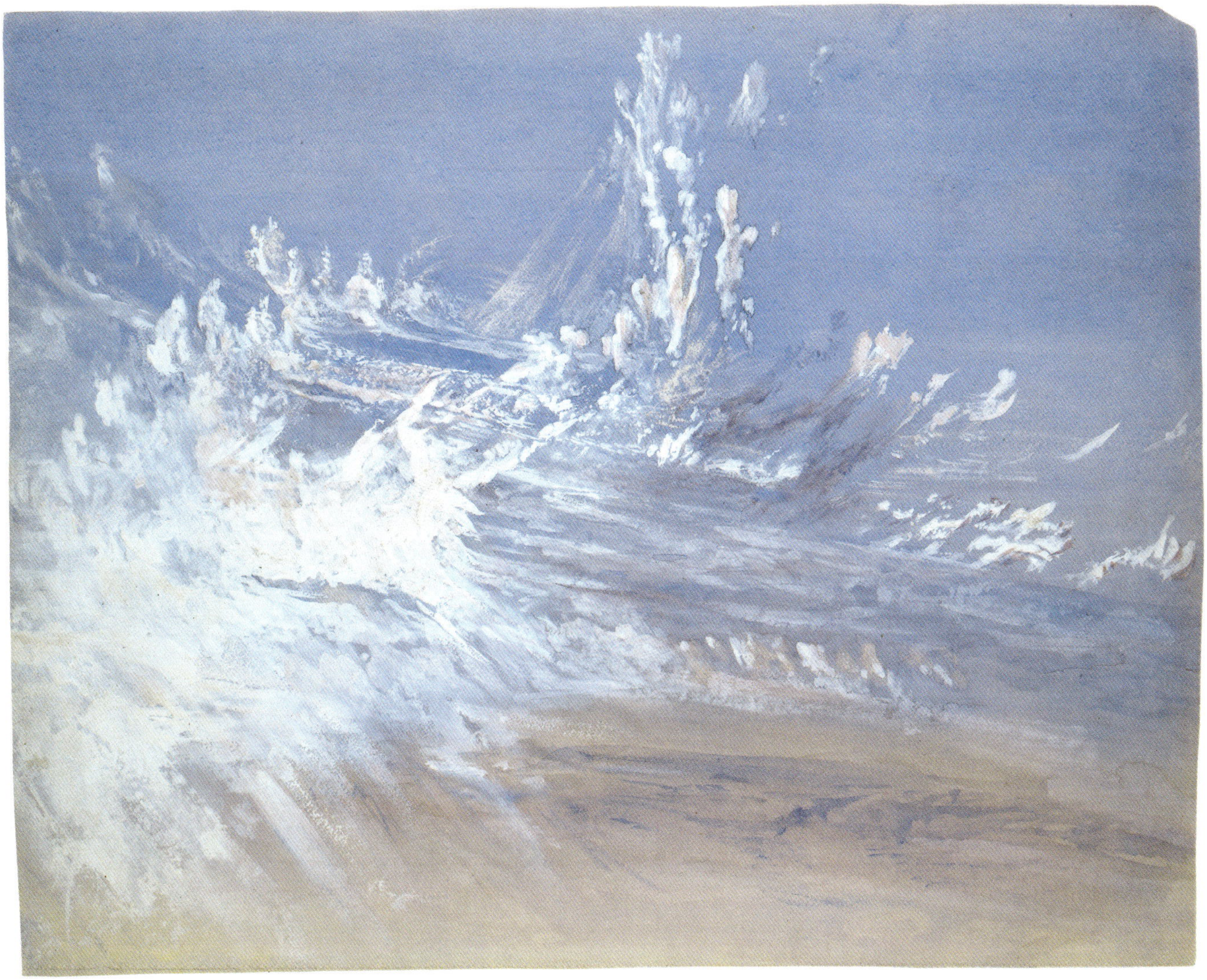

104

Mer de Glace, Chamonix, France 1860

Graphite, watercolour, bodycolour, pen and ink on grey paper; 42.1 × 33.1 cm
Whitworth Art Gallery, The University of Manchester (D.1968.3)
Inscriptions: graphite, *J. Ruskin Chamonix 1860*

This watercolour was made during Ruskin's stay in Switzerland from June to September 1860, following the publication of the fifth volume of *Modern Painters*. While there, he drafted *Unto this Last*, a work of political economy. The stay thus marks the opening of a new period in his intellectual life, which led him away from the study of art for its own sake, and his gathering preoccupation with economics and social questions. His interest in geology and mountain landscapes remained intense and continued to be explored and expressed in the drawings he made in this later period, of which this is one of the most breathtakingly beautiful. It shows a devastated confusion of boulders and vegetation beyond which is glimpsed the form of a glacier, seen as a diagonal gash of white bodycolour and marked by a jagged upper edge that signifies crevasses and standing columns of ice.

However, it may be recognized that a drawing of this type is less of a geographical record and investigation of the mechanisms of physical geography than it is an essay in the shapes, textures and colours that characterize the Alpine environment in summer. In this sense, it marks a shift in artistic purpose on Ruskin's part from scrupulous and selfless observation of an actual physical setting to something more subjective and aimed to achieve aesthetic satisfaction. The work was certainly studied directly from the motif, and yet was dependent in some degree on Ruskin's memories of paintings and drawings that he knew showing similar landscapes, such as a watercolour by J.M.W. Turner (fig. 7.3), which likewise shows the glacier running across the composition from the upper right to lower left – a drawing to which Ruskin had made reference in his 1851 pamphlet *Pre-Raphaelitism*.[1]

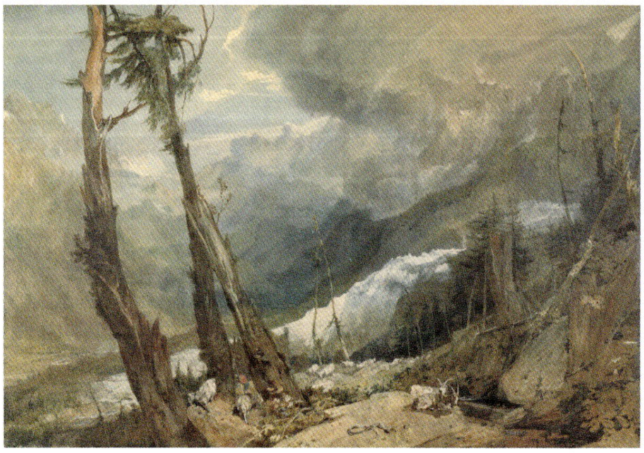

FIG. 7.3
J.M.W. Turner
Mer de Glace, in the Valley of Chamounix, Switzerland, 1803
Watercolour, graphite, gum, scraping out and stopping out
Yale Center for British Art, Paul Mellon Collection, New Haven (B1977.14.4650)

NOTES

1 Ruskin 1903–12, vol. 12, *Lectures on Architecture and Painting, Etc.*, p. 390.

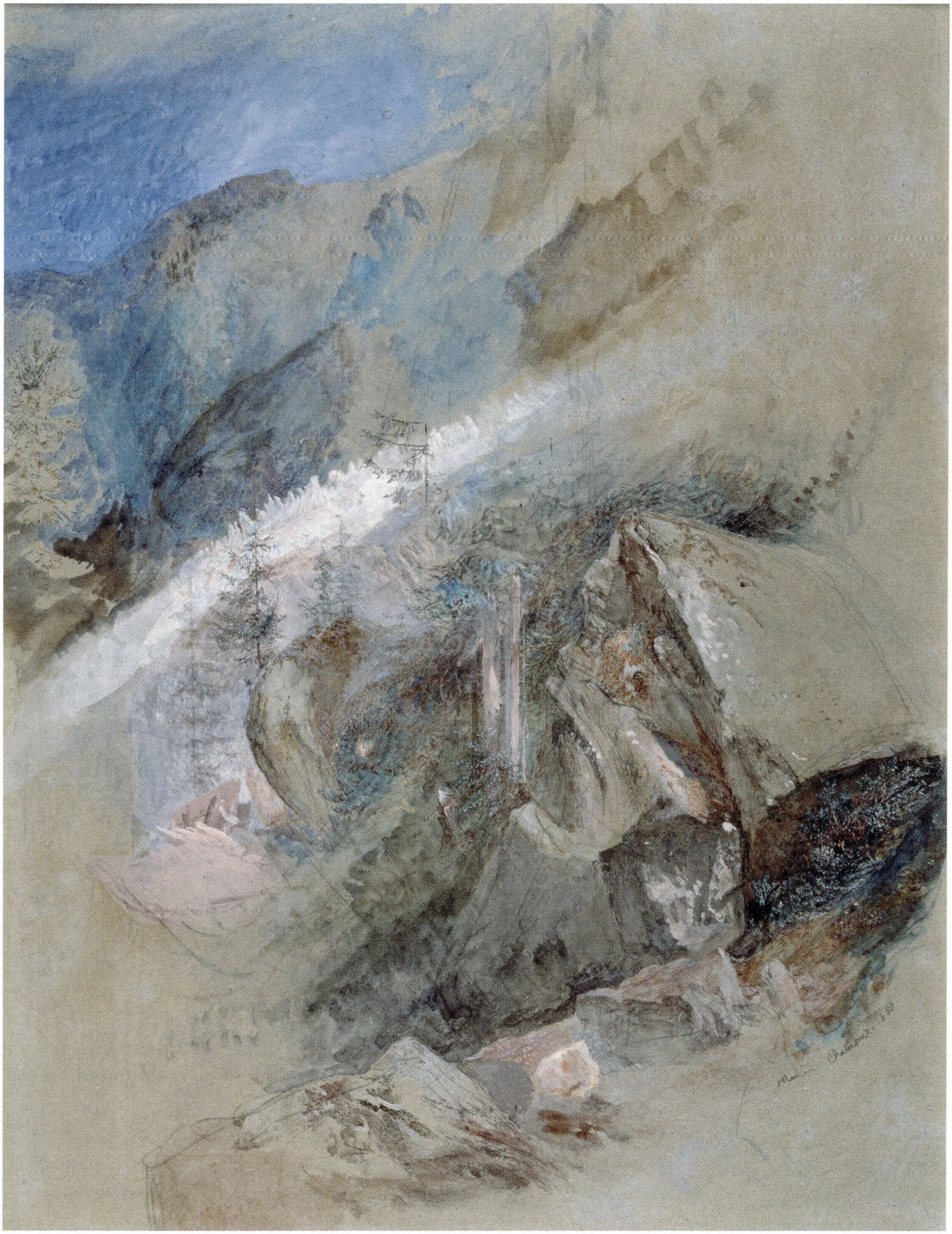

105

View from the Base of the Brezon above Bonneville 1862–63

Graphite, ink, watercolour and bodycolour on blue paper; 35.2 × 51.3 cm
Ruskin Foundation (Ruskin Library, Lancaster University) (RF 1174)
Inscriptions: graphite, verso, in a later hand, *Brezon – View from the Base of the Brezon before Bonneville – looking toward Geneva: The Jura in the distance: Salève on the left / (1862)*

This beautiful drawing, reminiscent of the landscapes of Flemish or Dutch painters of the seventeenth century, shows a northwest view along the Arve valley toward Geneva. The town of Bonneville is out of view to the right, while on the left is the village of La Roche-sur-Foron, seen from higher ground on the side of the Brezon. A spur of Mont Salève, close to Ruskin's temporary home at Mornex, appears in the distance on the left, while on the far horizon where the evening sun is sinking may be seen the Jura mountains, beyond the southern reach of Lake Geneva. Seldom did Ruskin ever treat an open or panoramic landscape with such rapture, and as such the work may be seen as a momentary expression of confidence and optimism.

According to Ruskin's editors E.T. Cook and Alexander Wedderburn, the large building in the lower left-hand part of the composition was the castle that he had thought of buying and converting into a house for himself. In *Præterita* Ruskin remembered this as having been in La Roche, while its architectural character seems to correspond to a description of the prospective purchase in a letter he wrote to his mother on 31 August 1862. It was, he said, "a true Savoyard château – notable for its lovely garden and orchard – and its unspoiled, unrestored, arched gateway between two round turrets, and Gothic-windowed keep." He had had second thoughts, however, as "on examination of the interior, [he found] the walls – though six feet thick – rent to the foundation, and as cold as rocks, and the floors all sodden through with walnut oil and rotten-apple juice – heaps of the farm stores having been left to decay in the ci-devant drawing-room," and so he "gave up all mediæval ideas, for which the long-legged black pigs (who lived like gentlemen at ease in the passage), and the bats and spiders who divided between them the corners of the turret-stair, have reason – if they knew it – to be thankful."[1]

NOTES

1 Ruskin 1903–12, vol. 17, *Unto this Last, Munera Pulveris, Time and Tide, with Other Writings on Political Economy, 1860–1873*, p. lv.

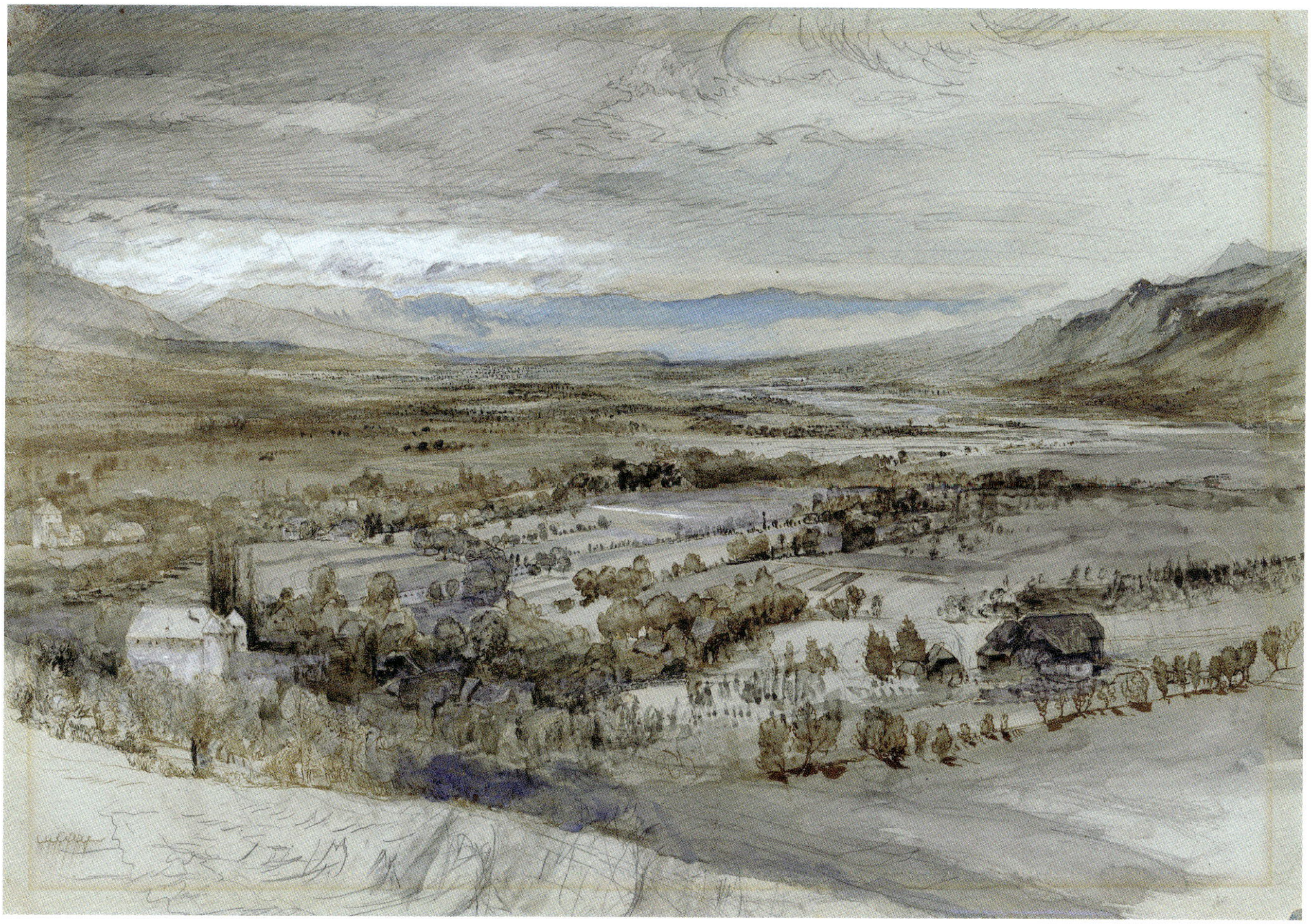

106

Dawn at Neuchâtel 1866

Watercolour over graphite on paper; 13.4 × 21 cm
Private collection
Inscriptions: *Vermilion darken / blue green stripe / shades to purple on left* [deleted] *right / relieving stripe / down into green*, verso, *Dawn. Neuchatel 9th May. 1866*

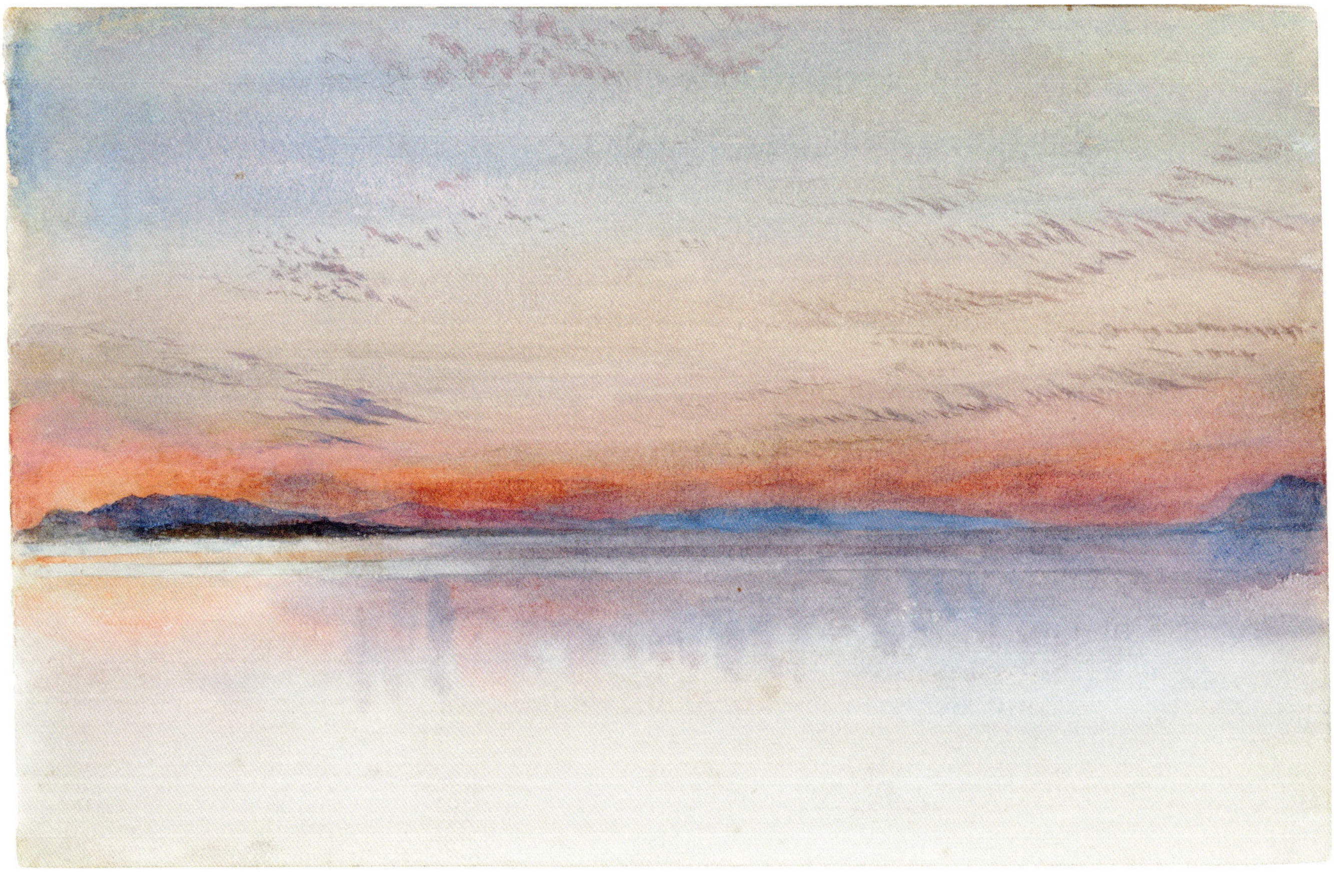

Ruskin had a particular love of the colours cast across the sky and the atmosphere at dawn. He habitually awoke early in the morning so as to observe the rising sun, and believed that there was much for students to learn from the subtle and transitory effects of luminescence and unfolding tints. In the manual *The Laws of Fésole*, published in parts in 1877–78 and intended as an expansion and successor to *The Elements of Drawing*, Ruskin besought his readers to follow a "standard of colour" that he regarded "an extremely safe one – the morning sky. Love *that* rightly with all your heart, and soul, and eyes; and you are established in foundation-laws of colour. The white, blue, purple, gold, scarlet, and ruby of morning clouds, are meant to be entirely delightful to the human creatures whom the 'clouds and light' sustain."[1]

Ruskin and a group of friends, travelling in Switzerland and France in the summer of 1866, arrived at Neuchâtel on 7 May, being conveyed – and with apparent contentment on his part – by train. As he described to his mother: "The approach to the lake by the new railroad line is the finest I have yet seen, though at all the best bits of it one plunges into a tunnel. But the comings out of tunnels were glorious, and the children [his cousin Joan Agnew, later Severn, and Constance Hilliard, the niece of Sir Walter Trevelyan] were quite overwhelmed when the blue lake opened with its Alps."[2] A few days later, however, the party was overtaken by misfortune, for Pauline Trevelyan fell ill and died. This tragic event, combined with the distress Ruskin felt at the interruption in his correspondence with Rose La Touche, forced upon him by her parents who had taken alarm at the relationship, left him in a depressed state of mind. On 21 May he wrote to C.A. Howell, then serving as his secretary in London: "I've had a rather bad time of it at Neuchâtel; what with Death and the North Wind; both devil's inventions as far as I can make out. But things are looking a little better now, and I have had a lovely three hours' walk by the lake shore, in cloudless calm, from five to eight this morning."[3]

Ruskin made at least three drawings of dawn rising on the lake at Neuchâtel during his stay there in May, all of which were done in a sketchbook that was subsequently broken up. *Dawn at Neuchâtel* (Fogg Art Museum, Cambridge, Massachusetts) represents a view southward across the lake toward the mountains of the Fribourg range (a view that he took again in the Ashmolean Museum's more complete watercolour *Afternoon in Spring, with South Wind, at Neuchâtel*). The present drawing, if the veracity of Ruskin's statement that it shows the lake at dawn is accepted, must have been taken from wherever the party was staying in Neuchâtel and with a view east looking into the wide expanse of the lake at its northeastern end, and with a mountain called Le Chasseral in the Swiss Jura on the left and the low hills rising to the south of the Bielersee and Seeland at the centre and on the right.

Drawings of this kind demonstrate a conscious or instinctive debt to the type of colour studies of coastal or lake landscapes that J.M.W. Turner had made in the 1830s and 1840s, of which Ruskin had a number of examples in his collection.[4] In these, the sun is often seen from a shoreline and over the sea, with a suggestion of a distant coastline, but no larger topographical indication as to where the drawing may have been made. In Turner's views, clouds frequently mask the sun with vaporous atmosphere tinged with reds and blues. Higher in the sky, bars or flecks of cloud catch the sunlight and show as pink strata in the wider cloudscape. Turner's very personal watercolours of the rising and setting sun exemplify an instinctive response to meteorological phenomena and qualities of atmosphere and light that Ruskin found thrilling to look at and that he consciously or unconsciously imitated in drawings such as the present.

NOTES

1 Ruskin 1903–12, vol. 15, *The Elements of Drawing, The Elements of Perspective, and The Laws of Fésole*, p. 417.
2 Ruskin 1903–12, vol. 18, *Sesame and Lilies, The Ethics of the Dust, The Crown of Wild Olives, with Letters on Public Affairs, 1859–1866*, p. xxxvi.
3 Ibid., p. xxxix.
4 See Wilton 1979, pp. 466–471, where nine marine studies are identified as having belonged to Ruskin or likely to have been in his collection.

107

a. *Study of Dawn: The First Scarlet on the Clouds* 1868

Watercolour and bodycolour over faint graphite lines on blue-grey paper; 13.8 × 18.8 cm
The Ashmolean Museum, Oxford. Presented by John Ruskin to the Ruskin Drawing School (University of Oxford), 1875 (WA.RS.ED.003)

b. *Study of Dawn: Purple Clouds* 1868

Watercolour and bodycolour over faint graphite lines on blue-grey paper; 15.3 × 22.3 cm
The Ashmolean Museum, Oxford. Presented by John Ruskin to the Ruskin Drawing School (University of Oxford), 1875 (WA.RS.ED.005)

These two delicate and enraptured studies of dawn skies – with another entitled *Study of Dawn: White Clouds* – were probably made in London from the windows of the Ruskin family home at Denmark Hill, the relative height of which in relation to neighbouring parts of south London allowed wide eastward panoramas toward the open countryside and clear air of Kent.

Ruskin was always conscious of the passing of time as measured by the succession of days. His personal motto was "To-Day," meaning that each day brought opportunities and was to be made best use of. In his diary he frequently marked entries with a number in a descending sequence, which referred to a notional number of days of life remaining to him. Furthermore, he was an habitual early riser, often recording the time that he was up – usually before dawn – in his diary. Ruskin disciplined himself to observe the sunrise, finding symbolic virtue of an almost sacramental kind in doing so, and recommending the practice as morally refreshing. Art students, as he wrote as an addendum to his catalogue of the Educational Series of drawings at Oxford, would be likely to find this a beneficial commencement to the day, and each person who remembers to "set aside a quarter of an hour of every morning ... for the observance of the sun-rise, and always to have pencil and colour at hand to make note of anything more than usually beautiful ... will find his thoughts during the rest of the day both calmed and purified, and his advance in all essential art-skill at once facilitated and chastised."[1]

NOTES

1 Ruskin 1903–12, vol. 21, *The Ruskin Art Collection at Oxford: Catalogues, Notes, and Instructions*, p. 106.

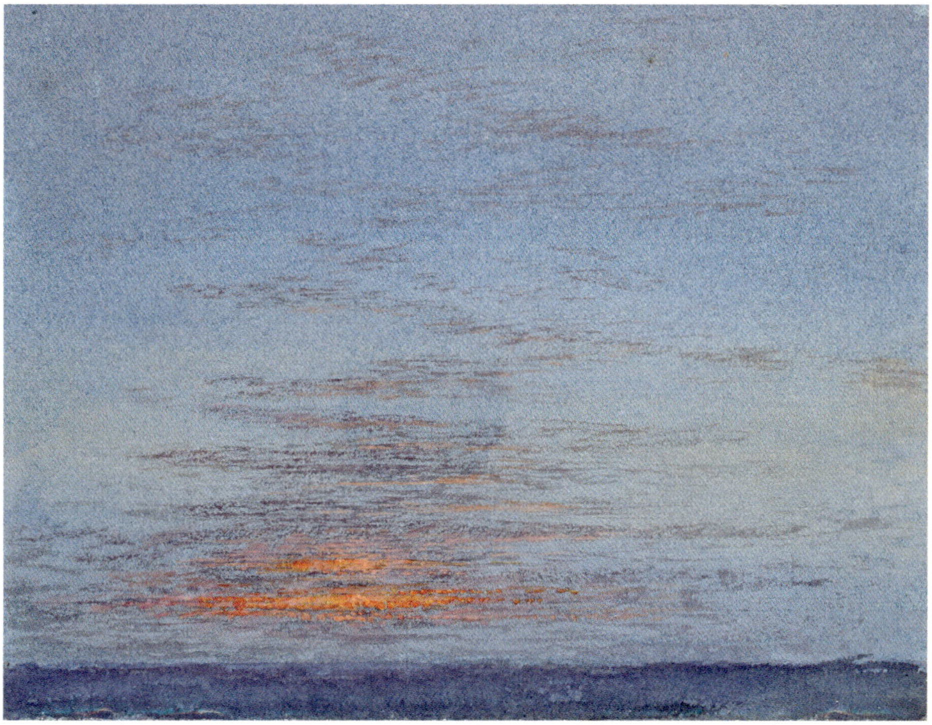

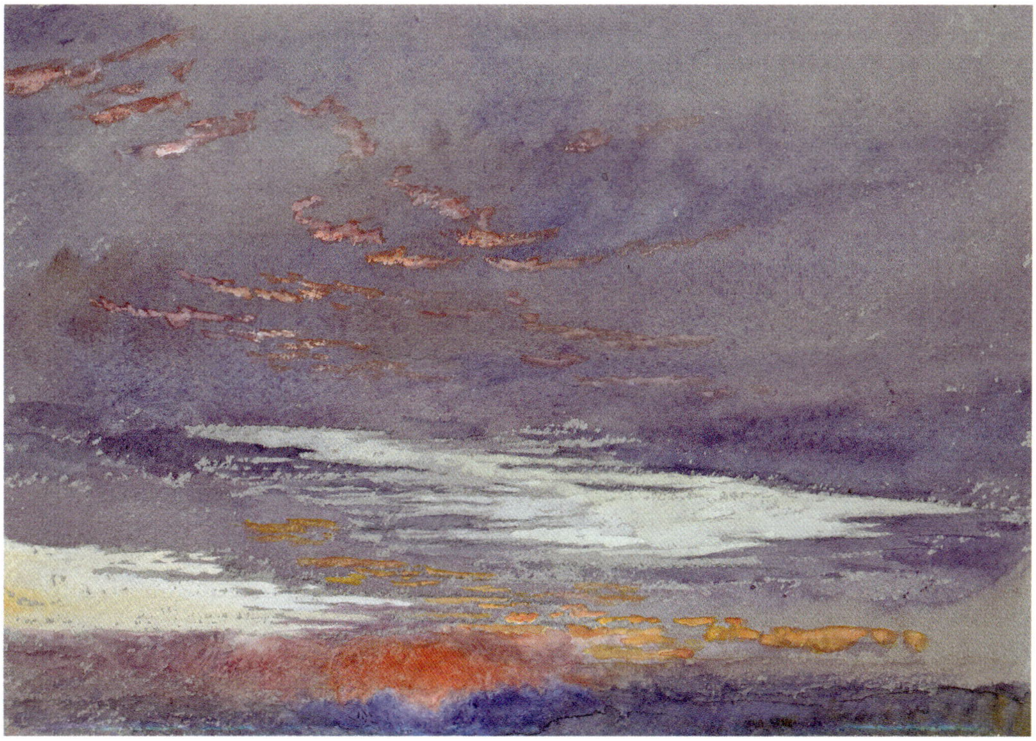

108

Dawn at Coniston 1873

Graphite, ink and watercolour on paper; 23.2 × 35.7 cm
Courtesy of Abbot Hall Art Gallery, Lakeland Arts Trust, Kendal, Cumbria, UK (LAT: 1998.0010)
Inscriptions: graphite, ...[?]*green purple* [?] ..., ink, *Dawn – Coniston – June 73*[twice] / *J Ruskin*

This ethereal watercolour shows the view across Coniston Water toward the Coniston fells. Mist rises from the glassy surface of the water, forming a wreath-like band across the sheet. The main body of mountainside on the lake's far shore is that known as the Old Man of Coniston, usually referred to by Ruskin as just "Old Man" or "Il Vecchio." The vantage point was somewhere close to Brantwood, the house on the eastern shore of Coniston Water that he had bought sight unseen in 1871 and that remained his home until his death in 1900.

Ruskin had loved the Lakes since childhood and found the countryside there an inspiration to his drawing. As he wrote to his friend Alfred William Hunt in anticipation of a visit that he was to make to see Ruskin in the early summer of 1873: "The scenery is – I think – the best in England ... there are more subjects in any twenty furlongs than in twenty miles of other country ... As for moor or mountain – I have rocks within two miles of me as fine at the St. Gothard."[1] It seems probable that Ruskin and Hunt worked together that summer, and certainly Ruskin commented on Hunt's drawings, beseeching him to give breadth and expression to his work. Hunt also made an early morning watercolour of Coniston Water. Titled *The Stillness of the Lake at Dawn* (1873, private collection), it likewise shows a view across the northern reach of the lake toward the Coniston Fells and dwells on the motif of mist rising from the surface of the water and the pellucid colour of the sunlit fells in the far distance.

NOTES

1 Violet Hunt Papers, Cornell University, quoted in New Haven Oxford 2004, p. 138.

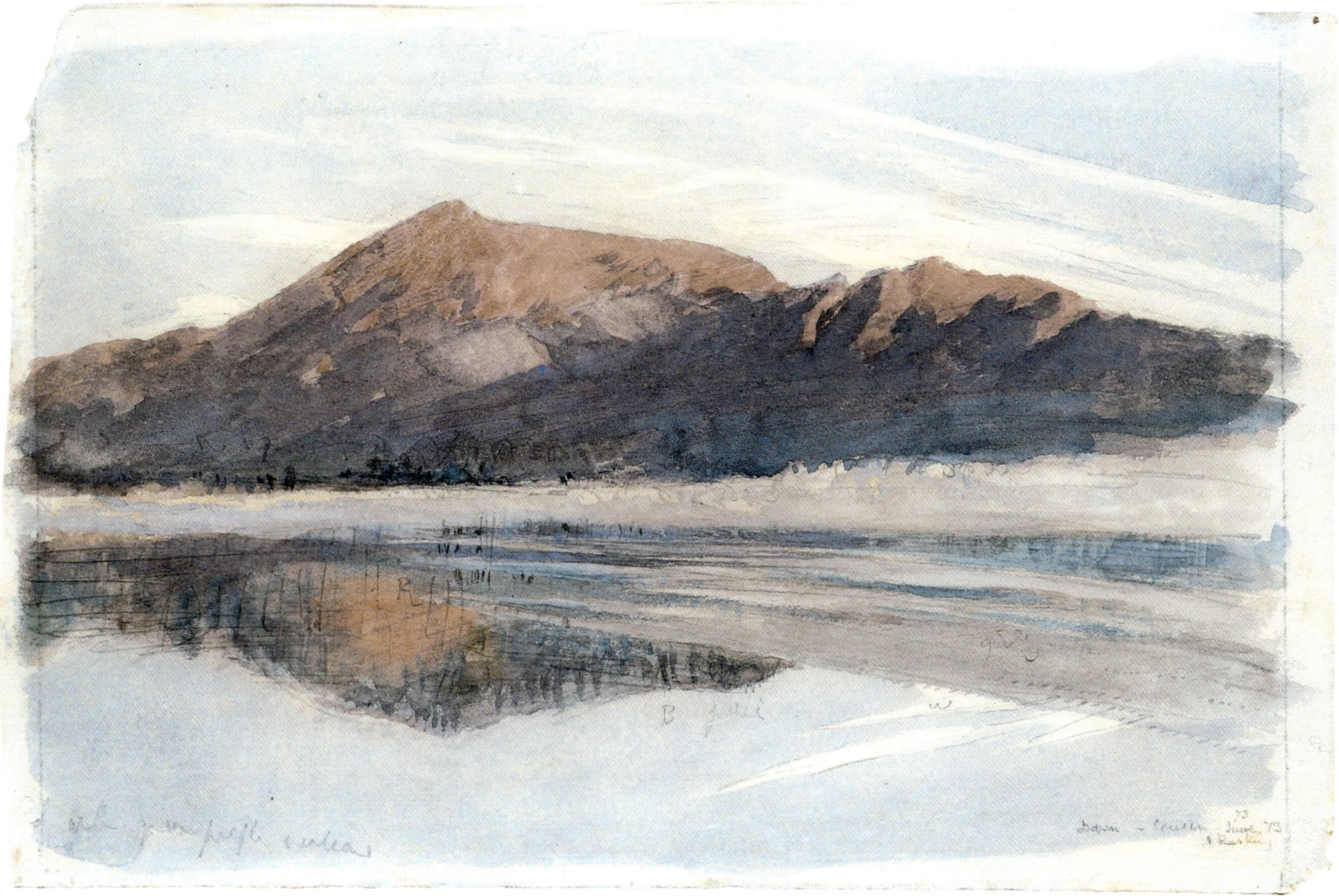

109

Etna from Taormina 1874

Watercolour touched with bodycolour on paper; 17 × 24.9 cm
The British Museum, London (1931.0618.1)
Inscriptions: *Etna. 1/2 past 4 morning. 26th April 1874. JRuskin.*

Ruskin travelled to Sicily in the spring of 1874, arriving at Palermo by steamer from Naples on 22 April. He then spent three days in Taormina, to which he went again by ship as far as Messina and from there by railway, before returning to Palermo, where he remained until 1 May. On Sunday 26 April he described the sight of the volcano at dawn as seen from his lodgings in Taormina: "This morning at ½ past 4, saw dawn on Etna: the most impressive and dreadful scene I ever yet saw in life."[1] The view is toward the south and along the east coast of the island, with the Bay of Naxos on the Ionian Sea on the left side. Etna is seen at a range of about twenty-two kilometres and rising to a height of nearly 3,000 metres.

The prevailing wind across the volcano is from the west, so that the smoke that drifts from its cone usually passes out over the sea. However, in the time that Ruskin observed the scene there was a change in direction of the wind so that in the present drawing a trail of smoke is shown forming a great vortex lying over the western and northern flanks of the volcano.

Ruskin's feeling of fear at the sight of the volcano is interesting. Nor was he alone in sensing the volcano as a baleful presence; Goethe and D.H. Lawrence were visitors to Taormina from the nineteenth and twentieth centuries who were similarly alarmed and fascinated by something that represented the potential for such cataclysmic destruction. Ruskin had surely read the chapter devoted to Etna in volume two of Charles Lyell's *Principles of Geology* (1830–33), which describes successive eruptions from ancient times to the present on the basis of historical accounts and geological evidence, and in which Lyell painted a prose picture of the volcano set against "delightful country ... covered with olives, vines, corn, fruit-trees, and aromatic herbs."[2] Furthermore, Ruskin was conversant with the theory of uniformitarianism, which posited that all the forms of landscape were the consequence of constant accumulative change, rather than periodic disruptions separated by long periods of stasis. In his book on geology *Deucalion*, he explained that although there were "demonstrable periods of the Earth's history, [they] interlace with each other, and gradate into each other – as the periods of a human life do."[3] Volcanoes, of which Ruskin had relatively little experience or knowledge compared to his close familiarity with Alpine physical geography, might seem to challenge the principle of smooth continuity of formation, but this understanding of them had been pioneered by geologists such as George Poulett Scrope, whose book *Considerations on Volcanos ... Leading to the Establishment of a New Theory of the Earth* (1825) made clear that – taken at a sufficiently long time scale – their evolution of form was to be considered something ceaseless and gradual, as was the case with any other landform.

NOTES

1 Ruskin 1956, vol. 3, p. 785.
2 Lyell 1847, p. 380.
3 Ruskin 1903–12, vol. 26, *Deucalion and Other Studies in Rocks and Stones*, p. 117.

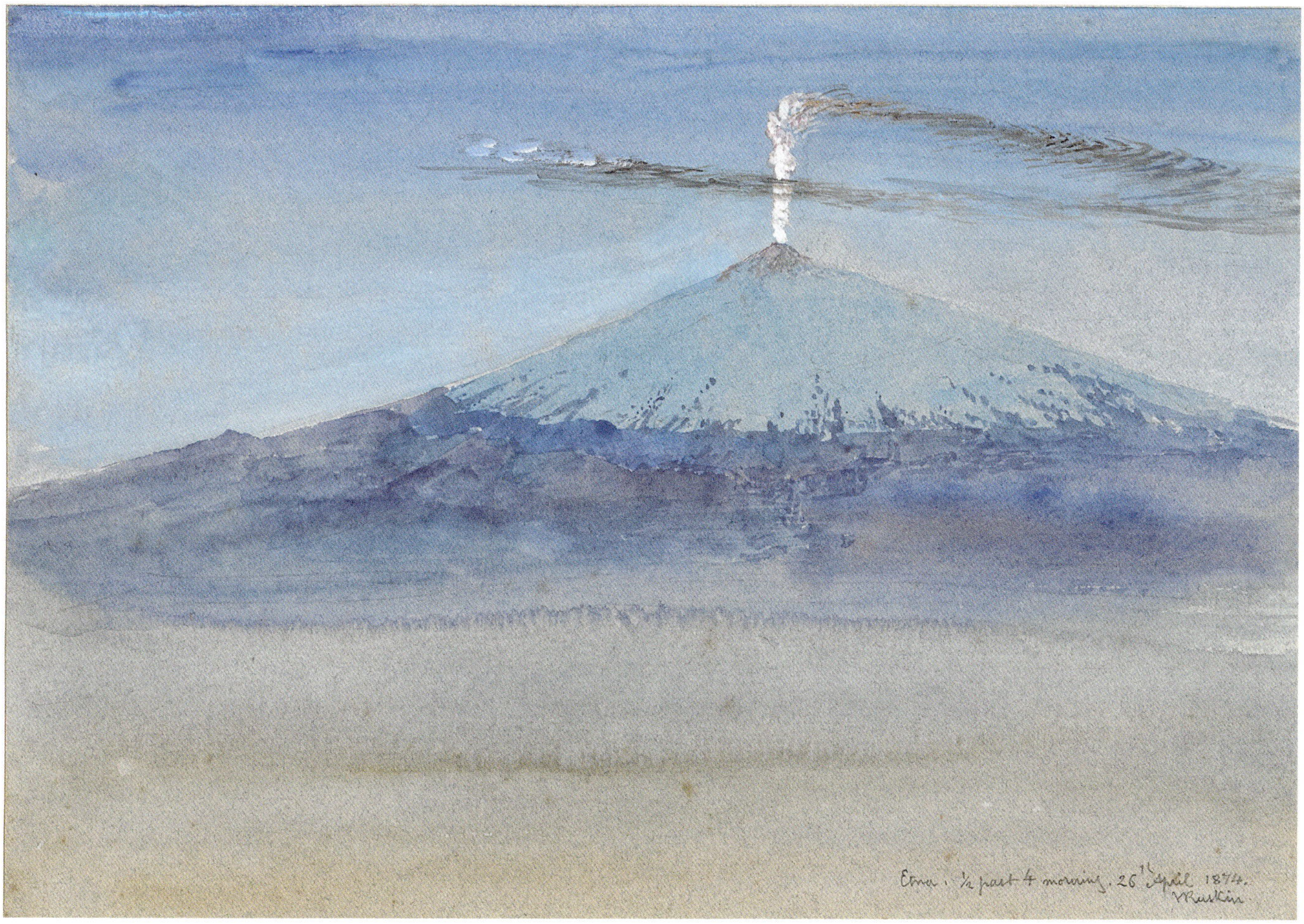
Etna. ½ past 4 morning. 26th April 1874.
J Ruskin

110

Junction of the Greta and Tees at Rokeby 1876

Graphite on white paper; 16 × 24 cm
Ruskin Foundation (Ruskin Library, Lancaster University) (RF 1085)
Inscriptions: graphite within image, *TEES / Greta*, black ink, *Greta and Tees*, graphite on original mount, *Junction of [Greta and Tees] / signed / March 17th. 1889. / Sketch on spot, with / Arthur & Joan, on last / posting expedition from / London to Brantwood. / I may retouch with colour / some day yet – (17th May 1889) / but write more for information / down streams. Greta – Tees*

This animated pencil study, done in May 1876 (although inscribed in 1889), shows a landscape that had long been dear to Ruskin and to generations of British landscape painters. The Greta joins the Tees at Rokeby, in Yorkshire's North Riding, with the village of Brignall close by. The house and grounds of Rokeby Park are on the south bank of the Tees about two and a quarter miles downstream of Barnard Castle. Ruskin, travelling with the Severns, was there from 2 to 4 May, staying at the inn at Rokeby (where in the visitors' book it was noted that the party was "very happy here" for those two days)[1] as part of what he explained in his later inscription on the mount was the "last posting [i.e. travelling by carriage rather than rail] expedition from London to Brantwood."

The place was familiar to Ruskin because since 1856 he had owned J.M.W. Turner's view of the same spot,[2] which he had given to the Oxford Drawing School the previous year. In his catalogue of the collection at Oxford, he described that drawing as "a faultless example of Turner's work at the time when it is most exemplary ... an unrivalled example of chiaroscuro of the most subtle kind: – obtained by the slightest possible contrasts, and by consummate skill in the management of gradation."[3] He was later to say that he felt that he had denied himself much in giving the Turner watercolour to Oxford,[4] and in his *Lectures on Landscape*, he stated that it was the best drawing by the artist that he had had in his possession.[5]

That Ruskin had visited Rokeby by way of homage to Turner is supported by his diary entry for 3 May, in which he expressed relief to find himself in a beautiful place and with the countryside radiant with spring, after a period in which he had suffered a relentless darkness of spirits: "Lovely at last; dew in Rokeby parks, and sun on budding branches ... Walked up Greta bed and found Brignal churchyard with my own Madonna herb all over the little chapel ... The woods all jewelled through with anemone and primrose, and perfect peace everywhere. Found Turner's view as I came back, accurately."[6]

NOTES

1 Ruskin 1903–12, vol. 21, *The Ruskin Art Collection at Oxford: Catalogues, Notes, and Instructions*, p. 11, note 2.
2 Turner's *Junction of the Greta and Tees at Rokeby* (Wilton 566) is now in the Ashmolean Museum, Oxford.
3 Ruskin 1903–12, vol. 21, p. 11.
4 See Ruskin 1903–12, vol. 13, *Turner, The Harbours of England, Catalogues and Notes*, p. 444.
5 Ruskin 1903–12, vol. 22, *Lectures on Landscape, Michael Angelo & Tintoret, The Eagle's Nest, Ariadne Florentina, with Notes for Other Oxford Lectures*, p. 16.
6 Ruskin 1956, vol. 3, p. 897.

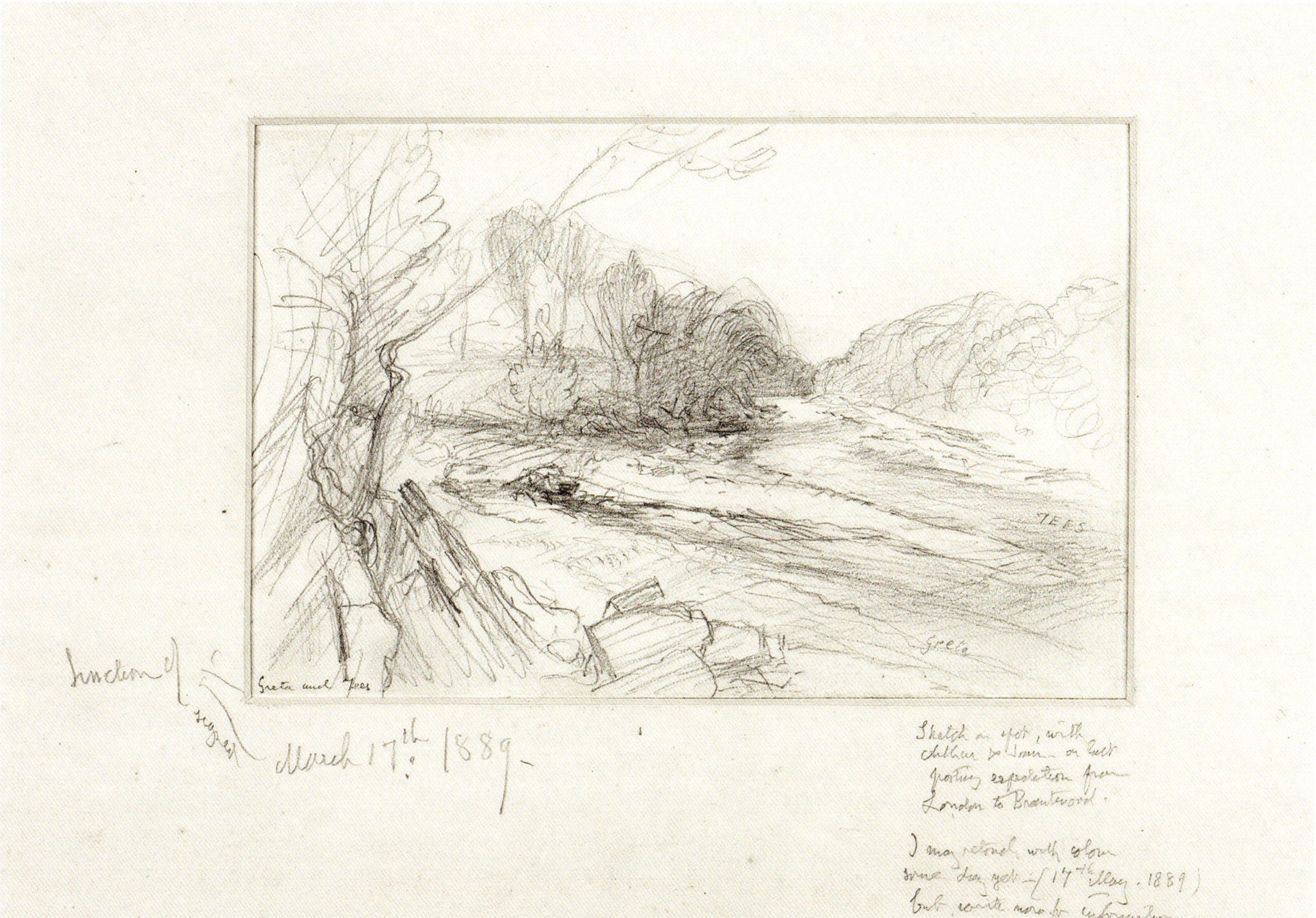
Junction of Greta and Tees
Greta and Tees
TEES
Greta
March 17th 1889
Sketch on spot, with
children to Joan on last
posting expedition from
London to Brantwood.
I may retouch with colour
some day yet – (17th May. 1889)
but write now for information
– down stream – Greta – Tees

III

Cloud Study – Ice Clouds over Coniston Water 1880

Graphite and watercolour on white paper; 20.5 × 38.5 cm
Ruskin Foundation (Ruskin Library, Lancaster University) (RF 902)

This was one of the drawings that Ruskin asked Arthur Severn and William Gershom Collingwood to translate into a set of five expanded diagrams to accompany his lecture "The Storm-cloud of the Nineteenth Century," given at the London Institution on two occasions in February 1884. Ruskin's editors E.T. Cook and Alexander Wedderburn described how the "coloured enlargements ... were thrown on a screen by the lime-light," which were painted in "Messrs. Newman's extra-luminous water-colours."[1] In a report of the lecture by Wedderburn, published in the April 1884 issue of *Art Journal*, he quoted Ruskin's description of the projected reproduction of the present drawing as a "dazzling maze of frosty filaments, a painted window in palpitation, its pulses of colour interwoven in motion, intermittent in fire, emerald and ruby, and pale purple and violet, melting into a blue that was not of the sky but of the sunbeam."[2] Woodblock engravings of the same set of five images were used to illustrate the article, and it was on this occasion that the alternative title of *An August Sky at Brantwood* was given to it (likewise the equally misleading title of "*A July Thunder-cloud in the Val d'Aosta*" for cat. 102).[3]

Ruskin's interest in cloud formations remained intense, with frequent diary notations recording meteorological conditions and cloud patterns. Increasingly, and as his own mental condition deteriorated, these observations became fearful and the source of anxiety, as if regarding the clouds as portents of grief. On 8 January 1880, for example, he described the dreadful weather that was then being experienced at Brantwood: "Deadly fog – [and] rain these three days, without a gleam; to-day, Manchester smoke, with the usual devilry of cloud moving fast in rags, with no wind."[4] Seven months later, by then the late summer and in conditions altogether more cheerful, he described "the most overwhelming, wonderful hours of increasing prismatic light," and the rich colours cast upon the expanses of the lake. There followed a rhapsodic passage describing "[a] sky interwoven with muslin and netting of divinest cirri cloud, over infinite shoals and sands of mackerel cloud; but all flying, failing, melting, re-appearing, twisting and intertwisting, faster than eye could follow ... ending in two great ranks of storm-cloud, lower, pale against higher, dark, or backing of dark; the latter with long locks and tresses, as of hair, at its edge; and both overlying the range of hills, exactly like the Hesperides dragon."[5]

NOTES

1 Ruskin 1903–12, vol. 34, *The Storm-cloud of the Nineteenth Century, On the Old Road, Arrows of the Chace, Ruskiniana*, p. xxvii.
2 "Mr Ruskin on 'The Storm-Cloud,'" *Art Journal* (1884), p. 107.
3 See Wildman 2009 for the dismissal of the two drawings made in preparation for the woodblock engravings, now each in the collection of the Ruskin Foundation at Lancaster University, as being by Ruskin.
4 Ruskin 1956, vol. 3, p. 980.
5 Ibid., p. 981. By the "Hesperides dragon" Ruskin was referring to the cloud effect in Turner's painting *The Goddess of Discord Choosing the Apple of Contention in the Garden of Hesperides* of 1806 (Tate, London).

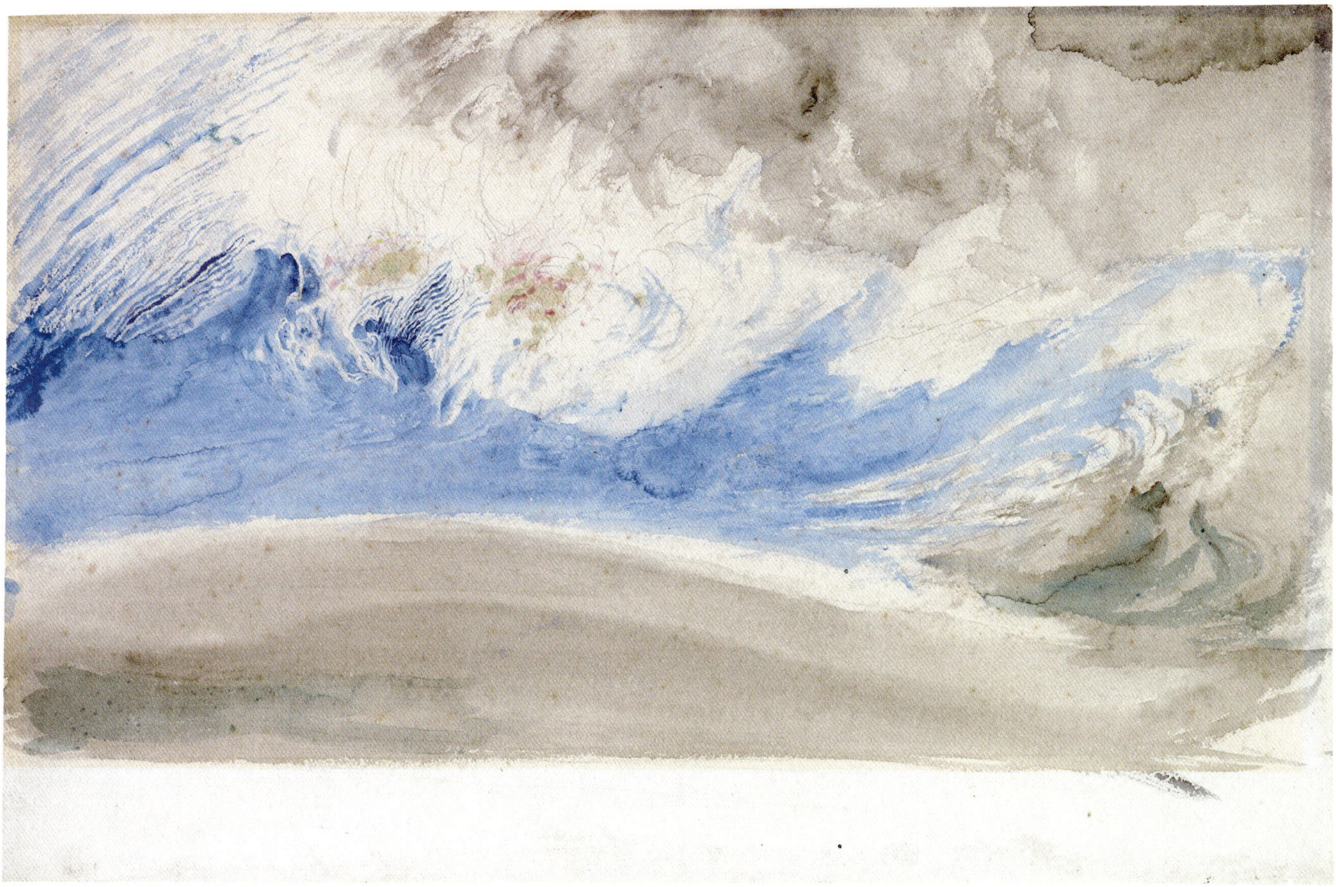

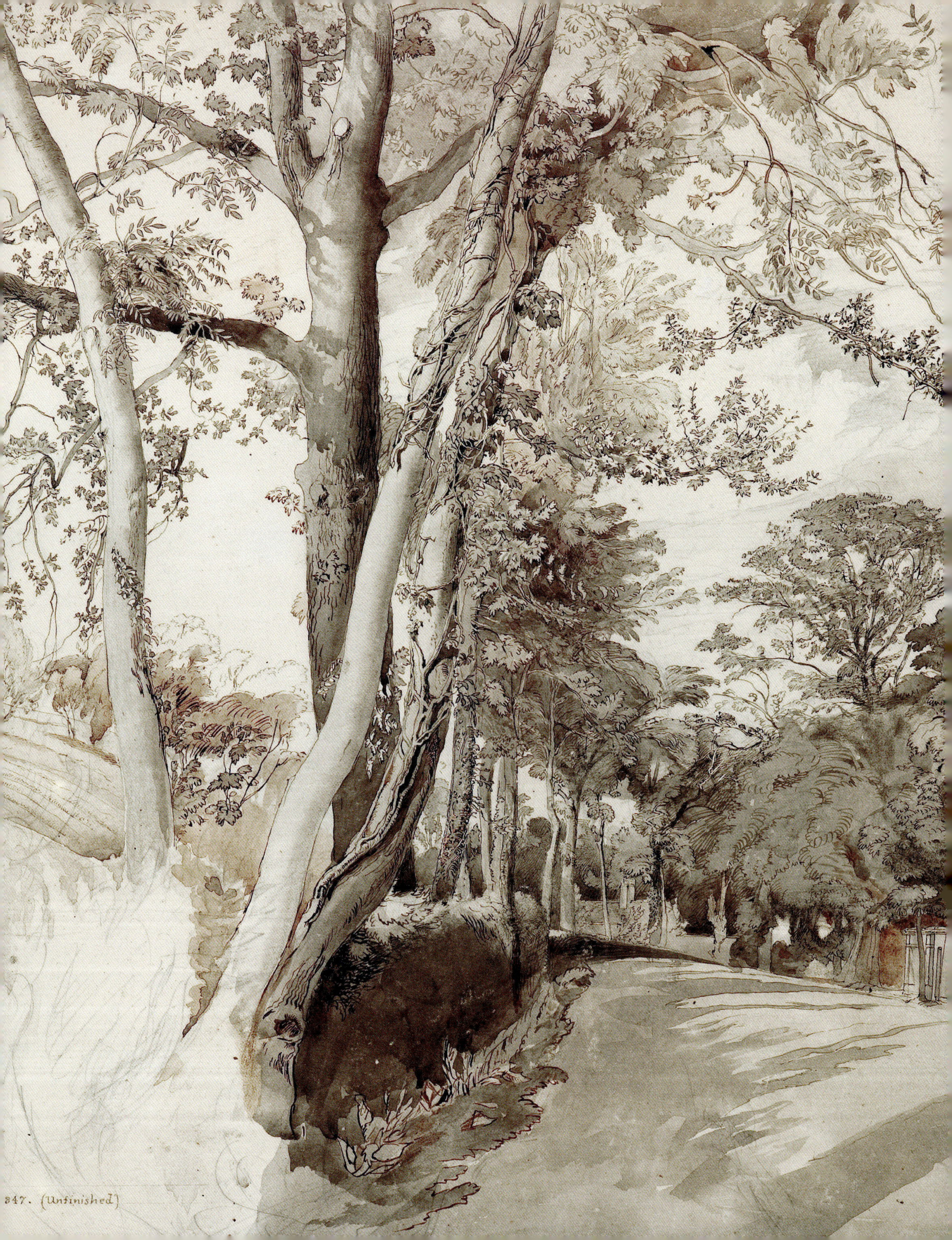

347. (Unfinished)

Nature Studies

112

Foliage on a Bank c. 1845–50

Graphite and pen and ink with brown and grey washes and bodycolour on paper; 22.1 × 16 cm
Private collection

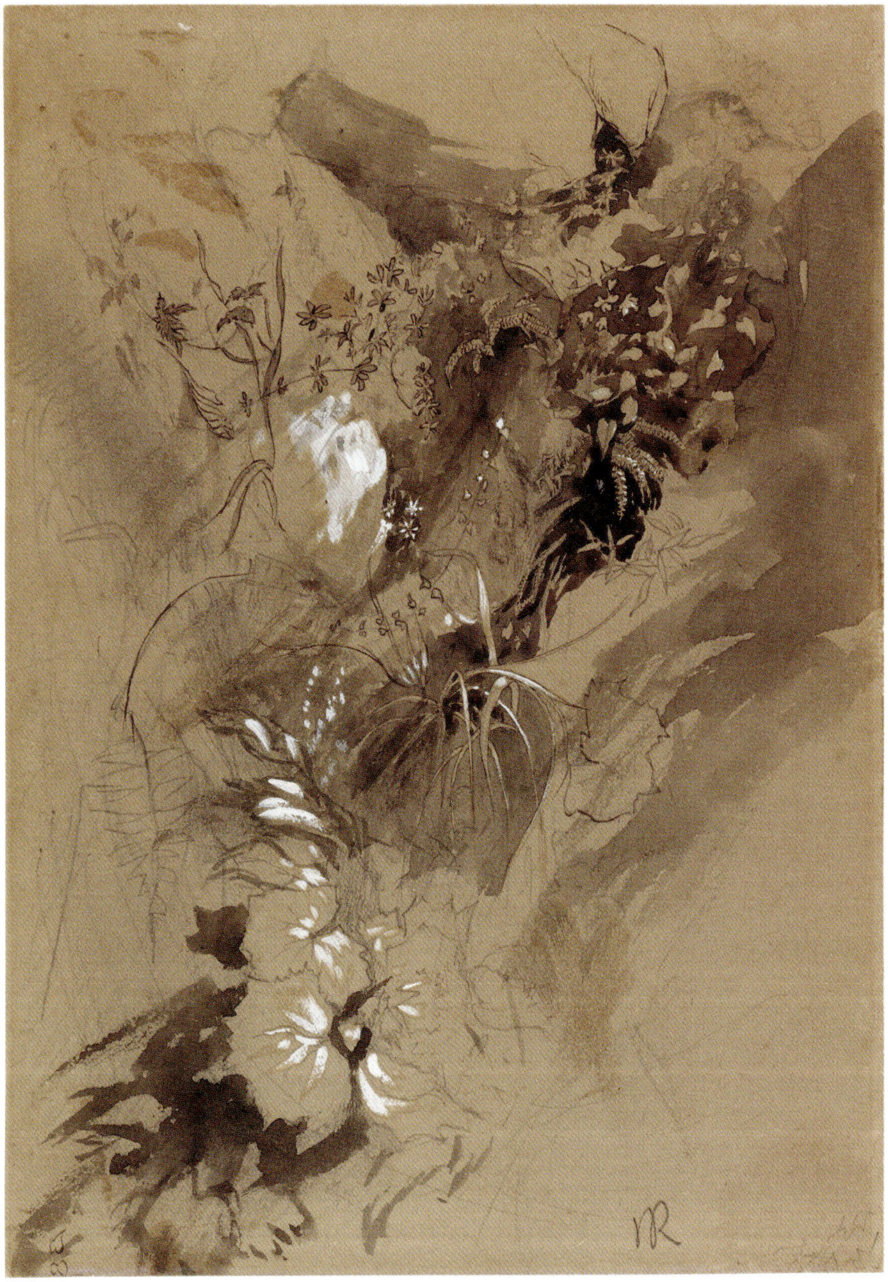

This drawing is an early example of the type of abstract foreground subject in which Ruskin always took delight. Leaves, grass, plant stems and flowers are crowded together and overlap against what appears to be a rutted bank. No clear indication has been given of the distance between the artist and what lay before him, but the mesmeric beauty of the composition and the fascination that it exerts upon the viewer owe much to the sense that the forms appear to be within arm's reach, yet remain inviolate to touch. A variety of media has been used to simulate the complexity of this microcosm of landscape – from the deep sepia washes of the upper-right and left foreground, which suggest the moistness of the soil from which the mass of plants have sprung, prompting memories of the delicious scent of freshly fallen rain, to the spidery ink threads of tendrils and stems, and the scintillating sparkle of white bodycolour glinting from dagger-like blades and lustrously reflecting from the glaucous surfaces of plantain leaves.

Ruskin had an instinctive predilection for the close inspection of natural forms, relying on the sharpness of his eyesight to recognize the varieties and condition of plants and flowers. In a footnote to the first volume of *Modern Painters* (1843), he conceded that as a consequence of differing qualities of vision some "who appear to generalize rudely or rashly are perhaps faithfully endeavouring to render the appearance which nature bears to sight of limited range [while] others may be led by their singular keenness of sight into inexpedient detail." This was followed by a broad categorization of artists according to their tendency to represent natural detail at greater or lesser distance, with Titian and Tintoretto being regarded as practitioners in whose art "the foreground is rarely more than five or six yards broad, and its objects therefore being only five or six yards distant are entirely detailed."[1] Whatever the imagined distance between the artist and the main body of the subject, certain parts would have been too small to have been made legible in detail, for as Ruskin wrote, "that which is nearness for the bank, is distance for its details; and however near it may be, the greater part of those details are still a beautiful incomprehensibility."[2] Animated with occasional points of razor-sharp detail within an overall looseness of composition, the present drawing simulates the very process of seeing.

Paul Walton has recognized a passage in the fifth volume of *Modern Painters* that conveys an analogous perception of nature as a living environment, constantly in flux and requiring close study so as to appreciate its variety and how all its parts blend together into patterns of infinite complexity: "The leaves of the herbage at our feet take all kinds of strange shapes, as if to invite us to examine them. Star-shaped, heart-shaped, spear-shaped, arrow-shaped, fretted, fringed, cleft, furrowed, serrated, sinuated; in whorls, in tufts, in spires, in wreaths, endlessly expressive, deceptive, fantastic, never the same from footstalk to blossom; they seem perpetually to tempt our watchfulness, and take delight in outstripping our wonder."[3]

Published in June 1860, and therefore following *The Origin of Species* by just seven months, the fifth volume of *Modern Painters* may be seen to be Darwinian in its observation of the multiplicity and competitive interdependence of nature.

NOTES

1 Ruskin 1903–12, vol. 3, *Modern Painters I*, p. 338, note.
2 Ruskin 1903–12, vol. 3, p. 338.
3 John Ruskin, quoted in Walton 2000, p. 54. The quotation comes from Ruskin 1903–12, vol. 7, *Modern Painters V*, p. 121.

113

Stone Pines at Sestri, Gulf of Genoa 1845

Graphite and pen and ink with washes and white bodycolour on off-white paper; 44.2 × 33.4 cm
The Ashmolean Museum, Oxford. Presented by John Ruskin to the Ruskin Drawing School (University of Oxford), 1875 (WA.RS.ED.022)

The Continental tour that Ruskin made from April to November 1845 was the first that he embarked upon without his parents. Volume one of *Modern Painters*, published two years previously, had principally been concerned with nature and how its truthful representation should inform works of art of all kinds if they were to be of value. Much of Ruskin's time in Italy in 1845 was to be spent looking at art and architecture as part of a deliberate campaign of self-education and in preparation for the projected second volume of *Modern Painters*, in which he intended to discuss the development of medieval and later art. Nonetheless, he continued to feel the need to be out of doors whenever possible and expressed his profound love of nature in ravishing landscape and nature drawings.

The present drawing was made shortly after Ruskin's arrival in Italy that spring. He interrupted his journey along the Ligurian coast for a day to make studies of the pine trees that grow on the shore at Sestri Levante, and on the evening of 30 April told his father that he had "been working all day like a horse, and have got a most valuable study of stone pine." The delight that he felt in finding himself in the south is clear from the further account he gave of the immediate setting: "rock to sit on – under the shade of an ilex – no wind – air all that's right – just as hot as it can be to admit of one's doing anything – and never uncomfortably so. No chills in the evening. Air all scented by the pines & wild flowers – and the birds singing so loud you can hardly hear the sea."[1]

The drawing ripples with the movement of branches, stems and leaves, and sparkles with reflected light. All conventions of composition are ignored, and only the slightest sense of a larger topographical context is offered by the glimpse of a distant headland. In 1878, when Ruskin presented the work to the Oxford Drawing School as part of the Rudimentary Series, he regarded it as having been made "with the utmost speed consistent with care."[2] As he looked back in *Præterita* on his progress as a draftsman, he saw the drawing as demonstration of the fact that he was by this time, "able to study from nature accurately in full chiaroscuro, with a good frank power over the sepia tinting,"[3] a method that owed much to his study of J.M.W. Turner's *Liber Studiorum*.

NOTES

1 Ruskin 1972, p. 46.
2 Ruskin 1903–12, vol. 21, *The Ruskin Art Collection at Oxford: Catalogues, Notes, and Instructions*, p. 297.
3 Ruskin 1903–12, vol. 35, *Præterita and Dilecta*, p. 340.

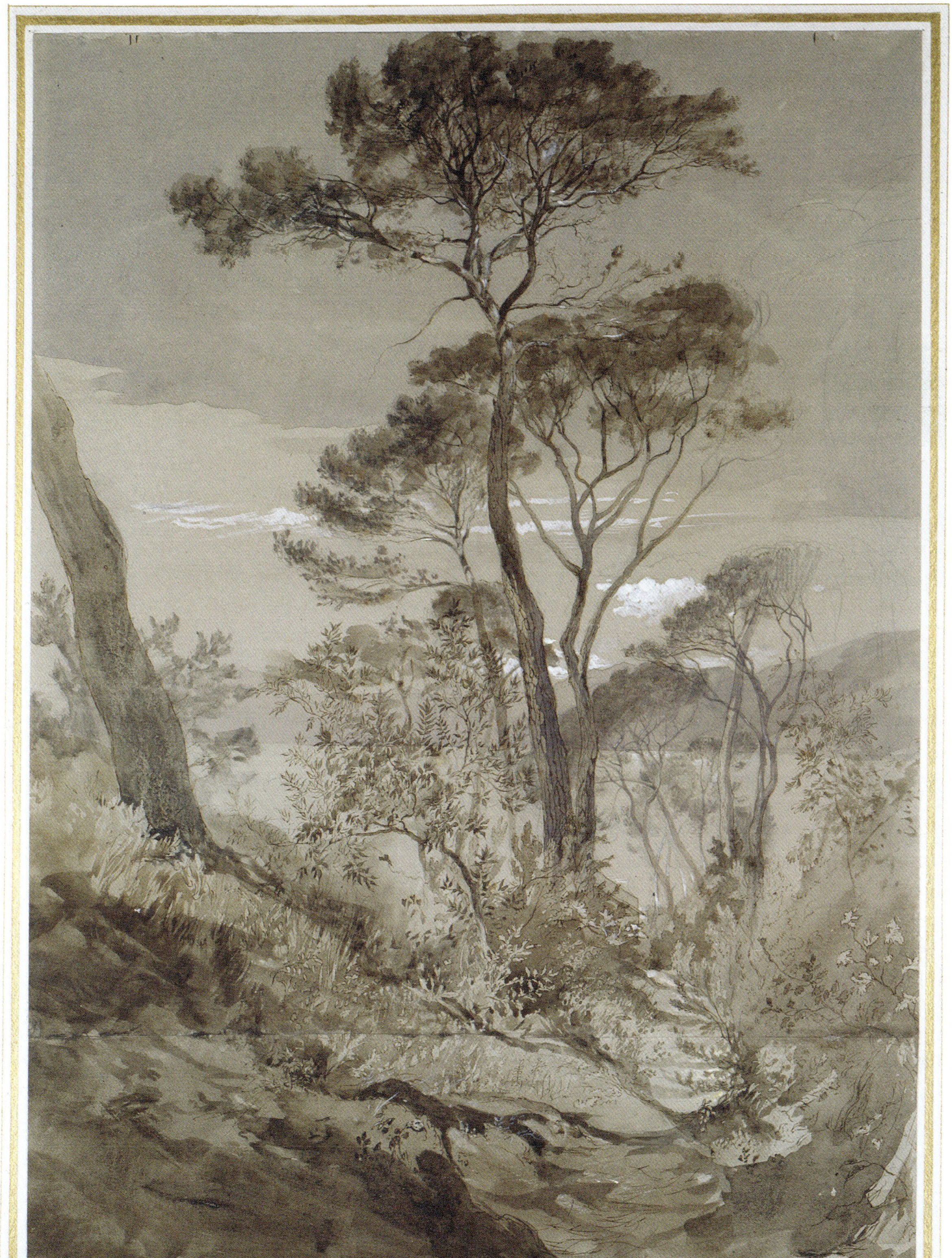

114

Trees in a Lane, perhaps at Ambleside 1847

Graphite, black and brown ink and ink wash on white paper; 44.5 × 57.2 cm
Ruskin Foundation (Ruskin Library, Lancaster University) (RF 1559)
Inscriptions: *Best way of studying Trees / with a view to knowledge of their leafage. / Young Shoots of the Oak and Ash, in Spring. / J.R. 1847. (Unfinished)*

In this, one of Ruskin's most beautiful and characterful early drawings, a line of trees is seen growing along a verge and beside a low wall that runs along the margin of a road – the surface of which forms the right-hand foreground before curving away and dropping downhill in the distance. The composition is utterly idiosyncratic and personal; a central oak, the dark trunk of which seems to divide the view into two separate spaces, is supported by the lighter-coloured stems of ash trees, forming a kind of cantilever on each side that in turn defines a fan-shaped spandrel made from further trees in near alignment. An extraordinary feeling of three-dimensionality is achieved by the cast of light from behind the spectator's left shoulder, so that the trunks are rounded and volumetric and the surfaces of their bark deliciously textured, while the smooth surface of the lane is defined by the diagonal fall of cast shadows.

The drawing owes its power to Ruskin's understanding of the psychology of the counterpoint of invitation and denial of opportunity to explore a physical environment about which the spectator longs for further knowledge. The place represented appears both as an actual landscape that one might hope freely to enter and explore, but also as one of which one may only dream, and which thus must remain impenetrable and pristine. The drawing's inscribed title makes clear that it was ostensibly intended as a didactic exercise – Ruskin was later to regard the differentiation of tree species and skill in the accurate representation of distinctive patterns of foliage and shapes of branches as vital for artists treating landscape and nature – but its beauty transcends any function of mere observation.

The drawing's usual title suggests that the lane and trees shown were found somewhere in the southern part of the English Lake District, although there is no larger topographical element to confirm this identification. In March 1847 Ruskin stayed for a period at Ambleside, seeking calm and distraction through work after the emotional disturbance that had overtaken him concerning his intended marriage proposal to Charlotte Lockhart. A letter to his father, dated 23 March, opens with the words: "I was certainly not well when I came down on the Lake, nor am I yet, perhaps; but I am only in the sort of illness which makes me look to nature with more thirst."[1] Later in the summer he moved on to Leamington Spa, where he sought further treatment for the depression that he was suffering, so it is possible that the countryside represented was in fact in Warwickshire.

NOTES

1 Ruskin 1903–12, vol. 36, *The Letters of John Ruskin, 1827–1869*, p. 70.

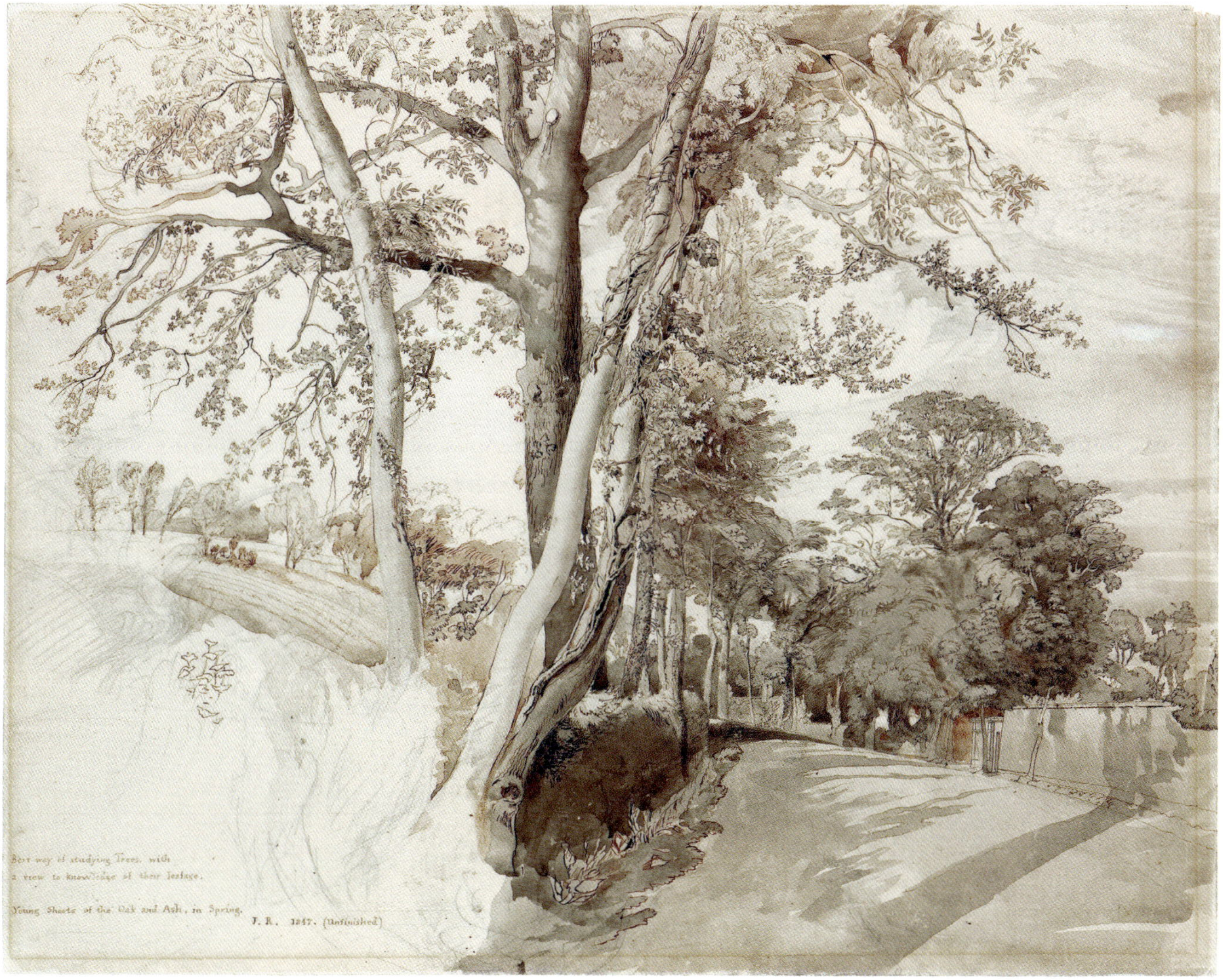
Best way of studying Trees, with
a view to knowledge of their leafage.
Young Shoots of the Oak and Ash, in Spring.
J. R. 1847. (Unfinished)

115

a. *Spanish Chestnut at Carrara, related to "The Elements of Drawing"* c. 1856–57

Pen and ink on paper; 10.1 × 12.3 cm
Private collection

b. *A Bough of Phillyrea, for "The Elements of Drawing"* c. 1856–57

Pen and ink on paper; 6.6 × 9.2 cm
Private collection

Ruskin's manual *The Elements of Drawing* was written as what E.T. Cook and Alexander Wedderburn have called "a kind of 'circular letter' in answer to requests for Ruskin's opinion and advice."[1] Ruskin prepared the texts during the winter of 1856–57, and three successive editions, published between 1857 and 1861, as well as pirated editions issued in the United States, were seized upon by a generation of enthusiastic amateur draftsmen and students seeking to become professional artists. In *The Elements of Drawing*, Ruskin specified particular aspects of the landscape and of nature that he believed merited close attention and study.

Ruskin loved to draw trees and seems to have thought of each specimen as having an individuality in terms of its own peculiar traits and predispositions, as well as characteristics determined by the circumstances of its immediate environment and history, a view expressed for example in the second letter of *The Elements of Drawing*, entitled "Sketching from Nature," in which he explained how the lines of a trunk and branches of a tree "show what kind of fortune it has had to endure from its childhood: how troublesome trees have come in its way, and pushed it aside, and tried to strangle or starve it; where and when kind trees have sheltered it, and grown up lovingly together with it, bending as it bent; what winds torment it most; what boughs of it behave best, and bear most fruit; and so on."[2]

The study here of a Spanish chestnut was worked up by Ruskin from a detail in his 1845 drawing *Spanish Chestnut at Carrara* (untraced). Another study deriving from that original, but just showing the sprays of leaves emerging from the gnarled and lightning-struck trunk, appeared as figure 24 in *The Elements of Drawing*.[3] In a draft passage deleted from the published text, as the drawing itself was omitted (along with a drawing by J.D. Harding with which he had previously intended to make comparison), Ruskin described his purpose in studying "a spray of real Spanish chestnut, thrown in similarly black profile against the white paper."[4]

NOTES

1 Ruskin 1903–12, vol. 15, *The Elements of Drawing, The Elements of Perspective, and The Laws of Fésole*, p. xv.
2 Ibid., p. 91.
3 Ibid., p. 114.
4 Ibid., pp. 114–115, note 1.

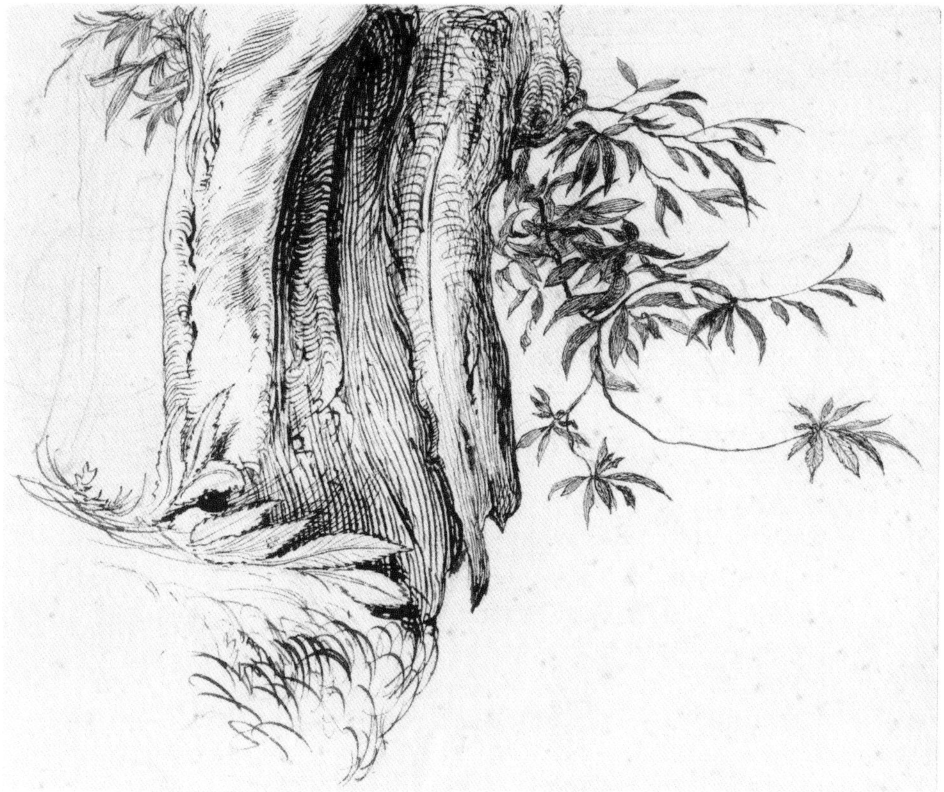

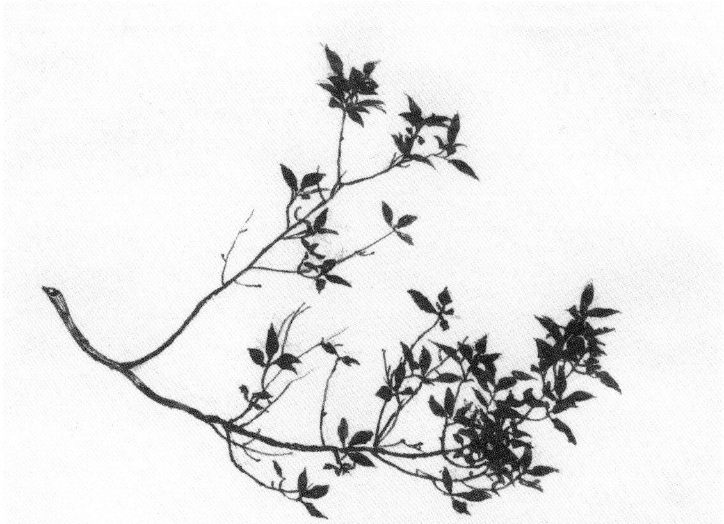

116

Study of Part of the Trees in Turner's "Crossing the Brook" c. 1856–57

Watercolour and bodycolour over graphite on pale brown wove paper; 44.6 × 32.4 cm
The Ashmolean Museum, Oxford. Presented by John Ruskin to the Ruskin Drawing School (University of Oxford), 1875 (WA.RS.RUD.294)

In addition to studying trees and their foliage in their natural setting, Ruskin was interested in the way artists had represented them. In the first volume of *Modern Painters*, he applauded J.M.W. Turner as "the only painter who ever drew the stem of a tree, Titian having come the nearest before him, and excelling him, in the muscular development of the larger trunks (though sometimes losing the woody strength in a serpent-like flaccidity), but missing the grace and character of the ramifications."[1] Elsewhere in the book, Ruskin asserted that "for three hundred years back, trees have been drawn with affectation by all the civilized nations of Europe,"[2] excepting only the two previously named artists, while in *The Elements of Drawing* he took swipes at Richard Wilson and Thomas Gainsborough, the former on the grounds that he "never conceives a tree as a round mass, but flat, as if it had been pressed and dried,"[3] and the latter for giving "nothing but meaningless touches; not even so much as the species of the tree, much less the variety of its leafage, being ever discernible."[4]

The present drawing was presumably made in the winter of 1856–57, at the time when Ruskin was sorting out the mass of paintings and drawings that had come to the nation as the Turner Bequest, and of which the work *Crossing the Brook* (fig. 8.1) was a part. Ruskin's drawing shows the trunks and foliage of the two exaggeratedly tall trees, indeterminate in species in Turner's painting but perhaps intended as Scots pines, which stand as a repoussoir on the left side of the strikingly Italianate composition. Ruskin used the same detail as the model for an engraved illustration in *The Elements of Drawing*, showing the crown of the pair of trees and the filigree of stems that supported the foliage – and in the process of drawing from Turner's painting, transforming the tree type into a more immediately recognizable umbrella pine.

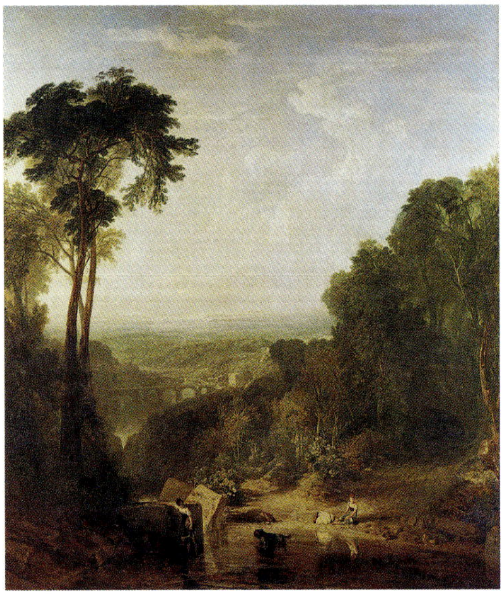

FIG. 8.1
J.M.W. Turner
Crossing the Brook, 1815
Oil on canvas
Tate, London (N00497)

NOTES

1 Ruskin 1903–12, vol. 3, *Modern Painters I*, p. 252.
2 Ibid., p. 585.
3 Ruskin 1903–12, vol. 15, *The Elements of Drawing, The Elements of Perspective, and The Laws of Fésole*, p. 93.
4 Ibid., p. 116.

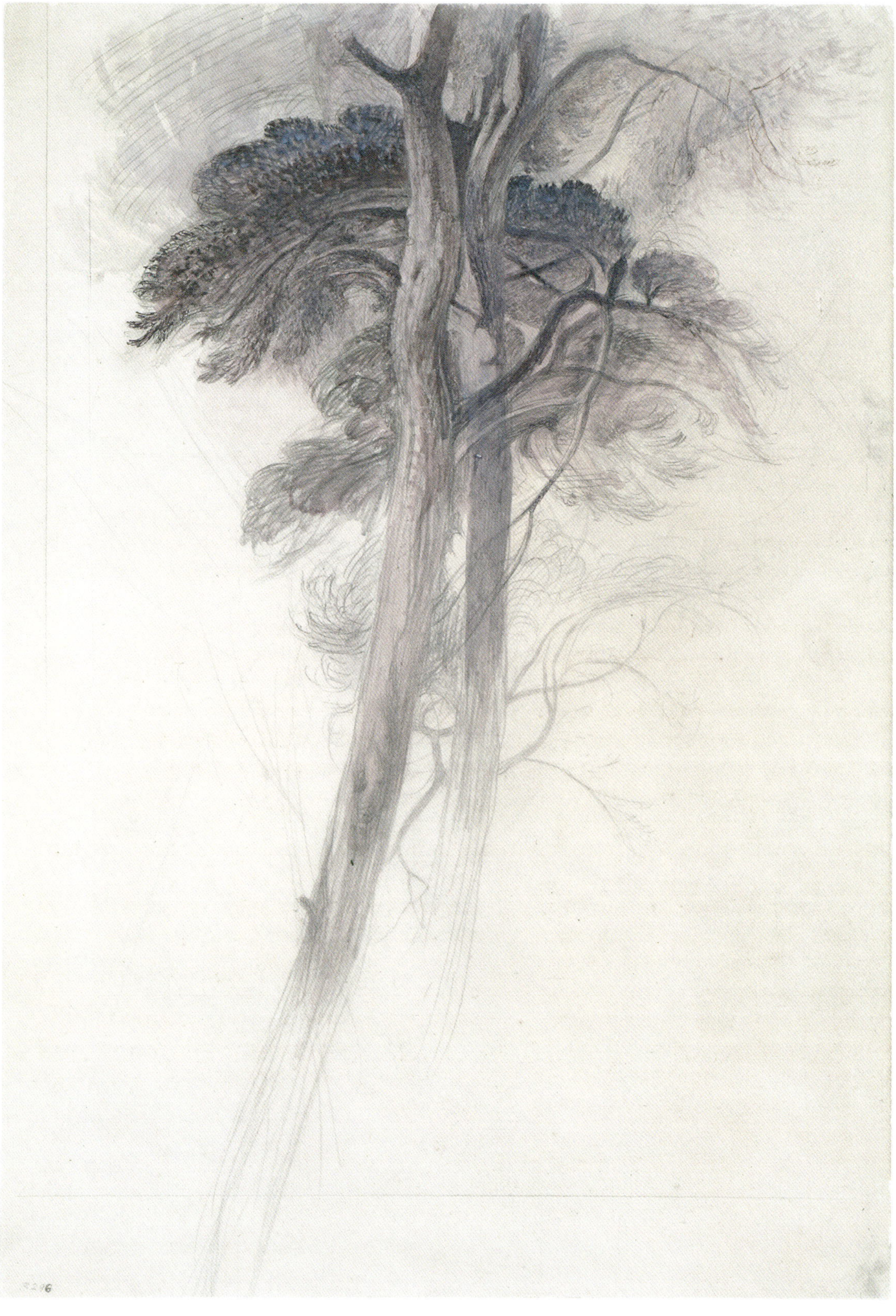

117

Prunus Persica 1857

Watercolour and bodycolour on paper; 10.2 × 9.4 cm
Private collection
Inscriptions: *J. Ruskin 1857*

This jewel-like botanical study shows a stem of flower buds from a peach tree. In it Ruskin has achieved a stupendous degree of actuality, despite the specimen that he has treated being so tiny and depicted at life size. Presumably a magnifying glass was used so that the creases in the outer surface of the yet unfurled petals might be studied and understood – likewise the structure of the stem and the cup-shaped brackets upon which the buds rest and the tip where a duo of young leaves are breaking forth. Ruskin showed all of this on a background of rich blue bodycolour, against which the stem seems to stand quite freely and as if within an undefined and infinite space.

The most careful attention has been paid to the lit and shadowed sides of the stem and the buds, giving an extraordinary sense of volume, so much so that one feels an urge to shift one's position in an attempt to see all around the specimen, as if it were an actual stem of peach buds viewed as part of some botanical display. Tiny flecks of varied bodycolour – light on dark and dark on light – give the forms of the plant a living quality and suggest the naturally occurring blemishes and random imperfections of something that is actually growing before our eyes. By such technique of fractured surface, achieved by the minute application of points of colour, Ruskin fulfilled his own appointed principle of "gradation," whereby across the surface there would be an infinite variety of degrees of intensity of colour and depth of tone, according to the varying fall of light and shadow. "No colour exists in Nature under ordinary circumstances without gradation," Ruskin stated in *The Elements of Drawing*, going on to cite the example of a birch trunk, in which "the rosy grey *must* be gradated by the roundness of the stem till it meets the shaded side; [while] similarly the shaded side is gradated by reflected light."[1]

The study of peach buds may well have been connected with *The Elements of Drawing*, published in June the same year. For example, it is similar in scale and format to the engraved illustration of "a young shoot of lilac,"[2] made after a drawing of Ruskin's and appearing in the manual. Many of the principles that are laid out in the book were in fact devised in the course of Ruskin's teaching at the Working Men's College, where students had frequently been set to the task of making close-up studies of botanical specimens.

NOTES

1 Ruskin 1903–12, vol. 15, *The Elements of Drawing, The Elements of Perspective, and The Laws of Fésole*, p. 147.
2 Ibid., fig. 6, p. 68.

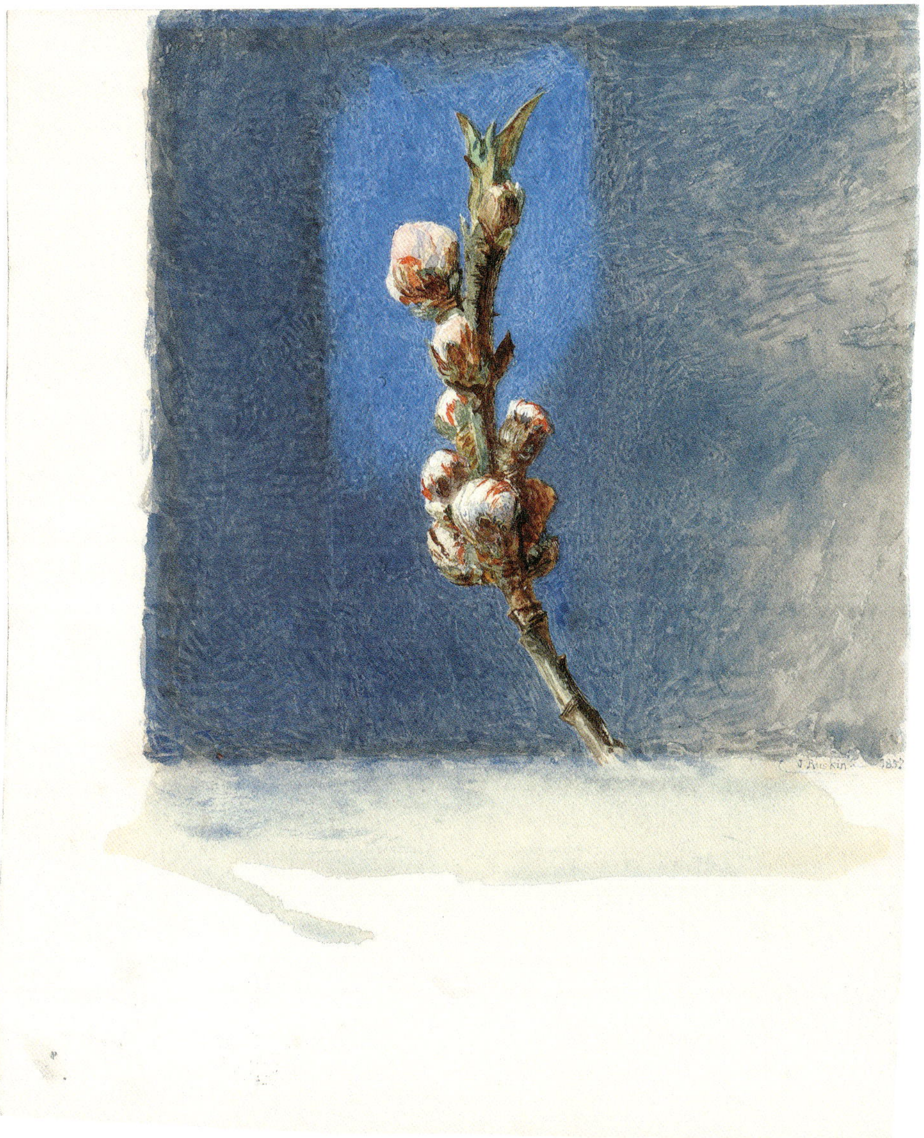

118

The Dryad's Waywardness: Oak Spray in Winter, Seen in Front c. 1858–60

Watercolour and bodycolour over graphite on blue wove paper; 22 × 26.7 cm
The Ashmolean Museum, Oxford. Presented by John Ruskin to the Ruskin Drawing School (University of Oxford), 1875 (WA.RS.ED.266)
Inscriptions: *By itself*

This is one of three studies of an oak spray made as illustrations to the fifth volume of *Modern Painters*.[1] The first part of the book, entitled "Of Leaf Beauty," was intended as a treatise on the beauty of vegetation and as such was a successor to the exegesis on the representation of mountain landscapes of the fourth volume. Ruskin's appreciation that everything that existed in the physical world – from plants and animals to the flow of water and even rock formations – was in a state of perpetual motion and transition leading inevitably to an unimagined and altered state caused him to look at all things in terms of their organic growth.

Trees became a particular preoccupation for Ruskin at this time and the object of intensive study. In 1857, in *The Elements of Drawing*, he had encouraged students to draw every kind of tree and take careful account of the particular characteristics of species. The account given of trees and their growth in *Modern Painters* and the lecture at the Royal Institution that he gave the following April on the theme "Tree Twigs" drew upon "the same close study of natural aspects combined with poetical fancy, and the same imaginative connexion of those aspects with ideas of morality and mythology,"[2] as wrote E.T. Cook and Alexander Wedderburn. Thomas Carlyle gave an account of this "lecture on Tree Leaves as physiological, pictorial, moral, symbolical objects," concluding with bewilderment but also delight that "Ruskin did blow asunder as by gunpowder explosions his leaf notions, which were manifold, curious, genial; and, in fact, I do not recollect to have heard in that place any neatest thing I likes so well as this chaotic one."[3] Therefore, in his study of trees, as in all his writings and the very patterns of his thought, a scatter of associations was made, and it does not seem odd in the context of an account of nature made on the basis of careful and even scientific observation to find a wood nymph invoked as the guardian of the natural world (the other two subjects that appear as illustrations to the fifth volume of *Modern Painters* were entitled *The Dryad's Toil* and *The Dryad's Crown*). Ten years later Ruskin had cause to defend the spiritual associations that he gave to flowers and vegetation, insisting that they were "nowise antagonistic to the theories which Mr. Darwin's unwearied and unerring investigations are every day rendering more probable. The aesthetic relations of species are independent of their origin. Nevertheless, it has always seemed to me, in what little work I have done upon organic forms, as if the species mocked us by their deliberate imitation of each other when they met: yet did not pass one into another."[4]

NOTES

1 The plate, made by R.P. Cuff, of the present drawing appears opposite p. 94 in Ruskin 1903–12, vol. 7, *Modern Painters V*.
2 Ruskin 1903–12, vol. 7, p. lviii.
3 Ibid., p. lix.
4 Ruskin 1903–12, vol. 19, *The Cestus of Aglaia and The Queen of the Air with Other Papers and Lectures on Art and Literature, 1860–1870*, p. 358, note.

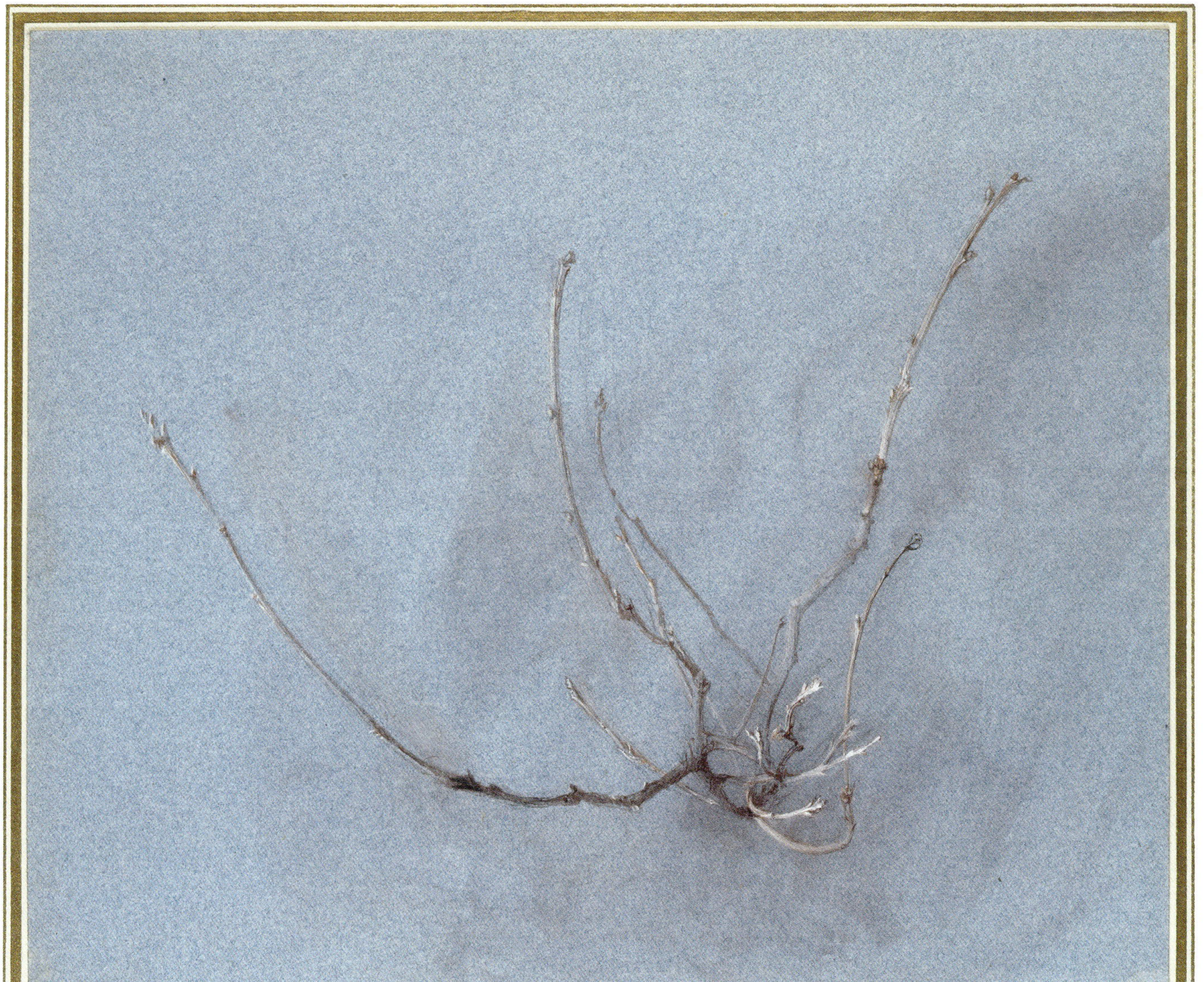
By itself

119

Juniper 1863

Watercolour over graphite with bodycolour on blue paper; 12.5 × 12.5 cm
Private collection
Inscriptions: *Juniper / J Ruskin 1863*

Ruskin wrote to his father from Mornex on 18 January 1863, arranging for this drawing to be sent to London to be mounted and framed. In his diary he made frequent observations about the early wildflowers that he came across on his walks and seems to have been reassured by them that the weather would eventually improve. Twelve years later he commenced the series of essays for *Proserpina. Studies of Wayside Flowers, while the Air was yet Pure among the Alps, and in the Scotland and England which my Father Knew.* Ruskin's specimen here is the Common Juniper, which is found in hill country. It has needle-like leaves that grow in whorls and fruit that gradually darkens in colour as it slowly ripens over a period of a year or more.

William Henry Hunt's drawings of flowers and fruit had long been the object of Ruskin's admiration. He and his father had acquired watercolours by Hunt for the family collection, and Ruskin often referred to the painter in his writings, especially recommending a method derived from Hunt's techniques to students in *The Elements of Drawing*. In 1879 he was the author of the catalogue of an exhibition of Hunt's works – along with those of Samuel Prout – at the Fine Art Society in London.

Ruskin's own nature drawings are in some degree dependent upon Hunt's example. He said of Hunt's flower studies that, "so far from being garlanded into any polite symmetry, his primroses fresh from the bank, and hawthorns white from the hedge, confess at once their artless origin in the village lane,"[1] and as such was celebrating them as genuine and unaffected products of an essentially English artistic vernacular. The legitimacy of the technique of using opaque colour and the mixing of white gouache was contested by conservative advocates of a traditional watercolour method, but Ruskin had no doubts that the placing of touches of bodycolour in mosaic-like patterns to simulate the constant variety and fluctuation of natural forms, which Ruskin called "gradation," was perfectly suited to the painting of nature studies. In drawings of his own, such as the present, he followed Hunt's example, as in "the way he used his body-colour; laying it first with extreme care in form and gradation."[2]

NOTES

1 Ruskin 1903–12, vol. 14, *Academy Notes, Notes on Prout and Hunt, and Other Art Criticisms, 1855–1888*, p. 378.
2 Ibid., p. 437.

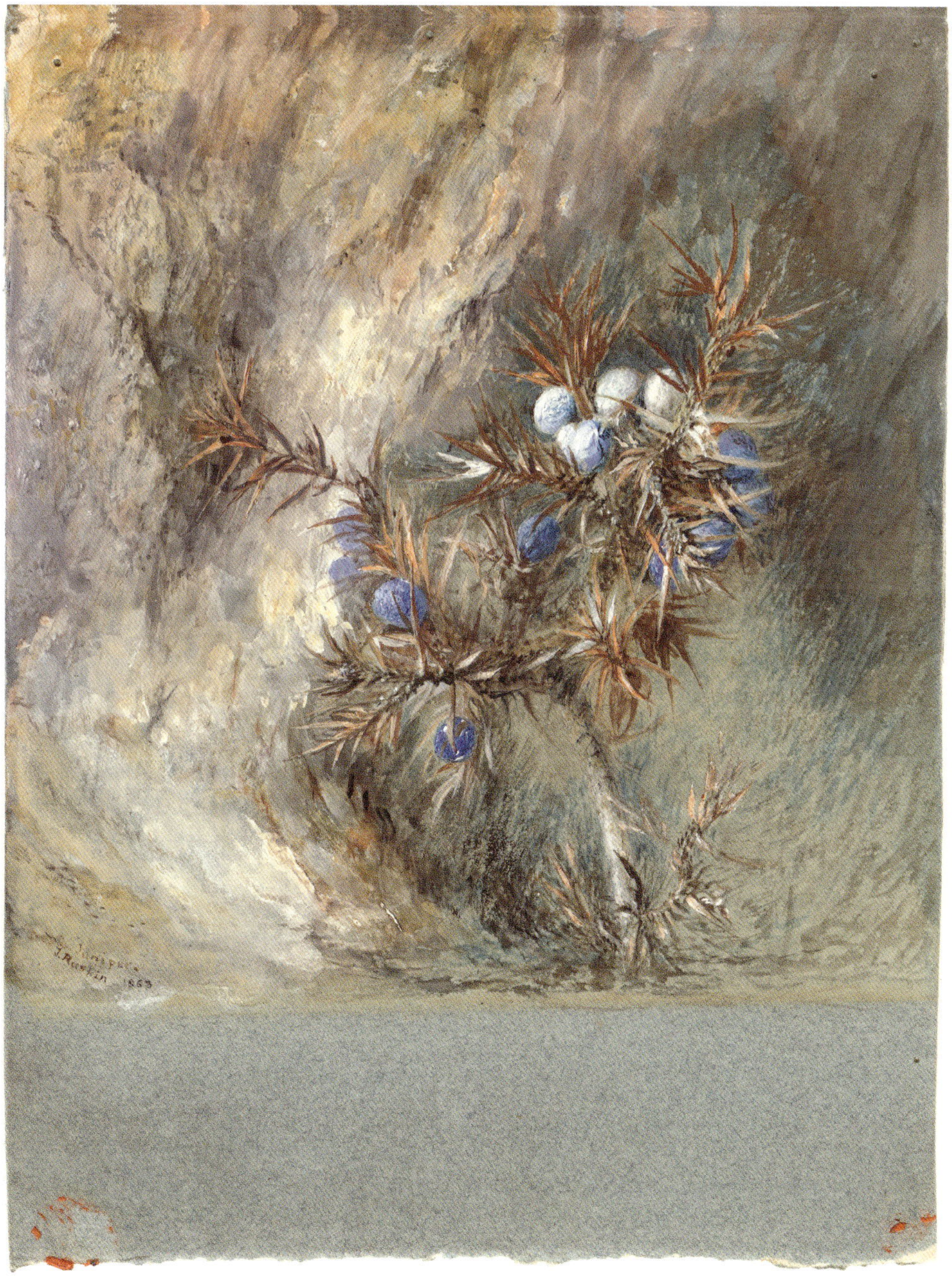
J Ruskin

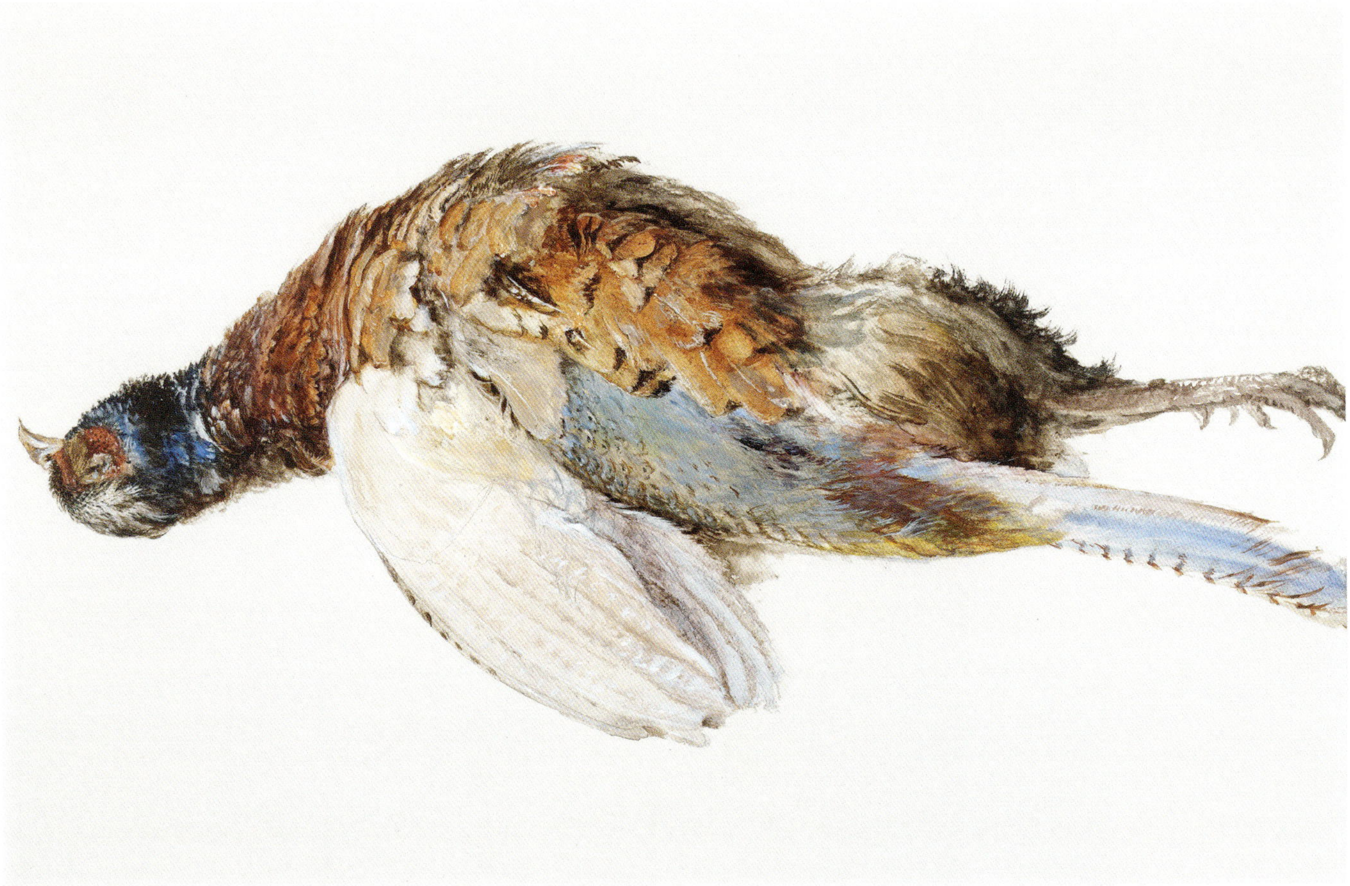

120

Dead Pheasant 1867

Graphite, watercolour and bodycolour on paper; 33 × 50.8 cm
Victoria and Albert Museum, London (D.394-1907)

A number of diary entries in January 1867 record Ruskin's work on a series of watercolours of birds – at least two of a pheasant, of which this was the largest and occupied him for several days; another of a partridge; and others of partridge, snipe, teal and mallard.[1] Indoor work such as this was necessitated by the terrible weather that affected London that winter but also by his need for distraction during an agonizing period when he waited for news of Rose La Touche and her promised response to his marriage proposal.

Ruskin was clearly fascinated by the minute variations of texture and colour in the feathers of these specimens, paying close attention as he did in each to the contrasts between different types of plumage on the birds. Nonetheless, the pheasant is treated with relative freedom in the handling of watercolour, so that the effect is somehow suggestive of Flemish still-life painting of the seventeenth century. His immediate purpose in making the study was however to test himself against J.M.W. Turner, two of whose watercolour studies of dead pheasants Ruskin had in his collection.[2]

NOTES

1 The drawing of the partridge is in the Ashmolean Museum, Oxford, while the mallard is in the British Museum, London.
2 For the Turner watercolour that served as the immediate prototype for Ruskin's study, now in the Whitworth Art Gallery, Manchester, see Wilton 1979, cat. 635.

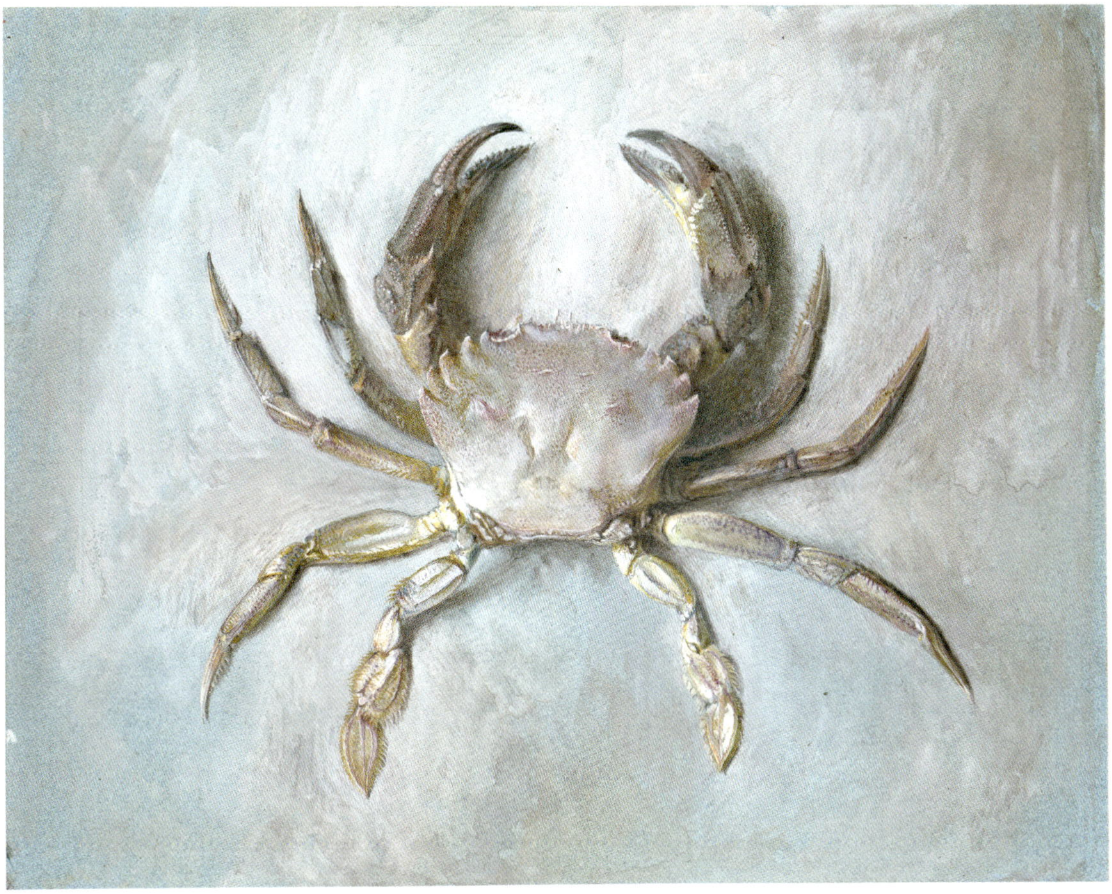

121

Study of a Velvet Crab 1870 (?)

Bodycolour over graphite on blue wove paper; 24.5 × 31.5 cm
The Ashmolean Museum, Oxford. Presented by John Ruskin to the Ruskin Drawing School (University of Oxford), 1875 (WA.RS.ED.199)

This beautiful and highly finished study of a crab was placed by Ruskin in the Educational Series of drawings given by him to Oxford, where it was displayed in the cabinet devoted to Elementary Zoology, in company with others of birds, cattle and fish.

Extraordinary for its single-minded observation of the forms of the specimen in question, and in which Ruskin found an abstract beauty of natural symmetry, it is also a most beguiling exercise in colour. In connection with this work, Nicholas Penny has observed that Ruskin "was as sensitive to the mixed colouring of shells as he was to that of marble."[1]

NOTES

1 Penny 1988, p. 46.

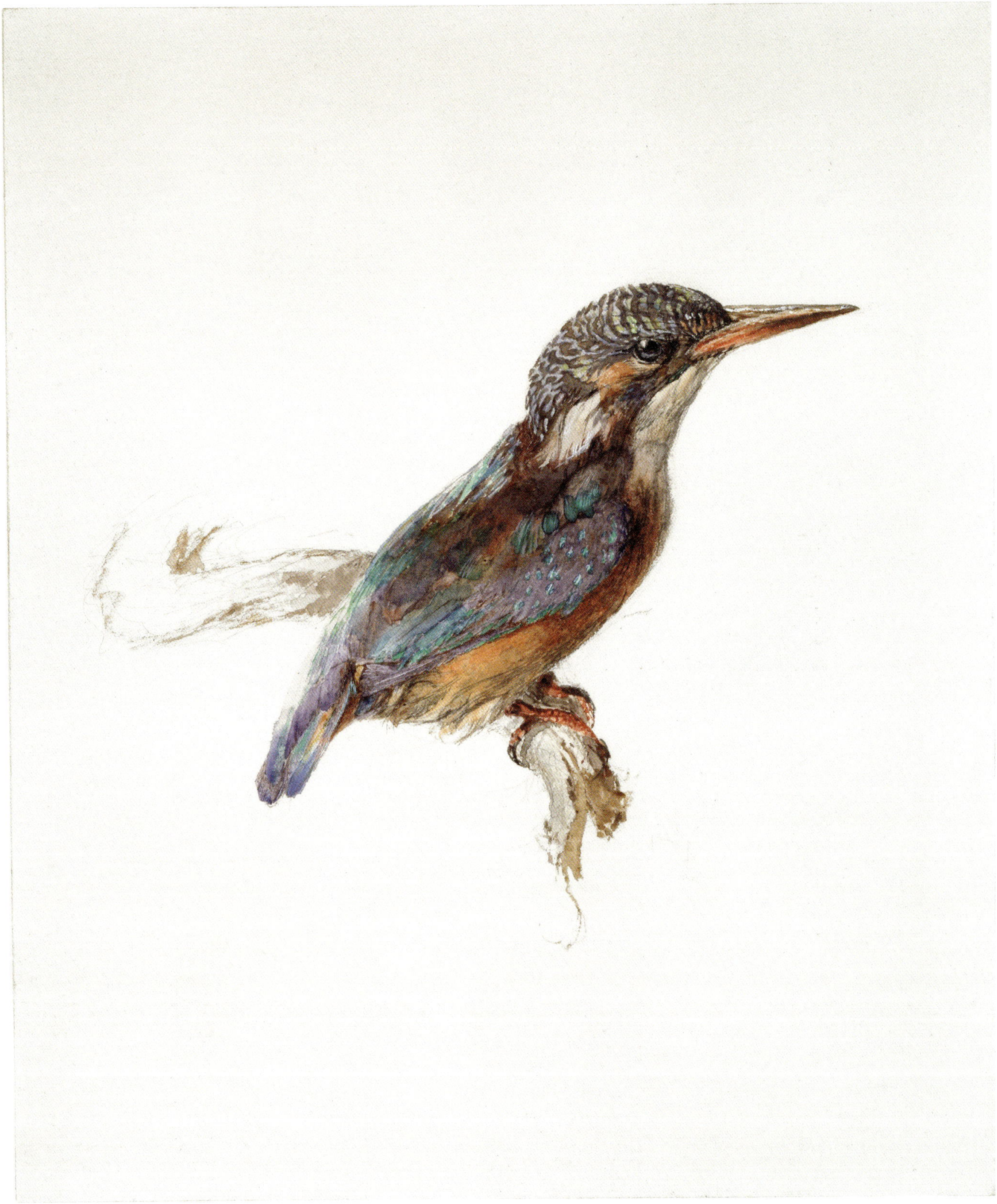

122

Study of a Kingfisher, with Dominant Reference to Colour probably 1871

Watercolour and bodycolour over graphite on wove paper; 25.8 × 21.8 cm
The Ashmolean Museum, Oxford. Presented by John Ruskin to the Ruskin Drawing School (University of Oxford), 1875 (WA.RS.RUD.201)

This is one of a series of five studies of a kingfisher that Ruskin included in the so-called Rudimentary Series of drawings that he presented to the Oxford Drawing School. It was placed in the ninth cabinet, devoted to "Exercises in Colour with Shade, on Patterns of Plumage and Scale." Others in the series showed enlarged details of the bird's plumage, while in addition there was a pen and chalk drawing of the whole bird as seen here, but with "dominant reference to shade."

In his Oxford lecture series "The Eagle's Nest," given in the Lent Term of 1872, Ruskin attempted to refute the purely scientific explanation as to the variations of species. He expressly contradicted Darwinian theory as to how the patterning of birds' plumage had evolved as a mechanism by which the species was perpetuated and that was linked to the particular characteristics of the variety of bird, preferring as he said that his listeners "should remain impressed with the effect which the lovely colour and fitful appearance of the bird have had on the imagination of men."[1] The gist of the lecture series was to explore "the relation of natural science to art," and among his anti-scientific maxims was that summarized by E.T. Cook and Alexander Wedderburn as stating that "anatomy will not help us to draw the true appearance of things."[2] Ruskin was in this period of incipient emotional crisis withdrawing from his youthful belief in the importance of attempting to understand whatever it was one looked at in scientific terms, and by using the power of observation to determine objective characteristics, to a more spiritual and unquestioning response to the forms of nature – one in which the sheer delight that he found in the beauty of colours and texture was predominant.

NOTES

1 Ruskin 1903–12, vol. 22, *Lectures on Landscape, Michael Angelo & Tintoret, The Eagle's Nest, Ariadne Florentina, with Notes for Other Oxford Lectures*, p. 256.
2 Ibid., p. xxxvi.

123

Cerastes Cornutus, Seen from Above, Drawn from Life c. 1871

Watercolour and bodycolour over graphite on pale brown wove paper; 12.2 × 14.4 cm
The Ashmolean Museum, Oxford. Presented by John Ruskin to the Ruskin Drawing School (University of Oxford), 1875 (WA.RS.ED.175b)

This drawing was presented by Ruskin to the Oxford Drawing School, where it was placed in the cabinet devoted to Elementary Zoology.

Ruskin had a horror of snakes that remained with him all his life, and was haunted by nightmares in which he was menaced by terrifying phantasms, such as occurred one night in November 1869 when he suffered:

> ... the most horrible serpent dream I ever had yet in my life [in which] ... the deadliest came out into the room under a door. It rose up like a Cobra – with horrible round eyes and had woman's, or at least Medusa's, breasts. It was coming after me, out of one room, like our back drawing room at Herne Hill, into another; but I got some pieces of marble off a table and threw at it, and that cowed it and it went back; but another small one fastened on my neck like a leech, and nothing would pull it off. I believe the most part of it was from taking a biscuit and glass of sherry for lunch, and partly mental evil taking that form.[1]

As is so often the case for people with phobias of this kind, Ruskin was also fascinated by the object of his terror, studying snakes in the London Zoological Gardens and in the wild in the gardens and on the fell at Brantwood. Drawings exist by him of adders, cobras and rattlesnakes. The present study shows a desert horned viper, a venomous snake from North Africa that has the habit of twisting itself into curved coils when preparing to strike and that rubs its scales together to make a rasping sound to warn of its presence. Ruskin's knowledge of snakes led to a lecture entitled "Living Waves," given in 1880 and subsequently combined with other themes into the volume *Deucalion*. This text was, he claimed, the first statement on "how a snake serpentines," and again he distanced himself from contemporary zoological science because he believed he had learnt more from looking at living specimens than "the anatomists [who] can't, for their life, look at a thing till they have skinned it."[2]

In his "Living Waves" lecture – which was accompanied by diagrams made by assistants based on his own studies – Ruskin explored the mythological associations of snakes and addressed the question of why so many people find such animals fearsome, and how they have come to represent "an entirely degraded and malignant human life." He concluded that "this head of the cerastes, and that of the rattlesnake, are in reality more terrific to you than the others, not because they are more snaky, but because they are more human, – because the one has in it the ghastliest expression of malignant avarice, and the other of malignant pride."[3]

NOTES

1 Ruskin 1956, p. 685.
2 Ruskin 1903–12, vol. 26, *Deucalion and Other Studies in Rocks and Stones*, p. xlii.
3 Ibid., p. 324.

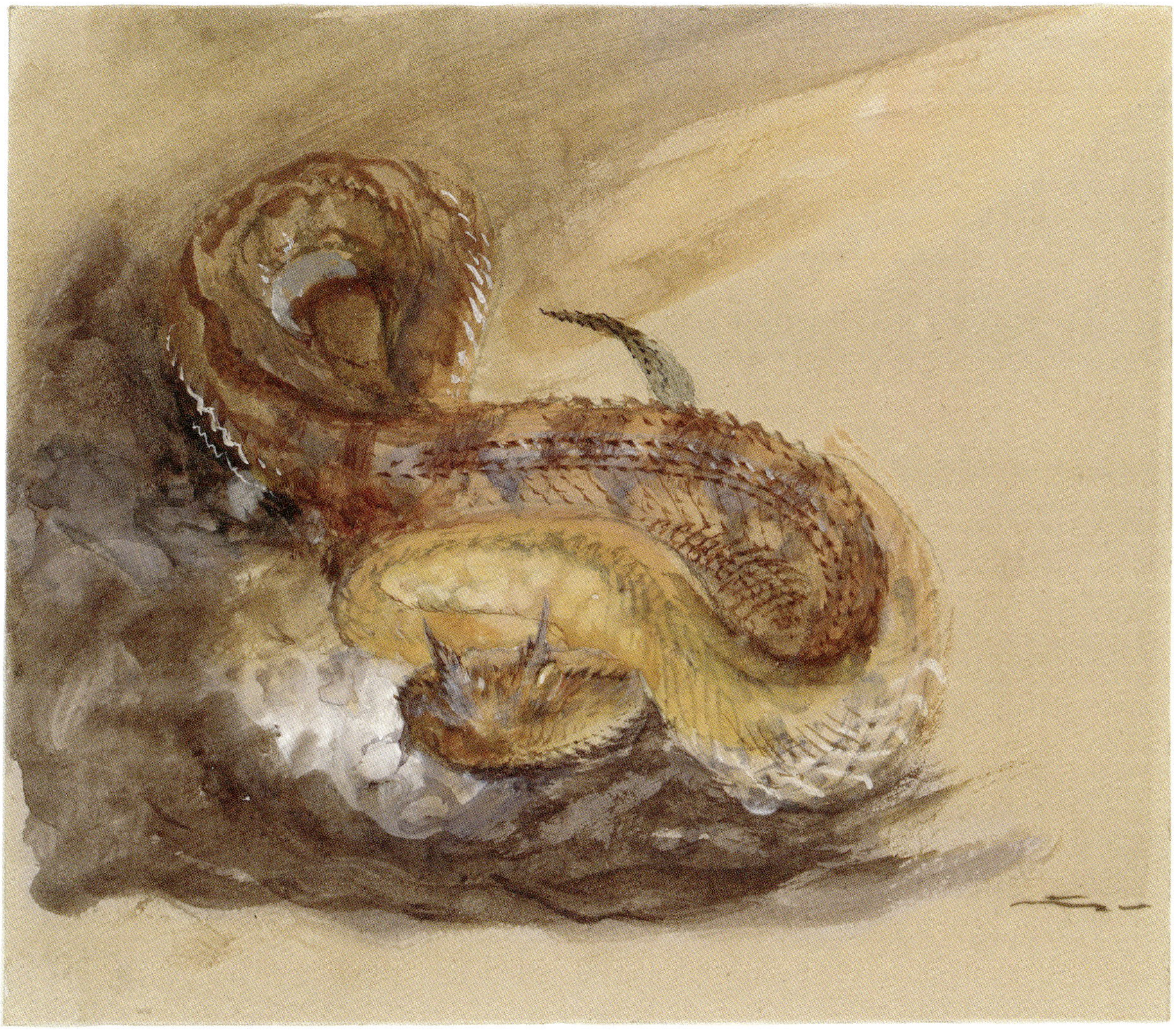

124

Blenheim Orange Apple c. 1873

Watercolour and bodycolour on heavyweight white wove watercolour paper; 11.7 × 16.5 cm (sight)
Private collection
Inscriptions: signed with initials *JR*, in an unknown hand on the mount, presumably following an original inscription by Ruskin, *Mrs. Stacey's present, 22 Nov. 73 / Red side first in shade, then in light. / Gamboge, Orange vermilion, Rose madder, Burnt umber, Cobalt, and Black (JR)*

This is one of a number of drawings that Ruskin made of apples in the 1870s. E.T. Cook and Alexander Wedderburn introduced a study of a Blenheim Orange apple as the frontispiece of the Library Edition of *The Elements of Drawing*, giving it the date 1873. The present drawing, which was once in the distinguished Cunliffe collection, may represent the same apple, if from a different angle, and is likely therefore also to have been made at the same time.

Although the drawing of apples was not among Ruskin's particular recommendations of objects for study in *The Elements of Drawing*, he may well have encouraged students at the Working Men's College to draw from fruit, following the example of William Henry Hunt who gave wonderfully volumetric renditions of plums, grapes, peaches, melons and apples by the use of stippled bodycolour and who was famous for the observation of blemishes and bruising on the surfaces of his examples. That Ruskin regarded the study of apples as a suitable exercise for the training of students is borne out by his having given such drawings of his own to Louise Blandy so that she might understand his technique and apply it in her own studies of fruit.[1]

NOTES

1 Ruskin's drawing of an apple, dated 29 November 1875, and Louise Blandy's of the same date, made in imitation of his original, were shown together in the exhibition *Ruskin and Oxford: The Art of Education*, Ashmolean Museum, Oxford, 1996 (see Oxford Sheffield 1996, cats. 15 and 16).

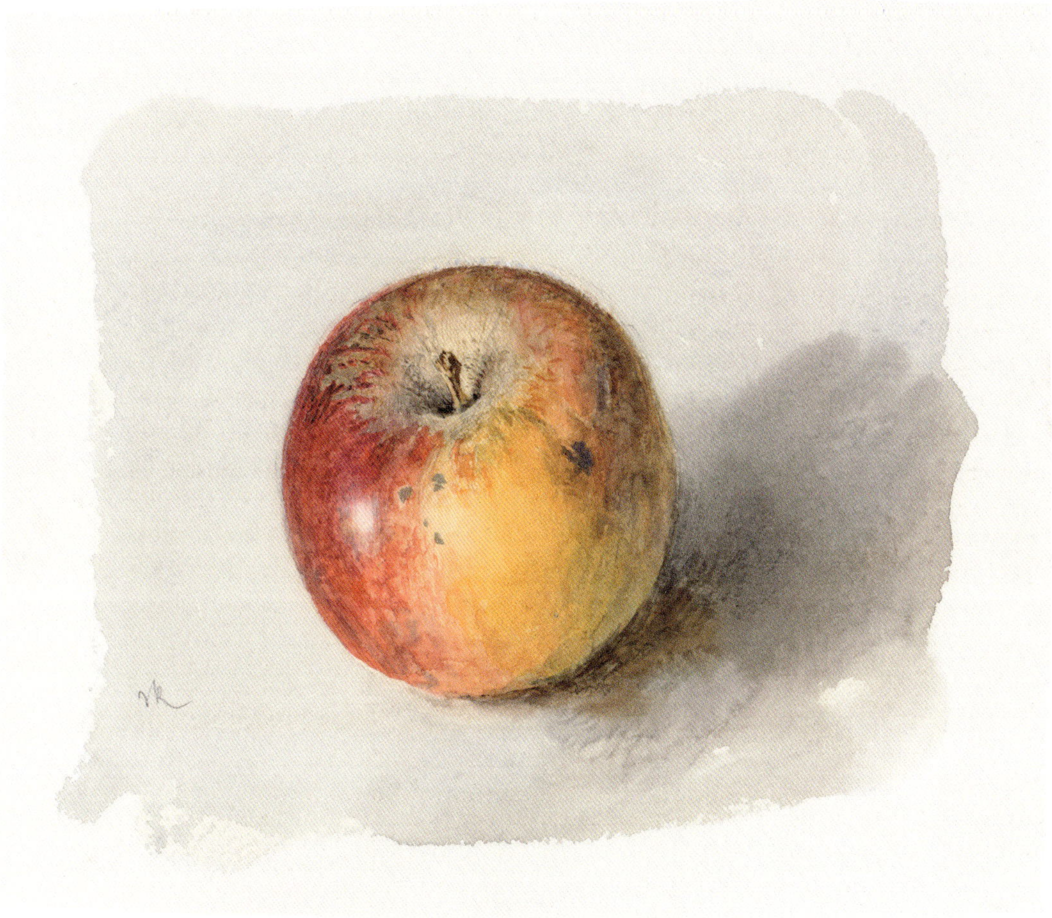

125

Study of a Peacock's Breast Feather 1873

Watercolour and bodycolour on paper; 28.9 × 19.8 cm
Collection of the Guild of St. George, Museums Sheffield (CGSG00046)

In the catalogue of the collections that Ruskin gave to the Guild of St. George and that were to be shown in the museum that he had built at Walkley in Yorkshire, Ruskin described this drawing as of "a single plume of peacock's breast, painted of its natural size." With it were displayed other drawings of peacock feathers, one of which showed parts of the feather at a magnification of three times.[1] Made in connection with Ruskin's Oxford lecture "The Robin," given in March 1873 and published as *Love's Meinie* later the same year, the corresponding passage of text provides a similarly scrupulous – not to say obsessive – account of such a specimen: "The extremity of the breast plumes parts slightly into two, as you see in the peacock's, and many other such decorative ones. The transition from the entirely leaf-like shape of the active plume, with its oblique point, to the more or less symmetrical dualism of the decorative plume, corresponds with the change from the pointed green leaf to the dual, or heart-shaped, petal of many flowers."[2]

Ruskin seems to have challenged himself to focus his attention with such exactitude as is seen in the present drawing, requiring total concentration and absolute precision of handling, and may have found in the task a kind of therapy and means of preserving himself from incipient dementia. Drawing feathers became an occasional recourse for him in the 1870s, referred to on one occasion in *Fors Clavigera* when he interrupted himself with the words: "And, in the meantime, I must stop writing because I've to draw a peacock's breast-feather, and paint as much of it as I can without having heaven to dip my brush in."[3]

NOTES

1 A photogravure plate was made as an illustration for *Love's Meinie*, which combined the present drawing with two studies of the enlarged filaments (Ruskin 1903–12, vol. 25, *Love's Meinie and Proserpina*, opposite p. 39).
2 Ruskin 1903–12, vol. 25, pp. 39–40.
3 Ruskin 1903–12, vol. 28, *Fors Clavigera, Letters 37–72*, p. 466.

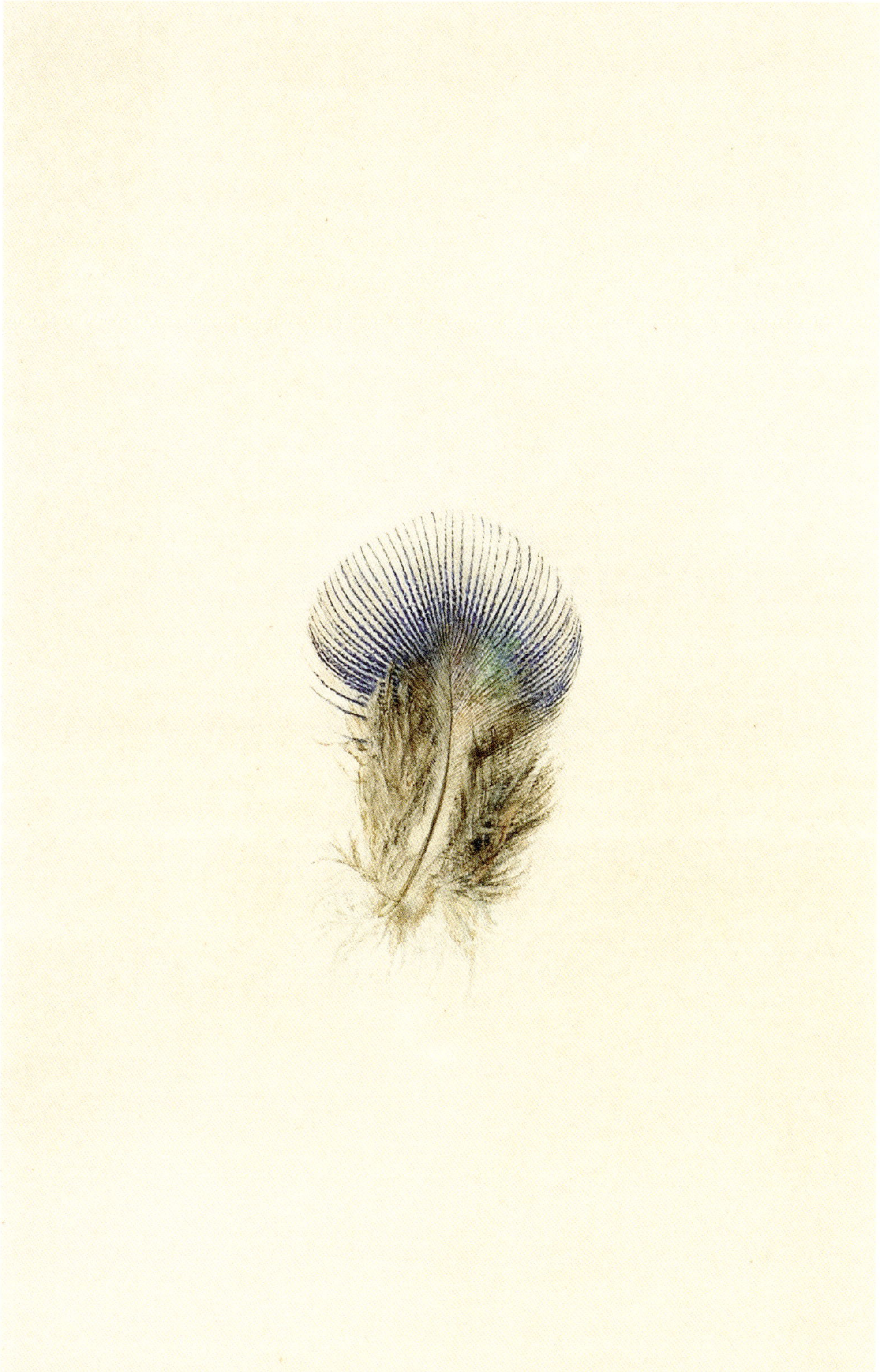

126

Three Feathers c. 1875

Pen and black ink and watercolour on cream paper; 22 × 15 cm
Private collection

Ruskin's particular interest in birds and their plumage was expressed in two extended exegeses – *Love's Meinie*, which was worked up from the texts of lectures given at Oxford and published in parts between 1873 and 1881, and *The Laws of Fésole*, a treatise on drawing and painting intended as a follow-up to *The Elements of Drawing* and issued in parts between 1877 and 1878. These texts include accounts of how feathers are formed and function, combined with descriptions of the beauty of their colours and patterns. Speaking, for example, of the feathers of "the domestic fowl and the partridge," he concluded that "there is nothing in arrangement of plumage approaching the exquisiteness of that in the vaulted roofs of their expanded *covering* wings; nor does anything I know in decoration rival the consummate art of the minute cirrus-clouding of the partridge's breast."[1] Occasional gibes at the theory of evolution are set within a larger attack on the manufacturing industry and utilitarianism.

The feathers in the present drawing appear to be those of a hen; this is suggested by their distinctive straggly filaments in their lower part and smoother and more regular patterning in their middle sections and in the banding of black and brown and their elegant blue tips. In October 1875, when staying with William and Georgina Cowper Temple at their country house, Broadlands, Ruskin described making a drawing of a "feather ... out of her hen's breast – picked up in poultry yard yesterday,"[2] to give to his hostess. This last drawing was later engraved by George Allen and used as an illustration for *The Laws of Fésole*.[3]

NOTES

1 Ruskin 1903–12, vol. 15, *The Elements of Drawing, The Elements of Perspective, and The Laws of Fésole*, p. 399.
2 Ruskin 1903–12, vol. 24, *Giotto and his Works in Padua, The Cavalli Monuments, Verona, Guide to the Academy, Venice, St. Mark's Rest*, p. xxi.
3 Ruskin 1903–12, vol. 15, opposite p. 365.

127

Fast Sketch of Withered Oak Leaves 1879

Watercolour, ink and graphite on paper; 14 × 18 cm
Collection of the Guild of St. George, Museums Sheffield (CGSG00150)
Inscriptions: *J Ruskin / Brantwood / 1879*

This drawing of a spray of dried oak leaves was made by Ruskin at Brantwood in the autumn of 1879. Another similar drawing, also in the collection of the Guild of St. George at Sheffield, bears the inscription "Dead leaves by John Ruskin (drawn by him in the presence of Miss Beever to show her his manner of work)." Susan Beever and her sister Mary lived close to Ruskin at a house called Thwaite, where they created a wonderful garden, and were both much loved members of the community. Ruskin and Susan became dear friends and exchanged delightful and whimsical letters, swapping information on things of mutual interest such as wildflowers and birds, about which Miss Beever was hugely well informed.

There is a freedom and instinctive quality in this drawing that makes it delicious. Finding in the contorted shapes and crackling textures of the leaves a sculptural character analogous to the decoration of a carved capital or a piece of wrought iron, Ruskin has used flashes of white bodycolour to make the whole thing glisten in its three-dimensionality and to give the impression of its trembling form being suspended in an undefined space. It may be regarded as the successor to earlier studies of stems and foliage, such as the studies of branches of dying chestnut leaves that he used to illustrate his lecture on "Tree Twigs" in April 1861. Once again, Ruskin may have had William Henry Hunt in mind when making this drawing – Hunt's studies of sprays of leaves were similarly organic in form and radiant with colour. The pair to the present drawing was included in the exhibition of works by Hunt and Samuel Prout that Ruskin helped organize in the last months of 1879, and that also included a selection of his own drawings.

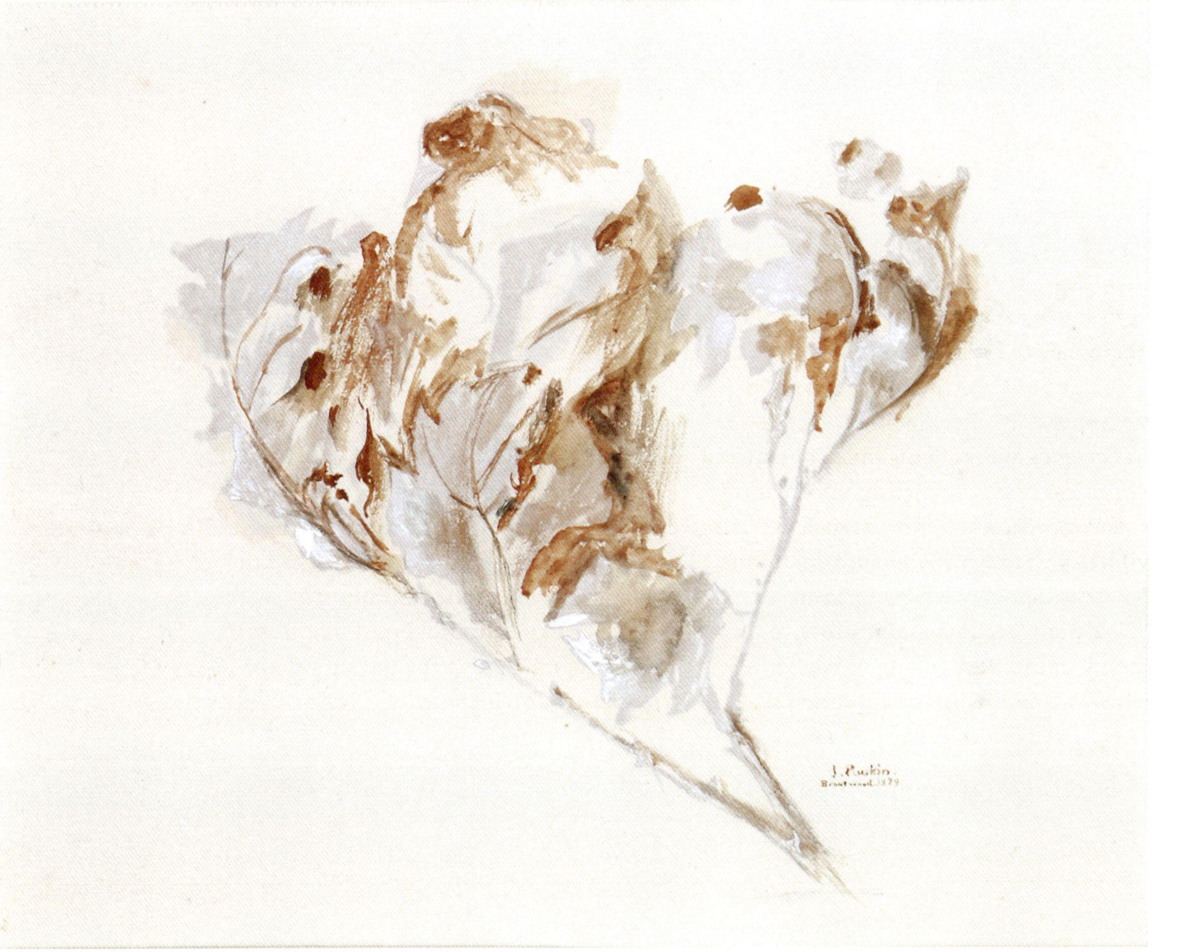
J. Ruskin.
Brantwood. 1879

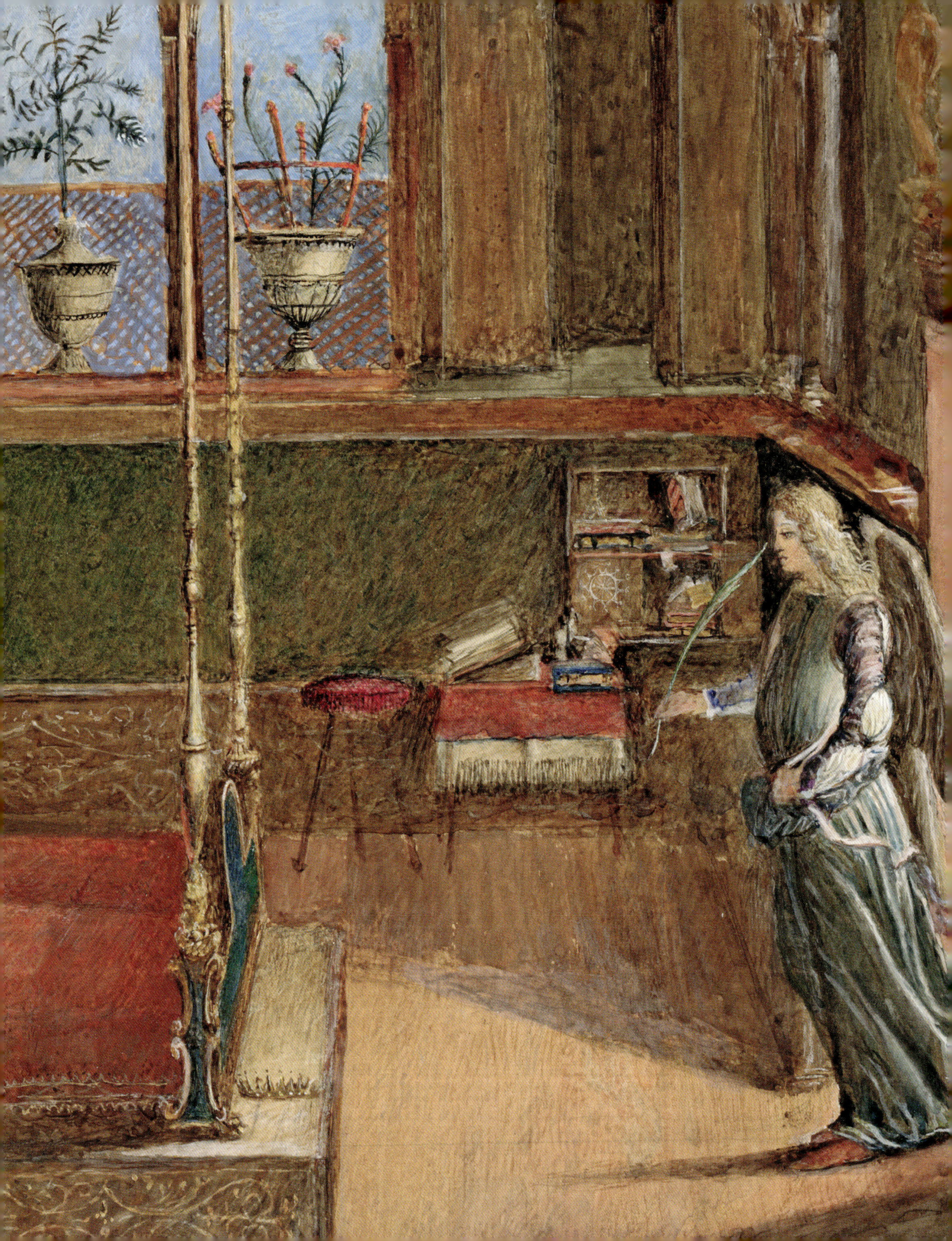

Figures

128

Copy of the Central Portion of Tintoretto's "Crucifixion" 1845

Graphite, black ink, watercolour and bodycolour on white paper; 27 × 53.5 cm
Ruskin Foundation (Ruskin Library, Lancaster University) (RF 1553)

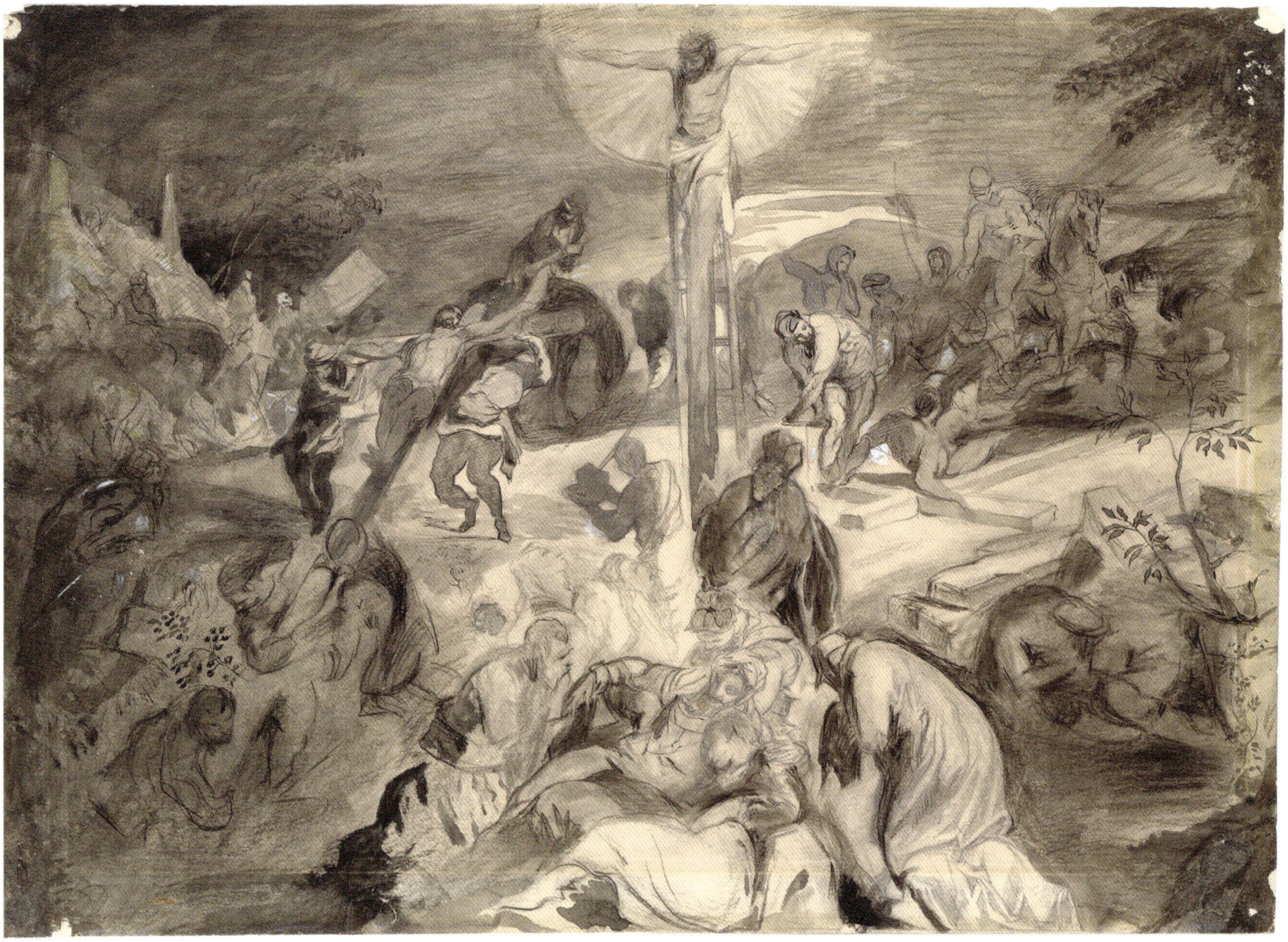

On 23 September 1845, while visiting the galleries of the Accademia in Venice with James Duffield Harding, Ruskin found himself overwhelmed by the work of "a man whom I never dreamed of – Tintoret. I always thought him a good & clever & forcible painter, but I had not the smallest notion of his enormous powers. Harding has been as much taken aback as I have, but he says he is 'crumbled up' while I feel encouraged & excited by the good art."[1] From that time forward,

Ruskin sought out paintings by Tintoretto wherever they were to be seen, shortly afterwards and while still in Venice finding his way to the Scuola Grande di San Rocco, an experience that he recalled in *Præterita* as a moment of epiphany: "But for that porter's opening [the door of the Scuola], I should ... have written *The Stones of Chamouni* instead of *The Stones of Venice* ... but Tintoret swept me away into the 'mare maggiore' of the schools of painting which crowned the power and perished in the fall of Venice; so forcing me into the study of the history of Venice herself; and through that into what else I have traced or told of the laws of national strength and virtue."[2]

In the second (and as it was then envisaged, final) volume of *Modern Painters*, in which Ruskin discussed the theory and power of imaginative art, Tintoretto became a hero, and this despite the fact that Ruskin's interests had previously focused on the Middle Ages, and notwithstanding his ongoing misgivings about the influence of Catholic dogma on the conduct of art.

In his copy of the San Rocco *Crucifixion*, Ruskin captured the dynamic frenzy and compositional complexity of the original work, with loosely blocked figures, shadowed peripheries, and a centrifugal subjection of all parts of the scheme to the central motif of the figure of Christ. Ruskin understood the mechanism whereby the artist had filled the composition "with such various and impetuous exertion, that the body of the Crucified is, by comparison, in perfect repose."[4] Furthermore, delighted as he always was by incidental detail in narrative subjects, he described the motif of a donkey feeding on palm leaves that remained strewn about from Christ's entry into Jerusalem. In the chapter entitled "Of Imagination Penetrative," Ruskin praised Tintoretto as a painter "whose intensity of imagination is such that there is not the commonest subject to which he will not attach a range of suggestiveness almost limitless; nor a stone, leaf, or shadow, nor anything so small, but he will give it meaning and oracular voice."[3]

Tintoretto's work in the Scuola di San Rocco began in the Sala dell'Albergo in 1564 with his commission-winning *St. Roch in Glory*. The *Crucifixion*, which is displayed on the same room's end wall, was commenced the following year. By the middle of the nineteenth century, these paintings were in perilous condition, dirty and discoloured, and in places badly affected by damp. By drawing them, Ruskin forced himself to trace their main lines and to search for lost pictorial detail. The studies are therefore an exercise in archaeological reconstruction as well as serving as a historical record of works of art in jeopardy. The experience of making them changed Ruskin's life, as he immersed himself in an art in which he found qualities of exhilaration and emotion.

NOTES

1 Ruskin 1972, p. 210.
2 Ruskin 1903–12, vol. 35, *Præterita and Dilecta*, p. 372.
3 Ruskin 1903–12, vol. 4, *Modern Painters II*, p. 262.
4 Ibid., pp. 270–271.

129

Copy of the Figure of a Girl in Van Dyck's "Portrait of Anna van Thielen, the Wife of the Painter Theodor Rombouts, and their Daughter Anna Maria" 1859

Graphite, pen and ink, sepia wash and bodycolour on paper; 51 × 35.5 cm
Brian Sewell, London
Inscriptions: *J. Ruskin after VANDYCK MUNICH 1859*

Prompted by a government commission into the organization of the National Gallery in London to which he had been asked to give evidence, Ruskin made a tour of German cities in 1859 to see picture galleries and museums there. Diary entries written in the course of his travels demonstrate that he was looking with interest at works of art that he might previously have been expected to dismiss. For example, in Dresden he admired Rembrandt's self-portrait with Saskia (c. 1635) and also found things to enjoy in Correggio's *Nativity* (1529–30). Much time was spent in contemplation of works by Paolo Veronese, the artist whose work *Solomon and the Queen of Sheba* (c. 1582) Ruskin had devoted a period of intensive study to the previous summer in Turin. As regards the Flemish Catholic painter Anthony van Dyck, Ruskin found his portrait of Queen Henrietta Maria (also in Dresden but now regarded as a studio copy) "ineffably beautiful in composition though far lower than Titian in mode of work."[1] However, doubts about the painter's true merits emerged in Ruskin's note on a *Lamentation of Christ* in Munich,[2] which he described as being of a "base form of picturesque – … forced and false, and without one atom of true feeling: but very captivating."[3]

Whatever Ruskin's misgivings may have been about Van Dyck's religious subjects, he was clearly delighted by the detail of a young girl that he found in the painter's portrait of a mother and daughter[4] – also in the Munich Alte Pinakothek. With characteristic attention to a peripheral, even incidental, motif within the larger composition, he observed the way in which the child's attention appears to have been caught by something outside the picture space, to which she turns her face although still clinging to her mother's arm, a distraction that may be imagined to have momentarily relieved the tedium of sitting quietly as the subject for the portrait.

NOTES

1 Ruskin 1956, vol. 2, p. 544.
2 There are in fact two paintings of the subject in the Alte Pinakothek in Munich, numbers 404 (c. 1616–17) and 606 (1634). The reference to the "white scroll on cross used a beautiful curving light" (Ruskin 1956, p. 547) indicates that it was the latter work that Ruskin was castigating.
3 Ruskin 1956, vol. 2, p. 547.
4 The sitter of the portrait (no. 599) has variously been identified as the wife of the Antwerp sculptor André Colyns de Nole or as the wife of the painter Theodor Rombouts. Corroboration of either identification depends on the correspondence of the work's pendant, also in the Alte Pinakothek in Munich, to known likenesses of either de Nole or Rombouts. In the 1986 catalogue of the Alte Pinakothek, a convincing case was made for that work being of the latter individual, and furthermore the two paintings are associated with entries in various inventories of collections in Antwerp. Rombouts married Anna van Thielen from Mechlin in 1627, and their daughter Anna Maria was born the following year. The girl appears to be about three or four years old in Van Dyck's portrait, suggesting a date of about 1632 for the work, which is consistent with its stylistic character.

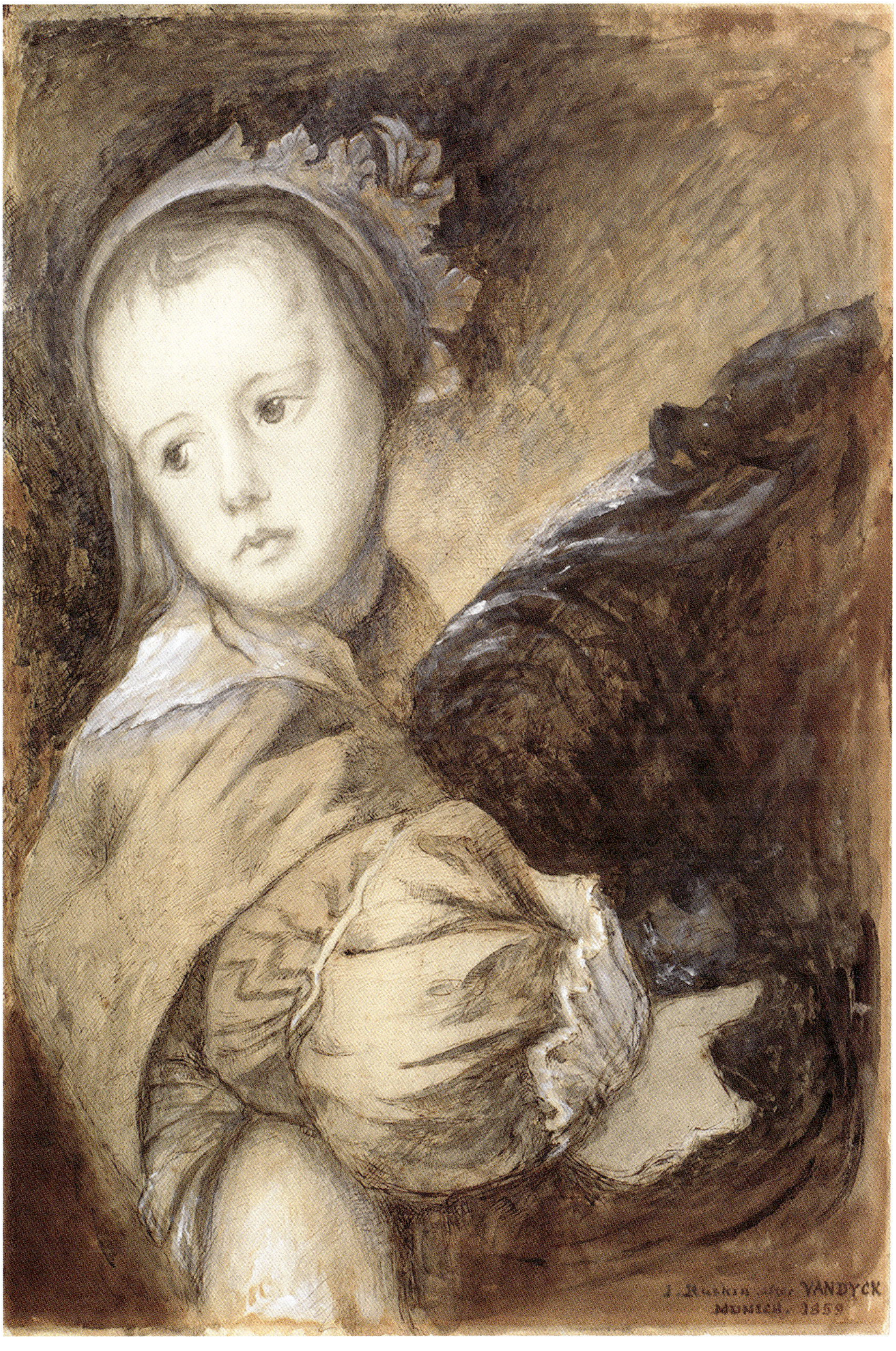
J. Ruskin after VANDYCK
MUNICH. 1859

130

Self-portrait, in Blue Neckcloth 1873

Watercolour and gouache on paper; 35.3 × 25.3 cm
The Morgan Library and Museum, New York. Purchased as the gift of the Fellows (1959.23)
Inscriptions: verso, graphite, presumably by Joan Severn, *Di Pa by himself*

The present self-portrait was made at the request of Charles Eliot Norton, Ruskin's American friend and eventually his literary executor. A terse diary entry for 29 January 1873, written from Brantwood – "Began portrait of self, for Norton"[1] – marks its commencement. Since 1859 Norton had been seeking to possess a portrait of Ruskin, in the first place commissioning one from Dante Gabriel Rossetti (a drawing was forthcoming in 1861, now in the Ashmolean Museum, Oxford, but was regarded as unsatisfactory). Norton later hoped that Edward Burne-Jones might produce something that would be fitting as a record of his friend, but gradually turned to the idea of encouraging Ruskin to draw self-portraits, believing that this would be a task that would comfort him, or at least prove a beneficial distraction, at times of depression or manic anxiety.

Ruskin was approaching his fifty-fourth birthday when he made this drawing of himself, and he clearly shows himself without self-flattery as a man in middle age. His sandy coloured hair, parted on the right side of his head (but seen here in mirror image), is swept back, while his whiskers and bushy eyebrows are unkempt. His face is furrowed with lines, particularly apparent on his forehead as he appears to lean forward toward the looking glass and seems to wrinkle his brow to open his eyes more widely. The drawing shows his face at close range so that it fills much of the sheet, with an indeterminate background of ochre and an indication of the lapels of his coat, a white shirt with collar turned up to his chin, and a stock of the blue that he habitually wore and that he seems to have believed complimented and brought out the remarkable and piercing blueness of his eyes. Looking so directly at his own physiognomy, and observing himself with searching candour as he stares directly into the reflected image of his own eyes, thus allowing us to gauge the intensity of his own self-awareness, Ruskin seems to suggest the acuity of eyesight, which remained with him all his life. In his directness of inspection, the drawing thus may be seen as a metaphor for what he regarded as a crucial human faculty.

This is one of a number of self-portraits by Ruskin that explore the way in which his features aged in the 1870s. A similar watercolour, perhaps by Ruskin himself or a copy of an autograph self-portrait drawing, was in the possession of Charles Fairfax Murray (the most likely alternative candidate for authorship of the work), and is now in the Tate collection. Ruskin is again seen wearing a blue stock and with hair drawn back from his forehead, while the background appears to show a part of Coniston Water and the lakeshore close to Brantwood.

NOTES

1 Ruskin 1956, vol. 2, p. 736.

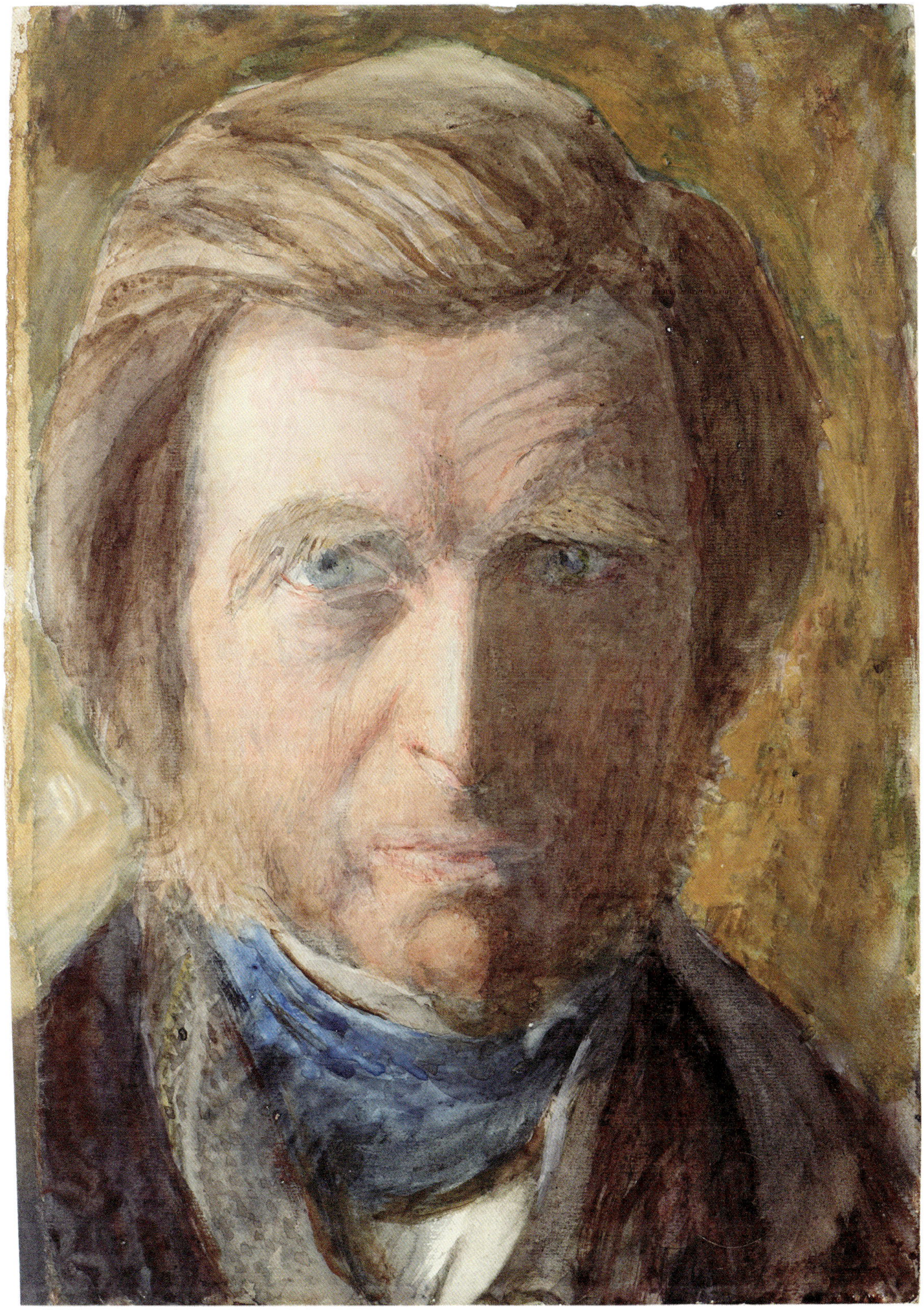

131

Self-portrait 1874

Graphite on white paper; 25.4 × 20.4 cm
Ruskin Foundation (Ruskin Library, Lancaster University) (RF 991)
Inscriptions: by C.E. Norton, graphite, *Ruskin (se ipsum) del.*, verso, graphite, *J. Ruskin. His own drawing of himself, 1873 or 4. C.E.N. Not a good likeness.*

During the winter of 1873–74 Ruskin moved aimlessly about England, finding it impossible to concentrate or even to distract himself from the agonizing suspense and uncertainty that he felt about his relationship with Rose La Touche, whom he was seldom allowed to see but with whom he continued intermittently to correspond. He spent the Christmas period at Margate and then returned to Oxford in the New Year of 1874, but found himself unable to continue with his teaching. He was at Brantwood by 23 February, then moved back to Oxford to lead the famous experiment whereby undergraduates of the university were taught how to build a road at Ferry Hinksey (in which the twenty-year-old Oscar Wilde participated), and eventually set out for Europe at the beginning of April.

The history of how the present drawing came to be made can be partially reconstructed from the letters that were exchanged between Ruskin and Charles Eliot Norton in the spring of 1874, commencing with an expression of intent by Ruskin to make a further record of himself for his American friend in a letter of 15 February, written from Corpus Christi College, Oxford, where he then had rooms. As he explained: "I came away here in the evening – and am going down to Brantwood, till the crisis [in Rose's health and state of mind] is over. I shall make you a little drawing of myself, positively before I go abroad."[1] In March Norton noted in a postscript to a letter written from his house Shady Hill in Cambridge, Massachusetts, that "it will be one of the best days in the year when I see the *Portrait*," and thanked Ruskin "for the promise of it." On 9 April, writing from Pisa, Ruskin reassured Norton that he had asked for "the two beginnings of myself I made for you" to be sent to him, going on to explain the difficulty he had with self-portraiture: "All that is good in me depends on terrible subtleties, which I find will require my very best care and powers of completion; all that comes at first is the worst. Continually I see accidental looks, which if I could set down you would like, – but I have been able to do nothing yet, only I let these failures be sent to show I have been trying."[2] Whether to be regarded as successes or failures, Ruskin's self-portrait drawings speak of a desire for self-knowledge and a belief that identity might be revealed in the specifics of physiognomy.

In the present drawing, all the twinkling engagement seen in the *Self-portrait, in Blue Neckcloth* (cat. 130) has gone, but instead a staring and manic fixedness of expression serves as a record of Ruskin at a grim time in his life. This was not how Norton remembered his friend from happier days – their first meeting had been in 1855 and their friendship confirmed on the occasion of an encounter on a boat on Lake Geneva the following year, while their most recent meeting appears to have been in the autumn and winter of 1872–73. In 1883, when Norton saw Ruskin

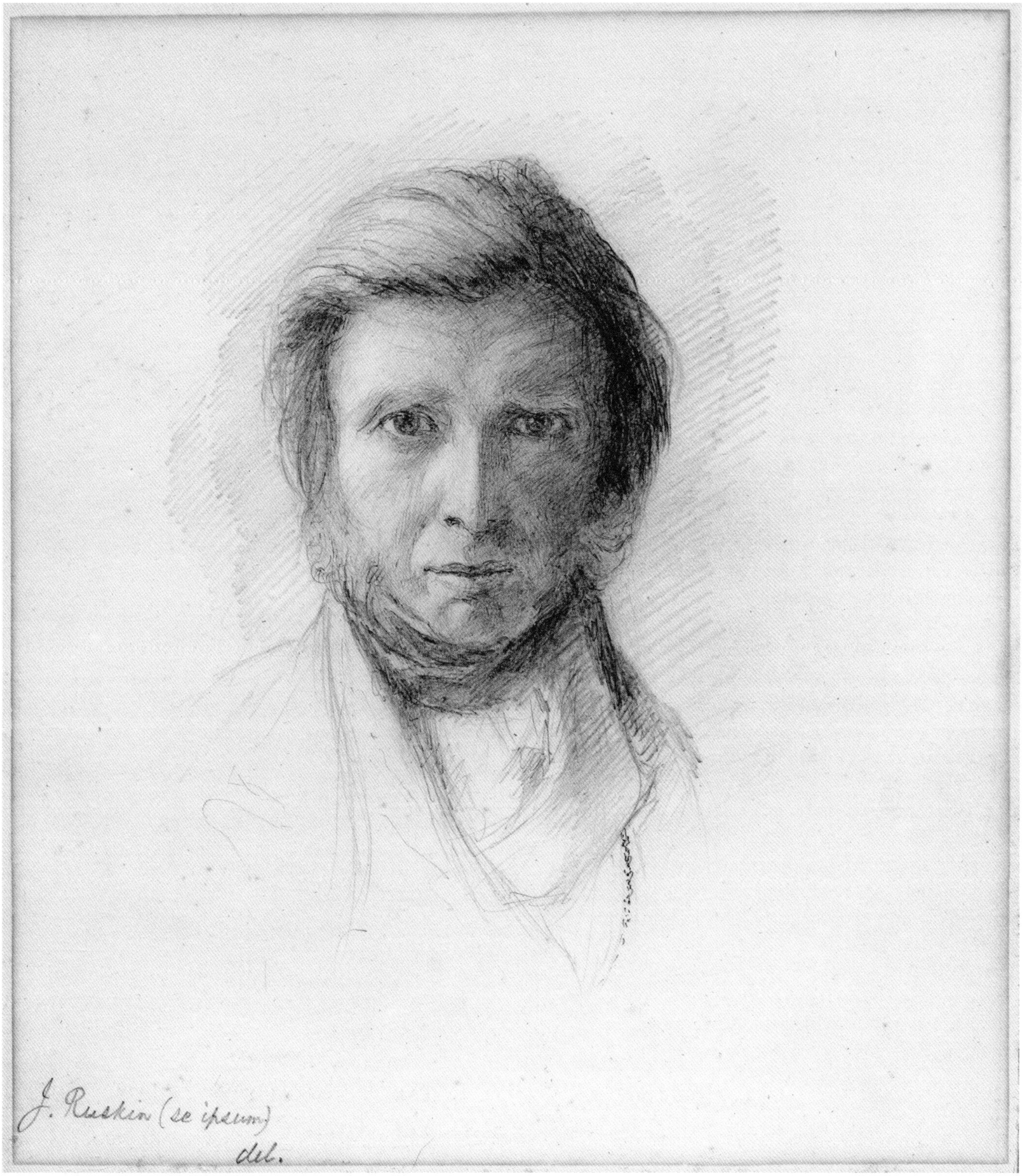
J. Ruskin (se ipsum)
del.

again when he visited him at Brantwood, he recalled how ten years previously he had been "a man in vigorous middle life, young for his years, erect in figure, alert in action, full of vitality, with smooth face and untired eyes."[3] Of the present drawing, however, he could only say that it was "not a good likeness."

Norton sought every opportunity to look at Ruskin's drawings when they were together in England or on the Continent, or in the course of his 1883 visit to Brantwood. Almost nobody else commented on Ruskin's work as a draftsman, and it seems to have been something of a surprise to him to find Norton so enthusiastic and admiring of the drawings. It was in fact his American friend's opinion that Ruskin had allowed himself to be led into too disparate a range of interests and areas of thought, and that he should be encouraged to concentrate on the matters upon which his reputation had been first established, essentially the study of art and architecture. Norton also felt that drawing and the intensity of observation that went with draftsmanship as practiced by Ruskin represented the very kernel of his genius. He besought Ruskin to draw, both because he felt that the process of observation would serve as a therapy that might preserve his sanity and because in the fullness of time a wider audience would come to appreciate the sheer beauty of his works and learn from them. Norton used the drawings that Ruskin gave him to instruct his students at Harvard and even proposed to use a purchasing grant to the university's Fine Arts department to commission further drawings from him – which if it had happened would have been a unique circumstance in Ruskin's career. Furthermore, Norton organized an exhibition of Ruskin's work, shown in Boston in 1879 and subsequently in New York. A fragment of a letter written on 10 July 1874, in which Norton speaks of the importance of Ruskin's works as a draftsman, mixes encouragement and admonition:

> Do you think I urge you draw and to give yourself to work that no man can do as well as you, in a light spirit? Not so: it is because I am sure your influence will be made deeper, more permanent, & more helpful by patient work of this kind, than by your impassioned and impatient appeals to men who will scoff at your words. You have sown seed; let the summer show where it has fallen, some at least will be found on good ground.[4]

NOTES

1 Ruskin Norton 1987, p. 308.
2 Ibid., pp. 311–312.
3 Ruskin 1903–12, vol. 33, *The Bible of Amiens, Valle Crucis, The Art of England, The Pleasures of England*, p. xlvii.
4 Ruskin Norton 1987, p. 320.

132

Drawing of Carpaccio's "Dream of Saint Ursula" from the "Legend of Saint Ursula" 1876

Watercolour and bodycolour over graphite on wove paper; 29.4 × 27.7 cm
The Ashmolean Museum, Oxford. Presumably presented by John Ruskin to the Ruskin Drawing School (University of Oxford), where it was first recorded in 1906 (WA.RS.WAL.09)

Ruskin saw Rose La Touche for the last time in February 1875; his account of her mania as he witnessed it on that occasion is distressing to read to this day.[1] She died on 26 May, aged twenty-seven, and the sense of loss that he experienced resonated through his every thought and action for years to come. For Ruskin, a long period of semi-inactivity at Brantwood followed, with his thoughts increasingly preoccupied with the image of dark clouds and black winds, as in for example his description to Charles Eliot Norton of "the plague of darkness – and blighting winds – perpetual – awful – crushing me with the sense of Nature & heaven failing as well as man."[2] In 1876, despite his re-election as Slade Professor of Fine Arts at Oxford, he felt unable to play any part in the life of the university, and he thus applied for a year's leave of absence, setting out in August for Venice, where he was to remain until May 1877. His mental health was deteriorating, and at Christmas 1876 he subsided into insanity. Haunted by thoughts of Rose, and with a mounting conviction that she still existed in some spirit world and might perhaps be seeking to communicate with him, he became obsessively interested in works of art that, to his deranged mind, seemed to give clues to some possible connection with her.

Ruskin's particular study that winter of Carpaccio's cycle of paintings telling the story of the virgin martyr St. Ursula was linked to his thoughts of Rose, as he made an analogy between the mythical Christian saint and his deceased beloved. As recounted in the *Legenda Aurea*, Ursula, the daughter of a British king, had been instructed to accept betrothal to a pagan prince by the angel of the Lord, who came to her in a dream. According to the legend, her only request was that her wedding should be postponed for three years (as Rose had asked Ruskin to wait for three years before she would say whether she would marry him) so that she might make a pilgrimage to Rome, but in the course of this journey, at Cologne, she and 11,000 virgin martyr companions were slaughtered for their Christian faith by Huns.

Of all the nine paintings in the St. Ursula cycle, which had been removed to the Accademia in 1812 following the Napoleonic suppression of the Scuola for which they had been painted, Ruskin's particular interest lay in the canvas entitled *The Dream of Saint Ursula*, a work that he had drawn from in 1869, and the elements of which he described in detail in Letter 20 of *Fors Clavigera*, of August 1872. Carpaccio had "taken much pains to explain to us ... the kind of life [St. Ursula] leads, by completely painting her little bedroom in the light of dawn, so that you can see everything in it." "At the door of the room an angel enters ... his body, like a mortal one, casting shadow from the light through the door behind, his face perfectly quiet; a palm-branch in his right hand – a scroll in his left. So dreams the princess, with blessed eyes, that need no earthly dawn."[3]

Ruskin explained to Charles Eliot Norton on 5 October 1876 how he had been given access to the painting by the museum directorship: "They have been very good to me in the Academy, and have taken down St. Ursula and given her to me all to myself in a locked room and perfect light. Im [sic] painting a small carefully toned general copy of it for Oxford."[4] In his drawing, Ruskin specified the motifs upon which the symbolical narrative of the original depended: the flood of light from heaven as the door is opened to admit the angel; the flowers standing in pots on the window ledge, representing earthly and heavenly love; and the Holy image lit by a smoking candle on the left wall. In *Fors Clavigera* Letter 71, written from Venice early in October 1876, he explained that the legend of Ursula was to be regarded as a metaphor, but in fact in the course of his agonizing and lonely sojourn in the city that winter, she increasingly became a subliminal reality to him, and he imagined himself to be receiving a bizarre system of coded messages – directed to him by the saint who in his febrile imagination morphed into a proxy for Rose herself. On Christmas Eve, Ruskin received by post a specimen of dried vervain from his friend Daniel Oliver at Kew Gardens, and as vervain was one of the two plants shown on the windowsill in Carpaccio's painting, this seemed to him to be a signal that Ursula/Rose was attempting to reassure him that she was watching over him from beyond the grave. Then an Irish woman he encountered in the street in Venice presented him with a pot of carnations as a Christmas present, and as these were the other flowers seen in the painting, Ruskin momentarily entered a state of frenzied elation, taking it as a sign that he should make amends with Rose's mother, having "received it as a direct command from St. Ursula."[5]

Ruskin was absorbed by the unthreatening and serene works of Carpaccio from the time that he first studied them in 1869 (and on which occasion he had made his first return to Venice for seventeen years). The importance to him of this discovery was expressed in a letter to Edward Burne-Jones, who was in fact the person who had recommended him to look at the early sixteenth-century artist's works in the first place, and which opens:

> My dearest Ned: – There's nothing here like Carpaccio! There's a little bit of humble-pie for you! Well, the fact was, I had never once looked at him, having classed him in glance and thought with Gentile Bellini, and other men of the more or less incipient and hard schools, – and Tintoret went better with clouds and hills. I don't give up my Tintoret, but his dissolution of expression into drapery and shadow is too licentious for me now. But this Carpaccio is a new world to me.[6]

Carpaccio therefore followed Fra Angelico and Tintoretto, and preceded Sandro Botticelli, as an artist to whom Ruskin would lay claim as his own.

NOTES

1 See Swett 1931, p. 118.
2 Ruskin Norton 1987, p. 354.
3 Ruskin 1903–12, vol. 27, *Fors Clavigera, Letters 1–36*, pp. 342, 344.
4 Ruskin Norton 1987, p. 387.
5 Ruskin 1956, vol. 3, p. 921.
6 Ruskin 1903–12, vol. 4, *Modern Painters II*, p. 356, note 3 from p. 355.

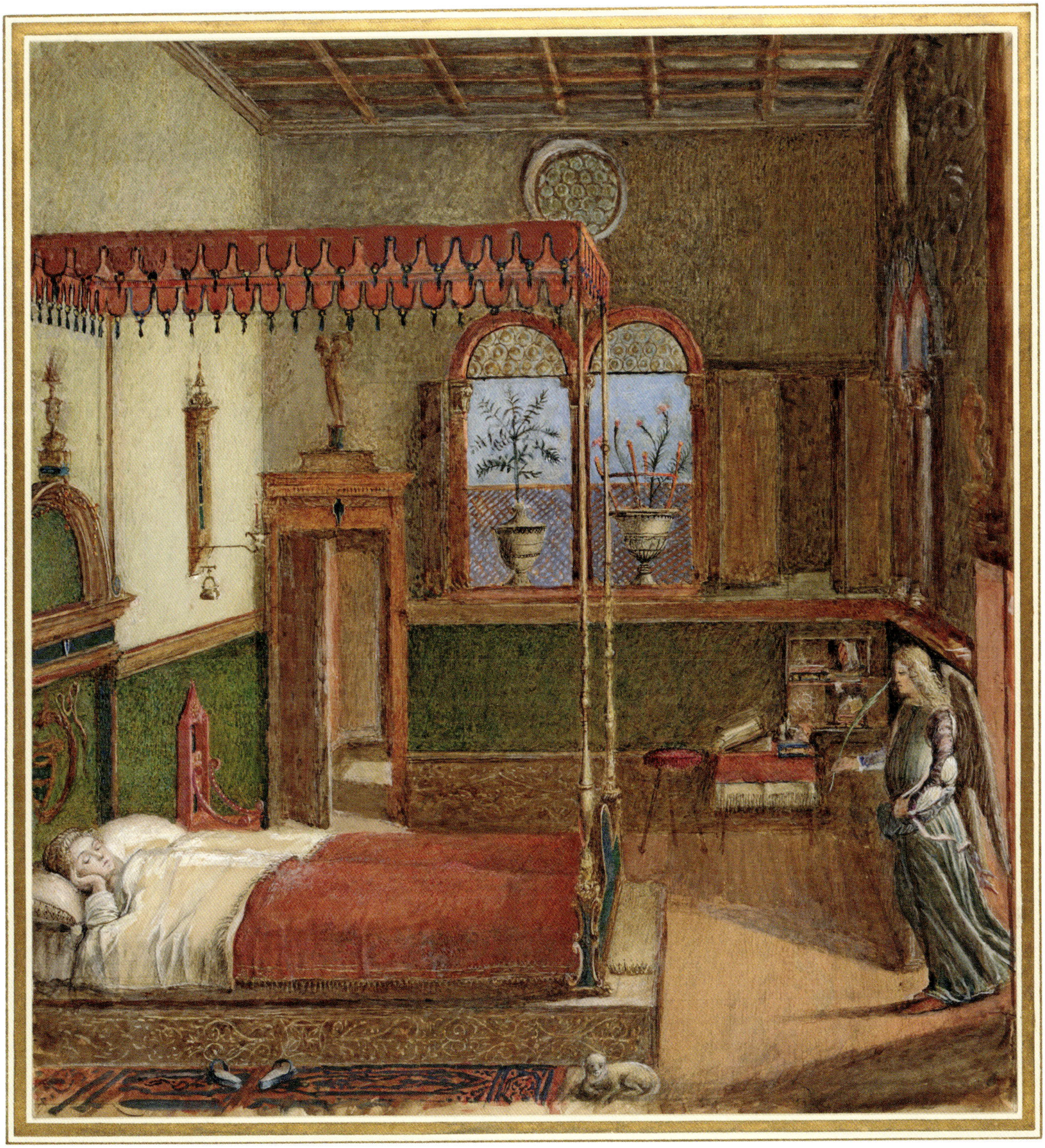

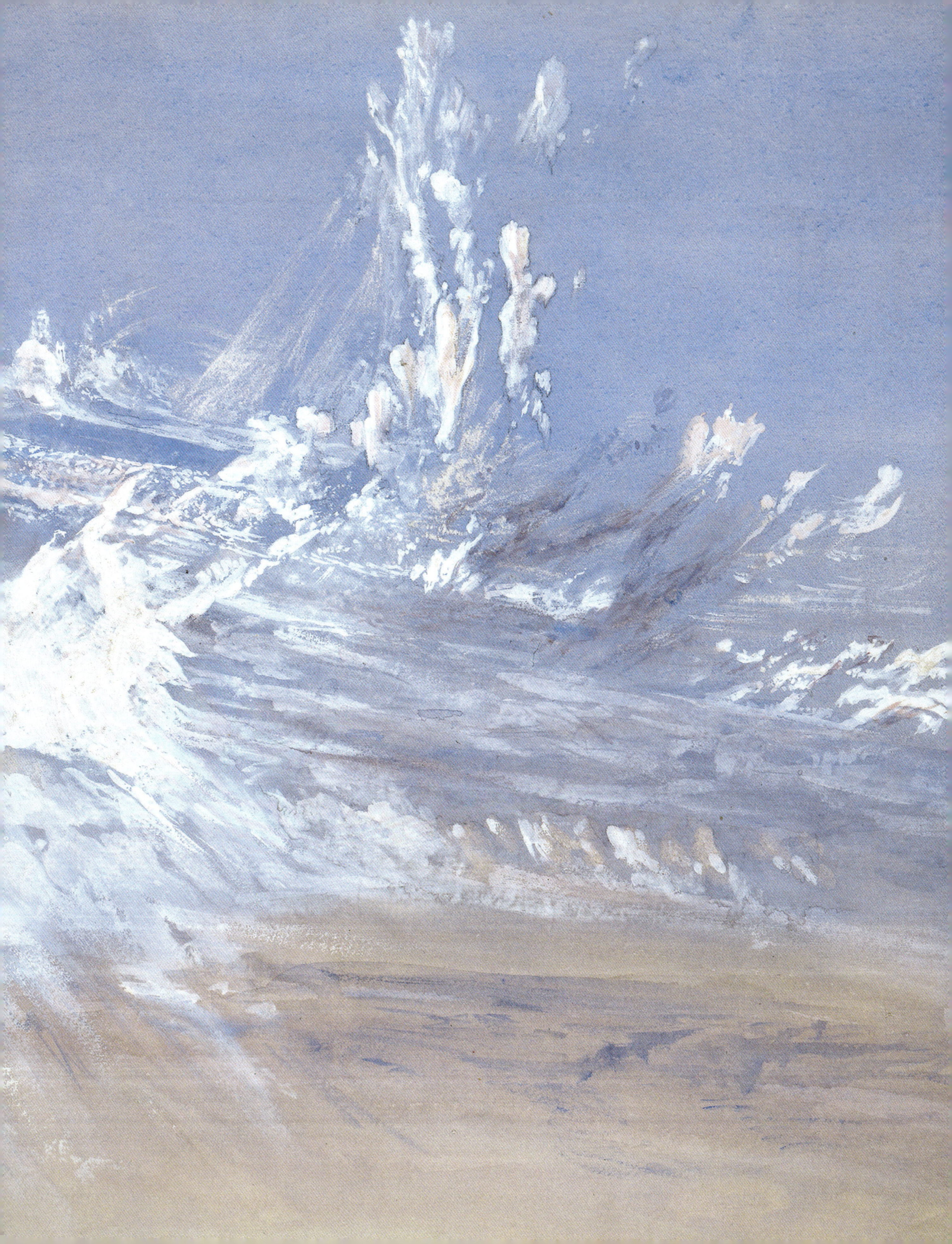

Chronology

CHRISTOPHER NEWALL

1819

Ruskin is born on 8 February at 54 Hunter St, Brunswick Square, London.

1826–27

The first of Ruskin's surviving juvenile studies in sketchbooks, now in the collection of the Yale University Art Gallery.

1828–29

He makes copies of maps in pen and ink.

1830

Ruskin and his father visit the summer exhibition of the Society of Painters in Watercolours for the first time.

1831

In the spring he commences weekly drawing lessons with Charles Runciman. Much time is devoted to exercises in perspective.

1832

For his birthday, he is given a copy of Samuel Rogers' *Italy*, with vignette illustrations by J.M.W. Turner, among others. This whets his appetite for travel to southern Europe.

In a letter to his father, dated 20 February, he describes making a landscape drawing based on memories of a place seen in Wales and in imitation of the watercolour technique of a cousin.

In May Ruskin's father makes his first purchase of a watercolour at the exhibition of the Society of Painters in Watercolours – a work by the president of the society, Anthony Vandyke Copley Fielding. Another drawing by Fielding is acquired the following year, and further purchases from the society's summer exhibitions take place over the following decade.

1833

Ruskin and his father study Samuel Prout's *Facsimiles of Sketches Made in Flanders and Germany* (1833), a volume of lithographic plates showing buildings and townscapes in a succession of northern European cities.

The family tours France, Germany, Switzerland and northern Italy. This marks Ruskin's first sight of the Alps, and in particular his first visit to the Alpine village of Chamonix, which in the years to come was to be the essential locus of his interest in mountains as a subject for art as well as objects of scientific study. On his return to London he embarks on an account of the journey, partly in verse and illustrated with his own drawings in vignette form.

1834

In June he commences a course of instruction in drawing in six lessons by Copley Fielding. The method advocated by Fielding was traditional, depending on successive washes of translucent colour to build up the volumes of the composition and upon the whiteness of the sheet to provide illumination. Ruskin would praise Fielding in the first volume of *Modern Painters* for his "faithful and simple rendering of nature," but in later life he looked back on the method that Fielding had introduced him to as facile and unchallenging.

He first becomes aware of David Roberts' landscape drawings and lithographic plates.

He publishes two essays in the *Magazine of Natural History*: the first an article on the colour of the waters of the Rhine; the second on the rock strata of the Mont Blanc massif, illustrated with engravings made after his own drawings.

1835

From June until December the Ruskin family tours France, Switzerland and Italy, including Venice. Ruskin makes many drawings of geological subjects and also of architecture and townscapes in the Alps and elsewhere. The media he uses varies from pen and ink line drawings to pure watercolour.

He experiments with oil painting but decides that for practical reasons watercolour is a preferable medium.

Cat. 103, detail

1836

He receives drawing lessons from Copley Fielding.

In October he writes a letter in response to an article by the Reverend John Eagles criticizing Turner's work in *Blackwood's Magazine* (the letter was sent on to Turner who recommended that it should not be published).

1837

He studies the lithographic plates in David Roberts' book *Picturesque Sketches in Spain*. Ruskin's father acquires a drawing of an architectural subject by Roberts, so that for the following couple of years Ruskin on occasions imitates Roberts' style of drawing, aiming for atmospheric space and subtle tinting.

He goes up to Oxford University as a "gentleman-commoner" at Christ Church. His skill as a draftsman is spoken of within the college, even by Henry George Liddell, who would later be the Dean. However, archaeologist Charles Newton criticizes an architectural study that he had asked to have made by Ruskin, on the grounds that its picturesque and ornamented character distracted from its usefulness as a record.

1839

In January Ruskin and his father acquire Turner's watercolour *Richmond Hill and Bridge, Surrey* (fig. 1.2), their first purchase of a work by the artist.

He studies the Windus collection of Turner watercolours.

1840

On the occasion of his twenty-first birthday, Ruskin's father gives him investments that produce an annual income of £200, money with which it is intended that further art purchases, especially drawings, are to be made.

The Turner watercolours *Gosport, Entrance to Portsmouth Harbour* (c. 1829, private collection) and *Winchelsea* (The British Museum, London) are purchased.

He is absent from Oxford for a period as a consequence of a breakdown that he had suffered at Easter.

On 22 June Ruskin attends a dinner at which Turner is present, possibly his first meeting with the artist.

In September the family sets out on a European tour. Ruskin prepares himself with sketchbooks in determination to make a complete pictorial record of their travels. Before departing, he seeks advice from artist friends including James Duffield Harding, Peter De Wint, David Roberts and Turner as to how he should set out to draw while away. The outward journey, the route of which is based on his desire to visit places where Turner had previously worked, takes them through France and into Italy.

In Rome he makes contact with George Richmond and other British artists then working in the city.

Ruskin's family travels on to Naples and further to the south.

1841

The family remains abroad until June. Their return journey brings them back to Rome and then on to Venice, where they stop for ten days, and then to Geneva.

Later in the summer Ruskin writes a poem entitled "The Broken Chain," set at Amboise and based on memories of the place from the time of his visit there the previous autumn, and accompanied by a watercolour that was a thoroughgoing imitation of Turner's style of work.

In November he commences drawing lessons with Harding, which are to continue over the following three years.

1842

In the spring he commissions two watercolours from Turner: *Lucerne from the Walls* (c. 1841, Lady Lever Art Gallery, Port Sunlight) and *Coblenz from Ehrenbreitstein* (1839, location unknown).

In the course of the summer, as described in *Præterita*, he finds himself wanting simply to draw what lies before him on the road to Norwood and at Fontainebleau.

From May to August he travels with his parents in France and to Chamonix, where they spend three weeks, and then moves on to Switzerland, Germany and Belgium, a tour that is intended as an opportunity for recuperation after the effort that he had made to pass his Oxford examinations. While travelling, he thinks about how he would prepare an expanded essay in which he would explain the importance and achievement of Turner and his particular significance in the context of British landscape painting.

1843

In May he publishes the first volume of *Modern Painters*, the sections of which are entitled "Of General Principles" and "Of Truth." Written in defence of Turner, but also (in its first edition) lavishing praise on contemporary watercolourists.

In celebration of the success of the book, Ruskin and his father buy a further group of Turner watercolours.

1844

Ruskin's father gives him Turner's oil painting *Slavers Throwing Overboard the Dead and Dying, Typhoon Coming On* (1840, Museum of Fine Arts, Boston).

Ruskin's lessons with Harding continue. Harding encourages him to study the plates of Turner's *Liber Studiorum* (1807–19).

In February he responds to a commission from Sir Robert Inglis, Conservative Member of Parliament for Oxford University, for a worked-up watercolour version of a drawing made at Amalfi in 1841 (the sketch is in the collection of the Ruskin Foundation at Lancaster University; the finished watercolour is in the Fogg Museum, Harvard University).

He exhibits a drawing at the "Graphic Society."

From May until August he travels in the Alps, spending a month in Chamonix. In the course of his return journey, he stays in Paris to study in the Louvre.

1845

From April to November he travels abroad for the first time without his parents, accompanied by his manservant John Hobbs. His purpose is to study historic schools of art, of which he was increasingly aware of his limited knowledge. He makes himself familiar with the newly expanding literature devoted to so-called "Primitive" art, including A.F. Rio's *Poetry of Christian Art* and texts by Franz Kügler and Gustav Waagen. In Florence he "discovers" the art of Fra Angelico. In Pisa he makes delicate line studies in pencil of the Camposanto frescoes. In Lucca, Pisa and Venice he draws Romanesque and Gothic buildings, using colour to convey the decoration of inlaid marbles and rich materials, finding himself ever-more conscious of the risk to such architecture through restoration or reconstruction. He breaks his tour with a stay at Macugnaga in the Piedmontese Alps, where he is joined by Harding. He later travels on to Faido to see the site of Turner's *The Pass at Faido, St. Gotthard* (Thaw Collection, The Morgan Library and Museum, New York), making his own drawings for purposes of comparison between his perception of the mountain landscape and that of Turner (they would eventually appear as illustrations in the fourth volume of *Modern Painters*, published in 1856).

Later in the year, when in Venice with Harding, his attention is drawn to the period now known as Mannerism, as he becomes fascinated by the art of Tintoretto – who, perhaps surprisingly, becomes the painter most roundly celebrated in the forthcoming second volume of *Modern Painters*.

In Venice he becomes interested in daguerreotype photographs of architectural subjects. While there, he has the opportunity to acquire a group of images, thus commencing what was eventually to be a large collection of photographs of landscape and architectural subjects.

1846

In April he publishes the second volume of *Modern Painters*, subtitled "Of the Imaginative and Theoretical Faculties," in which he discusses the historic art that he had seen the previous summer and explores ideas to do with the imagination in art.

From April to September he takes his parents to Italy to show them a selection of the works of art that had made such a great impression on him the previous year. Tension occurs as Ruskin's father feels that Ruskin's efforts, including as a draftsman, are not sufficiently focused and that too much is left incomplete or unresolved. The exhaustion that Ruskin suffers from work on *Modern Painters*, exacerbated by stress connected with disagreements with his father, leads to a period of mental instability and incipient breakdown. In the later months of the year, and into the following, Ruskin seeks to rest and gather his thoughts toward future projects.

In September a revised edition of the first volume of *Modern Painters* is issued, with passages of praise for the English watercolourists and members of the Society of Painters in Watercolours eliminated.

1847

In letters to *The Times* he complains about the damage being done to paintings in the National Gallery by incompetent restoration.

During the summer and autumn he spends a period in Leamington Spa, seeking relief from the depression that had overtaken him and drawing subjects from nature. Later, he travels to the Lake District and Scotland, staying for a period at Crossmount, where he makes studies of landscape foregrounds.

1848

From August to October Ruskin and Euphemia (known as "Effie"), whom he had married in April, travel in Normandy. He draws buildings by way of research for his projected book *The Seven Lamps of Architecture*, in which he was to use etched illustrations made on the basis of his own sketches. His preference at this time is to work in monochrome and with strong shadowing so as to allow the forms of buildings to be read three-dimensionally. Drawings of this type owe much to the study of daguerreotypes, in which the effect of contrast between lit and shadowed areas is often dramatic.

1849

In March he writes an essay on the art of Samuel Prout for the *Art Journal*.

From April to September he travels to the Alps with his parents but without his wife. In Chamonix and elsewhere in Savoy he makes many drawings of mountain landscape, focusing on glaciers, aiguilles, ravines and cascades. His understanding of the mechanisms of physical geography greatly advances.

1850

In October he travels with Effie to Venice to study architecture in the city in preparation for *The Stones of Venice*, and remains there until March of the following year. A succession of sketchbooks are filled with detailed notations on the buildings that attracted his attention, with close observation of the patterns and variety of mouldings and ornament, as well as of the profile and curvature of arches and arcades.

1851

In March he publishes the first volume of *The Stones of Venice*, subtitled "The Foundations." This is followed by the three parts of *Examples of the Architecture of Venice*, consisting of plates made from his own drawings, published in May and November.

In May he writes to *The Times* to defend the Pre-Raphaelites. He subsequently meets John Everett Millais.

In August he issues his pamphlet *Pre-Raphaelitism*, in which he argues that Turner and Millais are linked in their shared search for a way of representing nature truthfully.

In August he and his wife again set out for Venice, on a second research stay connected with *The Stones of Venice*, remaining there until June of the following year.

In December Turner dies in London. Ruskin is named as an executor of the painter's will (although he subsequently attempts to renounce this responsibility when Turner's family seeks to contest the terms of the bequest of works from the studio to the nation). Ruskin writes letters to his father beseeching him to buy whatever Turner drawings might be available, and especially Alpine subjects from the last ten years of the painter's life.

1852

In June Ruskin and Effie depart from Venice. He is not to return to the city for sixteen years.

1853

From June until October Ruskin and Effie, accompanied by Millais and for a period also by William Henry Millais and Ruskin's Christ Church contemporary Henry Acland, stay at

Brig o' Turk in the Scottish Highlands. Millais paints Ruskin's portrait (fig. 2.5).

The Stones of Venice, volume II ("The Sea-Stories") and volume III ("The Fall") are published in July and October.

In November Ruskin gives the "Edinburgh Lectures," in which he explores the idea of natural ornament in architectural decoration, in connection with which he and Millais make a series of drawings.

1854

In April Ruskin enters into a friendship with Dante Gabriel Rossetti.

From May until October he tours France and Switzerland with his parents. His thoughts are turning to what comes to be known as the "Swiss Towns Project," a history of Switzerland on the basis of the country's architecture, for which he intends to make a series of illustrations from etchings based on his own drawings. This endeavour is to preoccupy him intermittently over the following twelve years.

In October the Working Men's College is established by Frederick Denison Maurice; Ruskin gives lessons on landscape drawing each week until 1861.

In December his designs for architectural decoration for the Oxford Museum of Natural History are accepted.

1855

In June he commences *Academy Notes*, in which he reviews the works exhibited at the summer exhibitions at the Royal Academy and elsewhere.

1856

The third volume of *Modern Painters*, subtitled ("Of Many Things"), is published in January, while the fourth volume, subtitled ("Of Mountain Beauty"), is published in April.

From May until October he travels to Switzerland and there meets Charles Eliot Norton.

1857

He sends the watercolour *Study of a Block of Gneiss, Valley of Chamouni, Switzerland* [sic] (now known as *Fragments of the Alps*, fig. 6.1) to the American Exhibition of British Art at the National Academy of Design in New York (it subsequently travels on to venues in Philadelphia and Boston the following year).

In January he publishes a guide to the works from the collection of the Turner Bequest, then on display at Marlborough House.

In April he addresses students at St. Martin's School of Art on the "Value of Drawing."

In June he publishes *The Elements of Drawing*.

From July until October he tours Scotland with his parents.

1858

In May he completes his examination of the drawings in the Turner Bequest.

From May until September he travels in Switzerland and Piedmont, meeting the Pre-Raphaelite landscape painters John William Inchbold and John Brett.

1859

In July he travels in Germany with his parents, visiting Berlin, Leipzig, Munich and Dresden.

He exhibits drawings at the "Hogarth Club," an association in which he was enrolled as an "Artistic Member."

He sponsors John Wharlton Bunney to travel to the Alps to paint and draw Alpine scenery. The following year the same artist is employed to make copies of works of art in Venice.

In November he publishes *The Elements of Perspective*.

1860

From May until August he travels alone to Savoy and Switzerland.

In June he publishes the fifth volume of *Modern Painters*, the sections of which are entitled "Of Leaf Beauty," "Of Cloud

Beauty," "Of Ideas of Relation: Of Invention Formal" and "Of Ideas of Relation: Of Invention Spiritual."

In the summer he travels to Switzerland to recuperate but draws little.

1861

In March he gives forty watercolours by Turner to the University Galleries of Oxford University, followed in May by a gift of a further twenty-five to the Fitzwilliam Museum, Cambridge.

From September until December he travels to Chamonix and seems to recover pleasure in drawing. He considers the possibility of living permanently in Savoy.

1862

In May he sponsors Edward and Georgiana Burne-Jones' journey to Italy and joins them in Milan.

He settles at Mornex, near Geneva.

1863

He continues to live at Mornex until March. He then contemplates settling in Venice.

From September until November he travels in the Swiss and French Alps. He buys some land at Chamonix with a view to building a house for himself.

1866

His father dies.

From April until July he travels in France and Switzerland.

1867

From June until August he visits the Lake District.

1868

He stays in Abbeville and makes many drawings of the church of St. Wulfran.

1869

He exhibits several of his Abbeville drawings at the Royal Institution.

He travels to Venice and Verona, seeing each place for the first time since 1852 and making many drawings.

He is appointed as the first Slade Professor of Fine Art at Oxford University.

1870

In February he gives his inaugural lecture as Slade Professor.

He exhibits several of his Verona drawings at the Royal Institution.

He decides to establish the Oxford Drawing School.

1871

He suffers a mental breakdown.

He assists J.W. Bunney and his family to establish themselves in Venice, where Bunney remains until his death in 1882, working to make drawings of architecture and the decoration of buildings for the Guild of St. George.

Purchases Brantwood in the Lake District. He moves into the house a year later.

He provides funding for the Guild of St. George.

His mother dies.

1873

He is elected an Honorary Member of the Society of Painters in Watercolours, following a campaign led by the watercolourist Alfred William Hunt. From this time forward he becomes an occasional exhibitor at the society's summer and winter exhibitions.

Hunt visits him at Brantwood.

1875

He gives money and art collections to establish the Ruskin Drawing Mastership at Oxford University.

He founds the Museum of the Guild of St. George at Walkley.

1876

In August he travels to Venice, following a period of depression brought on by the death of Rose La Touche the previous spring. Ruskin intends to make a revised edition of *The Stones of Venice*, but in the event works on a variety of different projects, seeking distraction from obsessive and disturbed thoughts. He remains in Venice until the following year, suffering a severe mental breakdown in the winter.

1878

An exhibition of Ruskin's Turner drawings in conjunction with his own works is held at the Fine Art Society in London's New Bond Street.

He recruits Thomas Matthews Rooke as an architectural draftsman to be employed by the Guild of St. George to make drawings of buildings in France, Italy and England.

1879

He resigns the Slade Professorship.

The exhibition of his drawings previously shown at the Fine Art Society travels to Boston and New York.

He organizes an exhibition of works by Samuel Prout and William Henry Hunt at the Fine Art Society.

1880

He makes a tour of France, travelling with the amateur draftsman Hercules Brabazon Brabazon.

1882

He travels in Europe, spending periods in Savoy and Tuscany. He makes drawings aimed as illustrations for an intended nine-volume history of Christianity, the first part of which, *The Bible of Amiens*, had been published in 1880, but of which a further projected chapter was to be titled "Ponte Vecchio."

Following a correspondence involving matters to do with drawing, he is visited at Brantwood by Kate Greenaway.

1883

He resumes the Slade Professorship.

1885

He finally resigns the Slade Professorship at Oxford.

1888

He travels abroad for the last time.

1889

He make his last pencil studies, one a view of Calder Abbey, another a view on Langdale Pikes.

1900

Ruskin dies of influenza on 20 January at home at Brantwood.

BIBLIOGRAPHY

BAKER 2011
Baker, C. *English Drawings and Watercolours 1600–1900*. Edinburgh, 2011.

BLAU 1982
Blau, E. *Ruskinian Gothic: The Architecture of Deane and Woodward, 1845–1861*. Princeton, 1982.

BLOOM 1986
Bloom, H. *Modern Critical Views: John Ruskin*. New York, 1986.

BOYCE 1980
Boyce, G.P. *The Diaries of George Price Boyce*, ed. Virginia Surtees. Norwich, 1980.

BRADLEY 1955
Bradley, J.L. *Ruskin's Letters from Venice, 1851–1852*. New Haven, 1955.

BROOKS 1989
Brooks, M.W. *John Ruskin and Victorian Architecture*. London, 1989.

CAMBRIDGE NEW HAVEN 2009
Donald, D., and J. Munro, eds. *Endless Forms: Charles Darwin, Natural Science and the Visual Arts* (exh. cat.). Cambridge, Fitzwilliam Museum; New Haven, Yale Center for British Art, 2009.

CLARK 1964
Clark, K. *Ruskin Today*. Harmondsworth, 1964.

COLLINGWOOD 1893
Collingwood, W.G. *The Life and Work of John Ruskin*. London, 1893.

COLLINGWOOD 1903
Collingwood, W.G. *Ruskin Relics*. London, 1903.

COOK 1911
Cook, E.T. *The Life of John Ruskin*. 2 vols. New York, 1911.

DEARDEN 1999
Dearden, J.S. *John Ruskin: A Life in Pictures*. Sheffield, 1999.

EDINBURGH 1978
Holloway, J., and L. Errington. *The Discovery of Scotland: The Appreciation of Scottish Scenery through Two Centuries of Painting* (exh. cat). Edinburgh, National Gallery of Scotland, 1978.

FORBES 1900
Forbes, J.D. *Travels Through the Alps*, rev. W.A.B. Coolidge. London, 1900 [1843].

FOX TALBOT 1844
Fox Talbot, H. *The Pencil of Nature*. London, 1844.

FULLER 1988
Fuller, P. *Theoria: Art and the Absence of Grace*. London, 1988.

GRIEVE 1996
Grieve, A. "Ruskin and Millais at Glenfinlas." *The Burlington Magazine* 138, no. 1117 (April 1996), pp. 228–234.

HAYMAN 1982
Hayman, J., ed. *John Ruskin: Letters from the Continent, 1858*. Toronto, 1982.

HEWISON 1978
Hewison, R. *Ruskin and Venice*. London, 1978.

HEWISON 2000
Hewison, R., ed. *Ruskin's Artists: Studies in Victorian Visual Economy*. Aldershot, 2000.

HILTON 1985
Hilton, T. *John Ruskin: The Early Years 1819–1859*. New Haven and London, 1985.

HILTON 2000
Hilton, T. *John Ruskin: The Later Years*. New Haven and London, 2000.

HOUSTON CANBERRA LONDON 1989
Weaver, M. *The Art of Photography: 1839–1989* (exh. cat). Houston, Museum of Fine Arts; Canberra, Australian National Gallery; London, Royal Academy of Arts, 1989.

JACOBSON
Jacobson, K., and J. Jacobson. *Carrying Off the Palaces. John Ruskin's Lost Daguerreotypes*. London, forthcoming.

KEMPSTER ALTY 2008
Kempster, P.A., and J.E. Alty. "John Ruskin's relapsing encephalopathy." *Brain* 131, no. 9 (September 2008), pp. 2025–2525.

LANCASTER 2002
Wildman, S., and C.J. Gamble. *"A Perpetual Paradise": Ruskin's Northern France* (exh. cat.). Lancaster, The Ruskin Library, Lancaster University, 2002.

LANCASTER 2003
Hanley, K., and S. Wildman. *Ruskin's Romantic Tours 1837–1838* (exh. cat.). Lancaster, The Ruskin Library, Lancaster University, 2003.

LANCASTER 2006
Ruskin and the Daguerreotype (exh. cat.). Lancaster, The Ruskin Library, Lancaster University, 2006.

LANDOW 1985
Landow, G. *Ruskin*. Oxford and New York, 1985.

LASSAM 1979
Lassam, R. *Fox Talbot: Photographer*. Tisbury, 1979.

LEEDS 1993
Newall, C. *John William Inchbold: Pre-Raphaelite Landscape Artist* (exh. cat). Leeds, Leeds City Art Gallery, 1993.

LONDON 1960
Drawings by John Ruskin (exh. cat.). London, The Arts Council Gallery, 1960.

LONDON 1973
Parris, L. *Landscape in Britain, c. 1750–1850* (exh. cat.). London, Tate Gallery, 1973.

LONDON 1984
The Pre-Raphaelites (exh. cat). London, Tate Gallery, 1984.

LONDON 1985
Stainton, L. *British Landscape Watercolours, 1600–1860* (exh. cat.). London, The British Museum, 1985.

LONDON 2000
Hewison, R., I. Warrell and S. Wildman. *Ruskin, Turner and the Pre-Raphaelites* (exh. cat.). London, Tate Britain, 2000.

LONDON 2004
Staley, A., and C. Newall. *Pre-Raphaelite Vision: Truth to Nature* (exh. cat.). London, Tate Britain, 2004.

LONDON 2007
Rosenfeld, J., and Alison Smith. *Millais* (exh. cat.). London, Tate, 2007.

LONDON SHEFFIELD LUCCA 1993
Clegg, J. and P. Tucker. *Ruskin and Tuscany* (exh. cat). London, Accademia Italiana; Sheffield, Ruskin Gallery; Lucca, Fondazione Ragghianti, 1993.

LONDON WASHINGTON 1993
Wilton, A. *The Great Age of British Watercolours: 1750–1880* (exh. cat.). London, Royal Academy of Arts; Washington, D.C., National Gallery of Art, 1993.

LONDON WASHINGTON MOSCOW 2012
Barringer, T., et. al. *Pre-Raphaelites: Victorian Avant-garde* (exh. cat). London, Tate Britain; Washington, D.C., National Gallery; Moscow, State Pushkin Museum of Fine Arts, 2012–13.

LUTYENS 1965
Lutyens, M. ed. *Effie in Venice: Her Picture of Society and Life with John Ruskin 1849–1852*. London, 1965.

LUTYENS 1967
Lutyens, M. *Millais and the Ruskins*. London, 1967.

LUTYENS 1972
Lutyens, M. *The Ruskins and the Grays*. London, 1972.

LYELL 1847
Lyell, C. *Principles of Geology*. London, 1847 [1830].

MEYNELL 1940
Meynell, V., ed. *Friends of a Lifetime: Letters to Sydney Carlyle Cockerell*. London, 1940.

NEWALL 2007
Newall, C. "'Val d'Aosta': John Brett and John Ruskin in the Alps, 1858." *The Burlington Magazine* 149, no. 1248 (March 2007), pp. 165–172.

NEWMAN 1875
Newman, J.H. *Apologia pro vita sua: Being a History of His Religious Opinions*. London, 1875.

NEW HAVEN OXFORD 2004
Newall, C. *The Poetry of Truth* (exh. cat). New Haven, Yale Center for British Art; Oxford, Ashmolean Museum of Art and Architecture, University of Oxford, 2004.

NORTON 1913
Norton, C.E. *Letters of Charles Eliot Norton*. 2 vols. London and Cambridge, Mass., 1913.

OXFORD 2010
Harrison, C., and C. Newall. *The Pre-Raphaelites and Italy* (exh. cat). Oxford, Ashmolean Museum of Art and Architecture, University of Oxford, 2010.

OXFORD SHEFFIELD 1996
Hewison, R. *Ruskin and Oxford: The Art of Education* (exh. cat). Oxford, Ashmolean Museum of Art and Architecture, University of Oxford; Sheffield, Museums Sheffield and Mappin Art Gallery, 1996.

PENNY 1988
Penny, N. *Ruskin's Drawings in the Ashmolean Museum*. Oxford, 1988.

QUILL 2000
Quill, S., ed. *Ruskin's Venice: The Stones Revisited*. Aldershot, 2000.

RUSKIN 1903–12
Ruskin, J. *The Works of John Ruskin: Library Edition*, eds. E.T. Cook and A. Wedderburn. 39 vols. London, 1903–12.

RUSKIN 1956
Ruskin, J. *The Diaries of John Ruskin*, eds. J. Evans and J. Howard Whitehouse. 3 vols. Oxford, 1956.

RUSKIN 1972
Ruskin, J. *Ruskin in Italy: Letters to his Parents 1845*, ed. H.I. Shapiro. Oxford, 1972.

RUSKIN 1979
Ruskin, J. *Reflections of a Friendship: John Ruskin's Letters to Pauline Trevelyan 1848–1866*, ed. V. Surtees. London, 1979.

RUSKIN 1982
Ruskin, J. *John Ruskin: Letters from the Continent, 1858*, ed. J. Hayman. Toronto, 1982.

RUSKIN NORTON 1987
Ruskin, J., and C.E. Norton. *The Correspondence of John Ruskin and Charles Eliot Norton*, eds. J.L. Bradley and I. Ousby. Cambridge, 1987.

SCOTT 1805
Scott, W. *The Lay of the Last Minstrel.* London, 1805.

SHEFFIELD 1983
John Ruskin: An Arts Council Exhibition (exh. cat). Sheffield, Mappin Art Gallery, 1983.

STALEY 2001
Staley, A. *The Pre-Raphaelite Landscape.* New Haven and London, 2001.

SWETT 1931
Swett, L.G. *John Ruskin's Letters to Francesca and Memoirs of the Alexanders.* Boston, 1931.

TOURING CLUB ITALIANO 1974
Touring Club Italiano. *Guida d'Italia: Toscana.* Milan, 1974.

TOURING CLUB ITALIANO 1985
Touring Club Italiano. *Venezia.* 3rd ed. Milan, 1985.

UNRAU 1984
Unrau, J. *Ruskin and St. Mark's.* London, 1984.

VILJOEN 1956
Viljoen, H.G. *Ruskin's Scottish Heritage, a Prelude.* Urbana, Illinois, 1956.

WALTON 1972
Walton, P.H. *The Drawings of John Ruskin.* Oxford, 1972.

WALTON 2000
Walton, P.H. *Master Drawings by John Ruskin: Selections from the David Thomson Collection.* London, 2000.

WEAVER 1986
Weaver, M. *The Photographic Art: Pictorial Traditions in Britain and America.* Edinburgh, 1986.

WILDMAN 2009
Wildman, S. "*Coeli enarrant saepenumero*: New Light on Dark Clouds." *Ruskin Review and Bulletin* 5, no. 2 (autumn 2009), pp. 79–81.

WILTON 1979
Wilton, A. *The Life and Work of J.M.W. Turner.* London, 1979.

INDEX OF WORKS

A Bough of Phillyrea, for "The Elements of Drawing," c. 1856–57 (ca. 115b)

Aiguilles de Chamonix, 1849 (cat. 94)

Aiguilles de Chamonix, c. 1849 (cat. 97)

"A July Thunder-cloud in the Val d'Aosta," 1858 (cat. 102)

Baden, Switzerland, 1863 (cat. 51)

Basket and Lily Capital, St. Mark's, 1849–52 (cat. 7)

Ben Venue and the Trossachs over Achray, 1838 (cat. 86)

Blenheim Orange Apple, c. 1873 (cat. 124)

Byzantine Capitals, Convex Group, for "The Stones of Venice," c. 1851–53 (cat. 6)

Byzantine Ruin, Rio di Cà Foscari, Venice, c. 1851 (cat. 31)

Ca' d'Oro, Venice, 1845 (cat. 22)

Canal, Venice, 1877 (cat. 59e)

Cannaregio, Venice, 1877 (cat. 59d)

Capital 36 of the Ducal Palace, Venice, 1849–52 (cat. 8)

Casa Falier, Venice, 1877 (cat. 63)

Cerastes Cornutus, Seen from Above, Drawn from Life, c. 1871 (cat. 123)

Chamouni: Rocks and Vegetation, 1854 (cat. 80)

Church of St. Wulfran, Abbeville, 1868 (cat. 54)

Cloud Study – Ice Clouds over Coniston Water, 1880 (cat. 111)

Coast Scene near Dunbar, 1847 (cat. 69)

Copy of the Central Portion of Tintoretto's "Crucifixion," 1845 (cat. 128)

Copy of the Figure of a Girl in Van Dyck's "Portrait of Anna van Thielen, the Wife of the Painter Theodor Rombouts, and their Daughter Anna Maria," 1859 (cat. 129)

Cornice Decoration – for "The Stones of Venice," c. 1851 (cat. 9)

Crossmount, Perthshire; Study of Crag, Tree and Thistle, 1847 (cat. 71)

Dawn at Coniston, 1873 (cat. 108)

Dawn at Neuchâtel, 1866 (cat. 106)

Dead Pheasant, 1867 (cat. 120)

Design for a Window at the University Museum, Oxford, c. 1855–58 (cat. 13)

Design Studies for Capitals for the University Museum, Oxford, c. 1855–58 (cat. 12)

Diary Notebook or *Crossmount Sketchbook* (open at page of studies of funnels and sails, 1847), 1846–49 (cat. 70)

Drawing of Carpaccio's "Dream of Saint Ursula" from the "Legend of Saint Ursula," 1876 (cat. 132)

End View of the Pulpit in the Church of San Ambrogio, Milan, 1849 (?) (cat. 5)

Etna from Taormina, 1874 (cat. 109)

Farm Buildings in Switzerland, c. 1856–59 (cat. 46)

Fast Sketch of Withered Oak Leaves, 1879 (cat. 127)

Fisher Street, Carlisle, 1837 (cat. 37)

Foliage on a Bank, c. 1845–50 (cat. 112)

Fribourg, 1856 (cat. 45)

Fribourg. Rue de la Palme and Houses Beyond Pont de Berne, c. 1854 or 1856 (cat. 42)

Fribourg, Switzerland, 1856 (?) (cat. 41)

Fribourg. The Augustinian Convent. Distant View, c. 1854 or 1856 (cat. 44)

General View at Rheinfelden, 1858 (cat. 48a)

Geological Diary, 1835 (cat. 67)

Gorge at Ardon, 1854 (cat. 78)

Gorge at Ardon, 1854 (cat. 79a)

Gorge at Ardon, 1854 (cat. 79b)

Grütli, Uri-Rotstock from Lake Lucerne, 1858 (?) (cat. 100)

In the Pass of Killiecrankie, 1857 (cat. 81)

Junction of the Greta and Tees at Rokeby, 1876 (cat. 110)

Juniper, 1863 (cat. 119)

La Cascade de la Folie, Chamouni, 1849 or 1854 (?) (cat. 93)

Lateral View of the Façade of San Michele in Foro, Lucca, 1846 (cat. 26)

Lower Portion of the Façade of San Michele, Lucca, 1846 (cat. 27)

Lucerne, 1861 (?) (cat. 50)

Mer de Glace, Chamonix, 1849 (cat. 95)

Mer de Glace, Chamonix, c. 1849–54 (cat. 96)

Mer de Glace, Chamonix, France, 1860 (cat. 104)

Merton College and Magpie Lane, Oxford, 1838 (cat. 38)

Montagne de la Côte and Glacier des Bossons, c. 1849 (cat. 92)

Moss and Wild Strawberry, 1873 (?) (cat. 84)

Mountain Landscape, Macugnaga, 1845 (cat. 89)

Mountain Rock and Alpine Rose, 1844–49 (cat. 73)

Mountains of Villeneuve (Near the Eastern End of the Lake of Geneva), 1846 (cat. 90)

Northwest Porch of St. Mark's, Venice, 1877 (cat. 36)

Palazzo Agostini, Pisa, 1845 (cat. 21)

Palazzo Dario, Venice, 1845 (cat. 23)

Part of St. Mark's Basilica, Venice: Sketch after Rain, 1846 (cat. 24)

Part of the Façade of the Destroyed Church of San Michele in Foro, Lucca, as it Appeared in 1845, 1845 (cat. 20)

Part of the Façade of the Destroyed Church of San Michele in Foro, Lucca, Sketched in Colour, 1846 (cat. 25)

Pass of the Cenis, above St. Michel, or *Pine Forest on Mont Cenis*, 1854 or 1856 (cat. 99)

Piazza Sta Maria del Pianto, Rome, 1840 (cat. 39)

Ponte della Pietra, Verona, 1869–72 (cat. 55)

Prunus Persica, 1857 (cat. 117)

Rapid Studies of Effects from the Faulhorn, or *Studies of Alpine Peaks*, 1846 or 1854 (cat. 98)

Ravine at Maglans, 1849 (?) (cat. 74a)

Ravine at Maglans, 1849 (?) (cat. 74b)

Rialto Bridge, Venice, 1876 (cat. 59a)

Rialto Bridge, Venice, 1877 (cat. 59c)

Riva degli Schiavoni, the Ducal Palace and the Campanile of St. Mark's, 1870 (cat. 56)

Rock Study with Oxalis and Heather, mid-1880s (?) (cat. 85)

Rocks and Ferns in a Wood at Crossmount, Perthshire, 1847 (cat. 72)

Rosslyn Chapel, 1838 (cat. 1)

San Niccolo de Tolentini, Venice, 1876 (cat. 59b)

Santa Maria della Spina, Pisa (South Side Towards East End), c. 1846 (cat. 28)

Santa Maria della Spina, Pisa; East End, 1846–47 (cat. 29)

Self-portrait, 1874 (cat. 131)

Self-portrait, in Blue Neckcloth, 1873 (cat. 130)

Southwest Porch of St. Wulfran's, Abbeville, 1848 (cat. 4)

Southwest Portico of St. Mark's, Venice, c. 1849–50 (cat. 32)

Spanish Chestnut, at Carrara, related to "The Elements of Drawing," c. 1856–57 (cat. 115a)

Spiral Relief from the North Transept Door, Rouen Cathedral, 1882 (cat. 17)

St. Wulfran, Abbeville, Seen from the River, 1868 (cat. 53)

Stilted Archivolts, from a Byzantine Ruin in the Rio di Cà Foscari, Venice, 1849 (cat. 30)

Stone Pines at Sestri, Gulf of Genoa, 1845 (cat. 113)

Street Scene, Naples, 1840–41 (cat. 40)

Study for the General Chiaroscuro of the Sarcophagus and Canopy of the Tomb of Mastino II della Scala at Verona, c. 1869 (cat. 34)

Study of a Kingfisher, with Dominant Reference to Colour, probably 1871 (cat. 122)

Study of a Peacock's Breast Feather, 1873 (cat. 125)

Study of a Piece of Brick, to Show Cleavage in Burnt Clay, c. 1871 (cat. 83)

Study of a River Bank, Beauvais, 1846 (cat. 68)

Study of a Velvet Crab, 1870 (?) (cat. 121)

Study of an Acanthus Boss, Archivolt of the Central Door, San Marco, Venice, 1877 (cat. 16)

Study of Boulders, 1850s (cat. 75)

Study of Clouds in Turner's "Campo Santo, Venice," 1859–60 (cat. 103)

Study of Dawn: Purple Clouds, 1868 (cat. 107b)

Study of Dawn: The First Scarlet on the Clouds, 1868 (cat. 107a)

Study of Gneiss Rock, Glenfinlas, 1853–54 (cat. 76)

Study of Part of the Trees in Turner's "Crossing the Brook," c. 1856–57 (cat. 116)

Study of the Marble Inlaying on the Front of the Casa Loredan, Venice, 1845 (cat. 2)

Sunset on San Michele, Venice, 1877 (cat. 64)

The Augustinian Convent, Fribourg, 1854 or 1856 (cat. 43)

The Baptistery, Florence: Study of the Upper Part of the Right-hand Compartment on the Southwest Façade, 1872 (cat. 35)

The Bridge at Rheinfelden, 1858 (cat. 47)

The Dryad's Waywardness: Oak Spray in Winter, Seen in Front, c. 1858–60 (cat. 118)

The Fondamenta Nuove, Venice, 1877 (cat. 65)

The Glacier des Bois, c. 1843–44 (cat. 87)

The Glacier des Bossons, Chamonix, 1849 (cat. 91)

The Grand Canal, from the Ca' Tron to the Ca' d'Oro, 1876 (cat. 60)

The Grand Canal, from the Palazzo Bernardo to the Palazzo Dolfin-Manin, 1876 (cat. 61)

The Gryphon Bearing the North Shaft of the West Entrance of the Duomo, Verona, 1869 (cat. 10)

The Kapellbrücke at Lucerne, 1861 (cat. 49)

The Palazzo Contarini-Fasan, Venice, 1841 (cat. 19)

The Piazzetta and St. Mark's, Venice, 1835 (cat. 18)

The Ponte Vecchio and Lung'Arno, Florence, Looking Toward the Southeast, 1882 (?) (cat. 66)

The Rocky Bank of a River, 1853 (?) (cat. 77)

The South Side of the Basilica of St. Mark's, Venice, from the Loggia of the Doge's Palace, c. 1851 (cat. 33)

The Tomb of Frederick II in the Cathedral of Palermo, 1874 (cat. 14)

The Tomb of Ilaria del Carretto in the Duomo, Lucca, 1874 (cat. 15)

The Walls of Lucerne, c. 1866 (cat. 52)

Three Feathers, c. 1875 (cat. 126)

Trees in a Lane, perhaps at Ambleside, 1847 (cat. 114)

Val Anzasca, 1845 (cat. 88)

View from my Window at Mornex, Where I Stayed a Year, 1861–62 (cat. 101)

View from the Base of the Brezon above Bonneville, 1862–63 (cat. 105)

View from the Palazzo Bembo to the Palazzo Grimani, Venice, 1870 (cat. 57)

View of a Cliff-side with Buildings, 1861–63 (cat. 82)

View of the Bridge at Rheinfelden, 1858 (cat. 48b)

View of the Entry Post on the Bridge at Rheinfelden, 1858 (cat. 48c)

View of the West Front of the Duomo, Verona, Showing the Gryphon Sculpture, 1852 (?) (cat. 11)

View on the Upper Reach of the Grand Canal, Venice, 1876–77 (cat. 62)

Vineyard Walk, Lucca, 1874 (cat. 58)

Window at the Ca' Foscari, Venice, 1845 (cat. 3)

PHOTOGRAPHIC CREDITS

cats. 1, 6, 8, 9, 11, 17, 18, 22, 23, 27, 28, 30–32, 36–38, 40, 48, 52, 53, 58, 59, 62, 67, 70, 73, 74, 78, 79, 86, 87, 90, 95, 96, 105, 110, 111, 114, 128, 131; figs. 1.1, 1.7, 1.8, 2.1, 3.3, 3.4, 3.5, 3.10, 4.2, 4.3, 4.4, 4.5, 5.1, 5.2, 5.4, 7.1: Image courtesy of the Ruskin Foundation (Ruskin Library, Lancaster University)

cats. 3, 5, 120; figs. 2.8, 3.1: © Victoria and Albert Museum, London / V&A Images – All rights reserved.

cats. 4, 46, 50, 54, 55, 61, 63–65, 68, 71, 75, 82, 85, 88, 106, 112; figs. 3.7, 3.8, 3.12, 3.13: Photo Michael Cullen, Peterborough, Ontario

cats. 21, 56, 81, 97: © The Fitzwilliam Museum, Cambridge

cats. 33, 129: Photography Richard Valencia

cats. 41, 109; fig. 1.2: © The Trustees of the British Museum

cats. 42, 44; fig. 1.6: Courtesy K. and J. Jacobson, UK

cats. 69, 93, 94, 98; figs. 2.3, 2.4: © Birmingham Museums Trust

cats. 72, 80, 101, 108: Reproduced by courtesy of Abbot Hall Art Gallery, Lakeland Arts Trust, Kendal, Cumbria, UK

cats. 77, 89; fig. 2.6: Yale Center for British Art, New Haven

cats. 92, 100: The Alpine Club Photo Library, London

cat. 130: The Pierpont Morgan Library, New York

figs. 1.4, 1.5, 8.1: © Tate, London 2013

fig. 2.7: Delaware Art Museum / The Bridgeman Art Library

figs. 3.6, 6.1: Imaging Department © President and Fellows of Harvard College

p. 76: cat. 2, detail

p. 114: cat. 21, detail

p. 150: cat. 41, detail

p. 214: cat. 69, detail

p. 260: cat. 100, detail

p. 316: cat. 114, detail

p. 348: cat. 132, detail